Evangelical America

Evangelical America

An Encyclopedia of Contemporary American Religious Culture

TIMOTHY J. DEMY AND
PAUL R. SHOCKLEY, EDITORS

 ABC-CLIO™

An Imprint of ABC-CLIO, LLC
Santa Barbara, California • Denver, Colorado

Library of Congress Cataloging-in-Publication Data

Names: Demy, Timothy J., editor. | Shockley, Paul R., editor.
Title: Evangelical America : an encyclopedia of contemporary American religious culture / Timothy J. Demy and Paul R. Shockley, editors.
Description: Santa Barbara, California : ABC-CLIO, 2017. | Includes bibliographical references and index.
Identifiers: LCCN 2017010044 (print) | LCCN 2017020361 (ebook) | ISBN 9781610697743 (ebook) | ISBN 9781610697736 (hard copy)
Subjects: LCSH: Evangelicalism—United States—Encyclopedias. | United States— Religion—Encyclopedias.
Classification: LCC BR1642.U5 (ebook) | LCC BR1642.U5 E86 2017 (print) | DDC 277.3/08303—dc23
LC record available at https://lccn.loc.gov/2017010044

ISBN: 978-1-61069-773-6 (print)
      978-1-61069-774-3 (ebook)

21 20 19 18 17   1 2 3 4 5

This book is also available as an eBook.

ABC-CLIO
An Imprint of ABC-CLIO, LLC

ABC-CLIO, LLC
130 Cremona Drive, P.O. Box 1911
Santa Barbara, California 93116-1911
www.abc-clio.com

This book is printed on acid-free paper ∞

Manufactured in the United States of America

Contents

Topical List of Entries

Churches

Calvary Chapel (Costa Mesa, California)
Fourth Presbyterian Church
   (Bethesda, Maryland)
Moody Church (Chicago)
Park Street Church (Boston)
Tenth Presbyterian Church
   (Philadelphia)
Willow Creek Community Church
   (South Barrington, Illinois)

Denominations, Movements, and Groups

African American Evangelicalism
Baptists and Evangelicalism
Bible Conference Movement
Bible Presbyterian Church
Children of God
Counterculture, Evangelicals and
Cowboy Church Movement
Denominationalism and
   Evangelicalism
Evangelicalism
Harvard Evangelicals
Hispanic American Evangelicals
Homeschooling, Evangelicals and
Intelligent Design Movement
Jesus People Movement
Messianic Judaism
Missions, Evangelicals and
Neo-Evangelicalism
Pentecostalism (and Charismatic
   Movement), Evangelicals and

Reformed Tradition, Evangelicalism and
Vineyard Movement

Events and Trends

Contemporary Christian Music
Explo '72
Higher Education, Evangelicals and
Jesus Music
Key '73
Mass Media, Evangelicals and
National Day of Prayer

Ideas, Doctrines, and Controversies

Abortion, Evangelicals and
Bible, Authority of
Bible Exposition
Calvinism
Christian Apologetics
Christian Reconstructionism
Civil Rights Movement, Evangelicals and
Conversion
Dispensationalism
Emerging and Emergent Churches
Environment, Evangelicals and the
Eschatology
Ethics, Evangelical Theories of
Evangelism
Fine Arts, Evangelicals and
Foreign Policy, Evangelicals and
Fundamentalism
Gender, Evangelicals and
Hermeneutics
Human Rights, Evangelicals and

Christianity Today (1956)
Danvers Statement (1988)
Evangelicals & Catholics Together
    (1994)
The Genesis Flood (1961)
The Late Great Planet Earth (1970)
Moody Monthly (1900–2003)
Scofield Reference Bible (1909)
The Uneasy Conscience of Modern
    Fundamentalism (1947)

Organizations

Africa Inland Mission
American Scientific Affiliation
Ariel Ministries
Association for Biblical Higher
    Education
Association of Christian Schools
    International
AWANA Clubs International
Billy Graham Evangelistic Association
BSF International
Center for Bioethics and Human
    Dignity
Chosen People Ministries (formerly
    American Board of Missions to the
    Jews)
Christian Legal Society
Christian Medical & Dental
    Associations
Christians for Biblical Equality
Concerned Women for America
Conference on Faith and History
Council on Biblical Manhood and
    Womanhood
Creation Research Society
Cru (formerly Campus Crusade for
    Christ International)
Dallas Theological Seminary
Denver Seminary

Evangelical Christian Publishers
    Association
Evangelical Council for Financial
    Accountability
Evangelical Theological Society
Family Research Council
Fellowship of Christian Athletes
Focus on the Family
Fuller Theological Seminary
Gideons International
Gordon College
Gordon-Conwell Theological
    Seminary
The Gospel Coalition
Grace Theological Seminary
Institute for Creation Research
InterVarsity Christian Fellowship/USA
International Council on Biblical
    Inerrancy
Jews for Jesus
L'Abri Fellowship
Ligonier Ministries
Military Ministries
Moral Majority
National Association of Evangelicals
National Black Evangelical Association
Navigators
Nyack College and Alliance
    Theological Seminary
Officers' Christian Fellowship
Pacific Garden Mission (Chicago)
Parachurch Ministries
Princeton Evangelical Fellowship
Prison Fellowship
Promise Keepers
Sojourners
Women's Ministries
World Vision International
Wycliffe Global Alliance
Young Life
Youth for Christ International

Preface

The purpose of this encyclopedia is to provide users with an overview of American evangelicalism from the Second World War until the present (2016). Evangelicalism is a global phenomenon without geographic boundaries, but the experiences within evangelicalism are shaped by national borders and histories.

The encyclopedia is not exhaustive. Such a work would require several volumes. Rather, it aims to provide readers with information on some of the prominent individuals, institutions, and ideas of the movement in the past 75 years. In so doing, following the introduction and chronology of American evangelicalism since the beginning of the Second World War, the encyclopedia has alphabetical entries for 193 topics covering ideas, individuals, institutions, controversies, publications, and organizations within American evangelicalism since 1940. Within each alphabetical entry, there are cross references to other entries in the encyclopedia, as well as a brief reference list to guide the reader who desires greater in-depth information on the subject to current and relevant books, articles, and Web sites. In addition to the alphabetical entries, readers will find numerous sidebars that provide ancillary information on evangelicalism.

At the end of the encyclopedia readers will find an up-to-date bibliography for further study of American evangelicalism as a whole. Included at the end of the bibliography are pertinent Web sites. There are also primary source documents of American evangelicalism that elucidate some of the key ideas of the era and show diverse opinions on some topics.

American evangelicals span the ethnic and socioeconomic spectrum in the United States. Evangelicalism in the United States has a long history with theological roots dating from the Reformation era of the 1500s in Europe. Although most evangelicals are Protestant and found outside what has traditionally been known as Protestantism's mainline denominations (United Methodists, Presbyterian Church in the United States, Episcopal Church in America, United Congregational Church, Lutheran Church in America, etc.), there are individuals and groups of evangelicals in these denominations. Additionally, some American evangelicals self-identify themselves as being either Roman Catholic or Orthodox Christians.

Self-identification as an evangelical is one of the hallmarks of evangelicalism in America and draws on both the democratic spirit of individualism in many aspects of life in the United States and the theological perspective of a religious conversion or "born again" experience (drawing on the words of Jesus as recorded in the Gospel of John 3:1–21).

Evangelicalism is a vibrant and fluid movement. It is a religious river that flows through American society and draws from several religious tributaries—notable among them American Protestant fundamentalism of the first half of the 20th century, 20th-century American Pentecostal and Charismatic movements, American Baptist traditions, traditions of Reformed theology, Holiness theology, and the heritage of revivalism in the United States dating to the Great Awakening of the 1730s and extending through the ministry of Billy Graham and into the present. There is also a strong transatlantic connection between evangelicals in Great Britain and the United States, dating to the colonial era. Rich expressions of evangelicalism are also found in the religious experiences of Hispanic, Asian, and African Americans. Each of these groups has contributed to evangelicalism in America, and readers will find overlap between and among various types of evangelicals.

Introduction

Evangelicalism is not a uniquely American phenomenon. Manifestations of it are global. There are evangelicals, and in fast-growing numbers, in Africa, Asia, Latin America, and South America. What began as a transatlantic movement in the 1700s, with religious roots in the Reformation era of the 1500s, became an international movement by the 2000s. Evangelicals belong to many Protestant denominations and to thousands of nondenominational churches—independent churches or networks of churches that claim no affiliation, such as Southern Baptist, Episcopal, United Methodist, or Lutheran. Evangelicals span the economic spectrum and the educational spectrum. They also vote in every color of the political prism. One simply cannot say that an evangelical looks like *x* or *y* or *z*. But that is not to say that one cannot identify anything about evangelicals.

In 1989, British historian David Bebbington published a seminal volume on British evangelicalism titled *Evangelicalism in Modern Britain: A History from the 1730s to the 1980s*. In addition to noting the deep and wide transatlantic ties between evangelicalism in the British Isles and evangelicalism in the United States, Bebbington presented what has come to be called by historians of religion the "Bebbington Quadrilateral" or the "Evangelical Quadrilateral." What is meant by this is Bebbington's identification of four central elements, or characteristics, of the evangelical experience: (1) *biblicism*—a particular regard for the Bible (e.g., all essential spiritual truth is to be found in its pages), (2) *crucicentrism*—a focus on the sacrificial death atoning work of Jesus Christ on the cross, (3) *conversionism*—the belief that human beings need to be converted, and (4) *activism*—the belief that the gospel message needs to be expressed in effort such that it is proclaimed and applied.

As with most segments and aspects of American life and culture, American evangelicalism is far from monolithic. Using the imagery of Genesis 37:3, where readers learn of Hebrew patriarch Jacob's "coat of many colors," so too are evangelicals in the United States part of a multifaceted, multigenerational, and multiethnic religious culture. And evangelical America is changing demographically in rates equal to, if not surpassing, national trends. For example, Hispanic evangelicals are growing rapidly within American evangelicalism (and elsewhere). Politically, evangelicals are also diverse. Although the majority self-identify as moderate or conservative, broader and left-wing politics also have a steady and firm stance within evangelicalism, dating at least to the early 1960s. The same is true for social issues that are so often a part of political discourse and posturing in the United States.

Whereas one might rightly consider with American evangelicalism historian George M. Marsden that the American religious fundamentalism of the 1920s and beyond was "essentially a separatist and sectarian movement on the fringes of American church life and society," the same cannot be said for post–World War II American evangelicalism (*Fundamentalism and American Culture*, rev. ed., 2006, p. 231). Evangelicalism permeates American Protestantism and is found in every strata and pocket of American society. Thus, it is rightly described as religious culture, but it is not a subculture. Evangelicals are *not apart from* American society; they are *a part of* American society in all of its fullness. Identification with such inclusiveness was one of the hallmarks and aspirations of American evangelical leaders in the 1940s as the movement (then termed *neo-evangelicalism* to distinguish it from the earlier title of fundamentalism or evangelicalism) sought to intentionally and proactively influence American religious life beyond the churches and Sunday worshiping congregations.

One of the sociological distinctions of early 20th-century Protestant fundamentalism was the separatism and isolationism of the fundamentalists. Sometimes separation was imposed by the religious bodies and Protestant denominations upon fundamentalists, and at other times the expulsions, exiles, and exits were self-initiated in order to separate from what was considered by the fundamentalists to be individual and denominational biblical apostasy (a willful departure from truth), social modernism, and theological liberalism. What changed between American Protestant fundamentalism of the prewar years and American Protestant evangelicalism of the postwar years was not primarily the theology (though there were shifts in emphasis of some elements); it was the sociology and the willingness to interact with the broader American culture on a wide array of theological, political, and social items. This was indeed the clarion call of evangelical theologian Carl F. H. Henry's small landmark book published in 1947, *The Uneasy Conscience of Modern Fundamentalism*. In it Henry challenged readers to reclaim their Reformed, cultural, political, and intellectual history. He believed that evangelicals ceded too much to liberal theology and secular ideologies, and when faced with challenges, too often retreated into pietistic platitudes, attitudes, and conclaves.

The call to broader action and interaction was not accomplished without tensions, dissent, and controversy within evangelicalism, but the issues facing Americans as a nation and democracy were part of the evangelical agenda. At times evangelicals lead the causes; other times they came late to the causes, and at yet other times they were in step with non-evangelical citizens. One thing that differentiated the evangelicals, however, was their desire to act and a belief that they were acting from within a distinctively biblical and Christian worldview.

Yet, in contemporary American evangelicalism, there is also continuity with earlier expressions of the theologically conservative faith. There is a firm commitment to evangelism and proclamation of the Gospel, that which is seen as being at the core evangelicalism and the Christian faith. There remains commitment to the key doctrinal beliefs, the "fundamentals" of the faith; and liberal theological beliefs are deemed to be corrosive of Christian orthodoxy.

Spiritual formation and personal piety remain an essential element of evangelicalism. Evangelicalism has always been expressed in intensely individualistic terms—indeed, such individualism is at the center of the history of revivalism in America as well as in the democratic spirit of Americans. But for evangelicals, the individualistic impulse is much deeper. It is the fervently held belief that the historical fact of the death, burial, and resurrection of Jesus Christ was for individuals as much as for humanity. Finally, though specific practices or policies in the greater society have changed, evangelicals have remained committed in their opposition to secularizing trends in society deemed to be detrimental to or antagonistic toward Christianity. In the opposition, postwar American evangelicals, especially since the late 1970s, have been more willing to address specific social and policy concerns in conjunction with other religious groups doing so as cobelligerents. Two prominent illustrations of this are the mutual support many Protestant evangelicals and Roman Catholics give in shared opposition to abortion, and the mutual support of Israel that many evangelicals share with American Jews.

The editors of this volume believe that the terms *fundamentalism* and *evangelicalism* are not synonymous; nor are *fundamentalist* and *evangelical*. They overlap theologically, but socially, culturally, and politically there is more separation. How they are defined and understood depends a lot on the historical (and geographical) contexts into which they are placed in American history. How they are being studied—sociologically, historically, or theologically—matters a lot. The fundamentalist of the 1920s is not the evangelical of the 2010s. They share some core theological beliefs, but in the intervening 90 years significantly more direct participation in national politics and social concerns has taken place than previously. Whereas the fundamentalist of the 1920s would have looked largely to evangelism as the core ingredient in a recipe to solve personal and national problems, nearly a hundred years later evangelicals would see the solution as more complex and requiring more personal involvement by them. The fundamentalist believed that national revival would remedy national problems. Evangelicals also believe that, but they understand that revival is not the only solution.

The emergence of evangelist Billy Graham in the late 1940s, and his prominence in American religious life from the 1950s until his retirement from active ministry in 2005, made him one of the most recognized and heard people in modern history. As such, for half a century he was America's most visible evangelical. He was also at the core group of leaders seeking the revitalization of evangelicalism after the Second World War.

Through men such as Billy Graham, Harold John Ockenga, Carl F. H. Henry, Wilbur M. Smith, and Edward J. Carnell, fresh energy and thought was infused into the fundamentalism/evangelicalism of earlier years, with the rise of what was, for many years, termed *neo-evangelicalism*. There were still problems to be dealt with internally and externally, as well as prejudices to be overcome, but these evangelicals were optimistic and ready to fully engage a postwar America that was also undergoing transformation from what it had been prior to the Second World War. Now, a generation later, the *neo-* has been dropped and *evangelicalism* is the accepted term.

Not everyone under the evangelical umbrella agreed with the rise of neo-evangelicalism. Some individuals and institutions distanced themselves theologically and organizationally from the efforts of neo-evangelicals. Of these, some maintained the separatist fundamentalism of earlier years, whereas other picked and chose the elements of neo-evangelicalism they accepted or rejected.

Regional variations and trends within evangelicalism also exist and have played a part in shaping American evangelicalism and expressions of it today. The theological emphases are much the same, but worship styles and the relationships to various social and political issues vary greatly from one region to another (and one church to another). One should not expect that expressions of evangelicalism in Birmingham are identical to evangelicalism in Boston, San Francisco, Detroit, Houston, or Topeka.

What one finds in American evangelicalism is a horizontal slice of America, left and right, red and blue, Caucasian and not, lots of education and less education, wealth and poverty. As with any religious group, some members are well versed in their faith, and others, not; some are vocal and others, silent. Regardless of the individual evangelical's lot in life, each one believes that within the breadth of the evangelical tradition there is the is the potential to fully realize spiritual significance and growth, God's love, the forgiveness of sin, and eternal life through personal faith in the death, burial, and resurrection of Jesus Christ. By so believing, they are not only expressing and living their faith, they are participating in the democratization of religion in America, where there is a longstanding collective belief that every individual has the right to believe or not believe as he or she wishes. On a sociopolitical level, American evangelicalism is one manifestation of what many Americans of many religious traditions affirm when declaring, "In God we trust."

Chronology

1941	Founding of American Scientific Affiliation
1941	J. Vernon McGee begins the "Open Bible Hour" radio ministry
1941	Founding of InterVarsity Christian Fellowship/USA
1941	Founding of Young Life
1941	Founding of Awana Clubs International in Chicago, Illinois
1942	Founding of Wycliffe Global Alliance (formerly Wycliffe Bible Translators)
1942	Founding of National Association of Evangelicals
1943	Founding of Officers' Christian Fellowship
1945	Founding of Youth for Christ International
1947	Founding of Fuller Theological Seminary
1947	Founding of Accrediting Association of Bible Institutes and Bible Colleges
1947	Carl F. H. Henry publishes *The Uneasy Conscience of Modern Fundamentalism*
1947	Harold Ockenga coins the term *neo-evangelicalism*
1947	Billy Graham crusade ministry begins
1949	Billy Graham Los Angeles Crusade gains national attention
1949	Founding of the Evangelical Theological Society
1950	Founding of the Billy Graham Evangelistic Association
1950	Founding of Denver Seminary (formerly known as Conservative Baptist Theological Seminary)
1950	Founding of World Vision International
1951	Founding of Campus Crusade for Christ (now Cru)
1951	Founding of collegiate chapter of Navigators

1952	World Wide Pictures established as an arm of the Billy Graham Evangelistic Association to promulgate Christianity through film
1952	Bible Institute of Los Angeles changes its name to Biola College
1952	Talbot Theological Seminary, now Talbot School of Theology, established
1952	National Day of Prayer established by joint resolution of Congress
1952	Bill Bright authors gospel pamphlet "The Four Spiritual Laws"
1952	Death of Lewis Sperry Chafer
1954	Founding of Fellowship of Christian Athletes
1955	Founding of L'Abri Fellowship
1956	Founding of *Christianity Today* magazine
1956	Death of James ("Jim") Elliot
1957	Accrediting Association of Bible Institutes and Bible Colleges renamed American Association of Bible Colleges
1957	Billy Graham's New York City Crusade in Madison Square Garden is televised on primetime television
1960	Founding of Alliance Theological Seminary
1960	First publication of Billy Graham Evangelistic Association's *Decision* magazine
1961	Founding of Christian Legal Society
1961	Publication of *The Genesis Flood* by Henry Morris and John Whitcomb
1963	Founding of Creation Research Society
1963	Founding of National Black Evangelical Association (originally known as National Negro Evangelical Association)
1963	Founding of Trinity Evangelical Divinity School
1966	Publication of *Dispensationalism Today* by Charles C. Ryrie
1967	Death of Edward J. Carnell on April 25
1967	Founding of the Conference on Faith and History
1967	Publication of *New Scofield Reference Bible*
1968	Death of Charles E. Fuller

1969	Gordon Divinity School and Conwell Theological Seminary merge to form Gordon-Conwell Theological Seminary
1970	Publication of Francis Schaeffer's *Pollution and the Death of Man*
1971	Publication of Bill Bright's *Revolution Now!*
1971	Founding of Ligonier Ministries
1971	Founding of Liberty University
1971	Founding of Sojourners (formerly Sojourners Community)
1971–1972	Zenith of the Jesus People Movement
1972	Explo '72 event in Dallas, Texas, sponsored by Campus Crusade for Christ (now Cru)
1972	Founding of Institute for Creation Research
1973	"Chicago Declaration of Evangelical Social Concern"
1973	Key '73 event
1973	Founding of Jews for Jesus
1973	Publication of Hal Lindsey's *There's a New World Coming*
1973	*Roe v. Wade* U.S. Supreme Court decision legalizing abortion
1974	Founding of Evangelical Christian Publishers Association
1976	Harold Lindsell publishes *The Battle for the Bible*
1976	Charles Wendell ("Chuck") Colson founds Prison Fellowship
1976–1983	Publication of Carl F. H. Henry's *God, Revelation, and Authority* (6. Vol.)
1977	Founding of Ariel Ministries
1977	Publication of Ron Sider's *Rich Christians in an Age of Hunger*
1977	Founding of Regent University (formerly CBN University)
1977	Founding of Focus on the Family
1977	Evangelical Philosophical Society established
1977	Founding of International Council on Biblical Inerrancy
1978	"Chicago Statement on Biblical Inerrancy"
1978	Founding of Association of Christian Schools International
1979	Campus Crusade for Christ (now Cru) produces evangelistic movie *Jesus Film*

1979	Founding of the Moral Majority
1979	Founding of Evangelical Council for Financial Accountability
1979	Beverly LaHaye founds Concerned Women for America
1981	Biola College changes its name to Biola University
1981	Founding of Family Research Council
1982	Death of George Eld
1983	Charles Wendell ("Chuck") Colson founds Justice Fellowship
1984	Death of Francis Schaeffer
1985	First use of satellites by Billy Graham Evangelistic Association to broadcast throughout Great Britain from Sheffield, England
1985	Death of evangelical philosopher Gordon Haddon Clark
1985	Death of Harold John Ockenga
1986	American Board of Missions to the Jews changes its name to Chosen People Ministries
1986	Founding of Master's Seminary
1987	Death of Christian apologist Cornelius Van Til
1987	Founding of Council on Biblical Manhood and Womanhood, affirming a complementarian perspective of gender roles
1988	Founding of Christian for Biblical Equality, affirming an egalitarian perspective of gender roles
1988	Death of J. Vernon McGee
1989	Danvers Statement on complementarian perspective of gender roles released
1989	Billy Graham Evangelistic Association London Crusade broadcasts live to 250 locations across the United Kingdom and 300 locations in Africa
1990	Founding of Promise Keepers
1991	Billy Graham Evangelistic Association Crusade in Buenos Aires is transmitted via satellite and video to 20 Spanish-speaking countries in Central and South America
1991	Founding of the Discovery Institute
1994	Founding of Alliance of Confessing Evangelicals

1994   Publication of *Evangelicals & Catholics Together: The Christian Mission in the Third Millennium*

1994   Publication of Mark A. Noll's *The Scandal of the Evangelical Mind*

1994   Founding of the Center for Bioethics and Human Dignity

1995   Death of Richard ("Dick") Halverson

1995   Publication of *Left Behind* by Tim LaHaye and Jerry Jenkins

1996   Billy Graham Evangelistic Association launches Web site www .BillyGraham.org

1996   "Bill" Bright awarded Templeton Prize

1996   Publication of *Darwin's Black Box: The Biochemical Challenge to Evolution and The Edge of Evolution: The Search for the Limits of Darwinism* by Michael J. Behe

1998   Death of Harold Lindsell

2000   Billy Graham's son Franklin Graham named CEO of Billy Graham Evangelistic Association

2000   "The Cornwall Declaration on Environmental Stewardship"

2000   Death of James Montgomery Boice, pastor of Tenth Presbyterian Church, Philadelphia

2002   Death of W. A. Criswell, pastor of First Baptist Church, Dallas

2002   Death of Kenneth Kantzer

2002   Death of John F. Walvoord

2002   Founding of The Center for the Study of New Testament Manuscripts (CSNTM)

2003   Death of Carl F. H. Henry

2004   American Association of Bible Colleges renamed Association for Biblical Higher Education

2005   Founding of The Gospel Coalition

2006   Death of Henry Morris

2006   "Statement of the Evangelical Climate Initiative, Climate Change: An Evangelical Call to Action"

2008   Publication of *The Reason for God: Belief in an Age of Skepticism* by Timothy J. Keller

2011	Death of Mark O. Hatfield
2012	Death of Prison Fellowship founder Charles Wendell ("Chuck") Colson
2013	Death of Calvary Chapel Pastor Charles ("Chuck") Smith
2013	Death of Howard G. Hendricks
2013	Death of Edith Schaeffer
2013	Washington Bible College and Capital Bible Seminary acquired by Lancaster Bible College
2013	Death of C. Everett Koop
2016	Death of evangelical historian Robert G. Clouse
2016	Death of Tim LaHaye
2016	Death of Charles C. Ryrie
2016	Death of Thomas C. Oden
2017	Alvin Plantinga awarded Templeton Prize

A

ABORTION, EVANGELICALS AND

Evangelicals value human life, starting from the moment of fertilization. They ground their view of human dignity in God's creation of male and female in His own image. Consequently, most evangelicals oppose abortion. According to a 2013 Pew research survey, about three-quarters of white evangelical Protestants (73%) and more than half of black Protestants (53%, although the report did not distinguish between black evangelicals and black Protestants at large) believe abortion is morally wrong.

Although evangelicals point to Genesis and God's creation of humanity in His image as the foundation for their view of human life (1:27), they also point to additional scriptures. These include the psalmist's statement that he was woven in his mother's womb and is "fearfully and wonderfully made" (Psalm 139:14); the Sinai prohibition against murder (Exodus 20:13); God's statement that he knew Jeremiah even before forming him in his mother's womb (Jer. 1:5); and the taking of human life as overstepping the dominion that God gave to humans in ruling the earth (Genesis 1:26).

When the 1973 *Roe v. Wade* decision legalized abortion in the United States, an editorial in *Christianity Today* denounced the outcome, stating that the decision ran counter to the moral teachings of Christianity through the ages. The church fathers, including Augustine, Chrysostom, and Jerome, condemned abortion. Through the years as science has provided greater specificity about the moment at which human life begins, evangelicals have used more specific language to articulate that they view every human being, regardless of size or ability to produce, as worthy of protection.

Evangelicals prefer the label "pro-life" to "anti-abortion," as they see the former as the rationale behind opposing the action. Additionally, they may accept an abortion as being "pro-life" if it will save the life of the mother in cases in which both the mother's and the child's life would otherwise be lost. Yet they tend to be skeptical about how often such emergencies occur.

Many evangelicals contend that "life begins at conception." By "conception" they do not mean implantation, however, as most obstetricians do when they use the term. Though the medical definition of "conception" has evolved since the 1970s, most evangelicals' usage of this word has not. So when referring to "conception" in the context of abortion, evangelicals usually mean fertilization.

Because scientific textbooks state that life begins at fertilization, the focus of the debate has been shifting from arguments about when life begins to whether an embryo or fetus has the full rights and protections of personhood.

Regarding the 1973 *Roe v. Wade* decision, the Pew study reports that white evangelical Protestants are the only major religious group in which a majority (54%) favors overturning the law. Still, nearly half do not see doing so as the best approach to reducing the number of abortions.

Younger evangelicals are somewhat more conservative than older ones on this issue. White evangelicals under age 35 favor abortion restrictions by more than a two-to-one margin (71% among those under 25), whereas those over age 65 actually oppose more restrictions. Although there has not been complete agreement by evangelicals on the topic of abortion, the subject has been a major social issue for evangelicals and has served as a beginning point for many to pursue other social issues in the public, political, and policy arenas.

Sandra Glahn and Marnie Blackstone Legaspi

See also: Ethics, Evangelical Theories of; Sexuality, Evangelicals and

Further Reading

Davis, John Jefferson. *Evangelical Ethics*, 3rd ed. Phillipsburg, NJ: P&R, 2004.

Kilner, John F., Paige C. Cunningham, and W. David Hagers, eds. *The Reproduction Revolution: A Christian Appraisal of Sexuality, Reproductive Technologies, and the Family*. Grand Rapids, MI: Eerdmans, 2000.

Sproul, R. C., and Greg Bailey. *Abortion: A Rational Look at an Emotional Issue*. Lake Mary, FL: Reformation Trust, 2014.

AFRICA INLAND MISSION

Africa Inland Mission is a nondenominational missions organization founded by Scottish-American missionary Peter Cameron Scott (1867–1896) in 1895 during the height of the Protestant foreign missionary movement of the 19th and 20th centuries. Today, Africa Inland churches are found in almost every African country.

The Africa Inland Mission was originally conceived as a network of mission stations stretching from East Africa into the interior of the continent, where no missionary presence existed. Scott developed this strategy for African missions when he was recuperating from a tropical illness he contracted while serving with A. B. Simpson's Christian and Missionary Alliance in Dutch Congo. He took the opportunity to read about the history of missions and was probably influenced by the missiological ideas of Hudson Taylor, founder of the China Inland Mission, and inspired by Robert Moffat, pioneer missionary to Africa. Taylor emphasized adoption of host nation culture and dress (so long as the gospel is not compromised), and leading and calling by the Holy Spirit rather than formal missionary training. Moffat hoped to see missions established throughout the continent, but his work was largely confined to the south.

Unique Strategy

Scott's strategy was unique in that it was not sponsored by any economic venture and was therefore free to focus solely on the establishment of its missions' stations. As he sought to implement his plan, he encountered resistance from denominational leaders, so he formed his own Philadelphia Missionary Council in 1895. The Council was to raise funds and recruit volunteers to go to Africa, and the mission was to be largely self-governing. The work began in Kenya, with Scott at the helm (though he died within a year), establishing four stations there. After some difficulty, it continued and within 20 years, had expanded into four other nations. The significance of Scott's vision and ministry approach remains to the present, and the Africa Inland Mission is an example of evangelicalism's long-standing interest in global evangelism.

John D. Laing

See also: African American Evangelicalism; Missions, Evangelicals and; Social Action, Evangelicals and

Further Reading

Anderson, Dick. *We Felt Like Grasshoppers: Story of Africa Inland Mission.* Wheaton, IL: Crossway, 1994.

Gehman, Richard J. *From Death to Life: The Birth of the Africa Inland Church in Kenya, 1895–1945.* Ann Arbor, MI: C-M Books, 2014.

Miller, Catherine S. *Peter Cameron Scott, the Unlocked Door.* London: Parry Jackman, 1955.

Moreau, A. Scott, ed. *Evangelical Dictionary of World Missions.* Grand Rapids, MI: Baker Books, 2000.

AFRICAN AMERICAN EVANGELICALISM

African American evangelicalism refers to Christians of African descent in the United States who adopt doctrinal distinctives and express spiritual outlooks that support the importance of a conversion experience, advocate the central role of the Bible in the Christian life, express fidelity to Jesus Christ, emphasize the necessity of missionary work, and highlight the influence of the Holy Spirit. Black Christians of evangelical conviction, at least since the 1930s, have tended to hold conservative theological positions while generally, although not uniformly, embracing more progressive political orientations. Quantitative and qualitative scholarship has suggested African Americans across multiple generations remain some of the most religiously and spiritually active Christians when compared to the entire U.S. population, even as the percentage of African American "nones" (those who self-identify as having no religious preference) increases. Surveys have measured resounding convictions about biblical authority and the frequent practice of prayer, and scholarship has documented an abiding enchantment with and activist position toward the world.

Within the scope of American Christianity, African American evangelicals represent a substantial and vital influence. Although part of the story of African American evangelicalism has tracked along an unfolding narrative of slavery to freedom, such a generalization fails to underscore the cultural nuances, gender differences, class experiences, denominational traditions, and regional distinctions present within its rich history.

In an epoch defined by the broader contours of the Columbian Exchange, the Protestant and Catholic Reformations, the birth of capitalism, the onset of industrialization, and transatlantic slavery, ca. 1450–1850, racialized forms of religious thought and religious life defined the spiritual and material realities of white and non-white Christians. The complex entanglement of religion and race during the Atlantic Age marked whiteness as pure, innocent, and holy; and blackness as sinful, evil, and corrupt. Such associations, revealed collectively in the writings of scientists, economists, philosophers, and theologians, offered scriptural sanction for slavery and bondage and legitimated Anglo spiritual, political, and economic dominance. At the same time, enslaved (and free) populations of color eventually adopted the religion of the master class, yet through what religious studies scholar Derek Hicks terms "curative recalibration," retooled, repurposed, and reinterpreted biblical passages and ideas in the service of liberation and freedom. Christianity (the multiple forms of both Protestantism and Catholicism) in the modern world—in other words the multiple contexts in which African American Christianity was born—was thus fundamentally racialized and highly segregated. Some used Christian teachings to baptize unjust structures; others found rationales for emancipation in its doctrines.

A single racialized or religious idea or experience has never defined African American evangelicalism. Yet collectively, Christians of African descent in the Americas have long wrestled hermeneutics of oppression into expositions of liberation. In the 18th century, for example, Rebecca Protten (d. 1780), a free woman of color living on St. Thomas and part of the Moravian tradition, evangelized African-descended people of that Caribbean island. During the same era, black evangelicals who represented various Christian traditions achieved important contributions. Freeborn New Yorker John Marrant (1755–1791) converted to Christianity at a George Whitefield revival and received ordination in the Methodist Church, and Lemuel Haynes (1753–1833) fought in the American Revolution and pastored a white congregation in Vermont. The well-known Phillis Wheatley (1753–1784) affiliated with New England Congregationalism in Boston and penned lyrical meditations about religious matters as a free woman of color; the enslaved poet Jupiter Hammon (1711–1806) composed theologically sophisticated Calvinist verse.

During the antebellum period, black denominations took shape, such as the African Methodist Episcopal (AME) Church and the Methodist Episcopal Church. Abolitionist leaders and societal reformers like Henry Highland Garnet (1815–1882), Harriet Tubman (1822–1913), David Walker (1796–1830), and Maria Stewart (1803–1879) found inspiration for social action from Christian teachings, as did black missionaries such as David George (1742–1810), who preached in Nova

Scotia and Sierra Leone, and Lott Cary (1780–1828), who ministered in Liberia. Elsewhere, especially in the American South, other evangelicals of African descent practiced faith in white-controlled plantation congregations and in hush harbors or clandestine religious assemblies. Offering spiritual solace and identity affirmation, chanted sermons, spirituals, the ring shout, conjuring, and call and response coupled traditional African religious ritual and U.S. revivalism. Following the Civil War, black Christians of evangelical persuasion capitalized on newfound freedom and birthed new denominations such as the National Baptist Convention, and leaders like Henry McNeal Turner (1834–1915) and Daniel Alexander Payne (1811–1893) promoted educational ventures through missionary work and political activity. In addition, black Christians like Ida Wells-Barnett (1862–1931) condemned lynching, and black churchwomen such as Nannie H. Burroughs (1879–1961) drew on ecclesiastical networks to advocate for social and political change.

At the dawn of the 20th century, black evangelicals were integral to the early Pentecostal movement. William Seymour (1870–1922), for example, was a significant Pentecostal leader and powerful Azusa Street preacher, and published *Apostolic Faith*, a leading journal in the movement. Other black evangelical ministers in Pentecostalism included Charles Mason (1866–1961), founder of the Church of God in Christ (COGIC). The Great Migration, another signature event in the early 20th century, transformed African American evangelicalism. Black migrants brought religious traditions from the South and established Pentecostal congregations—the so-called "sanctified churches"—in locations such as Harlem, where people like Mother Rosa Horn, a Southern-born revivalist, led the Pentecostal Faith Church. Some ministers, including Mother Horn, broadcast sermon over the radio waves and distributed sermons and teachings on vinyl records, what religious studies scholar Lerone Martin calls "preaching on wax." During the Great Depression, black evangelical Christians such as Owen Whitfield offered a Pentecostal message to churches in Missouri, Arkansas, and Tennessee, and sometimes collaborated with white Christian allies like Claude Williams to emphasize a working-class gospel where authentic faith always translated into social action. Such action-oriented faith also inspired African American evangelical work in the Civil Rights Movement. Most readily exemplified by Martin Luther King, Jr., other black evangelical luminaries in the black freedom movement included individuals such as Mississippi activists Fannie Lou Hamer (1917–1977) and John M. Perkins (1930–), along with evangelist Tom Skinner (1942–1994). Hamer's political organizing and powerful songs, John Perkins's theologically inflected practice of localized community development, and Skinner's powerful preaching and writings demonstrated African American evangelical efforts toward fundamental social, religious, economic, and political change in U.S. society. In terms of education, the Southern Bible Institute, a once-segregated offshoot of Dallas Theological Seminary, began in 1927 but witnessed is largest growth in the mid to late 20th century. In Atlanta, Carver Bible College originated in the 1940s and grew steadily. Both institutions adopted evangelical teaching and promoted evangelical doctrines.

Educational Institutions Dedicated to Equipping Minorities

In spite of racial difficulties in America, evangelicals have educational ministries specifically dedicated to equipping minorities. For example, the mission statement of The College of Biblical Studies–Houston states: "The College of Biblical Studies–Houston provides biblically based education for the Body of Christ, with primary focus on African American and other ethnic minority groups, and equips its students with a biblical worldview for Christian service to the church and the world." Three of the most significant educational ministries are located in Texas:

The College of Biblical Studies in Houston
Rio Grande Bible Institute in Edinburg
Southern Bible Institute in Dallas

The post–World War II period and thereafter, compared to the rest of the 20th century, included monumental progress in American race relations and an increase in cross-racial evangelical fellowship and multiracial evangelical churches. Yet racial divides persisted, and economic and political conflict increased, which called for the continuation of black-led ministries to tackle societal injustices. Black parachurch organizations such as the National Black Evangelical Association (NBEA), founded in 1963, represented a coalition of black Christians who espoused conservative evangelical theology and attempted to strike a balance between doctrinal precision and justice-oriented social engagement. In addition, more recent developments within African American evangelicalism include the emergence of nationally recognized black megachurches such as Fred Price's Crenshaw Christian Center in California; Creflo Dollar's World Changers Church International in Atlanta; and Potter's House, T. D. Jakes's congregation in Dallas. Many of these churches adopt the prosperity gospel, another key aspect of African American evangelicalism, a series of teachings associated with neo-Pentecostalism that promotes self-realization, financial success, positive confession, positive thinking, divine healing, and financial success.

In contemporary times, numerous African American evangelical Christians have become leading commentators on social and cultural matters. Notable figures include Christena Cleveland, a social psychologist at Duke Divinity School and author of *Disunity in Christ* (2013); Brenda Salter McNeill, a pastor and professor at Seattle Pacific University and author of *Credible Witness* (2008) and *The Heart of Racial Justice* (2009); and former *Christianity Today* editor, essayist, and author Edward Gilbreath, whose 2006 book *Reconciliation Blues* chronicled white evangelicalism from a black perspective. His *Birmingham Revolution: Martin Luther King Jr.'s Epic Challenge to the Church* (2013) drew from the legacy of the black freedom struggle to advocate a renewed commitment to racial and economic justice. A growing number of black evangelicals have developed affiliations with traditions in Reformed Protestantism. This list includes political philosopher and Presbyterian Anthony Bradley, author of books on black masculinity, race and Christian higher education, and black popular culture; spoken word artist Propaganda, whose statements have spurred critical reassessments of long-cherished Puritan theologians and emphasized the practical outgrowth of intellectual theology; reformed rapper Shai Linne, whose records, such as *Lyrical Theology*, developed heady rhymes about Calvinism; and Caribbean minister Thabiti Anyabwile, who has published books on the history of black preachers and black liberation theology.

The broad history and diverse traditions represented within African American evangelicalism mark its history with a deep spirituality of survival and a body of teachings rich with theological reflection and social engagement. As a vital part of American religious history, African American evangelicalism reflects an enduring, prophetic presence into modern times.

Phillip Luke Sinitiere

See also: Civil Rights Movement, Evangelicals and; National Black Evangelical Association

Further Reading

The College of Biblical Studies. cbshouston.edu/mission.

Harvey, Paul. *Through the Storm, Through the Night: A History of African American Christianity.* Lanham, MD: Rowman & Littlefield, 2012.

Hawkins, J. Russell, and Phillip Luke Sinitiere, eds. *Christians and the Color Line: Race and Religion after* Divided by Faith. New York: Oxford University Press, 2013.

Hicks, Derek S. *Reclaiming Spirit in the Black Faith Tradition.* New York: Palgrave Macmillan, 2012.

Kidd, Colin. *The Forging of Races: Race and Scripture in the Protestant Atlantic World, 1600–2000.* Cambridge, UK: Cambridge University Press, 2006.

Martin, Lerone A. *Preaching on Wax: The Phonograph and the Shaping of Modern African American Religion.* New York: New York University Press, 2014.

Miller, Albert G. "The Construction of a Black Fundamentalist Worldview: The Role of Bible Schools." In *African Americans and the Bible: Sacred Texts and Social Textures*, edited by Vincent L. Wimbush (717–727). New York: Continuum, 2000.

Roll, Jarod, and Erik S. Gellman. *The Gospel of the Working Class: Labor's Southern Prophets in New Deal America.* Urbana, IL: University of Illinois Press, 2011.

AMERICAN SCIENTIFIC AFFILIATION

The American Scientific Affiliation was founded in 1941 to create an international professional organization fostering communication between those who are both scientists and Christians. Since its founding, it has taken a confident stance toward the natural sciences, currently stated as "a commitment to mainstream science, that is, any subject on which there is a clear scientific consensus." Notably, the leadership has distanced itself from "Creation Science" in its various forms, emphasizing rather a modern form of what has historically been known as the "two-book model" of knowledge: the book of special revelation (Scripture) and the book of general revelation (nature). Considerable alignment with most broadly accepted scientific theory is evident and utilized in publications for purposes ranging from "bridge building" to thoughtful natural resource stewardship consideration.

Its platform of faith ("Four Planks") noticeably omits terms such as "inerrancy" and "infallibility," instead using the phrase "divine inspiration, trustworthiness and authority of the Bible in matters of faith and conduct." And whereas some Christian organizations have apologetic agendas defending some aspect(s) of Christian belief, there is little of such an agenda—early on the ASA believed no single interpretation should be co-opted for scientific agenda, but rather that "there [be] a wide range of interpretation held among the membership. This is only natural and it is a very healthful situation." However, if one reads carefully the "The First Decade," one does sense a philosophical agenda, if not a scientific agenda, of "not getting in the way of science." Historical episodes of Galileo and Copernicus are given as example.

Current membership in the organization is about 2,000 and is open to anyone who holds a bachelor's degree in science and who agrees with its "Four Planks." Science is very broadly defined and includes history and mathematics. Membership is also open to philosophers and theologians.

Publications include the *Journal of the American Scientific Affiliation*, now published as *Perspectives on Science and Christian Faith*, and *God and Nature* (Web only). Affiliations include Christian Women in Science, Affiliation of Christian Geologists, Christian Engineers and Scientists in Technology, Christians in Science (UK), and the Canadian Scientific and Christian Affiliation. The organization illustrates the full spectrum of belief with respect to science and religion that is present in American evangelicalism.

Shawn Smith

See also: Creation Research Society; Science, Evangelicals and

Further Reading

American Scientific Affiliation. "Who Are We?" (n.d.). http://network.asa3.org/?page=ASA About-Who we are.
Everest, F. Alton. "The American Scientific Affiliation—The First Decade." *JASA* 3 (September 1951): 33–38. http://www.asa3.org/ASA/PSCF/1951/JASA9-51Everest.html.
Numbers, Ronald. *The Creationists: From Scientific Creationism to Intelligent Design*, expanded ed. Cambridge, MA: Harvard University Press, 2006.

ARIEL MINISTRIES

Ariel Ministries is a nonprofit organization that was founded by Arnold Fruchtenbaum (1943–) on December 1, 1977, in San Antonio, Texas. The main purpose of

Ariel Ministries is to "evangelize and disciple our Jewish brethren." Ariel Ministries holds to a dispensational theology and teaches the Scriptures from a Jewish perspective. The ministry currently has branches in the United States (San Antonio, Texas—home office, and Dallas/Fort Worth, Texas), Australia, Canada, Germany, Hungary, India, Israel, and New Zealand.

Fruchtenbaum was born on September 26, 1943, in Siberia, in the former Soviet Union. His paternal great-grandfather was a Hasidic leader in Poland at the start of World War II. In 1939, Arnold's father fled to the Soviet Union to avoid Nazi persecution, and there he met and married Arnold's mother. At the end of the war, the Fruchtenbaum family made their way west across Europe to New York.

In 1949, on their travel through Europe, a German Lutheran minister visited them. He was connected to the American Board of Missions to the Jews (ABMJ, now Chosen People Ministries) a Messianic Jewish ministry, which provided clothing and food packages to Jewish refugees. The minister informed them that when they arrived in New York, ABMJ could give them some assistance. Arnold's mother did not realize that this was a Messianic Jewish organization.

The Fruchtenbaum family arrived in New York City in 1951. In 1956, Fruchtenbaum's family was visited by Ruth Wardell from the American Board of Missions to the Jews. Arnold attended a meeting at this ministry, where there was a discussion about *Yeshua* (Jesus's Hebrew name) in the Old Testament. Fruchtenbaum had been taught that the Jewish people had their own Bible, the Tanakh, and the Gentiles had their Christian Bible, the New Testament. Ruth Wardell gave Fruchtenbaum a New Testament and asked him to see for himself whether *Yeshua* fulfilled the Messianic prophesies in the Old Testament. Fruchtenbaum became convinced that *Yeshua* had to be the Messiah of Israel, and he became a Christian.

Arnold Fruchtenbaum attended Shelton College in New Jersey and Cedarville College in Ohio, earning a BA in the biblical languages of Greek and Hebrew. In

Prominent Jewish Ministries

Within evangelicalism there are those who believe that God has a special plan for Israel (dispensationalists) and those who believe that the church has replaced Israel (covenant theology). But regardless of these two opposing views, there are a number of Jewish ministries that purposefully seek to evangelize, minister, and serve Jewish people, as Jesus Himself, or *Yeshua*, and the earliest formations of the church were decisively Jewish by identity and belief that Jesus is the predicted Messiah of Israel. These ministries include the following:

Ariel Ministries (1977)
Chosen People Ministries (1894)
The Friends of Israel Gospel Ministry (1938)
Jews for Jesus (1973)
Jewish Voice Ministries International (2001)

1966, he entered a Masters Program in Israel at The American Institute of Holy Land Studies. He next attended Dallas Theological Seminary while working for the American Board of Missions to the Jews, the very ministry where Arnold came to faith in the Messiah. In 1971, Arnold received a Master of Theology degree and moved to Israel, where he began a program to disciple new Jewish believers. His ministry grew, and in 1973 the Israeli government told him that they would not be renewing his visa. He returned to the United States, and in 1989 he received a PhD from New York University.

In 1977, Fruchtenbaum founded Ariel Ministries as a teaching ministry. A major work of the ministry is the 400-acre Camp Shoshanah located in the Adirondack Mountains, where he had attended a Bible camp for many years as a young man. Since 1973, there has been an intensive discipleship program every summer. In 2014, Ariel Ministries established a year-round teaching program at the camp. As a parachurch ministry, Ariel Ministries illustrates the long-standing relationship between evangelicals and interest in Jewish people (as well as the state of Israel) based on biblical and theological interpretations.

Jeffrey Gutterman

See also: Chosen People Ministries; Jews for Jesus; Messianic Judaism

Further Reading

Ariel Ministries. "A Brief History." (n.d.). ariel.org/ariel-history.htm.

Ariel, Yaakov. *Evangelizing the Chosen People: Missions to the Jews in America, 1880–2000.* Chapel Hill, NC: University of North Carolina Press, 2000.

Grace, L. Jesse. *Chosen Fruit: The Personal Life Story of Dr. Arnold G. Fruchtenbaum, Founder and President of Ariel Ministries.* San Antonio, TX: Ariel Ministries, 2015. http://www.ariel.org.

Wardell, Ruth, and Gutterman, Jeffrey. *Biography of "Ruth with the Truth" Wardell: Missionary to the Jewish People.* San Antonio, TX: Ariel Ministries, 2011.

ASSOCIATION FOR BIBLICAL HIGHER EDUCATION

The Association for Biblical Higher Education (ABHE) accredits credible, postsecondary institutions in North America whose courses of study center on programs in biblical studies and vocational ministry—historically known as Bible colleges or institutes. ABHE also provides professional development services, member reports, and software, and publishes the *Biblical Higher Education Journal*.

The Bible college and Bible institute movement of the late 1800s and early 1900s resulted in the formation of many Bible training institutions emphasizing vocational Christian service. In the 1930s, the Evangelical Teacher Training Association (ETTA) attempted to systematize training for Sunday school teachers through such Bible training institutions. This impulse toward systemization of educational standards

Prominent Evangelical Colleges and Universities

Biola University in La Mirada, California (1908)
Emmaus Bible College in Dubuque, Iowa (1941)
Grove City College, Grove City, Pennsylvania (1876)
Houston Baptist University in Houston, Texas (1960)
Liberty University in Lynchburg, Virginia (1971)
Moody Bible Institute in Chicago, Illinois (1886)
Oral Roberts University in Tulsa, Oklahoma (1965)
Regent University in Virginia Beach, Virginia (1977)
Union University in Jackson, Tennessee (1823)
Wheaton College in Wheaton, Illinois (1860)

culminated in the formation of the American Association of Bible Institutes and Bible Colleges (AABIBC) in 1947. The AABIBC was formed during the annual meeting of the National Association of Evangelicals (NAE) in Winona Lake, Indiana, to establish and implement educational standards for Bible colleges and institutes. This development corresponded with the increase in participation in postsecondary education and the formation of educational standards across higher education after World War II.

AABIBC was renamed the American Association of Bible Colleges (AABC) in 1957 and underwent additional name changes in 1973 and 1994. In 2004, it changed its name to the current Association for Biblical Higher Education (ABHE). The changes in the name of the organization reflect ongoing developments among Bible colleges and institutes—the expansion of curricula beyond vocational ministry programs, growing academic expectations and practices at such schools, and the broadening of the association's scope to include Canadian institutions. ABHE currently has around 150 members and 50 affiliate members out of an estimated total of more than 1,000 Bible training institutions in North America.

Joshua Michael

See also: Bible Institutes and Bible Colleges; Higher Education, Evangelicals and; National Association of Evangelicals

Further Reading

Ream, Todd. "Protestant Bible Institutes in the United States." In *International Handbook of Protestant Education*, edited by William Jeynes and David W. Robinson. Dordrecht: Springer, 2012.

Ringenberg, William C. *The Christian College: A History of Protestant Higher Education in America*, 2nd ed. Grand Rapids, MI: Baker Academic, 2006

ASSOCIATION OF CHRISTIAN SCHOOLS INTERNATIONAL

The Association of Christian Schools International (ACSI) is an evangelical organization for schools and education. It was founded in 1978 through a merger of three Christian school associations across the United States: The National Christian School Education Association, The Western Association of Christian Schools, and The Ohio Association of Christian Schools. In 1994, ACSI moved its international headquarters from La Habra, California, to Colorado Springs, Colorado. In addition to the international headquarters, ACSI uses regional offices located around the world.

ACSI is run by a president and a 36-member board, and these activities govern all of the organization's schools and publications. ACSI's mission is to enable Christian educators and schools worldwide to effectively prepare students for life, and they are recognized to offer school accreditation through the National Council for Private School Accreditation (NCPSA). The Department of Education does not recognize secondary educational accreditors. Additionally, ACSI publishes curriculum and other materials through Purposeful Design Publications and maintains several Christian education–related periodicals.

Regarding ACSI's significance for American evangelicalism, ACSI has advocated for a wide range of First Amendment–related legislations, especially those pertaining to Christian education curriculum, governance, educator professional legal liability assistance, government regulation, and financial assistance for private educational initiatives. Most notably, ACSI, in concert with a number of other Christian school representatives and students, sued the University of California system for maintaining what they believed to be "viewpoint discrimination" for unconstitutional policies and statements related to the evaluation of applicant qualifications. On October 12, 2010, *ACSI et al. v. Stearns et al.* was essentially ended after a partial summary judgment deemed the UC system's policies constitutional; the Ninth Circuit Court of Appeals affirmed the court's judgment; and the Supreme Court refused to review the case.

ACSI is a powerful organization for Christian education, with 24,000 schools across 100 countries around the world. In 2015, their total enrolled population was 5.5 million students.

Bryce Hantla

Further Reading

Association of Christian Schools International. "About ACSI." Teachers Transforming Nigeria 2017. Accessed May 27, 2015. http://acsinigeria.org/index.php/ACSI-Info/acsi-nigeria.html.

Association of Christian Schools International. "About ACSI and Membership." Accessed May 27, 2015. http://www.acsi.org/about-acsi-and-membership.

National Center for Science Education. "ACSI et al. v. Stearns et al." NCSE. April 25, 2009. http://ncse.com/creationism/legal/acsi-v-stearns.

AWANA CLUBS INTERNATIONAL

Awana is a global, nonprofit ministry with fully integrated evangelism and long-term Christian discipleship programs for children ages 2 to 18 that actively involve parents and church leaders. Each week, more than 2 million youth, 330,000 volunteers, and 260 field staff take part in Awana in more than 30,000 churches around the world. Offered through local churches, Awana seeks to minister to children in their own environment and encourage them in their faith journey.

Awana's founder was Lance Lathan (1894–1985), senior pastor of North Side Gospel Center in Chicago, Illinois. In 1941, Lathan collaborated with the church's youth pastor, Art Rorheim, to develop weekly clubs to appeal to both church and non-church youth, an idea considered innovative at the time. Other churches in the Chicago area soon learned about the effectiveness of the program, and in 1950 Latham and Rorheim founded Awana as a parachurch organization. The name Awana is an acrostic derived from the New Testament reference 2 Timothy 2:15 and the words "Approved Workmen Are Not Ashamed."

According to Awana's report, by 1960, 900 churches had started a program. By 1972, Awana began its first international club in Bolivia. Today, youth in 104 countries participate in Awana programs, and millions of adults are alumni. Awana serves churches from 100 different denominations and extends God's love to kids via orphanages, Christian schools, and a leper colony.

Globally, Awana gives young people from every cultural setting a place to belong, build confidence, and grow in their Christian faith. Awana continues to expand and make disciples by pursuing new locations and partnerships, including in prisons, refugee camps, slums, and other hard-to-reach places around the world. Under its current President and CEO Jack Eggar (since 1999), the global reach of Awana has grown rapidly, with a goal of reaching 10 million children with the gospel by 2020. Art Rorheim (1918–) continues to serve as the cofounder and president emeritus.

James Menzies

See also: Evangelism

Further Reading

Eggar, Jack D. *Great and Mighty Things: The Awana Vision for Equipping the Church to Reach Children and Youth for Christ.* Streamwood, IL: Awana Clubs International, 2004.
Rorheim, Art. *Mr. Awana.* Larkspur, CO: Grace Acres Press, 2010.

B

BAPTISTS AND EVANGELICALISM

The Baptist and evangelical families overlap, but there are Baptists who are not evangelicals, and many evangelicals who are not Baptist. And the degree of overlap depends on how one defines *evangelical*.

In a famous *Newsweek* cover story on "The Year of the Evangelical" (November 5, 1975), Southern Baptist ethics-agency head Foy Valentine placed his denomination squarely outside the evangelical camp. He was taking exception to *Christianity Today* editor Harold Lindsell's criticisms of President Jimmy Carter. Valentine declared in the article: "We are not evangelicals. That's a Yankee word. They want to claim us because we are big and successful and growing every year. But we have our own traditions, our own hymns and more students in our seminaries than they have in all of theirs put together. We don't share their politics or their fussy fundamentalism, and we don't want to get involved in their theological witch hunts" (p. 76).

Despite Valentine's protestations, a "conservative resurgence" was underway among Southern Baptists, one that replaced liberal seminary professors with avowed inerrantists and elected pro-life advocate Richard Land to succeed abortion-defender Valentine. In succeeding years, the denomination featured as platform speakers such Evangelicals as Evangelical Free Church pastor Charles Swindoll, Church of the Nazarene's James Dobson, and Presbyterian Dan Quayle.

There was some truth in suggesting that Southern Baptists (roughly equivalent in size to the other national Baptist bodies in America put together) drew from outside the camp, for their house publisher was not a resurgence enthusiast. When the 1970s *Broadman Bible Commentary* equivocated over the ravens' feeding Elijah in 1 Kings 17 and the ax head's floating in 1 Kings 19, publishing house William B. Eerdmans was there with a stronger affirmation in its *Keil & Delitzsch Commentary on the Old Testament*. And Zondervan, also of Grand Rapids, was the one to publish Harold Lindsell's *Battle for the Bible*, with a chapter taking elements of the Southern Baptist Church (SBC) to task.

Ironically, the Southern Baptists became a bastion of inerrancy while some of the formerly stalwart evangelical presses and institutions began to indulge roomier perspectives. A number of evangelical professors geographically from the north and west joined the faculties of Southern Baptist colleges and seminaries and continued their inerrantist scholarship and advocacy from new academic positions.

The core doctrinal statement of the Evangelical Theological Society says, "The Bible alone, and the Bible in its entirety, is the Word of God written and is therefore inerrant in the autographs. God is a Trinity, Father, Son, and Holy Spirit, each an uncreated person, one in essence, equal in power and glory." Baptists of several

Prominent Southern Baptist Seminaries

The Southern Baptist Convention operates six theological seminaries with the purpose to educate, equip, and train educators, missionaries, music leaders, and pastors in partnership with about 46,000 Southern Baptist churches, with the over-arching purpose being to faithfully live out the "Great Commission" in Matthew 28:18–20:

The Southern Baptist Theological Seminary (1859) in Louisville, Kentucky

Southwestern Baptist Theological Seminary (1909) in Fort Worth, Texas

New Orleans Baptist Seminary (1917) in New Orleans, Louisiana

Gateway Seminary of the Southern Baptist Convention (1944) in Ontario, California

The Southeastern Baptist Theological Seminary (1951) in Wake Forest, North Carolina

Midwestern Baptist Theological Seminary (1957) in Kansas City, Missouri

camps have signed this, some of them becoming president of the society: indeed, among the society's presidents have been David Howard of [Baptist General Conference] Bethel Seminary; Gerry Breshears of Western [Baptist Theological] Seminary; Gordon Lewis of Denver [Conservative Baptist] Seminary; and Bruce Ware, Craig Blaising, and John Sailhamer of Southern Baptist seminaries.

Corporately, Southern Baptists are not joiners; rather, they are averse to ecumenism. Thus they do not belong to the National Association of Evangelicals or the World Evangelical Alliance, though, of course, they agree with the heart of what these bodies affirm. Furthermore, they have broken ties with both the Baptist World Alliance and the Baptist Joint Committee on Public Affairs over differences in application. Nevertheless, individual Southern Baptist leaders are free to join the leadership of various evangelical parachurch groups. Southern Baptist Theological Seminary President R. Albert Mohler is a case in point, as he sits on the boards of Focus on the Family, The Gospel Coalition, and Together for the Gospel.

Nevertheless, Southern Baptists, as a denomination, are cobelligerents with a number of groups, even non-Evangelicals, depending on the cause. So it is not uncommon to find SBC leaders on panels with Catholics, Jews, Muslims, and even atheists when the cause is something like partial birth abortion or homosexual marriage. Also, the SBC Ethics and Religious Liberty Commission frequently files *amicus curiae* ("friend of the court") briefs with an intriguing range of co-belligerents. The Hobby Lobby case is an example, with the ERLC joining taking sides along with Missouri Synod Lutherans, Charles Colson's Prison Fellowship, and Liberty University, as well as a broad range of non-evangelical religious groups, including the Knights of Columbus, Mormons, the Rabbinical Council of North America, Krishna Consciousness, and Lukumi Babalu Aye (Santeria).

The American Baptist Churches, USA (formerly the Northern Baptists) are another matter. Since their split over slavery with Southern Baptists in 1845, they have been more susceptible to modernism and secularism and have seen a number of more conservative groups break away through the years, beginning with the Baptist Bible Union (later the General Association of Regular Baptists) in 1923, the Conservative Baptists in 1947 (from which split the Fundamentalist Baptist Fellowship in 1967), and Transformational Ministries (the former Pacific Southwest Association, encompassing Southern California, Nevada, Arizona, and Hawaii). This latest division came from concern that the denomination was slighting biblical authority in not enforcing its 1992 "American Baptist Resolution on Homosexuality" that "the practice of homosexuality is incompatible with Christian teaching." Indeed, the homosexuality-friendly Association of Welcoming and Affirming Baptists has found willing American Baptist congregations with which to identify.

As the Northern/American Baptists tacked left, leaving a train of more conservative breakaways in their wake, the Southern Baptists shed "moderates" and "liberals/progressives" who could not accept the renewed emphasis on biblical inerrancy in the denomination's agencies. Thus, the Alliance of Baptists formed in 1987, and the Cooperative Baptist Fellowship in 1991. Neither group applies the term *evangelical* to itself.

The 1990s saw similar Baptist conflicts in Europe. For years, "moderate" professors from SBC's American seminaries had finished teaching tours at a seminary in Ruschlikon, outside Zurich. There they served alongside professors of the European Baptist Union who were less than sympathetic to the inerrancy cause. Because Ruschlikon was significantly funded by the SBC Foreign Mission Board (now the International Mission Board), Southern Baptist conservatives were upset not only about theological influence but also about stewardship of mission monies. For instance, some were dismayed over the impact of casual approaches to the virgin birth taken by those who reasoned that the account appeared only in a single Gospel.

At the same time, conservative Southern Baptists resonated with the theology of a seminary founded by Second Baptist Church of Oradea, Romania. This school, now Emmanuel University, began as an underground Bible institute in the days of Communist ruler Nicolae Ceausescu, and allegiance to biblical inerrancy was central to its theology. With this sharp contrast before them, the Board defunded Ruschlikon, counting it less than fully evangelical.

Of course, Northern and Southern Baptists, and their offshoots, are not the whole story. A look back to the end of the 18th century reveals other diversities. Spurred by the missionary zeal of Englishman William Carey, who sailed for India in 1793, American Baptists established a Triennial Convention in 1814 for sending their own missionaries abroad. But some Baptists were never a part of this effort. The Primitive, or Hard-Shell, Baptists were ultra-Calvinist and minimized global missions, trusting God to save whom He would. Others, who came to be known as Landmarkers, were convinced that God's missionary plan rested in the historically-pedigreed local church and that denominations were not a proper New Testament entity. Continuing to this day, neither group has embraced the term *evangelical*, though they have preached the gospel of Christ crucified and risen to redeem sinners. On the other hand, Free Will Baptists, firmly non-Calvinist in perspective, are evangelical. The northern branch of this group merged with the Northern Baptist Convention, but the southern group is free-standing and evangelical.

In America, black Baptists are an interesting case. They typically embrace evangelical values, but they are less averse to cooperation with non-evangelicals than their Southern Baptist counterparts. A look at the member roll of the decidedly non-evangelical National Council of Churches (NCC) shows four black Baptist groups alongside the African Methodist Episcopal Church—the National Baptist Convention of America, the National Baptist Convention USA, the National Missionary Baptist Convention of America, and the Progressive National Baptist Convention.

Historically, this is understandable, as theological liberals were major participants in the American Civil Rights Movement, and many black Americans are leery of the politics of the Religious Right, often identified with evangelicalism. Still, gains in the homosexual agenda have revealed fault lines in the "mainline" churches, which predominate in the NCC, and within the NCC itself. For instance, the National Black Church Initiative, listing 34,000 member churches, cut ties with the Presbyterian Church, USA—an NCC stalwart from the beginning—over its accommodation of homosexuality. Similarly, supporters of the pro-traditional-marriage Proposition 8 in California were shocked at the number of black Christians who crossed accustomed political lines to vote for the measure. So in recent years, one has found a wide range of black Baptist leaders, from Jesse Jackson and Al Sharpton to more conservative pastors such as SBC president Fred Luter of New Orleans, Voddie Baucham of Houston, and E. V. Hill of Los Angeles. These latter three stand with other Baptist preachers whom evangelicals treasure, including John Bunyan, Charles Spurgeon, and Billy Graham.

Mark Coppenger

See also: The Battle for the Bible; Denominationalism and Evangelicalism; Evangelism; Graham, William F., Jr. ("Billy"); Inerrancy

Further Reading

American Baptist Churches USA. http://www.abc-usa.org/wp-contetn/uploads/2012/06/homsexuality1.pdf.

Chute, Anthony L., and Michael A. G. Haykin. *The Baptist Story: From English Sect to Global Movement*. Nashville, TN: B&H Academic, 2015.

Dockery, David. S. *Southern Baptists & American Evangelicals: The Story Continues*. Nashville, TN: Baptist Sunday School Board, 1994.

Dockery, David S., Ray Van Neste, and Jerry Tidwell, eds. *Southern Baptists, Evangelicals, and the Future of Denominationalism*. Nashville, TN: B&H Academic, 2011.

Evangelical Theological Society. "ETS Constitution." (n.d.). http://www.etsjets.org/about/constitution-A3.

Kidd, Thomas S., and Barry Hankins. *Baptists in America: A History*. New York: Oxford University Press, 2015.

THE BATTLE FOR THE BIBLE (1976)

The Battle for the Bible was a prominent book in the evangelical debate about the inspiration and inerrancy of the biblical text. In 1976, Harold Lindsell set off alarm bells in the evangelical world with *The Battle for the Bible*, defending biblical inerrancy. Lindsell took to task, in turn, individuals in the Lutheran Church—Missouri Synod, the Southern Baptist Convention (of which he was a member), Fuller Theological Seminary (where he once taught), and the Evangelical Theological Society (for which he'd served as president). Lindsell, with a PhD in history from New York University, appealed to Church history to help make his case.

Reaction to the book revealed a fault line. Among the enthusiasts were presidents Harold J. Ockenga (Gordon-Conwell Theological Seminary), John F. Walvoord (Dallas Theological Seminary), and Carl Armerding (Wheaton College). They were joined by Dallas pastor W. A. Criswell (former president of the SBC) and evangelist Billy Graham, who told *Time* magazine that the book was "one of the most important of our generation. Less charitable were presidents David Hubbard (Fuller Theological Seminary) and Duke K. McCall (Southern Baptist Theological Seminary). McCall dismissed Lindsell as one who "stirs up the snakes but kills none of them" with his "silly game with words." Nevertheless, the book helped launch the SBC's "conservative resurgence" in 1979 and helped stir the Evangelical Theological Society to expel, in 1982, a member who questioned an historical account in the gospels.

Carl F. H. Henry, also an inerrantist and Lindsell's predecessor as editor of *Christianity Today*, was concerned that the book would needlessly upset the evangelical unity for which he had strived. Some found Lindsell's painstaking effort to defend inerrancy (e.g., regarding the dimensions of a basin on the Jerusalem Temple grounds) pointless; others found it appropriate, persuasive, and divisive where it needed to be so. The volume brought to public awareness theological divisions within evangelicalism regarding beliefs about the inspiration and inerrancy of the Bible and helped set the stage for more than a decade of debate within American evangelicalism about the nature and authority of the biblical text.

Mark Coppenger

See also: Henry, Carl F. H.; International Council on Biblical Inerrancy; Theological Controversies within Evangelicalism

Further Reading

Dayton, Donald W. "The Battle for the Bible: Renewing the Inerrancy Debate," *Christian Century*, November 10, 1976, pp. 976–980. www.religion-online.org/showarticle.asp?title=1823.

Geisler, Norman L., ed. *Inerrancy*. Grand Rapids, MI: Zondervan, 1980.

Lindsell, Harold. *The Battle for the Bible*. Grand Rapids, MI: Zondervan, 1976.

Lindsell, Harold. *The Bible in the Balance*. Grand Rapids, MI: Zondervan, 1979.

BIBLE, AUTHORITY OF

The authority of the Bible is an essential doctrinal conviction within evangelical thought and life. Evangelicals readily affirm that Scripture alone serves as the rule, norm, and standard for all matters of faith and practice. They recognize, however, that the basis for Scripture authority is located in the nature of God and a firm belief in the verbal inspiration of the Scriptural texts. The Triune God, who is the transcendent Creator of all things, is entirely sovereign over all other authorities or powers. God alone has the right to rule over creation and judge creatures according to His purposes and will. Therefore, the Scriptures are the special verbal revelation given

---

Key Term in Evangelicalism: *Inspiration*

Inspiration is a term derived from the New Greek word *theopneustos*, meaning "God-breathed." Inspiration is used in theology to refer to the activity of the Holy Spirit whereby He actively guided human personalities and their individual styles to produce God's words in such a way that they are totally free from error, fully authoritative, and reliable in every way (e.g., matters of personal faith; geography; science) in their original writings (2 Timothy 3:16–17, 2 Peter 1:19–21, John 10:34–35, Matthew 5:17–18, 2 Peter 3:15–16). Evangelicals refer to this view of inspiration as *verbal*, that is, inspiration is extended to the very words of Scripture, and *plenary*, that is, to the whole of Scripture, namely, Genesis 1:1 to Revelation 22:20.

Key Term in Evangelicalism: *Translation theories*

One of the fundamental reasons why there are so many different translations of the Bible is due to the philosophies surrounding Bible translation: formal equivalence; dynamic equivalence; optimal equivalence. Some evangelicals believe that the Bible should be translated from the original Greek and Hebrew into contemporary languages, offering a word-for-word translation known as "formal equivalence." Formal equivalence seeks to be as transparent as possible with the original text (e.g., English Standard Version [ESV] and New American Standard Bible [NASB] translations). Others believe the Bible should be given a thought-for-thought translation ("dynamic or idiomatic equivalence"), granting greater accessibility to modern readers (e.g., New International Version [NIV] and New Living Translation [NLT] translations). Proponents of thought-for-thought seek to translate the meaning of a text in such a way that it makes the same impact on contemporary audiences as it made on its original readers. Optimal equivalence is a blending of both formal equivalence and dynamic equivalence by translating accurately from the earliest ancient manuscripts (employing formal equivalence) and offering the best of dynamic equivalence in order to make translation smooth and readable.

by God through select prophets and apostles in order to guide and instruct God's people concerning His divine will and desires. Given this conviction, Evangelicals simply affirm that what Scripture says, God says. Divine inspiration is the source of scriptural authority and every other doctrine that appeals to the Scriptures, for its basis depends on the assumption that all Scripture is given by God.

Evangelicals inherited a theology of Scripture handed down by the Protestant Reformers of the 16th century, who elevated the authority of Scripture over any ecclesiastical office or conciliar pronouncements. Although creeds and other statements of faith are helpful guides to understand Christian orthodoxy, they are always subservient to the authority of Scripture and open to revision based on clearer understanding and exposition of divine revelation. The same can be said for any other ecclesiastical or religious authority because evangelicals believe that the authority of Scripture derives from God, not from the church. So though the church confesses the authority of Scripture, Scripture's authority is intrinsic and not dependent on the confession of the church or any particular member. In this sense, the process of canonization in the church was not an attempt to impose authority on a set of documents, but a process of recognizing those texts that were already inspired and possess divine authority. At the same time, there have been other challenges to biblical authority based on personal religious experiences. Although evangelicals value spiritual experiences, no individual spiritual experiences supersede the authority of the Scripture. Instead, all religious experiences are judged in accordance with Scripture. The Bible as the Word of God offers the clear standards and criteria by which God judges people and the manner in which creatures can rightly approach a righteous God.

Evangelicals point to a number of biblical passages they believe are self-attesting references to the inspiration of Scripture, such as 2 Timothy 3:16 and 2 Peter 1:21. In both the Old and New Testaments, there are also various exhortations to obey the Word of God and diligently keep God's commands and instructions (Deuteronomy 4:5–6; James 1:22–25). Evangelicals contend that Jesus Christ and his apostles also expressed a high view of the authority of Scripture (Luke 24:25–27; John 5:45–47), and 2 Peter 3:15–16 even acknowledges the authority of the Pauline writings. Alongside this internal testimony of Scriptural authority, extra-biblical

Tyndale House, Cambridge

Tyndale House in Cambridge, England, is a donor-supported study center for scholars who seek to do biblical research on all aspects of the Bible. Tyndale not only houses one of the greatest collections for biblical research but also provides long-term accommodations for scholars. Their staff members are involved in lectures across the globe and also have a scholarly organization known as the Tyndale Fellowship and a leading research journal known as the *Tyndale Bulletin* (1956).

literature is sometimes used to corroborate particular aspects of the biblical text. These works, however, do not possess divine authority themselves and can only be used to corroborate the authority of the sacred Scriptures.

In the modern period, the rise of higher criticism has posited a significant challenge to the evangelical understanding of the authority of the Bible. Some streams of biblical scholarship have applied critical theories that call into question certain aspects of the historicity and reliability of the biblical texts. Evangelicals, however, continue to affirm the inspiration of Scripture and address these challenges with various apologetic arguments. Though there may be some apparent difficulty that is currently unexplainable, at some point the solution will become clear through further research, at least until the final consummation. Finally, evangelicals affirm that God, by means of the Holy Spirit, continues to use Scripture as the primary means to communicate His will and purposes to the church. Although the church carries out its ministry, it should routinely instruct the faithful in the Scripture and formulate its ministry based on Scripture. Evangelicals believe that the Scriptures alone are the final standard for all matters of faith and practice among evangelicals.

Stephen O. Presley

See also: The Battle for the Bible; Hermeneutics; Inerrancy; Theological Controversies within Evangelicalism

Further Reading

Carson, D. A., and John D. Woodbridge. *Scripture and Truth*. Grand Rapids, MI: Baker Academic, 1992.

Geisler, Norman L. *Inerrancy*. Grand Rapids, MI: Zondervan, 1980.

Packer, J. I. *God Has Spoken: Revelation and the Bible*. Grand Rapids, MI: Baker Academic, 1994.

Warfield, B. B. *Inspiration and Authority of the Bible*. Phillipsburg, NJ: P&R, 1980.

BIBLE CONFERENCE MOVEMENT

The Bible Conference Movement has been an interdenominational gathering of conservative evangelicals to study the Bible; it began in the 19th century in the United Kingdom and migrated to the United States after the American Civil War (1861–1865). Its influence affected evangelical approaches to studying the Bible up to the present. Its studies usually focused on Christian spirituality, missionary endeavors, doctrinal orthodoxy, and eschatology. These conferences played a key role in the development of fundamentalism and evangelicalism in North America. The conferences were organized and led by key conservative leaders across denominational lines. These conferences were thought to be the most significant influence leading to the development of the rise of the fundamentalist movement in the last quarter of the 19th century.

Significant Study Bibles

The first study Bible was the *Geneva Bible*, published in 1560, offering annotations, woodcut illustrations, maps, tables, and verse divisions. The *Scofield Study Bible*, originally published by Oxford University Press in 1909 with a cross-reference system, and published again in 1917 with extensive notes offering a dispensational understanding of the Scriptures, made a significant and historical impact on evangelicalism, with more than 2 million of the 1917 edition immediately sold. Other significant study Bibles include the *NIV (New International Version) Study Bible* (1985; transdenominational with evangelicalism), *MacArthur Study Bible* (2013; based on the teachings of popular Bible expositor John MacArthur), the *Reformation Study Bible* (1998; Reformed tradition), *Ryrie Study Bible* (1978; dispensational scholar from Dallas Theological Seminary), *Life in the Spirit Study Bible* (2003; Pentecostal/Charismatic), and *The Apologetics Study Bible* (2012; theme centered).

The American Bible Conference Movement began to emerge as early as the 1840s and continues to our present time. Believed to be a merger from earlier revival meetings and the influence of Plymouth Brethren "Bible readings" from Ireland, gatherings often began as private affairs that then allowed any interested person to attend. The gathering was for serious study of the Bible and fellowship, usually in a comfortable location and lasted for a week. The context was the post–Civil War Industrial Revolution, where a rising middle-class family could ride the train to these remote locations, usually on a lake or along a costal area. The annual conferences during summertime brought together well-known Bible teachers such as F. B. Meyer, G. Campbell Morgan, William G. Moorehead, James Hall Brookes, Cyrus I. Scofield, Nathaniel West, A. J. Gordon, Arno C. Gaebelein, William J. Eerdman, William B. Riley, A. T. Pierson, James M. Gray, George Needham, R. A. Torrey, and H. A. Ironside. The speakers often used the "Bible reading" approach to teaching, where they would follow key words from a concordance with only a few comments because they believed the Scriptures speak for themselves.

The most influential Bible conference was founded in 1875 and known as The Believers' Meeting for Bible Study, also known as the Niagara Conference, located at Niagara on the Lake, Ontario, Canada. The head of the Niagara Conference was the Saint Louis Presbyterian Pastor James Hall Brookes. Niagara became the model for most other conferences throughout the nation. Most conferences would start on a Wednesday evening and run through the following Tuesday night. On Sunday mornings, there would be a worship service and communion was served to those attending from a wide representation of Protestant denominations from North America. Each day would have two morning sessions, two afternoon sessions, and a single evening session. Because they were usually held at resorts, recreation would be mixed in during the times when no one was speaking.

The rise of theological liberalism in the United States parallels the rise of the Bible Conference Movement. As a result, James Brookes formulated a 14-point "Niagara Creed" in 1878. The creed spoke of the verbal inerrancy of Scripture, a Calvinist view of human depravity, salvation by grace through faith in the death of Christ, defended the personality and current work of the Holy Spirit in the lives of believers, the need for personal holiness, and the premillennial Second Coming of Christ, which was set against the dominate postmillennialism of the day. Controversy over the pretribulation rapture lead to the eventual decline of the conference and its last year was 1900 because of Hall's death in 1897 and declining attendance.

Later, toward the end of the 1800s, conservative mainline churches began holding Bible and prophecy conferences in their churches, mainly to promote dispensational premillennialism. The leaders of the Niagara Conference, in a desire to focus on Bible prophecy, helped to sponsor the first large Bible and Prophetic Conference that was held in 1878 at the Church of Holy Trinity (Episcopal) in New York City. The *New York Times* ran a special edition and printed all of the sermons from the conference. Conference speakers came from the following denominations: Presbyterian, Baptist, Episcopalian, Methodist, Congregationalist, and Dutch Reformed. Later, similar large conferences were held in Chicago, 1886; Allegheny, Pennsylvania, 1895; Boston, 1901; Chicago, 1914; and Philadelphia and New York, 1918. Virtually all the speakers at these large and impactful conferences were only dispensational premillennialists. It was through such exposure that dispensationalism was catapulted into the mainstream of fundamentalism and evangelicalism.

After World War I, it became common for conservative churches in America to sponsor a yearly Bible conference, often relating to Bible prophecy, but sometimes not. Such conferences appear to be dying out, but there are still many churches that have annual Bible conferences to focus on a particular biblical teaching.

The Bible Conference Movement has played a significant role in shaping conservative Christianity in America during the last 150 years. Bible conferences are seen as the catalyst for the founding of over a hundred Bible colleges and some seminaries. The dynamic of the Bible Conference Movement lead to an interdenominational interaction based on a common theology and has resulted in the foundation of many missionary societies and organizations and parachurch organizations.

Thomas D. Ice

See also: Bible Exposition; Dispensationalism; Eschatology; Premillennialism; Rapture

Further Reading

Beale, David O. *In Pursuit of Purity: American Fundamentalism since 1850.* Greenville, SC: Unusual Publications, 1986.

Bebbington, David W. *The Dominance of Evangelicalism: The Age of Spurgeon and Moody.* Downers Grove, IL: InterVarsity Press, 2005.

Marsden, George M. *Fundamentalism and American Culture*, 2nd ed. New York: Oxford University Press, 2006.

Pettegrew, Larry Dean. "The Historical and Theological Contributions of the Niagara Bible Conference to American Fundamentalism." ThD diss., Dallas Theological Seminary, 1976.

Sidwell, Mark. "Come Apart and Rest a While": The Origin of the Bible Conference Movement in America. *Detroit Baptist Seminary Journal* 15; 2010: 75–98.

BIBLE EXPOSITION

Bible Exposition is that field of study that seeks to determine the author's intended meaning of a biblical text and to communicate that meaning through expository preaching and teaching. Verse-by-verse Bible exposition and preaching have been hallmarks of evangelical teaching and preaching. To determine the author's intended meaning of a biblical text, an expositor uses the literal, grammatical, historical, cultural, literary system of hermeneutics. The literal approach means that each word has a plain, normal meaning while allowing for figurative language. The grammatical approach emphasizes the meaning of words (lexicology), the form of words (morphology), the function of words (parts of speech), and the relationships of words (syntax). The historical approach recognizes that each book of the Bible was written to a specific group of readers in a specific historical, geographical situation for a specific reason or purpose. The cultural approach takes into account the beliefs, languages, customs, and practices of the social groups mentioned in the Bible. The literary approach distinguishes the various genres of Scripture, understanding that the style and form of a passage influence how it is to be understood.

Having first determined the meaning of a biblical text, an expositor then seeks to communicate that meaning to an audience. This process is called expository preaching (or teaching). Expository preaching focuses on a specific text of Scripture and emphasizes its immediate context. Consequently, expository preachers routinely preach through entire books of Scripture rather than taking a topical approach to the Bible. Expository preaching is noted for its primary emphasis on the interpretation of a biblical text and secondary emphasis on the application of a biblical text.

Dallas Theological Seminary is the principal institution responsible for popularizing Bible exposition in the modern age. The seminary has a long history of producing graduates who practice Bible exposition in churches and schools throughout the world. These graduates have also produced a number of books advocating Bible exposition, most notably *Living by the Book* by Howard Hendricks and *Basic Bible Interpretation* by Roy Zuck. Dallas Theological Seminary is one of only a few institutions to offer a PhD in Bible Exposition.

Israel P. Loken

See also: Bible, Authority of; Dallas Theological Seminary; Hermeneutics

Further Reading

Hendricks, Howard G., and William L. Hendricks. *Living by the Book: The Art and Science of Reading the Bible.* Chicago: Moody Press, 2007.

Johnson, Elliott E. *Expository Hermeneutics: An Introduction*. Grand Rapids, MI: Zondervan, 1990.

Richard, Ramesh. *Preparing Expository Sermons: A Seven-Step Method for Biblical Preaching*. Grand Rapids, MI: Baker Books, 2001.

Robinson, Haddon W. *Biblical Preaching: The Development and Delivery of Expository Messages*, 3rd ed. Grand Rapids, MI: Baker Academic, 2014.

Zuck, Roy B. *Basic Bible Interpretation*. Colorado Springs, CO: David C. Cook, 1991.

BIBLE INSTITUTES AND BIBLE COLLEGES

Bible institutes and *Bible colleges* (sometimes referred to as Bible schools) are terms used to describe a particular kind of Protestant, evangelical educational institution in which, historically, the curriculum centered on the Bible, theology, and vocation ministry. Originating in the late 1800s, they occupied a distinct niche in American education and evangelicalism, though some of the original, unique characteristics of the movement have diminished. In contemporary usage, the term *Bible college* may refer to schools originating in that movement, current schools whose curriculum is built around the Bible, and/or Christian educational institutions outside the liberal arts tradition. *Bible institute* typically refers to such schools with one to two year courses of study only.

The impulse to establish such schools was precipitated by several factors. Religious motivations had longed played an important role in the founding of American educational institutions, dating from Colonial times. The period of renewed religious fervor and revivalism in the decades after the Civil War, sometimes known as the Third Great Awakening, was no different. Evangelists such as Dwight L. Moody (1837–1899) and A. B. Simpson (1843–1919) sought to mobilize Christians to participate in proclaiming the gospel and in practical ministry, particularly in urban areas. To this end, both established training institutes—Simpson established Nyack College in 1882 in New York City, and Moody established Moody Bible Institute in Chicago in 1889—where lay Christian church members could receive practical training in ministry, theology, and the Bible. Previous European antecedents included the Gossner Mission and the East London Missionary Training Institute, the latter of which was known to A. B. Simpson. Other institutes soon followed over the next few decades so that at least 40 Bible schools existed by 1920.

Students typically were non–high school graduates, past college age, who attended a Bible institute for one or two years and studied a limited curriculum centered on the English Bible. Women constituted a substantial portion of all students and were in the majority at some institutions. Emphasis was placed on Bible study, practical ministry, and personal spiritual growth. Students and faculty were expected to exhibit high standards of Christian conduct and spiritual-mindedness, and graduated with certificates or diplomas. Many of the early schools were small and struggled to survive more than a short time. For example, the Bethel Bible College in Topeka, Kansas, which was instrumental in the start of the Pentecostal movement lasted less than two years. A large number were operated out of churches and offered classes in the evening. Newer religious movements, such as the Holiness and Pentecostal movements, were particularly active in established training institutes.

The fundamentalist-modernist controversies of the 1920s provided additional impetus for evangelicals to establish new higher education institutions. Many evangelicals perceived that modernist ideas such as biological evolution were taking over existing secular educational institutions, and Christian seminaries were yielding to higher critical scholarship and liberal theology. This called into question secular education and the liberal arts model. For many evangelicals, the establishment of new schools that promoted Biblical authority and taught orthodox positions on these matters seemed required. Bible colleges in many cases assumed the roles of providing trained vocational ministers, which was a development beyond their original purposes, though fundamentalist seminaries were soon established as well.

Another factor in the development of Bible schools was dispensational premillennial eschatology. Premillennial beliefs became more widely known and accepted in the last decades of the 1800s through prophecy conferences such as the Niagara Bible Conference. Bible institutes proved an ideal fit for premillennial teachings. The emphasis on preaching the gospel in light of Christ's soon return meant that short, Bible-centered training was ideal for quickly producing Christians who were capable of proclaiming the gospel.

Related to this emphasis on the gospel was the growing belief that denominational boundaries interfered with the mission of proclaiming the gospel. Additionally, evangelicals in denominations that had grown more liberal found themselves sharing more in common with other fundamentalists than members of their own denomination. Most of the early Bible institutes were established as nondenominational schools. However, denominationally affiliated ones arose too among groups that withdrew from liberal denominations.

The growth in American education after World War II buoyed growth in Bible colleges and institutes as well. By 1960, nearly 250 such schools existed in the United States, with about half of them identifying themselves as Bible colleges. This reflected a common pattern in which Bible institutes expanded their programs and curricula and sought to enroll high school graduates, positioning themselves as a postsecondary educational option. Such changes precipitated a need for increased oversight and improved standards, which led to the formation of the Accrediting Association of Bible Institutes and Bible Colleges (AABIBC) in 1947 (now known as the Association for Biblical Higher Education—ABHE). This organization has served as the primary accreditation agency for Bible colleges and institutes since its founding.

By and large, these developments did not diminish the religious character of the schools. Students were expected to live according to strict codes of conduct and seek personal spiritual growth. The curriculum still focused on a degree in Biblical studies, and most graduates sought vocational ministry as pastors or missionaries. The contribution of these schools to Protestant missions in the 20th century was particularly noteworthy.

Today, there are more than 1,200 institutions in North America that can be classified as Bible colleges or institutes according to ABHE, the vast majority of which are unaccredited. The largest of these offer many degree programs and share more similarities with liberal arts universities than did their predecessors. Many more, however, remain modest in size and curricular scope, numbering a few hundred students or less. In particular, the unaccredited schools are typically very small and often associated with a single church or small network of churches. Recent trends in American higher education, including online education, diversifying student populations, and increased financial pressures, are affecting Bible colleges as well, resulting in the closure of some schools. Others have sought to leverage the online environment as a new platform for training Christian leaders.

Joshua Michael

See also: Association for Biblical Higher Education; Biola University; Higher Education, Evangelicals and; Moody, Dwight Lyman; Moody Bible Institute

Further Reading

Brereton, Virginia L. *Training God's Army: The American Bible School, 1880–1940.* Bloomington, IN: Indiana University Press, 1991.

McKinney, Larry J. *Equipping for Service: A Historical Account of the Bible College Movement in North America.* Fayetteville, AR: Accrediting Association of Bible Colleges and Institutes, 1997.

Ream, Todd. "Protestant Bible Institutes in the United States." In *International Handbook of Protestant Education*, edited by William Jeynes and David W. Robinson. Dordrecht: Springer, 2012.

BIBLE PRESBYTERIAN CHURCH

The new Presbyterian body that formed in 1936 from the fundamentalist–modernist conflict, ultimately known as the Orthodox Presbyterian Church (OPC), soon split into two factions: the OPC, focusing on classic Reformed theology and church life; the other, focusing on cultural battles (including abstention from alcohol) and premillennial theology (dispensationalism), that discerns the coming of Christ to be both necessary to save the world and imminent. The latter group, founded from division in 1938 as the Bible Presbyterian Church (BPC), was charismatically led by Carl McIntire and, like him, was fiercely pugnacious in its ethos and practice. It established its headquarters at McIntire's congregation in Collingswood, New Jersey.

The BPC established several agencies and edifices with grand purpose but diminishing existence as the parent body experienced further splits into ever-smaller pieces. These included the International Board of Presbyterian Foreign Missions, the American and the International Councils of Churches, two beach-front conference centers, Shelton College, Faith Theological Seminary, and a Florida retirement home. The second split took place in 1956 (dividing the BPC's 88 congregations), followed by others in later years as contentions traditionally turned outward toward liberals, compromising evangelicals, and Roman Catholics; and new Bible translations were turned inward as well. McIntire, exuding conviction, maintained leadership of the core continuing group until his death in 2002.

However, the BPC's enduring influence on church and culture has been significant. Francis Schaeffer, the first minister ordained by the BPC, became a missionary to Europe and later a well-known writer and filmmaker who analyzed philosophy, culture, and theology, then proposed intelligent Christian responses. Jay Adams, author of *Competent to Counsel*, became leader of the Nouthetic Counseling movement that challenged secular practices with Biblical principles. Although the theories and applications of both men brought controversy, they also changed the terms of thought and practice. Covenant College and Covenant Theological Seminary, both now of great strength and influence, were founded by the BPC before the 1956 split. Oliver Buswell, then president of Wheaton College, was a founding minister of the BPC. A prolifically popular Christian author, he later becoming first dean of Covenant College and of Covenant Theological Seminary. Both institutions left the BPC in the 1956 split, as did Adams, Buswell, and Schaeffer, with Schaeffer using the BPC as a negative model for his teachings urging love and unity within the church.

McIntire and the BPC engaged in strident anti-Communism, criticism of Supreme Court decisions, support rallies for the Vietnam conflict; and opposition to evolution, the National and the World Councils of Churches, and the United Nations. McIntire was a master of media, using pamphlets, *The Christian Beacon* newspaper, and radio talks—including a "pirate" radio station from a ship in international waters when the Federal Communications Commission shut down his radio station due to the "Fairness Doctrine"—to disseminate his strident messages. Leader of a small group becoming smaller, he yet succeeded, repeatedly, in claiming national attention.

With McIntire's life ended, and the BPC quieted to a group of 30 congregations, a heritage may be contemplated of meticulous doctrinal purity, and of personal power and pique, impossible to sustain. Yet the power of those Scriptural and doctrinal ideas that lay at the BPC's root grew some fruit that, despite all the turmoil of its planting and pruning, nurtured millions.

Mark A. Jumper

See also: Fundamentalism; Premillennialism; Reformed Tradition, Evangelicalism and; Schaeffer, Francis A. and Edith; Wheaton College

Further Reading

Bible Presbyterian Church. 2015. http://www.bpc.org

Dennison, Charles G. 1992. "Tragedy, Hope and Ambivalence: The History of the Orthodox Presbyterian Church 1936–1962." *Mid-America Journal of Theology* 8, no. 2: 147–59.

The Orthodox Presbyterian Church. 2017. http://opc.org/historian.html.

Ruotsila, Markku. 2012. "Carl McIntire and the Fundamentalist Origins of the Christian Right." *Church History* 81, no. 2: 378. *MasterFILE Premier*, EBSCOhost.

Sanderson, John W. 1976. "Buswell as Churchman." *Presbyterian* 2, no. 1–2: 109–130. *ATLA Religion Database with ATLASerials*, EBSCOhost.

BILLY GRAHAM EVANGELISTIC ASSOCIATION

The Billy Graham Evangelistic Association is a nonprofit organization that directs a range of domestic and international ministries, including Franklin Graham Festivals, Will Graham Celebrations, The Billy Graham Library, The Billy Graham Training Center at The Cove, SearchforJesus.net, the Billy Graham Rapid Response Team of crisis-trained chaplains, My Hope with Billy Graham television ministry, and others. Founded in 1950 by Billy Graham, the organization has been led by Franklin Graham since 2000. Formed in Minneapolis, Minnesota, the ministry employs more than 470 people worldwide and is headquartered in Charlotte, N.C., with additional offices in Australia, Canada, Germany and Great Britain.

At the mid-point of the 20th century, Billy Graham (1918–) was just months removed from the 1949 Greater Los Angeles Crusade that launched his ministry into national prominence. As a result of this sudden exposure, Graham was approached about beginning a nationwide Christian radio program. Though he dismissed the notion at first, he eventually agreed, if $25,000 could be raised in one night to begin the process of buying air time. That night in Portland, Oregon, the funds—an exceedingly large amount of money at the time—came in, and the radio program *Hour of Decision* was born.

In order to handle the unexpected influx of financial support for the ministry, Graham called George Wilson, his business manager at Northwestern Schools in Minneapolis, who immediately filed the paperwork to launch a nonprofit organization. Thus, in 1950, BGEA was formed for the purposes of broadcasting the Gospel of Jesus Christ. Over the next six decades, the ministry served as the organizational backbone of Graham's evangelistic outreaches and Crusades, as he preached to nearly 215 million people in live audiences across 185 countries and territories.

Hour of Decision

The Billy Graham Evangelistic Association (BGEA), famous for *Hour of Decision*, a weekly live half-hour radio broadcast hosted by Cliff Barrows (1923–2016), has sought to utilize media and technology in expansive, global ways, ranging from minute broadcasts, messages from his historic crusades available online, TV broadcasts, movies, and even online training. The association states that from their movies alone more than 2 million people have made personal decisions, receiving salvation from Jesus Christ.

Pluralism versus Exclusivity

Religious pluralism is the view that at some level every religion is true, offering a genuine and adequate point of contact with the Ultimate or true God (e.g., John B. Cobb (1925–); John Hick (1922–2012); Paul F. Knitter (1939–). In contrast, evangelicals embrace exclusivism, claiming that they only believe what Jesus Christ has claimed is true for salvation because they believe He is the Son of God (John 3:16) who came to redeem people from their sins as predicted in the Hebrew Scriptures in passages such as Isaiah 52:13–53:12.

At a time when many Christians were wary of motion pictures, Graham embraced movies as a method for sharing the Gospel, releasing the film *Mr. Texas* in 1951 and officially establishing World Wide Pictures (WWP) in 1952 as the motion picture division of BGEA. Over the next 55 years, WWP would produce and distribute more than 130 films, including many full-length movies.

In 1957, the ministry of the BGEA hit primetime television during the historic New York City Crusade in Madison Square Garden. For the first time, Graham's messages were broadcast live across the country on national television, giving ABC its highest ratings up to that point.

Graham also saw the value in books and magazines. He released six books in the first decade of BGEA and was part of founding the Christian publication *Christianity Today* in 1956. In 1960, Graham published the first issue of BGEA's *Decision* magazine, which has grown into a widely read Christian periodical with a circulation of some 400,000 today. Over the course of his ministry, Graham has written 32 books.

In 1985, the ministry first used satellites to broadcast meetings throughout Great Britain from Sheffield, England. In 1989, the Crusade in London was broadcast live to 250 locations across the United Kingdom and nearly 300 locations across Africa. In 1991, the strategy was expanded in Central and South America, as a Crusade in Buenos Aires was transmitted via satellite and video into 20 Spanish-speaking countries.

In 1996, BGEA launched the ministry's flagship Web site, www.BillyGraham.org. The site quickly became a portal to offer ministry updates and spiritual guidance. Today, hundreds of thousands visit the site every month. BGEA's Internet Evangelism ministry today has seen more than 4 million make commitments to Jesus Christ online.

One item that consistently concerned Graham was equipping today's evangelists in the developing world while developing the next generation of evangelists. To that end, the ministry held three massive conferences in Amsterdam's sprawling RAI Center, widely known as Amsterdam 83, Amsterdam 86, and Amsterdam 2000. These events, each officially titled the International Conference for Itinerant Evangelists, brought together thousands of evangelists from hundreds of countries for training and encouragement.

In 2000, Graham's son Franklin was named CEO of BGEA, and in 2001 he was named president of the organization. BGEA officially relocated to Billy Graham's hometown of Charlotte, N.C., in 2003, and the Billy Graham Library, designed to be an ongoing crusade, opened in 2007 on the same property.

In November 2013, more than 110,000 people made commitments to Jesus Christ through My Hope with Billy Graham, an evangelism effort of more than 26,000 churches in the United States and Canada that culminated with the broadcast of Billy Graham's video message, *The Cross*, in homes, churches and online across the two nations.

James Menzies

See also: Evangelism; Graham, William F., Jr. ("Billy"); Mass Media, Evangelicals and

Further Reading

Graham, Billy. *Just As I Am: The Autobiography of Billy Graham*. New York: HarperCollins, 2007.

"History." Billy Graham Evangelistic Association. (n.d.). Accessed April 21, 2017. https://billygraham.org/news/media-resources/electronic-press-kit/bgea-history/.

Rosell, Garth M. *The Surprising Work of God: Harold John Ockenga, Billy Graham, and the Rebirth of Evangelicalism*. Grand Rapids, MI: Baker Academic, 2008.

Wacker, Grant. *America's Pastor: Billy Graham and the Shaping of a Nation*. Cambridge, MA: Harvard University Press, 2014.

BIOLA UNIVERSITY

Biola University is a private, evangelical university located in La Mirada, California. Founded in 1908 in downtown Los Angeles, the Bible Institute of Los Angeles (BIOLA) was initially a small school offering a two-year curriculum focused on Bible and missions. In recognition of its broader liberal arts curriculum, the school changed its name in 1949 to Biola College. In 1952, the first graduate school, Talbot Theological Seminary (now Talbot School of Theology), was launched. The college moved from downtown Los Angeles to La Mirada, California, in 1959 and was renamed Biola University in 1981.

Biola University is known among evangelical colleges and universities as a theologically conservative institution. From 1910–1915, Biola's founders played a key role in publishing *The Fundamentals: A Testimony to the Truth* (commonly referred to as *The Fundamentals*). Today the school retains its conservative theological stance as exemplified in its adherence to the doctrine of Biblical inerrancy. In light of its desire to maintain fidelity to its conservative theology, the university requires every faculty member to sign a statement acknowledging agreement with the school's doctrinal position. The school is not tied to any particular Christian tradition. The majority of students come from nondenominational, Baptist, and Presbyterian churches.

The University is composed of six schools (Arts and Sciences, Business, Education, Intercultural Studies, Psychology, Theology) and offers more than 150 academic programs at the undergraduate, master's and doctoral level. In 1995, Biola launched the Torrey Honors Institute, an undergraduate honors program patterned after Oxford's tutorial system. In 2012, the Biola University Center for Christian Thought (CCT) was formed. CCT is a research center aimed at gathering top Christian scholars from around the world for research and publication. In 2013, the Biola University Center for Christianity, Culture and the Arts (CCCA) was formed for the purpose of fostering thoughtful engagement with the culture and the arts from an evangelical vantage point. In addition to these initiatives, the university is involved in the publication of four academic journals in the fields of philosophy, psychology, theology, and education.

These initiatives indicate the university's desire to fund an intellectually satisfying and culturally engaged form of evangelicalism while remaining true to historic commitments for a Bible-centered education that instills in its students a value for missionary work; these last two commitments being exemplified in the requirement that all undergraduates complete a minor in Bible and the school's annual missions conference, the largest annual student-run missions conference in the world.

Robert S. Covolo

See also: Bible Institutes and Bible Colleges; Higher Education, Evangelicals and; Talbot School of Theology

Further Reading

Draney, Daniel. *When Streams Diverge: The Origins of Protestant Fundamentalism in Los Angeles*. Eugene, OR: Wipf & Stock, 2008.

Marsden, George M. *Fundamentalism and American Culture: The Shaping of Twentieth Century Evangelicalism*. Oxford: Oxford University Press, 2006.

Williams, Robert. *Charted for His Glory: Biola University 1908–1983*. La Mirada, CA: Associated Students of Biola University, 1983.

BOICE, JAMES MONTGOMERY (1938–2000)

James Montgomery Boice (1938–2000) was a prominent Reformed theologian, Bible teacher, and successful inner city pastor of Tenth Presbyterian Church in Philadelphia from 1968 until his death in 2000. He was a well-known author and speaker in evangelical and Reformed circles. His messages continue to be heard on The Bible Study Hour radio broadcast.

Boice published more than 50 books, including a collection of hymns, served as Chairman of the International Council on Biblical Inerrancy for more than 10 years, and was a founding member of the Alliance of Confessing Evangelicals.

He received a diploma from The Stony Brook School (1956), a BA from Harvard University (1960), a BD from Princeton Theological Seminary (1963), a ThD from the University of Basel in Switzerland (1966), and a DD (honorary) from the Theological Seminary of the Reformed Episcopal Church (1982).

Dr. Boice was also a prodigious world traveler. He journeyed to more than 30 countries and taught the Bible in such countries as England, France, Canada, Japan, Australia, Guatemala, Korea, and Saudi Arabia. He lived in Switzerland for three years while pursuing his doctoral studies.

Boice once shared in a sermon that when he was a seminary student at Princeton in 1960, his father called to tell him about the sudden death of Donald Grey Barnhouse, then pastor of Tenth Church and Boice's pulpit hero. Boice related how, when he heard the news, he fell to his knees in his room and prayed for God to give him double the portion of Elijah if he was to take up the mantle of so great a man as Barnhouse.

When Boice assumed the pastorate of Tenth Church, there were 350 people in attendance. At his death a little more than 30 years later, the church had grown to a regular Sunday attendance in three services of more than 1,200 persons, and a total membership of 1,150 persons and became a model for ministry in America's northeastern inner cities. Under his leadership, the church established a preschool for children ages 3–5; a high school known as City Center Academy; a full range of adult fellowship groups and classes; and specialized outreach ministries to international students, women with crisis pregnancies, HIV-positive clients, and the homeless.

As an author, Boice wrote nearly 40 books on a number of Bible-related themes. Most of his books are expositional commentaries taken from his preaching. Title include *Psalms* (1 volume), *Romans* (4 volumes), *Genesis* (3 volumes), *Daniel, The Minor Prophets* (2 volumes), *The Sermon on the Mount, John* (5 volumes, reissued in one), *Ephesians, Philippians*, and *The Epistles of John*. Other popular volumes include *Hearing God When You Hurt, Mind Renewal in a Mindless Christian Life, Standing on the Rock, The Parables of Jesus, The Christ of Christmas, The Christ of the Open Tomb*, and *Christ's Call to Discipleship*. Boice also authored a 740-page theology for laypersons entitled, *Foundations of the Christian Faith*. Many of his books have been translated into other languages, such as French, Spanish, German, Japanese, Chinese, and Korean.

In 1974, Boice founded the Philadelphia Conference on Reformed Theology (PCRT). At the time, critics insisted that no one wanted to hear Reformed theology teaching, much less pay to attend such a conference. Nevertheless, the PCRT grew, with more than 2,000 people attending in 2010, and spurred a host of larger conferences such as the annual Ligonier Conference and the more recent Together for the Gospel.

For 10 years Dr. Boice served as Chairman of the International Council on Biblical Inerrancy, from its founding in 1977 until the completion of its work in 1988. ICBI produced three classic, creedal documents: "The Chicago Statement on Biblical Inerrancy," "The Chicago Statement on Biblical Hermeneutics," and "The Chicago Statement on the Application of the Bible to Contemporary Issues." The organization published many books, held regional "Authority of Scripture" seminars across the country, and sponsored the large lay Congress on the Bible I, which met in

Washington, D.C., in September 1987. Boice also served on the Board of Bible Study Fellowship.

Boice founded the Alliance of Confessing Evangelicals in 1994, initially a group of pastors and theologians who were focused on bringing a new reformation to the then 20th-century church. In 1996, the group published a document entitled "The Cambridge Declaration."

In 1996, Boice brought *The Bible Study Hour; God's Word Today* magazine; Philadelphia Conference of Reformation Theology, and other Bible teaching ministries under the auspices of the Alliance of Confessing Evangelicals, which also includes the *White Horse Inn* broadcast and *Modern Reformation* magazine, both founded by Michael Horton.

Boice died of liver cancer on June 15, 2000, at age 61. Two hours after receiving his diagnosis (on Good Friday) he delivered a sermon on the crucifixion of Jesus Christ. Several weeks later, Boice informed his congregation of his condition and asked, "If God does something in your life, would you change it? If you'd change it, you'd make it worse. It wouldn't be as good." His favorite benediction was said to have been from Romans 11:36: "For from him and through him and to him are all things." Boice was married to Linda Ann (McNamara) Boice, who continued to teach at the high school they cofounded following his death.

James Menzies

See also: Reformed Tradition, Evangelicalism and; Tenth Presbyterian Church

Further Reading

Boice, James Montgomery. "The Future of Reformed Theology." In *Reformed Theology in America: A History of Its Modern Development*, edited by David F. Wells. Grand Rapids, MI: Eerdmans, 2009.

Boice, James Montgomery, and Dennis T. Lane. *Whatever Happened to the Gospel of Grace? Rediscovering the Doctrines That Shook the World.* Wheaton, IL: Crossway, 2009.

Ryken, Philip Graham. *Ecclesiastes: Why Everything Matters.* Wheaton, IL: Crossway, 2009.

BRIGHT, WILLIAM R. ("BILL") (1921–2003)

William R. ("Bill") Bright (1921–2003) has been listed among the top influential evangelical leaders of the late 20th century. He was an American evangelist and founder of Campus Crusade for Christ (now Cru), a ministry to college students at the University of California. Bright authored *The Four Spiritual* gospel booklet (1952) and produced the evangelically based *Jesus Film* (1979). Bright was awarded the $1.1 million Templeton Prize for Progress in Religion in 1996 and donated the money to promote fasting and prayer.

Bill Bright was born in Coweta, Oklahoma. His mother had miscarried her last child, so when she became pregnant with Bill, she made a commitment to God. If God would allow the child to be born healthy, she would commit him to whatever service the Lord had in mind. In one sense, Bill Bright was called to the ministry before he was even born.

Bright graduated from Northeastern State University in Tahlequah, Oklahoma, with an Economics degree. As a student at Northeastern State University, he was initiated into the Zeta chapter of Sigma Tau Gamma fraternity and has subsequently been granted honorable alumni status to Alpha Gamma Omega Christ-Centered Fraternity. In his early 20s, he moved to Los Angeles and founded a company called Bright's California Confections.

Bright became a Christian in 1944, while attending the First Presbyterian Church, Hollywood, where he met Henrietta Mears, a wealthy and influential leader in the church. Mears taught a Sunday school class that was to become the greatest influence of Bright's theology and methodology. Mears believed in the inerrancy of the Scriptures but would invite liberal German theologians to her home to teach Bible studies. Mears wanted to expose her students to the most current scholarship available even if she did not agree with what was being taught.

Henrietta Mears was most concerned with winning people to Christ. Her Bible teaching was called lengthy but entertaining, and Bright encountered a Christianity he had never conceived of before: influential people attending hour-long Bible studies and striving to live for Christ. All this had a profound impact on Bright. In 1945, less than a year after moving to Los Angeles, he was converted under Mears's teaching. Mears continued to disciple Bright in her home.

Bright later attended Princeton and Fuller Theological Seminaries, though he never completed a degree at either. While a student at Fuller, he felt the call of God to help fulfill Christ's Great Commission (Matthew 28:19), beginning with students at University of California, Los Angeles (UCLA). This gave birth to Campus Crusade for Christ.

During the decades to follow, Bright and his wife, Vonette, remained faithful to the work, and the ministry expanded. In 2011, CCC reported 25,000 missionaries in 191 countries. Bright held five honorary doctorate degrees: a Doctor of Laws from the Jeonbuk National University of Korea, a Doctor of Divinity from

---

Key Term in Evangelicalism: *Saved*

The word *saved* is a popular, causal term for *salvation*. For evangelicals, salvation refers to God's deliverance of those who believe from spiritual death to spiritual life, from condemnation to declared righteousness, from separation unto the family of God, and a bestowal of numerous positional benefits at the moment of salvation and forevermore. Evangelicals historically believe that no one can be good enough to earn salvation by doing good deeds. Rather, salvation occurs when one receives the free gift of salvation by personally placing one's trust in Jesus Christ, believing that Jesus is the Son of God who died on the cross for one's sins and who rose bodily from the dead (John 3:16; Acts 16:31; Romans 5:8–10).

John Brown University, a Doctor of Letters from Houghton Seminary, a Doctor of Divinity from the Los Angeles Bible College and Seminary, and a Doctor of Laws from Pepperdine University. In 1983, he chaired the National Committee for the National Year of the Bible. Bright wrote more than 100 books and booklets, and thousands of articles and pamphlets distributed in most major languages by the millions.

Bright was a cofounder of the Alliance Defense Fund, which funds high-profile litigation cases on behalf of Christians' First Amendment rights, and he was also a cosignatory of the "Land" letter of 2002, outlining a just war rationale for the 2003 invasion of Iraq by President George W. Bush.

Bright's production the *Jesus Film* was released by Warner Brothers but was not a financial success, losing approximately $2 million. In 1988, Bright led a protest against the Martin Scorsese film *The Last Temptation of Christ*, offering to purchase the film's negative from Universal in order to destroy it.

Bright is perhaps best known for his *The Four Spiritual Laws*, a booklet that outlines four essentials of Christian salvation. CCC reports that more than 100 million copies have been distributed in all of the major languages of the world. The booklet summarizes four spiritual laws, with appropriate verses illustrating each. The four spiritual laws are as follows:

1. God loves you and offers a wonderful plan for your life.
2. Man is sinful and separated from God and cannot know God's love and plan for his life.
3. Jesus Christ is God's only provision for man's sin. Through Him you can know and experience God's love and plan for your life.
4. Each one of us must receive Jesus as Savior and Lord; then we can know and experience God's love and plan for our lives.

In 2001, Bright stepped down as leader of CCC, and Steve Douglass became president. Bill Bright died in 2003 after several years battling pulmonary fibrosis. More than 5,000 people attended the formal memorial service. He was survived by his wife, Vonette, sons Zachary and Brad, and four grandchildren.

James Menzies

See also: Cru (formerly Campus Crusade for Christ International); Evangelism

Further Reading

Bright, Bill. *Abundant Living: Who You Are in Christ*. Peachtree City, GA: NewLife, 2004.

Fleming, Travis. "An Analysis of Bill Bright's Theology and Methodology of Evangelism and Discipleship." PhD diss., The Southern Baptist Theological Seminary, 2006.

Richardson, Michael. *Amazing Faith: The Authorized Biography of Bill Bright, Founder of Campus Crusade for Christ*. Colorado Springs, CO: WaterBrook Press, 2001.

Turner, John G. *Bill Bright & Campus Crusade for Christ: The Renewal of Evangelicalism in Postwar America*. Chapel Hill, NC: The University of North Carolina Press, 2008.

BSF INTERNATIONAL

BSF International, formerly Bible Study Fellowship, is a nondenominational parachurch organization founded in 1952 by British-born Audrey Wetherell Johnson (1907–1984). Johnson had previously served as a missionary to China for 17 years. In 1942, when Japan invaded China, she and other missionaries were sent to a Japanese internment camp (Longhua Prison) until her release and deportation to England in 1945. She returned to China in 1948 to teach in the China Bible Seminary, but the Communist takeover by Mao Tse-tung forced this institution to close, and Johnson left China for California in 1950. Visiting friends in America before her intended return to England, she was a popular speaker on missions and her experiences in China.

In 1952, after speaking at a church service in San Bernardino, Johnson was approached by five ladies who requested a study of the New Testament book of Colossians. Out of this opportunity grew the fourfold methodology that would characterize BSF's curriculum: personal and prayerful Bible study without additional aids, and answering study questions; sharing and listening to answers in a group context; hearing a lesson taught by a Teaching Leader; and reviewing lesson notes. Johnson taught women and trained leaders for about six years, then moved to the Bay Area in 1958, having been invited to begin her brand of Bible studies there, to help follow up with converts from the Billy Graham Crusade that year. Johnson moved to Oakland and officially incorporated BSF in 1959–1960 with the help of her friend Alverda Hertzler. BSF's ministry expanded when Hertzler became convinced of the need to teach preschoolers and, with the help of Doreen Shaw and Martie Johnson, developed a three-year curriculum in 1963. Further, in 1966 BSF began offering men's classes under the leadership of Dr. Bob Stevens. Later, classes for young adults were added, as Johnson became interested in the work of Dr. Francis A. Schaeffer at L'Abri Fellowship.

From Southern California, BSF International spread across the nation, and today has chapters in more than 30 countries, with classes for women, children, men, and young adults. Its interests have always been to help people study the Bible individually and to advance the gospel globally; indeed, Johnson has referred to BSF as "ecumenical." BSF adheres to a conservative Evangelical doctrinal position, including the verbal plenary inspiration and inerrancy of the Scriptures, virgin birth of Christ, original sin, vicarious atonement, exclusivity of belief in Christ for salvation, and bodily return of Christ. It is currently headquartered in San Antonio, Texas. It is a significant parachurch ministry that seeks to encourage study of the Bible regardless of one's denomination or affiliation.

Stefana Dan Laing

See also: Bible, Authority of; L'Abri Fellowship; Schaeffer, Francis A. and Edith; Women's Ministries

Further Reading

Johnson, A. Wetherell. *Created for Commitment: The Remarkable Story of the Founder of the Bible Study Fellowship.* Carol Stream, IL: Tyndale House, 1982.

Lewis, Gregg, and Debra Shaw. *True to His Word: The Story of Bible Study Fellowship.* Colorado Springs, CO: Biblica, 2010.

C

CALVARY CHAPEL (COSTA MESA, CALIFORNIA)

Calvary Chapel is the founding church of an international network of evangelical congregations. In 1965, Calvary Chapel of Costa Mesa, California, was a church of 25 people. As of 2015, there are more than 1,600 local independent churches throughout the United States and worldwide that can trace their roots to the same Calvary Chapel of Costa Mesa. The founder of this movement was Charles ("Chuck") Smith (1927–2013). The church and network grew through Smith's efforts and those of some key individuals—Greg Laurie, Skip Heitzig, Mike MacIntosh, Don McClure, and Raul Ries.

Calvary Chapel began under the ministry of Chuck Smith. Smith was raised and ordained in the Four Square Gospel denomination. He served as pastor in various churches for about 17 years before he was asked to lead a small church, Calvary Chapel. Although the church was declining, growth came when Smith changed his preaching from topical to verse-by-verse expository sermons. He taught through every book of the Bible. Growth also came as his church began to minister to the "hippie" counterculture generation of the 1960s. Calvary Chapel Costa Mesa was transformed from a church of 25 to a church of thousands. The church focused on worship, fellowship, and biblical exposition.

Theologically conservative, Calvary Chapels affirm biblical inspiration, young earth creationism, a future nation of Israel, substitutionary atonement, the resurrection of Jesus, gifts of the Holy Spirit following conversion, and a pretribulational and premillennial return of Jesus.

Calvary Chapels experienced rapid growth while Smith was pastor. He was visionary, committed to teaching the Bible, and also relational with individuals. Smith invested time and energy in the lives of individuals, with a view to enabling them to start similar churches with the name of Calvary Chapel. One of the second-generation leaders was Greg Laurie (1952–), founder and pastor of Harvest Christian Fellowship (Riverside, California), with a church membership of about 15,000. Laurie is also the founder of the evangelistic Harvest Crusades, which has had an audience of more than 4 million. Another second-generation leader is Raul Ries, who was the founder and pastor of Calvary Chapel Golden Springs (California), with an attendance of 12,000. Ries is heard on more than 350 radio stations around the country. A few other significant second-generation Calvary Chapel leaders are Skip Heitzip, founder and pastor of Calvary Chapel Albuquerque (New Mexico), with an attendance of more than 15,000; Mike MacIntosh, founder and pastor (until 2015) of Horizon Christian Fellowship (California); and Don McClure, founding pastor Calvary Chapel Lake Arrowhead (California) and Calvary Chapel Redlands (California). McClure has also assisted in planting eight Calvary Chapels in the San Jose, California, region and founded Calvary Chapel Bible College (Murrieta, California).

Calvary Chapels are an example of the enormous growth of evangelicalism in the postwar era and of the willingness of evangelicals to address social, cultural, and countercultural ideas from a theologically conservative perspective. By so doing, Calvary Chapel has influenced American Christianity for the past 50 years.

David A. McGee

See also: Bible Exposition; Counterculture, Evangelicals and; Smith, Charles W. ("Chuck")

Further Reading

Bustraan, Richard. *The Jesus People Movement: A Story of Spiritual Revolution among the Hippies.* Eugene, OR: Pickwick, 2014.

"Calvary Chapel History." Calvary Chapel. (n.d.). Accessed October 13, 2015. http://calvarychapel.com/about/calvary-chapel-history/view/calvary-chapel-history.

Eskridge, Larry. *God's Forever Family: The Jesus People Movement in America.* New York: Oxford University Press, 2013.

Smith, Chuck, and Tal Brooke. *Harvest.* Costa Mesa, CA: The Word for Today, 2010.

Smith, Chuck, and Chuck Smith Jr. *Chuck Smith: A Memoir of Grace.* Costa Mesa, CA: The Word for Today, 2009.

CALVINISM

Calvinism is a widely held theological system with American evangelicalism. Rooted in the Swiss Reformation during the 16th century, grounded in the teachings of Ulrich Zwingli (1484–1531), and systematized by John Calvin (1509–1564), a biblical theologian, Calvinism is a theological system that centers on the Scriptures and emphasizes the sovereignty, goodness, glory, and unmerited grace of the one and only infinite and perfect Triune God. Although sometimes used synonymously with Presbyterianism, Calvinism is most often used to refer to a broader theological system and even a worldview, whereas Presbyterianism refers to a specific ecclesiological structure or church government. A worldview is the big picture that directs one's daily actions and behavior; it is the sum total of one's beliefs about this world, and consequently, a certain way of seeing and doing. Until John Calvin, no other Protestant Reformer predecessor systematized, that is, brought together in an orderly arrangement, the doctrines of Scripture. A doctrine is simply what the Bible teaches about a particular topic. Thus, Calvin brought the topics of the Bible together into an orderly arrangement that has continued to influence evangelicalism and beyond to this very day.

Best understood in view of Martin Luther's (1483–1546) ongoing reformation in Germany, Calvinism views salvation as the work of a sovereign God who is the sole agent of redemption and recipient of glory. The sovereignty of God establishes the basis not only for humanity's understanding of the world but also how the individual is to function in relationship to God. Luther primarily emphasized the doctrine of justification and the means through which people are granted salvation. In contrast, Calvinism began with the principle of God's sovereign nature and his commitment to self-revelation.

While Luther's Reformation was calling into question the practice of indulgences and the position of priests and Pope's as mediators of grace, Ulrich Zwingli went a step further by advocating the rule of Scripture and using it as the authoritative guide for the church's doctrine and practice. Zwingli, along with Heinrich Bullinger (1504–1575) and Johannes Oecolampadius (1482–1531), rejected the Catholic Church's incorporation of saintly worship in church liturgy, the doctrine of purgatory, and the invocation of the saints in prayer. However, Zwingli was unable to unite with Luther's German Reformation due in part to a sharp disagreement over the presence of Christ within the Eucharist. Consequently, Luther and Zwingli's movements would remain linked and yet ultimately distinct.

John Calvin continued Zwingli's work as a second-generation reformer and maintained his commitment to Scripture as the rule for faith and practice. For Calvin, true knowledge of God results in worship, affection, and devotion to him. As evidenced by the completion of the first draft of his *Institutes of Christian Religion* (1536), Calvin called the Christian church to reorient its practice around the glory of God and the pursuit of divine knowledge. This pursuit of God is made possible only by God and is the highest form of wisdom, the noblest of pursuits, and the chief end to which humanity was created. Calvin would have a profound influence on Switzerland, specifically within Geneva, where he would spend much of his time in ministry.

Calvin rejected the medieval practice of biblical interpretation, which permitted the allegorization, moralization, and spiritualization of the Scriptures, in favor of taking the Scriptures in their plain, normal, literal, and historical sense. In essence, Calvin, who was a biblical theologian, trained in grammatical-historical exegesis following his legal studies, embodied and emphasized one of the central truths of the Protestant Reformation, namely, *sola Scriptura*, that is, Scripture only. For all Christians, he believed that the Bible was to be the final and ultimate authority for both religious belief and practice.

Calvin also championed the one and only Triune God, namely, the Father, Son, and Holy Spirit, equal in power and glory, in One Person, sovereign over all. Sovereignty, for Calvin, meant that God, who is all self-sufficient, absolute, and independent from all things, is the personal Creator and sustainer of all things, possessing infinite and perfect power, righteousness, goodness, and holiness. Thus, all things work toward His perfect plan, purpose, and will; God's goals are never frustrated.

Calvin also emphasized a view of humanity that declares that every human person is created in God's image, possessing intrinsic value. Even though humanity's first parents, namely, Adam and Eve, possessed holiness, true knowledge,

---

Key Term in Evangelicalism: *Open theology*

Open theology, also known as open theism, is a controversial view in and beyond evangelicalism. Akin to process theology, but finding expression in Wesleyan theology, it presupposes the view that people are truly free. If God knows all things actual and potential, then people cannot be truly free. But because God loves people and earnestly desires that humans freely choose Him, His knowledge of the future is conditional on the decisions people make. God may know all things that are, but the future is yet to be. But He actively works with and responds to people as they forge the future. Passages discussed about this view include Genesis 6:6; 22:12; Exodus 32:14; Jonah 3:10; and Amos.

---

and righteousness, they also received a free will, which enabled them to choose to obey or disobey God. Tempted by the serpent, which is Satan, Adam and Eve freely chose disobedience against God, thus totally or completely corrupting their nature and all their future posterity—though the image of God and inherent value remains within.

The concept of grace is also foundational to John Calvin. Grace is an unmerited, underserved free gift to humanity. Although creation has been corrupted by the fall and humanity is totally depraved, God sustains and enables humanity's continued existence through common grace. But this grace is not salvific. The human will is free, but only in accordance with its inherently depraved constitution. People are therefore fundamentally incapable of choosing God and are powerless to save themselves. The solution must be found in God. In His gracious act of salvation, He serves as the sovereign and sole agent of redemption. He chooses to give saving grace to some, those He has predestined to receive it. The work of Jesus Christ on the cross is efficacious, removing the guilt and punishment of sin while also obtaining salvation for the elect. As a gift from a sovereign and omnipotent God, this grace is irresistible and persistent. All who have been chosen for salvation will receive it, and those who have been saved will persevere, remaining faithful until the end.

The Reformed teachings of John Calvin, consequently known and further delineated and developed into what is known as Calvinism, would continue to spread throughout Western Europe and the United States over the course of the subsequent centuries. From the Puritans in the Massachusetts Bay Colony and the teachings of Jonathan Edwards (1703–1758), America's first premier theologian, to Charles Hodge (1797–1878) and B.B. Warfield (1851–1921), both of Princeton Theological Seminary, and later John Gresham Machen (1881–1937), to the controversy of modern liberalism, which sought to adapt theological and religious ideas to contemporary thought and culture, to the establishment of Westminster Theological Seminary (1929), Calvinism has made a profound impact on Christianity across the world. Reformed churches are united around their belief in a sovereign

God who graciously interacts on behalf of His people to provide them with salvation. Present in Congregational, Presbyterian, Reformed, and Independent churches to this day, Calvinism continues to have a strong presence that transcends both denominational lines and certain evangelical theological systems such as Covenant theology and dispensationalism.

In essence, Calvinists uphold the beliefs that God is ultimately incomprehensible and that any attempts to define Him will ultimately prove futile. Affirming the centrality of the Scriptures and revelation, they also affirm that God wills to be known by His creatures, and He works to reveal His character and nature to them. From the Second Helvetic Confession (1562) to the Second Synod of Dort (1618) and the crafting of the Westminster Confession of Faith (1646), Calvinism has also emphasized the sovereignty of God and His gracious work of redemption. God is understood to be the sole agent of creation and redemption, condescending to reveal Himself to and redeem His creatures. Calvinists affirm that God created the world out of His inscrutable will and is completely self-sufficient, sovereignly ruling over a created world whose continued existence is dependent upon His divine will.

The Second Synod of Dort of 1618 attempted to resolve the emerging conflict among the Reformed community as the followers of Jacobus Arminius (1560–1609) challenged the theology of the Belgic Confession. Specifically focusing on the freedom of the human will, the Synod of Dort responded by clearly articulating five theological tenets of Calvinism: total depravity, unconditional election, limited atonement, irresistible grace, and perseverance of the saints. Although frequently communicated as five separate points of Calvinism, these points are best understood as an exposition of the Calvinist understanding of saving grace—though Calvinists today may not agree with all five tenets (e.g., Moderate Calvinists, who may embrace some but not all five points of Calvinism).

Although Calvinists emphasize theological study and a comprehensive understanding of the Scriptures, their goal is a biblically coherent worldview. For them, theological reflection and orthodoxy is to lead to orthopraxy. In other words, for Calvinists, the goal of Christian thought, life, and practice is godly living to the glory of God with a spirit of gratitude for the underserved favor that has been given to them by a good and sovereign God.

Daniel Hill

See also: Dallas Theological Seminary; Dispensationalism; Fourth Presbyterian Church; International Council on Biblical Inerrancy; Reformed Tradition, Evangelicalism and; Westminster Theological Seminary

Further Reading

Boice, James Montgomery, and Philip Graham Ryken. *The Doctrines of Grace: Rediscovering the Evangelical Gospel.* Wheaton, IL: Crossway, 2009.

Calvin, John. *Institutes of the Christian Religion*, edited by John T. McNeil; translated by Ford Lewis Battles. 2 vols. Philadelphia: Westminster Press, 1960.

Hansen, Collin. *Young, Restless, Reformed: A Journalist's Journey with the New Calvinists.* Wheaton, IL: Crossway, 2008.

Hart, D. G. *Calvinism: A History.* New Haven, CT: Yale University Press, 2013.

Kuyper, Abraham. *Lectures on Calvinism: The Stone Lectures of 1989.* Peabody, MA: Hendrickson, 2008.

McNeil, John T. *The History and Character of Calvinism.* Oxford: Oxford University Press, 1954.

CARNELL, EDWARD JOHN (1919–1967)

Edward J. Carnell (1919–1967) was a leading Christian theologian, apologist, and seminary president during the 1950s and 1960s. He authored nine books that had a profound impact on the nascent neo-evangelical movement in America.

Carnell was born June 28, 1919, at Antigo, Wisconsin, into the home of Herbert Carnell and Fannie Carstens. His father, a fundamentalist Baptist pastor, had migrated from England to America to study at Moody Bible Institute. Young Carnell's strict upbringing and his father's emphasis on avoiding temptation and separating from activities deemed to be sinful caused him to struggle with guilt much of his adult life.

In 1937, Carnell enrolled at Wheaton College, a respected Christian liberal arts college outside of Chicago, Illinois. His academic interests were awakened under the tutelage of Gordon H. Clark (1902–1985), his professor of philosophy. A staunch Calvinist and apologist, Clark instilled in young Carnell the importance of thinking logically.

Carnell was graduated with a BA in 1941and applied for admission to Westminster Theological Seminary (Philadelphia, Pennsylvania), an independent Presbyterian school founded in 1929 to be an alternative to the more liberal Princeton Seminary. At Westminster, Carnell studied under J. Gresham Machen (1881–1937), the famed Greek and New Testament scholar and under Cornelius Van Til (1895–1987), a renowned apologist. He earned the ThB and ThM degrees in 1944.

Carnell then matriculated simultaneously into Harvard Divinity School and Boston University, where he worked on ThD and PhD degrees, respectively. He successfully completed both programs in 1948.

While at Harvard, he was introduced to the writings of Reinhold Niebuhr (1892–1971), an American theologian and ethicist, whose book *The Nature and Destiny of Man* was ranked one of the top 20 nonfiction books of the 20th century. Carnell became a Niebuhr scholar and wrote his dissertation on the existentialism of Niebuhr in light of biblical revelation. D. Elton Trueblood (1900–1984), the Harvard chaplain, also impacted Carnell's intellectual development. From Trueblood, he adopted the verification approach to apologetics, which included forming a hypothesis and then testing it against logic, empiricism, and existentialism. At Boston University, Carnell studied under Edgar Sheffield Brightman (1884–1953), philosopher and theologian, from whom he embraced rational empiricism.

While working on his degrees, Carnell somehow found time to teach philosophy and apologetics at Gordon Divinity School in the neighboring town of Wenham, Massachusetts. He was dynamic and youthful, and the students loved him.

During this time, he also submitted a manuscript to Eerdmans that was accepted and published under the title *An Introduction to Christian Apologetics*. It won the Evangelical Book Award for 1948, which included a first-place prize of $5,000. With book and doctorates in hand from two prestigious schools, the 29-year-old scholar was acclaimed the most brilliant young apologist and theologian on the American religion scene.

Carnell was invited to join the faculty of Fuller Theological Seminary (Pasadena, California), which had opened its doors in 1947. The founders—Charles E. Fuller (1887–1968), a well-known evangelist, radio preacher, and wealthy orange grower from Southern California, and Harold Ockenga (1905–1985), the pastor of famed Park Street Church in Boston, Massachusetts—envisioned the school to be rigorously academic like Princeton, thoroughly orthodox like Westminster, but without an emphasis on separation from the world. Fuller graduates were trained to converse articulately with liberal theologians and secular thinkers, and to engage the culture. Carnell seemed like a perfect fit.

From 1948–1954, Carnell taught philosophy and apologetics. He was the most popular classroom teacher on campus. He authored several more books that established him as the leading evangelical theologian in America.

Carnell became known mainly for a new method of apologetics, which he called "critical realism." He started with the hypothesis that God exists. As a hypothesis, this had to be put to the test and either verified or falsified. First, it had to pass the test of reason, especially the Law of Contradiction. Every belief must be logical. Second, it had to pass the test of empirical adequacy. Evidence must confirm every truth claim. Third, the hypothesis had to pass the test of existential vitality. It must offer a sense of satisfaction. Every hypothesis had to pass the test of systematic consistency in order to be true.

Carnell believed Fuller Seminary needed an on-campus president. Harold Ockenga had served for six years as president in absentia and travelled occasionally from his church in Boston to Los Angeles to attend Board meetings. Otherwise, he was disengaged. Carnell lobbied to be president. In 1954, the Trustees inaugurated Carnell as the new president, a position he held until 1959. Under his leadership, Fuller grew in numbers and gained accreditation from the Association of Theological Schools, the first evangelical seminary ever to receive this status. Despite his many successes, Carnell soon discovered he loathed administration. He no longer had time to teach, write, read, or stay abreast of the latest scholarship. He could no longer satisfy his one passion—classroom teaching. Gradually he began to experience angst and insomnia. Before long he was fighting bouts with clinical depression. He turned to sleeping pills and barbiturates for relief.

In 1960, Carnell resigned the presidency and returned to teaching but found himself far behind the academic curve. His effectiveness in the classroom had waned. He tried to regain his scholarly edge but experienced loss of memory. His depression worsened, and he submitted to electric shock treatments. They were not successful.

On April 25, 1967, Carnell was scheduled to speak at a theology conference but failed to appear on the dais at the appointed hour. He was found dead in his hotel room of a barbiturate overdose. Although Edward John Carnell's career ended on a sad note, he influenced a future generation of apologists, including Francis Schaeffer, Os Guinness, Gordon Lewis, and Ronald Nash.

R. Alan Streett

See also: Christian Apologetics; Clark, Gordon Haddon; Fuller, Charles E.; Fuller Theological Seminary; L'Abri Fellowship; Neo-Evangelicalism; Schaeffer, Francis A. and Edith

Further Reading

Carnell, Edward J. *An Introduction to Christian Apologetics.* Grand Rapids, MI: Eerdmans, 1948.
Carnell, Edward J. *The Case for Orthodox Theology.* Philadelphia: Westminster, 1959.
Marsden, George M. *Reforming Fundamentalism: Fuller Seminary and the New Evangelicalism.* Grand Rapids, MI: Eerdmans, 1987.
Nelson, Rudolf. *The Making and Unmasking of an Evangelical Mind: The Case of Edward Carnell.* New York: Cambridge University Press, 1987.

CENTER FOR BIOETHICS AND HUMAN DIGNITY

The Center for Bioethics and Human Dignity (CBHD) was founded by Dr. Nigel M. de S. Cameron (1994) and sponsored in part and hosted by Trinity International University in Deerfield, Illinois. Evangelical theologian Harold O. J. Brown (1933–2007) and several legal and medical professionals as well as other scholars interested in bioethics worked with Cameron the prior year to launch the Center in conjunction with its first summer conference *The Christian Stake in Bioethics*.

During the early 1990s, the rapid expansion of possibilities in biotechnology, significant progress, and promises caused some academic and religious leaders to lament that religious and philosophical questions were not being addressed. They believed that bioethics had emerged with a distinctively secular perspective, and it was from this concern that the Center for Bioethics and Human Dignity was formed not only to offer a voice in the greater marketplace of ideas, ethics, and science but also to speak to American Christianity.

In addition to Web-published resources, audio-cast case studies, extensive bibliographies, and a bioethics podcast, physical resources include a 1,000-volume bioethics research library. The Center's significant production in two decades includes the quarterly journal *Dignitas*, an annual summer conference, 40 events or major speaking engagements, and 50 regional and six international conferences. Along with numerous ongoing, research programs, CBHD aspires to provide an extensive book series in publication either directly by or indirectly through partnerships and collaboration. The Center for Bioethics and Human Dignity offers an evangelical, scholarly voice that addresses issues of ethics, humanity, and potential consequences that can bring about both the best and worst in humanity.

Shawn Smith

See also: Abortion, Evangelicals and; American Scientific Affiliation; Christian Apologetics; Ethics, Evangelical Theories of; Philosophy, Evangelicals and; Science, Evangelicals and

Further Reading

Demy, Timothy J., and Gary P. Stewart, eds. *Genetic Engineering: A Christian Response.* Grand Rapids, MI: Kregel, 1999.

Foreman, Mark W. *Christianity & Bioethics: Confronting Clinical Issues.* Eugene, OR: Wipf & Stock, 2011.

Michael J. Sleasman. "Bioethics in Transition." *Dignitas* 21, no. 4 (Summer 2014).

Mitchell, Ben C. *Christian Bioethics: A Guide for Pastors, Health Care Professionals, and Families.* Nashville, TN: B&H, 2014.

CHAFER, LEWIS SPERRY (1871–1952)

Lewis Sperry Chafer (1871–1952) was the founder of Dallas Theological Seminary and a prominent 20th-century Bible teacher. He was born into the home of a pastor, Thomas Franklin Chafer, a graduate of the Auburn Theological Seminary and ordained Presbyterian cleric, though he served in several Congregational churches as well as two years (1870–1872) on the south/central Kansas prairie as a church planter. The home established by Thomas and Lomira was graced with three children, Lewis being the youngest. It appears to have been a stable, loving home filled with musical interests, although it was pierced with the health struggles that Thomas experienced. His career ended in his untimely death in 1882, a victim of tuberculosis, about the time of his son's spiritual awakening.

Financially insecure, Lomira kept her family together by teaching in Rock Creek, Ohio, the town of her upbringing and the location of Thomas's second parish; Thomas and Lomira were separated by that time, and he was in Kansas, where he labored apart from the family in the hope that the prairie would prove beneficial to his health. Later, Lomira moved to New Lyme, Ohio, as the children finished their elementary education, so they could attend the New Lyme Institute, a college preparatory school. When his siblings entered college, Lewis entered the preparatory school of Oberlin College, Oberlin, Ohio, in 1888 before entering the Conservatory of Music the following year studying harmony, voice, and piano (1889–1890 and the spring of 1891). Financial exigencies brought a conclusion to his college studies. However, he was later granted two honorary doctorates: one from Wheaton College, Wheaton, Illinois (1928), and the other from the Free Protestant Theological Seminary at Aix-en-Provence, France (1946).

In the early 1890s, Chafer labored in evangelistic meetings with several evangelists, principally Arthur T. Reed, as a baritone soloist and general worker. He sought additional music training at the Moody Bible Institute but found the educational level unhelpful. He did, however, make important connections in the evangelical music world, meeting Ira D. Sankey, George Stebbins, and George Root, among others. To supplement his meager income, he taught numerous music classes, organized the Chicago Minuette Club, and later served as business manager of the Ithaca (New York) Conservatory of Music.

In 1896, he married Ella Lorraine Case, having met her at Oberlin College and sharing mutual interests in Christian ministry. The two formed an evangelistic team, Lewis increasingly assuming the role of preaching, Ella playing the organ, and the two singing duets (Lewis was a baritone and Ella a contralto); their venue was a variety of churches. To provide some financial stability, they also served an assistantship in Painesville, Ohio, and in 1899 joined the staff of the Congregational Church, Buffalo, New York. This allowed them to combine itinerant ministry with local church ministry. It is in this context that he was formally ordained to the Congregational ministry in 1900 in the Franklin Association (Buffalo).

For yet unknown reasons, Chafer's widening circle of influence brought him to Northfield, Massachusetts, in 1901, where he purchased a home and farm, continued to itinerate in the fall and spring, and attended the annual conferences (Ella became the conference organist). Meeting prominent leaders and teachers through the Northfield Conferences only deepened his circle of friends and colleagues. However, in the fall of 1901, he attended the Northfield Training School and heard its director, C. I. Scofield, also pastor of the Northfield Trinitarian Congregational Church. The two connected and became intimates for the remaining years of Scofield's life; as well, Chafer became as Scofield's successor in the Bible conference/Bible training movement. He later wrote of hearing Scofield, "Until that time I had never heard a real Bible teacher." Scofield left Northfield to return to Dallas, Texas, in 1902; the Scofield reference Bible consumed his interests, and the Chafers continued at Northfield, teaching in the Mount Hermon School for Boys and itinerating (increasingly with Scofield). Reflective of liberal trends in his denomination, Chafer transferred his ministerial credentials to the Northern Presbyterian Church in 1906 and later to the Southern Presbyterian Church in 1912, holding credentials in the Dallas Presbytery at the time of his death.

Scofield later settled in Douglaston, New York, a New York City suburb, and that brought Chafer's increasingly uneasy Northfield connection to a conclusion. Moving to the New York area—to Orange, New Jersey—in 1915, Chafer assisted Scofield in the founding of the New York Night School of the Bible, having helped his mentor to establish the Philadelphia School of the Bible in 1913, where he served on the early faculty and created the initial curriculum. In succeeding years, the two often traveled together in conference ministry, Chafer emphasizing the spiritual life and Scofield eschatology. As Scofield's health declined, Chafer became more prominent.

Significant Dispensational Evangelicals

1. Lewis Sperry Chafer
2. John Nelson Darby
3. Arnold G. Fruchtenbaum
4. Elliott E. Johnson
5. Tommy D. Ice
6. H. A. Ironside
7. Tim LaHaye
8. Robert P. Lightner
9. John MacArthur
10. J. Dwight Pentecost
11. J. Randall Price
12. Charles C. Ryrie
13. C. I. Scofield
14. Robert L. Thomas
15. John F. Walvoord

His growing connection with Scofield brought a shift away from evangelistic ministry, though the passion for evangelism did not wane. Chafer was teaching both in an increasing number of conference opportunities (beginning in 1910, he directed the annual Southland Bible Conference in Florida) and in the classroom. The emphasis of his teaching seemed to focus on two themes: the spiritual life and eschatology from the perspective of a dispensational approach to Scripture reading. While teaching music at Northfield, he published *Elementary Outline Studies in the Science of Music*, edited *Northfield Seminary Songs*, and wrote several musical scores in *Selected Hymns for Music*. The movement from a musical career became evident in his later publications: *Satan* (1909) and *True Evangelism* (1911), Scofield writing the introduction to these volumes. *The Kingdom in History and Prophecy* (1915) was dedicated to his mentor, followed by *Salvation* (1917), *He That Is Spiritual* (1918), *Grace* (1922), and *Major Bible Themes* (1926). In 1947, he published an eight-volume systematic theology, the culmination of his classroom teaching.

In 1922, Chafer moved to Dallas, Texas, where he pastored Scofield's former church (1923–1926) and was appointed as General Secretary of the Central American Mission (1923–1925), a mission founded in 1890 under the direction of Scofield. He also served on the General Council of the mission from 1922–1930 and edited the mission's journal.

It is in this context that Chafer became the visionary for the founding of the Evangelical Theological College in 1924 (now the Dallas Theological Seminary). Despairing of educational weakness in the Bible training schools and disappointed by the liberal trends in the historic, mainline seminaries, his dream evolved from his travels in the second decade of the century. With no existent graduate school with a strong emphasis on the Bible itself for ministerial and missionary preparation, as well as no distinctly premillennial, dispensational institution, the Evangelical Theological College opened its doors, with its 13th student in a rented property, in October 1924. Chafer was appointed president of the fledging institution and remained in that post until his death in 1952. In June 1935, he endured a heart attack and four months later a ruptured appendix, restricting his work for two years. In 1945, Chafer suffered a second stroke and his health declined thereafter, likely a result of years of overwork, enormous stress, and the loss of his wife, Ella Lorraine Case Chafer, the previous year. With his weakening condition, John F. Walvoord, then professor of systematic theology, assumed many of the administrative responsibilities of the seminary and would eventually be Chafer's choice to lead the school.

John D. Hannah

See also: Dallas Theological Seminary; Dispensationalism; Higher Education, Evangelicals and; Walvoord, John F.

Further Reading

Hannah, John D. *The Uncommon Union: Dallas Theological Seminary and American Evangelicalism.* Grand Rapids, MI: Zondervan, 2009.

Marsden, George M. *Fundamentalism and American Culture, 1870–1925*, 2nd ed. New York: Oxford University Press, 2006.

CHICAGO DECLARATION OF EVANGELICAL SOCIAL CONCERN (1973)

The Chicago Declaration of Evangelical Social Concern is a 1973 confession and declaration of unified understanding on the issues of social justice. In the larger world of evangelicalism, the declaration sought to highlight and strengthen evangelical commitment to social issues. During Thanksgiving weekend in 1973, a group of evangelical scholars, theologians, and activists came together at Calvin College in Grand Rapids, Michigan, for a conference related to politics. Forty evangelicals gathered, including Carl F. H. Henry, Frank E. Gaebelein, Jim Wallis, John Perkins, Sharon Gallagher, Richard J. Mouw and Ron Sider. These men and women represented an array of traditions and theological viewpoints within evangelicalism. Their concern about the lack of social action among evangelicals made them determined to overlook their differences and unite for a cause. Their collaborative efforts resulted in the declaration.

The group's open dialogue resulted in a manifesto that addressed common beliefs and failures regarding economic justice, peacemaking, racial reconciliation, and gender concerns within the framework of the biblical narrative. As the weekend concluded, these men and woman wrote and signed the Chicago Declaration of Evangelical Social Concern. They pledged to change the model of passive, uncaring Christians. This declaration affirms the following tenets: full authority of the Word of God; God's total claim on the lives of his people; the requirement of God's love and justice within the world; the abundance of God's mercy and forgiveness to those who repent; the Gospel of Jesus Christ who, through the power of the Holy Spirit, provides freedom; the responsibility Christians possess as citizens; and Christ's imminent return to establish his kingdom.

The declaration includes the following confessions: the separation of Christians from issues of social justice around the world; failure to recognize God's claim on lives; the failure to engage and confront injustice suffered, especially by the poor and oppressed; silence about racism and discrimination against women; materialism and the misuse of the nations' wealth, which led men to prideful domination and women to irresponsible passivity.

As a result of this manifesto, Evangelicals for Social Action (ESA) was founded by Ron Sider in 1974. The tenants of the Chicago Declaration of Evangelical Social Concern served as the driving force for ESA's initiatives and decision-making.

Four years later, ESA was incorporated as an official national membership organization, and it hired staff and set up offices in Philadelphia, Pennsylvania. Those initial days included the composition of the ESA Update (later known as the ESA Advocate), establishment of local ESA chapters, and hosting two-day seminars regarding world hunger and economic justice.

ESA aligns with no specific political party. The organization remains committed to awareness both on the national level and the local level. ESA helps local churches integrate evangelism and social action. *PRISM* magazine replaced the *ESA Update* in 1993 and remains a leading publication on the issues of social justice around the world.

Bill Kallio served as executive director from 1981–1987. Founder Ron Sider has served in a variety of positions within the organization, including executive director and president. His advocacy for social justice ranged from writing more than 30 publications to engaging in political activism. The Declaration of Evangelical Social Concern began a movement among evangelical Christians that emphasized and affirmed restorative justice.

Sandra Glahn and Marnie Blackstone Legaspi

See also: Ethics, Evangelical Theories of; Henry, Carl F. H.; Mouw, Richard J.; Sider, Ronald James; Social Action, Evangelicals and; Wallis, Jim

Further Reading

"Chicago Declaration of Evangelical Social Concern." Evangelicals for Social Action. (n.d.). Accessed August 1, 2014. http://www.evangelicalsforsocialaction.org/about/history/chicago-declaration-of-evangelical-social-concern/.

"Declaration of Evangelical Social Concern." *International Review of Mission* 63, no. 250 (1974): 274–275.

Gasaway, Brantley W. *Progressive Evangelicals and the Pursuit of Social Justice.* Chapel Hill, NC: University of North Carolina Press, 2014.

Miller, Steven P. *The Age of Evangelicalism: America's Born-Again Years.* New York: Oxford University Press, 2014.

"The 1993 Chicago Declaration." (n.d.). The Center for Public Justice. Accessed August 1, 2014. http://www.cpjustice.org/node/928.

Rees, Paul S. 1974. "Prayer and Social Concern." *Reformed Journal* 24:1 (1974): 8–11.

CHILDREN OF GOD

The Children of God is the former name of a small, secretive group, whose name was changed to The Family, and now Family International, founded by David "Moses" Berg in 1968. The group began within the evangelical movement, but its theology and practices soon placed it outside evangelicalism. This group organizes into communes, and the size of The Family International is not known but has been estimated to be less than 15,000 members worldwide.

Early History—1960s and 1970s

On the heels of the Jesus revolution of the 1960s and 1970s, David Brandt Berg (1919–1994), also known in the group as Moses David, Mo, or Father David, became the leader of this controversial sect, largely drawing from the hippie community and the "Jesus Revolution." After his death, his organization was subsequently controlled by Karen Zerby, Steve Kelly, and Grant Montgomery.

To promote its religious perspectives, The Family produced a variety of publications as well as audio and video materials, the most famous being the "Mo Letters."

In 1949, Berg became pastor of a Christian Missionary Alliance Church in Arizona but left that church abruptly in 1951, allegedly due to a sex scandal, though Berg denied this. Berg moved to Huntington Beach, California, around 1968 and started a ministry at a coffeehouse formerly occupied by the parachurch youth ministry Teen Challenge. Berg and his followers at that time became known as Teens for Christ. In 1969, he left California, alleging that he been persecuted, and during this time also left his wife for Karen Zerby, claiming that he had received a prophecy that replacing his wife was God's will.

During the early days of the Children of God, Berg and his disciples concentrated on evangelism, with emphasis on the last days and the rejection of organized religion and the outside world. During the mid-1970s, the Children of God practiced an unusual and aberrant form of evangelism, called "Flirty Fishing," in which females of the organization used sex to win converts to their group. From "Flirty Fishing" came a number of births, and one case relating to child custody from this practice occurred in England, in which the Justice concluded that this became little more than prostitution.

Changes within the Organization in the 1970s and 1980s

From the late 1970s through 1981, the Children of God called themselves the Family of Love, and there was considerable emphasis on sexual love within the organization. Changes began to occur after 1982, and The Family, as it was then called, became involved in much evangelistic activity. The Family claims to have wrought through Christ an average of 200,000 conversions each month and have distributed approximately 30 million pages of literature. Additionally, a warning was issued regarding any sexual activity between adults and children. This became important because such prohibitions were not truly stated in previous communications from the organization to its members. Such warnings became necessary because previously Berg had encouraged various members of the organization to engage in sexual activity with each other and even to encourage children to be involved in sex. Amidst such sexual excesses and the possible prosecution for child endangerment, there were calls for the group to relocate internationally.

The Family in the 1990s—Post Berg

After David Berg died in October 1994, leadership in the organization fell to Karen Zerby. She and her new husband, Steven Kelly, began changing a number of rules, called "Fundamental Family Rules," to provide new guidance for the organization. The guidelines explain the relationship between the group's members and also set forth the giving practices expected of each person.

The Family International—2004 through 2015

The last name change for the Children of God is The Family International. The group now has a new emphasis on evangelism and does not appear to be involved in some of the more sexual and perverse aspects of its history.

Beliefs of the Children of God

David Berg established diverse beliefs of the Children of God. Regarding the Bible, Berg said that "some of the parts the Bible are no longer up to date." Another time Berg, challenging the teachings of the apostle Paul, wrote that Paul "was no more divinely inspired, nor infallible, then we are by His Spirit." In another instance, Berg indicated that he was the only one who could uncover the true teachings of the Bible and that he did so through his letters. An interesting perspective by Berg was that, when he was more intoxicated, he was able to more clearly understand the revelations of God through the Spirit.

Berg seems to have held to an Arian view of Jesus, believing that He had been created some time before the world was created. He also believed that the conception of Jesus came not by direct act of Holy Spirit, but by a sexual intercourse between

Mary and God the father; later, he seemed to teach that it was sex between Mary and the angel Gabriel.

The teaching of Berg on salvation is a mixture of orthodoxy and heresy. He taught that one can only be saved by faith, apart from works, but on the other hand believed that this law of love permitted one to do anything one pleased as long as it was done in love.

Berg taught that if one does not accept Jesus in this life, he or she will be able to do so in the afterlife. Consistent with his emphasis on sexual relations, Berg believed that sexual activity would occur in heaven. He believed a variation of the doctrine of purgatory, saying that individuals who do not accept the gospel in this lifetime would suffer for a while but, having learned their lesson, would then be able to embrace the truth and ultimately receive salvation.

H. Wayne House

See also: Counterculture, Evangelicals and; Jesus People Movement

Further Reading

Ajemian, Sam. *The Children of God Cult, aka The Family.* Seattle, WA: Amazon, 2005.

Eskridge, Larry. *God's Forever Family: The Jesus People Movement in America.* New York: Oxford University Press, 2013.

House, H. Wayne. "The Family/Children of God." *Charts of Cult, Sects, and Religious Movement.* Grand Rapids, MI: Zondervan, 2000.

Melton, John Gordon. "The Family International." Encyclopædia Britannica Online, s. v. Accessed May 20, 2015. http://www.britannica.com/EBchecked/topic/701799/The -Family-International.

CHOSEN PEOPLE MINISTRIES/AMERICAN BOARD OF MISSIONS TO THE JEWS

Chosen People Ministries is a nonprofit organization that has branches in 13 nations worldwide, with a focus on Christian ministry and evangelism among Jewish people. In the late 1800s, many European Jews were attracted to the United States because of economic opportunities and freedom to practice their Judaism. Many European Jews immigrated to New York City because it had an established Jewish population.

Chosen People Ministries was established in Brooklyn, New York, in 1894 as the Brownsville Mission to the Jews by Leopold Cohn (1862–1937). Leopold Cohn was born in East Hungary into an Orthodox Jewish family. Leopold studied and became a rabbi in Hungary. He was intrigued by the Messiah and set out on a quest to learn about this Messiah. He left his wife and family and arrived in New York in 1892. Shortly thereafter, Rabbi Cohn came to faith in *Yeshua*, Jesus, the Jewish Messiah. In 1894, he established the Brownsville Mission to the Jews. He wanted to share the Good News of Messiah with his Jewish brethren. The attendance at his meetings grew and grew, and more than 1,000 Jewish people accepted Yeshua as their Messiah.

Ministering to Orthodox Jews is difficult because of the history of Jewish persecution at the hands of so-called Christians. The growing attendance of the ministry did not go unnoticed by the large Orthodox community, and Rabbi Cohn and his family endured much verbal and physical persecution.

Cohn believed that the purpose of the ministry was not only to minister spiritually, but materially. The ministry would help the Jewish immigrants become self-supporting and a productive part of the American society. There were sewing classes that prepared young Jewish women to secure jobs in New York's garment industry. In these classes, the Gospel was shared.

He also opened a dispensary to treat Jewish immigrants who were in poverty and could not afford good health care. While physicians ministered to the physical needs of these people, others were attending to the spiritual condition of the Jewish people.

The Brownsville Mission to the Jews operated under that name from 1894 through 1896. In 1896, the Williamsburg Mission to the Jews was established, and it existed under that name until 1924. In 1924, the mission name was changed again to the American Board of Missions to the Jews. The ministry was renamed Chosen People Ministries in 1986, which is the name that it is known by today.

Leopold Cohn's son, Joseph Hoffman Cohn (1886–1953), took over the leadership of the ministry when his father died, and began to include some new technologies such as radio broadcasts to share the gospel.

In addition to the home office in New York City, offices have been established in Argentina, Australia, Canada, France, Germany, Hong Kong, Israel, New Zealand, Russia, South Africa, Ukraine, United Kingdom, and the United States of America. Their purpose is to "pray for, evangelize, disciple, and serve Jewish people everywhere and to help fellow believers do the same." The current president is Dr. Mitch Glaser.

Jeffrey Gutterman

See also: Ariel Ministries; Jews for Jesus; Messianic Judaism

Further Reading

Ariel, Yaakov. *Evangelizing the Chosen People: Missions to the Jews in America, 1880–2000.* Chapel Hill, NC: University of North Carolina Press, 2000.

Chosen People Ministries. (n.d.). https://www.chosenpeople.com/site/our-mission/.

Sevner, Harold A. *A Rabbi's Vision—A Century of Proclaiming Messiah.* Charlotte, NC: Chosen People Ministries.

Wardell, Ruth, and Jeffrey Gutterman. *Biography of Ruth with The Truth Wardell: Missionary to the Jewish People.* San Antonio, TX: Ariel Ministries, 2011.

CHRISTIAN APOLOGETICS

Christian apologetics is the rational and logical defense of Christianity. This discipline of theology explains *why* Christians believe what they believe. A Christian apologist is not someone who offers profuse apologies for the failings of the church. To the contrary, he offers a "reasonable defense" of the teachings and truth claims of the Christian faith. In fact, the word *apologetics* finds expression in biblical passages such as 1 Peter 3:15–16, where the Greek word for defense is used, namely, *apologia*. Rich in apologetic content even from the beginning and rise of Christianity, from Jerusalem to Athens to Rome and beyond, the significance of apologetics within evangelicalism has become even more popular as a post-Christian culture emerges in Western thought and culture whereby secularism, other world religions, philosophies, and the powers of media, film, and social media are competing for their truth claims to be recognized, valued, and embraced by the larger society. Thus, in this cacophony of truth claims, Christian universities like Biola University and Houston Baptist University and seminaries like Southern Evangelical Seminary in Charlotte, North Carolina (an evangelical seminary dedicated to Christian apologetics), have dedicated a tremendous amount of resources and scholarship to equip evangelicals with the skills to proclaim truth claims in the competing marketplace of ideas.

Influential Contemporary Evangelical Apologists

1. Paul Copan
2. Winfried Corduan
3. William Lane Craig
4. Norman L. Geisler
5. Os Guinness
6. Douglas Groothius
7. Gary Habermas
8. Timothy Keller
9. Greg Koukl
10. John Lennox
11. Josh McDowell
12. John Warwick Montgomery
13. J. P. Moreland
14. Nancy Pearcey
15. Ron Rhodes
16. Kenneth Samples
17. Mary Jo Sharp
18. R. C. Sproul
19. Lee Strobel
20. Ravi Zacharias

Key Term in Evangelicalism: *Apologetics*

Apologetics is a term derived from the Greek word *apologia*, which means "speech in defense" in passages like 1 Peter 3:15–16. Apologetics is a discipline in theology with two primary roles: (1) to provide answers to people's questions (e.g., Why does God allow suffering and evil?) and (2) to protect the historic integrity of Christian beliefs and Christians from possible compromise into false teaching or apostasy (Jude 3). There are at least nine major types of apologetic methodology within evangelicalism: classical, cultural, cumulative case, evidential, experiential, historical, imaginative, presuppositional, and relational.

On the primary level, the apologist defends the historical accuracy and philosophical soundness of such key doctrines as Creation, the Fall, the Trinity, the Incarnation, the Atonement, and the Resurrection. Though more specialized apologists will often defend doctrines that are distinctive to certain denominations (the Catholic transubstantiation; the Calvinist TULIP [total depravity, unconditional election, limited atonement, irresistible grace, preservation of the saints]; a literal six-day creation, etc.), the heart of apologetics concerns itself with the core doctrines that have been believed at all times by orthodox, creedal Christians.

On the next level, the apologist answers questions and criticisms posed both by skeptics seeking to disrupt the claims of the church and Christians struggling with aspects of the faith that are hard to understand: (1) If God is both all good and all powerful, then why does he not eradicate pain, suffering, and evil? (2) How can we accept the miracles recorded in the Bible when we now "know" that miracles break the laws of nature and are thus impossible? (3) How can we trust that the Bible is accurate and reliable if we do not have the original manuscripts, but copies of copies? (4) Don't the wars of religion and the Christian slaveholders of the Old South expose Christianity as false? (5) How can we accept the traditional Christian codes of sexual conduct when they violate our "natural" desires and orientations? (6) How can Christianity claim to be the one and only pathway to salvation when there are so many other religions in the world?

Finally, apologists seek not only to defend specific doctrines and answer specific questions but also to demonstrate that Christianity represents a unified and coherent worldview that speaks to all areas of human life and offers a consistent witness in the fields of theology, philosophy, ethics, politics, economics, psychology, sociology, science, health, the arts, and so on. In sharp contrast to secular-humanist universities that dismiss Christianity as a personal belief system that has no place in the academy, apologists offer the Christian worldview—with its teaching that man was made in God's image (and therefore possesses intrinsic worth and value) but is fallen (and therefore incapable of building utopia); that God is an ordered, rational God who created an ordered, rational cosmos; that we are not souls trapped in

---

Key Term in Evangelicalism: *Faith*

Faith is a term that means "reliance or trust." Though some evangelicals may claim faith is a leap into irrationality, evangelicals widely believe that faith complements reason and evidence (e.g., 1 Corinthians 15). Thus, faith is typically defined as the reliance on that which one has good reasons and evidence to believe is true and trustworthy.

---

bodies, but enfleshed souls; that divinity took on human flesh and dwelt among us; that the supernatural exists and that there is something outside of time and space—as central to the mission and purpose of the university.

Although apologists are often categorized together with evangelists, there is a subtle but vital distinction between their vocations. Whereas evangelists (who share the evangel: "good news") generally take for granted the existence of God, the need for salvation, and the authority of the Bible, apologists set themselves the task of defending such beliefs. In many ways, apologetics offers a kind of "pre-evangelism" that paves the way for the work of the evangelist. Generally speaking, apologists do not seek faith decisions from those who read their books or listen to their speeches. They seek only to present Christianity as a logical system of thought that deserves to be considered carefully and rationally. Once the apologist clears the ground, it is the job of the evangelist to challenge the listener to move from intellectual assent to personal commitment.

Apologetics in its modern form represents a concerted attempt to answer the challenges of the Enlightenment. In the 18th and 19th centuries, a sharp (but finally artificial) line was drawn between reason, logic, and science on one side, and faith, emotion, revelation, and religion on the other. Often referred to as the fact/value or secular/sacred split, this Enlightenment view of the world led to the privatization of all faith claims. It set new ground rules for intellectual discussion and public debate that excluded from consideration any systems of thought founded on revelation and necessitating reference to experiences and realities outside the confines of empiricism.

For the first two-thirds of the 20th century, most evangelicals contented themselves with guarding their religious space while allowing the academy, the public schools, the arts, the media, and the government to fall under the sway of secular humanism. It was in many ways the popular apologetic works of an Oxford/Cambridge professor, C. S. Lewis (1898–1963)—*The Problem of Pain* (1940), *The Screwtape Letters* (1942), *Miracles* (1947), and *Mere Christianity* (1952)—that inspired evangelicals to take a stand against the secular status quo and to defend the intellectual integrity and consistency of Christianity. In fact, there are more than eight different types of apologetics methods (e.g., cultural, evidential, classical, imaginative, relational, cumulative, historical apologetics, presuppositional). Below are some of the most significant:

The first American evangelical to make a concerted effort to explode the Enlightenment myth that Christian truth claims have no logical, objective content was Francis Schaeffer (1912–1984). In *The God Who Is There* (1968) and *Escape from Reason* (1968), Schaeffer argued that the West had sacrificed its once unified field of knowledge and made a sharp dichotomy between an objective, mechanistic downstairs reality in which reason and facts operate, but man loses his freedom; and a subjective, mystical upstairs where there is freedom and beauty, but no logical categories or binding rational structure. He offered the Christian worldview as a platform for reintegrating upstairs and downstairs. His use of cultural apologetics, wedding biblical worldview thinking to all of life, including the arts, the environment, the sciences, and sociology, brought unity to evangelicals who either resisted or never seriously considered the study of and interaction with Western thought and culture or who divided Christian thought from the rest of life (e.g., art, community, work).

Although the apologetics of Lewis and Schaeffer is literary in tone and frequently appeals to the imagination, American apologetics after Schaeffer took a practical, evidential approach. Arguably the first truly American work of modern apologetics is Josh McDowell's *More Than a Carpenter* (1977). In it, McDowell (1939–) took a three-pronged approach that has been frequently imitated: (1) He quotes the Bible often to back up his claims, but does not rely only on Scripture to prove his points; (2) he keeps the focus firmly on Christ Himself—particularly on His claims to divinity, His fulfillment of messianic prophecy, and the historicity of His death and resurrection; (3) he presents Christ as someone about whom we cannot be neutral by focusing on the reactions and testimonies of people, past and present, who have rejected or accepted Him.

Other apologetics like Norman L. Geisler (1932–), author or coauthor of more than 96 books, follows a classical approach to apologetics, as seen in his work *Christian Apologetics* (1976). This type of apologetic methodology, which was most often used in the history of Christian thought and practice, begins by using natural theology—that is, the disclosure of divine revelation via creation, human conscience, Godward longings, and human design—to establish the existence of God (e.g., cosmological argument, teleological argument, objective moral law argument, religious need argument). Once God's existence is affirmed, classical apologetics offer historical evidences that affirm the central truths of Christianity, such as the bodily resurrection of Jesus Christ.

Other significant works on apologetics include William Lane Craig's *Reasonable Faith* (1984, 1994, 2008), J. P. Moreland's *Scaling the Secular City* (1987), Ravi Zacharias's *Can Man Live Without God?* (1994), Gary Habermas's *The Historical Jesus* (1996), Lee Strobel's *The Case for Christ* (1998), and Timothy Keller's *The Reason for God* (2008). Peter Kreeft's whimsical but effective *Between Heaven and Hell* (1982) is written in the mode of Lewis; Charles Colson and Nancy Pearcey's *How Now Shall We Live?* (1999) and Nancy Pearcey's *Total Truth* (2004) develop the worldview focus of Francis Schaeffer. Pearcey, like Colson and Schaeffer, also offers a critique against secularism in such works as *Saving Leonardo: A Call to Resist the Secular*

Assault on Mind, Morals, and Meaning (2010) and *Finding Truth: 5 Principles for Unmasking Atheism, Secularism, and Other God Substitutes* (2015).

Louis Markos

See also: Biola University; Clark, Gordon Haddon; Colson, Charles Wendell ("Chuck"); Creation Research Society; Geisler, Norman L.; Intelligent Design Movement; L'Abri Fellowship; Philosophy, Evangelicals and; Plantinga, Alvin C.; Schaeffer, Francis A. and Edith

Further Reading

Archer, Gleason. *Encyclopedia of Biblical Difficulties.* Grand Rapids, MI: Baker Book House, 1982.

Bush, L. Russ, ed. *Classical Readings in Christian Apologetics. A.D. 100–1800.* Grand Rapids, MI: Academic Books, 1983.

Carson, D. A., ed. *Telling the Truth.* Grand Rapids, MI: Eerdmans, 2000.

Clark, Kelly James, ed. *Philosophers Who Believe.* Downers Grove, IL: InterVarsity Press, 1993.

Frame, John. *Apologetics to the Glory of God.* Phillipsburg, NJ: P&R, 1994.

Geisler, Norman. *Baker Encyclopedia of Christian Apologetics.* Grand Rapids, MI: Baker Book House, 1999.

Groothius, Douglas. *Christian Apologetics. A Comprehensive Case for the Christian Faith.* Downers Grove, IL: InterVarsity Press, 2011.

Guinness, Os. *God in the Dark.* Wheaton, IL: Crossway, 1994.

Guinness, Os. *Long Journey Home.* Colorado Springs, CO: Waterbrook, 2001.

Lewis, C. S. *Mere Christianity.* New York: Macmillan, 1960.

Lewis, C. S. *The Problem of Pain.* New York: Simon & Schuster, 1996.

McDowell, Josh. *Evidence That Demands a Verdict.* San Bernardino, CA: Here's Life, 1979.

McDowell, Josh. *More Evidence That Demands a Verdict.* San Bernardino, CA: Here's Life, 1981.

Schaeffer, Francis A. *The Collected Works of Francis A. Schaeffer.* Five volumes. Wheaton, IL: Crossway, 1985.

Swinburne, Richard. *The Coherence of Theism,* rev. ed. New York: Oxford University Press, 1977, 1993.

Van Til, Cornelius. *Christian Apologetics.* Phillipsburg, NJ: P&R, 1976.

Zuck, Roy, ed. *Vital Apologetics Issues.* Grand Rapids, MI: Kregel, 1996.

CHRISTIAN LEGAL SOCIETY

The Christian Legal Society, formed in 1961, is a 501(c)(3) nonprofit organization based in Springfield, Virginia, compromised of lawyers, judges, professors, scholars, law students, and others who concur with its stated objectives.

The objectives of the Christian Legal Society are straightforward: "To proclaim Jesus as Lord through all we do; to defend the religious liberty of all Americans through the legislatures and courts; to defend the religious liberty of students to gather on their campuses as Christian organizations; to promote justice for the poor, religious liberty, sanctity of human life, and biblical conflict resolution; to encourage Christian lawyers to view law as a ministry and help them integrate faith and their legal practice; to provide Christian lawyers a means of society and fellowship; to encourage and disciple Christian law professors and students; to provide a forum for discussing issues related to Christianity and the law; to encourage lawyers and law students to serve the poor and needy" (Christian Legal Society, n.d.).

The department of the organization that litigates is called The Center for Law & Religious Freedom, which consults, counsels, proffers amicus briefs, and litigates on behalf of clients on a pro bono basis. The Christian Legal Society's publications include *The Christian Lawyer, The Journal of Christian Legal Thought, CLS Bible Studies*, and *CLS E-Devotionals*. And, annually, the organization holds a convention with chosen speakers, seminars, and publication offerings to advance its stated objectives.

The most prominent cases litigated by the Christian Legal Society include a victory and defeated. The Christian Legal Society prevailed in *Beta Upsilon Chi Upsilon Chapter v. Machen*, 586 F.3d 908, 911–912 (11th Cir. 2009). The University of Florida refused to recognize the Beta Upsilon Chi fraternity because of its bylaws constricting membership to Christian men. The U.S. Court of Appeals for the Eleventh Circuit on appeal from the Northern District of Florida, Leon County, concurred with the Christian Legal Society. The University of Florida then changed its policy

Christian Legal Organizations

In view of the influence and impact of legal organizations such as the American Civil Liberties Union (1920) and the NAACP (National Association for the Advancement of Colored People) Legal Defense Fund (1909), the 1980s saw both the rise of the conservative Federalist Society (1982) and the rise and Christian legal movement. The Rutherford Institute (1982), for example, early on, defended freedom and the inherent rights of the unborn. But other legal advocacy groups also emerged, forming a conservative Christian legal community that often amalgamates evangelical, Roman Catholic, and politically conservative interests (e.g., religious liberty; sanctity of life; traditional family) such as the American Center for Law and Justice (1990). Other legal advocacy groups include the following:

> Alliance Defending Freedom (1994)
> Becket Fund for Religious Liberty (1994)
> Center For Law and Religious Freedom (1980)
> Legal Institute (1997)
> Liberty Counsel (1989)
> Liberty Institute (merger between Free Market Foundation [1972] and Liberty
>   National Legal Foundation [1985])
> Pacific Justice Institution (1997)
> Thomas More Law Center (1998)
> Thomas More Society (1997)

to allow recognition for the Christian fraternity. The issue at law thus rendered moot, the appeal was consequently dismissed.

The second most prominent case litigated by the Christian Legal Society is *Christian Legal Society v. Martinez*, 561 U.S. 661 (2011), where the U.S. Supreme Court held in a 5–4 decision that campus organizations at the Hastings Law School of the University of California cannot have recognition and funding unless they have an "all comers" membership policy, that is, student organizations must allow admission even to those opposing the stated purpose and/or beliefs of the organization. The existence and work of the Christian Legal Society illustrates the depth and breadth of evangelical engagement in American culture beyond the worshipping communities.

George Gatgounis

See also: Social Action, Evangelicals and

Further Reading

"About Us." Christian Legal Society. (n.d.). http://www.clsnet.org.
Schutt, Michael P. *Redeeming Law: Christian Calling and the Legal Profession.* Downers Grove, IL: InterVarsity Press, 2007.

CHRISTIAN MEDICAL & DENTAL ASSOCIATIONS

The Christian Medical and Dental Associations is an evangelical 501(c)3 organization comprised of the Christian Medical Association (CMA) and Christian Dental Association (CDA) and is a professional organization for Christian health care professionals and students. Founded in 1931 by students George Peterson and Kenneth Gieser at Northwestern University, Chicago, it has a present membership of about 18,000 and sponsors student ministries in medical and dental schools, addresses policies on health care issues, sponsors overseas medical evangelism projects, and provides a professional network for health care professionals. It also provides marriage and family conferences and continuing education opportunities, and distributes education and inspirational resources.

In addition to its global health care relief support, the organization provides opportunities for its health care professional members to assist in providing health care to the poor and needy in the United States. It also supports short-term mission programs involving international medical education and it has a specific ministry to pan-African Christian surgeons.

The society has adopted a number of individual ethics statements on many bioethical issues and topics pertaining to the provision of health care. Additionally, there are several scientific statements and public policy statements. The Christian Medical & Dental Associations is one of several professional organizations for evangelicals and illustrates the long-standing commitment of evangelicals to apply

Christian beliefs and spirituality in all aspects of personal, vocational, or professional activities.

Timothy J. Demy

See also: American Scientific Affiliation; Christian Legal Society

Further Reading

Christian Medical & Dental Associations. (n.d.). Accessed April 21, 2017. https://www
.cmda.org.

CHRISTIAN RECONSTRUCTIONISM

Christian Reconstructionism is a conservative evangelical movement that began in the mid-1960s in the United States and that seeks to return society to Puritan roots in accordance with the Mosaic Law of the Bible's Old Testament. Rousas John Rushdoony (1916–2001) was the founder of the movement and was aided by his son-in-law Gary North (1942–present) and theologian Greg Bahnsen (1948–1995).

Rushdoony's *Institutes of Biblical Law*, released in 1972, is considered the seminal work for the movement in which he expounded on the Ten Commandments as the law structure for all areas of society today. It includes an extensive history and interaction with the role of the Mosaic Law as the foundational base for Western law since the Reformation. Bahnsen released *Theonomy in Christian Ethics* in 1977 as a major defense of the use of Old Testament law today. He declared that Old Testament law carries over into the era of Christianity unless specifically abrogated and that a new Divine enablement for keeping the law is part of the New Covenant (Jeremiah 31:31–37) for Christians. North has written on a wide range of topics, including eschatology, survivalism, economics, history, and theology, and is the movement's major protagonist.

Reconstructionism is a version of Calvinist theology developed within a strong view of the sovereignty of God. There are at least three distinctive areas of theology blended together to compose the Reconstructionist mix: first, the presuppositional epistemology of Cornelius Van Til (1895–1987), which provides an absolute standard of truth through God's revelation in the Old and New Testaments of the Bible. Thus, the thoughts and intentions of mankind are rejected if they are not consistent with Scripture. This approach starts with the Bible as the framework through which Christians are called to think God's thoughts after Him as they endeavor to build a God-honoring society. Second, Reconstructionist believe that the Law of God, or Biblical Law, as codified in the Old Testament should be instituted as the law of the United States and every nation on earth before the return of Christ. *Theonomy* is the term coined by Greg Bahnsen in which he said, "The Christian is obligated to keep the whole law of God as a pattern for sanctification and that this law is to be enforced by the civil magistrate where and how the stipulations of God so designate." Third, Postmillennialism teaches that God's kingdom was established by Christ's victorious first coming. Thus, the kingdom has been established. Now, through the preaching of the gospel, the kingdom is advancing and will eventually lead to the conversion of a large majority of people at some point still in the future. Therefore, the world will have been conquered through the church, whose influence will lead to the millennial phase of the kingdom, which will last for a thousand years or more. After a brief apostasy, Christ will return to earth and history will end. Reconstructionists see theonomy as a means to advance the kingdom.

Reconstructionists believe that at some point in our current age the United States, and eventually the entire world, will become so transformed that we will see a radically different and much more righteous world than exists today. Radical change is expected within the spheres of the family, education, the church, civil government, economics, business, and law. They believe non-Christians will be excluded from a government under God's law. Education will be under the control of godly families producing God-honoring children. The Church will be totally Reformed, and all will be orthodox in theology and practice. Persistent heretics will be executed by the state. The civil government would be empowered to apply the death penalty for murder, gross negligence resulting in the death of another, rape, adultery, apostasy, homosexuality, bestiality, gross incorrigibility in children, idolatry, and perhaps Sabbath-breaking. In economics, society would be on the gold standard operating within a free market. There will be no fractional reserve banking or central bank. There would be tight limitations on debt, with no long-term debt like a 30-year mortgage. The tithe, not public taxes, would finance most social welfare. These are only a few examples of what Reconstructionists envision will be operative during the future millennial phase of the Kingdom.

The impact of the Reconstructionist movement is hard to assess because most Christians who are influenced by their views rarely accept the entire system. However, there is no doubt that this movement has had a great impact in formulating political and social ideology for the Christian Right. Reconstructionist ideology has greatly impacted the Christian school and home schooling movements within North America. Also, they have been the prime mover in the field of eschatology by spurring a revival of postmillennialism and introducing for the first time in American history among Evangelicals a significant acceptance of preterism, which sees most Bible prophecy as having already been fulfilled in the first century CE.

The Christian Reconstruction movement has been an influence for good as they have challenged conservative Christians to develop a worldview that involves all areas of life and to reengage in culture, society, and politics in support of biblical Christianity. However, their view of theonomy goes beyond the historic Christian view of using the Mosaic Law as wisdom in the Church Age, to demanding that a Christian is obligated to implement this law within the various spheres of life. Their postmillennialism and preterism does not line up with the biblical necessity of Christ's return to judge the world and remove most of the curse, as He remains on earth for a thousand years in order to provide for and oversee His millennial reign.

The fullness of Christ's kingdom will not arrive gradually, as Reconstructionists teach; instead, it will come through the sudden intervention of Christ's return to reign with His people in victory.

Thomas D. Ice

See also: Calvinism; Christian Apologetics; Eschatology; Homeschooling, Evangelicals and; Politics, Evangelicals and; Reformed Tradition, Evangelicalism and

Further Reading

Bahnsen, Greg. *Theonomy in Christian Ethics*, 3rd ed. Nacogdoches, TX: Covenant Media Press, 2002.

Gentry, Kenneth L., Jr. *He Shall Have Dominion: A Postmillennial Eschatology*, 3rd ed. Draper, VA: Apologetics Group, 2009.

House, H. Wayne, and Thomas Ice. *Dominion Theology: Blessing or Curse?* Portland, OR: Multnomah Press, 1988.

McVicar, Michael J. *Christian Reconstruction: R. J. Rushdoony and American Religious Conservatism.* Chapel Hill, NC: The University of North Carolina Press, 2015.

Rushdoony, Rousas John. *The Institutes of Biblical Law.* Phillipsburg, NJ: P&R, 1972.

CHRISTIANITY TODAY

Christianity Today (*CT*) is a leading evangelical publication. It was founded in 1956 through the work of Billy Graham and L. Nelson Bell, his father-in-law, and it was intended to be a serious-minded, scholarly periodical for evangelicals, avoiding both fundamentalist separatism (evidenced by *The Sword of the Lord*) and liberal theology (the mainline Protestant *The Christian Century*), but modeled after the intellectual tone of *The Christian Century* and transcending denominational lines. The magazine was to promote evangelical scholarship and scholars and bring intellectual respectability to evangelicalism. Along with the birth of the National Association of Evangelicals and the founding of Fuller Theological Seminary, *CT* can be seen as part of the rise of an evangelicalism of the 1940s and 1950s that sought to de-emphasize the separatism of fundamentalism and denominational ties while promoting conservative theology and cultural engagement.

Wilbur Smith, professor at Fuller Theological Seminary, had initially broached an idea for a scholarly, evangelical magazine to Graham, and after he decided he was unable to serve as the editor, Graham recruited Carl F. H. Henry, who took a leave of absence from Fuller Theological Seminary to serve as editor. Graham served as chairman of the board of trustees, and the magazine's offices were located in Washington, D.C. Soon leaving Fuller entirely, Henry served as editor in chief until 1968, and under his direction *CT* maintained a restrained, intellectual tone and covered politics and ethics in addition to theology and religion. The magazine depended for its financial support on J. Howard Pew and was initially delivered free of charge to Protestant pastors all across the country. Seeking to appeal to a

---

Prominent Evangelical Magazines

Many evangelical magazines that address evangelical concerns, news, and themes. Some of them, like *Christianity Today*, the leading evangelical magazine, have incredible influence. Many of them not only offer devotional, pastoral, and theological insights but also provocative debates and beneficial dialogue within and beyond the evangelical community.

Bible Study Magazine (2008)
CCM Magazine (1978)
Charisma (1975)
Christianity Today (1956)
The Gospel Magazine (1766)
Our Daily Bread (1956)
RELEVANT Magazine (2002)
Touchstone: A Journal of Mere Christianity (1986)
WORLD Magazine (1986)

---

broad spectrum of evangelicals, the magazine had soon surpassed *The Christian Century* in the number of subscriptions, though within several years it proved necessary to reduce the number of subsidized subscriptions.

Though Henry promoted conservative theology in *CT* during his tenure, many fundamentalists, as well as Bell and Pew, believed he was not conservative enough on social and political issues. Henry resigned under pressure in 1968 and was succeeded by Harold Lindsell. Under Lindsell, who had served as associate editor since 1964, *CT* became more outspoken on political questions and theological issues such as inerrancy. Inerrancy had by this time become a key point of contention between conservative and progressive evangelicals in seminaries, denominations, and evangelical organizations, and Lindsell's 1976 book *The Battle for the Bible* drew clear lines on the question. During this time, the magazine faced serious financial difficulties and required financial help from its backers to avoid bankruptcy. Kenneth Kantzer followed Lindsell as editor from 1978 to 1982 and maintained an emphasis on inerrancy.

The addition of Harold Myra in 1975 as president and publisher proved fruitful. Myra oversaw moving the magazine from Washington, D.C., to Carol Stream, Illinois, in 1977. Myra emphasized a businesslike approach and focused on broadening *CT* to a wider audience that reached 155,000 circulations by 1978, obviating the need for major subsidies, and launched other magazines as part of a family of publications targeted to specific audiences. The first of these other publications was *Leadership*, launched in 1980, and aimed at Christian ministers. Other titles followed in the next two decades, such as *Campus Life*, *Today's Christian Woman*, *Christian History*, and *Books & Culture*, though not all currently survive.

The expansion in titles led to the establishment of Christianity Today International (CTI), which serves as the umbrella organization under which the various publications and media platforms exist. Myra hired Paul Robbins as executive vice president in 1977, and the two jointly led the organization until they retired in 2007. *CT* had an early presence on the World Wide Web, launching as Christianity Online in 1994 before changing to ChristianityToday.com in 2000. As of 2015, ChristianityToday.org serves as the online home of CTI, providing Christian content for laypeople and ministers through magazines, blogs, ministry aids, articles, news, and analysis, and ChristianityToday.com is the digital home of *CT*. Currently, CTI produces six print publications as well as several digital titles.

Joshua Michael

See also: Graham, William F., Jr. ("Billy"); Henry, Carl F. H.; Lindsell, Harold

Further Reading

Board, Stephen. "Moving the World with Magazines: A Survey of Evangelical Periodicals." In *American Evangelicals and the Mass Media*, edited by Quentin J. Schultze. Grand Rapids, MI: Zondervan, 1990.

Marsden, George. *Reforming Fundamentalism: Fuller Seminary and the New Evangelicalism.* Grand Rapids, MI: Eerdmans, 1987.

Rosell, Garth M. *The Surprising Work of God: Harold John Ockenga, Billy Graham, and the Rebirth of Evangelicalism.* Grand Rapids, MI: Baker Academic, 2008.

CHRISTIANS FOR BIBLICAL EQUALITY

Christians for Biblical Equality (CBE), based in Minneapolis, Minnesota, is an international nonprofit organization of Christian men and women who affirm that the Bible, properly interpreted, teaches the fundamental equality of men and women regardless of ethnicity, economic status, or age. Prominent American evangelicals associated with the organization include Anthony Campolo, Millard Erickson, W. Ward Gasque, Stanley Gundry, Gretchen Gaebelein Hull, Catherin Clark Kroeger, Roger Nicole, Gordon Fee, Craig Keener, Ronald J. Sider, Aída Besaçon Spencer, and Ruth A. Tucker.

Disturbed by what they considered an incorrect hermeneutic that led liberals to reject Scripture and Christian organizations to exclude the free exercise of women's spiritual gifts, a group of evangelical leaders assembled in 1987 to publish their perspective in a new scholarly journal, *Priscilla Papers*. The group determined that a national organization was needed to provide education, support, and leadership about biblical equality.

The organization itself, Christians for Biblical Equality, was established the following year. Their mission is to promote an egalitarian perspective of gender roles and to challenge sex-based hierarchy. CBE bases their argumentation especially on Bible verses such as Galatians 3:28, which says, "There is neither Jew nor Gentile, neither slave nor free, nor is there male and female, for you are all one in Christ Jesus" (NIV, 2011).

CBE members believe "that men and women are equally created in God's image; equally responsible for sin; equally redeemed by Christ, and equally gifted by God's Spirit for service; and equally held responsible for using their God-given gifts." Thus the organization's mission statement affirms "the biblical truth that all believers—without regard to gender, ethnicity or class—must exercise their God-given gifts with equal authority and equal responsibility in church, home and world."

In terms of biblical instruction about submission in marriage, CBE believes that the Bible teaches mutual submission and that although "the Bible reflects patriarchal culture, the Bible does not teach patriarchy in human relationships." They also affirm that God distributes spiritual gifts without regard to gender, ethnicity, or class; believers must develop and exercise their God-given gifts in church, home, and world; believers have equal authority and equal responsibility to exercise their gifts without regard to gender, ethnicity, or class and without the limits of culturally defined roles; restricting believers from exercising their gifts on the basis of gender, ethnicity, or class resists the work of the Spirit; and believers must promote righteousness and oppose injustice in all its forms.

The organization's first major project was the creation of their statement, "Men, Women, and Biblical Equality," which laid out their Bible-based rationale for the shared leadership and authority of men and women in church, home, and society.

CBE is often described as the counterpart to the Biblical Council on Manhood and Womanhood (BCMW), the members of which self-identify as "complementarians." Thus the two distinct camps with statements on the issue of the role of women are CBE/egalitarians and BCMW/complementarians. The latter's paper is called the Danvers Statement on Biblical Manhood and Womanhood (1987), which states that men and women are "complementary, possessing equal dignity and worth as the image of God, and called to different roles that each glorify him." This group, which assigns male authority to male/female roles in the church and home, sometimes interprets CBE members as embracing a unisex ideal and/or of seeking to erase God-given male/female distinctions. The title of the book *Discovering Biblical Equality: Complementarity without Hierarchy* (IVP Academic, 2005), to which members of CBE contributed, reflects CBE's clarification of their belief that God made male and female different and complementary. The authors argue that sex differentiation is real and God-given, but that those differences do not suggest innate authority differences in male/female roles, whether in home, church, or society.

CBE's reach includes members from more than 100 denominations and 65 countries. The organization conducts annual, international conferences; publishes two periodicals, a blog, and a weekly e-newsletter; and hosts an online bookstore devoted to reviewing and promoting resources on gender and the Bible from an egalitarian perspective. CBE also has local chapters around the globe.

CBE's two print periodicals have won numerous honors for journalistic excellence. As of 2014, *Mutuality*, CBE's popular-market publication, had been recognized with

15 awards from the Evangelical Press Association (EPA); *Priscilla Papers* journal, the academic voice of Christians for Biblical Equality, had received 14. Because views of what the Bible says about gender roles have ramifications for church government, marriage counseling, and spiritual growth, CBE maintains a directory of egalitarian churches, counselors, therapists, and spiritual directors.

Sandra Glahn

See also: Council on Biblical Manhood and Womanhood; Theological Controversies within Evangelicalism

Further Reading

Cochrane, Pamela D. H. *Evangelical Feminism: A History.* New York: New York University Press, 2005.

Pierce, Ronald W. and Rebecca Merrill Groothius, eds. *Discovering Biblical Equality: Complementarity without Hierarchy.* Downers Grove, IL: IVP Academic, 2005.

CIVIL RIGHTS MOVEMENT, EVANGELICALS AND

Evangelicals and the Civil Rights Movement refers to the relationship between American evangelicalism—Christians adherents whose doctrinal convictions center on the conversion experience, biblical authority, a focus on Jesus Christ, missionary endeavors, and the impact of the Holy Spirit—and the modern freedom struggles of black Christians and other Christian people of color. Although some evangelicals advocated for social and political change as part of the long Civil Rights Movement dating to the 1800s, other Christian activists participated in justice initiatives in more recent freedom movements. The broader story of American evangelicals and justice-inspired social action covers many decades with nuanced, complex cultural and theological twists and turns.

The historical era that commenced around World War II (1939–1945), an era of profound growth and wide destabilization, ushered in significant geopolitical and cultural change that decisively shaped decolonization abroad in locations such as India and Africa, and freedom struggles more locally in the United States. In continuity with freedom fighters from earlier eras, civil rights supporters in the post–World War II period and thereafter supported both racial justice and economic democracy. One was not fully achievable without the other.

The birth of Koinonia Farm in 1942 by white Southern Baptist minister Clarence Jordan (1912–1969) bucked the racial order of Jim Crow in Georgia and elsewhere in the south with its commitment to Christian interracialism and economic equality. It also offended the sensibilities of southern white Christians who maintained rigid racial segregation using biblical arguments and cultural customs. Resistance to Koinonia came swiftly in the form of rhetorical attacks and acts of vandalism against the group's property and business interests. Around the same time, white evangelical Christians associated with publications like *Christianity Today*, organizations such as the National Association of Evangelicals (NAE), and an assortment of Christian colleges and seminaries debated vigorously over questions of racial justice. Some supported integration and cited injustice as sinful. Those part of the neo-evangelical movement who gestured in the direction of equality held uniformly the conviction that personal conversion provided the solution for social ills. Others, especially white Christians in Southern states such as Mississippi, energetically supported racial exclusion and defended segregationist practices on biblical grounds.

Elsewhere, evangelicals adopted more forceful and articulate positions in favor of racial justice and economic equality. One of those individuals, a white Christian named John Alexander, began publishing a small periodical *Freedom Now* (later called *The Other Side*) in the 1960s. The journal featured the likes of black evangelical leaders John M. Perkins (1930–), William Pannell, and Tom Skinner (1942–1994). Collectively, these voices emphasized racial and economic equality, cited biblical arguments for social justice, and advocated for the poor and oppressed. While writing for Alexander's publication, Perkins worked for social justice in his native Mississippi by founding Mendenhall Ministries to provide care and concern for local black residents and work on civil rights causes. Later, he started Voice of Calvary Ministries to address further the material needs of Mississippians, actions that along with Perkins's social justice work in California embodied his evangelically inspired outreach philosophy of redistribution of resources, relocation to areas of need, and reconciliation for unity.

Although black and white Christians played important roles in the larger story of evangelicalism and civil rights, Latino/a evangelicals also participated in freedom struggles. Reies López Tijerina (1926–2015), for example, engaged in civil rights activism as a leading Chicano freedom fighter. Armed actions in the late 1960s in response to centuries of Anglo oppression brought Tijerina to national attention. However, an abiding Pentecostal faith inspired his freedom crusades and commitment to communal organization, and encouraged blistering critiques of economic inequality across the United States. Meanwhile, Latino Mennonites—an evangelical group rooted in Anabaptism—engaged in missionary work on both sides of the U.S.–Mexico border, sponsored youth events, and participated in labor activism within the larger farmworker movements of the 1960s. Committed to peace and Christian service, Latino Mennonites sometimes joined with black Mennonite civil rights activists such as Vincent Harding (1931–2014) to advance causes of equality and justice.

Although white evangelicals have not been entirely absents from the larger freedom struggles of the modern Civil Rights Movement, as the account of Koinonia Farm illustrates, for example, on historical balance the tendency to spiritualize material inequality and individualize spirituality has rendered them complicit in the perpetuation of racial discrimination and economic injustice. However, today a larger number of Anglo evangelicals publish more justice-oriented books with evangelical publishers than at any other time in the movement's history; denounce injustice boldly from the pulpit; and sometimes comment or post on social media or in online forums on behalf of the marginalized. Nevertheless, both surveys and academic scholarship find that for evangelicals the go-to solution for racial injustice and economic inequality—contemporary concerns indelibly linked to the Civil Rights Movement—remains individual soul transformation instead of structural change, the cultivation of personal relationships above social reform, and prayer over protest. Through such a series of advancements forward and steps backward, the larger account of American evangelicalism and the Civil Rights Movement demonstrates the power and peril of American religion, both its shortcomings and strengths. In the end, understanding evangelicalism and the Civil Rights Movement is vital to understanding the sweeping scope of U.S. religious history and culture.

Phillip Luke Sinitiere

See also: African American Evangelicalism; National Black Evangelical Association; Social Action, Evangelicals and

Further Reading

Dupont, Carolyn *Renée. Mississippi Praying: Southern White Evangelicals and the Civil Rights Movement, 1945–1975*. New York: New York University Press, 2014.

Evans, Curtis J. "White Evangelical Protestant Responses to the Civil Rights Movement." *Harvard Theological Review* 102/2 (2009): 245–273.

Gasaway, Brantley W. *Progressive Evangelicals and the Pursuit of Social Justice*. Chapel Hill, NC: University of North Carolina Press, 2014.

Hawkins, J. Russell, and Phillip Luke Sinitiere, eds. *Christians and the Color Line: Race and Religion after* Divided by Faith. New York: Oxford University Press, 2013.

Hinojosa, Felipe. *Latino Mennonites: Civil Rights, Faith & Evangelical Culture*. Baltimore, MD: Johns Hopkins University Press, 2014.

Scott, Lindy. "Reies López Tijerina: The Visions and Obedience of a Pentecostal Activist." In *Los Evangélicos: Portraits of Latino Protestantism in the United States*, edited by Juan F. Martínez and Lindy Scott, 139–148. Eugene, OR: Wipf & Stock, 2009.

Swartz, David R. *Moral Minority: The Evangelical Left in an Age of Conservatism*. Philadelphia: University of Pennsylvania Press, 2012.

CLARK, GORDON HADDON (1902–1985)

Gordon Haddon Clark was an influential philosopher and thinker in evangelical circles from the reception of his PhD in 1929 until his death. Born in Philadelphia, Clark grew up in the Reformed branch of the Christian faith. His Reformed stance in evangelism would serve to distinguish his work and contributions as well as to foster controversy with colleagues.

Academic Career

Clark began his academic career as a professor at the staunchly evangelical Wheaton College. However, as mentioned, Clark's Reformed theology clashed with the

Personality Profile: Cornelius Van Til

Cornelius Van Til (1895–1987), who emigrated from Grootegast, Holland, at the age of 10, received his ThM in theology from Princeton Theological Seminary (1925) and PhD in philosophy from Princeton University (1927). Influenced by Abraham Kuyper (1837–1920) and B. B. Warfield (1851–1921), Van Til used idealist philosophical language to communicate a worldview mindset and apologetic approach that claims that God is the basis of all meaning. In order to make sense of everything, one presupposes God's whole revelation because the Creator–creation distinction (God Himself vs. what God has created) is so great. But only God can account for rationality and meaning. Thus, all other worldviews and interpretations of reality are ultimately incoherent.

beliefs upheld at Wheaton. From there, Clark gained a professorship at Reformed Episcopal Seminary and later taught at Covenant College. Again Clark's theological stance was not well received, but this time, by Cornelius Van Til, who found Clark's Calvinism lacking. The recently ordained Clark found himself in the middle of a controversy between himself and Van Til, who successfully sought to have Clark's ordination through the newly established Orthodox Presbyterian Church revoked. This controversy still ripples to this day, and the controversy itself led Clark to take a position at Butler University, where he became the Chair of the Philosophy Department, a position he held for 28 years. Clark wrote and taught up until his retirement, only a year before his death.

During his career, Clark published more than 30 books along with many articles. He also presided as president of the Evangelical Theological Society in 1965. In addition to his written contributions, Clark significantly influenced other major evangelical leaders and thinkers. Carl F. Henry was Clark's student when both were at Wheaton College, and Henry became a major advocate in the inerrancy debate and scholarship of evangelical thought. Additionally, Ronald Nash was a student of Clark's, though Nash and Clark would express great differences in their positions. Nash would become a leading evangelical philosopher. Finally, there is John Edward Carnell, who also learned from Clark at Wheaton and who would later help establish Fuller seminary and make his own unique contributions to Evangelical Christian Apologetics.

Beliefs and Intellectual Contributions

Clark's system was that of a "rational," or "deductive," presuppositionalism as opposed to Van Til's revelational presuppositionalism. Clark took the triune God of Scriptures as his starting point. He claimed the truth of the Bible as his "axiom," which he points out is never deduced and assumed without proof, thus justifying his position. Other classical apologists, like Norman L. Geisler, cite Clark's position as circular; Clark himself admits the same, but Clark's defense is that everyone's position is circular. Therefore, his position that Christianity is true stands as sound in relation to other religious positions due to internal consistency, which Clark demonstrates deductively with the laws of logic, particularly the law of noncontradiction.

However, Evangelical thinkers both Reformed and non-Reformed have severely criticized Clark in other areas of his philosophy. For example, Clark agreed with David Hume that a person's senses could deceive the person and therefore could not be trusted. Clark takes a skeptical stance toward any information gained via empirical means or through classical natural theology. He denied any necessary connections between a person's ideas and events, as well as disavowing any use for historical apologetics. In Clark's view, even if the resurrection of Jesus Christ could be absolutely proven as having happened, the empirical information would be ultimately useless because this evidence in no way proves why Jesus died, namely, for the sins of believers.

Consequently, Clark believed that apart from any divine illumination, a person would not be able to know anything for certain. Anything the person held as knowledge would be suspect. Therefore, the only place knowledge could begin is with the revealed Scriptures, the source of all knowledge. From this view came a denial of any use for the classical theistic proofs for the existence of God.

Positive Influences in Evangelicalism

Gordon Clark trained and influenced many leading leaders in evangelical thought. In his teaching and writing, Clark forced Evangelicals to rethink and refine both their theological and philosophical positions. Clark's apologetic method also offered a simplified, on-step test for truth rather than the multistep methods often employed by others. Clark also made advances in insisting on a rational religious belief as well as the acceptance of objective, propositional truth of Christianity.

Critiques of Clark

From the Reformed side, Clark's opponents have often been supporters of Cornelius Van Til and his revelational presuppositionalism. Often opponents accuse Clark of having elevated the human mind and logic above the revelation of God because Clark insisted on submitting the truth of Scripture to the tests of logic. Indeed, Clark saw logic as the "common ground" between the believer and nonbeliever, an idea many of his critics reject.

From the classical apologetics side, Clark's method was criticized as inconsistent. Clark rejected sense data, yet he encouraged people to read their Bibles, which is the gaining of knowledge through sensory data. Additionally, many have found his view of truth being that which is consistent as lacking strength because other systems could also be consistent in and of themselves. Clark's legacy is one that spans much of the 20th century. Despite criticisms, no one can deny the influence Clark had on evangelical thinking and methodology in apologetics.

Thomas McCuddy

See also: Christian Apologetics; Geisler, Norman L.; Reformed Tradition, Evangelicalism and; Schaeffer, Francis A. and Edith

Further Reading

Clark, Gordon H. *An Introduction to Christian Philosophy.* Dallas: Trinity Foundation, 1993.

Geisler, Norman. *Baker Encyclopedia of Christian Apologetics.* Grand Rapids, MI: Baker Academic, 1999.

Hoover, David P. *Gordon Clark's Extraordinary View of Men & Things.* Hatfield, PA: Interdisciplinary Biblical Research Institute. 2012.

CLOUSE, ROBERT G. (1931–2016)

Robert G. Clouse was a historian and Professor Emeritus of History at Indiana State University, Terre Haute, Indiana, where he taught from 1963. He received training and taught early modern European history, but he is best known for his historical treatment of millenarianism and evangelical theology and of Christianity's relationship to culture and politics.

Clouse was born in Mansfield, Ohio, in 1931. He began his undergraduate studies at Ashland College, Ashland, Ohio, before transferring to William Jennings Bryan University, Dayton, Tennessee, where he received his BA in 1954. Clouse completed a Bachelor of Divinity at Grace Theological Seminary, Winona Lake, Indiana, in 1957. He went on to the University of Iowa, Iowa City, Iowa, for graduate studies, earning first an MA in 1960, and then a PhD in history under the direction of Reformation scholar Robert M. Kingdon in 1963. It was while a graduate student at Iowa that he met two other evangelical students, Robert D. Linder and Richard V. Pierard, with whom he collaborated on several publishing projects related to Christianity and politics in the decade after completing his graduate work. Also in 1963, Clouse became an assistant professor of early modern Europe at Indiana State, where he remained throughout his career. He also served as a visiting professor at three institutions: Indiana University in Bloomington, Indiana; the University of Illinois; and Juniata College of Pennsylvania, where he was the J. Omar Professor of Christianity. He also served as an adjunct at several other colleges.

Clouse's scholarship often focused on the cultural and theological influences on the Christian church in history that shaped its current condition. In 1980, he authored *The Church in the Age of Orthodoxy and the Enlightenment,* in which he examined pietism and rationalism as reactions to inert Reformation orthodoxy between 1600 and 1800. He edited or authored four popular books on the history of millennial eschatology, beginning with the bestselling *The Meaning of the Millennium:*

Four Views in 1977. The book proved to be groundbreaking in that its format made a significant impact on evangelical publishing practices. For the first time, proponents of competing perspectives on a theological topic presented their views alongside one another positively, with space given for rebuttals of the other views. This multiview way of introducing a controversial topic led to a spate of publications that imitated Clouse's arrangement, including three Clouse again edited between 1981 and 1989: *War: Four Christian Views; Wealth and Poverty: Four Christian Views of Economics*; and *Women in Ministry: Four Views*.

In the midst of his most productive period of teaching and publication, in 1985, Clouse suffered a viral infection that threatened his life. He received a new heart at a time when transplants were still considered novel and survived the procedure by more than 30 years. After his recovery, he continued his teaching and service at Indiana State, and his leadership within the Conference on Faith and History, a society of evangelical historians. Clouse was one of the founders of that organization and served on its Executive Board from 1970 to 2004.

Liam J. Atchison

See also: Conference on Faith and History; Linder, Robert D.; Pierard, Richard V.

Further Reading

Clouse, Robert G. *The Meaning of the Millennium: Four Views.* Downers Grove, IL: InterVarsity Press, 1977.

Clouse, Robert G., Robert D. Linder, and Richard V. Pierard, eds. *The Cross and the Flag.* Eugene, OR: Wipf & Stock, 2007 [originally published, 1972].

Clouse, Robert G., Richard V. Pierard, and Edwin M. Yamauchi. *Two Kingdoms: The Church and Culture through the Ages.* Chicago: Moody Press, 1993.

Douglas, James Dixon, and Robert G. Clouse. *New 20th-Century Encyclopedia of Religious Knowledge.* Grand Rapids, MI: Baker, 1991.

Pierard, Richard V. "In Memoriam of a Founder of CFH: Robert G. Clouse." *The Conference on Faith and History Newsletter* 21, no. 5 (June 2016): 1. http://us9.campaign-archive1 .com/?u=7a777b1a3aaf717ae2274551d&id=bf8258f010.

COLSON, CHARLES WENDELL ("CHUCK") (1931–2012)

Charles Wendell ("Chuck") Colson (1931–2012) was founder of Prison Fellowship, the Colson Center for Christian Worldview, and *BreakPoint*, a weekday radio commentary of Christian perspective on news and culture, airing on 1,400 outlets nationwide, with an audience of 8 million. Prior to his conversion, he served as Special Counsel to President Richard Nixon (1969–1973). On March 10, 1973, 17 months before Nixon's resignation, he resigned from the White House to return to the private practice of law as Senior Partner at the law firm of Colson and Shapiro, Washington, D.C. However, he was retained as a special consultant by President Nixon for several more months.

Colson was born in 1931 in Boston, Massachusetts. After attending Browne & Nichols School in Cambridge (1949), he earned his BA, with honors, from Brown University (1953), where he was a member of Beta Theta Pi, and his JD, with honors, from George Washington University Law School, Washington (1959). He served in the Marine Corps from 1953–1955, becoming what was at the time its youngest captain. He began his political career in 1956, as the youngest administrative assistant in the Senate, working for Massachusetts Republican Senator Leverett Saltonstall.

Once known as President Nixon's "hatchet man" and described by the 1970s media as "incapable of humanitarian thoughts," Colson gained notoriety at the height of the Watergate scandal for his involvement with the infamous "Watergate Seven." Not long after his conversion, he plead guilty to obstruction of justice and in 1974 served seven months of a one-to-three year sentence in the federal Maxwell Prison in Alabama. He was the first member of the Nixon administration to be incarcerated for Watergate-related charges.

As Colson was facing arrest, his close friend, Raytheon Company Chairman of the Board Thomas L. Phillips, gave him a copy of *Mere Christianity* by C. S. Lewis, which led Colson to faith in Christ. He then joined a prayer group led by Douglas Coe and including Democratic Senator Harold Hughes and Republican congressman Al Quie. Following his release, he founded Prison Fellowship Ministries (1976), fulfilling a promise made to inmates that he would "never forget those behind bars."

His founding of Justice Fellowship in 1983 helped make Colson one of the nation's most influential voices for criminal justice reform. During his lifetime, he visited some 600 prisons in the United States and 40 countries, and built a movement that extended to more than 50,000 prison ministry volunteers. His advocacy for prisoners' religious rights led him in the 1990s to lobby legislators to support the Religious Freedom Restoration Act and the Religious Land Use and Institutionalized Persons Act. Colson and Justice Fellowship also brought about the passage of the Prison Rape Elimination Act in 2003.

Colson received 15 honorary doctorates and was awarded the Templeton Prize for Progress in Religion (1993), the world's largest annual award in the field of religion, a prize he donated to further the work of Prison Fellowship (as he did all his speaking fees and royalties). In 2008, he was awarded the Presidential Citizens Medal by President George W. Bush. Other awards included the Presidential Citizens Medal (2008, the second-highest U.S. civilian honor), the Humanitarian Award from Domino's Pizza Corporation (1991), The Others Award from the Salvation Army (1990), several honorary doctorates from colleges and universities (1982–1995), and Outstanding Young Man of Boston from the Chamber of Commerce (1960).

Colson wrote more than 30 books, and they have sold more than 5 million copies. His autobiographical book, *Born Again*, was one of the nation's bestselling books in 1976 and was made into a feature-length film. His 1987 book, *Kingdoms in Conflict* (republished as *God and Government*), was a directive to the Christian community on the proper relationships of church and state and positioned Colson as

Cultural Mandate

The cultural or creation mandate is the view that God desires Christians not only to engage culture but also to transform culture, as God is concerned about all people. Thus, Christians should strive to be like Jonah, who was believed to be used by God to change the Assyrians' ways in the capital city of Nineveh, a people group known for their horrific cruelty (Jonah 3:5–10). Jesus said to his disciples to be the "salt of the earth" and "the light of the world." In other words, followers of Christ are be people who prevent personal and cultural decay; enrich life in dynamic ways (e.g., advocating art that nourishes society in the most noble ways); restrain evil; and uphold virtue, goodness, and justice (Matthew 5:13–16). Consequently, this cultural mandate applies to all areas of life, such as the arts, civil duties, education, environment, entertainment, family, politics, and scientific research. In other words, the cultural mandate demands that the Christian faith is never to be privatized or personal, but holistically applied to every aspect of personal and cultural transformation.

an evangelical voice for balanced Christian political activism. His last book, *The Faith*, is an appeal to the Church to re-embrace the foundational truths of Christianity. In the early 1990s, he helped to write two documents called "Evangelicals & Catholics Together."

In his later years, Colson worked to develop Christian leaders who could influence culture. This effort culminated in The Chuck Colson Center for Christian Worldview, a research and training center launched in 2009. The Center provides online courses and serves as a catalyst for Christian organizations. In 2009, Colson also served as a writer of the "Manhattan Declaration," calling on Christians to defend the sanctity of human life, traditional marriage and religious freedom.

Colson once said that his remark "'I've been born again and given my life to Jesus Christ' kept the political cartoonists of America clothed and fed for a solid month." Colson's first marriage with Nancy Billings, in 1953, bore three children. This marriage ended in divorce in January 1964. Colson was survived by his wife of 48 years, Patty; children Wendell, Christian, and Emily; and five grandchildren. Colson's work in the prisons and his advocacy for evangelical social engagement moved the latter to prominence in late 20th-century American culture.

James Menzies

See also: Prison Fellowship; Social Action, Evangelicals and

Further Reading

Aitken, Jonathan. *Charles Colson: A Life Redeemed.* New York: Continuum, 2006.
Colson, Chuck. *Born Again.* Ada, MI: Chosen Books, 2008.

Colson, Chuck. Socrates in the City. (2016). www.socratesinthecity.com/speakers/chuck
    -colson.
Congressional Record Volume 158, Number 60, Wednesday April 25, 2012, E643-E644.
    https://www.gpo.gov/fdys/pkg/CREC-2012-04-25/html/CREC-2012-04-25-pt1
    -PgE643-3.thm.
Miller, Steven P. *The Age of Evangelicalism: America's Born-Again Years.* New York: Oxford
    University Press, 2014.
Prison Fellowship Ministries. "About Charles W. Colson." http://www.pfm.org.

CONCERNED WOMEN FOR AMERICA

Concerned Women for America (CWA) is a conservative Christian women's public policy organization with 501(c)(3) status in the United States. The organization, through prayer and activism, focuses on the following issues: the family, sanctity of life, religious liberty, education, sexual exploitation, national sovereignty, and support for Israel.

CWA monitors court decisions and offers experts to media. The organization keeps members informed about current issues such as legislation through its Web site, e-mails, print, and radio. In doing so, CWA provides information about what its principals deem to be biblical responses.

The doctrinal statement for CWA includes belief in the following: the Bible as the Word of God; the deity of the God-man, Jesus Christ; and the fallen nature of humanity. As a ramification of these beliefs, the statement says, "We believe it is our duty to serve God to the best of our ability and to pray for a moral and spiritual revival that will return this nation to the traditional values upon which it was founded."

Perhaps best known as the wife of Tim LaHaye—coauthor of the *Left Behind* series (Tyndale House) and cofounder of The Moral Majority—author Beverly LaHaye founded CWA in 1979. She did so in response to a television interaction she watched between interviewer Barbara Walters and second-wave feminist Betty Friedan. When Friedan stated that she spoke for American women, LaHaye felt Friedan's views misrepresented her and many she knew.

CWA has gone on record as opposing abortion, sex education in public schools, embryonic stem cell research, and pornography. It has also opposed feminism, as well as government-sponsored childcare for families in which both parents are employed. The organization does not oppose all forms of contraception, however. CWA supports teaching intelligent design in public schools and advocates school prayer.

The annual budget for CWA is approximately $6 million. About 18 percent of its budget is devoted to fundraising; 5.9 percent is administrative; and the rest goes to programs (source: charitynavigator.org). Politically, the organization usually aligns itself with the conservative wing of the Republican Party; their program for training students is called the Ronald Reagan Memorial Internship Program. However, CWA opposes all causes and policies by any political party that they deem to be unbiblical—such as gay rights.

The organization's Web site states that CWA is the nation's largest public policy organization with a "half million members." Though *woman* appears in the name, both men and women join, and there is no membership sign-up or fee. Rather, one joins by supporting CWA in some way.

A subset of CWA is The Beverly LaHaye Institute (BLI). Founded in 1999, it began as the think tank for CWA in order to "counter the prevailing ideologies and agendas of radical leftists and secular humanists." BLI provides research, analysis, and commentary to "undergird the Judeo-Christian foundation of American culture."

Within CWA, Young Women of America (YWA) is a student-oriented initiative geared toward high school and college campuses. YWA is intended to bring women together to promote conservative values.

Sandra Glahn

See also: LaHaye, Tim and Beverly; Politics, Evangelicals and

Further Reading

Concerned Women for America. (n.d.). Accessed April 25, 2017. https://concernedwomen
.org/about/.

Hunter, James Davidson. *Culture Wars: The Struggle to Define America.* New York: Basic Books, 1991.

Smith, Leslie Dorrough. *Righteous Rhetoric: Sex, Speech, and the Politics of Concerned Women for America.* New York: Oxford University Press, 2014.

CONFERENCE ON FAITH AND HISTORY

The Conference on Faith and History (CFH) is an international society of Christian historians founded in 1967. CFH offers professional and undergraduate biennial conferences at various locations, and throughout its history has published a journal, *Fides et Historia.* Since 1979, CFH has been an affiliated society of the American Historical Association (AHA), which reports CFH membership to be about 600 in 2016.

In the late 1950s and early 1960s, evangelical historians in the United States increasingly demonstrated the desire for a permanent organization for fellowship and mutual professional development. Some scholars attempted to address this dearth by hosting receptions at the regular meetings of the AHA. Finally, a group of young historians from public institutions, including Robert Linder of Kansas State University, Richard Millett of Southern Illinois, and Robert Clouse and Richard Pierard of Indiana State University, led efforts to form an organization at the December 1966 AHA annual meeting. Provisional officers were appointed the following year, with John W. Snyder of Indiana University serving as the first president and Linder as editor in chief of *Fides et Historia.*

According to the Constitution of the CFH as adopted in 2005, the purpose of the organization is sevenfold: "To encourage scholars to explore the relationship between Christian faith and historical studies; To provide a forum for discussion of philosophies, methods, and traditions of history and to foster research in the general area of faith and history; To encourage and advance teaching and research informed by Christian faith commitments; To bring before the larger historical community the concerns and perspectives of Christian historians; To sponsor international, national, and regional meetings; To publish *Fides et Historia*; To provide a context for mentoring and networking among historians from various Christian traditions." The founding documents of CFH included the word *evangelical* to identify what kinds of scholars received encouragement. Specifically evangelical membership distinguished CFH from its larger and older AHA co-affiliate, American Society of Church History.

Liam J. Atchison

See also: Clouse, Robert G.; Linder, Robert D.; Pierard, Richard V.

Further Reading

"Constitution of the Conference on Faith and History." March 31, 2005. http://www .faithandhistory.org/wp-content/uploads/2014/02/cfhconstitutionmarch2005.pdf.

Hart, D. G. "History in Search of Meaning: The Conference on Faith and History." In *History and the Christian Historian*, edited by Ronald A. Wells. (68–87). Grand Rapids, MI: Eerdmans, 1998.

Noll, Mark A. "The Conference on Faith and History and the Study of Early American History." *Fides Et Historia* 11 (Fall 1978): 8–18.

Pierard, Richard V. "A Note on the Origins of the Conference on Faith and History." *Fides Et Historia* 1 (Fall 1968): 23–24.

CONTEMPORARY CHRISTIAN MUSIC

Contemporary Christian Music is a genre of Christian music that has developed over the past 60 years that is similar to pop music. Initially developed to appeal to the youth as part of college and youth evangelism efforts, the contemporary Christian music industry has roots in the late 1960s and early 1970s Jesus Movement and its Jesus Music artists. Contemporary Christian music has grown into the largest segment of the growing Christian music industry. Billy Graham (more than 80 years old), arguably the greatest evangelistic preacher of all time, has always used a blend of the old hymns and contemporary music at his evangelistic crusades.

Christian Market

Recent (2015) research conducted by the Gospel Music Association (GMA) shows that 68 percent of Americans—215 million people—have listened to Christian or gospel music within the past 30 days. Contemporary Christian music is the largest segment of this industry: (1) Adult contemporary: 33.8 percent, (2) gospel:

17.6 percent, (3) praise and worship: 13.6 percent, (4) rock: 11.5 percent, and (5) Southern gospel: 5.5 percent.

The popularity of this genre can been seen in tour attendance. Jamtour is an annual concert tour featuring many of the top names in Christian music, including TobyMac, Third Day, Newsboys, Steven Curtis Chapman, Lecrae, Skillet, and more. The tour has outpaced any other tour's attendance for the past four years. In 2010, the tour was second to AC/DC, and surpassed sales in excess of 400,000 tickets, landing the multi-artist spectacular ahead of tours by such artists as John Mayer, Bon Jovi, Coldplay, and Taylor Swift for the first quarter of 2010. In 2014, sales of the top tours placed this principally contemporary Christian concert tour decisively ahead of the pop music megastars, with 557,112 in attendance, followed by Bruce Springsteen (341,314) and Beyoncé (331,882). In 2015, the tour shattered attendance records, with nearly 600,000 people at a total of 47 shows across the country. At Christian music's No. 1 tour in the world, Winter Jam, attendance surpassed such tours as Fleetwood Mac, Maroon 5, and Miranda Lambert, among others, according to Pollstar's 2015 First Quarter Year to Date Worldwide Ticket Sales Top 100 Tours chart.

Artists

Many of the top-selling Christian artists are dominated by contemporary artists, including groups and names such as Casting Crowns, MercyMe, Newsboys, Needtobreathe, Michael W. Smith, Hillsong United, and Jamie Grace.

An Example: Casting Crowns

Casting Crowns is the top-selling contemporary Christian and Christian rock band; it was started in 1999 by youth pastor John Mark Hall (1969–), who serves as the band's lead vocalist, as part of a youth group at First Baptist Church in Daytona Beach, Florida. The band members all serve in their local churches and have kept their church jobs while simultaneously developing one of the most successful careers in the history of Christian music. Casting Crowns' latest album, *Thrive*, arrived January 28. It debuted at No. 1 on Billboard's Top Christian Albums chart and No. 6 on the Billboard 200, selling 45,000 first-week copies, according to Nielsen SoundScan. The group's self-titled debut, released in 2003, has sold more than 1.9 million. In a little more than a decade, Casting Crowns has placed 12 titles on Top Christian Albums and racked up some impressive statistics. The band's 2005 sophomore album, *Lifesong*, spent two weeks at No. 1 on Top Christian Albums and has sold 1.4 million. *The Altar and the Door* (2007) spent 13 weeks at No. 1 and has sold 1.2 million. In 2009, *Until the Whole World Hears* spent 18 weeks at No. 1 and has sold 1.1 million. *Come to the Well*, released in 2011, spent 14 weeks at No. 1 and has sold 779,000 copies.

Katherine Pang

See also: Calvary Chapel; Fine Arts, Evangelicals and; Jesus People Movement; Parachurch Ministries

Further Reading

Allen, Ronald B. *The Wonder of Worship.* Dallas: Thomas Nelson, 2001.
Makujina, John. *Measuring the Music: Another Look at the Contemporary Christian Music Debate*, 3rd ed. Dahlonega, GA: Old Paths, 2016.
Miller, Steve. *The Contemporary Christian Music Debate: Worldly Compromise or Agent of Renewal? Worldly Compromise or Agent of Renewal.* Minneapolis, MN: Tyndale House, 1993.

CONVERSION

Evangelicals contend that conversion is the moment one becomes a Christian. Evangelicals derive their name from the Greek word *euangelion*, which means "good news" (or gospel). For evangelicals, receiving the free gift of eternal life given by Jesus Christ in the open arms of faith alone makes one a Christian. The gospel is thus: that all people have fallen short of the perfection God ordained for humankind when He formed humanity from the dust and commanded them to care for the earth and worship Him. Their lives, being made more and more futile by wrongdoing (sin), guilt, and fear, come to resemble death rather than life. Yet God was not satisfied to condemn his creatures or see humanity destroy themselves and so He devised a way to remove their punishment and shame, and also their imperfections and evils themselves. He accomplished this not with abstract concepts of philosophy or law, but by becoming a man, without losing any aspect of His deity (the God-man), living the life of perfection that people could not, teaching them about God's love by word and example, and commanding them to turn from their wickedness. Even though Jesus Christ was unjustly executed by the civil authorities, He allowed Himself to be punished and killed in order to be the final substitute for sin on behalf of sinners (Isaiah 52:13–53:12). What seemed like a defeat was instead a victory over evil. He proved His victory by returning to life, having been raised bodily from the dead, defeating both death and sin. He then instructed His followers to tell others that their sins can be forgiven and that their lives can be restored exclusively through Jesus Christ (John 3:16).

Evangelicals believe that because God used the death and resurrection of Jesus to restore or save humans from their own depravity, destruction, and eternal separation from God, no one can partake of His forgiveness merely by assenting to various theses or arguments about the existence of God and the reality of good and evil. Rather, because it is the very act of God sacrificing Himself that makes forgiveness possible, evangelicals believe that they must place their trust in Jesus Christ for salvation, believing that He is the Son of God, who died on the cross for their sins and rose bodily from the dead. In other words, although Jesus Christ's substitutionary work alone saves, people must place their trust in Jesus Christ's Person and His work in order to receive eternal life.

To be sure, evangelicals contend that it is not an individual's faith that is the cause of one's salvation. Rather, evangelicals believe that Jesus Christ saves people; He is to be the object of their faith. Therefore, Jesus Christ, not faith, is what saves a person, for salvation is not in doing something but in receiving the love gift of eternal life from God. Once they are "converted," sinners are transferred from death to life; guilt to forgiveness; despair to hope; from being God's enemy to being one of His children.

Although evangelicals differ on specific particulars in terms of what assurance of salvation looks like and whether salvation can be willfully forsaken and lost, there are normative truths that they claim one must know before salvation takes place: (1) He or she is a sinner in need of redemption (Romans 3:23); (2) the wages of sin is death (Romans 6:23); (3) Jesus Christ died on behalf of the sinner (Romans 5:8; 1 Corinthians 15:3); (4) sinners must place their faith in Jesus Christ alone (John 3:16; Acts 16:31). But it is not mere information that brings about eternal life. Rather, evangelicals assert that only at the personal moment of receiving Christ alone as Savior, which is by the Holy Spirit's effectual drawing the sinner to Himself, is the sinner converted from death to eternal life.

Because of their emphasis on conversion, evangelicals believe that no one becomes a Christian by accident of birth or by the decision of a family member or government. The New Testament book Hebrews 11:6 states, "Without faith it is impossible to please God." Thus, a person may attend church through childhood and even participate in its various activities and ceremonies yet still not be a Christian. Though church rituals often demonstrate various Christian truths and educate those who do not yet believe, they are not what makes one a Christian. Because it is their own individual wrongs, self-destruction, and nature that have separated people from God, evangelicals contend that people must turn aside from our wickedness by embracing the gospel, letting God soften their hearts of stone and give them new purposes and desires. This first moment of belief, where a person specifically and sincerely responds to the gospel and becomes a follower of Christ, is the moment of conversion.

Russell Hemati

See also: Calvinism; Christian Apologetics; Denominationalism and Evangelicalism; Emerging and Emergent Churches; Evangelism

Further Reading

Elwell, Walter A., ed. *Evangelical Dictionary of Theology.* Grand Rapids, MI: Baker Books, 2001.

Lightner, Robert P. *Sin, Savior, and Salvation: The Theology of Everlasting Life.* Nashville, TN: Thomas Nelson, 1991.

Luther, Martin. "Preface to the Letter of St. Paul to the Romans." Trans. Andrew Thornton. *Christian Classics Ethereal Library.* Grand Rapids, MI: Calvin College. Web. May 30, 2015.

Pentecost, J. Dwight. *Designed to Be Like Him: Understanding God's Plan for Fellowship, Conduct, Conflict, and Maturity.* Grand Rapids, MI: Kregel, 1966.

St. Augustine, *Confessions.* Trans. Henry Chadwick. Oxford: Oxford University Press, 1992. Note particularly Books I–IX.

COUNCIL ON BIBLICAL MANHOOD AND WOMANHOOD

Founded in 1987, The Council on Biblical Manhood and Womanhood is an organization of evangelical scholars, pastors, and leaders who represent "complementarianism," the view that men and women possess equal worth and dignity as the image of God and are called to different roles in the family and church that together glorify God. This view can be distinguished from egalitarianism in that it does differentiate the roles of men and women in the family and the church while denying that role difference entails difference in dignity and value. It is also different from patriarchalism in that it limits the claim of God-given role differences to family and church rather than seeing these as necessarily pervading all aspects of human society, and in that it affirms the equal dignity and value of women and men as being made in the image of God (Genesis 1:26).

After an informal meeting in Dallas, Texas, in 1987, the Council on Biblical Manhood and Womanhood was formally incorporated on December 2–3, 1987, in Danvers, Massachusetts. There it adopted a document outlining the group's position, now known as the Danvers Statement on Biblical Manhood and Womanhood. Key founding members included John Piper (its first leader), James Borland, Susan Foh, Wayne Grudem, H. Wayne House, Dorothy Patterson, and Ken Sarles. Other notable contributors include D. A. Carson, J. Ligon Duncan, Elisabeth Elliot, John Frame, Douglas Moo, Paige Patterson, Vern Poythress, Randy Stinson, and Bruce Ware.

In the Danvers Statement, the Council on Biblical Manhood and Womanhood expressed concern at the incursion of secular feminism among evangelicals. It noted growing cultural confusion about the God-given, complementary differences between men and women and the disruption of harmony in marriage and the church resulting from a homogenized view of men and women. Another motivating concern was the sense of ambivalence toward the value and dignity of women in the traditional roles of motherhood and vocational homemaking. Further, the Danvers Statement noted negative effects on the family (physical and emotional abuse) and the church (lack of Biblical fidelity in patterns of leadership, hermeneutical sophistry) that the group saw as arising from a higher commitment to feminism than to Scripture.

Specific evidence given of a negative effect of feminism included a rejection of the traditional understanding of Scripture as limiting the office of pastor to men. The group also attacked "gender-neutral" translations of the Bible, most notably making an extended critique of the translation process for updates made to the New

International Version (NIV) of the Bible. The group argued that the concern for gender-neutral language ends up revising the language of Scripture, removing words such as *he, him, brother, father, son*, and *man*, and in effect undercutting the affirmation of the verbal inspiration of Scripture.

Through the Danvers Statement, the Council on Biblical Manhood and Womanhood affirms the God-givenness of gender distinctions along with the equal value and dignity of men and women as persons in the image of God. Its members argue that this unity-in-diversity of men and women predates the Fall of Adam and Eve into sin and that its good and beneficial harmony was and remains distorted by sin. They insist that the Scriptures teach the equal value and dignity of men and women throughout while affirming role differences between men and women, including male spiritual leadership in the family and Covenant community. As a result, they argue that the dignity and value of women and men is affirmed and defended not only through emphasis on the ways in which men and women are the same (i.e., being made in the image of God) but also through appreciation of the value of their differing, yet complementary and mutually beneficial, role responsibilities in the family and church.

After publication of the Danvers Statement, the Council on Biblical Manhood and Womanhood's first major project was a collection of essays, *Recovering Biblical Manhood and Womanhood: A Response to Evangelical Feminism* (1991), named *Christianity Today's* Book of the Year in 1992. The group also published a Statement on Abuse in 1994 and in the same year launched its Web site (CBMW.org) and a print journal, *Journal for Biblical Manhood and Womanhood*.

The Council on Biblical Manhood and Womanhood has had influence in evangelical life through its creation of a venue for publication and scholarship for complementarian evangelical scholars. It has also had significant influence on several evangelical denominations, such as the Presbyterian Church of America. All six of the Southern Baptist seminaries require affirmation of the Danvers Statement as a condition of employment for faculty. Furthermore, the group has cosponsored academic debate and dialogue with the primary evangelical egalitarian group, Christians for Biblical Equality (founded in 1988).

Benjamin Blair Phillips

See also: Danvers Statement; Gender, Evangelicals and; Human Rights, Evangelicals and; Social Action, Evangelicals and; Theological Controversies within Evangelicalism

Further Reading

The Danvers Statement on Biblical Manhood and Womanhood, 1987.

Grudem, Wayne. *Biblical Foundations for Manhood and Womanhood.* Wheaton, IL: Crossway, 1991.

Piper, John, and Wayne Grudem. *Recovering Biblical Manhood and Womanhood: A Response to Evangelical Feminism.* Wheaton, IL: Crossway, 1991.

COUNTERCULTURE, EVANGELICALS AND
(1960s AND 1970s)

Evangelicals took part in and confronted all aspects of the counterculture movement in American society. Evangelicals were part of American life during those years and were not separate from it. They were influenced by and affected the ideas and activities of the era. Although most evangelicals were theologically, socially, politically conservative, they were not monolithic, and there were strong voices and activities on both the left and the right on every issue, from emerging environmental concerns to the war in Vietnam. There was fragmentation and realignment of evangelicals, especially among white evangelicalism. In the aftermath of the Second World War (1939–1945), American evangelicals projected a new voice in American religion that shed much of the social and ecclesiastical separatism and fundamentalism of the 1920s and 1930s.

Evangelicalism was on the rise numerically and visibly in American culture in the 1950s, and by the 1960s there were many strong evangelical institutions, organizations, and publications. Although many evangelicals rejected ideas and aspects of the 1960s, including the counterculture movement epitomized by such things as the antiwar movement, rock music, the drug culture, hippies, and radical politics, they also helped shape responses to those things in ways that would later inform single-issue activism, such as the debate over abortion, civil rights, sexuality, economic concerns, and gender issues.

Out of the political tumult of the 1960s and 1970s would arise the evangelical politics and movement of the Religious Right seen most clearly in the prominence of Jerry Falwell and the Moral Majority. However, there were dissenting evangelical voices such as Ron Sider, Jim Wallis and participants in the Sojourners community, Evangelicals for McGovern, and Evangelicals for Social Action.

Evangelicals such as Bill Bright and Hal Lindsey used the terminology and hopes of the counterculture movement in their evangelism and writings, such as Bright's *Revolution Now!* (1971) and Lindsey's *There's a New World Coming* (1973). Other writers such as Francis Schaeffer were among the first evangelicals to address ecology and the environment in *Pollution and the Death of Man* (1970) as Earth Day was inaugurated in 1970 and pollution became a national issue. Similarly, in 1973 a group of evangelicals publically called for a stronger evangelical commitment to social action and social justice with the 1973 Chicago Declaration of Evangelical Social Concern. Publications such as *Campus Life* (published by Youth for Christ International) and the *Hollywood Free Paper* of the Jesus People Movement used the language of the era to encourage change in the churches and society and to call for spiritual growth and spiritual revolution. Many churches had evangelistic outreach ministries such as coffee houses that sought to specifically minister to young people. The ministry of Campus Crusade for Christ (now Cru) flourished on college campuses, with speakers such as Josh McDowell and Hal Lindsey addressing hundreds of thousands of college students with talks on culture and Christian apologetics. So also did the international ministry of Francis and Edith Schaeffer at L'Abri sites in

Switzerland and the United States attempt to address the concerns, answer the intellectual questions, and encourage spirituality of those coming of age in the 1960s and 1970s. The work of all of these individuals, organizations, and many others continues to the present, energizing evangelicals on the left and the right.

The most visible participation of evangelicals in the counterculture movement came from the 1970s Jesus People Movement (also called at the time the Jesus Revolution and Jesus Freaks), located primarily on the West Coast of the United States and centered in the San Francisco Bay area, California's counterculture capital. Much of the Jesus People Movement had a strong evangelistic thrust, often with apocalyptic overtones proclaiming the soon fulfillment of Bible prophecy and events such as the rapture of Christians and the Second Coming of Jesus Christ. Out of this movement also came music from musicians such as Barry McGuire and Larry Norman that influenced secular and religious music to the present. The present-day politically active evangelical left can also be traced to the social and political activism of the 1960s and 1970s, during which evangelicals across the political spectrum articulated political positions based on their respective interpretation and application of Christian doctrine and the Bible.

Evangelical involvement in the counterculture shows that evangelicals were diverse and complex and would continue to be so in the ensuing decades to the present. The beginning of evangelical responses to many present-day concerns such as environmentalism, justice, gender, race, war, peace, and political activism arose out of evangelical engagement with the counterculture movement.

Timothy J. Demy

See also: Chicago Declaration of Evangelical Social Concern; Explo '72; Jesus Music; Jesus People Movement; Norman, Larry David; Politics, Evangelicals and; Schaeffer, Francis A. and Edith

Further Reading

Gasaway, Brantely W. *Progressive Evangelicals and the Pursuit of Social Justice.* Chapel Hill, NC: University of North Carolina Press, 2014.

Schafer, Axel. R., ed. *American Evangelicals and the 1960s.* Madison, WI: The University of Wisconsin Press, 2013.

Sutton, Matthew Avery. *American Apocalypse: A History of American Evangelicalism.* Cambridge, MA: Belknap Press, 2014.

Swartz, David R. *Moral Minority: The Evangelical Left in an Age of Conservatism.* Philadelphia: University of Pennsylvania Press, 2012.

COWBOY CHURCH MOVEMENT

The cowboy church movement is a transdenominational evangelical seeker church movement that originated by delivering an applicable message to a unique population at a specific point in history. The church began with Fellowship of Christian

Cowboys, which is a nonprofit interdenominational ministry that operates solely on the faith-funded support of individuals and companies who share a common desire to further the spread of the gospel of Jesus Christ to rural America.

In 1973, Wilbur Plaugher (1922–), the famous rodeo clown, and Mark Schricker (1938–2014), National Finals Rodeo calf roping and steer wrestling champion, started the Fellowship of Christian Cowboys, with the national office in Colorado Springs, Colorado. It is a faith-funded ministry designed to promote the gospel of Jesus Christ to rural America. By mid-century, rodeos attracted participation from contemporary working cattlemen and rodeo cowboys throughout the western United States and Canada. Rodeos became so popular by the mid-1900s that Hollywood produced rodeo-themed movies; Nashville published rodeo-themed songs; universities developed rodeo athletic programs; and rodeoing proved a large-scale, professional occupation. The cowboy, of course, stole the show within these performances as their central character. Several appreciated the model, namely Canadian cowboy minister Phil Doan, who began a cowboy church in Calgary, Alberta; and Harry and Joanne Yates, who started a church in Nashville, Tennessee by 1990. The cowboy church movement has had phenomenal growth.

Cowboy pastors, as they see it, emulate Jesus's example of using parables. Most pastors relate personal stories or provide real-life examples to explain Scripture and its application in 21st-century America. Cowboy pastors explain traditional churches have forgotten that Christians are supposed to know each other intimately and befriend strangers. They strive to make attendees feel welcome, even "at home," during services.

This church movement is part of the theologically strict and conservative seeker church movement. This indicates that lay leadership is essential to the vitality and function of each cowboy church. Members claim "real" worship means without pretensions or people trying to be something they are not. An authentic church is one whose leaders are open, honest, and transparent about their faith, struggles, and commitments. The community that cowboy Christians create through their religious performances and shared experiences, both within and away from the meeting-house, enables them to get through the difficult trials.

The cowboy church movement is unique. Their churches offer a "down-to-earth" environment, and their members ride horses and eat home cooking together; they

Key Term in Evangelicalism: *Testimony*

The word *testimony* is a casual term used by evangelicals to refer to one's personal, subjective experience of salvation or some aspect of one's spiritual life (Acts 10:30–33, 10:38–43, 26; 1 Peter 3:15–16). Testimonies are not only historically seen in evangelistic crusades, revival services, and worship services but also used in conversational evangelism and Christian apologetics, offering an explanation of hope, reasons for belief, intimacy with God, or a particular act or acts attributed to God.

also advocate conservative evangelicalism in such a way that is appealing to rural Americans, their context, and their ideals. The movement illustrates the breadth of evangelicalism and the desire evangelicals have to minister across the cultural spectrum.

James Towns

See also: Emerging and Emergent Churches; Evangelicalism; Evangelism; Warren, Richard Duane ("Rick"); Willow Creek Community Church

Further Reading

Bielo, James S. *Emerging Evangelicals: Faith, Modernity, and the Desire for Authenticity.* New York: New York University Press, 2011.

Bromley, David G., and Elizabeth Phillips. "Cowboy Churches." World Religions and Spiritualities Project. July 11, 2013. http://www.wrldrels.org/profiles/CowboyChurches.htm.

Hirschman, Dale. *The Cowboy Call: Living for Jesus in the Western World.* Mustang, OK: Tate, 2010.

McAdams, Jake R. "Can I Get a Yee-Haw and an Amen: Collecting and Interpreting Oral Histories of Texas Cowboy Churches." MA thesis, Stephen F. Austin State University, 2013.

CREATION RESEARCH SOCIETY

The Creation Research Society is an evangelical professional and academic association whose members believe in a six-day creation. It was founded in May 1963 primarily to provide a research and publication platform for scientific papers that endorsed and supported the views of biblical creationism. Originally conceived as the Creation Research Advisory Committee early in 1963, and headed by Walter E. Lammerts (1904–1996), a geneticist; William J. Tinkle, a geneticist; and Henry M. Morris (1918–2006), a hydraulic engineer, the society's 10 founding scientists had experienced problems publishing papers in other peer-reviewed technical journals, presumably increasingly controlled by evolutionary perspectives. In July 1964, it published the first quarterly issue of *Creation Research Society Quarterly*. Scientific fields represented both in membership and in publication include geology, general and specialized biological science (genetics, natural selection, taxonomy), and thermodynamics; and later included astronomy and physics. Within the quarterly flood, geology became a key component of the articles and other published literature. According the Duane Gish (1921–2013), in 1973, the research required to disprove evolution had already been done, but geologic work explaining the phenomenon had a long way to go. Instead of actualism, primary attention was given to the interpretation of geological data against the backdrop of catastrophism. The 1961 publication John C. Whitcomb (1924–) and Henry Morris's *The Genesis Flood* (1961) had a major impact on the early lines drawn in the Society; however, the authors left in 1970 to start the Institute for Creation Research. Members of these two organizations are among the key figures in the modern young earth creation science movement.

The society's membership is under 1,000, and there are two levels of membership: voting membership, requiring a post-graduate scientific degree; and sustaining membership. Both require adherence to their statement of belief. The statement contains specific truth claims key to the intersection of science and belief and includes the principle of literal, plain interpretation of history and science statements in Scripture; a six-day young earth creation, in which organic changes occur only within kinds created during these six days; the special creation of Adam and Eve along with their subsequent fall into sin; and a global Noahic flood.

CRS has expanded its focus over the decades. In addition to the journal, it has produced or published many books, textbooks, and primers. It provides modest support of the research itself, both with grants and the 1994 construction of the Van Andel Creation Research Center (VACRC) in north-central Arizona. Both of these resources are dedicated to creation-related research programs. Additionally, in order to support more popular articles, CRS has since 1996 published *Creation Matters*. Members also provide presentations to churches and other groups. VACRC is one of several organizations dedicated to the understanding of and research in science from an evangelical perspective. It also is a reminder that there is no single view of science among evangelicals.

Shawn Smith

See also: American Scientific Affiliation; Christian Apologetics; Environment, Evangelicals and the; Institute for Creation Research; Intelligent Design Movement; Morris, Henry; Science, Evangelicals and

Further Reading

Gish, Duane T. "A Decade of Creationist Research, [Parts I and II]." *Creation Research Society Quarterly* 12(1–2): 34–46.

Harrison, Peter. *The Territories of Science and Religion.* Chicago: The University of Chicago Press, 2015.

Livingstone, David N., D. G. Hart, and Mark A. Noll, eds. *Evangelicals and Science in Historical Perspective* (Religion in America Series). New York: Oxford University Press, 1999.

Moreland, J. P. *Christianity and the Nature of Science: A Philosophical Investigation.* Grand Rapids, MI: Baker Books, 1989.

Numbers, Ronald L. *The Creationists: From Scientific Creationism to Intelligent Design*, expanded ed. Berkeley, CA: University of California Press, 2006.

Rusch, W. H. 1982. "A brief statement of the history and aims of the CRS." *CRS Quarterly* 19(2): 149.

CRISWELL, W. A. (1909–2002)

A prominent Southern Baptist minister, Wallie Amos Criswell was born in Eldorado, Oklahoma, in 1909. He died in Dallas, Texas, as pastor emeritus of First Baptist Church in 2002. Young Wallie's early years were hard and lacking in luxuries of life. Criswell stated that the family lived on very little and that they were not poor—they just did not have any money. In the second grade, Criswell took elocution lessons. After graduating from school in Amarillo, Texas, he entered Baylor in the fall of 1927. Later he chose English as a major, and minors in philosophy, psychology, and Greek. In 1931, he entered the Southern Baptist Theological Seminary in Louisville, Kentucky, where he was awarded the Master of Theology degree in 1934. During the seminary days, Criswell met Betty Harris. She was a schoolteacher and played the piano where Criswell served in a student pastorate. Criswell married Miss Harris on February 14, 1935. W. A. Criswell earned the Doctor of Philosophy degree in 1937, with a major in New Testament interpretation. His dissertation was entitled "The John the Baptist Movement in Its Relation to the Christian Movement." Completion of formal education did not stop Dr. Criswell's study. He maintained a diligent study of Scripture approximately five hours a day, as well as a constant pursuit of material to substantiate his conservative theological position. He was the author of 54 books and spoke numerous times. Criswell accepted pastorate at First Baptist Church of Chickasha in 1937 with great zeal. In 1939, he and Betty Criswell welcomed their first and only child, a daughter whom they named Mabel Anne.

It was in Chickasha that Criswell's ability as a bible preacher improved. He became known for his exposition of Scripture.

The success story of Dr. W. A. Criswell at First Baptist Church of Dallas could sound like a chapter out of a Texas brag book. Criswell was outspoken on controversial issues in politics, theology, and segregation. Perhaps Criswell's greatest opposition came from the Association of Baptist Professors of Religion, which adopted a resolution against Criswell's interpretation of the Bible in his book *Why I Preach That the Bible Is Literally True*. Whether from friend or foe, Criswell has been described as a cross between Billy Sunday and King Kong.

Although Criswell had been asked through the years, he would not permit his name to be nominated for presidency of the Convention. He always declined because his first allegiance was to his local congregation; however, he finally acquiesced and was elected to two terms as president. Criswell was invited to speak to the annual

Key Term in Evangelicalism: *Infallibility*

The term *infallibility* is an older term in evangelicalism that essentially means "incapable of error." This word is used to describe the original autographs or documents based on their interpretation of 2 Timothy 3:16–17 and Peter 1:19–21. If God, who is the sum total of His infinite perfections, cannot err, than the original writings cannot be capable of error. God, who is perfectly powerful, sovereign, and good, can use finite, sinful people to record His words in such a way that they are absolutely free from mistakes, errors, or omissions (John 17:17).

Baptist Statewide Conference on Evangelism at Columbia, South Carolina, in February 1956. The speech caused a blast of controversy when the news media stated, "Criswell said that he not only strongly favored racial segregation but that it would be best for religious groups to 'stick to their own kind.'" Criswell proclaimed that forced desegregation was fundamentally undemocratic and unchristian and was quoted by the Associated Press as saying, "Integration is a thing of idiocy and foolishness. Any man who says he is altogether desegregated is soft in the head."

The first Sunday after Criswell was elected president of the Southern Baptist Convention, he made an address to the First Baptist Church of Dallas, Texas, on June 9, 1968, advocating integration. In the year 1968, there were several major events that were significant in the integration controversy. Some of the events were affirmatively constructive, and some were devastating. Criswell faced two issues that needed to be clarified. In his first sermon after being elected president of the SBC, Criswell revealed a paradigm shift as he preached a sermon entitled "The Church of the Open Door." He told of the battle that had been in his heart for several years concerning his position on segregation. Criswell stated that he did not want any embarrassment to come to the church or convention because of his former stand on segregation. This new outlook was encouraged by one of Criswell's friends, who spoke of the possibility of designed destruction, hurt, and embarrassment to the church because of a speech he had made earlier in 1956 in South Carolina before he changed his mind about segregation. The question still remained: Was Criswell a transformed person concerning race, or did he have a spiritual paradigm shift, or was this a political move to keep Dallas from becoming a second Little Rock?

W. A. Criswell discerned political signs of the times. He was able to envision the emergence of a new conservatism that would become the new Religious Right. Perhaps Criswell's most famous and revealing sermon came in 1985; it was entitled "Whether We Live or Die," and it addressed the issues: (1) the pattern for death of a denomination; (2) the pattern of death for an institution; (3) the pattern of death for a preacher and professor; and (4) the promise of renascence, and resurrection and revival. Criswell proclaimed that opposition to evangelical truths sprang from two sources. One was the publication of Darwin's *Origin of Species*, and the other was the vast inroads of German higher criticism and rationalism that explained away the miracles of the Bible and reduced the inspired Word to merely a human book. He concluded by stating, "United in prayer, preaching, witnessing, working, not around the higher-critical denial of Scripture, but around the infallible Word of God in Christ Jesus, we cannot fail."

Criswell's paradigm of preaching, speaking and writing can best be summarized as coming from a person who was firmly committed to the Bible and its application to daily life.

James Towns

See also: Baptists and Evangelicalism; Inerrancy

Further Reading

Criswell, W. A. "An Address by Dr. W. A. Criswell, Pastor, First Baptist Church, Dallas, Texas, to the Joint Assembly," *The Courier-Journal* (Louisville, Kentucky), February 23, 1956, p. 10. Accessed April 25, 2017. https://www.newspapers.com/newspage/108458555/

Criswell, W. A. "Whether We Live or Die." Sermon delivered June 10, 1958, at the Pastor's Conference o the Southern Baptist Convention in Dallas, Texas. Nashville: Southern Baptist Historical Library and Archives, videotape.

Criswell, W. A. *Why I Preach the Bible Is Literally True.* Nashville, TN: Broadman Press, 1969.

Keith, Billy. *W. A. Criswell: The Authorized Biography.* Old Tappan, NJ: Fleming H. Revell, 1973.

Towns, James. *The Social Conscience of W. A. Criswell.* Dallas: Crescendo Press, 1977.

CRU (FORMERLY CAMPUS CRUSADE FOR CHRIST INTERNATIONAL)

Formed in 1951 by William and Vonette Bright, Campus Crusade for Christ International (or "Cru," as it is known today in the United States) launched as a parachurch organization on the University of California, Los Angeles (UCLA) campus. The group exists to "fulfill the Great Commission [Matthew 28:16–20] in the power of the Holy Spirit by winning people to faith in Jesus Christ, building them in their faith, sending them to win and build others, and helping the body of Christ to do evangelism and discipleship."

Bright grew up on a ranch in Oklahoma to a Christian mother and a non-Christian father. After becoming a Christian in 1945, Bright briefly attended Princeton Theological Seminary before transferring to Fuller Theological Seminary in 1947. During his years in seminary, he also dated and married Vonette Zachary, who would become his lifelong partner in ministry. During his senior year at Fuller, Bright described an instance in the spring of 1951 "when God spoke to me in a sovereign, unique, supernatural way concerning my role in helping to fulfill His command." Friend and trusted Fuller seminary professor Wilbur Smith gave Bright the name for his newfound organization: Campus Crusade for Christ.

Shortly thereafter, Bright left Fuller Seminary, formed an advisory board for the fledgling ministry, and focused his attention on UCLA as the first area of outreach. According to Bright, within the first few months of activity, more than 250 UCLA students committed their lives to Jesus Christ. Soon, Campus Crusade formed groups on additional campuses. By the fall of 1952, Campus Crusade established ministries on several campuses, including the University of Southern California (USC), the University of California at Berkeley, Oregon State, and the University of Washington.

As he traveled across the country, Bright recognized the need for a "distilled essence of the gospel message" for ministry and outreach. This eventually led to the formation of the booklet entitled *Have You Heard of the Four Spiritual Laws?* According to Bright, "just as there are physical laws governing the physical universe (such as the law of gravity), so there are spiritual laws that govern the spiritual universe."

Bright encouraged Crusade staff members to use the spiritual laws in their evangelistic efforts. The four laws are as follows: (1) God loves you and offers a wonderful plan for your life. (2) Man is sinful and separated from God; thus he cannot know and experience God's love and plan for his life. (3) Jesus Christ is God's only provision for man's sin. Through Him you can know and experience God's love and plan for your life. (4) We must individually receive Jesus Christ as Savior and Lord. Then we can know and experience God's love and plan for our lives. According to its own estimates, Campus Crusade has distributed more than 100 million copies of the tract in all the major languages of the world.

In June 1972, Campus Crusade hosted EXPLO '72 in Dallas, Texas. The conference drew more than 85,000 people and offered specialized training for high school and college students, laymen and women, faculty members, and others involved in various ministries. In addition, roughly 1.3 million people attended EXPLO '74 in Seoul, Korea; finally, EXPLO '85 connected 600,000 Christians via satellite at 100 different locations throughout the world.

By 1958, Crusade began the process of establishing ministries overseas. Dr. Joon Con Kim from Fuller Theological Seminary served as Crusade's first international director, and by 1968, the ministry had plants in 32 countries.

In 1976, Bright partnered with movie producer John Heyman to create the *JESUS* film. Bright envisioned a biblically accurate film that could be used as an evangelistic resource. According to internal Campus Crusade statistics, the film has resulted in 66 million exposures to the Gospel, 12 million decisions for Christ, 5 million initial discipleship follow-ups, and 42,000 planted churches and preaching points since its 1979 release.

Although Campus Crusade had based its headquarters in Arrowhead Springs, California, since 1962, the organization shifted its international headquarters to Orlando, Florida, in 1991. In 1996, Bright received a $1 million award as the recipient of the Templeton Prize for Progress in Religion. Previous winners included Mother Theresa and Dr. Billy Graham. In his acceptance speech, Bright indicated that he would allocate the award funds "to educate leaders of the church worldwide to the spiritual benefits of fasting and prayer." In 2000, Bright received news that he was suffering from pulmonary fibrosis, an incurable and incapacitating lung disease. In 2001, Bright selected Steve Douglass to succeed him as president of the ministry. Bright died in 2003, at 81 years old, due to complications from the disease.

In 2011, the American branch of the organization changed its name from Campus Crusade for Christ to the abbreviated "Cru." The group discontinued the use of the term "crusade" because of its negative association with the medieval religious wars; furthermore, the ministry did not want its name to serve as a hindrance to evangelistic efforts, particularly among Muslims.

Cru has become the largest nonphilanthropic, evangelical parachurch organization in the United States, with worldwide revenues that surpassed $689 million in 2013. Today, Cru International maintains an operational staff of more than 27,000 members and 225,000 volunteers in 190 countries. The ministry has operational offices around the world, including in India, Hungary, Costa Rica, Singapore, South Africa, Germany, and the United States. Staff members raise their own financial support to cover the costs of their salary, training, and ministry. As of 2015, Cru had 5,300 campus ministries worldwide, with 2,088 in the United States. In addition to its campus outreach, Cru oversees a number of additional outreach programs, including the Josh McDowell ministry, Athletes in Action, and the Christian Embassies in Washington, D.C., and the United Nations. Cru also provides ministry for graduate students, faculty members, military personnel, and those in the inner city.

Brittany Burnette

See also: Bright, William R. ("Bill"); Evangelism; Parachurch Ministries

Further Reading

"Bill and Vonette Bright: Founders of Campus Crusade for Christ, International." (n.d.). Accessed April 1, 2015. http://www.cru.org/about/our-leadership/our-founders.html.

Bright, Bill. *Come Help Change the World.* Peachtree City, GA: Campus Crusade for Christ/ Bright Media Foundation, 1999.

Bright, Bill. "Have You Heard of the Four Spiritual Laws?" (2011). Accessed April 28, 2017. https://annointing.files.wordpress.com/2011/03/have-you-ever-heard-of-the-four -spiritual-laws.pdf.

Bright, Bill. "How You Can Help Fulfill the Great Commission." (n.d.). Cru.com. Adapted from How You Can Help Fulfill the Great Commission, Bill Bright. Copyright 1971, 1998 NewLife Publications, Campus Crusade for Christ. Accessed April 28, 2017. https://www.cru.org/content/dam/cru/legacy/2012/04/brighthowyoucanhelpfulfillthe greatcommission.pdf.

Bright, Bill. (n.d.). "How You Can Witness Effectively: The Message." Cru. April 28, 2017. https://www.cru.org/train-and-grow/transferable-concepts/introduce-others-to-christ .3.html.

Cru. "About Us." (n.d.). Accessed March 31, 2015. http://www.cru.org/about.html.

Goodstein, Laurie. "Campus Crusade for Christ Is Renamed." *New York Times,* July 20, 2011. http://www.nytimes.com/2011/07/21/us/21brfs-CAMPUSCRUSAD_BRF.html?_r=0.

Staggers, K. L. "Campus Crusade for Christ International." In *Dictionary of Christianity in America.* Daniel G. Reid, Robert Dean Linder, et al. Downers Grove, IL: InterVarsity Press, 1990. Logos Edition.

Turner, John G. *Bill Bright & Campus Crusade for Christ: The Renewal of Evangelicalism in Postwar America.* Chapel Hill, NC: University of North Carolina Press, 2008.

UPI (United Press International). "American Wins Templeton Prize for Religion," (March 6, 1996) Accessed April 28, 2017. www.upi.com/Archives/1996/03/06/American-wins -Templeton-Prize-for-religion/7110826088400/.

D

DALLAS THEOLOGICAL SEMINARY

Dallas Theological Seminary is a nondenominational evangelical seminary that has been one of the leading institutions of evangelical higher education in the United States. The roots of the Dallas Theological Seminary, a postgraduate institution committed to the preparation of Christian leaders, can be traced to the Bible Conference Movement of the late 19th and early 20th centuries. At least one historic feature of the school provides evidence of its trajectory: the embrace of the Gaebelein/Scofieldian assimilation of the Darbyite (following the eschatology of John Nelson Darby) nuancing of premillennialism, coupled with dispensationalism, poignantly evidenced in the fracturing dissolution of the Niagara Bible Conferences and the emergence of the Seacliffe Bible Conferences,.

Lewis Sperry Chafer (1871–1952), its visionary founder, was a product of the Bible Conference Movement; most particularly, he embraced the theological insights of his primary mentor, Cyrus Ingerson Scofield (1843–1921). Chafer met Scofield when the latter pastored the Congregational Church of Northfield, Massachusetts, at D.L. Moody's behest, and directed the Northfield Training School. There he came under Scofield's mentorship in 1901, having been in evangelistic ministry for a decade. He traveled with Scofield after 1910 under the extension auspices of the New York Night School of the Bible, cofounded the Philadelphia School of the Bible (1913), and served with Charles Trumbull, the author of the early hagiographic biography of Scofield (1921), in the offices of the *Sunday School Times* in Philadelphia, before moving to Dallas, Texas.

The vision for the Evangelical Theological College (1924), now Dallas Theological Seminary (1936), embraced three broad Bible conference distinctives in the post-Niagara conference era: premillennial dispensationalism, filtered through the lens of Scofield and Gaebelein; a mild embrace of Keswick sanctification theories; a firm embrace of the Augustinian and reformed approach to soteriology (sin and grace); and the Princetonian advocacy of the inerrancy of the biblical text. This did not place the institution in an awkward position within "Fundamentalism/Evangelicalism" in the early 1920s, but it did within "Evangelicalism" as it took shape in the 1940s and 1950s. At the same time, it brought to the surface differences within "Fundamentalism" as it took shape in the same decades. The differences between "Evangelicalism" and the seminary were theological and attitudinal in nature; with "Fundamentalism," it became largely attitudinal.

Dispensationalism

Dispensationalism is an evangelical system of theology that embodies three central concepts, namely, the consistent use of a plain, normal, literal, grammatical, historical-literary method of interpretation to the Scripture. They believe this inductive approach to the Scripture then leads one to recognize that not only does God have a distinct program for Israel and the Church, but also reveals God's overall purpose, namely, to glorify Himself (Ephesians 1:6, 12, 14). The word dispensationalism finds its origins in the Greek word "oikonomia" which means to administer, manage, or regulate the affairs of a household. Thus dispensationalists believe God has ruled over the timeline of human history in various ways as He progressively discloses revelation adapted to their particular needs over a specific period of time. While God Himself has not changed, the ways He has governed over the lives of people have changed. Those changes are called ages, economies, or dispensations. Other types of Dispensationalism include the recent development of progressive dispensationalism, and ultra-dispensationalism, which is an extreme version. Historically, dispensationalists have generally embraced seven dispensations by which God has governed human history:

1. Age of Innocence: Genesis 1:28–3:6
2. Age of Conscience: Genesis 4:1–8:14
3. Age of Civil Government: Genesis 8:15–11:9.
4. Age of Promise or Patriarchal Rule: Genesis 11:10–Exodus 18:27
5. Age of the Mosaic Law: Exodus 19:1–Acts 1:26
6. Age of the Church: Acts 2:1–Revelation 19:21
7. Age of the Millennium: Revelation 20:1–15

The components of the institution's definitional structure and ethos emerged in the initial decade of its existence, yet it became increasingly difficult to find a fit within evangelicalism. It was fundamentalistic, but not fundamentalist in rhetoric and posture while being separatistic socially and morally. It sought, in the original vision, to be denominational loyalists favoring the reformed tradition in its approach to soteriology, though modified by its rejection of definite atonement and reformed approaches to sanctification. It was the institutionalization of the Bible conference approach to the Scriptures at the graduate level of ministerial preparation with a hermeneutical approach to the Bible reflective of its embrace of dispensational, pre-tribulational, premillennialism that was eschewed by the mainline denominations. It was a "dove" that ultimately made a sacred ark out of contradictory pieces into an allegorical "Chinese puzzle"; it is an "American" institution.

Five presidents have served the seminary. Each shaped the school; each brought a defining persona to the office that is both a product of biblical insight and scriptural passion and, at the same time, was contextually time-locked. Chafer (served from 1924–1952) was a visionary whose passion for the grace of God as expressed in Bible proclamation and evangelism was the heart of the man. He was magnetic in the sense that he possessed an ability to graft students into his vision. He founded an institution with an array of supportive, secondary valves that he envisioned as essential bulwarks in the accomplishment of the two primary goals. Among these priorities were dispensationalism, as supportive of biblical grace, more so than covenantalism; a Princetonian inerrancy theory as a safeguard that preserved the magnificence of the gospel, and a mild Keswick theory of sanctification with Brethren activism as the proper response to grace. His strength was not in operations, but passion.

John F. Walvoord (served from 1952–1986) possessed administrative and organizational skills lacking in his predecessor and these were revealed throughout his presidency. In his tenure, the school emerged from obscurity to become a world-class institution with an enlarged campus, diversified student body, multiple degree programs, a scholarly faculty, and a huge budget. There was change, however, of a more subtle kind. Because of the expertise of Walvoord in the field of eschatology, his teaching, writing, and conference ministry, that emphasis greatly enlarged while other emphases continued. Walvoord saw eschatology as essential to the accomplishment of the school's mission, and the central importance of it greatly was increased, particularly in the view of observers. The school took on his personality and benefited from his accomplishments.

The Donald K. Campbell (served from 1986–1994) administration was sadly troubled with an economic downturn, faculty dissension within and without the confines of its creedal affirmations, and student body decline. A unique feature of Campbell's tenure was his attempt to eschew some of the public perceptions of the school as a narrow, inflexible institution. In seeking to broaden the image of the school, though not so the faculty, he sought to bring the school into the "broader" evangelical world. There is evidence to suggest that he was not pleased with some of the outcomes of his policies. In effect, his contacts with the larger evangelical world helped him to see benefits of enlarging the seminary's circle. He, like the other presidents, sought see the seminary's mission accomplished in a way the other had not. He was willing, for example, to allow diversity of opinion concerning dispensationalism and loosen the doctrinal requirements for entrance and matriculation.

In Charles R. Swindoll (served from 1994–2001), the school had its first non-academician at the helm. His pastoral compassions became foremost in the school's direction. Though he embraced the school's theology and mission statement, he placed more emphasis through his rhetoric on issues of moral and spiritual integrity than previous presidents. He wanted a "leaner," more focused school reflective of his personal passions.

With the current administration, under the direction of Mark L. Bailey, it is difficult to draw only tentative conclusions at this time. It seems that it can be argued that the current presidency is more uncertain about the propriety of the centrist direction than in the Campbell era and a greater interest in administrative details than the Swindoll era.

In conclusion, it may be argued that Dallas Theological Seminary is an anomaly within American evangelicalism and the root cause of this is its blended heritage of a variety of historical theological traditions. In a sense, it is a Chinese puzzle with a composite of beliefs, attitudes, relationships, and actions that has left outsiders appalled and insiders amused and amazed at times. It is an American institution etched by a utilitarian pragmatism and a common-sense approach, but it has remained true to its 19th-century epistemological origins. It is the Bible Conference Movement, the combination of revivalist spirit and fascination with the Bible, brought into an educational setting as a graduate institution. It is reformed but not enough for some; it is fundamentalist but not enough for some and far too much for others. Its dispensational adherence is blamed for social retreatism and its approach to the spiritual life has as holiness bent without Pentecostalism's motoric speech. It is a school that simply is not a comfortable fit in any particular form of evangelicalism. Perhaps that is its genius after all is said and done and it remains a strong presence within contemporary American evangelicalism.

John D. Hannah

See also: Bible Conference Movement; Bible Exposition; Chafer, Lewis Sperry; Dispensationalism; Higher Education, Evangelicals and; Ryrie, Charles Caldwell; Walvoord, John F.

Further Reading

Blaising, Craig A., and Bock, Darrell L., eds. *Dispensationalism, Israel, and the Church.* Grand Rapids, MI: Zondervan, 1992.

Hannah, John D. *The Uncommon Union: Dallas Theological Seminary and American Evangelicalism.* Grand Rapids, MI: Zondervan, 2009.

Marsden, George M. *Fundamentalism and American Culture, 1870–1925.* New York: Oxford University Press, 1980.

Marsden, George M. *Evangelicalism and Modern America.* Grand Rapids, MI: Eerdmans, 1984.

Sandeen, Ernest R. *The Roots of Fundamentalism: British and American, 1 Millennialism, 1800-1930.* Chicago: University of Chicago Press, 1970.

Walvoord, John F. *The Blessed Hope: The Autobiography of John F. Walvoord.* Chattanooga, TN: AMG Publishers, 2001.

DANVERS STATEMENT

The Danvers Statement is a 1989 evangelical document that presents what is known as complementarian perspective on the biblical interpretation of gender and roles between men and women. Concerned at the growth of what they took to be unbiblical teaching on the roles of men and women, a group including H. Wayne House, John Piper, and Wayne Grudem met in Dallas in 1987 to discuss a response. They were convinced that, according to the Bible, men and women were equal in dignity and worth, but that their roles were not identical. Their view on this issue was complementarian as opposed to egalitarian.

Later that year, they gathered in Danvers, Massachusetts, on the eve of a meeting of the Evangelical Theological Society, and adopted a theological position statement, one they had drafted in Dallas. Their Danvers Statement on Biblical Manhood and Womanhood became the cornerstone of the Council on Biblical Manhood and Womanhood (cbmw.org), which they established on the same occasion.

The next year, egalitarians formed a counterorganization, Christians for Biblical Equality (cbeinternational.org), which soon published a response to the Danvers Statement and a general declaration of their own. In turn, in 1991, the complementarians produced *Recovering Biblical Manhood and Womanhood: A Response to Evangelical Feminism*, with essays by such evangelical scholars (with diverse denominational connections, including Lutheran, Baptist, Presbyterian, Evangelical Free, and Orthodox) as D. A. Carson, John Frame, Thomas Schreiner, Wayne House, Ray Ortland, Vern Poythress, James Borland, John Frame, and Paige Patterson, as well as author Elisabeth Elliot. It won *Christianity Today's* Book of the Year award.

Through the years, the board of reference for CBE has included Anthony Campolo, Richard Foster, Roberta Hestenes, Alvera Mickelsen, Ron Sider, Millard Erickson, and Mary Stewart Van Leeuwen. The council for the contrasting CBMW has included J. Ligon Duncan, Daniel Akin, R. Albert Mohler, Mary Kassian, Bruce Ware, Kent Hughes, Beverly LaHaye, Douglas Moo, Mary Farrar, and Joshua Harris.

The Danvers Statement offers both rationale and affirmations, and concludes with the assessment, "We are convinced that a denial or neglect of these principles will lead to increasingly destructive consequences in our families, our churches, and the culture at large."

The rationale speaks of "widespread uncertainty and confusion," whose "tragic effects" include "unraveling of the fabric of marriage"; "distortions or neglect of the glad harmony portrayed in Scripture"; "widespread ambivalence regarding the values of motherhood [and] vocational homemaking"; "growing claims of legitimacy for sexual relationships which have biblically and historically been considered illicit"; "the upsurge of physical and emotional abuse in the family"; missteps in church leadership that "backfire in the crippling of Biblically faithful witness"; "hermeneutical oddities" and a "threat to Biblical authority"; and "apparent accommodation of some within the church to the spirit of the age at the expense of winsome, radical Biblical authenticity."

The affirmations, with Scripture references, include the image of God in both men and women; role distinctions in the created order; Adam's pre-Fall headship; the destructive effects of the Fall on relationships within church and home; the Old and New Testament witness to complementary roles; the effects of redemption in setting things aright; the authority of Christ and Scripture over these matters; and the countless ministries open to men and women alike.

Mark Coppenger

See also: Christians for Biblical Equality; Council on Biblical Manhood and Womanhood; Theological Controversies within Evangelicalism

Further Reading

Cochrane, Pamela D. H. *Evangelical Feminism: A History.* New York: NYU Press, 2005.

"The Danvers Statement." International Church Council Project (ICCP). (n.d.). Accessed April 28, 2017. www.churchcouncil.org/iccp_org/Documents_ICCP/English/17_Male Female_Distinctives_A&D.pdf.

Grudem, Wayne. *Countering the Claims of Evangelical Feminism.* Portland, OR: Multnomah Press, 2008.

Kassian, Mary. *The Feminist Mistake: The Radical Impact of Feminism on Church and Culture.* Wheaton, IL: Crossway, 2005.

Piper, John, and Wayne Grudem, eds. *Recovering Biblical Manhood and Womanhood: A Response to Evangelical Feminism.* Wheaton, IL: Crossway, 1991.

DENOMINATIONALISM AND EVANGELICALISM

American evangelicals exist inside and outside of Protestant denominationalism. Some denominations have evangelical theology at their core, and some denominations are broader in theological values and convictions but have strands of evangelicalism or minority groups of evangelicalism within them. Some of the reasons for evangelicals not being part of denominations can be traced to the Fundamentalist–Modernist Controversy in American religion in the 1920s and 1930s, during which time conservatives lost numerical strength and control of some denominations and were either expelled from them or split and founded new denominations or remained independent.

The National Association of Evangelicals includes around 40 member groups, representing, among others, the Presbyterians, Anglicans, Wesleyans, Pentecostals, Charismatics, Anabaptists, and the Salvation Army. The mission of the NAE is to "honor God by connecting and representing evangelical Christians." It is not designed to erase denominational differences, as if one could merge the Foursquare Church and the Anglican Mission in North America, two of their member groups. The same goes for the World Evangelical Alliance, whose members include the Wesleyan Church and the Presbyterian Church in America.

Nevertheless, many speak of a "pan-evangelical" perspective, and there is denominational mobility among evangelicals—those espousing gospel centrality and the authority of Scripture—with, for instance, the same family joining a Baptist church in one town, later a Presbyterian church in another, and subsequently a nondenominational community church in another. Furthermore, a single evangelical church may favor adult baptism by immersion but accept new members without rebaptism or even arrange a baptism for their newborns.

These phenomena are traceable to the Great Awakenings of the 18th and 19th centuries, when revival swept across the parish boundaries of established, state churches, emphasizing personal conversion and renewal rather than membership. Instead of counting other churches as alien, the emerging evangelical consensus was more apt to speak of the broader body of believers "variously denominated"—hence, denominations. It was, thus, a term of approbation, granting many groups membership in this "transdenominational" family.

As a movement not limited to individual denominations, Evangelicalism birthed many parachurch groups and nondenominational churches and schools. For some believers, parachurch loyalties are stronger and more non-negotiable than their church or denominational connections. So their attendance, giving, and ministry might be centered on Cru (Campus Crusade), Gideons, or Habitat for Humanity. Although their denominational alliances would be convictional, they might also be pragmatic, useful in raising prayer and financial support, even in competition with denominational missions causes.

One might also speak of evangelical "quasi-denominations" such as the Acts 29 Network, Vineyard Movement, and the Willow Creek Association, which includes thousands of churches from scores of denominations. In this environment, Christian celebrities are known not so much for their denominational affiliation as for their evangelical credentials. Thus, many are not aware that Chuck Swindoll served for decades as an Evangelical Free Church pastor, that Max Lucado serves in the Church of Christ, and that Carl F. H. Henry was Southern Baptist.

Then there are nondenominational (or antidenominational) denominations, such as the Church of Christ. With no national offices, their churches nevertheless support such colleges as David Lipscomb and Harding, which are readily identifiable with the Church of Christ. And professors from these schools are part of the Stone-Campbell Restorationist group within the Evangelical Theological Society.

An interesting manifestation of the transdenominational movement is the trend toward dropping denominational labels from church names, relegating these connections to Web site footnotes. For instance, though the majority of churches in the Chicago Metro Baptist Association (SBC) still use *Baptist* in their name, dozens do not. Instead, they choose the adjectives *Bible, Community*, and *Christian*. And instead of *Church*, some have gone with *Fellowship, Assembly, Temple, Cathedral, Center, Household*, and *Ministry*. Some are not even identifiable as churches, e.g., Project 146. Indeed, this can be true of a denomination itself, for the former Baptist General Conference, with Scandinavian roots, adopted the name Converge Worldwide in 2008.

Though the "mainlines" are not considered evangelical, there are evangelical renewal movements within them. The Institute for Religion in Democracy encourages the efforts of conservative activists in denominations such as the Presbyterian Church (PCUSA), the Episcopal Church, and the United Methodist Church, whose Good News Magazine and movement is a forum for Methodist renewal.

As for Episcopalians displeased with the direction of their church in America (ECUSA), they now have evangelical options in the form of the Anglican Church in North America (ACNA) and the Convocation of Anglicans in North America (CANA), which joined together in 2013 at the urging of the Global Anglican Future Conference (GAFCON). These developments began in the "Third World," where archbishops such as Peter Akinola of Nigeria and Gregory Venables of Argentina stood with like-minded evangelicals at the Lambeth Conference against the gay agenda at work in the Anglican churches of North America and Europe.

In 1965, Presbyterians upset at the initial draft of a new denominational confession formed the Presbyterian Lay Committee. Particularly troubling was the confession's clause "The Scriptures are nevertheless the words of men."

It's important to recognize that not all groups who have *evangelical* in their name are evangelical according to ETS standards. For instance, the Evangelical Lutheran Church of America and Garrett-Evangelical Seminary would not count themselves evangelical in the sense denoted by such Evangelical leaders as Billy Graham and Carl F. H. Henry.

The 2003 book *Why We Belong: Evangelical Unity and Denominational Diversity* gives voice to six representative denominations. Within the essays, several of the writers play off David Bebbington's (1989) four-part description of evangelicalism, with its "conversionism; missionary activism; biblicism; and Crucicentrism."

Gerald Bray cherishes his Anglican Church's "patience and willingness to tolerate a wide range of ideas" and its "outward looking" stance. Lutheran Doug Sweeney talks about his denomination's notion of God's "real, objective presence" in the world, and of the way this "incarnational" emphasis encourages the arts. Timothy Tennant lists nine reasons for his Methodism, including belief in prevenient grace, a missions DNA, and a tradition of great hymn singing. Pentecostal Bryon Klaus speaks of the Holy Spirit's outpouring of signs and wonders. Presbyterian Bryan Chappell notes their "regulated" worship on "covenantal" theology, and Baptist Timothy George speaks of "believer's baptism by immersion." Denominationalists, yes, but evangelicals all.

Mark Coppenger

See also: Baptists and Evangelicalism; Evangelicalism; Evangelical Theological Society; Reformed Tradition, Evangelicalism and

Further Reading

Bebbington, David. *Evangelicalism in Modern Britain: A History from the 1730s to the 1980s.* London: Unwin Hyman.

Chute, Anthony L., Christopher W. Morgan, and Robert A. Patterson. *Why We Belong: Evangelical Unity and Denominational Diversity.* Wheaton, IL: Crossway, 2013.

Marsden, George M. *Fundamentalism and American Culture, 1870–1925.* New York: Oxford University Press, 1980.

Marsden, George M. *Evangelicalism and Modern America.* Grand Rapids, MI: Eerdmans, 1984.

National Association of Evangelicals (NAE). (n.d.). "Mission and Work." Accessed April 28, 2017. https://wwwnae.net/about-nae/mission-and-work/.

DENVER SEMINARY

Denver Seminary is an independent evangelical graduate school of theology located in Littleton, Colorado. Although independent, its statement of faith reflects an historically Baptistic orientation. Accredited by the Association of Theological Schools, the Higher Learning Commission, and the Council for Accreditation of Counseling and Related Education Programs, it offers the MA, MDiv, and DMin degrees through its main campus in Colorado and satellite campuses in Washington, D.C.; and West Texas.

Denver Seminary was initially organized as the Conservative Baptist Theological Seminary in 1950 and became Denver Conservative Baptist Theological Seminary (CBTS) in 1982 and Denver Seminary in 1998. The school was originally proposed by a group of Colorado Conservative Baptist pastors, a group that had recently (1947) separated from the Northern Baptist Church as a result of the fundamentalist-modernist schism. Its first president was Carey S. Thomas, who presided until his death in 1956. Vernon Grounds then assumed leadership of the school and served as president until 1979 and as chancellor until 1993. Dr. Grounds, much beloved by both students and faculty, was to guide the seminary in its growth and transformation from a largely parochial institution into one with worldwide influence. His vision for the school is summed up in the following words: "Here is no unanchored liberalism, freedom to think without commitment. Here is no encrusted dogmatism, commitment without freedom to think. Here is a vibrant evangelicalism, commitment with freedom to think within the limits laid down in scripture."

In the late 1960s, the seminary acquired the campus of Denver's Kent School for Girls and was located directly across from the Cherry Hills Country Club, famous for its internationally acclaimed golf tournaments. The spacious property enabled the school to expand, with multiple building projects adding student apartments, a library, and additional classroom spaces. The property, because of its location on some of the most desirable real estate in Denver, also facilitated the school's move, in 2005, to its present location in Littleton and the construction of a state-of-the-art educational facility.

Denver Seminary's presidents and faculty are recognized as some of the most significant leaders within the Evangelical Movement. They include Dr. Vernon Grounds, Dr. Haddon Robinson (known as one of the most eloquent preachers of the 20th century), Dr. Bruce Shelly, Dr. Bruce Demarest, Dr. Gordon R. Lewis, Dr. Douglas Groothuis, and Dr. Craig L. Blomberg.

Today, Denver Seminary is an independent evangelical theological school offering studies that are both intellectually challenging and practically relevant to the realities of the contemporary world. Its student body has grown to more than 1,000 students annually, and its graduates serve in ministries around the world. Its roots reflect the Baptist tradition, with full-time faculty signing a baptistic statement of faith. Students, staff, and adjunct faculty sign the statement of faith used by the National Association of Evangelicals. Its graduates serve in conservative Baptist churches, evangelical Presbyterian churches, and numerous other evangelical missions, organizations, and churches around the world. Its goal is to prepare "men and women to engage the needs of the world with the redemptive power of the gospel and the life-changing truth of Scripture" and remains a strong force in American evangelical higher education.

Dayne E. Nix

See also: Baptists and Evangelicalism; Evangelicalism; Higher Education, Evangelicals and

Further Reading

CB America: A Church-Based Network of Missional Ministries. (n.d.). Accessed May 15, 2015. http://www.cbamerica.org.
Denver Seminary. (n.d.). April 28, 2017. http://www.denverseminary.edu.
Shelly, Bruce L. *Transformed by Love: The Vernon Grounds Story.* Grand Rapids, MI: Discovery House, 2003.
Wenig, Scott. "A Man for All Evangelicals." *Christianity Today* 54, no. 11 (November 17, 2010): 50.

DISPENSATIONALISM

Dispensationalism is a major system of theology in American evangelicalism. It derives its name from the way it divides human history into successive periods of divine administrations, or management. Though some believe it is a system of interpretation, this confuses one of its distinctives—the consistent, literal, plain interpretation of the Scripture, for its nature. Dispensationalists believe their theology is the result of a consistent, literal hermeneutic.

"Dispensation," translates the Greek word *oikonomos*, which means administration, stewardship, or house law. A dispensation, therefore, is a distinct and identifiable administration in the outworking of God's plan for human history (Epheisans 3:2; Colossians 1:25–26). God administers human history as a household, moving humanity through sequential stages of His administration. Each stage, or dispensation, is determined by the level of revelation the Lord has provided up to

---

Key Term in Evangelicalism: *Substitutionary atonement*

Substitutionary atonement, the most widely held view among evangelicals, refers to the belief that Jesus Christ sacrificed Himself in the place of sinners, not only to satisfy God's holy and righteous demands but also to provide the opportunity for people to have eternal life. In other words, Jesus Christ died as a substitute for sinners (Isaiah 53:5; 2 Corinthians 5:21; 1 Peter 2:24; Romans 6:23). Evangelicals reject other theories about the atonement such as accident, commercial, example, moral influence, recapitulation, and ransom-to-Satan theory.

that time in history. That revelation, usually in the form of a covenant, specifies man's responsibilities, tests regarding those responsibilities, and God's gracious provision of a solution when failure occurs.

Though each dispensation has distinct and identifiable characteristics, the truths and principles of God's revelation and plan for redemption are constant. Dispensationalists do not believe in different ways of salvation for different dispensations, i.e., obedience to the Law in the Old Testament in contrast to salvation by grace in the New Testament. They believe salvation is always by grace through faith alone in Christ alone. Prior to the cross, faith anticipated fulfillment of the divine promise of salvation through the work of the Messiah. Since the crucifixion of Jesus Christ, faith looks back to His finished, substitutionary atonement on the cross. Other characteristics are modified as God's revelation progresses, such as the practice of animal sacrifices or the observance of the Sabbath.

The dispensational understanding is that the current Church Age is a "parenthesis" between the 69th and 70th week of Daniel's prophecy in Daniel 9:25–27. In order for God's plan for Israel to move forward, the Church Age must be brought to completion, and Church Age believers caught up from the earth when Jesus Christ returns for them in the air. (The Latin Vulgate translated the Greek *harpazo* ("caught up") with *rapio*, from which "rapture" is derived; 1 Thessalonians 4:18).

Evangelical theologian and dispensationalist Charles C. Ryrie identified three foundational beliefs, or the sine qua non, of dispensationalism that characterized all dispensationalists from Darby to the mid-20th century. The first states that the Bible must be consistently interpreted on the basis of the plain, literal meaning of words, including the use of figures of speech. The second develops from the first, that God has a plan for ethnic and national Israel that is distinct from His plan for the New Testament Church. The third principle of dispensationalism is that human history is the outworking of an eternal plan of God that culminates in bringing maximum glory to Himself. The consistent application of a literal hermeneutic is what undergirds the other distinctives.

Dispensationalists sometimes differ as to the exact number of dispensations revealed in Scripture, but they usually list these seven:

1. Innocence: from Creation to the Fall
2. Conscience: from the Fall to the Flood
3. Human Government: from the Flood to Abraham
4. Patriarchs: from Abraham to Moses
5. Mosaic Law: from Moses to the Cross
6. Church Age: from the Day of Pentecost to the rapture
7. Millennial Kingdom: the literal 1,000-year reign of Jesus Christ following His Second Advent

Dispensational theology is mostly identified with God's prophetic timetable for humanity. Dispensationalism is one type of premillennial eschatology that usually emphasizes the rapture of all believers prior to Daniel's 70th week, also known as the Tribulation. The current Church Age focuses on the *Church* as the people of God, not on Israel. Yet for Daniel's prophecy of the 70th week to be literally fulfilled (Daniel 9:27), in the same way the initial 69 weeks were literally fulfilled (Daniel 9:25–26), the Church must be removed from the earth. Only then will God begin to fulfill all He promised to Israel in the Old Testament. The removal of the Church is called the rapture of the Church (1 Thessalonians 4:16–17), and many dispensationalists believe that the rapture precedes the last seven years of God's decreed timetable for Israel, known as the time of Jacob's trouble, or the Tribulation. These seven years, which are technically a completion of the age of the Mosaic Law, follow the rapture of the Church and conclude with the Second Advent. Thus, the doctrine of the pretribulation rapture is closely identified with dispensational theology.

Dispensationalism was first articulated as a consistent system of theology in the early 19th century by a former Anglican pastor and leader in the Plymouth Brethren movement in England, John Nelson Darby (1800–1882). However, the recognition of successive divine administrations of history can be traced back to the many church writers, including Clement of Alexandria (150–220), Augustine (354–430), Joachim of Fiore (ca. 1135–1202), Pierre Poiret (1646–1719), and Isaac Watts (1674–1748), each of whom suggested different dispensational divisions in their writings. William Watson details numerous examples of pre-Darby dispensationalists, and even those who held to a pretribulation rapture, in *Dispensationalism Before Darby*. Darby, though, is credited with being the first to thoroughly systematize dispensational theology.

Following Darby, dispensational theology was promoted by a number of central proponents, including Dwight Moody, James Hall Brookes, Cyrus I. Scofield, Lewis Sperry Chafer, J. Dwight Pentecost, Charles C. Ryrie, John F. Walvoord, Donald G. Barnhouse, Hal Lindsey, and Thomas Ice. Dispensationalism has received its most noted popularization through the *Scofield Reference Bible* (1909, 1917); the popular writings of Hal Lindsey and, later, Tim LaHaye; and Jerry Jenkins's *Left Behind* series. The thousands of students, pastors, and missionaries who graduated from schools like Moody Bible Institute, Dallas Theological Seminary, Talbot School of Theology, Grace Theological Seminary, and The Master's Seminary, among many others, have spread the teaching of dispensational theology. Both the early founders' form of dispensationalism, identified by some as classic dispensationalism (Darby to Chafer), and the so-called revised dispensationalism of Walvoord, Pentecost, and Ryrie are contiguous, embodying Ryrie's three essentials. All of these dispensationalists should probably be identified as "normative dispensationalists."

A new form of dispensationalism developed in the 1980s that is discontinuous from the earlier version, primarily in the area of hermeneutics, and the relationship of the Church to Israel. This controversial variation of dispensationalism has been labeled *Progressive Dispensationalism*. The three architects of this system are Craig A. Blaising, Darrel L. Bock (Southwestern Baptist Theological Seminary and Dallas Theological Seminary), and Robert L. Saucy (Talbot Theological Seminary).

The foundation of progressive dispensationalism is the addition of a new system of interpretation—complementary hermeneutics. On this basis, New Testament writers are said to have made complementary changes to Old Testament promises that added new information. The result of this is a system that differs markedly from normative dispensationalism: the kingdom of God is not necessarily a literal, earthly, geopolitical kingdom. Therefore, we are now living in an already inaugurated kingdom—Jesus is currently reigning in heaven from the right hand of God, seated on the throne of David; the New Covenant has already been inaugurated, though its blessings will not be fully realized until the millennial reign; and the Church is no longer completely distinct from Israel as taught by normative dispensationalists.

Since its inception, dispensationalism has had a profound impact on evangelical Christians, enabling them to understand the Scriptures more fully, challenging them to greater levels of both biblical study and evangelism, as well as establishing numerous Bible colleges and seminaries.

Robert L. Dean Jr.

See also: Bible Institutes and Bible Colleges; Dallas Theological Seminary; Eschatology; Hermeneutics; Premillennialism; Rapture; Ryrie, Charles Caldwell; Scofield, Cyrus Ingerson; Talbot School of Theology; Walvoord, John F.

Further Reading

Bateman, Herbert W. *Three Central Issues in Contemporary Dispensationalism: A Comparison of Tradition and Progressive Views.* Grand Rapids, MI: Kregel, 1999.

Boyer, Paul. *When Time Shall Be No More: Prophecy Belief in Modern American Culture.* Cambridge, MA: Harvard University Press, 1992.

Carpenter, Joel A. *Revive Us Again: The Reawakening of American Fundamentalism.* New York: Oxford University Press, 1997.

Marsden, George M. *Fundamentalism and American Culture: The Shaping of Twentieth-Century Evangelicalism: 1870–1925*, 2nd ed. New York: Oxford University Press, 2–6.

Ryrie, Charles C. *Dispensationalism Today.* Chicago: Moody Press, 1966.

Ryrie, Charles C. *Dispensationalism*, rev. and expanded ed. Chicago: Moody Press, 1995.

Watson, William C. *Dispensationalism Before Darby: Seventeenth-Century and Eighteenth-Century English Apocalypticism.* Silverton, OR: Lampion Press, 2015.

Weber, Timothy P. *Living in the Shadow of the Second Coming: American Premillennialism, 1875–1982*, enlarged ed. Chicago: The University of Chicago Press, 1987.

DOBSON, JAMES C., JR. (1936–)

James Dobson is the founder of the evangelical parachurch ministry Focus on the Family. Born in Shreveport, Louisiana, to Holiness pastor and evangelist James Clayton Dobson Jr. (1936–), with a strong family lineage of ministers, he was an only child who moved across Oklahoma and Texas, eventually moving to California to attend Pasadena College (now, Point Loma Nazarene University in San Diego,

California) in 1954. After graduating in 1958 with a bachelor's degree in psychology, Dobson met and married Shirley Deere in 1960. Subsequently, they moved to Los Angeles so that he could continue his studies at the University of Southern California, obtaining a PhD in the area of child development in 1967. After graduation, Dobson taught and researched at USC as a faculty member, building what promised to be an impressive academic career.

Because of his biblical upbringing and educational background and subsequent clinical experience in the field of child development and pediatrics, Dobson became discontented with American parenting styles that had become popularized in the 1960s by psychologists such as Benjamin Spock (1903–1998) and others. Dobson believed that this conception of the family lacked a biblical foundation and the discipline structures fundamental to the growth a healthy, psychologically sound family environment. The family, Dobson believed, was instrumental in setting boundaries in children's lives for behavior and attitudes that were allowable or not. His beliefs and observations about this method of parenting led him to publish his first book, *Dare to Discipline*, in 1970. Additionally, after publicizing his ideas through an initially small weekly radio broadcast in California, through which his political, evangelical, and biblical views were clearly articulated, Dobson worked to establish the nonprofit organization Focus on the Family.

Since its formation in 1977, Focus on the Family established its headquarters in Colorado Springs, Colorado, and has grown to more than 74 different ministries seeking to provide family-centered resources to parents, ministers, educators, and psychologists and those in healthcare professions. The wide array of resources on a broad spectrum of topics from an evangelically oriented and biblically based perspective helped establish Focus on the Family as one of the preeminent family organizations in the country from an evangelical perspective.

Dobson and other conservative political leaders at the time, such as Pat Robertson, Gerald Regier, and Gary Bauer, worked toward broadening their influence by enacting the Family Research Council (FRC), a public policy ministry based out of Washington, D.C., in 1983. The FRC works as a powerful lobbying entity in favor of conservative legislation, especially the sanctity of human life, life beginning at conception, religious liberty, school choice for parents, censorship of pornographic materials, and a heterosexual definition of marriage. Although often seen as the political arm of Focus on the Family, Dobson softened his involvement with the FRC while staying on as a board member.

In addition to his work with FRC, Dobson held a number of other important political appointments through the 1980s and 1990s, under both Democratic and Republican presidents. Dobson received a special commendation from President Carter in 1980 for his work on a task force that summarized the White House Conferences on the Family. Additionally, from 1982 to 1984, President Ronald Reagan appointed Dr. Dobson to the National Advisory Commission to the office of Juvenile Justice and Delinquency Prevention. Under President Reagan, who emphasized family values consistently throughout his presidency, Dobson was invited to the

White House on a regular basis to consult on family matters. Later, from 1986 to 1988, Dobson served as cochairman of the Citizens Advisory Panel for Tax Reform, in consultation with President Reagan, and served as a member and later chairman of the United States Army's Family Initiative. Dr. Dobson was appointed to Attorney General Edwin Meese's Commission on Pornography in 1985–86; and in the spring of 1987, Dobson was appointed to the Attorney General's Advisory Board on Missing and Exploited Children and to Secretary Otis Bowen's Panel on Teen Pregnancy Prevention. President George H. Bush also consulted with Dobson on family-related issues. Finally, even though Dobson had limited findings on the negative effects of gambling in general, due to political pressures and great resources from the multibillion-dollar gambling industry, Dobson researched the impact of gambling through his appointment to the National Gambling Impact Study Commission. These and other political action positions helped solidify the lasting influence that Dobson has had on American politics and the role Dobson has played as a staunch voice for family values and issues important to evangelicals in the United States.

Dobson is the author of more than 35 books, including *Dare to Discipline* (1977); *Love Must Be Tough* (1983); *The Strong-Willed Child* (1992); *The Complete Marriage and Family Home Reference Guide* (2000), a compendium of marriage, family and parenting; and *Bringing Up Boys* (2002) and *Bringing Up Girls* (2010). He has been a major figure in evangelicalism and in the resurgence of politically conservative values within parts of evangelicalism and the American public since the 1970s.

Bryce Hantla

See also: Focus on the Family; Parachurch Ministries

Further Reading

Buss, Dale. *Family Man: The Biography of Dr. James Dobson.* Wheaton, IL: Tyndale House, 2005.

Gilgoff, Dan. *The Jesus Machine: How James Dobson, Focus on the Family, and Evangelical America Are Winning the Culture War.* New York: St. Martin's Press, 2007.

Zettersten, Rolf. *Dr. Dobson: Turning Hearts toward Home: Insights from the Life of America's Family Advocate.* Nashville, TN: W Publishing Group, 1992.

E

ELLIOT, JAMES ("JIM") (1927–1956)

Philip James "Jim" Elliot (1927–1956) was a Christian missionary to the Quechua and Huaorani, also called the Auca, Indians in Ecuador. Along with four other missionaries, Jim Elliot was killed on the mission field in January of 1956 after spending four years in Ecuador. At the time of their deaths, the story of their martyrdom was covered by *Life* magazine in a 10-page spread that brought international attention to their work and martyrdom. Despite his death, Jim Elliot has had a tremendous impact on world missions, and his legacy has lived on into the 21st century.

Jim Elliot was born in Portland, Oregon in 1927, the third of six children. He enrolled in Wheaton College in 1945, pursuing studies in Greek in order to translate the Bible for missionary purposes. Elliot was devoted to his studies and passionate about using every moment of his life to bring glory to God. Elliot served as the president of the Foreign Mission Fellowship at Wheaton College and graduated with highest honors in 1949. While studying at Wheaton, he joined the wrestling team, convinced that it would prepare his body for the rigors of mission work.

Believing that he was divinely called to be a missionary, in 1950 Elliot spent his summer at the Summer Institute of Linguistics, which was led and sponsored by Wycliffe Bible Translators (now Wycliffe Global Alliance). After taking a mission trip to Mexico where he learned Spanish, Elliot decided to work as a missionary with indigenous tribes in South America, and he made plans to travel to Ecuador in order to evangelize the Quechua Indians.

Although he felt strongly that marriage might distract him from world missions, it was during his tenure at Wheaton College that Elliot would meet his future wife, Elisabeth Howard (1926–2015). They married in 1953 on Jim's 26th birthday. Together they would have one child, Valerie, born in 1955.

In February 1952, Elliot traveled to Ecuador with his friend Pete Fleming. They initially worked with the Quechua Indians at a mission station in Shandia. During this time, the violence of the Huaorani Indians escalated. The Huaorani had recently killed five people, and Shell Oil Company had evacuated the area as their employees were in danger. But the possibility of losing their lives did not deter Elliot and Fleming. Moving to the jungles near Quito, Ecuador, Jim and Pete were joined by Ed McCully, Roger Youderian and their pilot, Nate Saint. After spending considerable time with the Quechua Indians, the five missionaries determined that it was necessary to travel deeper into the jungle in order to teach the Huaorani. Although it was a dangerous endeavor, the missionaries felt the call to take the gospel of salvation to those who had never had a chance to hear it.

Using a small plane, the group attempted to make contact with the Huaorani people using a loudspeaker and passing down gifts via a small basket. They hoped that these gifts would help build bridges with the Huaorani peoples and allow them to form friendships despite their reputation for violence. The five missionaries would go on to build a camp not far from the Huaorani Indian village, near the Curaray River. Within less than a week, the group made contact with a small group of the Huaorani who had ventured into their camp and a man they named George, whom they allowed to ride on their airplane. Encouraged by these seemingly friendly encounters, the group radioed their wives the following Sunday morning, promising to contact them again later that evening at 4:30 p.m. However, that call never came. Through the combined efforts of the Ecuadorian Air Force and the United States Armed Forces, the bodies of the five missionaries were found downstream. They had been attacked by the Huaorani and stabbed to death by wooden spears and machetes.

Eventually, Elisabeth Elliot and Nate Saint's sister, Rachel, would return to the Huaorani Indians in 1959. There they discovered that "George" had lied to his fellow villagers, telling them that the missionaries intended to kill and eat them. This had caused the Huaorani to attack the missionary camp. The presence of Elisabeth and Rachel, along with other Christian missionaries, led to the conversion of many within the Huaorani village and a drastic decrease in violence.

Although Elliot and his four missionary friends were killed on the mission field, their memory and legacy continues. Elisabeth Elliot, Jim's wife, in particular had a profound impact on evangelical world missions throughout the 20th century and became a leading figure in evangelicalism in her own right. She published more than 20 books and became a conference speaker in high demand as well as a defender of the complementarian view of marriage and gender roles in Christian ministry and service. She also advocated sexual purity prior to marriage in her popular work *Passion and Purity*. She served as an adjunct faculty member for Gordon-Conwell Theological Seminary beginning in 1974, and from 1988–2001, hosted the radio program *Gateway to Joy*. She was also a contributor for the committee of the New International Version. Coupled together, Jim and Elisabeth Elliot's firm commitment to missions impacted evangelicalism and served as evangelical commitment to proclaiming the global message of Christianity as they understood it, regardless of personal consequences.

Daniel Hill

See also: Gordon-Conwell Theological Seminary; Missions, Evangelicals and; Wheaton College; Women's Ministries; Wycliffe Global Alliance

Further Reading

Elliot, Elisabeth. *Through the Gates of Splendor*. Wheaton, IL: Tyndale House, 1981.
Elliot, Elisabeth. *Shadow of the Almighty: The Life and Testament of Jim Elliot*. San Francisco: HarperCollins, 1989.

Long, Kathryn, and Carolyn Nystrom. "Martyrs to the Spear." *Christian History & Biography* 89 (Winter 2006): 43–45.

Saint, Steve. "Nate Saint, Jim Elliot, Roger Youderian, Ed McCully, and Peter Fleming—Ecuador, 1956: A Cloud of Witnesses." In *Martyrs: Contemporary Writers on Modern Lives of Faith*, edited by Susan Bergman. (142–154). San Francisco: HarperSanFrancisco, 1996.

EMERGING AND EMERGENT CHURCHES

The emerging and emergent church movement(s), which found expression around the turn of the 21st century, is an ecclesiastical, intellectual, and spiritual movement(s) that arose among a new and distinct sociological classification of young adults known as the "emerging adulthood" in the United States. The mindset of these emerging type of adults not only offers a new way of thinking in the midst of a society that may be described as post-Christian, but within evangelicalism they also offer new ways of doing church and engaging theological thought and life as they interact with the greater community with all its arts, politics, social discourse, history, and technological developments. Critical of both traditional and "seeker-sensitive" evangelical churches, this multifarious movement—difficult to conceptualize given its particular contextual strains—is surrounded by controversy and misunderstood by many.

The term "emerging," finds sociological expression in the groundbreaking research of Jeffrey Jensen Arnett. He concludes that the new type of adulthood, ranging from age 18–29, is too old to be categorized as adolescents, but not willing to embrace the normative responsibilities of adulthood as conceived by American culture in the 20th century with its values of personal affluence and the pursuit of the "American dream." Instead, emerging adults value the notion of embracing or constructing their own set of religious beliefs instead of receiving dogma. They prize sublimity, religious experiences, and integration of thought with life. They seek to develop a personal relationship with God but without participating in organized religion where abuses can occur, authorities remain unquestioned, and corruption overlooked. These younger generations pursue a wide range of personal and enriching experiences over material success. Their activities are strikingly reminiscent of Romanticism over and against the Enlightenment, or "Age of Reason," mindset that values logical thinking, empirical evidences, analytical tools, and didactic discourses. In fact, members of emerging adulthood consider the philosophical ideas of the Enlightenment to be philosophically and existentially bankrupt with their notion that we can create better people and better societies through scientific experimentation and discoveries, analytical thinking, and knowledge alone (also identified with modernism).

In an effort to impact the cultural shift from Enlightenment influences to a post-Christian society of growing secularism, therefore, church structure, Christian thought, and even the way evangelicals live life must be done differently. Thus, the emerging movement(s) contends that evangelical churches must contextualize their ministry to their situational setting in order to fulfill the Great Commission and be an agent of positive and qualitative enriching change for all involved.

Evangelical Population in America

According to Pew Research Center's "US Religious Landscape Study," released in May of 2015, evangelicals make up about 1 in 4 American adults, with only a loss of 1% since 2007 (25.4% in 2014 vs. 26.3% in 2007). Thus, evangelicals remain as the largest religious group in the United States, with about 62 million adult adherents. Though there seems to be an increase of 2 million since 2007, the number could be as high as 5 million.

In essence, emerging churches are opposed to the framework of both traditional evangelical churches and "seeker-sensitive" churches because of the embedded assumptions from the Enlightenment. Emerging churches reject the traditional approach of evangelicalism with its focus on individualism, systematic doctrinal formulations, didactic sermons, and passive participation in church worship as a listener. But they also reject what is known as "seeker-sensitive" churches. The "seeker-sensitive" church model movement seeks to create an ecclesiastic and aesthetic setting that is attractive and viable to the non-Christian. Therefore, for example, the church itself does not look much different from a conference center. No crosses. No stained glass. No organ. Thus, using marketing skills, excellent performances, and attractive advertisements, the seeker-sensitive church approach targets the greater community by discovering what concerns or needs people have and creates programs and opportunities to meet those needs on a very practical level. But for the emerging adult, this type of church model is "consumer driven," thus potentially reducing what it means to be human. Emerging adults hunger for rich experiences, opportunities for participation, and dynamic interpersonal relationships that go beyond the superficial. Both types of evangelical churches—whether the traditional church with its pews, white walls, and large pulpit, or the seeker-sensitive church with its performance-type services—are believed by the emerging movement to be based on modernistic assumptions and practices that have consciously, or even unconsciously, impacted the way the evangelical tradition with all of its successes and failures was formed or molded.

Emerging and emergent movements also arose in reaction to the traditional evangelical understanding of the nature of church community. This movement critiques the traditional evangelical and seeker-sensitive church for being more concerned with form than mission. In other words, these two types of Enlightenment-influenced church models are more focused on institutional authority and ecclesiastical preservation than on God's mission of impacting an ever-changing community with a Christlike disposition in every possible way. Thus, the unwillingness to adapt church polity to their surrounding community, engaging people where they are, and their sterility in thought and life led emerging adults to reconsider evangelical thought, life, and even the outside community differently.

The emerging church movement in the United States originated in a Young Pastor's Conference in the late 1990s. Organized by the Leadership Network (later called the Young Leader Network), which sought to bring young pastors together to discuss cultural change and how to address those changes, Mark Driscoll (1970–) gave a message discussing the cultural emergence of and identification with postmodernism among Generation X (a descriptive title of those people born between 1961–1981). Following his presentation, young pastors came together and formed the emerging movement.

The emerging movement is not a singular movement with an institutional focus or a singular set of doctrinal beliefs, but a varied movement that is difficult to describe in overarching terms because emerging churches are contextually driven given particular cultural contexts (e.g., gay and lesbian community; impoverished neighborhood; university area). Notwithstanding, emerging churches do question and challenge long-established assumptions and convictions, emphasizing how one's context affects the way one understands and embraces a particular theological belief or practice. Though emerging churches seek to dismantle Enlightenment influences in Christian thought and practice, they do not necessarily place a postmodern paradigm in its place. Further, emerging churches are highly communal as a church body (not individualistic) and generous to the community with their time, resources, and energy; they wholeheartedly welcome the "stranger."

Within the emerging movement, two types of emerging churches stand out, namely, "the relevants" and "the reconstructionists." These two types of emerging churches are not postmodern. The first are emerging churches that "minister *to* postmoderns," known as "relevants." They seek to restructure the aesthetics of the worship service while not changing their commitment to traditional evangelical theology or even the authority of the local church as an institution. For example, a worship service may look more like a coffee house than pews facing a lectern, yet the church may advocate a Reformed theology, stress a doctrinal statement, and practice Bible exposition.

And second, there are emerging churches that "minister *with* postmoderns," described as "reconstructionists." These types of emerging churches turn to expressions of church worship practiced by the first three centuries of the ancient early church. Christian worship is primarily seen in churches that meet in homes (known as house churches) or may even take place in monastic-type communities; families gather and serve together, meeting the needs of the community and following after Jesus Christ in a pattern that is described as "incarnational," meaning, a lifestyle of servanthood that exemplifies the way Jesus Christ lived, thought, and engaged people regardless of their past, status, or troubles. Some of these reconstructionist models may follow, to a lesser or greater degree, certain types of monastic orders of the Catholic Church such as that of Benedictine or Franciscan community. They may also value the Eucharist over and against a symbolic view of and casual treatment of the communion. Reconstructionist emerging churches advocate ancient liturgies and practices that relate to the whole person (e.g., physical needs, emotional needs, family needs, spiritual needs) while perhaps blending ancient forms of worship with contemporary expressions, technologies, and art mediums (e.g., industrial resins).

Emerging churches are not necessarily the same as emergent churches, for the latter integrates postmodern tenets such as deconstructionism into theological methodology and content, changing long-held doctrines and beliefs historically embraced by evangelicals. Thus, emergent churches that seek to "minister as postmoderns" are known as "revisionists." These emergent churches are perceived radical among traditional evangelicals for their use of postmodern deconstructionism to theology. In essence, deconstructionism involves a philosophical presupposition asserting that there is no meaning prior to language. In fact, meaning is inherently unstable, shifting never exhaustive, and ultimately nontransferable between author and audience. Thus, all meaning is relative to a particular context, culture, or situation. To be sure, deconstructionism does not seek to obliterate, negate, or ignore meaning. Rather, deconstructionists seek to reconstruct meaning, looking for the "difference," namely, that which is "overlooked," "neglected, "marginalized," or "left out." Therefore, emergent churches seeks to "revision" evangelical theology altogether because they contend that traditional evangelical assumptions and practices are embedded, if not determined, by a particular historical, cultural context of the Enlightenment with all of its modernistic contours.

In sum, emergent churches seek to deconstruct Christian orthodoxy as a way of being in the world rather than a set of fixed or certain religious beliefs about the world. Theological doctrines and descriptive terms do not sufficiently express totalizing truths, for they are language and contextually bound. Therefore, they recast theology as being an ongoing conversation about God and seek to use deconstructionism as a way to reconstruct itself in order to reach a post-Christian society. But as evidenced above, not all emerging churches are emergent. Thus, certain evangelicals can be described as emerging without being emergent. How and to what extent these emerging streams of evangelical thought develop and influence society or particular segments of society remains to be seen. Notable thinkers who have contributed to the emerging movements' attractiveness, influence, controversy, and growth include Tony Jones (1968–), Dan Kimball (1960–), Brian McClaren (1956–), and Doug Pagitt (1966–).

Paul R. Shockley

See also: Fine Arts, Evangelicals and; Hermeneutics; Reformed Tradition, Evangelicalism and

Further Reading

Arnett, Jeffrey Jensen. *Emerging Adulthood: The Winding Road from the Late Teens through the Twenties.* New York: Oxford University Press, 2004.

Belcher, Jim. *Deep Church: A Third Way between Emerging and Traditional.* Downers Grove, IL: InterVarsity Press, 2009.

Carson, Donald A. *Becoming Conversant with the Emerging Church: Understanding a Movement and Its Implications.* Grand Rapids, MI: Zondervan, 2005.

Driscoll, Mark. *The Radical Reformission.* Grand Rapids, MI: Zondervan, 2004.

Gibbs, Eddie, and Ryan Bolger. *Emerging Churches: Creating Christian Community in Postmodern Cultures.* Grand Rapids, MI: Baker House, 2005.

Hybels, Bill and Lynne. *Rediscovering Church: The Story and Vision of Willow Creek Community Church.* Grand Rapids, MI: Zondervan, 1995.

Kallestad, Walt. *Entertainment Evangelism: Taking the Church Public.* Nashville, TN: Abingdon Press, 1996.

Kimball, Dan. *Emerging Worship: Creating Worship Gatherings for New Generations.* El Cajon, CA: EmergentYS, 2004.

McKnight, Scot, "Five Streams of the Emerging Church." *Christianity Today* (January 19, 2007). http://www.christianitytoday.com/ct/2007/february/11.35.html.

Sweet, Leonard. *Post-Modern Pilgrims: First Century Passion for the 21st Century.* Nashville, TN: Broadman & Holman, 2000.

Webber, Robert E. *Ancient-Future Worship: Proclaiming and Enacting God's Narrative.* Grand Rapids, MI: Baker House, 2008.

ENVIRONMENT, EVANGELICALS AND THE

American evangelicals have been involved with concerns about the environment since the 1970s. This has increased significantly since the late 1990s but has also met with resistance from some evangelicals, primarily with respect to the topics of climate change and global warming. As with the American population as whole, there is no unanimity of opinion on the subject. Several evangelical organizations, position papers, and declarations have been created specifically addressing evangelical perspectives on environmentalism. Among the most prominent are the Evangelical Environmental Network, Young Evangelicals for Climate Action, and the Cornwall Alliance, the latter taking a dissenting view of climate change and global warming. Prominent statements include "The Evangelical Climate Initiative," "A Southern Baptist Declaration on the Environment and Climate Change," and "The Cornwall Declaration on Environmental Stewardship." Numerous books have also been published by evangelicals on the subject in recent years. One of the earliest works to address the topic was Francis A. Schaeffer's 1970 work *Pollution and the Death of Man*, written just as the environment was becoming a counterculture cause as well as a concern of mainstream America.

Evangelical understanding of the environment is perhaps one of the most misunderstood positions in moral thought, politics, and science. Although attention to the environment was not on the forefront of evangelicalism historically, given other concerns such as short life expectancy, fight against disease, famine, and safety, the Christian worldview with its Protestant ethic (e.g., Max Weber's *Protestant Ethics and the Spirit of Capitalism*) has contributed to Western economic development, freedom, health, science, and security whereby attention in recent years has turned to consider environmental issues on an unprecedented scale. But in areas across the world where basic human needs are still not met (e.g., clothing, food, healthcare, housing, water, transportation), environmental consciousness still remains low.

Notwithstanding the lack of attention that may have been given to the environment, which parallels the development of environmental consciousness in the greater marketplace of ideas (e.g., the recent development of environmental philosophy), the evangelical understanding of the environment is rooted in what they understand to be six major truth claims from Scripture, the ultimate source for their authority. Scripture claims in Genesis 1:26–28 and James 4:17 that Christians are to fulfill their responsibilities for caring for the land in a way that demonstrates their love of God and neighbors alike (Mark 12:28–34; 1 John 3:16–17).

First, The God of the Bible created the heavens and the earth and deemed it to be good (Genesis 1–2). The universe and all it contains is believed to be the product of God's mind, reflecting His creativity, intelligence, power, and will. All created beings have value. But the creation of creatures implies a clear Creator/creature distinction, namely, God, who is infinite and personal, created the heavens and earth; all life forms owe their creation to Him. Therefore, God is not the universe, but a created product from the mind of God, the Uncaused Cause, the Prime Mover, a Being who is Pure Actuality with No Potentiality.

But due to the fall of humanity (Genesis 3), whereby historic Adam and Eve yielded to temptation, abusing the good gift of free will, evil—that is, the corruption of what is good—entered into Eden and affected the natural world (Romans 8:18–22) in the most disastrous ways. Yet, the Creator/creature distinction remains. Thus, the divinization of the earth or the worship of any aspect or object of the created order is perceived as idolatry by Jews and Christians alike.

Evangelicals contend against a naturalistic worldview involving the denial of the immaterial, the supernatural, and God Himself; not only does such a view go against the natural witness of creation about God's existence, generating existential tension about human origins, identity, meaning, morals, purpose, and destiny, but it also commits the fallacy of reductionism, that is, focusing on aspect to the neglect of all related areas. Reducing humanity to mere materialistic elements combined with biological determinism generates problems about how to account for stewardship and abuses of environment given biological determinism (not free will agency), specified and irreducible complexity, objective moral duties, values, and accountability; in addition it also represents the exaltation of humanity and thus the greater possibility of greater abuse of power. But why exalt humanity, as they are nothing more than the accidental byproduct of time, energy, and chance? What makes them so special? Thus, evangelicals contend that a naturalistic worldview cannot adequately provide a strong enough foundation to generate a proper view of the environment or generate objective duties, values, and accountability. In fact, if humans refuse to acknowledge their place and responsibility in God's created order, they not only lower their humanity in view of rejecting the inherent value God has given, but they also can abuse nature, for if God does not exist, everything is permissible.

Others propose pantheism, namely, God is the universe, as a better moral foundation for the environment. Although the Creator/creature distinction is conflated and unity possesses meaning, the particulars of man have no meaning. But evangelicals believe that a pantheistic basis for the environment possesses similar problems as a naturalistic worldview, such as the fallacy of reductionism and no moral distinctions as concerns the creation order. The divination of or monistic conception of nature cannot adequately account for free will choices of creatures and the sufferings that accompany natural evil (e.g., hurricanes; tidal waves; volcanic eruptions).

In contrast, evangelicals such as Norman L. Geisler, Nancy Pearcey, and Francis A. Schaeffer claim that the Creator/creature distinction offers an anti-reductionistic alternative that not only affirms physical matter, human reasoning, the reality of the mind, and empirical evidences, but also provides the ontological foundations for moral values, duties, and accountability for a wise stewardship of the environment. They believe that empirical, materialistic, and rationalistic approaches to the environment are reductionistic compared to an evangelical view of the environment that can appreciate and integrate all three aspects. For example, evangelicals affirm knowledge acquired by the five senses because they believe God created them. But evangelicals disagree with an empirical only approach to the environment. Evangelicals embrace rational thinking because God created both the human mind and the world with a rationally knowable structure. But they reject a rationalism-only approach to the environment. Evangelicals affirm the material world and universe but reject materialism-only approaches. They can appreciate what biologists, foresters, philosophers, and scientists discover because God created all things and declared them to be good (Genesis 1:31). In other words, evangelicals contend that the phenomena of cosmos, nature, and all life can be better accounted for with an evangelical worldview offering a way of seeing and doing that encompasses a holistic view of the environment. They are able take into account the material order, rational knowable structures, and empirical evidences, but also provide a moral foundation that will generate objective values, duties, and accountability for wise stewardship and tender care of the environment. Instead of worshipping creation, they see this stewardship as an act of worship to the infinite and personal God they love.

Because evangelicals take free will seriously, over and against biological determinism, they are able to exercise sensitivity to biodiversity and ecological systems, respond to ecological tensions and traumas, preserve and defend life, and accept responsibility with biblical justifications that do not dehumanize people or exploit the environment. In fact, how one treats the environment demonstrates one's view of God and humans.

Moreover, the Creator/creation distinction with God being infinite and personal clears the path away from metaphysical obscurity given the technological age in which people now find themselves. They encourage people to explore nature, observe and study the created order, and see how nature points to God. Thus, they are concerned with those who find themselves in "virtual reality" never experiencing the challenges, the fascinations, and wonders of physical nature. There is the evangelical concern that this obscuring of reality creates existential tension within because these people are not experiencing the beauty and the complexities of the environment and their relationship to the created order as given by God; their lives are largely indoor, and nature is perceived to be a nearby park.

Second, God has disclosed aspects of Himself through creation (Psalms 139; Romans 1:19–20). The apostle Paul, for example, claims that creation itself bears witness to God's attributes. The activities and scene of nature provoke worship of God as one looks at the beauty, colors, and complexities of nature and follows these aspects to the Creator (Psalms 139:7–12). Therefore evangelicals believe in a good stewardship of the environment; to inhibit or destroy nature keeps people from receiving clear testimony of God's attributes, contributing to a distorted view of Him and His ways.

Third, evangelicals agree God specifically gave humans the task of being good stewards over His creation (Genesis 1:28, 2:15; Psalms 24:1). This stewardship involves three commands, namely, populate the earth, rule over creation, and take care of it. Being made in the image of God involves reflecting God's plans, priorities, and values. People are to represent God's interests, which involves creativity, intellect, and will (personality).

Though Christians have not been consistent in this area in view of sinfulness, frailties, and other shortcomings such as ignorance, the mandate to be a good steward is commanded by God. People are mirroring His image by caring for the environment like God cares for His people. This responsibility takes into account not only ecological systems and the delicate balances therein but also introducing invasive species into settings that can create forestry problems, ecological calamities, and a literal change of the ground for the worse (e.g., Chinese tallow trees in U.S. soil). Education is critical to helping people better understand what is most beneficial to their well-being, their land, and their future.

Evangelicals like Geisler claim that people like Lynn White Jr. are unfair to blame Christians for environmental crises by claiming Christians believe it is God's will for people to exploit nature for their own proper ends. Instead, evangelicals assert that the critics themselves have misunderstood the Hebrew precept to "subdue" the world and take "dominion" over it in Genesis 1:28. Although particular Christians may proclaim "domination" over nature given ignorance, personal bias, or certain contextual setting, evangelical scholars observe that this not on appropriate textual understanding of Genesis 1. Moreover, a "dominion"-type perspective does not cohere with the other teachings of the Bible about proper stewardship of the environment.

Though evangelicals disagree with biological egalitarianism, that is, giving equal value and rights to all life forms, they affirm that each individual bears the unique responsibility to care for creation that reflects His beauty and values. Therefore, to place humans on the same level as all other creatures negates this critical human responsibility.

Fourth, the God of the Bible cares for all animal life. Although humans are to be stewards of God's creation, given their unique gift set of creativity, imagination, and the powers of reason, possessing inherent value, no matter age, background, color, gender, or race, animals also possess value and thus are to be properly cared for. For example, the Ten Commandments give animals a day of rest (Exodus 20:10); the Mosaic Law offers specific instructions on treatment of animals (Deuteronomy 22:4, 6–7); and Balaam was rebuked by the angel of the Lord for beating his donkey (Numbers 22:32). Israelites were also commanded to give the land itself a Sabbath rest every seven years. Whatever the land produced was to be eaten not only by people but also livestock and wild animals (Leviticus 25:1–7). Jesus Christ said that God cares for birds (Matthew 6:26) and that God is concerned when a sparrow falls to the ground (Matthew 10:29).

Fifth, wise care for the natural world contributes to the health of people. Because God cares for the physical well-being of his people, as recorded in His care for the freed Israelites from Egyptian enslavement, Jesus's care of the physical lives of others and the commandment to commit oneself to the true good of others (*agape* love), evangelicals are to be concerned about endangered species, exploitation and contamination of natural resources, and the use of chemicals that may contribute to disease and death. The connection between human health and the environment is critical to loving others with greatness.

And sixth, evangelicals believe that this present environment is the best way to a best world achievable; nobody can prove otherwise. Thus, evangelicals believe one day God will remove the curse, and He will reign over the natural order, where everything will be in a state of harmony (Isaiah 11); nature will be completely restored. Revelation 21–22 gives a picture of a new heaven and new earth where there will be no more corruption, pain, and violence. God-given harmony and peace will transcend every aspect of the created order; evil will be eliminated.

Evangelical perspectives on the environment continue to be part of the robust discussions on the topic in American public life and bring another decidedly religious perspective to those of other faith traditions and within Christianity.

Paul R. Shockley

See also: Christian Apologetics; Ethics, Evangelical Theories of; Philosophy, Evangelicals and; Schaeffer, Francis A. and Edith

Further Reading

Beisner, Calvin E. *Where Garden Meets Wilderness: Evangelical Entry into the Environmental Debate.* Grand Rapids, MI: Eerdmans, 1997.

Bouma-Prediger, Steven. *For the Beauty of the Earth: A Christian Vision for Creation Care. Engaging Culture.* Grand Rapids, MI: Baker Academic, 2001.

Cornwall Alliance for the Stewardship of Creation. (n.d.). April 28, 2017. http://www.cornwallalliance.org.

Evangelical Environmental Network. (n.d.). April 28, 2017. http://www.creationcare.org.

Geisler, Norman L. *Christian Ethics: Contemporary Issues & Options*, 2nd ed. Grand Rapids, MI: Baker Academic, 1989, 2010.

Geisler, Norman L., and Ryan P. Snuffer. *Love Your Neighbor: Thinking Wisely about Right and Wrong.* Wheaton, IL: Crossway, 2007.

Pearcey, Nancy. *Finding Truth: 5 Principles for Unmasking Atheism, Secularism, and Other God Substitutes.* Colorado Springs, CO: David C. Cook, 2015.

Schaeffer, Francis A. *Pollution and the Death of Man: The Christian View of Ecology.* Wheaton, IL: Tyndale House, 1970.

White, Lynn, "The Historical Roots of Our Ecological Crisis." In *Ecology and Life: Accepting Our Environmental Responsibility*, edited by Wesley Granberg Michaelson. Waco, TX: Word Books, 1988.

ESCHATOLOGY

Eschatology is the doctrine of future things and has been an emphasis in American evangelical thought and teaching. Biblical prophecy can be defined as prewritten history. Many of the prophecies spoken of in the Bible have already transpired. Examples include Old Testament predictions regarding the Messiah's birthplace (Micah 5:2; Matthew 2:5–6), death through piercing (Psalms 22:16; Isaiah 53:5; Zechariah 12:10; John 19:34), unbroken bones (Exodus 12:46; Psalms 22:17, 34:20; John 19:32–33), crucifixion between thieves (Isaiah 53:12; John 19:18), and burial in the tomb of a rich man (Isaiah 53:9; Matthew 27:57–60). However, there are many biblical predictions that have not yet been fulfilled and therefore await a future fulfillment. The systematic study of these unfulfilled biblical prophecies constitutes the area of systematic theology known as eschatology. "Eschatology" is derived from two Greek words: *eschatos*, meaning "end" or "last," and *ology*, which means "the study of." Thus, eschatology involves the study of the last or end things as revealed in the Bible.

Although the Book of Revelation represents an important contribution to the subject of eschatology, there is much more to this subject than merely this vital book. In order to understand prophecy in its entirety, it becomes necessary to examine many other areas of Scripture as well, such as Genesis, Isaiah, Ezekiel, Daniel, Thessalonians, Romans, and so on. In fact, the Bible's first eschatological statement is found as early as Genesis 3:15, which predicts the Messiah's ultimate victory over Satan (Revelation 20:10). Systematic theology represents a biblical "round up" of all material on a given subject. In this sense, studying eschatology is akin to assembling pieces of a jigsaw puzzle. The goal of putting together such a puzzle is to assemble the random pieces into a meaningful or coherent whole. Similarly, eschatology involves gathering together the various relevant pieces found throughout the entire Bible and arranging them into a meaningful presentation concerning what the Bible predicts regarding the end of time.

At least *five* reasons make the subject of eschatology important. *First*, it represents the time in history when God attains His final victory. In other words, eschatology represents that future time when "God wins." God's purposes in history are *doxalogical* in that He works in history to glorify Himself. Because the believer's calling is to glorify God (1 Corinthians 10:31), eschatology should be a topic that is

---

Evangelical Views on the Rapture

The "rapture" refers to the "catching up" of the church resulting in her eternal union with Jesus Christ. While premillennialists, that is, those who believe Jesus Christ will return with Christians to establish a literal thousand-year kingdom are united on the timing of Jesus Christ's Second Coming to the earth (Second Advent), they are not united on when the church will be "caught up" to be with Him (John 14:3–11; 1 Thessalonians 4:13–17):

Midtribulationalism: Jesus Christ will rapture the church in the middle of the seven-year tribulation. Proponents include Gleason L. Archer, Norman B. Harrison, and Merrill C. Tenney.

Partial Rapturism: Only spiritually mature Christians will be raptured before the seven-year tribulation begins. Proponents include G. L. Lang and Ray Brubaker.

Posttribulationism: Jesus Christ will rapture the church following the seven-year of tribulation. Proponents include Robert H. Gundry, George E. Ladd, J. Barton Payne, and Alex Reese.

Pretribulationism: Jesus Christ will rapture the church before any aspect of the seven-year tribulation begins. Proponents include Lewis S. Chafer, J. Dwight Pentecost, Charles C. Ryrie, and John F. Walvoord.

---

foremost on the believer's mind since it represents God's ultimate vindication and glorification.

Second, eschatology is important given the vast amount of Scripture devoted to the subject. Roughly 27 percent, or over a quarter of the Bible, was eschatological at the time it was written. To ignore prophecy is to ignore over one-fourth of the Bible. If someone seeks to read and minister the whole counsel of God's Word (Acts 20:27), at some point he must interact with the Bible's prophetic and eschatological content.

Third, eschatology demonstrates the supernatural origin of the Bible. Because the Bible reveals history in advance, and many of its predictions have already come to pass, it is rational to conclude that the Scripture was inspired by an omniscient, or all-knowing, God. Thus, God often challenges skeptics to His authenticity by pointing to predictive prophecy. Notice God's declaration in Isaiah 48:3–5: "I declared the former things long ago and they went forth from my mouth, and I proclaimed them. Suddenly I acted, and they came to pass. Because I know that you are obstinate . . . Therefore I declared *them* to you long ago, before they took place I proclaimed *them* to you, So that you would not say, 'My idol has done them, and my graven image and my molten image have commanded them.'" Similarly, in John 13:19, Jesus said, "From now on I am telling you before *it* comes to pass, so that when it does occur, you may believe that I am *He*."

Fourth, eschatology rightly understood has a profound impact on the daily life of the believer. It has often been said that those who are the most heavenly minded are the least earthly good. In actuality, the exact opposite is true. Those who understand the eternal priorities of the next life, as revealed though the study of eschatology, are more likely to align the priorities of their present life in accordance with these eternal priorities. For example, Paul's knowledge of the future judgment seat of Christ shaped his ministry philosophy. After describing this future judgment (2 Corinthians 5:9), He proclaimed, "Therefore, knowing the fear of the Lord, we persuade men" (2 Corinthian 5:11). Thus, biblical descriptions of eschatological truths are typically connected to behavioral inunctions for the believer. For example, the any-moment-return of Christ is used in Scripture to encourage endurance in the midst of trials (James 5:8–9), as well as comfort the believer (John 14:1–3; 1 Thessalonians 4:13–18). Because the Second Coming conveys the idea of accountability, it is often tied to daily holy living. After describing Christ's return (1 John 3:2), 1 John 3:3 states, "And every one who has this hope *fixed* on Him purifies himself, just as He is pure." Similarly, after describing God's future destruction of the present earth (2 Peter 3:10), 2 Peter 3:11 exhorts, "Since all these things are to be destroyed in this way, what sort of people ought you to be in holy conduct and godliness."

Fifth, eschatology provides hope in a hopeless age. Due to the daily challenges associated with living in a fallen world, many live without hope. Against this dark background stands God's eschatological truth, which teaches that although things appear dark in the present, Satan will soon be overthrown, and Christ will return and usher in an age of unparalleled blessing and optimism for all of humanity. Without this eschatological point of view, it is easy to become discouraged over the current state of the world. Such optimism explains why Titus 2:13 identifies Christ's return as "the blessed hope." Similarly, Second Peter 1:19 refers to prophecy as "a lamp shining in a dark place" to which we "would do well to pay attention."

Biblical eschatology was the last of the major areas of systematic theology to be aggressively systematized and understood. Prophetic truth is designed by the Holy Spirit to become progressively more understandable as the world approaches the allotted time period when the prophecies will be fulfilled. Progressive revelation ceased with the closing of the biblical canon back in the first century (Jude 3; Revelation 22:18–19). However, progressive illumination, whereby the Holy Spirit enables the Church to comprehend ever-increasing degrees of already revealed biblical and prophetic truth, continues to be an ongoing reality. After receiving a prophetic vision about the future, Daniel was told, "But as for you, Daniel, conceal these words and seal up the book until the end of time; many will go back and forth, and knowledge will increase" (Daniel 12:4). Daniel then inquired into the vision's meaning and was once again told that the words were to be closed up and sealed *until* the time of the end. Daniel 12:8–9 reads, "As for me, I heard but could not understand; so I said, 'My lord, what *will be* the outcome of these *events*?' And He said, 'Go *your way*, Daniel, for *these* words are concealed and sealed up until the end time.'" Many incorrectly interpret this reference in Daniel 12:4 to how many in the last days "will go back and forth, and knowledge will increase" as an increase in travel and technology in the last days. However, the reference to going "back and forth" is also used in Amos 8:12 to refer to a vain search for spiritual knowledge during a time period when it is inaccessible. This verse says, "People will stagger from sea to sea, and from the north even to the east; they will go to and fro to seek the word of the LORD, but they will not find *it*." When this parallel passage is taken into account, going "back and forth" or "to and fro" refers to reading the eschatological sections of Scripture. As people will give themselves in the last days to reading and studying eschatological truth, Daniel predicts that God's obscure end time program will become increasingly understandable, especially as the time period for the predicted events draws ever nearer (Daniel 8:26b–27; 1 Peter 1:10–11).

This reality of progressive illumination explains why eschatology was the last of all the branches of theology to be developed and systematized. Here is a very rough outline of doctrinal history. The second century was the age of apologetics. The doctrine of God and especially the Trinity then took center stage in the third and fourth centuries. Anthropology then became the Church's focus in the early fifth century. The late fifth and then sixth and seventh centuries were characterized by an ecclesiastical interest in Christological matters. In the 16th century, the reformers focused on soteriological (the doctrine of salvation) concerns. Finally, the Church gave itself to correcting a mythical and mediaeval pre-Reformation eschatology. Thus, eschatology was the last of the branches of theology to be systematized because it was not designed to be progressively unsealed or illuminated by the Holy Spirit until just before the fulfillment of the predicted events.

Andrew M. Woods

See also: Dispensationalism; Israel, Evangelicals and; Premillennialism; Theological Controversies within Evangelicalism

Further Reading

Boyer, Paul. *When Time Shall Be No More: Prophecy Belief in Modern American Culture.* Cambridge, MA: Harvard University Press, 1992.

Chafer, Lewis Sperry. *Systematic Theology.* 8 vols. Dallas: Dallas Seminary Press, 1948. Reprint, [8 vols. in 4], Grand Rapids, MI: Kregel, 1993.

Hannah, John D. *Our Legacy: History of Christian Doctrine.* Colorado Springs, CO: NavPress, 2001.

Orr, James. *The Progress of Dogma.* Grand Rapids, MI: Eerdmans, 1952.

Payne, J. Barton. *Encyclopedia of Biblical Prophecy: The Complete Guide to Scriptural Predictions and Their Fulfillment.* New York: Harper & Row, 1973.

Pentecost, J. Dwight. *Things to Come: A Study in Biblical Eschatology.* Findlay, OH: Dunham, 1958. Reprint, Grand Rapids, MI: Zondervan, 1964.

ETHICS, EVANGELICAL THEORIES OF

Evangelical ethics in many ways parallels the ebb and flow of ethical theories, their popularity, and their practical impact in Western thought and culture. Although evangelicals are typically absolutists, that is, believing the Bible to be the supreme authority for thought, life, and practice because it is God's special revelation to humanity, they differ on what to do when two or more biblical commands come into conflict with one another in a world that is corrupted by evil. As a result, various evangelical models of ethics arose responding to the issue about whether biblical commands do come into conflict with each other and what to do when this happens in a given situation. These ethical models include Non-Conflict or Unqualified Absolutism, Conflict Absolutism, Graded Absolutism, and Aretaic Graded Absolutism. Although all views are within the range of biblical orthodoxy, some are argued to have more explanatory power than others.

Evangelicals are identified with deontological ethics. Deontological ethics states that an action is right if and only if it is in accord with a moral rule or principle. This rule-based approach affirms the moral rules or principles to be the ethical teachings of what is right and wrong, and good and bad, from the Bible. Because these commands are God given, they are believed to be not only objective features of the world but also always binding, and cannot be overridden by other moral or nonmoral issues. Thus, these commands are binding, obligatory, and necessary to follow regardless of the consequences personally or collectively. In fact, evangelical deontological ethics stands in great contrast to consequential ethics (outcome-based approach) that states an action is right if and only if it promotes the best consequences (e.g., happiness; pleasure).

Yet, what are Christians are to do when two or more biblical commands come into conflict with one another in a given situation (e.g., telling the truth vs. saving a human life from a certain physical abuse, persecution, or death)? As a result of this concern, evangelicals have embraced differing positions that can be historically traced back to three distinct but related theological streams of thought: Non-Conflict or Unqualified Absolutism (Anabaptist Tradition); Conflict Absolutism (Lutheran Tradition); Graded Absolutism (Reformed Tradition).

Non-Conflict or Unqualified Absolutism historically affirms that all moral conflicts are only apparent; they are not real. This view is valued for it claims that God will always spare the faithful for He will never place a believer in a situation where he or she will be required to sin or break a divine command. Moreover, God's absolutes are preserved. The Christian is called to trust and obey God no matter the situation.

But will God always spare the faithful? Are there any historical situations where third alternatives were not available? Does believing that God will intervene if the Christian does what is right beg the question? Will God have to perform a miracle each and every time? Are Christians to trust and obey that God will provide a way out of a particular dilemma each and every time? Can one commit a greater sin of omission in order to avoid what one believes to be a sin of commission? Is there not a hierarchy to biblical commands (e.g., love God, then love your neighbor)?

Conflict Absolutism states that when two or more biblical commands come into conflict with one another, one is obligated to follow the lesser evil. Because people live in a world corrupted by evil, moral conflicts are inevitable. But Christians are obligated to follow all biblical commands. Thus, when one chooses to break a command, one must choose the lesser evil such as lying in order to save a human life. But every time a biblical command is broken, the Christian, no matter how well intended, violated a biblical absolute. But God, out of his mercy and foreknowledge, provided a remedy for the believer, namely, restoration in fellowship unto God through the sincere confession of sin, that is, acknowledging to God that breaking this command(s) was wrong; sincere repentance takes place (1 John 1:9).

Conflict absolutism is valued among evangelicals because God's commands are considered to be absolute and unbreakable (Exodus 20:7; Psalms 19:7, 11, 119:4, 160); the evil, fallen world where people's nature is corrupted by sin generates these conflicts between God's commands. Moreover, when moral conflict occurs where the Christian is obligated to do the lesser evil, forgiveness of sins is available as a divine remedy.

Notwithstanding, conflict absolutism is faced with questions like how can there be a moral obligation to do evil? Because God is aware of these possibilities, surely He would grant exemptions or divine immunity if for some mysterious reason He does not provide a way to avoid breaking a command at all.

Graded Absolutism, following in the tradition of thinkers such as St. Augustine (354–430), Charles Hodge (1797–1878), and Norman Geisler (1932–), advocates the idea that when two or more universal ethical norms come into unavoidable conflict, the Christian's nonculpable duty is to follow the higher moral law. Similar in some ways to Sir William David Ross's (1871–1971) hierarchy of *prima facie* principles in his case for intuition ethics, this evangelical position maintains that one is personally guiltless if he or she follows the higher moral law in a particular situation. In other words, God grants an exemption to the lower moral law in view of one's duty to obey the higher moral law (e.g., love your brother vs. obeying government laws).

The graded absolutist position is valued because it preserves moral absolutes but places them in a hierarchical structure. Like conflict absolutism, graded absolutism recognizes that people live in a sinful world where moral conflicts occur. When moral conflicts are unavoidable, it recognizes maintaining the higher moral law over the lower moral law. No imputation of guilt if higher moral law if a lower moral absolute was "violated" because of God's justice and fairness. For example, a policeman who is positioned under a red light indicator motions the driver to come forward without the vehicle ever coming to a complete stop. The authority of the policeman supersedes the authority of the red light indicator. Likewise, a higher biblical command such as "saving a neighbor's life" supersedes a lower command such as "telling the truth." In fact, one might say that the Christian is not disobeying the lower law at all because the higher law exempts one from obedience to follow the lower command.

The graded absolutist position is faced with challenges like how can one know what is the higher moral law in a given situation? Does not each situation present its own set of concerns or issues? How certain are the graded absolutists that the Christian is divinely exempted from a lower command when biblical commands come into conflict with one another? What about people who use this approach for their own ends, believing that they are exempted from obedience to following commands? In other words, does graded model lend itself to antinomian abuse?

Interestingly, each of these three positions, namely, Non-Conflict or Unqualified Absolutism, Conflict Absolutism, and Graded Absolutism, historically parallel the greater philosophical ethical conversation beyond the realm of evangelical ethics. Immanuel Kant's (1724–1804) work drove the conversation of rule-based or deontological ethics in philosophical discourse until 1958, when Gertrude Elizabeth Margaret Anscombe (1919–2001) challenged proponents of Kantian ethics with her famous critique "Modern Moral Philosophy." She argued that one couldn't advocate moral laws apart from an objective Moral Law Giver. Instead of asking what one should do in a given situation, one should be asking, "What type of a person should I be?" In essence, her solution to them is that if Kantians want to have ethics without God, they need to return to Aristotle's (384–322 BCE) virtue ethics and build on his character-based approach as delineated in his significant work *Nicomachaean Ethics*. Virtue ethics claims that an action is right if and only if it is what the virtuous person would do. Thus, virtue ethic centers on character formation.

This rule-based mindset approach, which Kant's legacy drove, also impacted evangelical ethics. In other words, Kant's influence even governed the conversation among evangelicals. But following Anscombe's famous criticism, there is renewed interest in how to assimilate aspects of virtue ethics into deontological absolute approaches to offer a holistic approach that looks more like Jesus Christ since He was not only concerned with one's action but also one's character (e.g., Matthew 23). One such approach is known as Aretaic Graded Absolutism.

Aretaic Graded Absolutism is the integration of virtue theory and graded absolutism in such a way that when the Christian is obedient to God, the inner desire is to be obedient. By strengthening graded absolutism with virtue theory one is not only concerned with "doing," but also with "being." But if graded absolutism is left to itself, it suffers from difficulties such as not being able to readily handle "*gray areas*," where moral duties conflict, lends itself to antinomian abuse, and neglects character formation. But if graded absolutism is integrated with virtue theory into these weaknesses are replaced, in various degrees, with certain advantages such as assuming both virtue and moral obligations (deontology) have intrinsic value and are needed in order to have a robust and holistic moral system of ethics. It offers a balanced or well-orbed emphasis on both obedience to biblical commands and possessing a requisite disposition that reflects Christ. Aretaic Graded Absolutism offers a twofold inward motivational component whereby one seeks to foster their new disposition in delighting or taking pleasure in the pursuit of godliness.

Although all four models of evangelical ethics are within the range of biblical orthodoxy, it suffices to say that other areas of evangelical ethics are integrated, such as the role of natural law in the life of the believer and in governing decision-making in general. Natural law, which finds expression not only in the Catholic faith but also in the writings of early church (e.g., Origen) and Protestant Reformers (e.g., John Calvin), affirms the idea that God designed people to be moral. Thus, there are moral natural foundational principles that are not only right for all to follow, but at some level are also known to all. These natural, moral laws are applicable to everyone everywhere, for they are built into the fabric of human nature. Therefore, natural law claims that moral skepticism is make-believe, a mask of self-deception, and correlates with passages such as Romans 2:14–16.

Thus, though evangelical ethics is deontological, and its proponents can integrate virtue theory and natural law theory into their approaches, they are unequivocally opposed to consequential ethics or any type of ethical approach that erodes or takes away the inherent value of humanity or equal human rights, or that promotes a type of approach where hedonism, that is pleasure, becomes supreme, or some ethical approach that is based on sentiments or skepticism. Evangelical ethics is historically rigorous against a nihilistic worldview whereby nothing matters and everything is considered permissible because there is not ultimate accountability.

The rich legacy, controversies, and challenges evangelical ethicists face is seen in the activities and works of people like Charles Colson (1931–2012), James Dobson (1936–), Jerry Falwell (1933–2007), Norman Geisler, Francis Schaeffer (1912–1984), and Joni Eareckson Tada (1949–), and also in the institutions, parachurches, and societies that have come about that address, testify, and stand against certain moral positions such as the L'Abri Fellowship, Focus on the Family, Liberty University, the Moral Majority, the Council of Biblical Manhood and Womanhood, Prison Fellowship, and the National Black Evangelical Association.

Although evangelicals might differ on the handling of specific moral issues, they seek to stand with the victimized, the hurting, and the persecuted, whether it is the plight of the Jewish people, the life of the unborn, the physically challenged, human trafficking of women and young girls, divorce and family dysfunctionalism, human slavery, the uneducated, the oppressed, or the malnourished.

Paul R. Shockley

See also: Colson, Charles Wendell ("Chuck"); Council on Biblical Manhood and Womanhood; Dobson, James C., Jr.; Focus on the Family; Geisler, Norman L.; Henry, Carl F. H.; L'Abri Fellowship; Liberty University; Moral Majority; National Black Evangelical Association; Prison Fellowship; Schaeffer, Francis A. and Edith

Further Reading

Baucham, Voddie. *Family Driven Faith*. Wheaton, IL: Crossway, 2011.

Budziszewski, J. *What We Can't Not Know: A Guide*. San Francisco: Ignatius Press, 2011.

Davis, John Jefferson. *Evangelical Ethics: Issues Facing the Church Today*, rev. and expanded ed. Phillipsburg, NJ: P&R, 1985, 1993, 2004.

Geisler, Norman L. *Christian Ethics: Contemporary Issues and Options*, 2nd ed. Grand Rapids, MI: Baker Books, 1989, 2010.

Feinberg, John S., and Paul D. Feinberg. *Ethics for a Brave New World*, 2nd ed. Updated and Expanded. Wheaton, IL: Crossway, 1993, 2010.

Kaiser, Walter. *What Does the Lord Require? A Guide for Preaching and Teaching Biblical Ethics.* Grand Rapids, MI: Baker Books, 2009.

Rae, Scott B. *Moral Choices: An Introduction to Ethics*, 3rd ed. Grand Rapids, MI: Zondervan, 2009.

Schmidt, Alvin J. *How Christianity Changed the World.* Grand Rapids, MI: Zondervan, 2004.

EVANGELICAL CHRISTIAN PUBLISHERS ASSOCIATION

The Evangelical Christian Publishers Association (ECPA) is an international nonprofit trade organization comprised of member companies that are involved in the publishing and distribution of Christian content worldwide. ECPA's mission is "to equip our members so they can more effectively make the Christian message more widely known." ECPA works to strengthen Christian publishing by building networking, information, and advocacy opportunities within the industry and throughout multiple channels so that its members can more effectively produce and deliver transformational Christian content. Through its network of people and organizations, ECPA serves as a focal point of thought and activity for evangelical publishers throughout the world. Although its publishers are also business competitors, they share a common vision to produce transformational Christian content. ECPA provides member programs that advocate for the industry, including providing access to key data and research that informs strategic business decisions and offering opportunities to network and connect with industry colleagues, experts, customers, and vendors.

ECPA was organized on October 10, 1974, at a meeting of several Christian publishers and incorporated as a nonprofit association on March 16, 1976. The first board consisted of Dr. Robert L. Mosier (president), Hugh Barbour, William T. Greig Jr., Robert L. Kregel, Wilfred C. Frykman, Walter Poff, Muriel Dennis, and Doug Ross.

Popular ECPA programs include the annual ECPA Management Seminar and the CEO Symposium; the Gold Medallion Book Awards; the annual ECPA Lifetime Achievement Award; the ECPA Christian Collective exhibit at the Frankfurt Book Fair Christian; the ECPA International Rights Managers Committee, which produces

---

VeggieTales

VeggieTales is a popular, successful series of animated children's films, books, and music that teach biblical stories, themes, and lessons primarily from the Bible. Created by Phil Vischer (1966–), with the main characters of *VeggieTales* being computer-generated fruits and vegetables, they are now owned by DreamWorks Animation.

an International Rights Guide; the ChristianManscriptSubmissions.com online writer's service; and the weekly *Rush to Press* industry e-newsletter.

Dennis Hillman

See also: Evangelical Christian Publishers Association; Mass Media, Evangelicals and

Further Reading

Schultze, Quentin J., ed. *Evangelicals and Mass Media.* Grand Rapids, MI: Zondervan, 1990.
Schultze, Quentin J., and Robert Herbert Woods Jr., eds. *Understanding Evangelicalism and Media: The Changing Face of Christian Communication.* Downers Grove, IL: InterVarsity Press, 2008.

EVANGELICAL COUNCIL FOR FINANCIAL ACCOUNTABILITY

The Evangelical Council for Financial Accountability (ECFA) is an accreditation agency to promote fiscal integrity among member organizations. Founded in 1979, it comprises nearly 1,900 evangelical Christian organizations that qualify for tax-exempt, nonprofit status, and receive tax-deductible contributions. As of 2014, the collective annual revenue of ECFA member organizations is reported to be nearly $22 billion. Members include Christian ministries, denominations, churches, and other tax-exempt 501(c)(3) organizations. Members are required to submit a renewal document annually that includes a recent copy of the audited financial statement and answers to a number of questions related to the membership standards. Field reviews are conducted on a regular basis by ECFA representatives. Since its inception, ECFA has been based in the Washington, D.C., area, with offices presently in Winchester, Virginia.

The mission statement adopted by the ECFA is "Enhancing Trust in Christ-Centered Churches and Ministries."

In the 1970s, there was growing public and political concern over an increase of questionable fundraising practices in the nonprofit sector. At the same time, donors and governmental agencies expressed concern over the management of donations to achieve publicly stated objectives as presented in fundraising appeals. So in 1977, Senator Mark O. Hatfield, a member of the board of World Vision, told evangelicals that they needed to formalize some means for financial accountability, or government legislation would be required.

A group of representatives from more than 30 evangelical groups met in December 1977 to formulate a plan. At that meeting, Hatfield's chief legislative assistant told them that "a voluntary disclosure program" would "preclude the necessity of federal intervention into the philanthropic and religious sector." Two years later the ECFA was founded by the Billy Graham Evangelistic Association and the U.S. branch of World Vision.

Through its conference presentations, Web site, publications, and services, ECFA informs its members of board governance, accounting, financial, fundraising, and legislative matters of common concern.

James Menzies

See also: Billy Graham Evangelistic Association; Hatfield, Mark Odom; Mass Media, Evangelicals and; Parachurch Ministries; World Vision International

Further Reading

Hadden, Jeffrey K., and Charles E. Swann. *Prime Time Preachers: The Rising Power of Televangelism.* Boston: Addison-Wesley, 1981. http://www.ecfa.org/.

VanderPol, Gary F. "The Least of These: American Evangelical Parachurch Missions to the Poor, 1947–2005." ThD diss., Boston University School of Theology, 2010. http://open.bu.edu/bitstream/handle/2144/1337/vanderpol_gary_thd_2010.pdf.

EVANGELICAL THEOLOGICAL SOCIETY

The Evangelical Theological Society is a professional organization for evangelical pastors, students, and professors. It was founded in 1949 and describes itself as "a group of scholars, teachers, pastors, students, and others dedicated to the oral exchange and written expression of theological thought and research. The ETS is devoted to the inerrancy and inspiration of the Scriptures and the gospel of Jesus Christ" (http://www.etsjets.org/about).

At its founding the society started with a single doctrinal basis: "The Bible alone, and the Bible in its entirety, is the Word of God written and is inerrant in the autographs." In 1990, it added a clause to include the doctrine of the Trinity: "God is a Trinity, Father, Son, and Holy Spirit, each an uncreated person, one in essence, equal in power and glory." Anyone seeking membership must provide written agree with this two-sentence position.

ETS publishes a quarterly journal, the *Journal of the Evangelical Theological Society (JETS)*, an academic periodical featuring peer-reviewed articles as well as extended book reviews in the biblical and theological disciplines. ETS also holds national and regional meetings across the United States and Canada.

ETS was formed in an organizational meeting at a YMCA in downtown Cincinnati, December 27–28, 1949. Key leaders at the meeting were Edward R. Dalglish (chairman), George Ladd, and Burton Goddard, all faculty members of Gordon Divinity School in Boston. Clarence Bouma of Calvin Seminary was elected its first president. Also present at this meeting were representatives from approximately 20 theological institutions from as many different denominations, all holding an inerrant view of Scripture.

The purpose of ETS is stated in its constitution, "to foster conservative biblical scholarship by providing a medium for the oral exchange and written expression of thought and research in the general field of the theological disciplines as

Contemporary Evangelical Theologians

1. D. A. Carson
2. William Lane Craig
3. John Frame
4. Norman L. Geisler
5. Timothy George
6. Wayne Grudem
7. Alister McGrath
8. Al Mohler
9. Richard Mouw
10. J. I. Packer
11. R. C. Sproul
12. Kevin Vanhoozer

centered in the Scriptures" (http://www.etsjets.org/about), though in practice it has broadened this purpose to include exploration and research of all biblically related issues.

As in any scholarly society, a primary purpose of ETS meetings is the presentation of academic papers. From its outset, presentations made at ETS meetings were to address matters directly related to the study of the Bible from an exegetical, historical, and theological perspective, displaying the best of conservative biblical scholarship. These presentations provided a medium for both an oral exchange and written expression of thought for evangelicals, as well as fostered scholarship centered on the Scriptures.

Membership in ETS is available to anyone with a Master of Theology (ThM) degree or its equivalent, and who subscribes to the doctrinal statement on inerrancy and the Trinity. There is also an associate membership available for anyone without such a degree, though associate members are not allowed to vote. A student membership is available for half the price of full membership. Members do not need to belong to specific denominational or theological traditions and are not required to be affiliated with any particular school or seminary. Dues are paid yearly. The number of members in 2012 was 4,074 (2,309 full members, 586 associate members, and 1,179 student members).

The organization has experienced a number of doctrinal controversies in its nearly 70-year history. In the 1970s, the definition of "inerrancy," including questions about literal versus nonliteral language, and the possibility of errors, was a major debate resulting in the 1983 expulsion of Robert Gundry (professor of New Testament studies and Koine Greek, Westmont College, Santa Barbara, California) from the Society for his views on the historicity of some events in Matthew's gospel.

A five-year controversy over "open theism," the doctrine that future free will choices of individuals cannot be known ahead of time by God, divided the Society

Other Evangelical Academic Societies

There are several evangelical academic societies where scholarship is exchanged, issues are debated, and collaborations are made in order to advance evangelical scholarship, equip younger generations, and engage society at the highest levels of academics. Among them are the following:

The Evangelical Homiletics Society (EHS), established in 1997 for the sharing of ideas related to the art and science of biblical preaching. It publishes the *Journal of the Evangelical Homiletical Society* (*JEHS*).

The Evangelical Missiological Society (EMS), established in 1990 to advance the cause of world evangelization (1990)

Evangelical Philosophical Society (EPS), established in 1977, devoted to the pursuit of philosophical excellence in the church and the academy. It publishes *Philosophia Christi*.

International Society of Christian Apologetics (ISCA), established in 2006, promotes discussion that is relevant to the defense of the historic Christian faith. They publish *The Journal of the International Society of Christian Apologetics*.

The Society for the Arts in Religious and Theological Studies (2007) is an academic society interested in the dynamic relationships among the arts, theology, religion, and spirituality. Though associated with the American Academy of the Arts and Society of Biblical Literature, evangelical aesthetic theologians actively contribute (e.g., William Dyrness of Fuller Theological Seminary). They publish *ARTS: The Arts in Religious and Theological Studies*.

in the early 2000s. In 2003, discussions were held whether to expel Clark Pinnock (Professor Emeritus of Systematic Theology at McMaster Divinity College) and John Sanders (professor of religious studies at Hendrix College) for their position on open theism. Also in 2003, theologian and philosopher Norman L Geisler wrote an open letter of resignation from ETS. And in a surprising move, Dr. Francis Beckwith resigned as president of ETS in 2007 following his decision to be received into the Roman Catholic Church.

In spite of the controversies, ETS continues to be the flagship of theological thought and research devoted to the inerrancy and inspiration of the Scriptures and the gospel of Jesus Christ. ETS is a growing professional organization, and out of it has also arisen the Evangelical Philosophical Society.

James Menzies

See also: Higher Education, Evangelicals and; Inerrancy; Philosophy, Evangelicals and; Theological Controversies within Evangelicalism

Further Reading

The Evangelical Theological Society (ETS). (n.d.). "About the ETS." Accessed April 28, 2017. http://www.etsjets.org/about.

The Evangelical Theological Society (ETS). (1991). "Reports Relating to the Forty-Second Annual Meeting of the Society." *Journal of the Evangelical Theological Society*, 34(1):141.

Köstenberger, Andreas J. *Quo Vadis, Evangelicalism? Perspectives on the Past, Direction for the Future: Nine Presidential Addresses from the First Fifty Years of the Journal of the Evangelical Theological Society.* Wheaton, IL: Crossway, 2007.

Morrison, Douglas. *Has God Said? Scripture, the Word of God, and the Crisis of Theological Authority.* Eugene, OR: Wipf & Stock, 2006.

Strachan, Owen. *Awakening the Evangelical Mind: An Intellectual History of the Neo-Evangelical Movement.* Grand Rapids, MI: Zondervan, 2015.

Wiseman, John. "The Evangelical Theological Society Yesterday and Today." *The Journal of the Evangelical Theological Society*, 28:5 (1985): 5–28. http://www.etsjets.org/files/JETS -PDFs/28/28-5/28-5-pp005-024_JETS.pdf.

EVANGELICALISM

Evangelicalism, whether used with a capital "E" or a small "e," is a broad term referring to the most influential religious movements in American Christianity. It is not limited to a single religious denomination, ethic group, or social or economic class of Americans. In its broadest sense, this movement embodies the belief that, as revealed through the Bible, salvation is by grace through faith in Jesus Christ. David W. Bebbington, a noted British historian whose scholarship involves global evangelicalism, identifies four key distinctives of evangelicalism, known as *The Bebbington Quadrilateral*: crucicentrism (the centrality of the cross in preaching and teaching); conversionism (personally accepting the gospel, that is, the gift of grace by faith in Jesus Christ, and thus receiving spiritual life); biblicism (devoted to the Bible as God's word); and activism (the belief that the gospel should be expressed in effort). Evangelicals in general align themselves with the following respective theological tenets: (1) Jesus Christ as the sole source of salvation through faith in Him, as validated by His crucifixion and bodily resurrection; (2) personal or "experiential" faith and conversion with regeneration (spiritual life from spiritual death) by the Holy Spirit; (3) recognition that the Bible is the inspired Word of God and serves as the ultimate basis and authority for faith and Christian living; (4) commitment to biblical missions and the spreading of the gospel by words and works; (5). special focus on the person and work of the Holy Spirit in one's life (conversion), lifestyle (spiritual maturity), church (e.g., revival services), and society.

Evangelicalism by most accounts is the largest religious sector in the United States, but the influence of the movement cannot be wholly quantified by its numerical mass because, especially from the mid- to late 20th century, the United States has been regarded by the world as the seat of evangelical growth and as the heart of the continuing global phenomenon. Evangelicals are made up of mostly Protestant but also some Roman Catholic and Orthodox Christians, and both Western and non-Western churches are included in this category so long as they conform to the above key distinctives. Though defining evangelicalism is problematic, the background and development of evangelicalism over time, including key figures and major events and doctrines contributing to the movement, give information that sets this mindset, movement, and influence apart from others.

Background and Definitions

The word *evangelical* finds its linguistic roots in the Greek word transliterated as *euanggelion* but pronounced as "yoo-ang-ghel'-ee-on," and the Latin word *ēvangelium*, literally "God's good news." This Good News, or "Gospel," may refer to the entire Bible, the coming Messiah, the message itself, or the person bringing the message.

The genesis of evangelicalism centers in Protestantism because Martin Luther (1483–1546) referred to the *evangelische Kirche* (the "evangelical church" in German) in an attempt to distinguish Protestants from Roman Catholics. Serving as the slogan for the Reformation, Luther emphasized the Five *Solas*: (1) *sola scriptura*, "by Scripture alone"; (2) *sola fide*, "by faith alone"; (3) *solus christus*, "through Christ alone"; (4) *sola gratia*, "by grace alone"; and (5) *soli Deo gloria*, "glory to God alone." The first *sola* frame what modern evangelicals might call the source of the *evangel*, and the latter four *solas* form the message of the *evangel*. However, this very early manifestation of evangelicalism has developed over time and in different locations around the world while maintaining the above-referenced five key distinctives.

Five Fundamentals of the Christian Faith

The five fundamentals of the Christian Faith, also known as the "five points of fundamentalism," were adopted by a 1910 Presbyterian General Assembly in response to theological liberalism. Though never intended to reduce the essence of Christianity to an exclusive definitive five-point list or even a creed, the five fundamentals summarized are as follows:

1. The Inerrancy of the Scripture
2. The Virgin Birth of Jesus Christ
3. Substitutionary Atonement of Jesus Christ
4. The Bodily Resurrection of Jesus Christ
5. Authenticity of Miracles

Interestingly, in the 1920s the physical return of Jesus Christ (premillennialism) was exchanged for the authenticity of miracles.

Historical Development

Although many evangelical traditions trace their roots to Martin Luther (1483–1546) (e.g., the Evangelical Lutheran Church) or later John Calvin (1509–1564) (e.g., Presbyterian and other Reformed traditions), The First Great Awakening (ca. 1730–1755) is truly what began the movement that has shaped the face of American evangelicalism today. Concurrent with Pietism, a sister movement in continental Europe around the same time, evangelicalism in the United States emphasized the experiential "conversion." A series of historical figures such as John Wesley (1703–1791), Jonathan Edwards (1703–1758), Charles Finney (1792–1875), and others sparked Congregationalist revivals, but efforts by George Whitefield (1714–1770) also helped crystallize these revivals into a movement. Known as "New Lights," these evangelical revivalists often aligned with Revolutionary Patriots, which leads some evangelical historians to draw close associations between the movement and other Revolutionary political activities of the day.

The Second Great Awakening (ca. 1790s to 1830s) was promulgated by evangelicals in the northeastern United States, but the effects were also felt in the South, an area still heavily practicing chattel slavery. In the northeast, this revival laid the groundwork for later abolitionist and temperance movements, the female seminary movement, and the establishment of then-stoic theological institutions of higher education such as Harvard, Yale, and Princeton. In the South, revivalism led to circuit riders, the Southern Baptist denomination (a schism occurring in 1845 due to differences in opinion over appointing slave-owning missionaries, among other things), and other denominations separated by the Mason Dixon Line. Ultimately, the Civil War (1861–1865) fractured the United States, shattering some of the earlier Methodist ideas of perfectibility leading to theological or biblical defenses for their respective positions on slavery and the war in general, and caused long-lasting social effects that permeate even today.

After the Emancipation and Southern Reconstruction matured, early 19th-century industrialization and urbanization bred resentment within American culture due to complex economic and cultural factors. Nevertheless, this period marked a general divide between evangelicals who despaired of social reform. Many reshaped their theology toward a dispensational premillennialism (and its hope in a rapture) while others adopted a Social Gospel, believing that God redeemed not only individuals but also institutions. The late 19th-century records the rise of prominent seminaries and seminarians, such as Presbyterian theologians B. B. Warfield (1851–1921) and A. A. Hodge (1883–1886), who held firm to the evangelical biblical authority position of Inerrancy.

The early 20th century brought a complex "give and take" through the rise of what American religious conservatives termed "Modernism," which resulted in conflict within American Protestantism and a rise in evangelical fundamentalism. Largely as a result of the delayed popularity of Charles Darwin's *The Origin of Species* (1859), the impact of German higher criticism, and the mockery of evangelicals resulting from the court of public opinion related to the 1925 "Scopes Monkey Trial" (*The State of Tennessee v. John Thomas Scopes*), American attitudes within mainline Protestant denominations and even Baptist groups cast doubt on biblical authority. Evangelicals, at this time identifying more as fundamentalists, retreated from mainline Protestant denominations, breaking off and forming independent churches or separate denominations. Private colleges, Bible institutes, and conservative seminaries as well as related evangelical publishing houses began gaining ground through the middle part of the century. In response, conservative figures such as Harold J. Ockenga (1905–1985) pioneered a neo-evangelistic movement to encourage cultural, intellectual, and social engagement without a reactionary spirit, and yet not succumb to theological liberalism with its diminished view of the authority and nature of Scripture and the gospel message.

Evangelicalism maintained the position as a cultural undercurrent amid a tumultuous American society through the middle part of the century until reaching what many refer to as the Fourth Great Awakening (1960–1980). Led largely by Billy Graham's massively popular Crusades, religious enthusiasm in the United States rose through various media such as radio and television. However, Michael Lindsay (2007), in his book *Faith in the Halls of Power: How Evangelicals Joined the American Elite*, asserts that evangelicalism rose prominently into the public sphere again when President Jimmy Carter (1924–) (a Southern Baptist Sunday school teacher) referred to himself on the campaign trail in 1975 as "born again," sparking the prime movement into spaces of political, economic, and corporate influence in the United States. Jerry Falwell (1933–2007), James Dobson (1936–), Pat Robertson (1930–) and others became evangelical cultural, political, and social activists. For example, the Moral Majority (1979–1989) was a Christian Religious Right organization founded by Falwell. As a result, all three U.S. presidential candidates, Carter, Ronald Reagan (1911–2004), and John B. Anderson (1922–), stood on evangelical platforms. Moreover, denominations such as the Southern Baptist Convention began to move away from liberalism toward evangelicalism, whereby a conservative resurgence began (1985).

Political action groups such as the Family Research Council (FRC), established by James Dobson (1981), began to strategically work through the American political system from the 1980s through the 2000s. The evangelical platform became synonymous with certain political issues, and the United States saw an increased tension through a series of combative "culture wars." Evangelical activism began to peak through the 1990s, when book burnings, pro-life rallies, prayer in school, and homeschooling became issues of national concern. Overall, the evangelical contingent in the United States continues to work through many of the strategies and mechanisms established in the latter part of the 19th and early part of the 20th centuries, to continue striving for national influence on American culture.

In 2011, the Pew Research Forum, in a report titled *Global Christianity*, estimated that there are more than 285 million evangelical Christians worldwide, making up a total of 13.1% of the Christian population and 4.1% of the world population.

Moreover, in the United States, evangelicals make up approximately 26% of the total population, with Catholics (22%) and mainline Protestants (16%) following, along with other major religious sectors. Regardless of the actual numbers, the influence and continued prevalence of American evangelicalism are manifestly evident. Evangelicalism is a rich movement with tensions, complexity, and diversity in terms of its past, adherents, initiatives, religio-cultural heritage, and powers. Therefore, to understand the central figures, debates, and certain intellectual, cultural, and social values and movements in modern history, whether cultural, intellectual, political, or social, one must engage the distinctive aspects, influences, mindset, and origins of evangelicalism.

Bryce Hantla

See also: African American Evangelicalism; Baptists and Evangelicalism; Billy Graham Evangelistic Association; Carnell, Edward John; Christian Apologetics; Christian Legal Society; Dobson, James C., Jr.; Evangelism; Falwell, Jerry L., Sr.; Family Research Council; Focus on the Family; Foreign Policy, Evangelicals and; Fuller Theological Seminary; Fundamentalism; Graham, William F., Jr. ("Billy"); Henry, Carl F. H.; Hispanic American Evangelicals; Moral Majority; Neo-Evangelicalism; Ockenga, Harold John; Theological Controversies within Evangelicalism

Further Reading

Green, John C., James L. Guth, Corwin E. Smidt, and Lyman A. Kellstedt. *Religion and the Culture Wars: Dispatches from the Front.* Lanham, MD: Rowman & Littlefield, 1996.

Hunter, James Davison. *American Evangelicalism: Conservative Religion and the Quandary of Modernity.* Rutgers, NJ: Rutgers University Press, 1983.

Marsden, George. *Understanding Fundamentalism and Evangelicalism.* Grand Rapids, MI: Eerdmans, 1991.

Smidt, Corwin. *American Evangelicals Today.* Lanham, MD: Rowman & Littlefield, 2013.

Smith, Christian, Michael Emerson, Sally Gallagher, Paul Kennedy, and David Sikkink. *American Evangelicalism: Embattled and Thriving.* Chicago: University of Chicago Press, 1998.

EVANGELICALS & CATHOLICS TOGETHER

In 1994, evangelical Protestant Charles Colson and Roman Catholic priest Richard John Neuhaus served as coeditors on an ecumenical document entitled *Evangelicals & Catholics Together: The Christian Mission in the Third Millennium* (hereafter referenced as *ECT*). The document addressed the belief that there are common concerns, normally social issues, shared by evangelicals and Roman Catholics. Historically, it built on the common ground many evangelicals and Roman Catholics shared in opposing abortion from the mid-1970s forward and reflected cobelligerency advocated by evangelicals such as Francis Schaeffer, C. Everett Koop, and Charles ("Chuck") Colson. According to *ECT*, "The love of Christ compels

[Evangelicals and Catholics], and we are therefore resolved to avoid such conflict between our communities and, where such conflict exists, to do what we can to reduce and eliminate it." Although not overlooking the theological differences between Evangelicalism and Roman Catholicism, *ECT* maintained that with the coming of a new millennium, both groups remain "resolved to explore patterns of working and witnessing together in order to advance the one mission of Christ."

The document outlines five areas in which Roman Catholics and evangelicals state their unified positions. First, it universally affirms the Lordship of Christ and the Apostle's Creed. Moreover, *ECT* asserts that "[Christians] are justified by grace through faith because of Christ. . . . All who accept Christ as Lord and Savior are brothers and sisters in Christ. Evangelicals and Catholics are brothers and sisters in Christ." Second, both groups shared the same *hope* that "all people will come to faith in Jesus Christ as Lord and Savior." As such, Catholics and evangelicals alike must zealously undertake the Great Commission. Third, *ECT* admits that Catholics and evangelicals disagree significantly on matters such as the sole authority of the Scripture, the sacraments, Mariology, and apostolic succession. However, both groups desire to "search together . . . for a better understanding of one another's convictions." Fourth, both groups contend together against anti-Christian causes, including relativism, abortion, pornography, and anti-intellectualism. Likewise, *ECT* will contend together for religious freedom, social justice, and stable families. Finally, the document maintains that it is not advantageous "to proselytize among active adherents of another Christian community." Therefore, as evangelicals and Catholics witness together, they will engage one another graciously and forgive one another lovingly for past sins that have hurt either community.

At the time, several prominent evangelical scholars endorsed the document, including Dr. Bill Bright, Dr. Os Guinness, and Dr. James I. Packer. Likewise, numerous Roman Catholics also endorsed *ECT*, including John Cardinal O'Connor, Peter Kreeft, and Dr. Nathan Hatch. However, other notable evangelicals argued that *ECT* glossed over significant theological issues, particularly with regard to justification. For example, R. C. Sproul identified *ECT* as "the biggest crisis over the purity of the gospel" that he encountered in ministry. For Sproul, the heart of the gospel lies in *sola fide* (faith alone), and he remained gravely concerned that *ECT* dismissed the canons of the 16th-century Council of Trent, which anathematized *sola fide* justification. Other notable evangelicals such as James Kennedy and John MacArthur concurred and criticized the *ECT* statement.

In spite of numerous, subsequent statements to clarify the positions of *ECT* and its statement on justification (such as the 1995 "Statement by Protestant Signers to the *ECT*" and the 1998 work *The Gift of Salvation*), the document remains a source of tension between adherents and nonsignatories.

Brittany Burnette

See also: Colson, Charles Wendell ("Chuck"); Koop, C. Everett; Schaeffer, Francis A. and Edith; Theological Controversies within Evangelicalism

Further Reading

Canons and Decrees of the Council of Trent, Sixth Session, Chap. XVI, Canon IX. (n.d.). Accessed March 31, 2015. http://history.hanover.edu/texts/trent/trentall.html.

Colson, Charles, and Richard John Neuhaus, eds. *Evangelicals & Catholics Together: Toward a Common Mission.* Dallas: Word Publishers, 1995.

Eskridge, L. "Colson, Charles Wendell." In *Biographical Dictionary of Evangelicals*, edited by Timothy Larsen (Leicester, England; Downers Grove, IL: InterVarsity Press, 2003): 155.

"Evangelicals & Catholics Together: The Christian Mission in the Third Millennium." First Things. May 1994. https://www.firstthings.com/article/1994/05/evangelicals-catholics -together-the-christian-mission-in-the-third-millennium.

"The Gift of Salvation." *First Things* 79 (January 1998): 20–23. http://www.leaderu.com /ftissues/ft9801/articles/gift.html.

"Irreconcilable Differences: Catholics, Evangelicals, and the New Quest for Unity, Parts 1–3." 1995. Grace To You. http://www.gty.org/resources/Sermons/GTY54.

Sproul, R. C. *Are We Together?* Sanford, FL: Reformation Trust, 2012.

"Statement by Protestant Signers to ECT." January 19, 1995. http://www.leaderu.com/ect /ect2.html.

EVANGELISM

One of the most distinguishing aspects of evangelicalism is the proclamation and persuasion of the gospel message as commanded by Jesus Christ himself in Luke 20:1 and lived out by his disciples in such passages as Acts 8:4.

Although it is not possible to define evangelism in terms that would be acceptable to all evangelical bodies, nor even possible to give a definition that would be universally accepted by evangelicals, certain essential elements are common to almost all definitions. First, any definition of evangelism will recognize that it is an attempt to confront people with a personal invitation to an encounter with God. Second, the gospel message is redemptive truth. Third, one motive for evangelization is love for Christ. And fourth, the ultimate aim of evangelism is thus to make disciples who, in turn, will proclaim Christ to their sphere of influence.

Throughout church history, a plethora of definitions have abounded concerning a biblical approach to the evangelization of the nations. The earliest definition from New Testament times comes to us from Jesus Christ Himself as he gave what has been labeled the "Great Commission" of Matthew 28:18–20, which states, "Go therefore and make disciples of all nations, baptizing them in the name of the Father and the Son and the Holy Spirit." Evangelicals take the Great Commission very seriously. But they also understand and integrate the rich history of defining evangelism.

Origen declared in 220 CE that the gospel had not been preached to all nations because it had not reached yet the Chinese, the Ethiopians, or the most remote and barbarous tribes. In his 1520 definition, Martin Luther stated that not only will the gospel always be preached and that it has gone throughout the world, but it also cannot be proclaimed without causing offense and tumult. In the 1755 *Dictionary of the English Language*, Samuel Johnson wrote that to evangelize was to instruct people in the gospel or law of Jesus Christ.

In the 20th century, the definition of "evangelism" continued to be refined and expanded. For example, Methodist evangelist John R. Mott, author of *The Evangelization of the World in This Generation* (1900), who spearheaded a youth movement toward world evangelization, believed that the evangelization of the world means giving everyone an adequate opportunity to know Jesus Christ as Savior and become His disciple. Even the Church of England became concerned about evangelization when the Archbishops convened in 1918 and developed a definition that stated that to evangelize was to present Christ Jesus so that people come to trust God through Him, accept Him as Savior, and serve Him as King, in the fellowship of His church.

In 1966, evangelist Billy Graham hosted the first conference for evangelicals on World Evangelism in Berlin, Germany. From that gathering, the International Congress on World Evangelization met in Lausanne, Switzerland, six years later in 1973. During the Congress, the Lausanne Covenant was developed and approved by itinerant evangelists from all over the world. The definition for evangelism involved the "spreading the good news" that "Jesus died for our sins" and "was raised from the dead," and that evangelism itself is the "proclamation of the historical, biblical Christ as Savior and Lord," and "persuading people to come to Him personally so be reconciled to God" (Stott, 1975).

Southern Baptist pastor, professor, and evangelist C. E. Autrey led a delegation of more than 70 from the Southern Baptist Convention to the above-stated gatherings. From his involvement and commitment to evangelism, he defined "evangelism" using terms like "the outreach of the church by confrontation with the gospel of Christ" and "an attempt to lead people to a personal commitment by faith and repentance in Christ as Savior and Lord" (Autrey, 1966: 13).

Although no one definition of "evangelism" will be readily accepted by evangelicals, they do agree that a biblical concept of evangelism involves the sharing of the gospel of Jesus Christ throughout the world, inviting people to make a personal decision by receiving Jesus Christ as their Savior. For them, evangelism is the lifeblood of the Church, and thus it necessitates that some definition and practical approach be accepted and continued until God's sovereign plans over this world are complete.

J. Denny Autrey

Key Term in Evangelicalism: *Witnessing*

The word *witnessing* is a casual term used by evangelicals to refer to an activity, event, or conversation whereby a Christian shares the gospel or offers reasons or evidence that undergirds their Christian faith (Isaiah 55:11; John 9:25, 29–33; Acts 2:32–36; 8:35; Romans 10:14). Although witnessing is mostly defined as a verbal act, it can also be used to refer to a deed, action, or even a lifestyle that exemplifies Jesus Christ and the way he behaved toward others.

See also: Baptists and Evangelicalism; Billy Graham Evangelistic Association; Emerging and Emergent Churches; Missions, Evangelicals and

Further Reading

Autrey. C. E. *The Theology of Evangelism.* Nashville, TN: Broadman Press, 1966.

Coleman, Robert. *The Master Plan of Evangelism.* Grand Rapids, MI: Revell, 1964, 1964, 1993.

Mott, John R. *The Evangelization of the World in this Generation.* New York: Student Volunteer Movement of Foreign Missions, 1900.

Reid, Alvin. *Evangelism Handbook: Biblical, Spiritual, Intentional, Missional.* Nashville, TN: B&H, 2009.

Stott, John. "LOP 3—The Lausanne Covenant: An Exposition and Commentary by John Stott." (1975). Lausanne Movement. https://www.lusanne.org/content/lop/lop-3.

Sweeney, Douglas A. *The American Evangelical Story: A History of the Movement.* Grand Rapids, MI: Baker Academic, 2005.

EVANS, ANTHONY T. ("TONY") (1949–)

Anthony T. Evans, known as "Dr. Tony Evans," is a prominent African American evangelical leader, prolific author, founding pastor of Oak Cliff Bible Fellowship, founder and president of The Urban Alternative, and board member of Dallas Theological Seminary. His evangelical ministry is heard daily worldwide.

Evans is married to Lois, and they have four children.

Evans graduated from Carver Bible College with academic honors, receiving a BA in 1972. In 1976, he received an outstanding achievement award and academics honors from Dallas Theological Seminary, earning a master's degree in theology (ThM), and in 1982, a doctorate in theology (ThD) from the same institution. Evans

---

Prominent Evangelical Media Programs of Preaching and Teaching

Evangelicals have long embraced technology as a tool for disseminating their values, beliefs, and worldview. Among the many personalities and programs doing so are these:

The Alternative with Tony Evans
In Touch with Charles Stanley
Insight for Living with Chuck Swindoll
Grace to You with John MacArthur
Bible Answer Man with Hank Hanegraaff
Hour of Decision with Billy Graham
Thru the Bible with J. Vernon McGee
Love Worth Finding with Adrian Rogers
Turning Point with David Jeremiah

also received an Honorary Doctorate of Humane Letters from Eastern College in St. Davids, Pennsylvania, and an Honorary Doctorate of Divinity from Dallas Baptist University in Dallas, Texas. He has taught at Dallas Theological Seminary as an associate professor in pastoral ministries, evangelism, homiletics and black church studies.

In 1976, Evans founded a church in his home, with less than a dozen people at the first church service. He continues to serve that church, Oak Cliff Bible Fellowship (Dallas) as the senior pastor. Through Evans's leadership, Oak Cliff Bible Fellowship developed into an estimated 8,000-member church with more than 100 ministries in operation.

He founded and currently presides over the national and international ministry known as *The Urban Alternative*, a syndicated radio service that can be heard in more than 1,000 outlets daily throughout the United States and more than 100 countries globally. This broadcast can also be viewed on television stations and online at TonyEvans.org. Noted for his speaking skills and use of illustrations, he formerly was a speaker on the Promise Keepers' platform, as well as a regular speaker in evangelistic meetings and Bible conferences in the United States and internationally. Among other achievements, Evans was honored by Family Research Center with the Marian Pfister Anshutz Award in recognition of his dedication to protecting, encouraging, and strengthening the American family. Evans has authored more than 30 books.

Evans has served as chaplain for the NBA's Dallas Mavericks over the last three decades, the longest standing NBA chaplaincy on record. Additionally, he served as a chaplain of the NFL's Dallas Cowboys for a number of years. He is a board member of the National Religious Broadcasters Association and one of contemporary American evangelicalism's most prominent individuals.

Tracy L. Winkler

See also: African American Evangelicalism; Civil Rights Movement, Evangelicalism and; Dallas Theological Seminary; Dispensationalism; Evangelicalism; Evangelism; National Black Evangelical Association

Further Reading

Evans, Tony. *Kingdom Agenda: Life Under God.* Nashville, TN: W Publishing Group, 2013.
Evans, Tony. *Oneness Embraced: Reconciliation, the Kingdom, and How We Are Stronger Together.* Chicago: Moody Press, 2011.
Evans, Tony. *Theology You Can Count On.* Chicago: Moody Press, 2008.
Hannah, John D. *An Uncommon Union: Dallas Theological Seminary and American Evangelicalism.* Grand Rapids, MI: Zondervan, 2009.

EXPLO '72

Explo '72 (shortened for "spiritual explosion"), or the International Student Conference on Evangelism, held in Dallas, Texas, June 12–17, 1972, is considered the most significant event marking the height of the Jesus People Movement of the 1970s. The concept for Explo '72 was conceived three years earlier at the U.S. Congress on Evangelism in Minneapolis by Campus Crusade for Christ (now Cru) founder Bill Bright (1921–2003) while he was listening to a message from Billy Graham (1918–). Estimated attendance for the daytime events varied from 80,000 to 85,000, with the majority of the attendees from a conservative white background. Most were middle-class high school and college students, and there were fewer than 3,000 African American attendees. During the day, the students attended sessions and were dispersed throughout the metropolitan cities to share their faith. Evening events were held at the Cotton Bowl Stadium (Fair Park) and featured music and bands, well-known preachers and evangelists, and professional athletes representing different sports. Billy Graham, honorary chairman, spoke six times, including at the final event of an eight-hour-long Christian music festival.

Graham identified the purposes of Explo '72: (1) to dramatize the Jesus revolution; (2) to teach people how to "witness" for Christ; (3) to remind the church that the old-time Gospel is relevant to this modern generation; (4) to teach young Christians that true faith must be applied to the social problems of the world; (5) to enlist thousands of new recruits for missionary societies, seminaries, and Bible schools; (6) to assist the church in evangelism; (7) to evangelize the world in their generation; and (8) to say to the world that Christian youth are on the march.

The final event, held on Saturday, June 17, 1972, was labeled "The Christian Woodstock," and drew an estimated attendance between 100,000 and 200,000. *Newsweek* described the attendees as "militant Christians." Significant artists performing included Randy Matthews, Larry Norman, Johnny Cash, Andre Crouch

---

The Four Spiritual Laws

The Four Spiritual Laws is an evangelistic method developed in 1957 by the founder of Cru (originally Campus Crusade for Christ), Bill Bright (1921–2003). The pamphlet "Have You Heard of the Four Spiritual Laws?" has sold more than 100 million copies. Making it as simple as possible in order to reach the greatest number of people, given where they are, the gospel is organized into four points emphasizing God's love:

1. God loves you and has a wonderful plan for your life (John 3:16, 10:10).
2. Humanity is tainted by sin and is therefore separated from God. As a result, we cannot know God's wonderful plan for our lives (Romans 3:23, 6:23).
3. Jesus Christ is God's only provision for our sin. Through Jesus Christ, we can have our sins forgiven and restore a right relationship with God (Romans 5:8; 1 Corinthians 15:3–4; John 14:6).
4. We must place our faith in Jesus Christ as Savior in order to receive the gift of salvation and know God's wonderful plan for our lives (John 1:12; Acts 16:31; Ephesians 2:8–9).

and the Disciples, and Kris Kristofferson. The growth of Contemporary Christian Music may in part be credited to the influence of Jesus music at the event. The lasting impact of Explo '72 resulted in many attendees devoting themselves to full-time Christian vocations and service.

President Richard Nixon eagerly wanted an invitation to the event for the purpose of co-opting Explo '72 for political purposes, but Campus Crusade's staff declined his offer. The president did send a telegram referring to a needed change that "requires a deep and abiding commitment to spiritual values. It requires a moral awakening" (Turner, 2008: 228). Ironically, this was the week of the infamous Washington, D.C., Watergate Hotel break-in.

Fundamentalists denounced the rock music, long hair, and insufficient attire of some attendees. Other conservative Christian groups criticized Explo '72 for its ecumenical aspects that included both Protestant and Roman Catholic ministries, and for the use of rock music. Also attending were fringe Jesus movement groups such as the Children of God and the Christian World Liberation Front (now Spiritual Counterfeits Project).

Explo '72 hastened the growth rate of Campus Crusade nationally and internationally as a parachurch ministry. The event was life-changing for many attendees who believed it achieved the "spiritual explosion" originally envisioned by Bill Bright, and it stands as one example of evangelical ministry to youth and the counterculture of the 1960s and 1970s.

J. Craig Kubic

See also: Bright, William R. ("Bill"); Calvary Chapel; Children of God; Contemporary Christian Music; Counterculture, Evangelicals and; Graham, William F., Jr. ("Billy"); Jesus Music; Jesus People Movement; Jews for Jesus; Lindsey, Harold Lee ("Hal"); Norman, Larry David; Smith, Charles W. ("Chuck")

Further Reading

Bustraan, Richard. *The Jesus People Movement: A Story of Spiritual Revolution among the Hippies.* Eugene, OR: Pickwick, 2014.

Eshleman, Paul, and Norman Rohrer. *The Explo Story: A Plan to Change the World.* Glendale, CA: G/L Publications, 1972.

Eskridge, Larry. *God's Forever Family: The Jesus People Movement in America.* New York: Oxford University Press, 2013.

"Rallying for Jesus." *Life* 72(25): 40–45.

Turner, John G. (2008). *Bill Bright and Campus Crusade for Christ: The Renewal of Evangelicalism in Postwar America.* Chapel Hill, NC: University of North Carolina Press.

Woodward, Kenneth L. (1972). "The Christian Woodstock." *Newsweek* 79(25): 52.

F

FALWELL, JERRY L., SR. (1933–2007)

Jerry Lamon Falwell Sr. was a Baptist pastor noted for his role as a catalyst for the political consciousness and activism of evangelical Christians in the United States from the 1970s until his death in 2007. He and his twin brother, Gene, were born on August 11, 1933, near Lynchburg, Virginia, to Helen and Carey Falwell. His father and grandfather were atheists, but his mother was a devout Christian. Falwell followed his mother's course and became a Christian in 1952. Soon after, he transferred to Baptist Bible College in Springfield, Missouri, where he graduated in 1956. He married Macel Pate in 1958. Together, they had three children; Jerry Falwell Jr., now Chancellor of Liberty University; Jonathan Falwell, now senior pastor of Thomas Road Baptist Church; and Jeannie Savas, a surgeon in Richmond, Virginia.

After completing college, Falwell returned to Lynchburg, Virginia, in 1956. That year, he founded Thomas Road Baptist Church with 35 people. A significant factor in the church's remarkable growth was Falwell's commitment to knock on the doors of 100 homes each day in the hopes of sharing the Gospel message and inviting people to come to the church. At the same time, he began the *Old Time Gospel Hour* radio and television ministry. At the first anniversary service of the church, nearly 850 people were present. Eventually, the church grew to more than 22,000 members under Falwell's leadership. Originally part of the Baptist Bible Fellowship International, Falwell also became affiliated with the Southern Baptist Convention by dually aligning with the Southern Baptist Conservatives of Virginia Convention in 1996. Falwell founded and became chancellor of Liberty University (founded in 1971), which claims to be the largest Christian university in the world.

Theologically, Falwell was staunchly Baptist. He was committed to the authority and inerrancy of the Bible and is best known for his vigorous defense of what he understood to be biblical morality. Falwell was also intentionally an evangelist

---

Key Term in Evangelicalism: *Born Again*

Based on John 3:1–21, the term *born again* means "born from above," a "rebirth." Thus, "being born again" is an evangelical term that refers to receiving the gift of salvation from God by means of faith resulting in receiving eternal life, a spiritually new nature or transformation, and spiritual regeneration from spiritual death (Ephesians 2:8–9; 2 Corinthians 5:17).

throughout his ministry. Though he became an active voice in American national politics, he retained his focus on communicating the gospel of salvation through faith in Jesus Christ as the core of his ministry.

Over the course of his public ministry, Jerry Falwell moved from an isolationist form of Christian fundamentalism to a socially engaged form of evangelicalism. His early views were reflected in his reaction to the political and social engagement of pastors in the American Civil Rights Movement, most notably Martin Luther King Jr. (1929–1968). Falwell expressed distrust of such pastors, arguing that it was the job of preachers to see people come to personal salvation, not pursue political causes. Some of his concern was driven by his youthful opposition to the Supreme Court decision in *Brown v. Board of Education* (1958), which ended segregated schooling on the basis of race. Falwell's opposition moderated dramatically over time, as did his early focus on other social taboos traditionally associated with Christian fundamentalism in America, such as alcohol, dancing, and movie theaters. In his later life, Falwell affirmed the common civil rights of all American citizens, regardless of race, economic status, or sexual practices.

The Supreme Court decision in *Roe v. Wade* (1973), legalizing abortion in the United States, was a critical event in the transformation of Falwell's view of pastors and politics. By 1979, Falwell's concern over abortion, secularism, and other changing aspects of morality in American culture led him to found the Moral Majority, along with Paul Weyrich (1942–2008). This organization intended to bring together conservative Christians with politically like-minded Roman Catholics, Jews, Mormons, and Pentecostals in support of public policy and politicians the organization found to be pro-life, pro–traditional morality, pro–traditional family, pro-American, and pro-Israel. When the Moral Majority dissolved in 1989, Falwell stated his belief that its mission had been accomplished. Five years later, however, he founded the Faith and Values Coalition (now the Moral Majority Coalition) to take up the agenda of the old Moral Majority.

Jerry Falwell died on May 15, 2007, in Lynchburg, Virginia. Beyond his role as the founding pastor of a major church and Christian university, he was a leading figure in bringing evangelicals and other conservative Christians into the American political process as an organized voting bloc. The genius of Falwell's political vision was its orientation toward rebuilding what he saw as the moral strengths of America.

Benjamin Blair Phillips

See also: Baptists and Evangelicalism; Bible, Authority, of; Billy Graham Evangelistic Association; Fundamentalism; Inerrancy; National Black Evangelical Association; Politics, Evangelicals and

Further Reading

Falwell, Jerry. *Listen, America!* Garden City, NY: Doubleday, 1980.
Falwell, Jerry. *Strength for the Journey: An Autobiography.* New York: Simon and Schuster, 1987.

Falwell, Macel. *Jerry Falwell: His Life and Legacy.* New York: Simon and Schuster, 2008.

Harding, Susan. *The Book of Jerry Falwell: Fundamentalist Language and Politics.* Princeton, NJ: Princeton University Press, 2001.

Sutton, Matthew. *Jerry Falwell and the Rise of the Religious Right: A Brief History with Documents.* Boston: Bedford/St. Martin's, 2012.

FAMILY RESEARCH COUNCIL

The Family Research Council (FRC) is a nonprofit, Christian public policy ministry that is based in Washington, D.C. Its primary purpose is to facilitate conversation and promote legislation centered on the establishment of traditional, Judeo-Christian family values. Among the values the Council affirms are the sanctity of life (with life beginning at conception), religious liberty, humane elder care, school choice for parents, and a man–woman definition of marriage. The Council was founded in 1983, three years after President James ("Jimmy") Carter hosted the 1980 White House Conference on Families. At this conference, James Dobson (1939–), an influential Christian family psychologist and speaker, led a strategy session, with eight conservative public figures, to develop a Washington-based think tank to advocate on behalf of family values.

The Council's first president, Gerald P. Regier (1945–), was present at the 1980 White House meeting. Regier's initial efforts through the Council were in favor of pro-life legislations, and he focused on developing legal briefs, offering media commentary, and securing appointments on government panels in support of the Council's identified values.

In 1988, Gary L. Bauer (1946–), former Under Secretary of Education and domestic policy advisor to President Ronald Reagan, became president of FRC. Bauer established a national headquarters in Washington, D.C., and a national distribution center in Holland, Michigan, which were instrumental in growing the influence of the Council. That same year, Bauer partnered the Council with Focus on the Family, a ministry effort begun by Dobson. The two organizations worked together as a powerful lobbying entity until 1992, when they became independent again after an IRS inquiry into their varying tax-exempt statuses. In 1992, the Council also formed a legislative affiliate, Family Research Council Action.

Kenneth L. Connor, prominent Florida attorney and national pro-life leader, took over as president in 2000 and brought a more academic focus to the Council's educational aims through a scholarship program, the Witherspoon Fellowship. In 2003, Tony R. Perkins (1963–), a Louisiana politician who forged the nation's first covenant marriage law, became president. The Council actively opposes judicial activism. There have also been widespread efforts throughout its history for the Council to reach beyond the bounds of evangelical denominations to Protestant mainline and Roman Catholic churches and organizations in order to come together on common causes.

The primary aim of the Council is to initiate public discussion surrounding traditional Judeo-Christian value structures, and it maintains an active publishing agenda in a wide range of Internet-, paper-, and radio-based media, including social media, email-based updates, blogs, press releases, policy statements, amicus briefs, pamphlets, and a radio broadcast called *Washington Watch*. Through their legislative affiliate, the Council has hosted a Values Voter summit each fall in Washington, D.C., since 2006. The Council's distinctly evangelical, biblical stance on same-sex attraction and their affirmation of man–woman marriage has drawn widespread support from other social conservatives, as well as criticism. As a politically conservative Washington think tank, the Family Research Council has enacted policy and given evangelicals a voice in favor of widely held conservative opinions on publically debated issues of political relevance.

Bryce Hantla

See also: Abortion, Evangelicals and; Dobson, James C., Jr.; Focus on the Family; Human Rights, Evangelicals and; Politics, Evangelicals and

Further Reading

Bauer, Gary. *Our Hopes, Our Dreams: A Vision for America.* Colorado Springs, CO: Focus on the Family, 1996.

Gilgoff, Dan. *The Jesus Machine: How James Dobson, Focus on the Family, and Evangelical America Are Winning the Culture War.* New York: St. Martin's Press, 2007.

Smith, Lauren Edwards, Laura R. Olson, and Jeffrey A. Fine. "Substantive Religious Representation in the U.S. Senate: Voting Alignment with the Family Research Council." *Political Research Quarterly* 63:1 (2010): 68–82.

FELLOWSHIP OF CHRISTIAN ATHLETES

Fellowship of Christian Athletes (FCA) is an international nondenominational ministry to student and professional athletes. Initially chartered by Eastern Oklahoma A&M basketball coach Don McClanen (1925–) on November 10, 1954, FCA has grown to become one of the most influential parachurch evangelical ministries in the world. McClanen partnered with former athlete and Presbyterian minister Louis H. Evans Sr. (1915–1981), Presbyterian minister Roe H. Johnston (1922–2007), and Baseball Hall of Fame member Branch Rickey (1881–1965) to formalize his initial vision to use the influence of athletes and the platform of athletics to promote the Christian faith. McClanen saw popular athletes endorsing commercial products and thought that a similar strategy might be used to have well-known athletes and coaches who were Christians proclaim their faith publicly to spiritually influence young athletes.

FCA has had several phases of development. Initially, the organization used large speaking engagements to rally support through popular professional and collegiate athletes, reaching more than 90,000 people through these rallies the first year. Then in 1956, FCA held its first sports camp at Estes Park, Colorado, with 256 athletes and coaches participating in the event.

In 1966, FCA expanded its presence on school campuses by using in-school "Huddles," which is one of the few surviving Christian student organizations meeting on public middle school and high school campuses. Huddles legally host worship services and Bible studies on public school grounds because they are entirely student initiated and led. Most schools, however, require a school-employed sponsor to monitor school facilities during events.

FCA's influence has not remained isolated in America. With its World Headquarters (National Support Center, since 2010) located in Kansas City, Missouri, FCA has begun to grow globally. In 2013, FCA divided the globe into 12 "super regions" to strategically reach both the United States and the world through its sports-based ministry model.

Through the influence of athletes and coaches, in 2013, FCA hosted 423 camps across 38 states and 25 countries, bringing in more than 59,000 attendees; additionally, campus-based Huddles reach more than 450,000 students on more than 9,000 campuses across the United States. The popularity and breadth of FCA's work demonstrates one way that evangelicals have sought to use popular culture in conjunction with evangelistic goals.

Bryce Hantla

See also: Cru; Evangelism; Hendricks, Howard G.; Parachurch Ministries

Further Reading

Atcheson, Wayne. *Impact for Christ: How FCA Has Influenced the Sports World.* Grand Island, NE: Cross Training, 1994.

Blazer, Annie. *Playing for God: Evangelical Women and the Unintended Consequences of Sports Ministry.* New York: New York University Press, 2015.

Fellowship of Christian Athletes. "History." Fellowship of Christian Athletes, 2014. http://www.fca.org/about-fellowship-of-christian-athletes/history/.

Hoffman, Shirl James. *Good Game: Christianity and the Culture of Sports.* Waco, TX: Baylor University Press, 2010.

Seward, Mickey. "60 Years and Counting." Fellowship of Christian Athletes. December 30, 2013. https://www.fca.org/magazine-story/2013/12/30/60-years-and-counting.

FINE ARTS, EVANGELICALS AND

The number of evangelicals creating and performing in the realm of fine arts as an expression of evangelical spirituality and a commitment to culture at large is increasing on the individual, collegiate, and organizational levels. Beyond academic programs, organizations such as the Brehm Center and The Christian Performing Artists' Fellowship encourage and nurture evangelicals in the arts.

Evangelical understanding and practice of the fine arts has significantly changed from a 16th-century spirit of Protestant iconoclasm involving suspicion and hostility, separation from culture, and exclusive focus on the centrality of the Scriptures, personal piety, and evangelism. Today, the fine arts are perceived by a growing number of evangelicals as a discipline of rigorous study, qualitative cultural engagement, and a way of life. This change of thinking, doing, and living within evangelicalism has found expression in the following five ways.

First, the call was made by "pioneering" evangelicals to engage the fine arts because they are spiritually significant; they are the outworking of one's worldview. Flowing out of 19th-century revivalism, the emergence of German Higher Criticism, and the growing plight of modernism, two separate cultures emerged, namely, the secular community and the evangelical community. Thus, two parallel communities were formed with their own financial resources, institutions, mores, and personalities.

But due to the pivotal influence of evangelical thinkers such as Francis and Edith Schaeffer (1912–1984 and 1914–2013, respectively) and Dutch art historian Hans Rookmaaker (1922–1977), direction was shifted to rethinking the evangelical relationship to the arts. Francis A. Schaeffer, who responded to the sensitivities of the 1960s countercultural movement and who was personally deeply moved by the arts, showed the evangelical community how the fine arts can be appreciated and investigated, and be reflective of one's foundational and personal beliefs about God, reality, truth, knowledge, ethics, humanity, and evil. By exploring the arts, one can uncover one's foundational beliefs of seeing and doing. Schaeffer also demonstrated how the arts could be used in Christian apologetics, everyday living, and legacy building.

Consequently, evangelicals are now engaged in a robust dialogue of thought, practice, engagement with society, and a way of life that transcends historic boundaries, maintains moral integrity, and offers thoughtful dialogue that speaks to both the beauty and brokenness of humanity, reasons to hope, and a certain sensitivity to surroundings, voices overlooked, and the imagination.

Historically evangelicals have centered their attention on the centrality of the Scriptures. Thus, when evangelicals are confronted with the fine arts, they look to the Bible and discover that it does not offer a discourse on theological aesthetics. The Scripture does not disclose a didactic treatment of the arts, but the instructions given, the stories recorded, the symbols carved, the celebrations observed, and the worship experienced are aesthetically rich and community centered.

The Bible, like other activities, offers a way of observing, creating, evaluating, and engaging the arts that integrates both the divine prohibition of making any kind of idol, image, or any other God substitute (Second Commandment; Exodus 20:4–6) and the reflective gift of creativity (Genesis 1 and 2). People are His images who are called on to reflect His beauty in what they create and critique (Genesis 1:26–28), as depicted in Jesus's work as a craftsman, the construction of the Tabernacle and Temple, the making of choice wine, and even the science and art of fishing on the Sea of Galilee. Just as God created the universe, evangelicals believe humans are capable of reflecting His image in what they create.

Second, younger generations experienced displeasure with the reactionary stance to the arts, the reductive spirit of evangelicalism, and the anemic aesthetic projects created by evangelicals within that separate culture.

Though the cultural wars between evangelicals and secularism continue, there is a growing movement of younger evangelicals, from Generation X to the Millennials, who are dissatisfied with the combativeness, separation, and reductionistic mindset of certain evangelical circles. This is especially acute in view of their embeddedness within a visually saturated society, the captivating brilliance of the fine arts in secular arenas, and the degree to which local churches have become unappealing, colorless, and restrictive with their architecture, imagery, sacred space, and songs. Functionality, separatism, and even the sensational have displaced sacredness, thoughtful engagement, and reflective beauty.

These factors compelled evangelicals to study in secular universities over and against Christian institutions that were lacking, unappreciative of the arts, or underfunded. Many evangelicals have not only gained degrees in art criticism, history, and philosophical aesthetics (e.g., Daniel A. Siedell, the author of *God in the Gallery: A Christian Embrace of Modern Art*) but have taken artistic, intellectual, spiritual, and theological risks. Thus, they have opened doors by becoming curators, historians, philosophers, and practitioners, transcending the sacred/secular divide. Other notable thinkers and practitioners of theological aesthetics include Jonathan A. Anderson, Jeremy Begbie, Mark Coppenger, Robert S. Covolo, William A. Dyrness, Holly Ordway, Jim Parker, W. David O. Taylor, and Jogvan Zachariassen.

20 Significant Films with Evangelical Themes

1. *The Hiding Place* (1976)
2. *Left Behind* (2000)
3. *Luther* (2003)
4. *Passion of the Christ* (2004)
5. *The Chronicles of Narnia: The Lion, Witch, and Wardrobe* (2005)
6. *The End of the Spear* (2005)
7. *Amazing Grace* (2006)
8. *One Night with the King* (2006)
9. *Billy: The Early Years* (2008)
10. *Fireproof* (2008)
11. *The Blind Side* (2009)
12. *Courageous* (2011)
13. *Soul Surfer* (2011)
14. *God Is Not Dead* (2014)
15. *Heaven Is For Real* (2014)
16. *Son of God* (2014)
17. *War Room* (2015)
18. *Ben-Hur* (2016)
19. *God Is Not Dead 2* (2016)
20. *Risen* (2016)

Third, evangelicals have turned from the separation of the arts to becoming culture-makers who contribute, engage, and enrich society. They now seek to create fashion, films, images, prints, sculptures, and songs that display excellence, not kitsch. Fine art pieces celebrated in the evangelical community were often expressively religious and overly sentimental. Many were criticized as displaying poor taste and skills; they will never be art pieces that stand the test of time. Thus, from the anemic qualities of evangelical fine art in contrast to the technical excellence and intellectual, religious, and spiritual depth that flowed out of the Renaissance and Reformation, and even Modernity, many have stepped into the vacuum, creating and celebrating architecture, art, dance, fashion, films, images, and music. They are entering into the "art world" and drawing attention on what might be overlooked, intentionally or unintentionally, by even artists themselves.

Driven by their faith experience, Christians such as Craig Detweiler, Makoto Fujimura, Steve Halla, and Mary McCleary are artists or practitioners, that is, creators of cultures, who seek to use their God-given gifts of creativity and imagination to connect to everybody; they are not mere evangelicals who are interested only in imitation. Rather, they seek to create excellent art that is conversant with or informed by their faith.

Fourth, instead of separating from culture, evangelicals are now hoping to challenge and influence people's assumptions about their view of the world, humanity, values, and decision-making. Through the fine arts, personal and culture transformation is possible. Like Plato observed, story telling, the visual, and the song have the potential to subvert the status quo, the establishment, and evoke personal and societal change that will qualitatively nourish lives.

And fifth, a growing number of evangelicals like Nancy Pearcey are seeking to offer an alternative, namely, a better vision to the reductionistic spirit of secularism that exposes existential tensions; instead, these evangelicals offer an enduring hope that appeals to the whole of one's life and is existentially relevant, morally beneficial, and logically coherent. But they contend that the arts have to be constructed in such a way that is aesthetically, intellectually, and spiritually captivating, gripping, or fascinating. Consequently, a growing number of evangelicals are finding themselves now part of the "art world," as evidenced by the value ascribed to their work by secular artists, curators, institutions, studios, and patrons alike.

Even evangelical philosophers are exploring how the aesthetic insights of thinkers like Aristotle, Plato, Aquinas, Immanuel Kant, Leo Tolstoy, Friedrich Nietzsche, John Dewey, and Monroe Beardsley can contribute to theological aesthetics without intellectual and spiritual compromise. Hans Urs Von Balthasar (e.g., *The Glory of the Lord*, 7 volumes) and Nicholas Wolterstorff (e.g., *Art in Action: Toward a Christian Aesthetic*) are held in high esteem as Christian examples of people who have offered the highest scholarly contributions to the relationships among the arts, culture, philosophy, and theology.

The relationship between evangelicals and the fine arts is one of change, difficulties, neglect, and surprise. But beginning sometime in the last four decades of

Theology and Film

Evangelical scholars have recently entered into the dynamic interrelationships of theology and film, especially because the major storytellers today are filmmakers. Recognizing how the visual is powerfully influencing society, shaping values, evoking certain social attitudes, and communicating powerful ideas, scholarship in this field is growing. Recent works in this area include the following:

Faith, Film, and Philosophy: Big Ideas on the Big Screen, edited by R. Douglas Geivett and James S. Spiegel (2007)

Reframing Theology and Film: New Focus for An Emerging Discipline, edited by Robert K. Johnson (2007)

Scripture on the Silver Screen by Adel Reinhartz (2003)

---

the 20th century, a growing practice of and value for the fine arts has emerged whereby art galleries are opening in churches; investing in artists and thinkers in scholarly programs in places like Biola University, Fuller Theological Seminary, The King's College, and Union University; and creating a theological aesthetics study group in organizations such as the Evangelical Theological Society, involving artists, pastors, philosophers, and theologians.

Paul R. Shockley

See also: Christian Apologetics; Emerging and Emergent Churches; Philosophy, Evangelicals and; Schaeffer, Francis A. and Edith

Further Reading

Anderson, Jonathan A., and William A. Dyrness. *Modern Art and the Life of Culture: The Religious Impulses of Modernism.* Downers Grove, IL: InterVarsity Press, 2016.

Duke, Barrett. "A Call to Evangelical Engagement in the Arts." Canon & Culture. February 6, 2014. http://www.canonandculture.com/a-call-to-evangelical-engagement-in-the-arts/.

Gasque, Laurel. *Art and the Christian Mind: The Life and Work of H. R. Hans Rookmaaker.* Wheaton, IL: Crossway, 2005.

Pearcey, Nancy. *Saving Leonardo.* Nashville, TN: B&H, 2010.

Siedell, Daniel A. *Who's Afraid of Modern Art? Essays on Modern Art & Theology in Conversation.* Eugene, OR: Cascade, 2015. http://www.christianperformingart.org.

FOCUS ON THE FAMILY

Focus on the Family is a nonprofit, multimedia organization founded in June 1977 by psychologist Dr. James Dobson. Dr. Dobson's vision for this family-based ministry began while he was completing his PhD studies in child development at the University of South Carolina. During his tenures at Children's Hospital in California and USC School of Medicine, he authored several books regarding the collapse of the traditional family and its effect on child development and culture.

The foundation of Focus on the Family rests on its six pillars of belief. These beliefs include the preeminence of evangelism so that humans can embrace the love and sacrifice of Jesus Christ; the permanence of marriage between a man and woman as a sacred covenant ordained by God; the value of children as a heritage and blessing from God's hand; the sanctity of human life because all humanity is created by God in His image, regardless of age (preborn or aged) or disabilities; the importance of social responsibility to be a voice in God-ordained social institutions; and the value of male and female as individually and intentionally created in God's image.

Within the first years, Focus on the Family began a radio broadcast and soon recorded and produced a seven-part film series, Focus on the Family. This series remains one of the organization's most popular outreach tools. During the 1980s, Focus published their first periodical, *Focus on the Family* magazine, while the radio program's listening audience increased and the program expanded to include international audiences.

In 1983, Dobson launched the Family Resource Council, a lobbying voice in Washington, D.C., dedicated to promoting the sanctity of life and religious freedom. Five years later, FRC merged with Focus on the Family and become the latter's political voice within the press and media. Due to leadership changes within Focus, FRC became a separate nonprofit organization in 1992.

During the 1990s, Focus developed an Internet presence, and Dr. Dobson lent his expertise to political issues affecting the family. In the decade that followed, Focus

Significant Evangelical Web Sites

Tim Challies: www.challies.com

Tom Constable's Expository Notes: www.soniclight.com

Dallas Theological Seminary's Hendricks Center for Christian Leadership and Cultural Engagement. www.dts.edu

Desiring God Ministries: www.desiringgod.org

FamilyLife Today: www.familylifetoday.com

Focus on the Family: www.focusonthefamily.com

The Gospel Coalition: www.gospelcoalition.org

Ligonier Ministries: www.ligonier.org

Bible.Org and home for the New English Translation (NET Bible): www.Bible.org

In Touch Ministries: www.intouch.org

Ravi Zacharias International Ministries: www.rzim.org

Reasonable Faith: www.reasonablefaith.org

Stand to Reason: www.str.org

continued to expand its international influence while also making leadership changes. Don Hodel began overseeing the day-to-day operations as president in May of 2003, and Dobson became chairman of the board. Jim Daly, Dobson's protégé, replaced Hodel about two years later. Dobson left all official affiliation with the organization in February 2009. With the leadership changes, the organization has pulled back from its political focus and returned to its emphasis on strengthening bonds of marriage and parenting.

Focus on the Family radio ministries include Adventures in Odyssey, a worldrenowned radio program for children that illustrates moral and biblical principals through memorable characters. Focus magazine publications include *Thriving Family*, designed to help families flourish, as well as *Thriving Pastor*, helping pastors and church staff remain relevant to their congregations. Focus Leadership Institute educates leaders on how to promote healthy families, grow churches, and contribute to society. *Enfoque a la Familia* equips Hispanic and Spanish-speaking families.

Focus on the Family ministers to individuals and couples without children with its Wait No More adoption and orphan-care initiative. Be A Voice provides resources on the sanctity of human life, training citizens to be a voice within their sphere of influence. TrueU and The Truth Project apologetics program help youth to become confident in their beliefs, equipping them to stand strong in their daily life with respect to their values and beliefs.

The Web site ministries of Focus on the Family include TrueTolerance.org, which helps parents navigate conversations relating to LGBTQ issues that their children are facing in public schools; Heartlink, which offers information about abortion, contraception, and ultrasound programs; Plugged In, which serves as a media-review site for movies, video games, and television programs in order to help parents navigate their children's culture; and Pure Intimacy, which provides online resources for those needing assistance handling sexuality, intimacy, and LGBTQ questions.

Focus's traditional stance on marriage causes it to be a target of differing viewpoints. Soulforce, an organization seeking nonviolently to be a voice for the LGTBQ community, organized a 700-person picket at Focus headquarters in Colorado Springs, Colorado, in May of 2005. The event concluded with the arrest of the picketers as they attempted to deliver more than 10,000 letters to Dr. Dobson and Focus on the Family staff. Soulforce and Focus on the Family continued to have an adversarial relationship until leadership changes in 2005. Then, under the direction of Daly, for the first time Soulforce was invited to visit Focus headquarters to converse about beliefs. Although Focus remains consistent in its stance on marriage, the organization has shifted in its approach. Focus on the Family illustrates the enormous reach of parachurch ministries in American Christianity and the intensity of evangelical commitments to social and cultural values it considers biblically centered or biblically derived.

Sandra Glahn and Marni Blackstone Legaspi

See also: Parachurch Ministries; Social Action, Evangelicals and

Further Reading

Bailey, Sarah Pulliam. 2011. Christianity Today. July 1. http://www.christianitytoday.com/ct
/2011/july/focus-on-the-family.html?order=&start=1.

Buss, Dale. *Family Man: The Biography of Dr. James Dobson.* Carol Stream, IL: Tyndale House,
2005.

Focus on the Family (n.d.). April 28, 2017. http://www.focusonthefamily.com/about_us
/guiding-principles.aspx.

History of Family Research Council. (n.d.). April 28, 2017. http://www.frc.org/historymission.

FOREIGN POLICY, EVANGELICALS AND

Foreign policy is a course of action that is adopted by one nation in its dealings with other states and that supports a nation's objectives. Evangelical churches and leaders of the United States have never spoken with one voice politically, nor have they always been organized and in sufficient numbers to exercise calculated influence in foreign affairs. Nevertheless, evangelicals share definable interests that come from a common faith and international experiences, and they have asserted these interests throughout American history by providing information and advice that has influenced policy formulation and decision-making at a national level. There have been at least two broad historical epochs in which evangelicals exercised influence in foreign affairs. The first was the modern missionary movement that grew out of the Second Great Awakening, beginning around 1800, that brought both the Gospel message and democratic impulses to foreign nations. The second era came with the resurgence of evangelicalism in the 1960s, in which an even greater expansion of missions was accompanied by increased cooperation among evangelicals to facilitate morality in American foreign policy.

Early American evangelicals were drawn to missions and were evangelists of both the Christian faith and democratic principles. At the beginning of the last decade of the 18th century, membership in America's Protestant churches was at its lowest point. Around this time, isolated spiritual stirrings began to occur in some parts of the United States, at first in New England but most significantly along the frontier. From small beginnings, this movement began to grow and take shape until it exercised a significantly lasting influence on all American life. This movement, known as the Second Great Awakening, grew along with the new nation in such a manner that historians often observe that rejuvenated Christians and churches established an evangelical consensus. Evangelical Christianity and democratic idealism became the hallmarks of America and Americans in the 19th century. This development is significant because evangelicals stressed the importance of a personal religious experience that resulted in evangelism and works of charity. It followed that they took a keen interest in missions. In 1810, new England Church leaders established the American Board of Commissioners for Foreign Missions as the first interdenominational sending agency. Establishment of other missions boards followed, and the number of American missionaries in countries around the world grew to a modest

5,000 by the end of the century. However, 19th-century missionaries were not only involved in evangelism and the teaching of the Bible and theology. They also established schools and hospitals and confronted beliefs and customs that were contrary to Christian education and scientific knowledge. Although agency leaders often warned missionaries not to be involved in political disputes, it was inevitable that they would bring their worldview into play at every opportunity. These foreigners brought democratic ideals as well as the gospel to people across the globe. As products of the evangelical consensus, they represented an unofficial extension of American foreign policy in far-flung lands. According to political scientist Mark Amstutz (pp. 53–59), their program was fourfold: advance understanding of human dignity; promote literacy and technical skills by establishing educational institutions; provide humanitarian relief; and build civil society. Missionaries have made contributions to official American foreign policy in both direct and indirect ways by using their expert knowledge of foreign peoples to advocate morality and informed action or restraint on the part of their government. Beginning in the 19th century and continuing through the mid-20th century, it was not uncommon for the U.S. government to tap missionaries for their knowledge of foreign lands and people. Cooperating with American officials sometimes worked well for the humanitarian ends of missionaries but more often put them in awkward, or even dangerous, positions when authorities in the host country became suspicious of the true motives of missionaries.

As the 19th century drew to a close, the evangelical consensus began to wane. In the Protestant churches, Darwinism and theological liberalism began to cause a split in denominations. At the same time, a confluence of issues at home, such as new immigration, industrialization, and urbanization, crippled the ability of the Protestant establishment to be able to shape the culture. Theological liberalism began to dominate the mainline churches while the fundamentalists who represented the old biblical faith left in large numbers and established churches, seminaries, and mission agencies. At first, these theological conservatives were skittish about cooperation and social action, behaviors that characterized their liberal opponents. In the 1940s, some fundamentalist church leaders called for a new evangelicalism that would retain the basics of the evangelical faith while restoring the evangelical impulse to improve society by exercising social consciousness. The establishment of the National Association of Evangelicals (NAE) in 1943 created an organization where evangelical churches and denominations could work together on common concerns. The NAE established an office in Washington, D.C., to promote causes that were important to evangelicals, including foreign policy issues. For example, the NAE was instrumental in ending missionary debriefing on the part of the Central Intelligence Agency. Beginning in the 1960s, the influence of the NAE grew with the resurgence of evangelicalism and waning of the mainline churches in America. In 1986, the NAE launched its Peace, Freedom and Security Studies program as an effort to offer a moral framework to guide foreign policy goals. In 2004, more than 90 evangelical leaders joined the NAE in adopting a document called "For the Health of the Nation: An Evangelical Call to Civic Responsibility." The document contained seven principles to guide political action at home and abroad, including religious freedom, the sanctity of life, compassion for the poor, and peaceful conflict resolution. Another organization that speaks to foreign policy issues is the 16-million-member Southern Baptist Convention through its Ethics & Religious Liberty Commission that lobbies on public policy issues including global and humanitarian concerns. In addition to these larger organizations, a number of smaller evangelical parachurch organizations have been involved in influencing American foreign policy, many of them reflecting the agenda of the Christian Right. Some of these organizations were the Christian Coalition, Focus on the Family, and the Family Research Council, which often shared foreign policy concerns of non-evangelical conservative groups. Specific issues that have been common to evangelical groups addressing foreign policy are religious freedom, global poverty and relief, human trafficking, and support for Israel.

Liam J. Atchison

See also: Human Rights, Evangelicals and; Israel, Evangelicals and; National Association of Evangelicals; Politics, Evangelicals and

Further Reading

Amstutz, Mark R. *Christian Ethics & U.S. Foreign Policy.* Grand Rapids, MI: Zondervan, 1987.

Amstutz, Mark R. *Evangelicals and American Foreign Policy.* New York: Oxford University Press, 2013.

Matthews, Arthur Hugh. *Standing Up, Standing Together: The Emergence of the National Association of Evangelicals.* National Association of Evangelicals, 1992.

Moore, Russell. *The Kingdom of Christ: The New Evangelical Perspective.* Crossway, 2004.

Murch, James DeForest. *Cooperation without Compromise: A History of the National Association of Evangelicals.* Eerdmans, 1956.

FOURTH PRESBYTERIAN CHURCH (BETHESDA, MARYLAND)

Fourth Presbyterian Church, Bethesda, Maryland, commonly known as "Fourth Church," has been a prominent spiritual and evangelical presence in the Washington, D.C., area since its founding in 1828. Its history is marked by long-term pastorates, long-term growth (to more than 2,700 members), innovative outreach, and strong Biblical leadership of international influence.

The Presbyterian Church USA split into Old School and New School branches in 1837, with Fourth joining the New School body that emphasized evangelistic outreach, revivals, and a more relaxed view and practice of strict Calvinism. Its Sunday school children were twice invited to visit with presidents at the White House. Fourth commenced a Sunday school for African American children in 1839, against violent opposition, and supported the founding of the First Colored Presbyterian

Church in 1842 (now Fifteenth Street Presbyterian Church). That church moved into Fourth's former building in 1850 and has been at the center of Washington, D.C.'s African American culture and advocacy ever since.

During the Civil War, Pastor Dr. John C. Smith became the city's first clergyman to volunteer as a chaplain, serving at hospitals. Southern sympathizers were known to "slam their pew doors and stamp out" of Fourth's worship when prayers were made for the U.S. president (Edington, 1961: 236). Fourth Church closed for several months in 1862–1863 to serve as a hospital. Its other closure occurred during the influenza epidemic of 1918.

The church grew in health and strength as it built new buildings (now in its fourth location), added members, supported less fortunate congregations in the Washington, D.C., area, and engaged in vigorous foreign mission activities. Pastor Dr. James Miers ministered on the technological cutting edge with a radio presence by Fourth that began in 1929 and continues to the present.

Richard Halverson, active in men's ministry and the National Prayer Breakfast movement, became senior pastor in 1958. He came from First Presbyterian Church of Hollywood, California, a center of evangelical influence through Henrietta Mears, their famed Christian Education director who founded Gospel Light publications and personally influenced the ministry formation of Bill Bright (founder of Campus Crusade for Christ) and evangelist Billy Graham.

Fourth Church gave intentional witness and action during the tumultuous 1960s. It formally protested the 1963 Supreme Court decision disallowing prayer in schools. It also opposed the adoption of the *Confession of 1967* by its parent denomination, the United Presbyterian Church (UPC), decrying the liberal theology in that document that displaced Biblical grounding. Fourth's people moved rapidly to help heal torn neighborhoods after the riots of 1968.

Pastor Halverson left Fourth in 1981 to become chaplain of the U.S. Senate. He was succeeded in 1983 by Dr. Rob Norris, who also came from ministry at the Hollywood congregation. Fourth Church chose to emphasize its evangelical identity and mission by changing its denomination to the Evangelical Presbyterian Church (EPC) in 1986. Dr. Norris's Gospel-centered preaching and teaching brought continued growth and outreach, including housing the initial Washington, D.C., campus of Reformed Theological Seminary, and leadership in the Gospel Coalition.

Fourth Church has long welcomed its share of prominent Washingtonians. Formal friends of the church have included Dr. Francis Collins (head of the Human Genome Project); Senator Mark Hatfield; Ambassador Jeanne Kirkpatrick; Senator Tom Kleppe; journalist Doyle McManus; U.S. Vice President Dan Quayle; and columnist George Will. Prominent members of Fourth have included Secretary Jack Kemp (U.S. Secretary of Housing and Urban Development; U.S. representative and architect of the Kemp-Roth Economic Recovery Tax Act of 1981; Republican candidate for vice president, 1996); Michael McManus (leader of Marriage Savers); columnist Cal Thomas; and Dr. Frank Young (Commissioner, U.S. Food and Drug Administration), who later became a pastor at Fourth.

Fourth Church, long displaying dynamic congregational life and witness, remains a catalyst and pace setter for orthodox belief, Reformed theology, mission outreach at home and abroad, and worldwide evangelical leadership.

Mark A. Jumper

See also: Halverson, Richard ("Dick"); Politics, Evangelicals and; Reformed Tradition, Evangelicalism and

Further Reading

Edington, Frank E. *A History of the New York Avenue Presbyterian Church.* Washington, D.C.: New York Avenue Presbyterian Church, 1961.

Hall, Russell. (n.d.). *Hall's Index of American Presbyterian Congregations.* April 28, 2017. http://www.history.pcusa.org/collections/online-catalogs/halls-database-american-presbyterian-congregations/halls-index.

Kurtz, Grace W. *The Story of the Fourth Presbyterian Church, Sesquicentennial Edition 1828–1978.* South Hackensack, NJ: Custombook, 1978.

FULLER, CHARLES E. (1887–1968)

Charles Edward Fuller (1887–1968) was an American Christian clergyman, radio evangelist, and founder of Fuller Evangelical Seminary. Born in Los Angeles, California, Fuller graduated from Pomona College in 1910 and entered the family citrus-packing business in southern California, where he worked until 1918. He was married to Grace Leone Payton and they had one son, Daniel. Fuller's father, Henry, a prosperous orange grower, set up the Emmanuel Missionary Fund in 1918 with initial assets of about $100,000 to support missionary work.

After being converted at a 1916 evangelistic meeting under the preaching of Paul Rader, Fuller studied at the Bible Institute of Los Angeles (now, Biola University), later becoming chairman of the board. Initially a Presbyterian, he became a Baptist minister in 1925 at Calvary Church in Placentia. Influenced by Rader, Fuller began the radio program entitled *The Pilgrim's Hour* during the late 1920s and broadcast over several local Southern California radio stations. By 1935, the voice of Dr. Fuller was a familiar sound in the Western states.

On October 3, 1937, Fuller aired his first *Old Fashioned Revival Hour* radio broadcast from a studio in Hollywood, California, over the 13 stations of the Mutual Network. He soon established the Gospel Broadcasting Association to sponsor his *Old Fashioned Revival Hour* programs. The program, a weekly Sunday broadcast, aired from 1937 to 1968 over the Mutual Broadcasting Network, supported solely by listeners' contributions.

In 1941, the program was moved to the Long Beach Municipal Auditorium in Long Beach, California, where thousands of servicemen, en route to the Pacific theater during World War II, attended the broadcast. From 1941 to 1958, Fuller and his *OFHR* musicians traveled throughout North America, holding citywide rallies that were often broadcast live. By the mid-1940s, Fuller was heard via his live broadcasts and recorded transcriptions over nearly 600 stations and by an estimated 20 million people each week, surpassing in size most popular network shows, including *Bob Hope* and *The Charlie McCarthy Show*. With help from his wife, Grace, affectionately referred to by Dr. Fuller as "Honey," the show evoked an "old-fashioned" atmosphere reminiscent of the revival style of Fuller's (and his listeners) youth. Fuller's sermons typically focused on the work of Jesus Christ on the cross; the dangers of God's wrath; a literal hell for the lost; human sinfulness; and the necessity of accepting Jesus Christ as personal savior before dying.

From 1941 through 1958, audiences attended services that were broadcast live from the Auditorium. By 1955, 1 million broadcast transcriptions had been made. Fuller and his associates of the *Old Fashioned Revival Hour* appeared in the Long Beach Municipal Auditorium for the last time on January 12, 1958, when the program was moved to Hollywood and again produced in a studio for 30-minute broadcasts. The broadcasts were noted for their music, featuring the Old Fashioned Revival Hour Choir and quartet, accompanied by organist George Broadbent and pianist Rudy Atwood. The choir made several popular recordings in the 1940s and 1950s.

Beginning in 1951, the program was carried on the ABC Radio Network and heard on more than 650 radio stations; it was later picked up by the CBS radio network as well. His last broadcast was December 1968. Although the *Old Fashioned Revival Hour* broadcasts have ended, their appeal continues. As of 2015, rebroadcasts stream weekly on the Internet and are also heard on radio stations in many cities in the United States.

In 1943, the Fuller Evangelistic Foundation was organized and, by absorbing the assets of his father's Emmanuel Missionary Fund and the assistance of National Association of Evangelicals President Harold J. Ockenga, Fuller created the Fuller Theological Seminary (named in honor of his father) in Pasadena to train evangelical Christian pastors, missionaries and evangelists. In 1944, Fuller purchased five acres near the civic center and city library in Pasadena, hoping to open the Fuller Seminary of Missions and Evangelism by the fall of 1945. Lake Avenue Congregational Church, in downtown Pasadena, agreed to let the school use their educational facilities until Fuller could build. Unfortunately, by late spring 1946, plans had to be postponed due to postwar building costs.

By April of 1947, Fuller put a bid on a five-acre estate in one of the most luxurious sections in Pasadena; a 32-room mansion, built by a member of the Cravens tobacco family, reputed to be the most expensive home ever built in Pasadena, having a cost of about a $500,000 in 1929. Fuller bid only the assessed value of $145,000. The entering class consisted of nearly 40 students from schools such as Harvard, Dartmouth, Berkeley, and the University of Southern California.

Fuller's son, Daniel, served the seminary as dean and professor of hermeneutics. Designed as a training school for evangelists and missionaries, as well as an evangelical response to both fundamentalism and mainline, liberal seminaries, Fuller Seminary grew to become the largest, nondenominational, Protestant seminary in the world.

Charles Fuller died in March 18, 1968, shortly after his final broadcast of the *Old Fashioned Revival Hour*. He is buried at Forest Lawn Memorial Park in Glendale, California. The Long Beach Municipal Auditorium was demolished in the 1960s, but a plaque marks the site of Fuller's broadcasts.

James Menzies

See also: Biola University; Fuller Theological Seminary

Further Reading

"Charles Fuller." (n.d.). Institute for the Study of American Evangelicals. Wheaton College. April 28, 2017. http://www.wheaton.edu/ISAE/Hall-of-Biography/Charles-Fuller.

Fuller, Daniel P. *Give the Winds a Mighty Voice: The Story of Charles E. Fuller*, reprint ed. Salem, OR: Wipf & Stock, 2015.

Hangen, Tona J. *Redeeming the Dial: Radio, Religion, and Popular Culture in America.* Chapel Hill, NC: The University of North Carolina Press, 2002.

Marsden, George M. *Reforming Fundamentalism: Fuller Seminary and the New Evangelicalism.* Grand Rapids, MI: Eerdmans, 1988.

Old Fashioned Revival Hour: Dr. Charles E. Fuller, "History." (n.d.). April 28, 2017. https://www.biblebelievers.com/OFRH/history.html.

Viola, Frank, and George Barna. *Pagan Christianity? Exploring the Roots of Our Church Practices* (Carol Stream, IL: Tyndale Momentum; Revised, 2008).

FULLER THEOLOGICAL SEMINARY

Fuller Theological Seminary, embracing the School of Theology, School of Psychology, and School of Intercultural Studies, is an evangelical, multidenominational, international, and multiethnic seminary in Pasadena, California, with several regional campuses in the Western United States. In 2016, it was the nation's largest seminary.

Fuller Seminary was founded in 1947 by radio evangelist Charles E. Fuller and Harold Ockenga, pastor of Park Street Church in Boston. According to the school Web site, their mission is "Under the authority of Scripture we seek to fulfill our commitment to ministry through graduate education, professional development, and spiritual formation. In all of our activities, including instruction, nurture, worship, service, research, and publication, Fuller Theological Seminary strives for excellence in the service of Jesus Christ, under the guidance and power of the Holy Spirit, to the glory of the Father."

In the mid-1940s, Charles Fuller had a popular radio broadcast, *The Old Fashioned Revival Hour*, with an estimated audience of 20 million worldwide. But he was seeking ways to expand his message by a school on the West Coast to train young evangelists and missionaries. Ockenga, a pastor and theologian in his own right, shared Fuller's vision but encouraged him to broaden it. The church not only needed evangelists, it needed pastors who were intellectually sound, culturally aware, and firmly evangelical. The seminary's founders sought not to break from, but to reform, the fundamentalism of the day from its separatist and perceived anti-intellectual stance. At first the faculty held to theologically and socially conservative views, though tensions arose in the late 1950s and early 1960s as some faculty became uncomfortable with staff and students who did not agree with Biblical inerrancy, and resigned.

In May 1947, Fuller and Ockenga met with four other evangelical scholars in downtown Chicago, Illinois, to pray and discuss starting a new seminary. With Ockenga contributing his scholarly proficiency to Fuller's astute business sense, the seminary—named for Charles Fuller's father, Henry Fuller—planned to open its doors in September 1947 at the Cravens Estate in Pasadena. They later discovered that city zoning ordinances prohibited the estate's use for instruction, so Fuller Seminary's inaugural group of 39 students began attending classes in the kindergarten Sunday school rooms of Lake Avenue Congregational Church—sitting in child-sized chairs as they learned from a charter faculty of theology.

Ockenga served as the seminary's first president (1947–1954), traveling across country to carry out his duties in Pasadena while continuing to serve as pastor of Park Street. He laid a strong foundation for the seminary's emphasis on excellence in scholarship and contributed to the establishment of the school, becoming a leading voice in evangelicalism.

In a few years the student body grew, and in 1953 the seminary, with an enrollment of 250 students, moved to the newly constructed Payton Hall on Oakland Avenue, its first building at the center of the Pasadena campus.

Throughout its history, Fuller has had five presidents: Harold John Ockenga (1947–1954 and 1960–1963), Edward John Carnell (1954–1959), David Allan Hubbard (1963–1993), Richard J. Mouw (1993–2013), and Mark Labberton (July 1, 2013—current). Labberton had previously served Fuller as Director of the Lloyd John Ogilvie Institute of Preaching and retains his position as Lloyd John Ogilvie Associate Professor of Preaching alongside the presidency. Mouw remains at Fuller as Professor of Faith and Public Life.

Responding to the needs of those unable to relocate to Pasadena, in 1973 the seminary opened the first of its regional campuses in Seattle, Washington, and Irvine, California. One year later, a third regional campus opened in Menlo Park, California, and by 1979, regional campus programs were operating in six cities in the Western United States. Today, Fuller's regional campuses are located in Orange County and the Bay Area in California, Washington, Arizona, and Texas.

Fuller has approximately 4,000 students from 90 countries and 110 denominations, with 41,000 alumni serving across the globe, and offers 18 degree programs, including seven master's degrees and 11 advanced degrees. Fuller is accredited by the Association of Theological Schools in the United States and Canada and the Western Association of Schools and Colleges.

Fuller's School of Theology is the oldest school and offers the following degrees: Master of Divinity (MDiv), Master of Arts (MA) in Theology, MA in Theology and

Ministry, Doctor of Ministry (DMin), Doctor of Philosophy (PhD) in Theology, and Master of Theology (ThM).

Fuller's School of Psychology was established in 1964 with the opening of the Pasadena Community Counseling Center as its first phase, followed in 1965 with the school's first class of 29 students and the inaugural deanship of Lee Edward Travis. In 1972, the American Psychological Association granted approval to the school's clinical PhD program, making it the first seminary-based graduate school of psychology to be accredited by the APA. The program expanded further with the addition of a second doctoral degree, the PsyD, in 1987, coupled with the move of the Marriage and Family master's program from the School of Theology to the School of Psychology. Another significant step came in 1991 with the establishment of the Lee Edward Travis Institute, a research unit within the school bringing together faculty, students, and other collaborators to explore topics across the behavioral sciences spectrum.

The School of Intercultural Studies was founded as the School of World Mission in 1965. As the seminary recognized a growing need for training in world evangelism, Donald A. McGavran, founder of the Institute of Church Growth, was asked to be dean, and the new School of World Mission began offering master's degrees in missiology. The School of Intercultural Studies now offers an MA in Intercultural Studies (in English and Korean language), an MA in Global Leadership (earned primarily online), a ThM in Missiology (in English and Korean), a Doctor of Ministry in Global Ministries (in Korean), a Doctor of Missiology, and a PhD in Intercultural Studies.

Fuller's School of Psychology opened in 1965 and is the first seminary-based psychology program to receive accreditation from the American Psychological Association. The School consists of two departments: Clinical Psychology and Marriage and Family. Research in the School of Psychology takes place within the context of the Travis Research Institute. Distinctive centers have been established for biopsychosocial research; the study of stress, trauma, and adjustment; research in psychotherapy and religion; and child and adolescent development research. The School of Psychology offers the following degrees: MA in Family Studies, MS in Marital and Family Therapy, Doctor of Psychology in Clinical Psychology (PsyD), and Doctor of Philosophy (PhD) in Clinical Psychology.

Fuller admits evangelicals from both conservative and liberal perspectives and has frequently been at the center of debates among religious and secular intellectuals on issues ranging from politics to religion, science, and culture. The school has taken a stand on various social causes, with students and faculty expressing diverse views.

James Menzies

See also: Henry, Carl F. H.; Neo-Evangelicalism; Ockenga, Harold John

Further Reading

Carpenter, Joel A. *Revive Us Again: The Reawakening of American Fundamentalism.* New York: Oxford University Press, 1997.

Fuller Theological Seminary. "About—Our History." (n.d.). April 28, 2017. http://fuller.edu /about/history-and-facts/our-history/.

Marsden, George M. *Reforming Fundamentalism: Fuller Seminary and the New Evangelicalism.* Grand Rapids, MI: Eerdmans, 1988.

Strachan, Owen. *Awakening the Evangelical Mind: An Intellectual History of the Neo-Evangelical Movement.* Grand Rapids, MI: Zondervan, 2015.

FUNDAMENTALISM

The term "fundamentalist" began to gain currency with the specification of five biblical fundamentals (the "Five Point Deliverance" in Presbyterian terms) that surfaced in the early 20th century: the verbal inerrancy of Scripture, the divinity of Jesus Christ, the virgin birth, substitutionary atonement, and the physical resurrection and bodily return of Christ. Concerned about the secularization of Western Civilization, efforts within the church to accommodate modernism, and the strength of rivals to Protestant orthodoxy, traditionalists rallied around these doctrines in the early decades of the 20th century.

In this connection, Christian philanthropist brothers Lyman and Milton Stewart funded a multivolume collection of 90 essays designed to counter the objectionable

The Fundamentals

Used as both a resource against theological liberalism and a guide to discern truth from heresy, the five fundamentals of the Christian faith are derived from a widely circulated collection of books known as *The Fundamentals: A Testimony to the Truth* (1910–1915), edited by Amzi Clarence Dixon (1854–1925), Louis Myer (1862–1913), and Reuben Archer Torrey (1856–1928). Originally published as a 12-volume set, they `contain 90 essays by 64 different authors, including B. B. Warfield (1851–1921) from Princeton Theological Seminary; W. H. Griffith Thomas (1861–1924), principal of Wycliffe Hall at the University of Oxford; and G. Campbell Morgan (1863–1945), pastor of Westminster Chapel in London. The costs, underwritten anonymously by the two Stewart brothers, Lyman (1840–1923), who was a cofounder of Union Oil, and his brother Milton, were freely distributed to well more than 300,000 Christian missionaries, pastors, theologians, and workers. This significant collection of essays impacted the evangelical landscape in unprecedented ways, offering scholarly and well-written affirmations of the traditional historical faith while giving a rigorous but irenic challenge to theological liberalism.

trends. Produced from 1910 to 1915, and edited by A. C. Dixon and R. A. Torrey, *The Fundamentals* were sent without charge worldwide to over a million Christian leaders. Articles addressed "higher criticism" and a range of "isms"—Darwinism, socialism, Romanism (Roman Catholicism), Mormonism, and Eddyism (named for Mary Baker Eddy, founder of Christian Science). Other essays urged evangelism, apologetics, and worldwide missionary effort, and defended a range of doctrines such as the Atonement and the Trinity.

The books offered testimonies not only from believers such as cricket sensation C. T. Studd but also in the form of "tributes to Christ and the Bible by brainy men not known as active Christians" (e.g., Ben Franklin, Napoleon, Shakespeare) (Torrey, Dixon, et al., 2000). Writers came from a range of denominational camps (e.g., Baptist, Presbyterian, Methodist, and Anglican) and included both religion professors (e.g., from Princeton, Moody, and Oberlin) and pastors (e.g., from New York's Marble Collegiate and London's Metropolitan Tabernacle, St. Paul's, and Westminster Chapel.)

Soon many came to the conviction that biblical orthodoxy was not enough. They were convinced that circumstances demanded a more militant posture. An additional standard emerged, "biblical separation," later summarized by the World Congress of Fundamentalists, meeting in Edinburgh in 1976. But their light, fundamentalism, "exposes and separates from all ecclesiastical denial of that Faith, compromise with error, and apostasy from the Truth" (Jones et al., n.d.). So although fundamentalism first focused on the internal reform of churches and denominations that had absorbed various strains of modernism, subsequent fundamentalists broke away from standing denominations, declaring their churches to be "independent."

A corollary to separation stipulated that the serious believer "earnestly contends for the Faith once delivered" (Jones et al., n.d.) because, in essence, "[f]undamentalism is militant orthodoxy set on fire with soulwinning zeal" (Beale, 1985). Theirs was a crusading posture, reflected in cartoons from the era in *Sunday School Times* and the Moody Bible Institute periodical. For instance, one pictures a modern man bowing before a statue of a monkey, with the caption "Ancestor Worship."

Some of this thinking found its way into law, and in 1925, an east Tennessee biology teacher was charged with presenting evolution. The ensuing Scopes Trial proved to be a major embarrassment to fundamentalism, as ACLU founder, Clarence Darrow, made something of a mockery of William Jennings Bryan's prosecution, to the delight of modernists. Bryan won, but it was a costly victory in terms of public relations. The unfortunate impression was deepened by the 1955 play *Inherit the Wind*, which took liberties with history to hammer fundamentalists. In this vein, the arts and media have typically given fundamentalists a hard time, portraying them as judgmental spoilsports and hypocrites, with mangled grammar, racist mutterings, secret affairs, and hateful utterances.

By the late 1940s, some who had tracked with the fundamentalists on their concerns with doctrinal integrity began to express reservations over tone and tactics, suggesting that there were "rocks on both sides." The effort to distance oneself from theological error and worldliness could result in gratuitous insularity and cultural ineffectuality. Leaders like Harold John Ockenga and Carl F. H. Henry proposed an alternative "neo-evangelical" approach, more conversant with society, more irenic in manner.

The split came into sharp relief when Billy Graham, who was totally devoted to evangelism and to the fundamentals of the faith, invited less conservative clergy to join in his citywide crusades, giving them seats on the platform and allowing them to solicit crusade converts for their own congregations. Fundamentalists broke with Graham and even broke with those who didn't break with Graham—"second order separation" (Callaway, 2013: 320).

Over the years, the expression was widely used as a pejorative term describing militancy and anti-intellectualism. Nevertheless, many wore it as a badge of honor.

To the ire of evangelicals, some Roman Catholics have used the term "fundamentalist" to cover inerrantists and other conservative Protestants of every stripe. For instance, Karl Keating, head of Catholic Answers, has penned *Catholicism and Fundamentalism: The Attack on "Romanism" by "Bible Christians."* The book applies the disparaging label to those who raise objections to such doctrines as papal infallibility, the perpetual virginity and bodily assumption of Mary, purgatory, indulgences, priestly celibacy, and a sacramental view of the Lord's Supper.

Secularists and theological liberals have often grouped Christian fundamentalists with fundamentalists and other "extremists" of every stamp, so that even Billy Graham appears in the same book with Black Panther Huey Newton, the Ku Klux Klan's David Duke, and "unabomber" Theodore Kaczynski.

In his influential book *Christ and Culture*, H. Richard Niebuhr supplies a rubric for sorting out the various paths Christians have taken to engage with or disengage from society. He labels one "Christ Against Culture" (Niebuhr, 1996: 45) and associates it with such figures as the Church Father Tertullian (who asked rhetorically, "What has Athens to do with Jerusalem?" and who wrote scathingly of the theater) and Menno Simon, of the Anabaptist camp. Similarly, this motif finds expression in the homeschooling movement and various latter-day versions of teetotalism, including disdain for credit cards, the celebration of Halloween, attendance at movies, or the use of contraception—all alert to the scriptural watchword 2 Corinthians 6:17: "Wherefore come out from among them, and be ye separate, saith the Lord, and touch not the unclean *thing*; and I will receive you." So whether or not one calls him- or herself a fundamentalist, there are fundamentalist strains throughout the Christian world, evangelicals included.

Mark Coppenger

See also: Bible Institutes and Bible Colleges; Evangelicalism; Henry, Carl F. H.; Neo-Evangelicalism; Ockenga, Harold John; Theological Controversies within Evangelicalism

Further Reading

Beale, David. O. (1985) "S.B.C.: House on the Sand?" International Testimony to an Infallible Bible. Accessed April 28, 2017. www.itib.org/articles/house_on_sand2.html.

Callaway, Tim W. *Training Disciplined Soldiers for Christ.* Nashville, TN: Westbow Press, 2013.

Carpenter, Joel A. *Revive Us Again: The Reawakening of American Fundamentalism.* New York: Oxford University Press, 1989.

Jones, Bob, III, Manley, J. P., Paisley, Ian R. K., and Yearick, David D. (n.d.). "We Believe." International Testimony to an Infallible Bible. Accessed April 28, 2017. www.itib.org /believe.html.

Marsden, George M. *Understanding Fundamentalism and Evangelicalism.* Grand Rapids, MI: Eerdmans, 1990.

Marsden, George M. *Fundamentalism and American Culture*, 2nd ed. New York: Oxford University Press, 2006.

Niebuhr, H. Richard. *Christ and Culture.* New York: HarperCollins, 1996.

Sutton, Matthew Avery. *American Apocalypse: A History of American Fundamentalism.* Cambridge, MA: Belknap Press, 2014.

Torrey, R. A., A. C. Dixon, et al. *The Fundamentals: A Testimony to Truth*, reprinted in four volumes. Grand Rapids, MI: Baker, 2000.

"We Believe." International Testimony for an Infallible Bible. Accessed April 28, 2017. www .itib.org/believe.html.

Weber, Timothy P. *Living in the Shadow of the Second Coming: American Premillennialism, 1875–1982*, enlarged ed. Chicago: The University of Chicago Press, 1987.

G

GEISLER, NORMAN L. (1932–)

Norman Leo Geisler (1932–) is a Christian apologist, a neo-Thomistic philosopher, and a systematic theologian. He has taught these subjects on the college or graduate level for more than 50 years. Geisler has authored or coauthored more than 90 books and cofounded two nondenominational seminaries and two professional societies. He has lectured in all 50 states and 26 countries on six continents

Education

Geisler received a diploma from William Tyndale College in 1955, attended the University of Detroit from 1956–1957, and received a BA in philosophy from Wheaton College in 1958. In 1960, he was awarded an MA in theology from Wheaton Graduate School, and in 1964, he received a Bachelor of Theology degree from William Tyndale College. He began graduate work in philosophy at Wayne State University Graduate School in 1964 and continued that work at the University of Detroit Graduate School, from 1965–1966, and Northwestern University, Evanston, Illinois, in 1968, before receiving a PhD in philosophy from Loyola University, Chicago, Illinois, in 1970.

Professional Experience

Geisler was an assistant professor of Bible and apologetics at Detroit Bible College from 1963–1966, an associate professor of philosophy at Trinity College from 1970–1971, and Visiting Professor of Philosophy of Religion at Trinity Evangelical Divinity School from 1969–1970. He was then promoted to Chairman of Philosophy of Religion at Trinity Evangelical Divinity School from 1970–1979 before accepting a position as Professor of Systematic Theology at Dallas Theological Seminary from 1979–1988. In 1989, Geisler became the Dean of the Liberty Center for Research and Scholarship in Lynchburg, Virginia, a position that he held until 1991.

Along with Ross Rhoads, Geisler was cofounder of the Southern Evangelical Seminary in 1992, where he remained as dean until 1999, before serving as president from 1999–2006 and then returning to the position of dean for 2006–2007.

He was a cofounder of the Veritas Evangelical Seminary and has been the Distinguished Professor of Apologetics and chancellor there, beginning in 2007, and Visiting Professor of Apologetics at Southern Evangelical Seminary since 2014. Norman Geisler was also a cofounder, as well as the first president of both the

Evangelical Philosophical Society (EPS) (1974) and the International Christian Apologetics Society (ISCA) (2006).

Geisler as Christian Apologist

Geisler is a classical apologist as opposed to an evidentialist apologist (both traditions exist within evangelicalism). The classical apologists argue that there is a need to establish a framework of a theistic universe before one can use historical evidences (such as the historicity of Jesus of Nazareth and his birth, death, and resurrection). Classical apologists argue that it is of little value to speak of God raising Jesus from the dead until one has philosophically established that the world is part of a theistic universe in which there is a God capable of performing miracles.

Geisler is the author or coauthor of more than 90 books, including many specifically written to defend the traditional Christian faith, such as these: *Baker's Encyclopedia of Christian Apologetics*, *I Don't Have Enough Faith to Be an Atheist*, *When Skeptics Ask*, *Christian Apologetics*, *The Big Book of Christian Apologetics*, and *Answering Islam: The Crescent in Light of the Cross*. He has engaged in over two dozen public debates on topics such as the existence of God, creation versus evolution, ethics, and the resurrection of Jesus.

Geisler as Systematic Theologian

Geisler is a conservative evangelical scholar who has taught theology for more than 50 years and written hundreds of scholarly and popular articles, a four-volume systematic theology, a general introduction to the Bible, and popular surveys of the Old and New Testaments. He is known as an ardent defender of the full inerrancy

---

Personality Profile: Ravi Zacharias

Ravi Zacharias (1946–), who was called by Charles Colson the greatest apologist of our time, is a prolific evangelical author, philosopher, theologian, and cultural apologist. Founder of the Ravi Zacharias International Ministry (RZIM) in 1984, he was born in India and became a Christian following an unsuccessful attempt at suicide at the age of 17. He has studied under Norman L. Geisler and been impacted by thinkers like C. S. Lewis and Malcolm Muggeridge. Zacharias has traveled the world, speaking at universities, government settings, and other public platforms, proclaiming the coherency of the Christian worldview and its unique ability to answer all the ultimate questions of life such as origin, identity, meaning, and destiny that is logically coherent, empirically adequate, and existentially relevant. *Can Man Live Without God?* (1994, 1996) is one of his most famous works. His 2006 biography is titled *Walking From East to West: God in the Shadows*.

of the Bible, being one of the cofounders and framers of the "Chicago Statement on Biblical Inerrancy." To explain his beliefs, Geisler was the editor of the book *Inerrancy* and coauthor of *Defending Inerrancy* and *From God to Us*.

Geisler contends that he is a "moderate Calvinist" as outlined in his book, *Chosen But Free* (cited in Allen, 2014). He rejects the classical Calvinist tenets of unconditional election, limited atonement and irresistible grace, yet retains modified versions of total depravity and perseverance of the saints.

Geisler as Neo-Thomistic Philosopher

With respect to the discipline of philosophy, Geisler is strongly associated with the tradition of Thomism, that is, a philosophical system derived from that of Thomas Aquinas (1225–1274). Geisler received his PhD in philosophy from Loyola University, Chicago, Illinois, with a dissertation on the reality of religious transcendent experience, making strong use of Thomas Aquinas's use of analogy to support a language for the communication of the experience of the believer and as a method for testing that experience.

He has also authored many books on philosophy, including *Introduction to Philosophy: A Christian Perspective, Philosophy of Religion*, and *Thomas Aquinas: An Evangelical Appraisal*, as well as many journal articles and popular articles.

R. Don Deal

See also: Christian Apologetics; Philosophy, Evangelicals and; Theological Controversies within Evangelicalism

Further Reading

"About Norman Geisler." *Dr. Norman Geisler.* NGIM.org. Accessed May 29, 2015. http://www.ngim.org.

Allen, Bob. "'Traditional' Southern Baptists counter Calvinism." Baptist News Global (June 9, 2014). Accessed April 29, 2017, https://baptistnews.com/article/traditional-southern-baptists-counter-calvinism/.

Cowan, Steven B., and Stanley N. Gundry, eds. *Five Views of Christian Apologetics.* Grand Rapids, MI: Zondervan, 2000.

Geisler, Norman L. *Baker Encyclopedia of Christian Apologetics.* Grand Rapids, MI: Baker, 1999.

Geisler, Norman L. *Christian Apologetics*, 2nd ed. Grand Rapids, MI: Baker Academic, 2013.

GENDER, EVANGELICALS AND

Gender issues in America have affected evangelicalism along with the larger culture since the 1960s. The American evangelical response has been diverse, especially since the 1980s. Evangelicals affirm that Genesis records that God made humanity in the divine image—male and female he made them (1:27). The terms *man, woman, male,* and *female* are categories of sex differentiation. Gender, on the other hand, is the organization of the relationship between the sexes by social category. Thus, the gender categories corresponding to man/male and woman/female are *masculine* and *feminine*. In addressing what evangelicals believe about gender, then, we are asking what they believe about masculinity and femininity and male/female social roles.

Evangelicals are united in their belief that God made the sexes different by design—an idea derived from Genesis 1:27. Indeed, both complementarians and egalitarians believe in the complementary relationship of males and females as a beautiful part of God's plan. In fact, evangelical believers also agree that male/female differences extend beyond mere sex differentiation.

Although most evangelicals oppose liberal and radical feminism, only the most traditionalist evangelicals have opposed women being in the workforce. Most evangelicals believe women's employment is acceptable to God—especially in the helping professions—as long as these women are not neglecting their family responsibilities. In evangelical missions, historically women have had a strong presence, although denominations—with the exception of Pentecostals—have been divided on the issue of ordination.

Where egalitarians and complementarians differ greatly on the gender question is in their view of what the male/female roles are, especially as these relate to authority and power. Egalitarians do not see hierarchy or male leadership as God's intention or design in the male/female relationship. They do not believe that males, by design, were made to rule women, or husbands to lead wives. Consequently, they welcome women at all levels of pastoral leadership. Both groups hold to the inerrancy of Scripture; they differ, however, on interpretation.

Both groups believe Adam was created before Eve. But they differ in what they consider the ramifications of this reality. Egalitarians tend to see the creation of Adam and Eve solely as a historical event with various cultural applications. They also argue that marriage texts should not be used to determine gender roles for the unmarried. Complementarians, on the other hand, tend to see the fact that Adam was created first as a principle with transcultural applications. So, for example, many complementarians (e.g., Focus on the Family, the Love and Respect ministry) teach that men were designed uniquely to receive women's respect, whereas women were designed uniquely to receive men's affectionate love. Those holding this view base their thinking in part on the differing commands given to husbands and wives in Ephesians 5. That is, husbands are told to love (*agapeo*) their wives while wives are instructed to submit to and respect their husbands. Also, the husband is called the "head," and the wife is called the "body." (Some pair "head" with "submit" when delineating roles.) These categories are viewed as stemming from an inherent design for male leadership.

In an effort to combat what they perceive as confusion about set gender roles, which many complementarians consider a contributing factor to homosexuality, some churches have designed "biblical manhood and womanhood" curricula and created classes in order to instruct members about gender.

Within the complementarian camp, one finds a broad range of views about women and their roles in the church, home, and society. Some, believing the Bible teaches men were made to rule women by nature, in accordance with God's creation, think women should never be in authority over men in any context, especially a public one. Thus, a female president would, in their view, violate God's intended creation order. Others believe that because the New Testament writers never mention restrictions on women in society at large, and because Deborah judged Israel (Judges 4), females are restricted from such roles only in the home and church.

Some complementarians understand the apostle Paul as saying that man's creation order (1 Timothy 2:13) sets him in authority over woman for all time. Some even see eternal subordination in the male/female relationship. They base this on seeing a similar eternal subordination in the Father/Son relationship in the Trinity. A few complementarians, however, are uncomfortable drawing human analogies from the nonhuman relationships inside the Godhead. Most egalitarians consider such teaching heresy, as it ascribes to the Son less authority than the Father.

Traditionalists follow the church fathers' view of women as being more easily deceived than men—this being the church's most enduring rationale given for women's limitations or "differing roles" in church and home. Complementarians may hold to the same restrictions, but their underlying reasons behind those restrictions differ from those of the traditionalists.

Shrinking globalization has introduced many to the idea that culture shapes views of male/female roles more than was once thought (e.g., a female roofer in Kenya is doing "women's work," whereas a female roofer in America is viewed as doing "men's work"). Additionally, gender studies as an academic field has brought new approaches both to the biblical text and to how evangelicals view supporting documents that have informed the text. For example, Strabo (ca. 2 BCE) wrote of female temple servants in Aphrodite's Temple in Corinth. But contemporary scholars note that he is speaking of something that happened 400 to 700 years prior to his own writing. Such scholars are thus more likely to speak of how Strabo represents women rather than to repeat Strabo's statement as reality.

Such a shift in the approaches to gendered texts has also caused scholars to reconsider traditional approaches to the New Testament. For example, knowing the difficulty a woman might have in initiating divorce in ancient Palestine, scholars are taking another look at the Samaritan woman whom Jesus encountered (John 4) and questioning the typical view of her as promiscuous, having had five husbands and living with a sixth. It is more likely, such scholars say, that she was abandoned and/or widowed five times, and finally given to a man with more than one wife. Infertility is one possible cause (Cf. 1 Samuel 1). Scholars versed in gender studies similarly point out that the "men" (*anthrōpos*) in Ephesus who were teaching false doctrine could very well have included women (1 Timothy 1:3).

Gender scholars have also used their tools of analysis to look at how Bible translations have changed over time. For example, the King James Version says a woman should not "teach or usurp authority over the man" (1 Timothy 2:12), whereas more recent translations render the text with the more restrictive "exercise authority" (New American Standard Bible, English Standard Version, New English Translation); "assume authority" (New International Version); or even "have authority" (New

Living Translation, Holman Christian Standard Bible). Such scholars note that translations have become more conservative in some renderings of gendered texts since the rise of contemporary feminism.

A moderating effect of a biblical view of gender is the recognition that one must determine what is always true about men's and women's social interactions. In order to be truly biblical, such ideas must transcend time and culture. American evangelicals have been part of the gender debates and culture wars in America without uniformity but with strong convictions about how gender should be understood in society.

Sandra Glahn

See also: Christians for Biblical Equality; Council on Biblical Manhood and Womanhood; Infertility, Evangelicals and; Women's Ministries

Further Reading

Baucham, Richard. *Gospel Women: Studies of the Named Women in the Gospels.* Grand Rapids, MI: Eerdmans, 2002.

Pierce, Ronald W., Rebecca Merrill Groothuis, and Gordon Fee. *Discovering Biblical Equality.* Downers Grove, IL: InterVarsity Press, 2004.

Piper, John, and Wayne Grudem, eds. *Recovering Biblical Manhood and Womanhood: A Response to Evangelical Feminism.* Wheaton, IL: Crossway, 1991.

Saucy, Robert L., and Judith K. TenElshof, eds. *Women and Men in Ministry: A Complementary Perspective.* Chicago: Moody Press, 2001.

Sumner, Sarah. *Men and Women in the Church: Building Consensus on Christian Leadership.* Downers Grove, IL: InterVarsity Press, 2003.

Winston, George and Dora. *Recovering Biblical Ministry by Women.* Longwood, FL: Xulon Press, 2003.

THE GENESIS FLOOD (1961)

The Genesis Flood sparked an entire creationist movement regarding the origins of the earth within evangelicalism that began in the late 20th century. Hydrological engineer Henry Morris, PhD, and theologian John Whitcomb, ThD, coauthored *The Genesis Flood* in 1961. The book remains in print more than 50 years later. To best grasp its impact, one should understand the intellectual climate that it entered.

For the vast majority of the history of Christianity, most Christians built their history primarily on records, taking primary cues from Genesis. Naturalistic and anti-miraculous philosophies transformed this tradition in the 18th century by insisting that certain earth features like extensive and thick rock layers required long ages to form. Tension between naturalism's defenders (found both within and outside Christendom) and dissenters reached a crescendo in the mid-1800s. A cadre of English geologists welcomed Noah's Flood in their answers to geologic mysteries. These "scriptural theologians" published papers that pinpointed flaws in naturalistic/gradualistic geologic interpretations, but their message simply failed to reach as wide a readership as Flood-denying persuaders like Scottish lawyer Charles Lyell did. By the next generation, slow-and-gradual concepts dominated geology, even among evangelicals, until 1961.

The Genesis Flood explained how catastrophic processes solve geologic mysteries. For example, because "almost all of the sedimentary rocks of the earth . . . have been laid down by moving waters" (Morris and Whitcomb, 1961: 124), why not consider catastrophic flooding as the primary cause of earth layers? This confronted the gradual erosion model of Lyell and his protégé Charles Darwin. Morris and Whitcomb highlighted signs of catastrophe that Lyell and Darwin overlooked, including nearly continent-sized continuous sedimentary rock layers and fossil beds representing countless rapidly entombed animals. Their discussion of rapid and recent mountain formation and deep and recent burial of organics to form coal measures and oil reservoirs represented a radical rethink of naturalistic notions.

The Genesis Flood confronted the mythologizing of Genesis with its clear biblical case that Genesis describes a literal globe-covering Flood only thousands of years ago. Its marriage of observational science and responsible exegesis kick-started an evangelical surge toward believing Genesis straightforwardly, without the burden of reinterpreting text to fit secular ideas.

Readers of *The Genesis Flood* saw that science not only posed no threat to Genesis as history but actually bolsters it. Within a few years, Christian scientists and theologians organized their attempts to reinterpret geology, astronomy, biology, and other disciplines from the perspective of a recent creation and global Flood. To this end, Henry Morris cofounded the Creation Research Society that has published its quarterly journal from 1964 to this day. *The Genesis Flood* sparked a groundswell of support that led to a modern creation movement that peaked in the 1980s but continues reaping the benefits of original research by credentialed evangelical scientists now three generations later. Though gradualist and naturalist voices still prevail among evangelicals heavily swayed by cultural traditions, creation scientists continue to present new evidence through the parachurch ministries of Answers in Genesis, the Institute for Creation Research, Creation Ministries International, and many others, which all find their roots in *The Genesis Flood*.

Brian Thomas

See also: American Scientific Affiliation; Intelligent Design; Institute for Creation; Morris, Henry; Science, Evangelicals and

Further Reading

Morris, Henry. *Scientific Creationism.* Green River, AK: Master Books, 1974, 1985.

Morris, Henry, and John C. Whitcomb. *The Genesis Flood: The Biblical Record and Its Scientific Implications.* Phillipsburg, NJ: Presbyterian and Reformed, 1961.

Mortensen, Terry. *The Great Turning Point.* Green River, AK: Master Books, 2004.

Numbers, Ronald. L. *The Creationists: From Scientific Creationism to Intelligent Design.* Cambridge, MA: Harvard University Press, 2006.

Roberts, Michael. *Evangelicals and Science.* Santa Barbara, CA: Greenwood, 2008.

GIDEONS INTERNATIONAL

Gideons International is an international Christian evangelical organization known for distributing Bibles to military personnel, college students, medical offices, prisons, and in hotel rooms around the world. The organization was founded in 1899 in Janesville, Wisconsin, and is led by and comprised of non-clergy.

The Gideons were founded by Samuel E. Hill (1867–1936), John H. Nicholson (1859–1946), and William J. Knights (1853–1940), and derives its name from the biblical character Gideon as depicted in the Old Testament book of Judges, Chapter 6. Samuel Hill was the first president of the organization, and after convening in prayer with Knights and Nicholson, they selected the name "Gideons," and thus the organization was born. The earliest members were all traveling businessmen; they spent much of their time in hotels, and so the practice of distributing Bibles, or just portions of the New Testament, came naturally to them.

In the more than 100 years since Gideons International placed the first Bible in a hotel room, more than 2 billion Bibles and New Testaments have been placed in other rooms around the world. Bibles that have been translated into more than 90 languages can be found worldwide, with the Gideon label inside. Today, Christians and non-Christians alike have the option to send greeting cards from the Gideon Web site to honor a loved one or simply to spread God's word. Although the first 1 billion Bibles took more than 90 years to distribute, the second billion were distributed in only 14 years. The third billion is in the process of distribution today, and 80 million Bibles are distributed annually in many languages. The organization's longevity and narrowly focused work illustrates evangelical commitment to evangelism and the centrality of the Bible in evangelicalism.

Jeffrey M. Shaw

See also: Evangelism; Parachurch Ministries

Further Reading

Henderson, Joe. *Sowers of the Word: A 95-Year History of the Gideons International, 1899–1994.* Peabody, MA: Gideons International, 1995.

GORDON COLLEGE

Gordon College is an evangelical nondenominational Christian college of the liberal arts and sciences located north of Boston in Wenham, Massachusetts. The school offers 38 majors, 42 concentrations, and 11 interdisciplinary and preprofessional minors as well as graduate programs in education and music education. Gordon has an undergraduate enrollment of about 1,700 students and 400 graduate students representing more than 50 Christian denominations.

In 1889, Adoniram Judson Gordon (1836–1895), pastor of Clarendon Street Church (Boston) and prominent clergyman of the late 1800s, founded the school,

Boston Missionary Training Institute, in the Fenway–Kenmore neighborhood of Boston in the basement of his church, to train Christian missionaries for work in what was then the Belgian Congo. Progressive at its inception in 1889, the school admitted both men and women of various ethnicities. It was renamed Gordon Bible College in 1916 and expanded to Newton Theological Institution facilities along the Fenway, into a facility donated by Martha Frost in 1919. Frost, a widowed Bostonian with several properties in the city, provided a significant philanthropic gift. In 1921, the school was renamed Gordon College of Theology and Missions.

School growth surpassed the Fenway facilities, and in the late 1940s, James Higginbotham, a student pastor at Gordon Divinity School, approached Frederick Prince about selling his Wenham estate to Gordon. Prince sold the 1,000-acre estate to Gordon for a very small sum and donated a large sum to construct what would become the Prince Memorial Chapel. In 1955, Gordon moved to Wenham, Massachusetts, selling its old facilities to Wentworth Institute of Technology. In 1958, Gordon College instituted a core curriculum. In the 1950s, it launched its first study abroad program, European Seminar.

In 1962, the school changed its name to Gordon College and Divinity School. In 1970, the Gordon Divinity School separated from the College to merge with the Conwell School of Theology, once part of Temple University, to form the Gordon-Conwell Theological Seminary in Hamilton, Massachusetts.

Barrington College, founded in 1900 as the Bethel Bible Institute in Spencer, Massachusetts, later relocated to Dudley, Massachusetts, and then to Providence, Rhode Island. It took the name Barrington after the campus was moved to Barrington, Rhode Island, in 1959. Barrington merged with Gordon College in 1985, forming a United College of Gordon and Barrington.

The New England Association of Schools and Colleges (NEASC) has accredited Gordon since 1961. The music program is accredited by the National Association of Schools of Music (NASM) and the social work program is accredited by the Council on Social Work Education (CSWE). The Department of Education of the Commonwealth of Massachusetts recognizes Gordon College's teacher-education program under the Interstate Service Compact. Gordon is a member of the Annapolis Group and of the Christian College Consortium. It is also a member of the Council for Christian Colleges and Universities (CCCU).

Gordon College offers undergraduate degrees from 38 majors, 42 concentrations, and 15 interdisciplinary and preprofessional minors and graduate degrees in education and music. The Graduate Education program offers the MEd degree. The Graduate Music program offers an MMEd degree, licensure-only options, and workshops. Gordon College is one of the nation's oldest evangelical colleges.

James Menzies

See also: Gordon-Conwell Theological Seminary; Wheaton College

Further Reading

"A. J. Gordon Heritage Project." (n.d.). Gordon College. April 29, 2017. http://www.gordon
    .edu/ajgordon.
"History of Gordon." (n.d.). Gordon College. April 29, 2017. http://www.gordon.edu/history.
Sargent, Mark. "Essays about Gordon." (n.d.). Gordon College. April 29, 2017. http://tinyurl
    .com/l29xfn8.

GORDON-CONWELL THEOLOGICAL SEMINARY

Gordon-Conwell Theological Seminary is an evangelical seminary located in Hamilton, Massachusetts, with satellite campuses in Boston, Massachusetts; Charlotte, North Carolina; and Jacksonville, Florida. According to the Association of Theological Schools, Gordon-Conwell ranks as one of the largest evangelical seminaries in North America in terms of total number of full-time students enrolled.

The Preamble of the school's Mission Statement affirms "Gordon-Conwell Theological Seminary is an educational institution serving the Lord and his Church. Its mission is to prepare men and women for ministry at home and abroad. The Seminary undertakes this task as a training partner with the Church so that what is learned on campus may be complemented by the spiritual nurture and the exercise of ministry available through the Church" (http://www.gordonconwell.edu/about/Mission-and-Purpose.cfm).

Gordon-Conwell Seminary arose from the combined labors of two men. Russell Herman Conwell (1843–1925), pastor of Grace Baptist Temple in Philadelphia, began tutoring sessions in his study. As the classes grew, the members of the church urged him to begin a school, called Temple College (chartered in 1888). Beginning with just seven students a study, what became known as Temple University graduated more than 10,000 students within 25 years. Russell's vision for the school was "to establish a progressive, Orthodox theology, vigorously biblical, and yet in close touch with the modern culture." Conwell wanted to make "education possible for all young men and women who have good minds and a will to work" (http://www.gordonconwell.edu/about/Our-History.cfm).

In 1889, out of a desire to train men and women for Christian service, Adoniram Judson (A. J.) Gordon (1836–1895), pastor of Boston's Clarendon Street Baptist Church, founded the Boston Missionary Training Institute, to be "undenominational, broadly evangelical, practical, spiritual, humble and unworldly, and consecrated to the benefit of the 'Regions Beyond.'" The school would be a place "of equipping men and women in practical religious work and furnishing them with a thoroughly biblical training" (http://www.gordonconwell.edu).

After the death of Gordon in 1895, the school's name was changed to the Gordon College of Theology and Mission. The school eventually moved to the Fenway section of Boston. In 1931, the graduate theological course of the college officially became Gordon Divinity School. In the 1950s, the Divinity School and the College move to the Princemere estate in Wenham, Massachusetts.

When Temple University came under the jurisdiction of the state of Pennsylvania, the theology school was reduced to a religion department. Leaders determined to continue Conwell's vision and founded the Conwell School of Theology in 1960 through the initiative of Mr. J. Howard Pew and Rev. Billy Graham.

Under the leadership of Billy Graham, Harold John Ockenga, and J. Howard Pew, who saw the need for a strong, evangelical seminary in the Northeast, Gordon Divinity School and the Conwell School of Theology merged in 1969 to form Gordon-Conwell Theological Seminary. Dr. Ockenga became the first president; Rev. Graham served on the board of trustees; and Mr. Pew provided much of the early funding.

The vision for the school was to "establish within a strong evangelical framework, an independent, interdenominational seminary whose constituents are united in the belief that the Bible is the infallible, authoritative word of God . . . consecrated to educating men and women in all facets of gospel outreach" (http://www .gordonconwell.edu/about/Our-History.cfm).

Significant changes took place in 1969. The founders purchased a former Carmelite seminary in South Hamilton, Massachusetts, for $1 million, and the school was moved to the current Kerr building, the only academic structure on the wooded 119-acre campus. The first new building, the Goddard Library, was constructed in 1971.

The merger brought to Gordon-Conwell a number of distinguished professors. During his tenure, Ockenga strengthened the faculty, built a new administrative team, and recruited new trustees. In 1976, the historic commitment of A. J. Gordon and Russell Conwell to theological education was honored with the opening of a second campus, the Center for Urban Ministerial Education (CUME), in Roxbury, Massachusetts.

CUME is the main campus and has a program offered exclusively through part-time night and weekend classes. The Charlotte program, founded in 1992, offers courses on weekends and evenings, as well as weeklong intensive courses. The Jacksonville campus, opened in February 2006, was originally an extension of the Charlotte campus, though now it is the fourth campus for Gordon-Conwell.

Gordon-Conwell has students from more than 90 denominations and from more than 40 countries; it is part of the Boston Theological Institute, a consortium of nine theological schools in the Greater Boston area and the Carolina Theological Consortium, a consortium of four theological schools in North and South Carolina. Notable present and former faculty members include John Jefferson Davis, Harold John Ockenga, Dennis Hollinger, Walter C. Kaiser Jr.; David F. Wells, Roger R. Nicole, Haddon Robinson, and Gordon Fee. It remains a leading evangelical seminary with a worldwide influence.

James Menzies

See also: Higher Education, Evangelicals and; Ockenga, Harold John

Further Reading

Gordon-Conwell Theological Seminary. (n.d.). April 29, 2017. http://www.gordonconwell.edu.
Rosell, Garth M., ed., *Vision Continues, The Centennial Papers of Gordon-Conwell Theological Seminary*. South Hamilton, MA: Gordon-Conwell Theological Seminary, 1992.

THE GOSPEL COALITION

The Gospel Coalition, or TGC, is a broad network and fellowship of evangelical churches from the Reformed theology tradition. It was cofounded in 2005 by Christian pastor D. A. Carson, who serves as Research Professor of New Testament at Trinity Evangelical Divinity School in Deerfield, Illinois, and Tim Keller, founding pastor of Redeemer Presbyterian Church in Manhattan, which he started in 1989. For more than 20 years, Keller has led a diverse congregation of young professionals that has grown to a weekly attendance of more than 5,000. He also serves as chairman of Redeemer City to City, which starts new churches in New York and other global cities, and publishes books and resources for faith in an urban culture. In more than 10 years, Redeemer City to City has helped to launch more than 250 churches in 48 cities.

The purpose of TGC is to encourage Christians and influence culture through its Web site, conferences, publications, and other projects and initiatives. It has a strong Calvinist focus, with an emphasis on cultural transformation. Its annual conference are attended by thousands of people and its Web site receives millions of "hits" each year and is one of the most prominent evangelical Web sites on the Internet. The Gospel Coalition works across denominational, ethnic, and class lines in efforts to revitalize the contemporary church.

Some of the prominent pastors involved in TGC include Alistair Begg, Bryan Chapell, Mark Dever, Kevin DeYoung, Ligon Duncan, Kent Hughes, Erwin Lutzer, Albert Mohler, Ray Ortlund, John Piper, and Philip G. Ryken. Its presence on the Internet and popularity with younger evangelicals makes it one of the most prominent evangelical ministries in America.

James Menzies

See also: Calvinism; Reformed Tradition, Evangelicalism and

Further Reading

"Bio: Timothy Keller." (n.d.). Accessed April 29, 2017. http://www.timothykeller.com/author/.
"Overview." The Gospel Coalition. Accessed April 29, 2017. https://www.thegospelcoalition .org/about/overview.
"Faculty, D. A. Carson, PhD." (n.d.). Trinity Evangelical Divinity School. Accessed April 29, 2017. http://divinity.tiu.edu/academics/faculty/d-a-carson-phd/.

GRACE THEOLOGICAL SEMINARY

Grace Theological Seminary (Grace Seminary), located in Winona Lake, Indiana, along with Grace College, serves as the primary educational institution for the

Fellowship of Grace Brethren Churches. The fellowship numbers 250 churches in the United States and nearly 3,000 worldwide. Evangelical in doctrine, the college and seminary serve the larger evangelical community, with a focus on a rigorous study and application of the Bible and biblical principles, their application to contemporary Christian life, and worldwide service. The seminary's view of eschatology is grounded in premillennialism and dispensationalism.

The seminary was established in 1937 in Winona Lake, Indiana, the headquarters of the evangelist Billy Sunday (the Fellowship would later acquire many of the Billy Sunday buildings, including the famous Billy Sunday Tabernacle). In association with Grace Seminary, the fellowship of Grace Brethren Churches was established as a separate denomination in 1939 and traces its roots to the Pietists and Anabaptists of Germany who, under the leadership of Alexander Mack, were convinced through their study of the Bible that believer's baptism and observance of biblical principles should guide the Christian life. Their stand resulted in local persecution, and the group completed its emigration to America in 1729, settling in Ephrata, Pennsylvania. Known as the Brethren, or German Baptists, the group experienced a number of divisions between 1729 and 1937, usually over application of biblical principles to the ever-changing contemporary life.

Grace Seminary was established as a result of a theological dispute within the Brethren Church (an offshoot of the Church of the Brethren), which had established a seminary at Ashland, Ohio. The era was characterized by fundamentalist disputes, especially over the historic Christian doctrines of the virgin birth and the inspiration of the Bible. Professors Alva J. McClain and Herman Hoyt came into conflict with the Ashland Seminary administration over their teaching of these doctrines (taking the historic conservative view) and were fired. In 1937, they moved to Winona Lake and began Grace Seminary. The seminary, college, and fellowship of churches trace their roots to this event.

Today, Grace Seminary has evolved to meet changing times. While staying true to the Grace Brethren statement of faith, which includes the Brethren practices of baptism by triune immersion and inclusion of the love feast within communion, the administration has developed innovative approaches to serve the larger evangelical community. Distance education and the development of commuter campuses have brought ministry education to an ever-expanding and diverse clientele. Grace Theological Seminary remains a strong force in American evangelical higher education.

Dayne E. Nix

See also: Higher Education, Evangelicals and

Further Reading

Etling, Harold. *Our Heritage: Brethren Beliefs and Practices.* Winona Lake: BMH Books, 1975.

"The FGBC Story." (n.d.). Fellowship of Grace Brethren Churches (FGBC). Accessed May 15, 2015. http://www.fgbc.org/about/our-story.

Grace College & Seminary. (n.d.). Accessed May 15, 2015. http://www.grace.edu.

Kent, Homer A., Sr. *Conquering Frontiers: A History of the Brethren Church.* Winona Lake: BMH Books, 1972

GRAHAM, WILLIAM F., JR. ("BILLY") (1918–)

William ("Billy") Franklin Graham Jr. (1918–) was born to William and Morrow Graham and christened into a Scottish Presbyterian family in Charlotte, North Carolina, and he referred to himself as a country boy who was raised on a dairy farm.

Growing up in Mecklenburg County, North Carolina, Graham was a skeptic of religion and Christianity, but after attending a revival one evening in hopes of seeing a fight, Graham heard the Gospel presented through a sermon preached by Baptist fundamentalist evangelist Dr. Mordecai Ham (1877–1961). At a subsequent meeting during the revival, Ham's message brought about an understanding on Graham's part about his own need for salvation, and in 1934, when he was almost 16 years old, Graham committed his life to Christ (the decision card on which he wrote his name on November 1, 1934, is kept in the Billy Graham Library, in Charlotte, North Carolina).

Graham began his higher education at Bob Jones College in 1936 but felt that it was too strict. So in 1937, he transferred to Florida Bible Institute (now Trinity College of Florida), where Dr. John Minder called on him to preach. After presenting an eight-minute sermon that was compiled from at least four other "borrowed" sermons he had previously heard, he began to feel God's call on his life to preach. In 1938, Graham gave his life over to Christian ministry. Graham graduated from the Florida Bible Institute and was ordained as a minister in the Southern Baptist Convention. Later, he attended Wheaton College, where he earned a Bachelor of Arts degree in June 1943.

It was while he was at Wheaton that he met Ruth Bell (1920–2007), the daughter of medical missionaries who had served in China. On Friday, August 13, 1943, Graham and Ruth were married at Gaither Chapel in Montreat, North Carolina. They eventually had five children, all of whom are currently serving in various ministries around the world.

In 1943, Graham took his first ministerial position as pastor of the Village Church of Western Springs (now Western Springs Baptist Church), Illinois, and he also began to preach in different venues. In 1945, he became the first full-time evangelist of Youth for Christ, which was an organization that sought to help youth and war veterans live for God. Due to the notoriety that his preaching brought him as he began to develop his own preaching style, Graham became the interim president of Northwestern Schools in Minneapolis, Minnesota, at age 29. Although he was frequently traveling across the United States and in Europe after the war ended, Graham worked to help fix the school's financial issues and also aided in growing enrollments.

In 1949, Graham preached at the Los Angeles Crusade, which was scheduled to last for three weeks. However, the venue was extended to longer than eight weeks, and Graham's popularity brought overflow crowds into the tent that had been erected in downtown Los Angeles for the event. It was at this crusade that Graham's international notoriety would be solidified. He was a key figure in the rise of neo-evangelicalism and was one of the cofounders of the evangelical publication *Christianity Today*.

In 1950, Graham determined to spread his ministry to a global scale with long-term impact, so he began a radio broadcast, called *The Hour of Decision*, that had a national scope. Out of this effort, Graham founded the Billy Graham Evangelistic Association (BGEA), headquartered in Minneapolis, Minnesota (later relocated to Charlotte, North Carolina in 2003). Ardently working to bring people together, the mission of the BGEA was to advocate for uniting Christian missions with help from every Christian denomination. Thus, *The Hour of Decision* radio program was broadcast to more than 800 radio stations when it began in 1950. Additionally, Graham launched television broadcasts of his evangelistic outreach through BGEA, and many of these recordings are replayed on Christian television networks today. BGEA also initiated a syndicated newspaper column titled "My Answer," and many newspapers both across the United States and around the world maintain the column to this day. Finally, BGEA runs a magazine called *Decision*, which has a circulation of

Prominent American Evangelists before Billy Graham

Although Billy Graham (1918–) is the most famous evangelist in American history, given his famous crusades, relationship to Reverend Martin Luther King Jr., and ministry to a number of U.S. presidents, there are number of evangelists who preceded and contributed in various ways to evangelicalism and American life:

Jonathan Edwards (1703–1758)
George Whitefield (1714–1770)
Dwight L. Moody (1837–1899)
Billy Sunday (1862–1935)
Charles Harrison Mason (1866–1961)
William Joseph Seymour (1870–1922)
Mordecai Fowler Ham Jr. (1877–1961)
Robert P. Shuler (1880–1965)
Bob Jones Sr. (1883–1968)
Aimee Semple McPherson, or "Sister Aimee" (1890–1944)
Ida B. Robinson (1891–1946)
Kathryn Johanna Kuhlman (1907–1976)
James Francis Marion Jones (1907–1971)
Torrey Maynard Johnson (1909–2002)
Oliver B. Greene (1915–1976)

more than 425,000, a number that qualifies the magazine as one of the most widely circulated periodicals in the world.

Graham began attracting massive interest at his Crusades, events at which Billy and his Crusade Team would host worship services in large forums such as ballparks and other outdoor venues. In March 1, 1954, Graham and his team got the opportunity to preach an international Crusade in London, England. Graham delivered 72 sermons at Harringay Arena, North London, and by the end of their 12 weeks, the Crusade had reached more than 2 million people with the Gospel of Christ. In fact, Graham recounts that thousands of decisions for Christ were made during that time.

The largest recorded crowd for one of Graham's Crusade meetings was in 1973 in Yoido Plaza, Seoul, Korea, where more than 1 million people sat and stood to hear Graham's evangelical message and to sing songs for the service. Graham's ministry through the BGEA has taken him all over the world, including the former Soviet Union during the years of the Cold War; he's preached to some of the largest gatherings recorded in modern Christian history.

15 Personalities Shaping Evangelicalism Today—Their Influence Is Unmistakable

1. Matt Chandler (1974–), lead teaching pastor at The Village Church in Dallas, Texas
2. William Lane Craig (1949–), Christian apologist, philosopher, and theologian
3. Wilfredo De Jesus (1965–), "Pastor Choco," head pastor of New Life Covenant Church in Chicago (Assemblies of God)
4. Louie Giglio (1958–), founder of Passion Movement
5. Franklin Graham (1952–), president and CEO of Billy Graham Evangelistic Association and Samaritan's Purse
6. Craig Groeschel (1967–), founder and senior pastor of Life Church
7. Bill Hybels (1951–), founding and senior pastor of Willow Creek Community Church and founder of the Willow Creek Association
8. T. D. Jakes (1957–), bishop and senior pastor of The Potter's House
9. Tim Keller (1950–), founding pastor of Redeemer Presbyterian Church in New York City
10. Albert Mohler (1959–), president of The Southern Baptist Theological Seminary
11. Lecrae (1979–), an American Christian hip-hop artist
12. John Piper (1946–), founder of Desiring God Ministries
13. Alvin Plantinga (1932–), analytic Christian philosopher
14. Andy Stanley (1958–), senior pastor of North Point Community Church
15. Rick Warren (1954–), senior pastor of Saddleback Church in Lake Forest

Consistent with his unifying disposition, Graham frequently opposed and spoke out against racism and segregation. In fact, Graham and Martin Luther King Jr. (1929–1968) met during the Montgomery Bus Boycott. Soon thereafter, Graham was calling for nonsegregation legislation in New York City during a Crusade, and Graham invited King to join him on stage on July 18, 1957, in Madison Square Garden. Although it was not something at the time that made him popular as a Southern Baptist minister, Graham insisted on holding integrated revivals, and King praised his efforts for striving for unity and justice in the United States.

Although he did not frequently interject political opinions and strived for non-partisan unity throughout his lifetime, Graham was frequently sought out as a spiritual advisor to several presidents. From President Truman to President Obama, American presidents have sought out Billy Graham for either spiritual counsel or friendship, or both. Graham's biographer notes that he was likely closest in friend-ship to President Lyndon B. Johnson.

Graham's wife, Ruth, passed away in 2007 but is survived by her husband, five children, 19 grandchildren, and even more great-grandchildren. One of Graham's sons, Franklin Graham (1952–), is currently the head of BGEA and continues on the ministry that his father began in 1950. Anne Graham Lotz (1948–) founded AnGeL Ministries and travels the world as an American Christian evangelist.

In addition to his children's ministries, Graham established the Billy Graham Library in June 2007, located in Charlotte, North Carolina. This library highlights Graham's many years of international evangelism work through the Crusades. Whea-ton College also honored Billy Graham's life and ministry by establishing The Billy Graham Center in September 1980, which displays the work of the BGEA as well as other evangelical organizations from around Graham's same era of ministry.

Graham has written more than 35 books, many of which have won awards, including *Peace with God* (more than 2 million copies sold in 38 languages, revised and expanded in 1984), *World Aflame* (*New York Times* bestseller), *Angels: God's Secret Agents*, *The Holy Spirit*, and *Just as I Am*. Graham is the most prominent American evangelical and is internationally recognized and respected as a global religious personality.

Bryce Hantla

See also: Baptists and Evangelicalism; Billy Graham Evangelistic Association; Carnell, Edward John; Evangelism; Falwell, Jerry L., Sr.; Foreign Policy, Evangelicals and; Fuller Theological Seminary; Fundamentalism; Henry, Carl F. H.; Neo-Evangelicalism; Ockenga, Harold John; Theological Controversies within Evangelicalism

Further Reading

Graham, Billy. *Just as I Am*. New York: HarperOne, 1997.
Martin, William. *A Prophet with Honor: The Billy Graham Story*. Grand Rapids, MI: Zonder-van, 2007.

Moore, Edward L. *Billy Graham and Martin Luther King, Jr.: An Inquiry into White and Black Revivalistic Traditions.* PhD diss., Vanderbilt University, 1979.

Wacker, Grant. *America's Pastor: Billy Graham and the Shaping of a Nation.* Cambridge, MA: Harvard University Press, 2014.

"William (Billy) F. Graham, Jr." 2016. Billy Graham Evangelistic Association. Accessed August 25, 2016. https://billygraham.org/about/biographies/billy-graham/.

HALVERSON, RICHARD ("DICK") (1916–1995)

Richard Halverson was a prominent evangelical pastor and chaplain of the U.S. Senate. His wide influence encompassed both trailblazing and highly traditional venues. His personal background, both evangelical and mainstream Presbyterian, presaged those two venues as he gained his BS from Wheaton College in 1939, and his BTh (equivalent to the modern MDiv) from Princeton Theological Seminary in 1942.

Halverson's nontraditional work began in 1942 as managing director of Forest Home Christian Conference Grounds in Forest Hill, California. Forest Home had been founded in 1937 by Henrietta Mears, a giant of worldwide evangelical influence from her position leading Christian Education at First Presbyterian Church, Hollywood. Halverson's brief pastoral works in Kansas City, then central California, led him to "the belief that God was leading me into a ministry with men who were outside the church and unreached with the Gospel" (Kurtz, 1978, p. 194).

Halverson then went to Hollywood. He notes: "The invitation to join the staff of Dr. Louis Evans, Sr., at the First Presbyterian Church in Hollywood, California [as Pastor of Leadership Education in 1947], was not an invitation to a conventional ministry. It was understood that I would pursue the specialized work to which it seemed God was calling. The eight-and-a-half years at Hollywood were devoted in great part to a ministry with small groups and individual contacts. Except for teaching two adult classes on Sunday morning and participating in the morning and evening services, my part in the ministry was quite unconventional" (Kurtz, 1978, p. 194).

Halverson, while at Hollywood, also commenced work with two significant "parachurch" ministries just as such organizations were gaining prominence. From 1956 to 1995, he served as a board member of the International Prayer Breakfast Movement, led by Abraham Vereide (Kurtz, 1978, p. 194), founder of Goodwill Industries, with every U.S. president since Eisenhower attending the annual prayer breakfast. He also served on the board of World Vision, an evangelical relief organization, from 1956 to 1983.

Halverson then accepted an unexpected invitation to take a conventional role as senior pastor of Fourth Presbyterian Church, Bethesda, Maryland, serving from 1958 to 1981. At first unused to such service, he felt free to encourage indigenous, locally developed programs by which the church found its successes by God's guidance through experience—including the importation of small group dynamics into larger congregational life (Kurtz, 1978, pp. 195–196). The church thrived and grew, expanding its sanctuary and other buildings to accommodate its needs. Halverson's parachurch leadership also grew, including the chairmanship of World Vision,

1966–1983, and Concern Ministries, a Washington, D.C., charitable foundation. Two prominent Presbyterian pulpits in Washington were filled by alumni of First Presbyterian Church Hollywood in the 1970s: Halverson at Fourth, and Louis Evans Jr. at National. Perhaps the highlight of Halverson's time at Fourth was leading its sesquicentennial celebration in 1978.

Halverson accepted an invitation in 1981 to serve in a supremely traditional place—the U.S. Senate—as chaplain. He ministered there till 1995, when declining health led to his retirement at 79, followed by his death just months later. He was survived by Doris Grace Seaton, his wife of 52 years; three children, including Rev. Richard C. Halverson Jr.; and nine grandchildren. Senate Majority Leader Dole stated, "As many of my colleagues said upon Dr. Halverson's retirement, from Senate staffers to elevator operators to police force members to electricians, it would be impossible to tell how many lives Dr. Halverson touched here on Capitol Hill. . . . Perhaps our colleague, Senator Nunn, said it best earlier this year when he called Dr. Halverson 'our friend, our colleague, our mentor, our adviser and, most of all, our example'" (U.S. Senate, 1996, p. 2). Senate Minority Leader Daschle said, "Through his religious belief, emanating every morning as he came to this Chamber, we all felt a little stronger, we all felt a little better, we all felt perhaps a little wiser, we all felt a little more able to work with each other. His contribution to his country and to this body will last for a long, long time" (U.S. Senate, 1996, pp. 2–3).

Halverson received four honorary doctorates, including from Wheaton College and Gordon College. He authored 16 inspirational books, including *Gospel for the Whole Life* and *We the People*. Speakers at his memorial service, held at Fourth Presbyterian, included Senator Mark O. Hatfield, Mr. Doug Coe, and Dr. Billy Graham (U.S. Senate 1996, 29ff). Condolences came from numerous former U.S. presidents and other national leaders.

Dick Halverson long occupied a pinnacle of national spiritual influence based on his ability to fulfill both trailblazing and traditional roles, founded on a firm evangelical faith. His spiritual leadership was personally supportive and focused on relieving human need rather than being publicly confrontational or politically programmatic. He affirmed the engraving on the National Archives building: "The Past Is Prologue," stating, "The better we understand our past, the more certain we are to fulfill our God-appointed destiny in the future," and he concluded by saying that that future should be met with "the preeminence of Christ, the centrality of the Bible, the sense of family, and outreach" (Kurtz, 1978, p. 197).

Mark A. Jumper

See also: Fourth Presbyterian Church; Politics, Evangelicals and

Further Reading

Kurtz, Grace W. *The Story of Fourth Presbyterian Church: A Past to Remember—A Future to Mold.* Trenton, NJ: Custom Book, 1978.

Princeton Theological Seminary. *The Richard C. Halverson Manuscript Collection*. Princeton, NJ: Princeton Theological Seminary Libraries, Special Collections.

U.S. Senate Document 104–15. *Memorial Tributes Delivered in Congress—Richard C. Halverson 1916–1995—United States Senate Chaplain*. Washington, D.C.: U.S. Government Printing Office, 1996.

HARVARD EVANGELICALS

Harvard Evangelicals, more recently termed the "Cambridge Evangelicals," was the informal term given to a group of young scholars studying at Harvard University and Boston University in the 1940s who later became leaders in the evangelical movement. Many of them were under the influence of Harold John Ockenga (1905–1985), the pastor of Park Street Church in Boston and a leading figure in evangelicalism, the National Association of Evangelicals, and the Evangelical Theological Society. Ockenga served as a model and mentor for these young scholars, and they in turn became some of the leading evangelicals from the 1950s–1990s.

Part of the emphasis of post–World War II evangelicals was the desire to give an intellectual defense of Christian orthodoxy and to engage the broader American culture and its social issues from a biblical perspective, but with academic credentials that were recognized and respected beyond the evangelical world. There was also a strong desire to back away from the prewar militancy and separatism of Protestant fundamentalism of the 1920s and 1930s.

Individuals identified as among the Harvard Evangelicals were Carl F. H. Henry (1913–2003), Edward J. Carnell (1919–1967), Kenneth Kantzer (1917–2002), George Eldon Ladd (1911–1982), and Samuel Schultz, Merrill Tenney, John Gerstner, Burton Goddard, Roger Nicole, Gleason Archer, Paul King Jewett, Jack P. Lewis, J. Harold Greenlee, and Terrelle Crum.

The Harvard Evangelicals were part of the larger postwar evangelical movement, specifically those known as New Evangelicals, or Neo-evangelicals, terms that show that evangelicalism was not and is not monolithic in theology, sociology, and perspectives on social and political issues. The Harvard Evangelicals became some of the renowned authors, scholars, and voices of evangelicalism, and were prominent in evangelical institutions, publications, and organizations such as Wheaton College, Fuller Seminary, Trinity Evangelical Divinity School, Gordon Conwell Theological Seminary, Evangelical Theological Society, *Journal of the Evangelical Theological Society*, and *Christianity Today*.

Timothy J. Demy

See also: Christianity Today; Evangelical Theological Society; Henry, Carl. F. H.; Higher Education, Evangelicals and; Ockenga, Harold John

Further Reading

Henry, Carl F. H. *Confessions of a Theologian: An Autobiography*. Waco, TX: Word Books, 1986.

Marsden, George. *Reforming Fundamentalism: Fuller Seminary and the New Evangelicalism.* Grand Rapids, MI: Eerdmans, 1988.

Miller, Steven P. *The Age of Evangelicalism: America's Born-Again Years.* New York: Oxford University Press, 2014.

Strachan, Owen. *Awakening the Evangelical Mind: An Intellectual History of the Neo-Evangelical Movement.* Grand Rapids, MI: Zondervan, 2015.

HATFIELD, MARK ODOM (1922–2011)

Mark Hatfield was an evangelical Baptist politician, political scientist, and educator. He was known as a political moderate during an era of growing conservatism within the Republican Party in the United States. Hatfield frequently alluded to his Christian faith as the primary influence on his political ideology and actions. He often opposed fellow Republicans on the basis of his conscience, most notably in his opposition to American involvement in the Vietnam War during his tenure as United States Senator from Oregon.

Hatfield was born in Dallas, Oregon, in 1922. His father was a railroad worker, and his mother was a schoolteacher. Hatfield graduated with a BA from Willamette University, Salem, Oregon, in 1943 and then joined the United States Navy as a lieutenant. He saw action in the battles of Iwo Jima and Okinawa during World War II. After the war, the veteran returned briefly to Willamette to study law but left to pursue a master's degree in political science at Stanford University, graduating in 1948. He joined the faculty at Willamette University as an assistant professor of political science in that same year and remained on the faculty through 1956. After his retirement from politics in 1997, Hatfield joined the faculty of George Fox University, Newberg, Oregon, an institution affiliated with the Quakers. There he served as the Herbert Hoover Distinguished Emeritus Professor of Politics. He was also an eponymous lecturer in the Hatfield School of Government at Portland State University.

While still teaching as a college professor, Hatfield ran for the Oregon House of Representatives and won in 1950, and voters later elected him to the Oregon Senate in the 1954 elections. In his first attempt in a statewide election in 1956, he edged out his opponent to become Oregon's youngest secretary of state, and similarly became the state's youngest governor in 1959, serving two terms. In 1966, he was elected to the United States Senate, serving five terms and retiring in 1997. After Republicans had regained control of the Senate in the 1980 elections, Hatfield became the chair of the powerful Appropriations Committee.

In 1966, while governor of Oregon, Hatfield gained national attention for being the only governor in the United States to refuse to sign a resolution by the National Governor's Conference supporting the Johnson administration's Vietnam War policies. He opposed that war as he also later opposed the 1991 Gulf War, though he consistently expressed his support for American troops. He led in opposition to nuclear weapons and energy produced by nuclear fission. As an evangelical, Hatfield was pro-life but expressed disappointment that Christians, especially his evangelical colleagues in the Senate, often promoted civil religion, which he believed to be too general and lacking in theological substance. While a senator, he mentioned this concern as the keynote speaker for the National Prayer Breakfast in February 1973, which both President Richard Nixon and evangelist Billy Graham attended. In the address, he publicly called on political leaders to eschew civil religion and repent in obedience to the biblical God. Hatfield was famously misconstrued by the press to be explicit in his condemnation of the war, but his actual remarks were enough to infuriate members of the Nixon administration. Predictably then, Hatfield opposed any legislation he saw as an effort to support civil faith, such as government-sponsored school prayer, rather than act in obedience to a just and righteous God. He also expressed concerns that the Nixon administration was manipulating Graham. Although Hatfield was critical of Nixon's unethical behavior leading up to and during the Watergate investigations, he was unable to escape increased scrutiny of politicians in the post-Watergate era: in 1991 the Senate Ethics Committee, in investigations that went back to 1984, twice rebuked the senator for receiving inappropriate gifts.

On balance, Hatfield was a respected legislator among his peers during his lifetime. He received many public honors in his home state after his retirement from the Senate. He died in Portland after a long illness in 2011. He was a pioneer among evangelicals seeking political office in the postwar era and did much to encourage others to pursue the same course.

Liam J. Atchison

See also: Politics, Evangelicals and

Further Reading

Eells, Robert, and Bartell Nyberg. *Lonely Walk: The Life of Senator Mark Hatfield.* Portland, OR: Multnomah Press, 1979.

Fendall, Lon. *Stand Alone or Come Home: Mark Hatfield as an Evangelical and a Progressive.* Newberg, OR: Barclay Press, 2008.

Hatfield, Mark O. *Conflict and Conscience.* Waco, TX: Word Books, 1971.

Hatfield, Mark O. *Between a Rock and a Hard Place.* Waco, TX: Word Books, 1976.

Hatfield, Mark O. *Against the Grain: Reflections of a Rebel Republican.* Ashland, OR: White Cloud Press, 2001.

HENDRICKS, HOWARD G. (1924–2013)

Howard G. ("Prof") Hendricks (1924–2013) was a professor, speaker, pastor, and popular author in the discipline of Christian education and leadership.. Hendricks was married to Jeanne, his wife, for more than 66 years, and their heritage includes four children, six grandchildren, and two great-grandchildren.

Born in Philadelphia, Pennsylvania, Hendricks was raised by his grandparents. Hendricks came to faith in Jesus Christ early in life. A man named Walt, who had a sixth-grade education, was his Sunday school teacher. Walt's influence was so contagious that 12 people out of 13 in his class entered into full-time Christian vocational ministry.

Hendricks graduated with a Bachelor of Arts from Wheaton College in 1946, and a Master of Theology (ThM) graduate degree from Dallas Theological Seminary in 1950. He entered the pastoral vocation by serving at McKinney Memorial Church in Fort Worth, Texas, and taught part-time for Dallas Theological Seminary. Hoping to begin a PhD, he enrolled at Yale University; however, in the fall of 1952, President John F. Walvoord of Dallas Theological Seminary asked Hendricks if he would defer his studies by teaching homiletics and theology. Hendricks taught at Dallas Theological Seminary until he retired in 2011.

Hendricks was the driving force behind the seminary's Christian education courses, the development of the seminary's Master of Arts in Christian Education, and the seminary's Center of Christian Leadership. He was a proponent of studying the Bible analytically, which led him to produce a required course in Bible study methods and hermeneutics, that is, the science and art of interpreting the Bible, for beginning Dallas Theological Seminary graduate students. Eventually, Hendricks converted this course into a book called *Living by the Book*, which has influenced not only thousands of his seminary students but also students at other academic institutions such as Cedarville University, College of Biblical Studies–Houston, Bible Institute, Cairn University (formerly Philadelphia Biblical University), Liberty University, Moody Bible Institute, Multnomah University, Trinity Evangelical Divinity School, and Word of Life. The hermeneutical method that a significant number of evangelical pastors, teachers, and missionaries apply when studying the Bible can be directly connected to the influence of Hendricks's approach to analyzing the Bible.

Hendricks's influence extends beyond the academic borders to millions of laypeople on daily and weekly bases. Former students and graduates of Dallas Theological Seminary who are popular radio preachers include Charles ("Chuck") Swindoll, Tony Evans, and David Jeremiah.

From the mid-1970s to the mid-1980s, Dr. Hendricks was the chaplain of the Dallas Cowboys, a professional football team of the National Football League. During that time, the Dallas Cowboys—composed of legendary head coach Tom Landry, Hall of Fame quarterback Roger Staubach, Hall of Fame running back Tony Dorsett, and Pro Bowl players such as Randy White, Ed ("Too Tall") Jones, and Drew Pearson—were known as "America's Team." For a period of about eight years, Hendricks spoke and ministered to some of the most recognizable sports figures in professional athletics. During these years, Hendricks was also a prominent speaker for Campus Crusade for Christ (now Cru). Through the 1990s and early 2000s, he continued as a prominent speaker for Promise Keepers and other key Christian conferences.

As an influential leader in the evangelical movement, numerous organizations appointed Hendricks to their board or advisory board. To name a few: The Navigators, Promise Keepers, Multnomah College and Seminary, Walk Thru the Bible

Ministries, and Fellowship of Christian Athletes. Hendricks also wrote more than 20 books in the areas of Christian education, Christian leadership, discipleship, and hermeneutics. Two of his more famous books are *Teaching to Change Lives* and *Living by the Book*. Both have been (or still are) required reading for most introductory hermeneutics and Christian education courses of many evangelical colleges and seminaries.

In the late 1980s, Dallas Theological Seminary added the Center for Christian Leadership, which Hendricks chaired until his retirement in 2011. His influence continues to be visible, with students at colleges and seminaries reading his books, his previous students teaching over the airwaves, and a new generation of students yet to be known who were influenced by him in the late 2000s. Hendricks's most significant contribution to contemporary American religious culture was his teaching and mentoring of 10,000+ graduate seminary students at Dallas Theological Seminary and ministry to thousands of other students and young adults through parachurch ministries.

David A. McGee

See also: Bible Exposition; Chafer, Lewis Sperry; Dallas Theological Seminary; Dispensationalism; Evans, Anthony T. ("Tony"); Fellowship of Christian Athletes; Higher Education, Evangelicals and; Promise Keepers; Swindoll, Charles R. ("Chuck"); Walvoord, John F; Wheaton College

Further Reading

Glahn, Sandra L. "A Lasting Legacy." *Kindred Spirit*, 37, no. 1 (2013).

Hannah, John D. *An Uncommon Union: Dallas Theological Seminary and American Evangelicalism*. Grand Rapids, MI: Zondervan, 2009.

Hendricks, Howard G. *Teaching to Changes Lives*. Colorado Springs, CO: The WaterBrook Multnomah, 1987.

Hendricks, Howard G., and William D. Hendricks. *Living by the Book*. Chicago: Moody Press, New Edition, 2007.

Lawson, Michael S., and Carisa A. Ash. "Howard Hendricks: A Teacher Who Changes Lives." *Christian Education Journal* 1, no. 2 (Spring 2004): 63–71.

HENRY, CARL F. H. (1913–2003)

Carl F. H. Henry was one of the most influential and prominent evangelical theologians of the later half of the 20th century and early 21st century. Widely hailed as the "dean of evangelical theologians" (or, as the *New York Times* obituary read, the "Brain of the Evangelical Movement"), Carl Ferdinand Howard Henry was born into one of New York City's German immigrant families in 1913. His parents were nominally Christian, with little faith to speak of. His upbringing was Episcopal, but he dates his conversion from 1933, when he responded to the claims of the gospel, thanks to the witness of a persistent young evangelist named Gene Bedford.

In high school, he made a promising start as a journalist, serving as a reporter for several New York–area newspapers, later editing one. But after his conversion, he turned to theological and philosophical studies, where he earned four postgraduate degrees. By the time of his death in 2003, he had written or edited more than 40 books, taught in a range of colleges and seminaries, and helped found a magazine (*Christianity Today*), an organization (National Association of Evangelicals), and a seminary (Fuller Theological Seminary).

Henry's work is best understood as, first, a defense of biblical authority and evangelical doctrine against challenges within and without the church. In this connection, he faulted existentialism, mysticism, scientism, Marxism, higher criticism, and the secular models of man and creation spawned by Freud and Darwin. He gainsaid theologians who, seeking accommodation with these schools of thought, proposed mediating approaches such as neo-orthodoxy, which did well to puncture the groundless cultural optimism of liberalism and stress the transcendence of God, but which faltered in their attenuated view of the Bible's accuracy.

His second major project was to help reverse the self-imposed cultural isolation which had overtaken biblical conservatism. In his 1947 book, *The Uneasy Conscience of Modern Fundamentalism*, Henry urged believers to renew their thoughtful activism in the public square, to shake off their other-worldly paralysis, an overreaction to the "social gospel," and to adopt a less strident tone, offering positive as well as negative counsel. Henry contended that the "apostolic Gospel" of Protestant conservatism stood "divorced from a passion to right the world" (Henry, 1947: 39) a passion it had exhibited abundantly in the 19th century, as in the Abolitionist Movement.

Henry's education and his service to educational institutions were considerable. He earned a BA and an MA in theology at Wheaton, a BD (now MDiv) and ThD at Northern Baptist Theological Seminary, and a PhD in philosophy at Boston University. He also did coursework at the University of Chicago, and Loyola University (Chicago), and research at the University of Cambridge in England, where he undertook his magisterial, six-volume *God, Revelation and Authority*. On the other side of the lectern, he was a professor at Northern, Eastern, and Fuller Seminaries and a visiting professor at Trinity Evangelical Divinity School and Gordon-Conwell Theological Seminary.

Not confined to the "ivory tower," he was continually involved in gospel projects and public theology. While at Fuller, he helped organize the Rose Bowl Sunrise Service in Pasadena. Then, in 1956, he left Fuller for Washington, D.C., to serve as founding editor of *Christianity Today*, an alternative to the more liberal *Christian Century*. While at the helm of *Christianity Today*, and in league with Billy Graham, he chaired the 1966 Berlin World Congress on Evangelism, with 1,200 evangelists in attendance. Later in life, he served as Lecturer-at-Large for World Vision and Prison Fellowship.

Henry sought to lead biblical conservatives from overreliance on emotion toward a greater appreciation for intellection. He insisted that the Bible was a book of propositional truth from which doctrinal and moral truths flowed. This led critics to call him a "rationalist," insensitive to literary genres, paradoxicality, and accommodations to personal and cultural circumstances. Their dismissive voices grew in the years following his death, and in some camps, his views were counted passé. But others have rushed to his defense, insisting that he was indeed cognizant and appreciative of the ways in which poetry, parable, and such were intrinsic to the Bible. They've engaged the gainsayers, suggesting that enthusiasm for speech act theory, postmodernism, and other intellectual developments has clouded their understanding of and respect for Henry's contribution. Furthermore, although Henry did say that the Christian faith generates and sustains the most reasonable of worldviews, he never supposed that one reasons oneself to conversion.

Though an inerrantist with respect to the Bible, Henry did not make this the litmus test for being counted an evangelical (for this would have excluded F. F. Bruce). Neither was it sufficient, as Jehovah's Witnesses embrace the doctrine. Nevertheless, inerrancy was important to the fullest expression of evangelicalism—indeed, orthodoxy. As for the line demarcation, Henry said that an evangelical was "one who believes the evangel. The Good News is that the Holy Spirit gives spiritual life to all who repent and receive divine salvation proffered in the incarnate, crucified and risen Redeemer. The Christian message is what the inspired Scriptures teach— no more, no less—and an evangelical is a person whose life is governed by the scriptural revelation of God and His purposes" (Henry, 1976–1983: 23)

Though an American and a Baptist, his reach among evangelicals (and in defining evangelicals) was shown in his 1966 book *Fundamentals of the Faith: From Contemporary Evangelical Thought*. Therein, he published articles from Methodist, Presbyterian, and Anglican as well as Baptist scholars—and from overseas voices in Germany, Switzerland, and Australia. In this same ecumenical vein, he served as the president of both the Evangelical Theological Society and the American Theological Society. (Both Henry and Billy Graham were consistently criticized not only for their theological conservatism but also their willingness to work with those less conservative.)

Although Henry was adamant on the primacy of special, biblical revelation, he struck a middle position on general revelation and natural law. He distanced himself from Karl Barth by speaking of a created order whose outline even nonbelieving people might discern. On the other hand, he objected to the enormous confidence that such thinkers as Thomas Aquinas and Hugo Grotius placed in fallen man's ability to grasp natural law to such an extent that the Bible's moral counsel was redundant.

Though his initial study and work was among Northern (American) Baptists, Henry began his relationship with Southern Baptists when he moved to Washington to edit *Christianity Today*. There he joined Capitol Hill Baptist Church, dually aligned at the time with the Northern and Southern conventions. Thereafter, he served the Southern Baptist Convention in a number of ways: In 1985, as member of the denomination's resolution committee, he penned the statement on gender complementarianism; in 1993, he served on a committee charged with identifying threats to orthodoxy, such as annihilationism, process theology, and feministic hermeneutics, while reaffirming commitment to, among other doctrines, penal substitutionary atonement and the direct creation of Adam and Eve as real persons; also in the 1990s, he served the Ethics and Religious Liberty Commission, known for its firm stands against abortion and the homosexual agenda.

He and his wife of more than 60 years, Helga, a missionary child whom he met at Wheaton, were parents of Paul Henry, who was into his fifth term as a U.S. congressman from Michigan when he died of cancer, and Carol, a professor of music.

Centers named in his honor stand at Trinity Evangelical Divinity School, Union University, and Southern Baptist Theological Seminary. Few evangelical theologians have had as great an influence on American evangelicalism as has Henry. His legacy is enormous, and his writings remain relevant to American evangelicalism and theological thought in the present century.

Mark Coppenger

See also: Baptists and Evangelicalism; Bible, Authority of; *Christianity Today*; Evangelicalism; Evangelical Theological Society; Graham, William F., Jr. ("Billy"); Inerrancy; Neo-Evangelicalism; Premillennialism; *The Uneasy Conscience of Modern Fundamentalism*; World Vision International

Further Reading

Henry, Carl F. H. *The Uneasy Conscience of Modern Fundamentalism.* Grand Rapids, MI: Eerdmans, 1947.

Henry, Carl F. H. *God, Revelation, and Authority.* 6 vol. Waco, TX: Word Books, 1976–1983.

Henry, Carl F. H. *Confessions of a Theologian: An Autobiography.* Waco, TX: Word Books, 1986.

Henry, Carl. *Carl Henry at His Best: A Lifetime of Quotable Thoughts.* Foreword by Charles Colson. Portland, OR: Multnomah, 1989.

Marsden, George M. *Reforming Fundamentalism: Fuller Seminary and the New Evangelicalism.* Grand Rapids, MI: Eerdmans, 1987.

Miller, Steven P. *The Age of Evangelicalism: America's Born-Again Years.* New York: Oxford University Press, 2014.

Patterson, Bob E. *Carl F. H. Henry.* Waco, TX: Word Books, 1983.

Thornbury, Gregory. *Recovering Classic Evangelicalism: Applying the Wisdom and Vision of Carl F. H. Henry.* Wheaton, IL: Crossway, 2013.

Wright, Doyle, G. *Carl Henry: Theologian for All Seasons.* Eugene, OR: Wipf & Stock/Pickwick, 2010.

HERMENEUTICS

The term *hermeneutics* refers to the general study of the theory of interpretation as it applies particularly to the Biblical text. This includes the entire process of reading and interpreting Scripture, as well as the application of any specific rules or methodologies. The study of hermeneutics is closely related to practice of exegesis, which is more narrowly understood as the application of specific principals, methods, and strategies of interpretation. Thus, although the study of hermeneutics includes applied exegetical methods, it also considers the general theological and philosophical perspectives that inform any particular methodology. In general, study of hermeneutics involves analyzing the complex relationship between an author, a particular text, and the original and subsequent readers of the text. Evaluating this dynamic relationship includes giving significant attention to the intentions of the author (both the human and divine Author) and what they hoped to communicate through their text. At the same time, the precise linguistic, grammatical, and syntactical features of any passage should be studied intensely. Finally, some consideration must be given to the original readers of the text and the way they might have understood the author's communication. This last feature is also helpful for discerning the way that the text applies to a contemporary audience. Of course the study of any text, including its author and audience, also assumes that the meaning of a text is accessible and that there are both good and bad interpretations of the text. Evangelicals readily affirm that no interpreter comes to Scripture from a purely objective and neutral vantage point. Anyone who reads scripture applies some kind of hermeneutic, whether he or she acknowledges it or not. Evangelicals are vigilant that they do not impose meaning on scripture, but instead work to understand the meaning expressed in the writings by God through the particular prophets and apostles.

Evangelicals recognize that their views on hermeneutics participate in conversation about Biblical interpretation that spans the life of the church. In the early days of the church, Christians emphasized reading Scripture in continuity with the rule of faith. This rule was a theological summary of the work of God in Christ and the Spirit. Scriptural interpretation, therefore, gave great attention to the person and work of Christ and the ongoing ministry of the Spirit as it was expressed in the Scriptures. Ancient Scripture readers readily applied a variety of methods of interpretation, especially the practice of typological and allegorical reading. The literal interpretation, however, was not lost, which is evidenced in the so-called distinction between the Alexandrian school that emphasized the allegorical sense and the Antiochene school that stressed the literal sense. During the time of the medieval church, these hermeneutical debates culminated into the development of what is known as the fourfold method of interpretation including the literal, allegorical, tropological, and anagogical sense of Scripture. The Protestant Reformers largely rejected this strict classification and argued that Scriptural interpretation was not nearly this complicated. They emphasized the general perspicuity, or clarity, of Scripture and the single meaning of a text within its original historical context. This emphasis on the historicity of the text prepared the way for the rise of higher criticism in contemporary hermeneutics. Many modern Biblical scholars reject the divine inspiration of the Scripture and study the texts like any other historical document. They apply a variety of critical theories that have further isolated the historical and literal interpretations of the texts.

For its part, Evangelical hermeneutics is indebted to this stream of dialogue and debate in the history of Biblical interpretation. For Evangelicals, any hermeneutical theory must function in harmony with a robust view of the inspiration, inerrancy, and authority of Scripture. Scripture is given by God and entirely truthful in all that it affirms. From the earliest days of the church, any applied method of interpretation functioned under the assumption of the inspiration of Scripture. In related fashion, Evangelicals also emphasize the perspicuity, or essential clarity, of Scripture, and the importance of the internal testimony of the Spirit as a guide for interpretation. Only those who are indwelt with the Spirit of God are adequately positioned to receive and interpret Scripture rightly, particularly as it pertains to the person and work of Christ. At the same time, Evangelicals also emphasize the importance of the internal consistency of divine revelation. Because all Scripture has been given by God, this verbal revelation is entirely consistent, and therefore Scripture is the best interpreter of Scripture. Certainly extra-biblical documentation can be helpful for clarifying the meaning of Scripture, but it does not hold priority over inspired Scripture.

More specifically, Evangelicals most commonly interpret scripture using a historical-grammatical method of exegesis, which stresses the important of the original historical context of the writings and the careful analysis of its literary features. This also implies that the Bible should be interpreted according to its literal sense, properly understood, with an emphasis on the authorial intention (especially the divine Author). Certainly the Spirit of God used the unique personalities of the writers, who employed various kinds of literary devices and strategies. These include figures of speech and other literary forms that should be understood according to their particular genres and conventions. Evangelicals also acknowledge that in certain cases the divine Author can intended a fuller meaning, or what is known as *sensus plenior*, that is not always evident to the human authors. These instances are common among prophetic and typological passages that correspond to the person and work of Christ. Finally, for Evangelicals Biblical authority is essential for hermeneutics. Any application of a hermeneutical theory also demands that the interpreter submit to the teachings of Scripture derived from the process of interpretation. The most important application of the hermeneutical process is when the faith and practice of the interpreter or the audience are brought into harmony with the teaching of Scripture.

Stephen O. Presley

See also: Bible, Authority of; Bible Exposition

Further Reading

Kaiser, Walter C., Jr., and Moisés Silva. *Introduction to Biblical Hermeneutics: The Search for Meaning.* Grand Rapids, MI: Zondervan, 2007.

Köstenberger, Andreas J., and Richard Patterson. *Invitation to Biblical Interpretation: Exploring the Hermeneutical Triad of History, Literature, and Theology.* Grand Rapids, MI: Kregel Academic, 2011.

Osborne, Grant R. *The Hermeneutical Spiral: A Comprehensive Introduction to Biblical Interpretation.* Grand Rapids, MI: Baker Academic, 2007.

Ramm, Bernard. *Protestant Biblical Interpretation: A Textbook of Hermeneutics.* Grand Rapids, MI: Baker Academic, 1980.

Zuck, Roy B. *Basic Bible Interpretation: A Practical Guide to Discovering Biblical Truth.* Colorado Springs, CO: David C. Cook, 1991.

HIGHER EDUCATION, EVANGELICALS AND

Evangelicals have had a long and varied association with higher education, with greater emphasis being placed on it in the last 75 years in the United States. Due in part to the primacy of the written and printed word in Protestantism since the Reformation, and especially the role of the sermon and the Bible in worship and study, literacy has been important for evangelicals. Primary and secondary education has been viewed as integral to Christian education and spiritual formation, and to the many churches and denominations of which evangelicals have been and are participants or spiritual heirs. Anglican, Reformed, and Lutheran traditions have strong emphases on education, but on the whole, that has not been bridged into evangelical institutions of higher education other than seminaries and a few colleges. However, there are notable institutions of higher education among some evangelical and theologically conservative denominations. Evangelicals have been more engaged in individual higher education endeavors than in institutional endeavors.

Since the colonial days, America has had a large concentration of evangelical colleges, universities, and seminaries, but the history has been fragmented. In part this is due to the loss of denominational influence and power by Protestant conservatives during the Fundamentalist-Modernist religious controversy of the 1920s and 1930s, and in part, it is due to an emphasis by American evangelicals on evangelism rather than education in the first half of the 20th century. With respect to higher education and denominational affiliation, many fundamentalists and evangelicals were either forced out of or left their denominations in disputes over theology, missions, and what the conservatives believed to be encroaching liberalism and a departure from Christian orthodoxy. In so doing, they also severed ties with denominational colleges and universities and lacked resources to establish educational alternatives.

At the same time, the evangelical emphasis on Bible institutes and Bible colleges was motivated by a desire to train students for various aspects of Christian ministry and missions. Often this arose out of the revivalistic and evangelistic impulses of the era, such as with the work of Dwight L. Moody (1837–1899) and the establishment of Moody Bible Institute.

Critiques of evangelical higher education have come from within the evangelical culture. In 1994, highly respected evangelical historian Mark A. Noll published a critique of American evangelical scholarship sharply criticizing evangelicals for their lack of developing a comprehensive worldview and fully engaging the culture and academia. In the work *The Scandal of the Evangelical Mind*, he noted that there was not a single Christian research university. His evaluation was not new, and evangelical leaders since the 1940s had encouraged the establishment of a world-class evangelical research university. Such an establishment was long the dream of leaders such as Carl F. H. Henry, Harold John Ockenga, and Bill Bright, and met with several false starts over the decades primarily because of lack of sustained funding and endowment. On an individual level, many evangelicals receive graduate and doctoral degrees at renowned universities in the United States and abroad and have done so since the 1940s.

More recently, externally there have been attempts at legislation in some American states to revoke the accreditation of any Christian higher education institution that does not accept the worldview of the secular state and which teaches distinctly Christian values. Though some institutions have opted for the safer secular route, traditional Christian higher education institutions still thrive and are still being started across the country. Some scholars argue that evangelical institutions of higher education are detrimental to a true liberal education and are the result of a defensive stance to protect long-held religious traditions and promote a series of narrow legalistic views and doctrines. Evangelicals counter that fact, stating that evangelical institutions seek to defend the historic Christian faith over and against other institutes that promote different values and worldviews, and this should come as no surprise and be of no offense in a tolerant and pluralistic society.

In America, several institutions have risen to the forefront of evangelical education. Wheaton College in Illinois has a long history in evangelicalism, dating from 1860, and more recently Liberty University in Lynchburg, Virginia, founded in 1971, remains popular. In addition to denominational schools such as the seminaries of the Southern Baptist Convention, like Southwestern Baptist Theological Seminary and The Southern Baptist Theological Seminary, other institutions such as Dallas Theological Seminary, The Master's Seminary, Gordon-Conwell Theological Seminary, Talbot School of Theology, Trinity Evangelical Divinity School, Beeson School of Divinity, Westminster Theological Seminary, Reformed Seminary, Calvin Theological Seminary, and Fuller Theological Seminary are among the major centers of evangelical theological scholarship across the spectrum of evangelicalism. A host of smaller schools continue the evangelical traditions, and schools such as Southern Evangelical Seminary in North Carolina as well as Biola University in California have graduate programs specializing in apologetics and philosophy.

Defenders of evangelical higher education continue to reaffirm that the entire movement was designed to offer liberal arts education from a Christian worldview. Evangelicals contend that in a pluralistic society, such a foundation should be seen as one of the many possible foundations for the liberal arts and should therefore be included and protected as other institutions.

Evangelical universities, seminaries, and Bible colleges continue to thrive in the midst of challenges. Many institutions have created branch campuses throughout the country (and overseas) and, like most institutions, are creating online educational opportunities. Evangelicals continue to start, support, and encourage involvement in higher education more so than in previous years and across all disciplines and professions.

Thomas McCuddy

See also: Bible Institutes and Bible Colleges; Gordon College; Harvard Evangelicals; Henry, Carl F. H.; Liberty University; Moody, Dwight Lyman; Moody Bible Institute; Wheaton College

Further Reading

House, G. K. "Evangelical Higher Education: History, Mission, Identity, and Future." *Journal of Catholic Education* 6, no. 4 (2003). http://digitalcommons.lmu.edu/ce/vol6/iss4/6.
Mayers, Marvin. *Reshaping Evangelical Higher Education.* Grand Rapids, MI: Zondervan, 1972.
Noll, Mark A. *The Scandal of the Evangelical Mind.* Grand Rapids, MI: Eerdmans, 1994.
Stroop, Christopher. "Special Report: Have Evangelical Colleges Succumbed to 'Theological Paranoia'?" *Religion Dispatches.* (January 19, 2016). http://religiondispatches.org/special-report-have-evangelical-colleges-succumbed-to-theological-paranoia/.

HISPANIC AMERICAN EVANGELICALS

Hispanic evangelicalism in the 21st century has found significant expression in American evangelicalism, and Hispanic evangelicalism has become a movement that is influencing Latino Americans in unprecedented ways. Some of its representatives, weary of cultural change, traditional values being mocked, dysfunctional families, and a people group being marginalized, are not only generating a type of Hispanic evangelical movement but are also affecting American life with social initiatives, gospel crusades, and the arts.

Reverend Samuel Rodriguez (1969–) is considered by CNN, Fox News, NBC/Telemundo, *Time* magazine, and *The Wall Street Journal* to be the most influential contemporary Hispanic evangelical leader. Rodriguez is known for merging Billy Graham's passion for evangelism with Martin Luther King Jr.'s aim for social justice activism. Seven directives drive his ministry: life, family, compassionate evangelism, stewardship, justice, education, and youth. Several ministries have birthed from Rodriguez's directives, including ministries geared toward ending human trafficking, helping people see their equality and value in the eyes of God, empowering evangelicals to surface as key voices in all spheres of society, and various other ministries. Rodriguez is president of the National Hispanic Christian Leadership Conference (NHCLC), established in 2001 and now considered the nation's largest Hispanic Christian organization, representing more than 40,000 churches and evangelicals ranging in the millions. As the leading spokesperson for the Hispanic Evangelicals and a conservative Republican, Rev. Samuel Rodriguez has been a featured speaker at the White House for topics on social justice and Latinos. Consequently, he has consulted with members of both the Senate and House of Representatives. Rodriguez is also the recipient of several awards such as the Martin Luther King Jr.

Leadership Award on Racial Equality. He is an accomplished writer and author, and is currently the senior pastor of New Season Christian Worship Center in Sacramento, California. Samuel and his wife, Eva, have been married 24 years and are the parents of three children.

Wilfredo De Jesús, also known as Pastor Choco, is pastor of New Life Covenant Church in Chicago, Illinois, which is one of the fastest growing churches in Chicago and the largest Assemblies of God Church in America. Pastor Choco became the senior pastor of New Life Covenant Church in 2000. Under his pastorate, the church has grown from 120 worshippers to 17,000 each week. De Jesús was named one of *Time* magazine's 100 most influential people in the world. New Life Covenant Church has more than 130 ministries and is heavily involved in the community, offering a wide array of ministries to those in need. For example, they have rehabilitation centers for prostitutes and drug addicts, help to those who are trying to find a way out of gangs, and a homeless shelter for women and children. Pastor Choco also dedicates himself to developing others in pastoral leadership through his Jumpstart Pastors and Leaders school, which hosts churches throughout the United States for a three-day conference. De Jesús formerly served as vice president of Social Justice for the National Hispanic Christian Leadership Conference. He has been featured on the cover of The Latino Reformation and *Time* magazine, and has authored *Amazing Faith: How To Make God Take Notice* (2012) and *In the Gap: What Happens When God's People Stand Strong* (2014). De Jesús resides in Chicago with his wife, Elizabeth, and their three children.

Luis Palau (1934–), a prominent Hispanic evangelical leader likened to Billy Graham (1918–), is a Christian evangelist who has shared the gospel of Jesus Christ with more than 25 million people in 70 nations, and has had more than a million recorded converts. Luis hosts a radio program that is heard in both English and Spanish in 42 countries. He has authored a total of 50 books, including *God's Grace* (2007), *High Definition Life* (2005), *God is Relevant* (1997), and *The Only Hope for America* (1996). Billy Graham played a significant role in Palau's life, and like Graham, Palau's dream is to see millions discover the benefits of conversion. He continues his ministry through the Luis Palau Association, which has more than 100 full-time staff in four continents, including three of his own sons.

Damond A. Horton, an author, speaker, artist, and preacher, has served as National Coordinator for Urban Student missions at the North American Mission Board (NAMB). He has also served as executive director at ReachLife Ministries, which is a partner of the well-known Christian hip-hop label Reach Records. Horton is a church planter by heart and has used his communication skills as a rap artist to engage the hip-hop culture. He does this by communicating biblical principles to an urban setting. Horton is also recognized for his passion for urban apologetics, wherein he addresses theological missteps such as the prosperity gospel and liberation theology, both of which are prevalent in the Latino evangelical churches. Horton carries a very influential voice among American Hispanics today through his preaching and seminary teaching. He earned his BS in biblical studies from Calvary Bible College and his master's degree in Christian studies from Calvary Theological Seminary. He is currently pursuing a PhD at Southeastern Baptist Theological Seminary while serving as pastor of Reach Fellowship, a church plant in Long Beach, California. He has authored three books: *G.O.S.P.E.L.* (2012), *DNA: Foundations of the Faith* (2013), and *Bound to be Free: Escaping Performance to be Captured by Grace* (2016). He and his wife, Elicia, have three children, two daughters and one son.

J. L. Escobar, also known as Brother Jay, founded TrueVoices in January 2012. Escobar wanted to create a platform in which people could meet in everyday common places and use the arts to communicate a Christ-centered message that will positively impact lives. From his vision, he created the first TrueVoices event in his hometown, South Bronx, New York. TrueVoices allows Christian artists to express their faith bodily through the arts, and this platform for Christian poetry and performing arts has now taken root in much of the culture across the nation. There are now TrueVoices events being held in Chicago; New Jersey; Washington, D.C.; Cincinnati; and Philadelphia. TrueVoices sponsors monthly poetry clubs for people ages 16–24, as well as TrueVoices Outdoors, which emphasizes reaching people through the spoken word in everyday places. TrueVoices hosts an annual conference named Proclaim that is rated as the largest Christian poetry and performing arts event on the East Coast. Escobar's focus extends to all ethnicities and people groups.

Hispanic evangelicalism is emerging in the United States in recent years because of key leaders such as the ones mentioned above. They are offering an evangelical voice not only to the Hispanic community but also to society as a whole by meeting people's practical needs and creating a national organization for Hispanic evangelicals through gospel crusades, hip-hop, and opportunities to reach young people through the arts in urban settings. As a result, Hispanic evangelicals are the largest growing ethnic group within American evangelicalism.

Matias Perez

See also: Evangelicalism; Fundamentalism; Graham, William F., Jr. ("Billy"); Social Action, Evangelicals and; Sojourners

Further Reading

Ballor, Jordan J., and Robert Joustra, eds. *The Church's Social Responsibility: Reflections on Evangelicalism and Social Justice.* Grand Rapids, MI: Christian Library's Press, 2015.

Gasaway, Brantley. *Progressive Evangelicals and the Pursuit of Social Justice.* Chapel Hill, NC: The University of North Carolina Press, 2014.

Palau, Luis. *The Luis Palau Story: An Autobiography.* Grand Rapids, MI: Revell, 1980.

Soong-Chan Rah. *The Next Evangelicalism: Freeing the Church from Western Cultural Captivity.* Downers Grove, IL: InterVarsity Press, 2009.

Soong-Chan Rah. *Many Colors: Cultural Intelligence for a Changing Church.* Chicago: Moody Press, 2010.

HOMESCHOOLING, EVANGELICALS AND

Evangelical homeschooling education has been growing since the 1980s, when many evangelical Christian parents, in reaction to the secularization of the public education system, started educating their children at home with their own chosen curriculum and their own personal values. The conflict between home and school occurs primarily in terms of the secular humanistic worldview of the public schools compared to the conservative Christian worldview of most homeschoolers. Although not all homeschooling families choose to do so for religious reasons, often citing educational goals or health issues, many homeschooling families wish to incorporate Christian thought into all the sciences and humanities, not just add a "Bible class" into their curriculum.

With its inception in the 1980s, evangelicals that chose to homeschool faced much well-documented opposition. Socially, homeschooling parents faced peer pressure from other parents who neither shared evangelical values nor understood the purposes of reacting against the public education system. Homeschooling children were often criticized as antisocial or abnormal children due to "lack of socialization." TV shows and movies in the 1980s and 1990s would use homeschooled children as the strange, awkward stereotype.

In addition to social pressure, parents faced litigation from the state. Districts that refused to acknowledge homeschooling as a legitimate educational system would charge homeschooling parents with truancy violations. Many homeschooling families were taken to court, where they had to fight for their right to educate their own children.

Eventually, the homeschooling families would win, and today the homeschooling movement grows nearly unhindered. For example, in North Carolina, the homeschooling associations won a major battle in the state supreme court, and now regulations are the most lenient in the entire country. This means parents have total freedom in how they choose to educate their children. Other states impose light regulations such as requiring homeschooling children to take standardized tests, or parents to submit records as evidence of education, but at the present time, Evangelicals enjoy nearly unrestricted liberty in the realm of homeschooling, something unknown just 30 years ago.

When it comes to homeschooling, evangelicals have a wide range of curriculum choices to replace the public school options, and the number continues to grow. Curriculum choices lie on a spectrum from most rigorous and structured, to loose, "life lessons" curricula. On the stricter end is material like Classical Conversations, which, like many similar classical-styled curricula, seeks to educate children in the classical manner, using the trivium and emphasizing rote memory. The trivium is comprised of grammar, logic, and rhetoric, and was the method of choice during the medieval period. For over a thousand years, the trivium and its complement, the quadrivium of arithmetic, geometry, music, and astronomy, provided a classic, liberal arts education. Such education is growing among evangelical homeschooling families, especially those connected with reformed theology.

The more middle-ranged curriculum, which would mirror more of the public school system of education, includes material produced by Apologia Press as well as Abeka. Both curriculums and those like them look and feel most like the form of traditional education, and such materials are even used by accredited private Christian schools.

On the other end of the spectrum are the less structured, more life-style methods of education called "unschooling." These families may not even opt for any formal curriculums, instead choosing to learn skills in life through working with family members and traveling to educational venues like museums and planetariums, as well as studying and reading what is perceived as most useful and enjoyable. Such methods have been utilized not just by evangelicals but also by parents whose children possess severe learning disabilities that prevent them from learning in the traditional fashion.

The results of the evangelical homeschooling movement are controversial. On the one side, critics have painted a picture of brainwashed, uneducated children living in compounds and having no contact with the outside world. Numerous blog articles cite specific instances of mothers who were deceived by the homeschooling movement and had terrible experiences with their children. However, on the other hand, many evangelicals cite test scores as a predominate benchmark of the success of the homeschooling movement, as test scores seem to be the primary benchmark for the public school system. On average, homeschooled children perform about two grade levels above their peers. Additionally, research has surprisingly shown that academic achievement is generally unrelated to socioeconomic status, unlike achievement in the public school. In fact, many well-respected colleges cater to homeschooling students because of the typical high performance found within the pool of students.

Evangelicals began homeschooling in order to raise their children as they chose, educate them according to the truth of Scripture, and fight the secular worldview exclusively promoted through the secular public school system. But evangelicals are not alone, as a growing portion of the homeschooled population is not religious in nature. The homeschool movement itself is not slowing down, but growing in influence, and the quality of education continues to increase and stand as a legitimate means of educating children.

Thomas McCuddy

See also: Higher Education, Evangelicals and

Further Reading

Apple, Michael W. *Gender, Religion and Education in a Chaotic Postmodern World.* Dordrecht: Springer, 2013.

Bauer, Susan Wise, and Jessie Wise. *The Well-Trained Mind: A Guide to Classical Education at Home.* New York: W.W. Norton, 2009.

Brown, Teri J. *Christian Unschooling.* Naperville, IL: Sourcebooks, 2003.

Jeynes, William. *International Handbook of Protestant Education.* Dordrecht: Springer, 2012.
Sherfinski, Melissa. "Contextualizing the Tools of a Classical and Christian Homeschooling Mother-Teacher." *Curriculum Inquiry* 44, no. 2 (January 7, 2015): 169–203.

HUMAN RIGHTS, EVANGELICALS AND

American evangelicals have been activists in human rights with varying levels of intensity and commitment. Although there has been a long-standing theological commitment to human rights and specific declarations of evangelical support dating to the mid-1950s, human rights as a cause has often been issue specific within the domain of human rights, rather than broad lobbying for all human rights. Evangelicals have also been criticized by some for ambivalence or lack of activism in the realm of human rights. However, evangelical theologians such as Carl F. H. Henry (1913–2003) and John Warwick Montgomery (1931–) have long included human rights as part of their writing and work. In recent decades, evangelical voices from the left of the political spectrum have consistently spoken against abuses in human rights by many nations, including the United States. Evangelical support for religious freedom has been very strong, as has evangelical activism against human trafficking. A number of evangelical organizations such as the National Association of Evangelicals and Evangelicals for Human Rights have garnered evangelical support for human rights.

Evangelical support for human rights is grounded in Judeo-Christian values and an understanding of every person being created in the image of God (*imago Dei*), as found in Genesis 1:27. For evangelicals, rights are understood as being divinely given prerogatives based on human dignity and grounded in the belief that human beings are created in the image of God and bear that image in a world marred and distorted by sin. It is the responsibility of governments to uphold the rights of every individual. Evangelicals acknowledge that the issue of diversity rights is enormous, and accept the framework of the development and recognition of the human rights framework as being generational; that is, having been developed in international

---

Dealing with Doubt and Disappointment with God

Os Guinness, *God in the Dark: The Assurance of Faith Beyond a Shadow of Doubt* (1996)

Gary Habermas, *Dealing with Doubt* (1990)

Alister McGrath, *Doubting: Growing through the Uncertainties of Faith* (1990, 2006)

Kenneth Richard Samples, *Without a Doubt: Answering the 20 Toughest Faith Questions* (2004)

Philip Yancey, *Disappointment with God: Three Questions No One Asks Aloud* (1988, 1992)

law and practice in stages. Among the many topics evangelicals have addressed that relate directly and indirectly to human rights are race relations, torture, religious freedom, immigration, prison reform, abortion, euthanasia, international trade, status of women, treatment of aboriginal and native peoples, AIDS, medicine, health care, legal and court procedures, political processes and voting, housing, animals, environmental concerns, sexual orientation, education, water and natural resources, slavery, and human trafficking.

Evangelicals believe that human rights are of monumental social, legal, political, and theological importance, and that to live as a Christian in the modern world and fully engage in political discourse and action, one must take seriously the promotion of human rights and the application of biblical truth to every area of life.

Timothy J. Demy

See also: Foreign Policy, Evangelicals and; Henry, Carl F. H.; Sider, Ronald James

Further Reading

Montgomery, John Warwick. *Human Rights & Human Dignity*, rev. ed. Edmonton: Canadian Institute for Law, Theology & Public Policy, 2007.

Nichols, Joel A. "Evangelicals and Human Rights: The Continuing Ambivalence of Evangelical Christians' Support for Human Rights." *Journal of Law and Religion* 24:2 (2008–2009): 629–692.

Witte, John, Jr. *God's Joust, God's Justice: Law and Religion in the Western Tradition.* Grand Rapids, MI: Eerdmans, 2006.

INERRANCY

Debate about the inspiration and inerrancy of the Bible was prominent in American evangelicalism in the 1970s and 1980s, and emerged again in the second decade of the 21st century. Inerrancy is the idea that the Scripture does not err in anything that it teaches, be it about the physical origins of the world, the history of God's acts in the world, or God's revelation of His will and ways. Inerrancy is usually understood to apply to the original manuscripts of the Biblical books. It does not rule out the presence of scribal errors in copies of the Biblical texts, nor does it affirm the accuracy of any particular translation of the original Hebrew and Greek texts of Scripture into other languages.

Inerrancy affirms the truth-telling function of the Bible without denying that it conveys truth through different kinds of literature and literary devices. Rather than requiring technically precise philosophical or scientific language, it is consistent with the range of ordinary human language, including the use of metaphor, parable, hyperbole, poetic imagery, sarcasm, and other literary devices. Inerrancy is also understood to be consistent with interpretive or loose quotation and uncommon grammar.

Inerrancy is sometimes equated with infallibility and sometimes distinguished from it. Authors who distinguish the two often affirm that the Bible is infallible with

Handling Bible Difficulties

Although evangelicals widely believe that the original autographs, that is, the original manuscript documents, are completely without error, contending that the originals are preserved in the copies (there is less than 1% of textual variance between copies), evangelicals differ on how to handle Bible difficulties such as differing accounts of the same event (e.g., the death of Judas Iscariot). Three views dominate: the abstract approach by B. B. Warfield (1851–1921); the harmonistic approach by Norman L. Geisler (1932–); and the moderate harmonistic approach by Everett F. Harrison (1902–1999). Although admitting that there are difficulties, the abstract approach states that the weight of evidence for inspiration and inerrancy is so great that no matter the difficulty of the textual issue in the Bible, the evidence favors reliability. The harmonistic approach uses conjecture to resolve difficulties, whereas the moderate harmonistic approach seeks to relieve those difficulties but attempts to restrain conjecture to only the information that is currently available.

respect to doctrine and morality, but allow that it can contain historical or scientific errors. Evangelicals have typically insisted that inerrancy extends beyond doctrine and morality to all that the Bible affirms, noting that Christianity's status as a historical faith means that historical error would ultimately undercut theological doctrine, as would errant assertions that implicate God's status as Creator of heaven and earth.

As a doctrine, evangelicals note that inerrancy arises from the Bible's affirmation of its own nature. All Scripture is "God-breathed" (2 Timothy 3:16), and because "it is impossible for God to lie" (Hebrews 6:18), one should conclude that "every word of God is pure" (Proverbs 30:5). In one of the most direct Biblical statements to this effect, Christ prayed that God would sanctify His followers by the truth, and added "Your word is truth" (John 17:17).

Evangelicals also appeal to the way in which Christ's use of Scripture demonstrates His confidence in its truthfulness. In a dispute with the Pharisees, Jesus argued that because Scripture as a whole "cannot be broken" (John 10:35, i.e., it speaks truthfully), then each of its affirmations must be true (John 10:35). In another setting, He also implied the truthfulness of the whole of Scripture when He affirmed that not the smallest part would "pass away" (Matthew 5:17–18).

Though affirmation of the inerrancy of Scripture is a hallmark of contemporary evangelical thought, it has been affirmed by Christian theologians since the second century. Irenaeus of Lyons (ca. 130–ca. 200 CE) affirmed that "the Holy Scriptures are perfect, because they are spoken by the Word of God and the Spirit of God" (*Adversus Haereses* 2.47). Augustine of Hippo (354–430 CE) wrote, "No one of those authors has erred in any respect in writing" (*Epistolae* 82.1.3). In the Middle Ages, Anselm (1033–1109) advanced an argument for the complete truthfulness of the Bible that was based on the deity of Christ and Christ's affirmation of the truthfulness of the Scriptures. Anselm wrote, "Therefore, just as it is necessary to affirm that He was truthful, so no one can deny the truth of anything contained in these testaments" (*Cur Deus Homo*, II. 22). Thomas Aquinas (1224–1274) also insisted, "The sacred Scriptures must manifest the truth correctly, without error of any kind" (*Summa Theologica*, I.1.10, ad.1).

The Reformer John Calvin (1509–1564) taught that the Bible is the "pure word of God" (*Institutes of the Christian Religion*, IV.8.9). In the early modern era, John Wesley (1703–1791) preached that "If there be one error in Scripture, there might as well be a thousand. If there was any error in this book, it did not come from the God of truth" (*The Journal of John Wesley*, 6:117).

In the 20th century, the rejection of the truthfulness of the Bible by both mainline Protestant scholars and secular writers in the United States led to renewed evangelical emphasis on the doctrine of inerrancy. Monographs on the subject peaked in the mid-1970s with Francis Schaeffer's *No Final Conflict* (1975), Harold Lindsell's *The Battle for the Bible* (1976), and Carl H. F. Henry's six-volume work *God, Revelation, and Authority* (1976–1983).

Ultimately, evangelical scholarship on inerrancy led to the convening of the International Council on Biblical Inerrancy in Chicago in the fall of 1978. This conference

---

Resources Evangelicals Widely Use to Deal with Bible Difficulties

Gleason P. Archer, *New International Encyclopedia of Bible Difficulties* (2001).

Norman Geisler and Thomas Howe, *The Big Book of Bible Difficulties: Clear and Concise Answers from Genesis to Revelation* (2008).

Walter C. Kaiser Jr., Peter H. Davids, F. F. Bruce, and Manfred Brauch, *Hard Sayings of the Bible* (1996).

---

published the Chicago Statement on Biblical Inerrancy, signed by more than 300 evangelical scholars. The body of the statement includes a short summary of the doctrine, an extended set of paired affirmations and denials, and a concluding exposition of the doctrine. The International Council on Biblical Inerrancy disbanded in 1988 after producing further statements on the interpretation of the Bible (1982) and principles for applying the Bible (1986).

The period from 1970–2000 also saw several denominations, such as the Missouri Synod Lutherans, reaffirm the doctrine of inerrancy. Most notably, the Southern Baptist Convention, America's largest Protestant denomination, began a multidecade process of restoring the commitment of its six seminaries to the inerrancy of the Bible. At the 2000 Baptist Faith and Message Convention, the description of the Bible as "truth, without any mixture of error" (Southern Baptist Convention, n.d.) was affirmed as an inerrancy statement.

Evangelical insistence on the inerrancy of Scripture has functioned apologetically as a primary defense of the unique authority of Scripture for Christianity. Tradition, Creeds, and the teaching of any individual are subordinate to the Scripture in that they can err, whereas Scripture cannot. This affirmation does not, however, mean that such sources are to be automatically rejected as fatally flawed. Instead, they have value as they accurately reflect what the Bible itself teaches. As a practical matter, evangelicals have argued that rejection of the complete truthfulness of the Bible leaves each Christian and Christian group to decide for themselves which parts of the Bible to believe and which to reject. The inevitable result of this, it is asserted, is that individuals and groups that find themselves convicted or discomforted by various teachings in the Bible will more readily reject those teachings of Scripture as being in error.

The doctrine of the inerrancy of Scripture has wide-ranging impact on evangelicals. Inerrancy motivates evangelical scholarship aimed at establishing the original text of the Bible, a field of study known as textual criticism. Evangelical affirmations of inerrancy mean that the study of biblical interpretation continues to be a productive area of scholarship for evangelicals. It also drives evangelical biblical scholars to continue to test interpretations of Scripture against the text itself and to pursue the study of difficult texts in the Bible.

Finally, the doctrine of the inerrancy of Scripture tends to foster humility among evangelicals. Because Scripture alone is considered to be inerrant, evangelicals are more apt to distinguish between the text of Scripture itself and human interpretations of the Bible, including their own. This helps evangelicals be open to critique and new scholarship but also remain resistant to abandoning the teachings of the Bible where they conflict with contemporary cultural values and agendas.

Benjamin Blair Phillips

See also: Authority, Bible of; *The Battle for the Bible*; Bible Conference Movement; Bible Exposition; Bible Institutes and Colleges; Christian Apologetics; Criswell, W. A.; Geisler, Norman L.; Henry, Carl F. H.; Hermeneutics; Institute for Creation Research; Lindsell, Harold; Schaeffer, Francis A. and Edith; Theological Controversies within Evangelicalism

Further Reading

Beale, Gregory K. *The Erosion of Inerrancy in Evangelicalism: Responding to New Challenges to Biblical Authority.* Wheaton, IL: Crossway, 2008.

Blomberg, Craig. *Can We Still Believe the Bible? An Evangelical Engagement with Contemporary Questions.* Grand Rapids, MI: Brazos Press, 2014.

Bruce, F. F. *The New Testament Manuscripts: Are They Reliable?* Grand Rapids, MI: Eerdmans, 2003.

The Chicago Statement on Biblical Inerrancy. (n.d.). The Evangelical Society. Accessed April 29, 2017. http://www.etsjets.org/files/documents/Chicago_Statement.pdf.

Geisler, Norman. *Biblical Errancy: An Analysis of Its Philosophical Roots.* Eugene, OR: Wipf & Stock, 2004.

Geisler, Norman. *Defending Inerrancy: Affirming the Accuracy of Scripture for a New Generation.* Grand Rapids, MI: Baker Books, 2012.

Hannah, John D. *Inerrancy and the Church.* Chicago, IL: Moody Press, 1984.

Henry, Carl F. H. *God, Revelation, and Authority.* 6 vols. Waco, TX: Word Books, 1976–1983.

Linnemann, Eta. *Historical Criticism of the Bible: Methodology or Ideology: Reflections of a Bultmannian Turned Evangelical.* Grand Rapids, MI: Kregel, 2001.

Merrick, J., and Stephen Garrett, eds. *Five Views on Biblical Inerrancy.* Grand Rapids, MI: Zondervan, 2013.

Southern Baptist Convention. "Basic Beliefs." (n.d.). Accessed April 29, 2017. http://www.sbc.net/aboutus/basicbeliefs.asp.

Wallace, Daniel B., ed. *Revisiting the Corruption of the New Testament: Manuscript, Patristic, and Apocryphal Evidence (Text and Canon of the New Testament).* Grand Rapids. MI: Kregel, 2011.

INFERTILITY, EVANGELICALS AND

Evangelicals are generally pro-marriage, and they believe children are a gift—even if not *the* gift. Thus, for them infertility can be a particularly painful crisis.

Infertility is the inability to conceive or carry a baby to term after one year of unprotected intercourse. Secondary infertility is the diagnosis couples receive when they have had one or more children but are unable to conceive or carry to term again.

More than half of all couples who seek medical treatment will go on to have a bio-logical child. The percentage of those who go on to have children is significantly lower among those who do not pursue treatment. A disproportionate number of evangeli-cals fall in the latter category. Some believe seeking medical treatment for fertility issues represents a lack of faith. Others recognize the significant moral issues related to assisted reproductive technologies (ARTs) and choose to stay away from fertility clinics, which usually engage in practices that might violate their consciences.

Since the Old Testament days of Sarah and Abraham; Jacob, Rachel, and Leah; and Hannah and Elkanah, infertility has affected God's people. In fact, it appears to have been a common affliction among the righteous. Evangelicals, particularly non-Pentecostals, generally consider infertility to be one of the results of The Fall and not necessarily the fault of the sufferer. Nevertheless, many still hesitate to seek med-ical attention.

Until the 1980s, Christian perspectives regarding infertility were difficult to find in written and spoken word. Within the past three decades, however, numerous resources and ministries have been created to minister to the infertile. Evangelicals do face numerous ethical considerations if they pursue medical treatment, because of their belief that life begins at fertilization. Some Christians believe that produc-ing a semen sample by masturbation is morally wrong. Most believe that when mas-turbation is performed with a good goal of having a child or helping determine a diagnosis, there is no harm unless the husband is lustful in the process.

Because fertility drugs are designed to improve the normal ovarian process of pro-ducing an egg, most evangelicals have no qualms about using them. The same is true for intrauterine insemination (IUI), as long as the husband's sperm is used. With IUI, the doctor uses a catheter to place specially treated sperm into a woman's uterus.

Another treatment for infertility is called in vitro fertilization/embryo transfer (IVF-ET). IVF-ET involves removing eggs from the wife, mixing them with sperm in a culture dish, and then transferring the embryo(s) into the uterus. This is the procedure of choice for patients with damaged fallopian tubes, and it is often the best treatment in egg-donor programs and for couples with severe male-factor infer-tility. IVF-ET bypasses the cost and risk of some surgeries, such as laparoscopies, laparotomies, and tubal repairs.

Although the Roman Catholic Church deems ARTs morally unacceptable because they separate the procreative from the unitive act of sex, Protestants generally do not disapprove of such procedures—providing a third party is not involved and one commits to giving every embryo the best possible chance to live. This can hap-pen by having the clinician expose the husband's sperm only to the number of eggs the wife is willing to carry to term if all eggs fertilize.

Freezing embryos, known as cryopreservation, can save money, as it may pre-vent couples from having to do multiple IVF cycles. Yet because a high percentage of frozen embryos die in the freeze/thaw process, most evangelicals have reserva-tions about this process. Although most agree that freezing embryos is better than discarding them, these believers would prefer for couples to avoid getting into such a situation in the first place. If freezing is chosen, evangelical ethicists usually counsel that the infertile couple remain fully committed to transferring all embryos into the uterus at some point, regardless of whether the couple has a child or children from an earlier attempt.

One of the most significant moral concerns of Christians in regard to ARTs is the multitude of fertilized eggs that fail to develop to maturity. Far more fertilized eggs die after unsuccessful attempts at implantation than actually develop into live-born babies. Equally disturbing is the number of early embryos that remain frozen and unused after a couple has had a successful IVF attempt involving cryopreservation. Although the moral status of the frozen embryo is a subject of debate, most evangelicals consider life to begin at the time of fertilization. Therefore, embryo donation, rather than destruction through thawing and discarding or use in research, is considered the lesser of two evils.

The process of using donor eggs, donor sperm, or a surrogate is referred to as third-party reproduction, and it is opposed by most religions. The Christian Medical Association has determined that third-party reproduction is inconsistent with God's design for the family, with the exception of gestational surrogacy.

With gestational surrogacy, an embryo is transferred to the womb of a woman who serves as its "host." The surrogate is not genetically related to the child and is thus only providing a "host womb" for the baby. When given the choice between allowing cryopreserved embryos to die or having them transferred to a gestational surrogate, evangelicals generally favor the latter because of their high view of human life, even at the one-cell stage.

Traditional surrogacy, which evangelicals generally oppose, involves a third-party female being inseminated with the husband's sperm. If the surrogate conceives, the child is genetically hers, but she agrees to place the child with the couple. The media has covered may stories about surrogates keeping the babies, but the more common occurrence is the infertile couple changing their minds, leaving the surrogate with a child.

Embryos can be tested for numerous genetic conditions and to determine the sex of the baby. Although these options are available, evangelicals do not consider them ethical if done with the intent to eliminate "substandard" embryos or for sex selection.

The three potential outcomes for infertile couples are to have a live birth, to adopt, or to remain childfree. Adoption is quite popular among evangelicals. In the past decade, however, it is becoming increasingly common for infertile couples also to opt to live without children.

Sandra Glahn

See also: Sexuality, Evangelicals and

Further Reading

The Christian Medical and Dental Associations. (n.d.). Accessed Month Day, Year. Accessed April 29, 2017. http://www.cmda.org.

Glahn, Sandra, and William Cutrer. *The Infertility Companion: Help and Hope for Couples Facing Infertility.* Grand Rapids, MI: Zondervan and the Christian Medical Association, 2004.

Glahn, Sandra, and William Cutrer. *When Empty Arms Become a Heavy Burden: Encouragement for Couples Facing Infertility.* Grand Rapids, MI: Kregel, 2010.

Saake, Jennifer. *Hannah's Hope: Seeking God's Heart in the Midst of Infertility, Miscarriage, and Adoption.* Colorado Springs, CO: NavPress, 2005.

INSTITUTE FOR CREATION RESEARCH

The Institute for Creation Research is a Biblical-creationist organization dedicated to research, education, and communication in support of scientific creationism. Biblical creationism is distinguished from scientific creationism in that the former holds to creationism on the basis of a literal reading of Genesis 1–11, especially the creation of the universe in six literal days and a literal, cataclysmic, worldwide flood (Genesis 7–8). Scientific creationism attempts to build a scientific case for a creationist perspective and against naturalistic evolution. Its significance in evangelicalism has been widespread, but not unanimously accepted.

The Institute was created by Dr. Henry Morris (1918–2006) in April 1972 in the wake of the breakup of the Creation Science Research Center. The institute was originally a division of Christian Heritage College, now San Diego Christian College, although with separate finances. The Institute claimed that it was the first creationist organization to have a staff of full-time scientists doing active research, writing, and teaching in the field of scientific creationism. These activities were designed to implement its strategy, which rejected legislative action in favor of education as the best approach to promoting creationist understandings of physical and biological origins. Publication was the main focus of the Institute, through its *Acts & Facts* newsletter and the founding of Christian Life Publishers, later Master Books. Its best-known monograph was Dr. Henry Morris's *Scientific Creationism* (1974), which became a standard text on the subject.

Lack of funds for experimental research was an early and persistent challenge for the Institute, as scientific research grants were generally unavailable to it. Early field research focused on thrust fault and "out-of-place fossil" studies, such as the apparent side-by-side dinosaur and human footprints near Glen Rose, Texas. It was hoped that these studies would provide a catalyst for the rejection of the standard geologic age model in favor of a Biblical creation/flood model. Much of this work was done by Dr. Stephen Austin, a visiting geologist (PhD in sedimentary geology, Penn State) and Dr. Henry Morris (PhD in hydraulic engineering, University of Minnesota). These studies were supplemented by two unsuccessful expeditions to Mt. Ararat in Turkey to find remains of Noah's Ark, led by Dr. John Morris (PhD in geological engineering, University of Oklahoma). By the mid-2010s, the Institute listed nine science researchers on its staff.

The teaching focus of the Institute for Creation Research was originally carried through its relationship with Christian Heritage College, but in 1981 the Institute separated from the College and founded its own graduate school with the goal of being a genuinely and exclusively Christian and creationist program. Its goal was to train graduate-level science educators and researchers as an alternative to the evolution-dominated science programs in universities and most religious schools. The California Department of Education's Office of Private Post-Secondary Education granted the Graduate School "approved" status. This status was revoked in 1990 but restored by a federal court order two years later. The program was terminated in 2010 when the Institute moved to Dallas, Texas, due to the program's inability to gain accreditation under Texas law. The graduate program has since been replaced by the Institute for Biblical Apologetics, which offers non-accredited online and DVD-based certificate, undergraduate, and graduate-level diplomas.

Benjamin Blair Phillips

See also: American Scientific Affiliation; *The Genesis Flood*; Institute for Creation Research; Intelligent Design Movement; Morris, Henry; Science, Evangelicals and

Further Reading

Institute for Creation Research. (n.d.). Accessed April 29, 2017. http://www.icr.org/.
Johnson, Philip. *Darwin on Trial.* Downers Grove, IL: InterVarsity Press, 1991, 2010.
Morris, Henry M. *History of Modern Creationism.* San Diego, CA: Master Books, 1984.
Numbers, Ronald L. *The Creationists: From Scientific Creationism to Intelligent Design.* Cambridge, MA: Harvard University Press, 2006.
Whitcomb, John C. *The Early Earth—An Introduction to Biblical Creationism*, 3rd ed., rev. ed. Winona, IN: BMH Books, 2011.

INTELLIGENT DESIGN MOVEMENT

Intelligent Design (ID) is a movement within science and the philosophy of science that argues that there is overwhelming evidence within nature that both humanity and the world were fashioned by a Designer who transcends space–time reality. Though often accused of being six-day creationists in disguise, ID theorists generally accept that the universe and planet earth are billions of years old. They merely contend that Darwinian evolution alone—undirected time and chance working via natural selection—cannot account for the world people observe. Far from setting science against religion, they see no inconsistency in positing both fixed laws of nature and a Designer who intervenes in nature. ID has also been accused of falling into the "God of the gaps" fallacy (Barnes, 1933), namely, whenever Christians cannot find a natural explanation for something, they fill in the knowledge gap with God. ID theorists, however—not all of whom are Christians and many of whom avoid identifying the Designer—contend that their conclusions are based on what people *know* about nature, not on what they do not know.

Although ID remains controversial, even among evangelicals, an increasing number of scientists have conceded that the fact that our universe had a beginning (the Big Bang) and that it is fine-tuned to an almost infinite degree of precision (the anthropic principle) points strongly to an intelligent Designer. In an attempt to avoid the theistic implications of the Big Bang, a number of scientists, including Stephen Hawking (1942–), have posited the existence of an infinite number of universes (the multiverse theory) for which they can offer no empirical evidence; ID theorists highlight such theories as revealing an unshakeable commitment to both philosophical and methodological naturalism that drives science and excludes a priori any possibility of a Designer.

The level of controversy increases when the focus shifts from physics and cosmology to paleontology, biology, and chemistry. As proof that Darwinian evolution, with its iconic branching tree and its hypothesized common descent, cannot account for the fossil evidence, ID theorists point to the Cambrian explosion (also known as the "biological big bang"). Extensive research of the Cambrian layer has shown that during a brief period of geological time about 600 million years ago, nearly all animal phyla appeared suddenly. Rather than verifying an evolution *toward* the various phyla (as the Darwinists expected), the Cambrian explosion has revealed an abrupt appearance of fully formed phyla followed by variations *from* the phyla. Meanwhile, on the microscopic level, ID theorists point to the almost unfathomable complexity of the DNA, each strand of which is frontloaded with more information than a supercomputer, as proof that our universe contains not only matter and energy, but information.

ID first caught the public eye in 1991 with the publication of Phillip E. Johnson's *Darwin on Trial*. Johnson (1940–), a lawyer and now retired UC Berkeley law professor, rejected the Darwinian distinction between the *theory* of evolution (which is always being modified) and the *fact* that evolution occurred. That so-called fact, Johnson argued, rests not on empirical science but a naturalistic philosophy that *demands* a material explanation for life. To maintain this artificial and inaccurate distinction, Darwinists co-opted the word "evolution"—using it to mean both microevolution (observed adaptation within species) and macroevolution (the unproven assumption that one species can evolve into another by physical processes alone).

Johnson's book was followed in 1996 by Michael Behe's *Darwin's Black Box*. Behe (1952–), a biochemist from Lehigh University, began his case for ID by acknowledging Darwin's own admission that if any biological system could be found that could not have evolved through a series of slow steps, Darwinism would be disproved. If a chemical or biological system could be identified that could not be formed by a gradual process in which each step possessed survival value, then that system would be "irreducibly complex" and would offer concrete evidence for the existence of an intelligence that transcended the unconscious, nonpurposeful system of natural selection. Behe identified just such a system in the bacterial flagellum, a microscopic, multipart machine that works like an outboard motor to propel the organism.

1998 brought a third support for ID in mathematician and philosopher William A. Dembski's pioneering book *The Design Inference*. Dembski (1960–) based his argument on a careful distinction between complex patterns (such as one finds in crystals) and "specified complexity"—a recognizable design or pattern that has meaning apart from the phenomenon itself. If one sees in the face of a mountain the rough outlines of a face, we dismiss it as the result of natural weathering forces; but if we see four distinct faces that clearly resemble four Presidents (specified complexity), we conclude the image is not random, but designed. We encounter exactly this type of specified complexity in our cells and DNA.

More recently, ID has been driven forward by the work of Stephen C. Meyer (1958–), whose *Signature of the Cell* (2009) explored in detail how the complexity of the DNA necessitates an intelligent Designer. Other key books in the ID movement include Lee Strobel's *The Case for the Creator* (2004; an excellent overview of the various areas of ID), Tom Woodward's *Doubts about Darwin* (2004; offers a history of the movement), Jonathan Wells's *Icons of Evolution* (2000; exposes the way disproven Darwinian icons, like the branching tree, continue to lodge themselves in the modern imagination), and *Unlocking the Mysteries of Life* (a 2002 DVD that documents the scientific conference that helped initiate ID).

It is incorrect to conflate creationism with intelligent design. Unlike ID, which asserts that the specified and/or irreducible complexity people observe is not adequately explained by undirected natural causes, creationism—and not the intelligent design movement—presupposes the scientific authority and reliability of Genesis as its starting point and then attempts to harmonize empirical data to it. In essence, creationists not only contend Genesis chapters 1 and 2 claim a literal six-day scientific account of creation, but they also claim the existence of a Garden of Eden, a, historical Adam and Eve, original sin, and a universal worldwide flood.

The Discovery Institute

Established in 1991 by Bruce Chapman (1940–), a past American ambassador for the United Nations, the Discovery Institute is a nonprofit secular think tank composed of board members, fellows, and donors representing a number of religious (e.g., Catholic; Jewish; Protestant including evangelicals) and nonreligious traditions (e.g., agnosticism). They are known for advocating religious liberty, separation of church and state, and the legitimacy of faith-based institutions in a pluralistic society. But their Discovery's Center for Science and Culture is perhaps best known because they have challenged the theory of evolution as an undirected process for the best explanation for the all designs one observes in both the universe and of living things; a naturalistic worldview is inadequate to account for these designs. Rather, they argue that the best explanation for specified complexity and irreducible complexity empirically detected is an intelligent cause. The intelligent design movement and scientific creationism (e.g., Henry Morris; Creation Research Institute) are not to be conflated or confused. Evangelical fellows for the Discovery Institute include William Lane Craig (1949–), William A. Dembski (1960–), J. P. Moreland (1948–), and Nancy Pearcey (1952–).

But ID proponents may or may not be Christians or be those who believe in the divine inspiration of the Bible. Moreover, intelligent design ideas are not even recent. Early accounts of intelligent design versions are articulated as early as Anaxagoras (ca. 510–428 BCE), Plato (428/427—348/347 BCE), and Aristotle (385–322 BCE), and are embraced by almost all founders of modern science. Thus, although evangelicals may be proponents of ID, not all ID proponents are Christians or even necessarily religious.

Therefore, although ID is an ancient idea, its recent challenges to Darwinian macroevolution are significant in view of its accomplished advocates, advancements, and arguments among both the religious and the nonreligious not only in the public marketplace of ideas but also in the very halls of private and public academia.

Louis Markos

See also: American Scientific Affiliation; Christian Apologetics; Geisler, Norman L.; Institute for Creation Research; Morris, Henry; Schaeffer, Francis A. and Edith; Science, Evangelicals and

Further Reading

Barnes, Earnest W. *Scientific Theory and Religion.* Cambridge: Cambridge University Press, 1933.

Behe, Michael. *Darwin's Black Box: The Biochemical Challenge to Evolution.* New York: Free Press, 2006.

Dembski, William. *The Design Inference: Eliminating Chance through Small Probabilities.* Cambridge Studies in Probability, Induction and Decision Theory. New York: Cambridge University Press, 1998.

Johnson, Philip. *Darwin on Trial.* Downers Grove, IL: InterVarsity Press, 1991, 2010.

Meyer, Stephen C. *Signature in the Cell: DNA and the Evidence for Intelligent Design.* New York: HarperCollins, 2009.

Strobel, Lee. *The Case for the Creator: A Journalist Investigates Scientific Evidence That Points toward God.* Grand Rapids, MI: Zondervan, 2004.

Wells, Jonathan. *Icons of Evolution: Why Much of What We Teach about Evolution Is Wrong.* Washington, D.C.: Regnery, 2002.

Woodward, Thomas. *Doubts about Darwin: A History of Intelligent Design.* Grand Rapids, Baker, 2007.

INTERNATIONAL COUNCIL ON BIBLICAL INERRANCY

The International Council on Biblical Inerrancy (ICBI) was founded in 1977 to clarify and defend the doctrine of biblical inerrancy. In the 1970s and 1980s, American evangelicals were embroiled in an internal controversy regarding the authority, inspiration, and inerrancy of the Bible, and ICBI was one of the major responses supporting biblical inspiration and inerrancy. The Council sponsored three major "summits," each producing an important statement. Numerous books and articles were published for popular and academic reading during the controversy, most

The Center for the Study of New Testament Manuscripts (CSNTM)

The Center for the Study of New Testament Manuscripts is a nonprofit organization that was established on September 13, 2002, by Dr. Daniel B. Wallace, a New Testament scholar and textual critic at Dallas Theological Seminary. Using the latest technology available, CSNTM seeks to digitalize, preserve, and study ancient New Testament manuscripts. Working with more than 40 institutions over four continents, they have so far produced more than 350,000 images of New Testament manuscripts, advancing New Testament studies in unprecedented ways. In fact, they have discovered more than 90 New Testament ancient manuscripts.

notably Harold Lindsell's 1976 book *The Battle for the Bible*. Debate subsided in the 1990s but since 2005 has arisen once again in a new generation of evangelicals.

Summit I met in Chicago on October 26–28, 1978. Over 300 Christian leaders, theologians, and pastors attended and adopted the Chicago Statement on Biblical Inerrancy, consisting of 19 articles with brief exposition. Dr. Jay Grimstead, one of the organizers of the ICBI, described the statement as "a landmark church document" created "by the then largest, broadest, group of evangelical protestant scholars that ever came together to create a common, theological document in the 20th century. It is probably the first systematically comprehensive, broadly based, scholarly, creed–like statement on the inspiration and authority of Scripture in the history of the church" (Dallas Theological Seminary [DTS], n.d.).

The ICBI convened Summit II on November 10–13, 1982, in Chicago to discuss guidelines for principles of interpreting the Bible. Approximately 100 people attended and adopted the Chicago Statement on Biblical Hermeneutics, comprising 25 articles and a brief exposition. The final ICBI conference, Summit III, met on December 10–13, 1986, in Chicago. The participants adopted the Chicago Statement on Biblical Application, composed of 16 articles with a separate introduction.

The "Chicago Statement on Biblical Inerrancy" is an eight-page document that opens with a summary statement of five declarations. The summary reads:

1. God, who is Himself Truth and speaks truth only, has inspired Holy Scripture in order thereby to reveal Himself to lost mankind through Jesus Christ as Creator and Lord, Redeemer and Judge. Holy Scripture is God's witness to Himself.

2. Holy Scripture, being God's own Word, written by men prepared and superintended by His Spirit, is of infallible divine authority in all matters upon which it touches: it is to be believed, as God's instruction, in all that it affirms; obeyed, as God's command, in all that it requires; embraced, as God's pledge, in all that it promises.

3. The Holy Spirit, Scripture's divine Author, both authenticates it to us by His inward witness and opens our minds to understand its meaning.

4. Being wholly and verbally God-given, Scripture is without error or fault in all its teaching, no less in what it states about God's acts in creation, about the events of world history, and about its own literary origins under God, than in its witness to God's saving grace in individual lives.

5. The authority of Scripture is inescapably impaired if this total divine inerrancy is in any way limited or disregarded, or made relative to a view of truth contrary to the Bible's own; and such lapses bring serious loss to both the individual and the Church.

Following the Statement are 19 Articles of Affirmation. The document's closing four pages, entitled, "III. Exposition," elaborates on six points. (A.) Creation, Revelation and Inspiration; (B.) Authority: Christ in the Bible; (C.) Infallibility, Inerrancy, Interpretation; (D.) Skepticism and Criticism; (E.) Transmission and Translation; and (F.) Inerrancy and Authority.

The 1978 "Chicago Statement on Biblical Hermeneutics" contains 25 Affirmations and Denials. Its opening statement reads in part:

> The work of Summit I had hardly been completed when it became evident that there was yet another major task to be tackled. While we recognize that belief in the inerrancy of Scripture is basic to maintaining its authority, the values of that commitment are only as real as one's understanding of the meaning of Scripture. Thus, the need for Summit II. For two years plans were laid and papers were written on themes relating to hermeneutical principles and practices (Packer, n.d.).

The "Chicago Statement on Biblical Application" opens, "This statement is the third and final in a trilogy of Summits sponsored by the International Council on Biblical Inerrancy. Summit I (October 26–28, 1978) produced the Chicago Statement on Biblical Inerrancy. Summit II (November 10–13, 1982) resulted in the Chicago Statement on Biblical Hermeneutics. This last conference, Summit III (December 10–13, 1986), drafted the Chicago Statement on Biblical Application. With this statement the proposed scholarly work of ICBI has been completed, for the doctrine of inerrancy has thus been defined, interpreted, and applied by many of the leading evangelical scholars of our day" (http://Library.dts.edu/Pages/TL/Special/ICBI.shtml).

The statement is followed by 16 Articles of Affirmations and Denial:
  I.   The Living God
  II. The Savior and His Work
  III. The Holy Spirit and His Work
  IV. The Church and Its Mission
  V.   Sanctity of Human Life
  VI. Marriage and the Family
  VII. Divorce and Remarriage

VIII. Sexual Deviations
IX. The State under God
X. Law and Justice
XI. War
XII. Discrimination and Human Rights
XIII. Economics
XIV. Work and Leisure
XV. Wealth and Poverty
XVI. Stewardship of the Environment.

The final four pages consist of an Introduction, Approaching Contemporary Problems, and New Vistas along Old Paths.

The intensity and scope of the debate regarding inerrancy and the breadth of the debate within American evangelicalism as evidenced by the efforts of ICBI illustrates the strong commitment of American evangelicals to their understanding of Christian doctrine and the Bible.

James Menzies

See also: The Battle for the Bible; Bible, Authority of; Inerrancy; Lindsell, Harold

Further Reading

Dallas Theological Seminary (DTS). (n.d.). "Records of the International Council on Biblical Inerrancy." Accessed April 29, 2017. Library.dts.edu/Pages/TL/Special/ICBI.shtml.

Geisler, Norman. *Inerrancy.* Grand Rapids, MI: Zondervan, 1980.

Geisler, Norman, and William C. Roach. *Defending Inerrancy: Affirming the Accuracy of Scripture for a New Generation.* Grand Rapids, MI: Baker Books, 2012. http://library.dts.edu/Pages/TL/Special/ICBI.shtml.

Kantzer, Kenneth S. *Applying the Scriptures.* Dulles, VA: Academie Books, 1987.

Packer, J. I. "The Chicago Statement on Biblical Hermeneutics." Alliance of Confessing Evangelicals (n.d.). Accessed April 29, 2017. http://www.alliancenet.org/the-chicago-statement-on-biblical-hermeneutics.

Radmacher, Earl, and Robert Preus. *Hermeneutics, Inerrancy, and the Bible: Papers from ICBI Summit II.* Dulles, VA: Academie Books, 1984.

INTERVARSITY CHRISTIAN FELLOWSHIP/USA

InterVarsity Christian Fellowship/USA (InterVarsity USA) is an evangelical organization that aims to establish and advance Christianity on college campuses. Initially chartered in the United States in November 1941 by Stacey Woods and two other staff members, who were all working in both the United States and Canada, InterVarsity was begun in England in 1877 by students at the University of Cambridge. These students began prayer and Bible study meetings and started discussing their faith with other students, despite some university officials' resistance. Because similar groups began appearing on other university campuses in England, these independent groups eventually formed the British InterVarsity, from *inter* (meaning "between") and *varsity* (the British term for "college-level students").

Having heard about the British movement, Canadian college students asked for assistance to begin their own InterVarsity chapters on college campuses in Canada. Thus, British InterVarsity sent Howard Guinness, who led his cabinmate to Christ on the voyage over, to Canada in 1928 to begin this effort. By 1937, college campuses in the United States began requesting assistance to start InterVarsity ministries. So in 1938, Stacey Woods and two other Canadian staff met with students on the University of Michigan campus and began working toward articles of incorporation for chapters in the United States, and in 1941, InterVarsity USA was established.

Globally, InterVarsity USA became the founding member of the International Fellowship of Evangelical Students (IFES), whose other charter members are Australia, Britain, Canada, China, France, Holland, New Zealand, Norway, and Switzerland; and now, more than 150 countries are members of this federation of national Christian student movements. Because of the international and missional emphasis of InterVarsity USA, IFES works through InterVarsity chapters to call every student impacted by its ministry to a global mission–mindedness. As of 2015, InterVarsity USA, through IFES, sent out almost 2,500 students on 300 international mission trips across 17 countries. Additionally, another 2,100 students participated in mission trips within the United States.

In the United States, perhaps one of the most prominent influences that InterVarsity has had on American evangelical life is its early commitment to multiethnic ministry, beginning as early as 1945 in the United States, when a staff member invited black students to a Bible study. Subsequently, there was an incident related to the desegregation of the Bible study, and the Board passed a resolution forbidding racial segregation at InterVarsity events, with a view toward unity in the Body of Christ. In line with this emphasis, InterVarsity's international federation of missions networks, through the IFES, ensures a global perspective to modern practices in evangelism and discipleship.

Like many campus organizations in the latter part of the 20th and early part of the 21st centuries, InterVarsity USA has been embroiled in legal battles regarding nondiscrimination policies established by university systems or by InterVarsity itself. Concurrent with their early progressive alignment against racial segregation, InterVarsity denied a noncelibate homosexual student a leadership position at Grinnell College in 1996–1997. Similarly, Middlebury College and Whitman College threatened to take recognition away from InterVarsity USA on their campuses due to restrictions placed on homosexual students in leadership. Again, in 2011, InterVarsity was unrecognized by an executive antidiscrimination order drafted by Charles B. Reed, the chancellor of the California State University system, one of the largest university systems in the United States. This executive order required all student organizations to sign a policy agreeing to not discriminate against student leaders in any of the normally protected classes within the U.S. legal system. Because

InterVarsity USA stated that they would not allow non-Christian leaders in any of their 23 chapters in the California State system, their recognition as a student organization was taken away from them, stripping them of several financial and logistical privileges afforded to all student organizations with campus facilities. In 2015–2016, InterVarsity reported that there were "1,011 chapters on 667 campuses" in the United States. Additionally InterVarsity Press is a major publisher of Bible Study resources, theological reference materials and textbooks, small group studies, and other Christian works that they produce not just for their campus fellowships, but also for mass distribution. Through these various ministries and the scope of their publishing, InterVarsity USA ministers to college students across not only the United States but also the world, and illustrates the breadth of parachurch ministries in American religious life.

Bryce Hantla

See also: Christian Apologetics; Cru; Evangelism; Fellowship of Christian Athletes; L'Abri Fellowship; Parachurch Ministries; Philosophy, Evangelicals and; Princeton Evangelical Fellowship

Further Reading

Hunt, Keith, and Gladys Hunt. *For Christian and the University: The Story of InterVarsity Fellowship of the USA: 1940–1990.* Downers Grove, IL: InterVarsity Press, 1991.

MacLeod, A. Donald. *C. Stacey Woods and the Evangelical Rediscovery of the University.* Downers Grove, IL: IVP Academic, 2007.

Woods, Stacey C. *The Growth of a Work of God: The Story of the Early Days of the Inter-Varsity Christian Fellowship of the United States of America as Told by Its First General Secretary.* Downers Grove, IL: InterVarsity Press, 1978.

ISRAEL, EVANGELICALS AND

American evangelicals have had long-standing support for Israel and were active in late 19th- and early 20th-century endeavors to establish a national homeland for Jews. In recent years, evangelicals have not been a unified as previously, with there being growing criticism among some evangelicals of the State of Israel and growing support for the establishment of a Palestinian state. Traditional evangelical support for a restoration of the Jews to the land of Israel goes back to England in the late 1500s (Francis Kett, ca. 1547–1589) and the early 1600s (Sir Henry Finch, d. 1625). As a result of Bible study, many English and American Puritans in the 1600s came to strongly believe that the Jewish people would be restored to their homeland in the last days and become a nation again. This viewpoint was known as "restorationism." Restorationism was the view of a majority of Puritans in the 1600s in the New England colonies, as represented by American colonial minister Increase Mather's (1639–1723) first book, *A Dissertation Concerning the Future Conversion of the Jewish Nation.*

The 19th century witnessed strong evangelical support in both Great Britain under the leadership of Anthony Ashley Cooper and Lord Shaftsbury (1801–1885) and in the United States by William E. Blackstone (1841–1935); their biblical faith led to attempts to influence their governments in the political realm to reestablish the state of Israel. Although evangelical support for the restoration of Israel began to decline in the late 1800s in Great Britain under the onslaught of liberalism, it grew stronger in the United States due to the adoption by most evangelicals of dispensationalism, which was seen as an answer to the more liberal views of the Bible arising out of German higher criticism in biblical studies that was adopted by most American Protestant denominations. Non-evangelical pastors began to emphasize what was termed "the social gospel," and conservatives doubled down on studies of and emphasis of the biblical text while disdaining critical influence. This period also saw the rise of Bible institutes in every major metropolitan area in North America, all teaching strongly that Israel would one day, likely soon, be reestablished as a nation in order to fulfill Bible prophecy.

By the early 20th century, premillennialism had become the standard view of almost all evangelicals, as it was bolstered by the release of *The Scofield Reference Bible* in 1909. Evangelicals, many of whom were scattered throughout the mainline denominations, were solidified in their restorationist views as a result of the notes in Scofield's study Bible. Virtually every North American Bible college and a number of Christian liberal arts schools like Wheaton College and Gordon College also held and taught restorationism. As evangelicals began to establish seminaries, schools like Dallas Theological Seminary (1924) added their strong voice as advocates of restorationist beliefs. By World War I, most evangelicals were strong supporters of the Balfour Declaration issued by the British government, calling for the creation in Israel of a Jewish homeland in November 1917. The Balfour Declaration was then incorporated into the British Mandate over Palestine and became settled international law in 1922.

As the modern state of Israel struggled under Great Britain, evangelical support grew greatly in the United States as it experienced a slow decline in Great Britain. After World War II and the Holocaust that killed at least 6.2 million Jews in Europe, the United States became the world's power and eventual leader of efforts to restore the Jewish homeland, thus replacing Great Britain. President Harry Truman, who had evangelical Christian leanings, went against most of his administration and led the fight for passage of the partition of Palestine and the creation of a Jewish state in what is now called Israel. Thus, on May 14, 1948, Israel officially became a nation, and the United States was the first nation to recognize it as a sovereign nation. However, the United States did not support Israel militarily during their war for independence. Nevertheless, in order to bring to an end the Suez Crisis in the fall of 1956, the United States pledged to help Israel militarily. This began the Israel–United States relationship that has been very strong ever since. American evangelicals and fundamentalists have provided almost uniform support since the founding of Israel in 1948. Many evangelicals see the founding of the modern state of Israel as a fulfillment of Bible prophecy relating to the end times, especially in the aftermath of the 1967 Six-Day War. There has been great support from within the North American evangelical community for Israel since 1948.

The last two decades have seen the rise of strong evangelical organizations designed to provide support for the modern state of Israel within the United States. The largest and most influential is Christians United For Israel (CUFI), founded in 2006 and led by its founder, Pastor John Hagee of San Antonio, Texas. CUFI has a large annual conference, has founded campus chapters on more than 300 university campuses, sponsors important people for trips to Israel, conducts many conferences and seminars to promote support for Israel, and has a lobbying presence in most state capitols and in Washington, D.C.

Yet, evangelical support is not monolithic, and there has been a growing anti-Israel sentiment among some younger evangelicals in the past 15–20 years, as well as the beginnings of broader erosion of evangelical support for Israel in North America. The establishment of organizations such as Christ at the Checkpoint reflects the shift of some from support of to antagonism against Israel. Such dissent shows that American evangelicalism contains a spectrum of political, social, cultural, and theological viewpoints. In spite of this shift, especially within academia and among the laity, recent polls indicate that evangelical support for Israel is still in the low 80 percent range. Some observers note that contemporary decline in evangelical support for Israel mirrors the decline in influence of the literal-grammatical-historical interpretation of the Bible, which is also in decline among evangelicals. American support for Israel has always risen or fallen in relation to the degree of biblical influence in the culture. Whether supporting or not supporting Israel, American evangelicals remain strong in their views about Israel, and such views are related to how evangelicals interpret and apply the biblical text in the outworking of their Christian experience.

Thomas D. Ice

See also: Foreign Policy, Evangelicals and; Premillennialism

Further Reading

Amstutz, Mark R. *Evangelicals and American Foreign Policy.* New York: Oxford University Press, 2014.

Borg, David. "The End of Evangelical Support for Israel?" *The Middle East Quarterly* 21, no. 2 (Spring 2014). http://www.meforum.org/3769/israel-evangelical-support.

McDermott, Gerald R., ed. *The New Christian Zionism: Fresh Perspectives on Israel and the Land.* Downers Grove, IL: IVP Academic, 2016.

Schmidt, David W. *Partners Together in This Great Enterprise: The Role of Christian Zionism in the Foreign Policies of Britain and America in the Twentieth Century.* Maitland, FL: Xulon Press, 2011.

Showers, James. "Eroding Evangelical Christian Support for Israel: That Cause and Cure." Paper presented at the December 2015 Pre-Trib Study Group Conference. http://www.pre-trib.org/data/pdf/Showers-ErodingEvangelicalCh.pdf.

JESUS MUSIC

Jesus Music is a style of music, identified by its use of guitar and apocalyptic lyrics, that was used during worship by members of the Jesus Movement in the late 1960s and 1970s. It found expression among those who had identified themselves as hippies, those involved in drugs, and others who were reacting to dysfunctionalism in the home; authority structures in society; war and corruption; the pursuit of materialism and its inability to bring forth fulfillment, meaning, and purpose; and no final answers in contemporary thought to the greatest questions in life.

As the decade of the 1960s was ending, the youth of the United States were growing frustrated with the social and political structures in existence. One result was the growth of the hippie movement, characterized by communal groups that made use of organic food, various eastern religions, and hallucinogenic drugs. The youth involved in this movement were displeased with the conservative mindset of mainstream America and sought to break those ties.

This cultural shift extended to the youth of the church as well. Mainstream denominations struggled to continue their tradition of conservativism within a disintegrating society. As a result, many youth became frustrated with the worship practices of their parents and experimented with the offerings of society.

The Jesus Movement began as a series of nonrelated youth outreach ministries in southern California. Most writers attribute the beginnings of the movement to Lonnie Frisbee (1949–1993) and Church Smith (1927–2013). Together, the duo reached thousands of teenagers and young adults through evangelistic efforts. The ideas of a casual type of Christianity, different from that of their parents, quickly spread along the West Coast and soon were transplanted into Middle America.

The movement was not complicated or difficult to understand. Its primary goal was to tell people about the love of Jesus and the end times as predicted in the Book of Revelation. Being an evangelical movement meant that street ministry, Christians approaching everyday people on the street to talk about these things, was one of the strongest methods of communication. Such an approach was not new to Christianity, but certainly not practiced by the majority of churches in the country.

Simplicity was also a key element to some of the music being created by the movement. Often, the music was similar in style to that of the popular artists of the time such as the folk singer, Joan Baez (1941–). Like many folk singers of the time, the singers of the Jesus Movement used the guitar as their primary instrument. The use of the guitar found its roots in the folk music of the United States that used acoustic instruments, those of the "common man." The rise in popularity of this instrument among youth movements was due to its perceived "authenticity," a simple instrument for being clearly understood.

As folk music was important to this new generation of Christians, so also was the ever-developing rock style that was played throughout the country. Late 1960s rock was heavily influenced by the Beatles, free thought, and drugs. In fact, many of the early converts to this new community were members of rock bands. One such performer was Chuck Girard (1943–) of the Hondells surf band, who left the surf scene to search for a spiritual awakening. After experimenting with drugs and meditation, he and a friend visited Calvary Chapel in Costa Mesa and became Christians. Girard formed a band that became the first successful Christian rock band, Love Song. The group maintained the folk-rock style of the early 1970s, which used guitars and drums and made use of close harmonies borrowed from the surf rock style. In addition, this type of music utilized smooth, lyrical melodies like those heard in the popular style.

Another pioneering band at this time was Agape (1968–1974), whose members were Fred Caban, Mike Jungman, and John Peckhart. The music of their first album blends pieces ranging from a straightforward blues style ("Blind") to the more effects-driven psychedelic rock, which is often applied to the band. The band gained recognition less for the quality of their music and more for their innovation in the realm of Christian music. Through the efforts of this band, the other side of the Christian popular music coin was formed. The smoother folk style would later develop into what has become adult contemporary, and the folk-rock blend would establish the rock elements of contemporary Christian music.

One other musical development from this evangelistic movement is the youth musical. With the acceptance of these new artists by thousands of youth throughout the country, composers saw a new interest by the youth to share their faith. It was then in the early 1970s that musicals written for amateur groups began appearing. Perhaps the musical with the greatest impact was the musical *Godspell* (1971), whose script and music were written by John-Michael Tebelak and Stephen Schwartz, respectively. Much of the text was taken from the Bible while other portions of text were taken from hymns. The popularity of this work, along with others like *Jesus Christ Superstar* (1971), created an interest in the creation of youth musicals.

These musicals were transported easily into the local church when many of the new bands were still not fully accepted into regular worship. The benefit of musicals written for church performance was that there was an understanding of limited resources and less concern for the professional end result of other productions. Many of the songs focused on the ministry of Jesus and how his life could be applied to that of youth. Social awareness was an important issue, as evidenced by the activities of the 1960s, and this was taken in by the youth of the 1970s. In addition, many of these works called for the use of guitar, an instrument that was quite far from being considered a traditional worship instrument. Composers understood how to attract youth through the music by using syncopation and faster rhythms that created a rock style that was similar to styles heard on the radio.

Although the Jesus Movement began on the West Coast of California, it quickly spread throughout the United States and in Europe, and engaged youth in reconsidering what it meant to be a Christian at a tumultuous and creative time. Music became a prominent element in the lives of those involved in the movement and was a tool used to reach thousands of teenagers and young adults with the gospel of Jesus Christ. Jesus Music borrowed heavily from the popular styles heard on the radio and ushered in the contemporary Christian music style that has grown into a mainstream market. By using familiar instruments, simple melodies, rock rhythms, and clear texts, Jesus Music not only impacted thousands of lives in a very difficult era in society with its creativity, use of Scripture, and message of hope, but also created a legacy that continues today.

Jason Runnels

See also: Calvary Chapel; Counterculture, Evangelicals and; Dispensationalism; Evangelism; Fine Arts, Evangelicals and; Jesus People Movement; L'Abri Fellowship; Norman, Larry David; Parachurch Ministries; Premillennialism; Rapture; Schaeffer, Francis A. and Edith; Smith, Charles W. ("Chuck")

Further Reading

Eskridge, Larry. *God's Forever Family: The Jesus People Movement in America.* Eugene, OR: Pickwick, 2014.

Gersztyn, Bob. *Jesus Rocks the World: The Definitive History of Contemporary Christian Music.* 2 vols. Santa Barbara, CA: Praeger, 2013.

Pederson, Duane. *Larger than Ourselves: The Early Beginnings of the Jesus People.* Hollywood, CA: The Hollywood Free Paper, 2015.

Stowe, David W. *No Sympathy for the Devil: Christian Pop Music and the Transformation of American Evangelicalism.* Chapel Hill, NC: University of North Carolina Press, 2011.

JESUS PEOPLE MOVEMENT

The Jesus People Movement began on the West Coast of the United States. It was a movement of hippie Christians, in the late 1960s and 1970s, who sought to transform individual lives, the church, and American culture. Based on evangelism and their understanding of the teachings of Christianity, which were restorationist, they sought to practice simple Christianity as they understood it to have been experienced in the first century. There was also a strong emphasis on the ongoing possibility of miracles and what is known as "sign gifts," such as speaking in tongues and other manifestations believed to be the working of the Holy Spirit. The strong emphasis on the Holy Spirit can be traced to the earlier Pentecostal and Charismatic movement in 20th-century American religious history. The movement was transdenominational within Protestantism and also included Roman Catholics. It was highly evangelistic, and its members often espoused millennialism in the theology, such as the premillennial views of Hal Lindsey's *The Late Great Planet Earth* (1970).

Members of the movement were called Jesus People or Jesus Freaks. The former term was used by a newspaper reporter in an interview with leader Duane Pederson (1938–), former editor of one of the movement's publications, the *Hollywood Free Paper* (modeled on other counterculture newspapers of the era). The latter term, Jesus Freaks, was first used pejoratively but soon came to be accepted without bias. There was no single leader or founder, but there was a constellation of key figures, churches, and organizations, among them Charles ("Chuck") Smith (1927–2013) and his ministry at Calvary Chapel, Costa Mesa, California. Others included Jack Sparks, the Christian World Liberation Front, and Lonnie Frisbee (1949–1993). Building on the restorationist strand, some prominent members later became priests in the Eastern Orthodox Church.

The movement eventually spread throughout North America, Central America, and Europe before its demise in the early 1980s. Prominent centers were in the San Francisco Bay area, Seattle, Detroit, and Los Angeles. At least one worshipping community, Jesus People USA, continues to exist in Chicago; and in the United Kingdom, there is Jesus Army, now known as Jesus Fellowship. Some Jesus People lived in communes or common houses, such as the Shiloh Youth Revival Centers founded by John Higgins in 1968, and in this way, shared in some of the broader counterculture commune phenomenon.

The high point of the movement was in 1971 and 1972. In the summer of 1972, Campus Crusade for Christ (now Cru) organized a five-day festival in Dallas at the State Fair Grounds and Cotton Bowl, called Explo '72, that was one of the most visible activities of the Jesus People, garnering about 80,000 people.

In most things such as politics social issues, the movement was countercultural and reflected the deep divide within American society that emerged in the

---

Singers and Groups That Came out of Jesus Music in the 1970s

Significant singers and groups that came out of Jesus Music in the 1970s include Love Song (1976), The Way (1971), Larry Norman (1947–2008), Barry McGuire (1935–), Second Chapter of Acts (1973), and Randy Stonehill (1952–). In the mid-1970s, Bob Bennett (1955–), Roby Duke (1956–2007), and Keith Green (1953–1982) became significant names. Other styles and pioneers soon emerged: Christian folk genre, with Children of the Day (1970), John Fischer (1947–), Noel Paul Stookey (1937–), Karen Lafferty (1948–), Phil Keaggy (1951), Scott Wesley Brown (1952–), and Kelly Willard (1956–); R&B gospel genre, with Andraé Crouch (1942–2015) and the Disciples, and Sweet Comfort Band (1974–1984; 2013), which blended R&B with Christian rock and jazz; Christian country rock genre, with Daniel Amos (1974), Gentle Faith (1974), Talbot Brothers (1976); and Christian hard rock genre with Petra (1972), Resurrection (1972), and Servant (1976).

turbulent 1960s. Many evangelical organizations were an outgrowth of the movement and era or had tangential affiliation with its adherents such as Jews for Jesus, Campus Crusade for Christ (Cru), Calvary Chapel, and the Vineyard Movement. In 1972, the movement disassociated itself with the Children of God movement and its authoritarian excesses, practices, and beliefs.

The Jesus People Movement significantly changed evangelical culture, even though it was short-lived, in that it brought an informality to worship in many churches, including the use of praise music, guitars and drums, and an intentional shift away from liturgical worship. Two of the most lasting legacies of the movement are its contribution to contemporary Christian music and its influence on evangelical youth involvement in cultural issues.

Timothy J. Demy

See also: Calvary Chapel; Children of God; Contemporary Christian Music; Counterculture, Evangelicals and; Jesus Music; Jews for Jesus; Lindsey, Harold Lee ("Hal"); Norman, Larry David; Smith, Charles W. ("Chuck")

Further Reading

Bustraan, Richard. *The Jesus People Movement: A Story of Spiritual Revolution among the Hippies.* Eugene, OR: Pickwick, 2014.

Eskridge, Larry. *God's Forever Family: The Jesus People Movement in America.* New York: Oxford University Press, 2013.

Miller, Steven P. *The Age of Evangelicalism: America's Born-Again Years.* New York: Oxford University Press, 2014.

Nichols, Stephen J. *Jesus Made in America: A Cultural History from the Puritans to the Passion of the Christ.* Downers Grove, IL: InterVarsity Press, 2008.

JEWS FOR JESUS

Jews for Jesus is a nonprofit organization that was formally incorporated in September 1973 by Martin (Moishe) Rosen (1932–2010). It arose as a parachurch evangelistic ministry primary to Jews and as part of the evangelical participation in and response to the counterculture movement of the 1960s and 1970s. The current executive director is David Brickner. Moishe Rosen, a Jewish believer in Jesus, was a prolific trainer of missionaries. A majority of the current missionaries to the Jews in North America were instructed by Moishe Rosen or by someone whom he trained. When people inquire about how long the ministry has been in existence, the answer given is "Jews for Jesus has been around since 32 CE, give or take a year."

Moishe Rosen started in ministry by working for the American Board of Missions to the Jews (ABMJ; currently Chosen People Ministries). From 1960 to 1974, Moishe was in charge of the Los Angeles office of ABMJ. While there, his efforts resulted in unprecedented growth of that branch. The ministry method that Moishe developed consisted of publicly proclaiming the gospel in the streets, accompanied by people handing out thought-provoking tracts. Weekly Bible studies were held at the mission to disciple those Jews who had already made a profession of faith. In June 1966, Moishe Rosen was appointed director of missionary training for ABMJ and was transferred to New York City.

In 1969, Moishe was asked to take to the streets of New York to reach the growing young counterculture that had risen up, starting on the college campuses. Moishe saw a great mission field and realized a new approach would be extremely effective in reaching the Jewish hippies. Moishe Rosen wrote amusing but effective gospel messages that this generation would more readily accept. These tracts became known as "broadsides" that the Jews for Jesus workers have handed out by the millions over the past four decades.

In the summer of 1970, ABMJ transferred Moishe to San Francisco, where he developed a method called "confrontational ministry." Their mission statement was and still is "We exist to make the messiahship of Jesus an unavoidable issue to our Jewish people worldwide." Moishe and his associates would take to the streets with placards and tracts that they would hand out personally to individual people. Some staff workers at ABMJ had informally given this group the name Jews for Jesus, which the media picked up and soon began using.

Internally, ABMJ was fully committed to giving their full support to the concept of media evangelism. By contrast, Moishe was dedicated to the "confrontational ministry approach." Both were proving to be very effective, but the ministry chose to separate from Moishe and his workers. In September 1973, Jews for Jesus became a separate, independent ministry. Both ministries grew and currently have branches throughout the world.

Currently, Jews for Jesus has branches in Germany, Hungary, Ukraine, Switzerland, South Africa, England, Russia, France, Australia, Israel, and Canada. In the United States, there are branch offices in San Francisco (the international headquarters), Florida, Chicago, New York, Los Angeles, and Washington, D.C.

Jeffrey Gutterman

See also: Ariel Ministries; Chosen People Ministries; Counterculture, Evangelicals and; Jesus People Movement; Messianic Judaism

Further Reading

Ariel, Yaakov. *Evangelizing the Chosen People: Missions to the Jews in America, 1880–2000.* Chapel Hill: University of North Carolina Press, 2000.

Jews for Jesus. Accessed April 29, 2017. https://jewsforjesus.org/about.

Rosen, Moishe and Ceil. *Witnessing to Jews: Practical Ways to Relate the Love of Jesus.* San Francisco: Purple Pomegranate Productions, 1998.

Rosen, Ruth. *Called to Controversy: The Unlikely Story of Moishe Rosen and the Founding of Jews for Jesus.* Nashville, TN: Thomas Nelson, 2012.

Sevner, Harold A. *A Rabbi's Vision: A Century of Proclaiming Messiah: A History of Chosen People Ministries, Inc.* Charlotte, NC: Chosen People Ministries, 1994.

K

KAISER, WALTER C., JR. (1933–)

Walter C. Kaiser Jr. (1933–) is the Colman M. Mockler President Emeritus and Distinguished Professor of Old Testament and Ethics at Gordon Conwell Theological Seminary. Focusing on Old Testament biblical exposition, theology, and criticism as well as the development of the study of Old Testament ethics, Kaiser has been a highly influential figure in evangelical scholarship throughout the 20th century.

Graduating from Wheaton College with a degree in bible in 1958, Kaiser went on to earn his PhD (1973) in Mediterranean studies from Brandeis University. After spending two years teaching at Wheaton College and Trinity Evangelical Divinity School, Kaiser became a faculty member at Trinity Evangelical Divinity School in 1966 before becoming the vice president and academic dean of Trinity, where he served from 1980–1992. In the fall of 1993, Kaiser joined Gordon-Conwell Theological Seminary and became the first Colman M. Mockler Distinguished Professor of Old Testament. He would later assume the presidency of Gordon-Conwell (1997–2006) while retaining his previous position. Kaiser also served as the president of the Evangelical Theological Society in 1977. In addition to writing numerous articles, he has served as a co-translator for 1st and 2nd Samuel in the New International Version of the Bible (1972) and is the author of more than 40 books.

One of Kaiser's significant contributions to the field of Old Testament studies has been in the development of his methodological and theological framework for understanding the Old Testament as well as its usage by the writers of the New Testament. Specifically, Kaiser is noted for the development of "promise-fulfillment theology." In *Toward an Old Testament Theology* (1978), Kaiser argues that the dominant and unifying theme throughout the Old Testament is the concept of promise and fulfillment. Believing that this is the primary concept in which the Old Testament has been organized, Kaiser argues that the object and content of the Abrahamic Covenant is identical to the promise and object of the Davidic Covenant: the seed through whom all of the nations will be blessed and the Messianic Kingdom will be established. As the authors and writers of the Old Testament continue to progressively reveal the purpose and plan of God throughout the subsequent centuries, God continues to reveal greater details into the nature of the promise, without shifting its content. As such, the Old Testament writers are unified around the task of revealing the details of God's promise and the manner in which it will find fulfillment.

Additionally, Kaiser has made significant contributions to the fields of textual criticism and biblical theology. During the first few decades of the 20th century, critical scholars typically dominated these fields. Historical and form critics discredited the validity of the Hebrew Bible in favor of other sources from the ancient Near

East. Kaiser entered into the academic discussion as one of the few evangelical voices. He criticized the documentary hypothesis, arguing that it does not give the same voice to the text of the Hebrew Bible that it has given to other ancient Near East documents. Additionally, he found the promise-fulfillment theme to be unique to the Hebrew Bible and its dominant theme. He acknowledges that similarities between Ancient Near East documents and the Hebrew Bible exist, but identifies that these similarities are exaggerated while key differences are ignored. However, at the same time, Kaiser called evangelicals to pursue excellence in their engagement of Old Testament scholarship. His work has led to a renewed interest in the field of Biblical theology among evangelicals.

Kaiser is also noted for reviving the field and study of Old Testament ethics. In his work *On Old Testament Ethics* (1983), he attempts to build a bridge between the character and nature of God as revealed in the Hebrew Bible and the manner in which the people of God are called to live. Kaiser also addresses the contemporary relevance that such passages provide for the modern reader while situating Old Testament ethics within his theology of promise. Providing insights into difficult passages of Scripture while also addressing passages that the modern reader might find offensive, Kaiser argues that the ethical commands of the Old Testament contain universal principles that are applicable to the modern community.

In conclusion, Walter Kaiser has tremendously impacted Old Testament scholarship, particularly within the evangelical community in the field of biblical studies and Biblical Theology. His excellence in scholarship and commitment to the authority of the Bible has revived the study of the Hebrew Bible within the evangelical community and has challenged the presuppositions of critical scholarship. Kaiser has consistently challenged evangelical and Christian colleges to remember their commitment to the biblical text and its import to the spiritual life and pastoral ministry.

Daniel Hill

See also: Gordon-Conwell Theological Seminary; Higher Education, Evangelicals and; Premillennialism; Trinity Evangelical Divinity School

Further Reading

Kaiser, Walter C., Jr. *Toward an Old Testament Theology.* Grand Rapids, MI: Zondervan, 1978.
Kaiser, Walter C., Jr. *Toward Old Testament Ethics.* Grand Rapids, MI: Zondervan, 1991.
Kaiser, Walter C., Jr. *Mission in the Old Testament: Israel as a Light to the Nations.* Grand Rapids, MI: Baker Academic, 2000.
Kaiser, Walter C., Jr. *The Promise Plan of God: a Biblical Theology of the Old and New Testament.* Grand Rapids, MI: Zondervan, 2008.

KEY '73

Key '73 was a mass, interdenominational evangelism campaign by American Christian groups with the goal of "calling our continent to Christ in 1973." The campaign was sparked by Carl F. H. Henry's editorial "Somehow Let's Get Together" in

Christianity Today in 1967 and occurred in the midst of a period of other global initiatives focused on global evangelism, such as the 1966 Berlin Congress, Explo '72, and Lausanne '74. In response to Henry's article, a number of evangelical leaders met later in 1967 in Rosslyn, Virginia, near the Francis Scott Key Bridge, and began developing a plan for a North American evangelism campaign in partnership with other Christian groups and organizations.

Though conceived and initially led by evangelicals, subsequent meetings sought participation from across the spectrum of American Christianity. Major Lutheran, Methodist, and Baptist denominations participated, as did evangelical parachurch organizations such as the Billy Graham Evangelistic Association, Youth for Christ, and Campus Crusade, and many local Roman Catholic archdioceses. Denominations at the ends of the spectrum of American Christianity refused to participate. Liberal bodies such as the National Council of Churches, Episcopal Church, United Presbyterian Church, and United Church of Christ took issue with the prominence of evangelicals in leadership and the conservative social views and theology of the campaign. Fundamentalist bodies refused to participate because the campaign emphasized ecumenical beliefs and included religious groups they considered apostate. In all, more than 140 Christian organizations participated in the campaign.

The campaign featured national mass media efforts, culminating in the televised film *Faith in Action*, large urban religious rallies, Bible distribution by the American Bible Society, and local small group meetings. The campaign did not achieve its initial expectations, with many observers judging it a failure. Key '73 only raised a quarter of its $2,000,000 fundraising goal, which meant the bulk of its planned media campaign could not be carried out. In many cases, individual denominations ended up directing their funds toward their own efforts during the campaign. Disagreements between evangelical and liberal participants over theological emphasis, media content, and social action highlighted the differences rather than the cooperation between American Christian groups. The campaign was also assailed for promoting an American civil religion (in part due to the prominence of Billy Graham and his close relationship with then-President Richard Nixon). On the other hand, almost 100 million copies of all or part of the Bible were distributed, and many people made professions of faith at rallies while others became involved in one of the thousands of small groups. On the whole, Key '73 did not lead to ongoing interaction between mainline denominations and evangelicals, nor did it precipitate a new era of cooperation among evangelical bodies.

Joshua Michael

See also: Christianity Today; Evangelism; Explo '72; Graham, William F., Jr. ("Billy"); Henry, Carl F. H.

Further Reading

Henry, Carl F. H. "Looking Back at Key 73: A Weathervane of American Protestantism." *Reformed Journal* 24:9 (1974): 6–12.

Kemper, Deane A. "Another Look Back at Key 73: A Response to Carl Henry." *Reformed Journal* 25:1 (1975): 15–20.

"Key 73: A Continental Call," *Christianity Today*, November 19, 1971.

Newman, William M., and William V. D'Antonio. "'For Christ's Sake': A Study of Key '73 in New England." *Review of Religious Research* 19:2 (1978): 139–153.

KOOP, C. EVERETT (1916–2013)

Charles Everett Koop, MD (1916–2013) was a pediatric surgeon and public health administrator and a strong evangelical voice in bioethics. He served as a vice admiral in the Public Health Service Commissioned Corps and as the 13th Surgeon General of the United States under President Ronald Reagan from 1982 to 1989.

Koop was born in Brooklyn, New York, the only child of John Everett Koop (1883–1972), and Helen (née Apel) Koop (1894–1970). He attended Dartmouth College in 1933 on a football scholarship, majoring in zoology. He gave up football after an eye injury and a warning from an ophthalmologist that he was endangering his future as a surgeon. He earned his AB in 1937.

Koop returned to New York to enter Cornell University Medical College. A year later, he and Elizabeth ("Betty") Flanagan were married. They had four children, Allen (1944–), Norman (1945–), David (1947–), and Betsy (1951–). Elizabeth passed away in February 2007, after nearly 70 years of marriage. On April 17, 2010, he married Cora Hogue.

Koop earned his MD degree from Cornell Medical College in 1941 and that summer took a yearlong internship at the Pennsylvania Hospital in Philadelphia, starting his surgical residency the following year. At the end of his residency in 1945, at age 29, he accepted appointment as the first surgeon-in-chief at Children's Hospital of Philadelphia. He established the nation's first neonatal surgical intensive care unit in 1956 and, with help from surgeon Morio Kasai, established the biliary atresia program in the 1970s. He also established the pediatric surgery fellowship training program at Children's Hospital.

While a surgeon in Philadelphia, Koop performed groundbreaking procedures on conjoined twins and invented techniques common today for infant surgery. He invented anesthetic and surgical techniques and participated in the separation of several sets of conjoined twins whose condition was considered hopeless. He gained international recognition in 1957 by the separation of two female infants conjoined at the pelvis and again in 1974 by the separation of twins conjoined at the spine.

Koop is best known for his work on four health issues: abortion, tobacco, AIDS, and the rights of the handicapped. Throughout these controversies, Koop saw himself as faithful to the professional principles and religious beliefs that guided him throughout his career.

Guided by his faith and professional commitment to saving lives, Koop became an outspoken opponent of abortion. As Koop explained, he conceived of abortion as a moral issue that could only be resolved through moral inquiry and reform. In the wake of the Supreme Court's 1973 decision, *Roe v. Wade*, Koop began to speak publicly about his fears that abortion devalued human life and would loosen the moral strictures against other care-dependent members of society. He expressed his concerns in *The Right to Live, The Right to Die*, published in 1976, and in *Whatever Happened to the Human Race?* (1979), a project produced in cooperation with theologian Francis Schaeffer in 1978.

Regarding tobacco use, in his 1988 Report of the Surgeon General, Koop proclaimed that nicotine was as addictive as heroin or cocaine. This action caused Congress to pass legislation requiring health warning labels on cigarettes packs in 1984.

Koop wrote the government's policy on AIDS and in 1988 took unprecedented action in mailing information to every U.S. household. He stated, "My position on AIDS was dictated by scientific integrity and Christian compassion. . . . My whole career has been dedicated to prolonging lives, especially the lives of people who were weak and powerless, the disenfranchised who needed an advocate: newborns who needed surgery, handicapped children, unborn children, people with AIDS" (https://profiles.nlm.nih.gov/ps/retrieve/Narrative/QQ/p-nid/84).

Regarding the handicapped, Koop took a special interest in the April 1982 case of a child born in Bloomington, Indiana, diagnosed with Down syndrome and esophageal atresia with tracheoesophageal fistula. Six days later, after disagreements among the court, parents, and physicians about whether or not to treat the baby, the infant died, having been denied surgical treatment to correct his esophageal atresia and tracheoesophageal fistula. As a pediatric surgeon, Koop and his colleagues had operated on 475 such babies, with ever-increasing survival rates. During his last eight years in active practice, Koop never lost a full-term baby on whom he had operated to correct esophageal atresia. It was due to this background that he became actively involved in championing policies to protect the rights of newborns with defects, which led to Congress passing the Baby Doe Amendment.

Koop resigned as surgeon general in October 1989, a month before the official end of his second term, to become chairman of the National Safe Kids Campaign, an effort to reduce accidents among children. During the 1990s, Koop continued to speak widely on health care reform and promoted the use of the Internet for disseminating health information. Dr. Koop died at the age of 96 on February 25, 2013, at his home in Hanover, New Hampshire. Koop's significance for the evangelical community is significant as a public voice of social and bioethical concerns and as an evangelical who rose to prominence in the government and public visibility.

James Menzies

See also: Abortion, Evangelicals and; Politics, Evangelicals and; Schaeffer, Francis A. and Edith; Social Action, Evangelicals and

Further Reading

"The C. Everett Koop Papers." (n.d.). Profiles in Science: U.S. National Library of Science. Accessed April 29, 2017. https://profiles.nlm.nih.gov/ps/retrieve/Narrative/QQ/p-nid/84.

Koop, C. Everett. *Koop: The Memoirs of America's Family Doctor.* New York: Random House, 1991.

Koop, C. Everett, and G. Timothy Johnson. *Let's Talk: An Honest Conversation on Critical Issues: Abortion, Euthanasia, AIDS, Health Care.* Grand Rapids, MI: Zondervan, 1992.

L'ABRI FELLOWSHIP

L'Abri (French for "shelter"), which emerged out of the family home of Dr. Francis (1912–1984) and Edith Schaeffer (1914–2013) in January of 1955, was a spiritual shelter for those in spiritual need. Today, L'Abri is global, with branches in places such as Australia, Brazil, Canada, England, Holland, Korea, Massachusetts, Minnesota, and Sweden. This historically evangelical ministry, though not marketed with advertisements and flyers, has made a significant impact on thousands of lives, seeking to meet people where they are and lead them to where they need to be. L'Abri strives to help individuals, within a Christian community setting, to find honest and satisfactory intellectual and existential answers about such topics as God, reality, truth, evil, humanity, and Christianity's application to society in all of its forms (e.g., the arts).

This ministry, which was named L'Abri by Francis Schaeffer, almost ended nearly when it began in the early months of 1955. Soon after the Schaeffer family returned to Champéry, Switzerland, from the United States, their youngest child, Frank, was afflicted by polio; their home was nearly destroyed by a terrifying avalanche of ice and mud (January); and then they received a letter of expulsion from the Swiss authorities for March 31 that same year. The reason for their expulsion was the religious influence they had had on the citizens in the village of Champéry, a place that was strongly Roman Catholic.

But through a series of unexpected events, their expulsion was annulled. Notwithstanding, the Schaeffer family was obligated to move to the nearby Protestant canton of Vaud and purchase property there. Then through another set of unexpected events, they made their home in the small village of Huémoz and purchased Chalet Les Mélèzes. This three-level chalet became the focal point for L'Abri. From this chalet, one could look across the Rhone Valley and see the mountaintops of the Dents du Midi. Within a few weeks of their move to Huémoz, one of their three daughters, Priscilla, began attending the University of Lausanne. There she invited students, by word of mouth, up to Chalet les Mélèzes for the weekend. From those invitations, L'Abri began its ministry to young people raised in secularism (post-Christians). Word began to spread of a place where people could ask honest questions and receive honest answers. Even American military soldiers stationed in Germany and young women, from many nationalities, who attended finishing schools frequented L'Abri.

In view of the ministry to which the Schaeffers believed God called them, they established four founding prayer principles, namely: (1) to only let God know of their financial and material needs; (2) that God will specifically bring the people He wants to bring to them; (3) that God will plan their work and unfold His plan to them through daily guidance; (4) that God will send the people they need to assist them with the work of their ministry.

Even after 50 years of work L'Abri continues to provide a place for people to ask questions and come to discover how Christianity as a worldview possesses explanatory power, existential relevance, empirical evidences, and logical consistency. In other words, Christianity was not presented by L'Abri staff as something of blind, irrational faith, but as that which is historical, real, true, and viable. Moreover, they sought to discuss how the Christian worldview relates to every area of life, including the arts, economics, environment, gender, philosophy, psychology, science, and sociology. Thus, L'Abri became a shelter where the Christian faith was taken seriously against the growing grip of secularism in Europe.

The historical emphasis of L'Abri is fourfold: (1) Christianity is objectively true, and the Bible is God's written word to humanity. Thus, biblical Christianity can be rationally defended. Honest questions are welcome. (2) Because Christianity is true, it speaks to all of life. Thus, L'Abri seeks to develop a holistic Christian worldview involving such spheres as the arts, politics, sciences, and philosophy. (3) True spirituality is evidenced in people who by grace are free to be fully human. Thus, L'Abri claims that there is no need to try to work out a spirituality on some higher level or in some negative way. (4) Because the reality of the sin following the fall of Adam and Eve is taken seriously (until Jesus Christ returns), everyone is affected by the "disfigurement of sin." Although the "place of the mind" is emphasized, L'Abri is welcome to anyone.

---

10 Significant Parachurch Ministries in Today's World

Parachurch ministries, which have significantly emerged in the 20th century, now numbering in the thousands, are organizations, paid and/or volunteer, that do not work within, but come alongside the church to address a particular area or need.

1. Answers in Genesis (1994)
2. Billy Graham Evangelistic Association (1950)
3. Christian Research Institute (1960)
4. Compassion International (1952)
5. Cru (formerly Campus Crusade for Christ) (1951)
6. Focus on the Family (1977)
7. MOPS International (1973)
8. Navigators (1933)
9. Prison Fellowship (1976)
10. Youth with a Mission (1960)

Through all the experiences the L'Abri staff faced, such as personal successes and failures, challenging circumstances, and the relationships made with people from all over the world who were curious, dogmatic, gifted, perplexed, skeptical, or troubled, with all sorts of worldviews, fragmentations, and divided beliefs, they grew in qualitative ways, making interpersonal connections that generated resources to benefit future generations. Consequently, coupled with the earnest desire to present Christianity as "total truth," L'Abri built an extensive library of books and recordings that could be tailored to meet individual needs.

When a person seeks to stay at L'Abri, he or she is given job responsibilities and a certain time of study throughout the week. L'Abri hosts chapel services, lectures, high tea, and other community connecting projects. Classical music can be heard played in the background, and conversations continue late in the night.

The Schaeffers' written works, which total more than 30 (with several being award winning), and their audio lectures, tours, and videos popularized L'Abri to evangelicals and others alike. By the mid-1970s L'Abri's status changed somewhat, with it becoming a popular "tourist" spot for Christians traveling in Europe. Moreover, the generational needs of people have changed too. Notwithstanding, L'Abri has branched out in the world and continues today, seeking to meet the needs of the present and next generation with a Christian worldview that connects evangelicalism to culture in dynamic and holistic ways.

Edith Schaeffer detailed the history, development, challenges, and changes of L'Abri in the following works: *L'Abri; The Tapestry: The Life and Times of Francis and Edith Schaeffer; With love, Edith: The L'Abri Family Letters 1948–1960*, and *Dear Family: The L'Abri Family Letters: 1961–1986*.

Paul R. Shockley

See also: Abortion, Evangelicals and; Calvinism; Christian Apologetics; Colson, Charles Wendell ("Chuck"); Falwell, Jerry L., Sr.; Fine Arts, Evangelicals and; International Council on Biblical Inerrancy; Koop, C. Everett; Missions, Evangelicals and; Parachurch Ministries; Schaeffer, Francis A. and Edith

Further Reading

Burson, Scott R., and Jerry L. Walls. *C. S. Lewis and Francis Schaeffer: Lessons for a New Century from the Most Influential Apologists of Our Time.* Downers Grove, IL: InterVarsity Press, 1998.

Duriez, Colin. *Francis Schaeffer: An Authentic Life.* Wheaton, IL: Crossway, 2008.

Follis, Bryan A. *Truth with Love: The Apologetics of Francis Schaeffer.* Wheaton, IL: Crossway, 2006.

Hankins, Barry. *Francis Schaeffer and the Shaping of Evangelical America.* Grand Rapids, MI: Eerdmans, 2008.

Morris, Thomas V. *Francis Schaeffer's Apologetics: A Critique.* Chicago: Moody Press, 1976.

Parkhurst, Louis G., Jr. *Francis Schaeffer: The Man and His Message.* Wheaton, IL: Tyndale House, 1985.

Schaeffer, Edith. *The Tapestry: The Life and Times of Francis and Edith Schaeffer.* Waco, TX: Word Books, 1981.

Schaeffer, Francis A. *The Complete Works of Francis A. Schaeffer.* 5 volumes. Wheaton, IL: Crossway, 1985.

Schaeffer, Edith. *L'Abri*, expanded ed. Wheaton, IL: Crossway, 1992.

LAHAYE, TIM AND BEVERLY (1926–2016 AND 1929–)

Tim and Beverly LaHaye have been influential as individuals and as a married couple in American evangelicalism since the 1960s. Very few marriages have influenced American evangelicalism like Tim and Beverly LaHaye's. Their desire to uphold their belief in supremacy of the Bible and the Second Coming of Jesus, and to influence American culture for Christ, has resulted in the establishment of a college, a scientific institute, two political think tanks, a national women's organization, and a bestselling book series that has sold more than 63 million copies. Additionally, the LaHayes established many of these ministries during a period of their lives when most people begin to think about retirement.

Tim LaHaye

Born in 1926, LaHaye, around the age of 9, came to faith in Jesus Christ at his father's funeral. He understood from his uncle, the presiding pastor of the funeral, that Jesus would return, resurrect LaHaye's dad, translate LaHaye during the rapture, and that they would be reunited again—for eternity. This teaching and understanding influenced Tim and his desire to teach the rapture and Second Coming of Jesus for the remainder of LaHaye's life.

At the age of 17, LaHaye enlisted in the United States Air Force and served in Europe as a machine gunner on-board a bomber during World War II. On completing his military service, LaHaye enrolled and graduated from Bob Jones University in 1950. After serving as a pastor in South Carolina and Minnesota, he moved his family to San Diego, California, in 1956 to serve as the senior pastor of Scott Memorial Baptist Church (now Shadow Mountain Community Church) until 1981. LaHaye also earned the Doctor of Ministry degree from Western Conservative Baptist Seminary.

During that time, LaHaye saw his congregation grow from 300 to 3,000. He founded the Christian Unified School District in 1965 and cofounded, with Art Peters and Henry Morris, Christian Heritage College (now San Diego Christian College) in 1970. Additionally, LaHaye and Dr. Henry Morris cofounded the Institute for Creation Research in 1970. Around this time, Tim also began his writing ministry, and in 1966, he wrote the *Spirit-Controlled Temperament*; in 1971, the *Transformed Temperaments*; and in 1976, he coauthored with Beverly *The Act of Marriage*, which has since sold more than 2.5 million copies.

In 1979, LaHaye was influential in encouraging Jerry Falwell to start the Moral Majority—a prominent American political organization that was closely associated with the Republican Party. Around this time, 1981, LaHaye resigned as senior pastor of Scott Memorial Baptist Church, appointed David Jeremiah as his successor, and focused his attention on politics and writing. During that same year, he founded the Council for National Policy, which is dedicated to limited government, traditional values, and strong national defense.

Throughout the late 1970s and 1980s, LaHaye concentrated his efforts on the political process. He formed two coalitions—the American Coalition for Traditional Values, which he founded in 1984, and Coalition for Religions Freedom, which was a precursor to American Coalition for Traditional Values. LaHaye's political involvement increased through the Moral Majority, which assisted Ronald Reagan in becoming the 40th president of the United States. In 1988, at age 62, LaHaye was appointed cochair of the Jack Kemp for President Committee, although later he resigned because of his biblical opposition toward Roman Catholic theology.

LaHaye's interest in biblical prophecy was reignited when he believed the doctrine of the pretribulational rapture was wavering among American Evangelicals; thus, in 1992, he published the book *No Fear of the Storm* (now *Rapture under Attack*). In 1993, at the age of 67, LaHaye founded the Pre-Trib Research Center. What followed would make LaHaye one of the most famous authors in the 20th century.

In 1995, nearing the age of 70, LaHaye and Jerry Jenkins coauthored a novel titled *Left Behind*. The book begins with the pretribulational rapture of Christians and what is to follow for those individuals who remain and endure the seven-year period called the tribulation. The popularity of the book exploded by word of mouth, and what resulted between 1995 and 2007 was that LaHaye and Jenkins published 12 bestselling novels, sold more than 63 million copies; in addition, their books form the storyline of four blockbuster movies. In 2014, a rerelease of *Left Behind*, the movie, came out.

The Left Behind series grossed over $650 million in sales for Tyndale House Publishers. At age 81, LaHaye was estimated to have earned $50 million, but LaHaye subsequently donated millions of dollars to Liberty University to build the LaHaye Ice Center, LaHaye Recreation and Fitness Center, and the Tim LaHaye School of Prophecy.

Beverly LaHaye

Born in 1929, Beverly LaHaye was married to Tim LaHaye in 1947. She attended Bob Jones University, and she and Tim are the parents of four children, nine grandchildren, and 15 great-grandchildren.

In 1978, Beverly LaHaye had finished watching an interview of Betty Friedan, the founder of the National Organization for Women, and was concerned that Friedan was not representing accurately the majority of women she knew who were God-fearing and pro-family, and who promoted Judeo-Christian values. This interview led her to organize her first meeting concerning the Equal Rights Amendment (ERA) in San Diego, California, with more than 1,200 in attendance.

35 Books That Significantly Influenced American Evangelicalism

1. Dietrich Bonhoeffer, *The Cost of Discipleship* (1937)
2. Corrie Ten Boom, *The Hiding Place* (1971)
3. F. F. Bruce, *The New Testament Documents: Are They Reliable?* (1943)
4. Oswald Chambers, *My Utmost for His Highest* (1935)
5. G. K. Chesterton, *Orthodoxy* (1908)
6. Charles Colson, *Born Again* (1976)
7. James Dobson, *Dare to Discipline* (1970)
8. Elizabeth Eliot, *Through Gates of Splendor* (1957)
9. Richard Foster, *Celebration of Discipline* (1978)
10. Carl F.H. Henry, *The Uneasy Conscience of Modern Fundamentalism* (1947)
11. Patrick Johnstone, *Operation World* (1964)
12. D. James Kennedy, *Evangelism Explosion* (1970)
13. Tim LaHaye and Jerry B. Jenkins, *Left Behind* (1995)
14. C. S. Lewis, *Mere Christianity* (1952)
15. Hal Lindsey, *The Late Great Planet Earth* (1970)
16. John MacArthur, *The Gospel According to Jesus* (1988)
17. Josh McDowell, *Evidence That Demands a Verdict* (1972)
18. Donald McGavran, *Understanding Church Growth* (1970)
19. Henry Morris and John Whitcomb, *The Genesis Flood* (1961)
20. Mark A. Noll, *The Scandal of the Evangelical Mind* (1994)
21. J. I. Packer, *Knowing God* (1973)
22. J. Dwight Pentecost, *Things to Come* (1958)
23. Frank Peretti, *This Present Darkness* (1986)
24. John Piper, *Desiring God* (1986)
25. Alvin Plantinga, *God and Other Minds* (1967)
26. Francis A. Schaeffer, *The God Who Is There* (1968)
27. C. I. Scofield, *The Scofield Reference Bible* (1909; 1917)
28. John Stott, *Basic Christianity* (1958)
29. Charles Swindoll, *Grace Awakening* (1990)
30. J. R. R. Tolkien, *The Lord of the Rings* (1954)
31. A. W. Tozer, *The Knowledge of the Holy* (1961)
32. A. W. Tozer, *The Pursuit of God* (1948)
33. Rick Warren, *The Purpose Driven Life* (2002)
34. John Wilber, *Power Evangelism* (1985)
35. Philip Yancey, *What's So Amazing About Grace* (1997)

Concerned Women for America (CWA) incorporated in January of 1979 with President Carter's pronouncement that 1979 would be The International Year of the Child. CWA immediately strategized to expose the concern over the abortion issue to the United Nations. The organization grew, and by 1981, CWA had grown to more than 100,000 members.

Throughout the 1980s, CWA provided legal representation not only for mothers but also fathers. In addition, CWA concerned itself with Supreme Court confirmations, objectionable public school curriculum, deviant sexual behavior such as homosexuality, and refugee needs in Central America. As the membership grew and Beverly LaHaye found herself more often in the capital of the United States, CWA decided to relocate the headquarters to Washington, D.C., in 1985.

The influence of CWA enlarged as President Ronald Reagan spoke at CWA's Fourth Annual Convention in 1987, and Beverly LaHaye met with President Violeta Chamorro of Nicaragua in 1990. Throughout the 1990s, CWA continued to press the United State government to reduce deviant sexual behavior and affirm the sanctity of an unborn child. In 1999, at its 20-year anniversary, CWA establish the Beverly LaHaye Institute—designed to research women and family issues. During the 2000s, CWA continued to advocate sanctity of life issues, defense of the family, traditional marriage, proper education, religious liberty, elimination of sexual exploitation, and the nation of Israel.

Tim and Beverly LaHaye have led the American political and evangelical landscape in more positive directions. Their firm belief that the Bible is the verbally inspired, inerrant word of God; that salvation is only through faith in the death, burial, and resurrection of Jesus of Nazareth; and that Jesus is coming back again has influenced both the religious and public arenas in the United States and the world.

David A. McGee

See also: Falwell, Jerry L., Sr.; Liberty University; Moral Majority; Rapture

Further Reading

LaHaye, Beverly. *Who but a Woman?* Nashville, TN: Thomas Nelson, 1984.

LaHaye, Beverly, and Terry Blackstock. *Seasons under Heaven.* (Season Series). Grand Rapids, MI: Zondervan, 2010.

LaHaye, Tim, and Jerry Jenkins. *Left Behind.* (Series). Wheaton, IL: Tyndale House, 1995.

LaHaye, Tim, and Timothy Parker. *The Book of Revelation Made Clear.* Nashville, TN: Thomas Nelson, 2014.

LANCASTER BIBLE COLLEGE

Lancaster Bible College (LBC) was founded in 1933 as Lancaster School of the Bible. The campus sits on 100 acres in Lancaster, Pennsylvania. It has been nondenominational and coeducational from its inception, and is unaffiliated with any particular church or denomination in its governance.

The founder and first president of LBC, Henry J. Heydt (1904–1987), studied at Moravian College and Theological Seminary in Bethlehem, Pennsylvania, earning an undergraduate degree in 1927 and a Bachelor of Divinity in 1930. After graduation, he pastored a Moravian congregation but left a few years later, disappointed that liberal theology and higher critical ideas had captured the American seminaries and filtered into many denominations, including his own.

The Fundamentalist–Modernist Controversy was raging in the early 1900s, and Heydt became convinced that he should begin a school based on biblical, orthodox Christian doctrine. Strongly influenced by the Bible college movement of the 1880s–1930s, and with a deep conviction in the sovereignty of God and scriptural authority, in 1933, Heydt founded Lancaster School of the Bible, with no financial backing and in the midst of the Great Depression. He also planted a church, Lancaster Tabernacle, later named Lancaster Gospel Center, which he pastored concurrently with his LBC presidency (1933–1953).

He established the college as an evening institute, beginning with 14 evening students and eight daytime students. Heydt maintained a strong interest in Jewish evangelism and was a long-time member of the American Board of Missions to the Jews (now Chosen People Ministries), publishing several monographs on the subject, including *Studies in Jewish Evangelism* (1951) and *The Chosen People: The Question Box II* (1976). When he resigned his presidency, he moved to New York and focused his efforts more intensely on the American Board of Missions to the Jews.

Since 1933, LBC has seen five presidents, each of whom expanded the campus and its programs. Its second president, William J. Randolph, began the push toward accreditation, which was continued by its third president, Stuart E. Lease, and finalized by its fourth, Gilbert A. Peterson. The school has grown from 22 to nearly 2,000 students at its main campus as well as six additional satellite campuses in Pennsylvania, Maryland, Virginia, Indiana, Florida, and Tennessee. LBC is accredited by the Middle States Commission on Higher Education (MSCHE) and the Association for Biblical Higher Education. It offers both undergraduate and professional master's degrees. In recent years (2013), LBC acquired the academic programs of Washington Bible College and Capital Seminary, merging the two as Capital Seminary and Graduate School, geographically housed at the Greenbelt, Maryland, location near Washington, D.C. Through the seminary and graduate school, LBC offers three doctoral and seven master's degrees. LBC holds to a classic evangelical theology, affirming the verbal plenary inspiration and inerrancy of the Scriptures, and a pretribulation rapture, followed by a literal, earthly millennial reign of Christ. Since the college's founding, its mission consistently remains to offer a biblically centered education that encourages and prepares students for ministry, both nationally and globally.

Stefana Dan Laing

See also: Bible, Authority of; Bible Exposition; Bible Institutes and Bible Colleges; Dispensationalism; Evangelicalism; Evangelism; Inerrancy; Premillennialism; Rapture

Future Reading

Ariel, Yaakov. *Evangelizing the Chosen People: Missions to the Jews in America, 1880–2000.* Chapel Hill, NC: University of North Carolina Press, 2000.

Figart, Thomas O., and Margaret G. Uhler. *A Godly Heritage, 1933–1983: A History of Lancaster Bible College.* Lancaster, PA: Lancaster Bible College, 1983.

Glerum, Stephen. *Stones of Remembrance.* Lancaster, PA: Lancaster Bible College and Graduate School, 2008.

Heydt, Henry J. *Studies in Jewish Evangelism* (1951).

Heydt, Henry J. *Comparison of World Religions* (1967).

Heydt, Henry J. *The Chosen People: The Question Box II* (1976).

Nichols, Stephen. "The Founding, the Vision, the Times." *Echo* (Fall, 2013): 24–27.

THE LATE GREAT PLANET EARTH (1970)

The Late Great Planet Earth was an international bestseller published in 1970 that articulated one biblical view of the end of human history that is known in Christian doctrine as eschatology. It was the first religious book to break into the secular publishing market and become a bestseller. Authored by Harold Lee ("Hal") Lindsey (1929–) with C. C. Carlson, *The Late Great Planet Earth* popularized dispensational premillennial theology beyond the religious market, bringing the Bible prophecy concept of the rapture of Christians. The biblical premise of the book was based on an interpretation of 1 Thessalonians 4:15–16, which Lindsey and many evangelicals believe is a central passage for the doctrine of the rapture. The book brought that doctrine into popular American culture. The phenomenal success of the book assisted in reshaping the religious publishing industry and popularized evangelical eschatology for an entire generation of Cold War and Vietnam-era Americans.

The theology of the book was not new, but Lindsey popularized it at a moment in American history when there was great social and political turmoil and unrest. His presentation to a nonreligious audience in the aftermath of the turbulent 1960s; the Six-Day War in Israel; and the youth countercultural movement, including the rise of the Jesus People, enabled the doctrine of the rapture and the framework of dispensationalism to spread into broader American culture. In the 1970s and 1980s, the rapture became the subject of numerous books, films, songs, posters, paintings, and bumper stickers. Lindsey's book resonated in conservative Protestant churches as well as among Christian counterculture members such as those in the Jesus People movement. As an author, speaker, and representative of American evangelicalism, and specifically, premillennial dispensationalism, Lindsey's sales were unsurpassed in his genre until the rise of prophetic novels by Tim LaHaye and Jerry Jenkins of the 1990s *Left Behind* series, which were grounded in the same theology and emphasized events in Bible prophecy such as the rapture, the tribulation, and the battle of Armageddon.

Lindsey's writings are not technical or academic, and although some within evangelical academia distanced themselves from some of his theological generalizations and speculation, he found a large audience, especially among teens and young adults. Lindsey was able to write to a young and nonreligious audience and present his views on prophecy and current events in a manner that made sense to readers and in which they understood his teaching to apply to them and their world. It was the most popular religious book published in the 1970s.

Timothy J. Demy

See also: Dispensationalism; Eschatology; Jesus People Movement; Lindsey, Harold Lee ("Hal"); LaHaye, Tim and Beverly; Rapture

Further Reading

Boyer, Paul. *When Time Shall Be No More: Prophecy Belief in Modern American Culture.* Cambridge, MA: Belknap Press, 1992.

Carpenter, Joel A. *Revive Us Again: The Reawakening of American Fundamentalism.* New York: Oxford University Press, 1997.

Lindsey, Hal, with C. C. Carlson. *The Late Great Planet Earth.* Grand Rapids, MI: Zondervan, 1970.

Sutton, Matthew Avery. *American Apocalypse: A History of Modern Evangelicalism.* Cambridge, MA: Belknap Press, 2014.

LEWIS, C. S., AND EVANGELICALISM

C. S. Lewis was an Anglo-Irish author, professor, and Christian apologist. Strange as it may seem, one of the great heroes of American evangelicals was an Englishman, born in Ireland, who taught literature at both Oxford and Cambridge, was a loyal member of the Church of England, and smoked and drank with great regularity. Though he spent the first half of his life as a committed atheist, Clive Staples Lewis (1898–1963) grew to be the greatest Christian apologist of the 20th century. The popular success of his *The Problem of Pain* (1940), which explained in commonsense layman terms how an all-good, all-powerful God could allow pain and suffering in our world, led the BBC to invite Lewis to give a series of broadcast talks on the Christian faith to inspire hope during the Nazi bombing of London. The talks—which found evidence for the existence of God in our in-built sense of right and wrong—argued that Jesus could not have been only a good man, but must have been either a deceiver, a madman, or the Son of God. These talks, which defended the moral imperatives and theological teachings of Christianity, were later collected and published as *Mere Christianity* (1952).

Lewis also wrote a spirited, if at times obscure, defense of the supernatural, *Miracles* (1947), in which he argued that naturalism is self-refuting and that moderns are too quick to dismiss the possibility of divine intervention in our world. Two of his most original works, *The Screwtape Letters* (1942) and *The Great Divorce* (1946), offer incisive analyses of the nature of sin and temptation and of heaven and hell by allowing us to overhear an infernal correspondence between a senior tempter and his nephew, and then to accompany a group of sinners who are allowed to take a bus ride to heaven, where their saved friends and relatives try to convince them, even now, to forsake their sin and rebellion and embrace the grace of Christ. Lewis is perhaps best known for his seven Chronicles of Narnia, magical tales that sweep the reader away to the world of Narnia, a land of talking animals and living trees ruled over by Aslan the Lion, whom Lewis identified as the Christ of Narnia: that is to say, what the Second Person of the Trinity might have been like had he been incarnated in a world of talking animals. In addition to replaying the gospel story, the Chronicles offer timeless insights into the nature of good and evil and how our choices shape and define who we are.

Lewis has exerted a strong and ever-increasing impact on American evangelicals for a number of reasons: (1) As both an apologist and a highly-respected professor, Lewis demonstrated that a Christian could and should love God with his mind as well as his heart (see Mark Noll's *The Scandal of the Evangelical Mind*). (2) By challenging modern prejudices against the supernatural, Lewis paved the way for American apologists, such as Josh McDowell (*Evidence that Demands a Verdict*) and Lee Strobel (*The Case for Christ*; *The Case for Faith*), who would go on the offensive and present Christianity as a logical, systematic worldview capable of being defended rationally. (3) While inspiring evangelicals to engage their intellects, he taught them as well that it was proper and godly to use their imaginations. (4) He encouraged his readers to take a nonpartisan stance in which the core teachings that all believing Christians share (what Lewis called "mere" Christianity) would be privileged over denominational distinctions.

Louis Markos

See also: Christian Apologetics; L'Abri Fellowship; Geisler, Norman L.; Noll, Mark A.; Philosophy, Evangelicals and; Plantinga, Alvin C.; Schaeffer, Francis A. and Edith

Further Reading

Burson, Scott R., and Jerry L. Walls. *C. S. Lewis and Francis Schaeffer: Lessons for a New Century from the Most Influential Apologists of Our Time*. Downers Grove, IL: InterVarsity Press, 1998.

Lewis, C. S. *The Abolition of Man*. New York: Macmillan, 1947.

Lewis, C. S. *Miracles: A Preliminary Study*. New York: Macmillan, 1947.

Lewis, C. S. *Surprised by Joy: The Shape of My Early Life*. New York: Harcourt Brace Jovanovich, 1955.

Lewis, C. S. *Mere Christianity*. New York: Macmillan, 1960.

Lewis, C. S. *A Grief Observed*. New York: Bantam, 1976.

Lewis, C. S. *The Problem of Pain*. New York: Simon & Schuster, 1996.

Lewis, W. H. ed. *Letters of C. S. Lewis*. New York: Harcourt Brace Jovanovich, 1966.

MacSwain, Robert, and Michael Ward, eds. *The Cambridge Companion to C. S. Lewis*. (Cambridge Companions to Religion). New York: Cambridge University Press, 2010.

McDowell, Josh. *Evidence That Demands a Verdict*. San Bernardino, CA: Here's Life, 1979.

McGrath, Alister. *C. S. Lewis—A Life: Eccentric Genius, Reluctant Prophet*. Carol Stream, IL: Tyndale House, 2013.

Mills, David, ed. *The Pilgrim's Guide: C. S. Lewis and the Art of Witness*. Grand Rapids, MI: Eerdmans, 1998.

Noll, Mark. *The Scandal of the Evangelical Mind*. Grand Rapids, MI: Eerdmans, 1994.

Strobel, Lee. *The Case for Christ*. Grand Rapids, MI: Zondervan, 1998.

Strobel, Lee. *The Case for Faith*. Grand Rapids, MI: Zondervan, 2000.

LIBERTY UNIVERSITY

Founded in 1971 in Lynchburg, Virginia, by Jerry Falwell (1933–2007), Liberty University is an accredited evangelical liberal arts university that seeks to instill students with the values, skills, and knowledge that will enable them to impact the world. The university offers more than 450 degree programs, ranging from the certificate to doctoral level. It is the largest private, nonprofit university in the nation, the largest university in the state of Virginia, and the largest Christian university in the world, with more than 13,000 residential students and 100,000 students enrolled online.

Serving as the pastor of Thomas Roads Baptist Church, a church he founded in his hometown in 1956, Jerry Falwell desired to establish a center where evangelical, Christian youth would be equipped to make a positive change in the United States and the broader world. The school began as Liberty Baptist College in 1975 and received its full accreditation in 1980 from the Commission on Colleges of the Southern Association of Colleges and Schools. Liberty would proceed to receive its full accreditation as a university by 1985. In this same year, Liberty University initiated a distance-learning program, which would form the foundation for its online education program, one of the first of its kind. Jerry Falwell would go on to serve as president and chancellor of Liberty University until his death in 2007. He was succeeded by his son Jerry Falwell Jr. (1962–).

Liberty University's educational and degree programs have expanded rapidly over the past few years. It has added a law school, which received its full accreditation from the American Bar Association in 2010. They have also received accreditations from the Commission on Accreditation of Athletic Training, Accreditation Council for Business Schools and Programs, National Council for Accreditation of Teacher Education, Accreditation Board for Engineering and Technology, Accreditation of Allied Health Education Programs, Commission on Collegiate Nursing Education, and the American Osteopathic Association Commission on Osteopathic College Accreditation. These accreditations signify that Liberty University has met and even exceeded some of the high standards placed on collegiate education in the United States.

One of Liberty University's most significant contributions to American education has been in the field of distance and online education. During the close of the 20th century and the first few years of the 21st century, Liberty was struggling financially due to a decrease in enrollment. Yet, at the same point in time, their distance-learning program was growing at a rate of nearly 20 percent each year. After meeting with Michael Clifford, Jerry Falwell unrolled a five-year plan that would transform the landscape of Liberty's educational system. Over the course of the next few years, Liberty would increase the number of classes and degrees that they offered online, which had direct impact on increasing their enrollment. Today, Liberty University offers student the ability to utilize online education for more than 250 degree majors.

Throughout the past few decades, Liberty University has been no stranger to controversy. In 1994, the school was facing financial issues arising from significant debt and received a $400,000 loan from the News World Communications and Women's Federation for World Peace, organizations operated by Sun Myung Moon (1920–2012), the founder of the Unification Church, and his wife, Hak Ja Han. Some questioned the move because of the perception of many evangelicals of the Unification Church's status as a non-Christian cult. Additionally, Liberty University has been a strong proponent of young earth creationism.

Liberty alumni are present and leading in multiple fields including, but not limited to, journalism, athletics, business, and politics. Liberty University is one of the nation's most prominent evangelicals colleges.

Daniel Hill

See also: Baptists and Evangelicalism; Bible, Authority of; Dispensationalism; The Gospel Coalition; Inerrancy; Israel, Evangelicals and; LaHaye, Tim and Beverly; Moral Majority; Politics, Evangelicals and; Premillennialism; Science, Evangelicals and

Further Reading

Falwell, Jerry. 1985. "Training Leaders for the Twenty-First Century." *Fundamentalist Journal* (December 1985): 10.

Glader, Paul. "The Unlikely Innovator." *Christianity Today* 58, no. 8 (October 2014): 60–64.

Kennedy, John W. "Liberty Unbound: How Jerry Falwell's Ambitious Sons Have Led the Lynchburg University to Financial Success and a Burgeoning Student Body." *Christianity Today* (September 1, 2009).

Stripling, Jack. "How Liberty U. Became an Unexpected Model for the Future of Higher Ed." *Chronicle of Higher Education* 61, no. 24 (February 27, 2015): 19.

LIGONIER MINISTRIES

Ligonier Ministries is an evangelical parachurch ministry rooted in the Reformed tradition of theology and addressing contemporary cultural and theological issues. Ligonier Ministries began in 1971 in Ligonier, Pennsylvania, 60 miles southeast of

Pittsburg. Robert Charles Sproul (R. C. Sproul), founder and leader of Ligonier Ministries, earned his Bachelor of Arts from Westminster College, Master of Divinity from Pittsburg Theological Seminary, Doctorandus from the Free University of Amsterdam, and Doctor of Philosophy from Whitefield Theological Seminary. Sproul was asked to establish a study center to bridge the gap between Sunday school and seminary; thus, he founded Ligonier Valley Study Center in Ligonier, Pennsylvania, in 1971. In 1984, as Sproul's teaching and speaking ministry expanded, the offices were moved to Orlando, Florida, and were renamed Ligonier Ministries. Under the leadership of Sproul, Ligonier Ministries has expanded from a local gathering of believers in Ligonier, Pennsylvania, to a potential listening audience of more than 100 million people worldwide.

Ligonier Ministries in the past 40 years has established a radio program called *Renew Your Mind*, a publication titled *Tabletalk*, Reformation Bible College, Ligonier Academy of Biblical and Theological Studies, a publishing company, and a music division. Ligonier has hosted regional and national conferences, and has published more than 500 books from 100 different authors. R. C. Sproul has written more than 90 of those books.

The theological perspective of Ligonier Ministries is Reformed theology with an emphasis on the holiness of God, the sinfulness of man, the substitutionary atonement of Christ, and the justification of sinners by faith alone in Christ alone through the awakening work of the Holy Spirit. Sproul is a devoted believer in all five points of Calvinism. Infusing Sproul's systematic and biblical theology is his love for historical theology. Sproul is greatly influenced by Martin Luther, John Calvin, and Jonathan Edwards, and incorporates church history into his many speaking engagements. Some of his influential books in the area of theology and Biblical studies are *Holiness of God*, *Dust to Glory*, and *Foundations*.

In addition to Sproul's theological and biblical emphasis, Ligonier Ministries has also underscored apologetics—a defense of the Christian faith. Sproul is a classical apologist who was influenced by John Gerstner (1914–1996). Although he is an ardent Calvinist, he is not a supporter of presuppositional apologetics—an apologetics approach often closely aligned with Reformed theology. Sproul has also written in the areas of philosophy, science, and world religions. Some of his influential books in the area of apologetics and philosophy are *Defending Your Faith*, *Not a Chance*, and *The Consequences of Ideas*.

In a time period when theological books and conferences were designed for young believers in the faith or for scholars, Sproul, through Ligonier Ministries, has sought to bridge the gap between Sunday school and seminary. His depth of knowledge of the Bible, theology, and philosophy combined with his superb pedagogical skills has gained him a broad audience and illustrates the commitment of many evangelicals to address contemporary social, cultural, and theological concerns in the United States and globally.

David A. McGee

See also: Christian Apologetics; Parachurch Ministries; Reformed Tradition, Evangelicalism and

Further Reading

Ligonier Ministries. (n.d.). Accessed April 29, 2017. http://www.ligonier.org.
Sproul, R. C. *The Holiness of God.* Wheaton, IL: Tyndale House, 1985.
Sproul, R. C. *Not a Chance.* Grand Rapids, MI: Baker Academic, 1994.
Sproul, R. C. *The Consequences of Ideas.* Wheaton, IL: Crossway, 2000.
Sproul, R. C. *Defending your Faith.* Wheaton, IL: Crossway, 2003.

LINDER, ROBERT D. (1933–)

Robert Dean Linder (1933–) is a historian and University Distinguished Professor of History at Kansas State University, Manhattan, Kansas, where he has taught since the mid-1960s. Linder has taught and written extensively on various aspects of the history of Christianity and has published scholarly and popular books on civil religion and the relationship of evangelicalism to late 20th- and early 21st-century politics in the United States.

Linder was born in Salina, Kansas, in 1933. After completing an undergraduate degree at Emporia State University, Emporia, Kansas, in 1956, he went on to the University of Iowa, Iowa City, Iowa, for graduate studies, earning first an MA and then a PhD in history under the direction of noted Calvin scholar Robert M. Kingdon in 1963. Linder focused on the politics of 16th-century Calvinist Pierre Viret in his doctoral and postdoctoral research, which led to the publication of his first book, *The Political Ideas of Pierre Viret*, in 1964. It was at Iowa that Linder forged a lifelong collaborative connection with then–fellow doctoral students Richard V. Pierard and Robert G. Clouse, evangelicals who also became teaching historians.

Following the completion of his doctorate and advanced study at the University of Geneva, Linder began his history teaching career at William Jewell College, Liberty, Missouri, in 1963. In 1965, he became an assistant professor at Kansas State, where he has remained since. Linder has influenced his discipline and the broader community through publications and leading the religious history graduate program at Kansas State.

The relationship between Christianity and politics has remained the primary research focus and the topic of popular books throughout Linder's career. He has authored or edited more than 18 books as well as scores of journal and encyclopedia articles. Beginning in 1988, Linder added Australian evangelical history to his repertoire, often breaking new ground in an arguably neglected aspect of that nation's history. Linder was a charter member of the Conference on Faith and History (CFH), a professional society of evangelical historians, and served on its executive council from 1968 to 1978. In 1967, he became the first editor of the CFH journal, *Fides et Historia*, remaining as editor-in-chief until 1988. In 2003, Kansas State awarded Linder the lifetime title of University Distinguished Professor, the highest honor the university confers on faculty members. His work illustrates the depth and breadth of evangelical engagement in academia and the rise of evangelical historians as well as historians who study evangelicalism.

Liam J. Atchison

See also: Conference on Faith and History

Further Reading

Clouse, Robert G., Robert Dean Linder, and Richard V. Pierard. *Protest and Politics: Christianity and Contemporary Affairs.* Greenwood, SC: Attic Press, 1968.

Linder, Robert D. *The History of the Church.* London: Candle Books, 2002.

Linder, Robert Dean. *The Reformation Era.* Westport, CT: Greenwood Press, 2008.

Linder, Robert Dean, and Richard V. Pierard. *Twilight of the Saints: Biblical Christianity & Civil Religion in America.* Downers Grove, IL: InterVarsity Press, 1978.

Wells, Ronald, ed. *History and the Christian Historian.* Grand Rapids, MI: Eerdmans, 1998.

LINDSELL, HAROLD (1913–1998)

Harold Lindsell was a professor, editor, and author who is most well-known for his defense of Biblical inerrancy. Lindsell was born in New York City on December 22, 1913. In 1938, he graduated from Wheaton College, where he was influenced by the Presbyterian theological scholar Gordon H. Clark and became friends with Carl F. H. Henry. Subsequently, he completed a master's degree at University of California, Berkeley in 1939 and a PhD in history at New York University in 1942. He taught at Columbia Bible College in South Carolina as a professor of church history and missions, and was ordained into the Southern Baptist Convention at First Baptist Church in Columbia, having converted from the Presbyterianism of his upbringing and education because of the issues of adult baptism and ecclesiology. From 1944–1947, he served as a faculty member at Northern Baptist Theological Seminary in Chicago, Illinois, joining Carl F. H. Henry, who had taught there since 1940.

On Henry's recommendation, Lindsell was invited by Harold Ockenga to join the faculty of Fuller Theological Seminary as one of its original members in 1947, along with Henry, Wilbur Smith, and Everett Harrison. Lindsell taught church history and missions initially and as the registrar because of his administrative talents. He later took on the role of faculty dean from 1951–1961 and served as vice president from 1961–1964. In his role as dean, he was instrumental in helping Fuller achieve accreditation by the Association of American Theological Schools in 1957.

The vision of Fuller as a mediating point between separatist fundamentalism and secularizing liberalism meant that it faced criticism from both sides, and Lindsell, in his capacity as an administrator, helped defend the "new evangelicalism" of the seminary against both more conservative fundamentalists and liberals during the 1940s and 1950s. However, the growth of the seminary had necessitated a larger pool of faculty, and the addition of new faculty who advocated more limited claims for Biblical inerrancy alarmed Lindsell and other faculty members. Contrary to faculty members who maintained that the Bible was inerrant only in matters of faith and practice or in its teaching on salvation and theology, Lindsell maintained that the Bible's inerrancy extended to every detail, from theology to history and science. His focus on inerrancy as the anchor of "new evangelicalism" increasingly identified him with the conservative faculty at the seminary. The late 1950s and early 1960s saw increasing tension among the faculty on a variety of issues, and Lindsell, as dean and as vice president, was very involved in these debates.

The 1963 ascension of the progressive David Hubbard to the presidency led to the departure of some conservative faculty members and contributed to Lindsell's departure. Lindsell resigned his vice president's position in February of 1964 to become an associate editor at *Christianity Today*, where Henry was serving as editor in chief. After serving as associate editor from 1964–1968, he succeeded Henry in the fall of 1968 and served as the editor in chief until the spring of 1978, when he retired and Kenneth Kantzer assumed the editorship. Under Lindsell's direction, the magazine had increased its circulation to more than 150,000 subscribers by the time he retired, though it avoided bankruptcy in the early 1970s only through financial subsidies from board members and donors. Under Lindsell's direction, it remained a vocal voice affirming conservative evangelical positions, notably on inerrancy, and adopted a more outspoken attitude on social and political issues than it had under Henry.

It was during his time as editor that Lindsell authored his best-known book, *The Battle for the Bible*, in 1976. In it, he identified recent attempts to qualify inerrancy by pastors and theologians in evangelical denominations (such as the Southern Baptist and the Lutheran Church Missouri Synod), schools (including Fuller Seminary), and evangelical organizations and contended that the ongoing debate among evangelicals on inerrancy was of critical importance. Lindsell argued that accepting a qualified inerrancy would undermine other essential Biblical doctrines and sought to alert conservatives to the dangers posed by accepting the possibility of errors in the Biblical texts. He maintained his position that the Bible was without error in every respect and therefore infallible, and further argued that this position on inerrancy should define who was rightly called an evangelical. The book received a wide reading, even outside of evangelical circles, and generated substantial discussion among evangelicals. Lindsell published a follow-up work entitled *The Bible in the Balance* in 1979, to respond to critiques of the earlier book and to call conservative evangelicals who believed in inerrancy but were not vocal on the issue, such as Henry, to take a more public stand.

Lindsell authored over 20 books, including the *New Harper Study Bible* (1991). In 1971, he served as the president of the Evangelical Theological Society. He and his wife, Marion, married on June 12, 1943, and had four children. Lindsell died on January 15, 1998, in Laguna Hills, California.

Joshua Michael

See also: The Battle for the Bible; Fuller Theological Seminary; Henry, Carl F. H.; Inerrancy; Neo-Evangelicalism

Further Reading

Lindsell, Harold. *The Battle for the Bible*. Grand Rapids, MI: Zondervan, 1976.
Marsden, George. *Reforming Fundamentalism: Fuller Seminary and the New Evangelicalism.* Grand Rapids, MI: Eerdmans, 1987.

LINDSEY, HAROLD LEE ("HAL") (1929–)

Harold Lee ("Hal") Lindsey is a prominent evangelical author who first came to national prominence with the 1970 bestseller *The Late Great Planet Earth* (written with C. C. Carlson). Lindsey was born in 1929 and raised in Houston, Texas. He was reared in a nominal Protestant family but rejected religious thought and life and, after graduation from high school, entered the University of Houston. His university time was followed by service in the United States Coast Guard and then work as a tugboat captain on the Mississippi River and waters surrounding New Orleans. After averting a major collision at sea in the fog with a large freighter, receiving only a glancing blow just behind the bow of the ship, Lindsey began to reevaluate his spiritual life and convictions. Later, through reading a Gideons *New Testament* and through dialogue with a lay preacher, Lindsey experienced a decisive conversion to evangelical Christianity. He left his maritime trade and returned to Houston. After several months there, he enrolled in Dallas Theological Seminary, an evangelical seminary and graduate school with a staunch conservative heritage of premillennial eschatology.

On graduation from seminary in 1962, Lindsey joined the staff of the parachurch organization Campus Crusade for Christ (now Cru). Serving as a campus minister on college campuses in California, and primarily at the University of California, Los Angeles, Lindsey was greatly involved in many of the activities of the Jesus People Movement of the late 1960s and early 1970s. His interaction with the secular and religious counterculture on college campuses led him to develop sermons and talks on Bible prophecy and its relevance to contemporary culture. When students asked Lindsey for easy-to-understand information on biblical prophecy, he wrote *The Late Great Planet Earth*. In the years following its publication, Lindsey continued to be a prolific and lasting presence in evangelical publishing with such titles as *Satan is Alive and Well on Planet Earth*, *The Liberation of Planet Earth*, *There's a New World Coming*, *The Road to Holocaust*, and others. He was also involved in making evangelical evangelistic films based on his teachings, and he hosted the program *International Intelligence Briefing* on the Trinity Broadcasting Network until 2006, at which time he started a new program, *The Hal Lindsey Report*.

Lindsey's writings and other efforts have been criticized as being too sensational in his attempts to align current events with Bible prophecy. Critics especially attacked his 1981 book *The 1980s: Countdown to Armageddon*. Lindsey helped popularize dispensational premillennialism in the latter quarter of the 20th century at a time when evangelicalism was growing significantly in the United States, and its influence was being felt beyond the churches and in the political and cultural lives of many Americans.

Timothy J. Demy

See also: Dallas Theological Seminary; Dispensationalism; Eschatology; Jesus People Movement; *The Late Great Planet Earth*; Rapture

Further Reading

Boyer, Paul. *When Time Shall Be No More: Prophecy Belief in Modern American Culture.* Cambridge, MA: Belknap Press, 1992.

Carpenter, Joel A. *Revive Us Again: The Reawakening of American Fundamentalism.* New York: Oxford University Press, 1997.

Lindsey, Hal. *The Events That Changed My Life.* Santa Ana, CA: Vision House, 1977.

Lindsey, Hal, with C. C. Carlson. *The Late Great Planet Earth.* Grand Rapids, MI: Zondervan, 1970.

Sutton, Matthew Avery. *American Apocalypse: A History of Modern Evangelicalism.* Cambridge, MA: Belknap Press, 2014.

MACARTHUR, JOHN F., JR. (1939–)

John F. MacArthur Jr. (1939–) is pastor of Grace Community Church, Sun Valley, California. He was born in Los Angeles, California, to Irene and Jack MacArthur. MacArthur, a stalwart American evangelical leader, is best known for his verse-by-verse bible exposition and pulpit ministry, his *MacArthur Study Bible* (2013), and his internationally syndicated radio program, *Grace to You*. John MacArthur is married to Patricia MacArthur and has 4 children and 17 grandchildren. A definitive scholar in the field of theology, with a pastoral focus, MacArthur attended Bob Jones University but transferred to Los Angeles Pacific College (now, Azusa Pacific University) and obtained a Bachelor of Arts degree. Later, he graduated with honors with a Master of Divinity from Talbot School of Theology in 1963. MacArthur has been given two honorary degrees, a Doctor of Letters from Grace Graduate School in 1976 and a Doctor of Divinity from Talbot School of Theology in 1977.

MacArthur's ministry began in Burbank, California, where he served from 1964 to 1966 as associate pastor of Calvary Baptist Church. From 1966 to 1969, MacArthur served as faculty representative for his alma mater, Talbot School of Theology. From there, MacArthur was brought on in 1969 to serve as pastor of the nondenominational Grace Community Church, where he currently serves as lead teaching pastor. Since the beginning of his ministry at Grace, MacArthur has taken special care in his teaching ministry to devote attention to a close reading of the Scripture, developing the background and historical context of each passage.

In 1985, MacArthur took over as president of Los Angeles Baptist College, and soon after coming to the college, MacArthur and the board of directors agreed to shift the school into becoming nondenominational and to change the name to The Master's College, now an accredited, liberal arts Christian college. Two years later, MacArthur founded The Master's Seminary in 1986 because he envisioned a seminary program that would train men for ministry in the context of a local church; the seminary obtained regional accreditation in 1988. Although a relatively small seminary with only 1,400 graduates since its inception, The Master's Seminary continues to stand firm in its conservative doctrinal alignment, especially in regard to its position on inerrancy and other related doctrines.

In 1969, in conjunction with his preaching ministry, MacArthur started recording his sermons on cassette tapes and set up *Grace to You*, a nonprofit organization, to help him promote his print and other media. In 1977, MacArthur began broadcasting his sermons through *Grace to You* in Baltimore, Maryland, which has grown into gaining international syndication with hundreds of thousands of listeners on a weekly basis.

From a theological perspective, MacArthur holds a number of notable positions that have been influential in the American evangelical tradition. Most notably, MacArthur is a Calvinist who sparked some controversy in the 1980s with his position on Lordship Salvation, citing Hebrews 12:14 as evidence that only those who persist will be saved. MacArthur is a staunch young-earth creationist, as expressed in *The Battle for the Beginning*, in which he vociferously argues against placing faith in science, as this defies faith in God and the Bible. In line with his anti-evolutionary science position, MacArthur is a proponent of nouthetic counseling, a method of counseling that has caused some controversy in psychological circles because it establishes the Bible as being sufficient for counselors to help others cope with mental illness and depression. Additionally, MacArthur defends a premillennial and pretribulational rapture of the church but also believes that the law applies in some ways to Christians in the current age, so he is not a strict dispensationalist. In line with other dispensationalists, however, MacArthur is a firm cessationist (he does not believe that charismatic gifts are practiced today as they were in the New Testament), having written three books and multiple other resources on the issue. Finally, MacArthur is complementarian in his stance on women and authority in the church.

MacArthur is regarded as one of the most prolific evangelical American authors in modern history, publishing more than 100 individual books over a period of 43 years that have been translated into more than two dozen languages. Some of his more prominent books include his *Twelve Ordinary Men* and *Twelve Ordinary Women*, *The Gospel According to Jesus*, *The Truth War*, and *Strange Fire*, ranging in topics including expository preaching, parenting, discipleship, politics, leadership, theology, and personal finance. In addition to individual books, he has published more than 70 Bible and commentary series, including the *MacArthur New Testament Commentaries*, *MacArthur Bible Studies* on books of the Bible, and *MacArthur Study Series* on topics related to the Bible. Most notably, the *MacArthur Study Bible* serves as the cornerstone resource of all of MacArthur's ministry.

Bryce Hantla

See also: Bible Exposition; Calvinism; Christian Apologetics; Council on Biblical Manhood and Womanhood; Master's Seminary; Missions, Evangelicals and; Pentecostalism (and Charismatic Movement), Evangelicals and; Rapture; Talbot School of Theology

Further Reading

MacArthur, John F., Jr. *The Gospel According to Jesus*. Grand Rapids, MI: Zondervan, 1988, 1994.

MacArthur, John F., Jr. *Right Thinking in a World Gone Wrong: A Biblical Response to Today's Most Controversial Issues*. Eugene, OR: Harvest House, 2009.

MARSDEN, GEORGE M. (1939–)

George M. Marsden (1939–) is the Francis A. McAnaney Professor of History Emeritus at The University of Notre Dame. Considered one of the most proficient and influential figures in evangelical scholarship of the last generation, Marsden's work deals with the interactions between Christianity and American culture, especially in regards to fundamentalism, evangelicalism, and higher education.

On completing studies at Haverford College and Westminster Theological Seminary, Marsden went on to earn a PhD (1965) in American history from Yale. Marsden held posts at Calvin College (1965–1986) and Duke Divinity School (1986–1992) before coming to The University of Notre Dame (1992–2008). He holds honorary doctorates from Valparaiso University and Westminster Theological Seminary, and has been a visiting professor at a number of schools including University of California, Berkeley; University of St. Andrews; and Harvard Divinity School. A celebrated historian, Marsden has received a number of honors and awards including the Bancroft Prize, the Merle Curti Award, the Grawemeyer Award, the Eugene Genovese Prize, the Philip Schaff Prize, the Annibel Jenkins Prize, and the John Pollock Award. He has served in editorial roles at *Christian Scholars Review* (1970–1977) and *The Reformed Journal* (1980–1990). In addition to edited works and numerous chapters and articles, he is the author of 10 books.

One of Marsden's monumental achievements has been his leading role as a historian of fundamentalism and evangelicalism. At a time when the tendency among religious historians was to characterize fundamentalism as merely an anti-intellectual reaction slated to disappear with modernity's advances, Marsden's groundbreaking *Fundamentalism and American Culture: The Shaping of Twentieth-Century Evangelicalism 1870–1925* presented a very different picture of fundamentalism. Marsden's work, carefully tracing the role of common sense realism, Baconian scientific method, dispensational premillenialism, and the Wesleyan holiness on the complex social, political, and intellectual movement that came to be known as fundamentalism, changed forever the way the movement was viewed. Marsden's sequel to *Fundamentalism and American Culture*, titled *Reforming Fundamentalism: Fuller Seminary and the New Evangelicalism*, provided an historical account of the tensions involved in Fuller's founding and establishment, thereby elucidating evangelicalism's struggle to emerge out of fundamentalism. In so doing, Marsden corrected the tendency both within and outside the academy to conflate or miss altogether the distinction between these two movements. Marsden's final work on the subject, *Understanding Fundamentalism and Evangelicalism*, offered a collection of essays further articulating the relationship of these movements and their leaders to politics and science.

A second striking contribution has been Marsden's historical assessment of the changing place of religion in the American academy. In the introduction to *The Secularization of the Academy*, and again in his substantial monograph *The Soul of the American University: From Protestant Establishment to Established Nonbelief*, Marsden chronicles the shift from the dominance of Protestants in higher education to the current abandonment and exclusion of any religious perspective. His extensive, richly documented, and careful account of the various sources and movements funding this change substantiated his contention that the current exclusion of committed religious scholarship in the academy is out of step with its avowed pluralistic commitments. In turn, Marsden's *The Outrageous Idea of Christian Scholarship* teased out what the return of religious scholarship to the academy might mean. Addressing both skeptical academics questioning the validity of religiously informed scholarship, as well as Christian scholars seeking clarity, the volume answered detractors while further elaborating how Christian scholars might take up their academic pursuits in light of their religious commitments.

Lastly, Marsden has also been noted for his historical work on early American philosopher, theologian, and pastor Jonathan Edwards. His extensive historical biography, *Jonathan Edwards: A Life* is considered the most important biography ever produced on Edwards. The numerous accolades the volume received are a witness to Marsden's qualification as a top historian with an ability to balance a sympathetic yet critical posture while weaving various (intellectual, psychological, social, cultural, religious, etc.) influences into a convincing narrative. As in his work with fundamentalism and evangelicalism, his biography of Edwards pushed past one-sided views to retrieve a complex man whose thought—formed as it was by his social and spiritual milieu—demonstrated a desire to articulate his religious experience and conservative theological views in light of contemporary cultural and intellectual challenges. As such, Marsden's Edwards is a fitting forefather to these movements.

In conclusion, Marsden's work has played a significant role not only in making fundamentalist and evangelical forms of Protestantism a proper subject of academic pursuit but also in how those both inside and outside of these movements have come to understand the movements. Similarly, Marsden's assessment of higher education and suggestions for Christian scholarship set the agenda for Christian colleges and scholars across North America. A Christian himself and a longtime member of the Christian Reformed Church, his example of how to do excellent scholarship as a religious person has served as a model for other Christian scholars.

Robert S. Covolo

See also: Evangelicalism; Higher Education, Evangelicals and

Further Reading

Marsden, George M. *Reforming Fundamentalism: Fuller Seminary and the New Evangelicalism.* Grand Rapids, MI: Eerdmans, 1987.

Marsden, George M. *The Soul of the American University: From Protestant Establishment to Established Nonbelief.* New York: Oxford University Press, 1996.

Marsden, George M. *The Outrageous Idea of Christian Scholarship.* Oxford: Oxford University Press, 1997.

Marsden, George M. *Jonathan Edwards: A Life.* New Haven, CT: Yale University Press, 2004.

Marsden, George. M. *Fundamentalism and American Culture: The Shaping of Twentieth Century Evangelicalism*, 2nd ed. New York: Oxford University Press, 2006.

Miller, Steven P. *The Age of Evangelicalism: America's Born-Again Years*. New York: Oxford University Press, 2014.

MASS MEDIA, EVANGELICALS AND

Evangelicals have had a longstanding use of mass media and capitalized on its ability to reach large numbers of people. As mass media transformed into networked media, evangelical use of it kept pace and is well established. In the broadening availability and democratization of digital media since the 1990s, and with the rise of the citizen-journalist, small groups and individuals (evangelicals among them) have been able to establish a wide range of low-cost media endeavors reaching millions of people, using video, film, gaming, and social media in the expanding world of media that moves beyond the radio and television technology of the 1940s–1980s. Evangelicals joined the media revolution in full force as media users and media makers.

As an extension of the heritage of revivalism dating back to the nation's earliest days, evangelicals quickly embraced technology and mechanisms to increase listening, watching, and participating audiences. Thus in the post–World War II years, with the rise of American evangelicalism as a vocal and visible segment of American Protestantism, evangelicals and evangelists across the evangelical, charismatic, and Pentecostal spectrum were quick to utilize radio, television, and the Internet. Evangelicals such as Charles E. Fuller (1887–1968), Jerry Falwell (1933–2007), Billy Graham (1918–), and scores of others acquired broadcasting time on secular stations and networks and others such as Pat Robertson (1930–) created their own networks.

In the 1940s, in the aftermath of the bitter Fundamentalist–Modernist religious debates in many Protestant denominations, there was a backlash by "mainline" denominations against the rapidly growing evangelical movement. Many Protestant leaders in these denominations argued that the radio time should not be sold or given as public service time to fundamentalists and evangelicals because these preachers were not denominationally regulated. However, the radio audiences of

WMBI

WMBI, otherwise known as Moody Radio (90.1 FM), has sought to expose the greatest number of people to the gospel since 1926, when it first came on the air in Chicago. Now Moody Radio extends around the world, with hundreds of outlets offering evangelical messages, stories, teaching, and other programs. It presently has three HD digital signs and six program services available by means of the Internet.

evangelicals were enormous. For example, Charles Fuller's *Old Fashioned Revival Hour* purchased 50 percent more airtime than the next largest secular broadcaster on the Mutual Broadcasting System (one of only three national radio broadcasting systems).

In 1943, the Federal Council of Churches supported extremely restrictive regulations against evangelicals desiring airtime and persuaded the three national networks (NBC, CBS, and the Mutual Broadcasting System) to adopt the restrictive regulations; every evangelical was taken off national radio and limited to local and independent stations.

More than 150 evangelical broadcasters joined together in 1944 and formed the National Religious Broadcasters association to gain credibility for evangelicals and fight the ban. In 1949, the newly created ABC radio network reversed the ban on paid radio broadcasting, and the other networks soon followed. The airwaves were opened again to evangelicals, and they fully embraced the technology (and television as it gained popularity in the 1950s and beyond).

From those initial beginnings, evangelicals are today a prominent presence in the media industry, with companies such as the Salem Radio Network and Salem Media Group successfully competing for market share. Evangelical radio, including satellite, web streaming, and podcasting, is divided into two formats— contemporary Christian music and preaching/teaching. From radio waves to television, to cyberspace, postwar evangelicals have capitalized on technology to disseminate their beliefs nationally and internationally, becoming consumers and creators of mass media.

Timothy J. Demy

See also: Contemporary Christian Music; Fuller, Charles E.

Further Reading

Hangen, Tona J. *Redeeming the Dial: Radio, Religion, and Popular Culture in America.* Chapel Hill, NC: The University of North Carolina Press, 2002.

Schultze, Quentin J. *Televangelism and American Culture: The Business of Popular Religion.* Eugene, OR: Wipf & Stock, 2003.

Schultze, Quentin J., and Robert H. Woods Jr., eds. *Understanding Evangelical Media: The Changing Face of Christian Communication.* Downers Grove, IL: InterVarsity Press, 2008.

Ward, Mark, Sr. *Air of Salvation: The Story of Christian Broadcasting.* Grand Rapids, MI: Baker Books, 1994.

MASTER'S SEMINARY, THE

Founded in 1986 in Los Angeles, California, by Dr. John MacArthur (1939–), the renowned pastor of Grace Community Church, conference speaker, popular Christian author, radio and TV preacher with Grace to You media ministry, the mission of The Master's Seminary is to advance the kingdom of the Lord Jesus Christ by equipping godly men to be pastors and/or trainers of pastors for excellence in service to Christ in strategic fields of Christian ministry. Offering graduate-level biblical, theological, and pastoral training, The Master's Seminary is designed to equip men for ministry within the local church.

Following his graduation with honors from Talbot Theological Seminary, John MacArthur became pastor of Grace Community Church in Sun Valley, California. Following a verse-by-verse style of Bible preaching known as biblical exposition, whereby one examines and proclaims from the Hebrew and Greek grammar and syntax within its historical and literary context what the Scripture state, the church grew to a capacity of 3,000 people. In 1985, MacArthur became president of The Master's College (formerly named the Los Angeles Baptist College), a liberal arts Christian college, and then in 1986, he established The Master's Seminary to equip pastors and Christian missionaries for full-time ministry. John MacArthur is also president and Bible teacher for Grace to You, which promotes his various ministries such as his audio messages, books, conference speaking, and other opportunities of ministry.

As founding president, Dr. John MacArthur has retained a steadfast focus on training men for Biblical exposition while also assisting in the development of their

---

Prominent Evangelical Seminaries

Evangelical seminaries and divinity schools (the latter are associated with universities) are graduate-level institutions that educate and equip students for professional roles in ministry (e.g., missionary, pastor, teacher). They not only place a strong emphasis on understanding biblical languages, books of the Bible, and theology, but also the importance of character formation, servant-leadership, and practical skills of ministry. Some of the most prominent evangelical seminaries and divinity schools in America are listed here:

Beeson Divinity School (1988)
Covenant Theological Seminary (1956)
Dallas Theological Seminary (1924)
Denver Seminary (1950)
Fuller Theological Seminary (1947)
Gordon Conwell Theological Seminary (1969)
The Master's Seminary (1986)
Southern Baptist Theological Seminary (1859)
Southwestern Baptist Theological Seminary (1908)
Talbot School of Theology (1952)
Trinity Evangelical Divinity School (1897)
Western Seminary (1927)
Westminster Theological Seminary (1929)

spiritual life. The Master's Seminary received its first regional accreditation in 1988 from the Western Association of Schools and Colleges. The school originally only offered a Master of Divinity but has since expanded its degree programs to include a Diploma of Theology, Bachelor of Theology, Master of Theology, Doctor of Ministry, and Doctor of Theology. Students matriculating through the Master of Theology are able to choose an emphasis in Old Testament, New Testament, biblical exposition, or theological studies. Students enrolled in the Doctorate of Theology degree program are able to choose an emphasis in Old Testament, New Testament, or theological studies.

In 1990, the faculty of The Master's Seminary began publishing a semiannual journal entitled the *Master's Seminary Journal*, which addresses issues in biblical exposition, theology, and pastoral ministry. Additionally, since 1998, The Master's Seminary annually hosts The Richard L. Mayhue Lecture Series, which addresses theological issues during spring chapel, is presented by various faculty members. This series is then published in the fall issue of the *Master's Seminary Journal*.

The Master's Seminary is conservative theologically and strongly holds to the inerrancy of Scripture, affirming the Chicago Statement on Biblical Inerrancy. Seeing implications in expository preaching, personal holiness, the life of the local church, and global missions, the school believes that commitment to the truthfulness and sufficiency of Scripture is of paramount importance. The school has a thorough doctrinal statement, which the faculty members are called to sign and fully embrace. The Master's Seminary affirms the doctrine of biblical inerrancy, a Reformed soteriology, and a premillennial, dispensational eschatology.

Beginning with an inaugural class of 95 students and four full-time faculty members, the seminary now boasts almost 400 students and 20 full-time faculty. True to its mission, more than 85 percent of all alumni are currently serving in full-time ministry across the globe, and the school remains a strong institution of American evangelical higher education.

Daniel Hill

See also: Bible Exposition; Calvinism; Dispensationalism; Hermeneutics; International Council on Biblical Inerrancy; MacArthur, John F., Jr.; Premillennialism; Rapture

Further Reading

MacArthur, John, Jr. *Pastoral Ministry: How to Shepherd Biblically.* Thomas Nelson, 2005.

MacArthur, John, Jr., and the Master's Seminary Faculty. *Rediscovering Expository Preaching: Balancing the Science and Art of Biblical Exposition.* Nashville, TN: W Publishing Group, 1992.

Mayhue, Richard. "A Short History of The Master's Seminary." *Master's Seminary Journal* 3, no. 1 (March 1, 1992): 1–3.

Mayhue, Richard. "Avoiding the Unavoidable: Protecting The Master's Seminary for Future Generations." *The Master's Seminary Journal* 24, no. 1 (Spring 2013): 1–4.

MCDOWELL, JOSH (1939–)

Josh McDowell is an evangelical evangelist and apologist with a focus on college students. Born Joslin McDowell in Michigan in 1939, Josh was raised in a conflicted environment of church-going and parental abuse at the hands of an alcoholic father. By the time he enrolled in a community college in Battle Creek, McDowell counted himself an agnostic and had no use for Christianity. Nevertheless, he responded to a challenge to examine the claims of the faith, a challenge delivered by a small, Christian, student-faculty group who'd impressed him.

As McDowell studied the matter, he came to the conviction that Christianity was true and that the supporting evidence was overwhelming: "If I were to remain intellectually honest, I had to admit that the Old and New Testament documents were the most reliable documents in all of antiquity." And by extension, as McDowell tells it in the opening chapter of his 1986 book *More Than a Carpenter*, he came to believe that Jesus "was all he claimed to be."

Trusting in Christ, McDowell became a believer, and the change was dramatic. Over the decades of his life, he became one of the church's foremost apologists for the faith, delivering tens of thousands of talks to tens of millions of people in well over a hundred countries. McDowell's plans to pursue a law degree gave way to enthusiasm to commend Jesus to a doubting world. In this connection, he transferred to Wheaton College to complete his bachelor's degree, which he followed with an MDiv at Talbot School of Theology. In 1964, he began to travel and speak for Campus Crusade, and in due course, he established Josh McDowell Ministry, which became a division of Cru (the U.S. division of Campus Crusade for Christ International).

When recounting the change that came to his life after conversion, McDowell listed the reception of mental peace in place of continual agitation of spirit, the calming of an explosive temper, and freedom from hatred, most dramatically for his father, whom he was able to lead to Christ.

Models of Christian Apologetics

Classical Apologetics: A prominent strategy in the history of the church methodologically, this approach to apologetics begins by using natural theology in order to establish theism. Once theism is established, then one can show historical evidences that support Christianity. Major proponents include Norman L. Geisler and Frank Turek.

Evidential Apologetics: The starting point for this approach is a broad range of historical evidences (e.g., archeology; the bodily resurrection of Jesus Christ; the historical reliability of the Gospels). As a result one argues for both theism and Christianity. One major proponent is Josh McDowell.

Historical Apologetics: Also called "resurrection apologetics," this methodology begins by showing the historicity of the New Testament documents. Once one demonstrates that the New Testament documents are historically reliable, then one can move

(continued)

to the historical record of the miracles of Christ, with particular attention given to the deity and resurrection of Jesus Christ. Thus, after one affirms that Jesus Christ is the Son of God, then whatever He affirms is true. Jesus affirms the truth of Scripture. Thus, the Scripture is true.

Relational apologetics is particularly used with those who embrace a postmodern worldview or mindset. Thus, one begins by sharing the personal narrative of having a love relationship with Jesus Christ. Jesus is the embodiment of truth. Thereafter, one can offer evidential, historical, and logical evidences.

The experiential approach appeals to personal experiences with God or Christianity. Thus, this view can involve a mystical religious experience, a divine encounter, or other type of experiences such as "conversion," a "changed life," or some type of testimony where God did something special. Thereafter, the person might be drawn to say, "I want what you have!"

The cumulative case approach is an informal strategy whereby one demonstrates that Christianity provides the best explanation of data, using probabilities. This view can stack up all the arguments, evidences, the existential, and experiences and ask what is more likely the case (e.g., atheism vs. Christianity). William Lane Craig and Richard Swinburne use this approach.

This approach, pioneered by Francis A. Schaeffer, uses a presuppositional foundation that argues that only biblical Christianity posits a foundation that is strong enough to support sinful society and produce God-given values, meaning, and significance, as He is here and not silent (God is both infinite and personal). Other worldviews/cultures cannot adequately nor consistently handle the sinfulness of humanity, the intrinsic value of creation (including humanity), and the nature of the external world, or even produce values that correspond to how things actually are (designed). Os Guinness, Nancy Pearcey, and Ravi Zacharias are major proponents of this view.

Imaginative apologetics use symbolic stories as a central apologetic strategy in their depictions of absolutes, evil, goodness, sacrifice, the power and corruption of temptation, and virtues such as loyalty and love. Thus, using the power of imagination, brilliant story telling, and irony/paradox, they seek to communicate biblical concepts and teachings in a compelling way. This approach finds its source in the literary genius of the creative group of apologetics in England: G. K. Chesterton (1874–1936), C. S. Lewis (1898–1963), Dorothy Sayers (1893–1957), and J. R. R. Tolkien (1892–1973).

Presuppositionalism is a school of thought in apologetics within Reformed theology, pioneered by evangelical philosophers Cornelius Van Til (1895–1987) and Gordon Clark (1902–1985), and clarified, modified, and advanced by thinkers like John M. Frame (1939–). In essence, its proponents claim that Christians must first presuppose the Christian worldview and demonstrate from that position its logical coherence. Apart from a Christian worldview, one cannot properly understand such things as meaning and morality without having those required epistemic conditions met. Given the vast distinction between God and His creation, there is no neutral ground to contend for the Christian faith. The best one can do is undercut objections to the Christian faith, showing how incoherent and unsatisfactory they are.

Given his bitter home experience, he has urged parents to exercise the "Seven A's" in relationships with their children—Affirmation (authenticating their feelings), Acceptance (with unconditional love), Appreciation (holding them in esteem), Affection (in appropriate word and touch), Availability (with sufficient presence), Approach (keeping channels open), and Accountability (with loving boundaries).

This sort of easily remembered formulation is characteristic of his work. For example, one sees in *Right from Wrong* repeated use of the rubric "Precepts, Principles, Person" for testing moral truth. And his most famous, and frequently updated, book, *Evidence That Demands a Verdict*, is replete with side-by-side comparisons, sometimes in table form, bite-sized notes and quotes, and historical taxonomies.

In the course of his travels, McDowell became increasingly aware of the destitute peoples abroad, and in 1991, he established Operation Carelift "to meet the physical and spiritual needs he discovered in orphanages, hospitals, schools, and prisons in the countries of the former Soviet Union." Nearly $50 million in supplies were provided through this ministry, for nearly a million of the recipients' children. For this, McDowell received an honorary doctor of pediatrics from the Russian Academy of Medicine.

McDowell has authored or coauthored scores of books that have appeared in more than 100 languages. *World* magazine selected his 1972 book, *Evidence That Demands a Verdict* as one of the 20th-century's top 100, along with George Orwell's *1984*, C. S. Lewis's *Mere Christianity*, Thomas Kuhn's *The Structure of Scientific Revolutions*, Anne Frank's *The Diary of a Young Girl*, and Allan Bloom's *The Closing of the American Mind*.

Evidence That Demands a Verdict marshals a wide range of data to support the claim that the Christian faith is compelling—the "cumulative case" approach. For instance, McDowell writes of the Bible's historical and archaeological qualifications, the "trilemma" that Jesus must be "Lord, Liar or Lunatic," the fulfillment of Old Testament prophecies in the New Testament, and the impact of Christianity on individual lives. And in subsequent work, he critiques world religions, such as Islam and Hinduism; "secular religions" such as agnosticism and Marxism; groups such as Jehovah's Witnesses and Mormons; and the occult, such as witchcraft and astrology. His ministry has also been replete with special events, some of which turned into campaigns: Six Hours with Josh, Why Wait?, Counter the Culture, Right From Wrong, and Beyond Belief to Convictions.

He and his wife, Dottie, have been married for more than 40 years, with four children, and 10 grandchildren. Son Sean earned a PhD in apologetics at Southern Baptist Theological Seminary, and together, father and son have written several books, including *Evidence for the Resurrection*, *The Bible Handbook of Difficult Verses*, *The Unshakable Truth*, *77 FAQs About God and the Bible*, and *10 Commitments for Dads*. McDowell has been an outspoken evangelical apologist for Christianity since the 1960s.

Mark Coppenger

See also: Apologetics; Cru; Evangelism; Parachurch Ministries

Further Reading

"Josh's Bio." Josh McDowell Ministry. (July 15, 2016). https://www.josh.org/about-us/joshs-bio/.

McDowell, Josh. *The New Evidence That Demands a Verdict.* Nashville, TN: Thomas Nelson, 1999.

McDowell, Josh. "Compare: Precepts, Principles, Person." Josh McDowell's Official Blog. (May 27, 2010). http://joshmcdowell.blogspot.com/2010/05/compare-precepts-principles-person.html.

McDowell, Josh. "My Story." Cru. (n.d.). Accessed April 29, 2017. https://www.cru.org/how-to-know-god/my-story-a-life-changed/my-story-josh-mcdowell.html.

McDowell, Josh. "Trilemma (Lord, Liar, Lunatic?)" YouTube. (n.d.). Accessed April 29, 2017. https://www.youtube.com/watch?v=clNG5YQbmwI.

McDowell, Josh, and Bob Hostetler. *Right from Wrong: What You Need to Know to Help Youth Make Right Choices.* Dallas: Word Publishing, 1994.

MCGEE, J. VERNON (1904–1988)

John Vernon McGee was a popular evangelical radio teacher during the 1940s–1980s and one of many evangelicals to utilize mass media after the Second World War. McGee was an ordained Presbyterian minister (PCUS), pastor of a nondenominational church, and Bible teacher best known for his *Thru the Bible* radio broadcasts heard on more than 800 stations in America and Canada—four in the Dallas area alone—and via satellite and the Internet throughout the world.

McGee was born in Hillsboro, Texas. He graduated with his Bachelor of Arts in 1930 from Southwestern University (Memphis, Tennessee); Bachelor of Divinity in 1933 from Columbia Theological Seminary; Master of Theology in 1937 from Dallas Theological Seminary; and a Doctor of Theology in 1940 from Dallas Theological Seminary.

McGee's first pastorate was in Midway, Georgia. He went on to serve in Presbyterian churches in Decatur, Georgia; Nashville, Tennessee (Second Presbyterian); and Cleburne, Texas (First Presbyterian, 1936–1940), before moving with his wife to Pasadena, California, where he accepted a position at the Lincoln Avenue Presbyterian Church (1940–1948).

The McGees moved in 1949 from Pasadena to Los Angeles, where he became the pastor of the Church of the Open Door, continuing as pastor until 1970. McGee also served as head of the English Department and chairman of the Bible Department at the Bible Institute of Los Angeles (Biola University) and was a visiting lecturer at Dallas Theological Seminary. In 1962, he cofounded and taught at the Los Angeles Bible Training School.

McGee's radio career started in 1941 with a Sunday afternoon program called the *Open Bible Hour*. In 1967, he began Thru the Bible, in the five-year format it's in today. The 30-minute programs are designed to guide listeners through the Old and New Testaments in five years.

After retiring from the Church of the Open Door three years later, he focused on the rapidly growing radio ministry. Originally recorded reel to reel, the programs gradually become digital. They can be purchased on CD or downloaded free from Thru the Bible's Web site. At the time of his death, the program aired in 34 languages. Today, it's in more than 100 languages and is broadcast on Trans World Radio throughout the world every weekday.

The ministry has about 20 employees and is housed in a nondescript building with no signage. There is no homage paid to Dr. McGee, beyond one photo in the cafeteria. His desk and pulpit, and the reel-to-reel tape player he originally recorded on, remain on display in the building.

In a systematic study of each book of the Bible, McGee took listeners from Genesis to Revelation in a two-and-a-half-year "Bible bus trip," as he called it. After retiring from the pastorate in January 1970, and realizing that two and a half years was not enough time to teach the Bible, McGee completed another study of the entire Bible in a five-year period.

"Bus riders" who make up *Thru the Bible's* audience are comprised mostly of the elderly who no longer make it to church, homeschoolers who use the program as their Bible study, and truck drivers and jail inmates. Another large part of the audience is listeners in foreign lands, who could be persecuted for practicing their faith. In non-English-speaking countries, producers translate the broadcasts and read the scripts.

Dr. McGee always planned to be the voice of *Thru the Bible* even posthumously. He and his board of directors were steadfast in their desire to continue the teachings long after he passed away. They did not want to risk "watering down" his original messages by handing things over to a successor.

McGee continued speaking after retirement, including while battling cancer, from which he fully recovered. A heart problem surgically corrected in 1965 (at which time doctors gave him six months to live) resurfaced, and he died in his sleep at age 84 on December 1, 1988. *Thru the Bible* continues to air on more than 800 radio stations in North America, is heard in more than 100 languages, and is broadcast worldwide via radio, shortwave, and the Internet.

As Thru the Bible president and longtime friend of McGee said, "It doesn't really matter that he's no longer here with us in person. What is important is that people are reading the Scriptures and are learning its truths. That's what mattered to Dr. McGee when he was alive and that's what still matters to us today." The ministry continues in the present. McGee's popularity as an evangelical radio voice illustrates how evangelicals embraced mass-media communications in the post–World War II era when the radio waves and later television communications were broadened to religious broadcasters and listeners beyond the prewar audiences.

James Menzies

See also: Mass Media, Evangelicals and

Further Reading

Delgado, Berta. "A Voice from the Heavens: J. Vernon McGee Guides Listeners through the Bible—from Beyond." Dallas Morning News. 2004. Accessed April 29, 2017. http://religionblog.dallasnews.com/2007/10/post-58.html/.

Hangen, Tona J. *Redeeming the Dial: Radio, Religion & Popular Culture in America.* Chapel Hill, NC: The University of North Carolina Press, 2002.

McGee, J. Vernon. *Genesis through Revelation.* (Thru the Bible 5 Volume Set). Nashville: Thomas Nelson, 1983.

Thru the Bible Radio Network. (n.d.). Accessed April 29, 2017. http://www.ttb.org/contentpages/21718/f744e18c-4e81-44c3-b6ce-c0231c0ec9f8/Dr.J.VernonMcGee.aspx.

Tomaso, Bruce. "More on Texas Pastor, Long Dead." *Dallas Morning News.* (October 2007). https://www.dallasnews.com/life/faith/2070/10/10/post-58.

MESSIANIC JUDAISM

Messianic Judaism is a movement of Jewish people for whom Jesus of Nazareth is the Messiah. It is a movement that is contested within Judaism and by some within Christianity, although accepted within evangelicalism for its shared doctrinal beliefs with evangelicals. The Messianic Jewish Movement is a response to the beliefs, worship, and lifestyle practices of Jews who accept Christian beliefs about Jesus of Nazareth as the promised Messiah of the Hebrew Scriptures (Old Testament).

There are various definitions of Messianic Judaism. Some erroneously believe that it is a syncretic movement that combines Christianity with Judaism. Syncretism is the blending of common aspects of different belief systems to present a unity that makes these differing systems inclusive. Others contend that Messianic Judaism is a movement of Jewish people who have accepted *Yeshua* (Jesus's Hebrew name) as their Messiah.

The English word "Messiah" comes from the Hebrew word *Moshiach*, which is translated in Greek as *Messias*. Its literal meaning is "anointed one" or "chosen one." It is questionable to many Jewish people whether one can be Jewish and believe in *Yeshua*. They state that no one can truly be Messianic because they believe that the Messiah has not yet come. They consider a Jew who believes in *Yeshua* to be a Christian and no longer a Jew (as does the Israeli legal system and its courts).

Who Is a Jew?

There is no definitive definition as to who is or is not a Jew. There is a religious definition, which is that anyone practicing one of the three main branches of Judaism—Orthodox, Conservative, or Reform—is a Jew. There is also a nationalistic definition—that is, one who is a citizen of Israel. There is also an ethnic identification by birth that is not contingent on practice of the faith or citizenship.

According to Messianic Jews and evangelicals, the Scriptures answer the question "Who is a Jew." The answer is that God made a covenant with Abraham and defined the lineage of the Jewish people. God declared in Genesis 17:19 that Sarah would bear a son, Isaac. Abraham had other sons, but Isaac was the chosen seed to whom the Covenant would be passed. In Genesis 25:23, Rebecca is informed that Jacob will be the chosen seed. In Genesis 28:13–15, Jacob is assured by God that he is the one through whom the Covenant made with Abraham will be kept. From these Scriptures, one rightly concludes that what is required for someone to be Jewish is for one to be a descendant of Abraham, Isaac, and Jacob. Being Jewish is a matter of birth.

Who Is a Christian?

Evangelicals note that the New Testament states in Romans 10:9–10 that if one confesses *Yeshua* as Lord and believes in their heart that God raised Him from the dead, then they will receive the free gift of salvation. Evangelicals believe that no one is born a Christian. One must choose to be a Christian.

Who Is a Messianic Jew?

A Messianic Jew is a descendant of Abraham, Isaac, and Jacob who believes that *Yeshua* is the Jewish Messiah. The Messiah is a Jewish belief. However, Jewish people who do not accept *Yeshua* as their Messiah consider a Jew who believes in *Yeshua* to be a Christian and no longer a Jew. Messianic Jews counter that a Jewish person who receives *Yeshua* has accepted the complete plan that God has for His Chosen People, the Jewish people. Thus, for them, following *Yeshua*, the Jewish Messiah, is a very Jewish thing to do.

The origin of the Messianic Jewish Movement can be traced back to the first followers of *Yeshua HaMoshiach*, Jesus the Messiah, in the early part of the first century CE. This movement existed mainly in Israel until the end of the fourth century CE, when the Christian faith had erased most of its Jewish origins. From the time of *Yeshua*'s ministry there have always been Jewish people who have believed that *Yeshua* is the promised Messiah. The first church was completely Jewish. From the fourth century on, those Jews who believed in *Yeshua* joined churches, and many were assimilated into a church that usually did not include the Jewish traditions and customs.

At the beginning of the 19th century, the modern Messianic Movement arose in the Eastern European nations. The latter years of the 19th century and the early part of the 20th century saw a great increase in the number of Jewish people who came to faith in Messiah. The rise of Nazism annihilated much of the Jewish and Messianic Jewish population of Europe. In the late 1960s and the 1970s, the Messianic Movement grew in the Western hemisphere. There was the development of Messianic congregations where Jewish believers could worship *Yeshua* and maintain their Jewish customs and traditions.

The modern Messianic Movement is worldwide. There are approximately, 250,000–350,000 Messianic Jews in the United States, 10,000–20,000 in Israel and more than 350,000 throughout the world. There are more than 400 Messianic congregations in the United States and 100–150 in Israel. Some of the larger associations of Messianic congregations are Messianic Jewish Alliance of America (MJAA), Union of Messianic Jewish Congregations (UMJC), Chosen People Ministries (CPM), Ariel Ministries, and Jews for Jesus. Messianic Judaism illustrates some of the social and cultural diversity found within American evangelicalism, as well as varied worship styles within it.

Jeffrey Gutterman

See also: Ariel Ministries; Chosen People Ministries; Jews for Jesus

Further Reading

Ariel, Yaakov. *Evangelizing the Chosen People: Missions to the Jews in America, 1880–2000.* Chapel Hill, NC: University of North Carolina Press, 2000.

Fruchtenbaum, Arnold G. *Jesus Was A Jew.* San Antonio, TX: Ariel Ministries, 2010.

Fruchtenbaum, Arnold G. *The Remnant of Israel: The History, Theology, and Philosophy of the Messianic Community.* San Antonio, TX: Ariel Ministries, 2011.

Goldberg, Louis, ed. *How Jewish Is Christianity? Two Views on the Messianic Movement.* Grand Rapids, MI: Zondervan, 2003.

Rudolph, David, and Joel Willetts, eds. *Introduction to Messianic Judaism: Its Ecclesial Context and Biblical Foundations.* Grand Rapids, MI: Zondervan, 2013.

MILITARY MINISTRIES

Evangelical churches and organizations have long recognized that military members and their families have unique challenges and needs. Service by military members in wartime and peace, as well as long separations from families, spouses, and children, often results in loneliness and intense questions of an existential and spiritual nature. Families of military members stationed overseas also face unique challenges due to isolated locations and challenging military requirements.

Local evangelical churches in military communities, both at home and abroad, have long served the spiritual needs of military members and their families stationed in those communities. Many churches have ministries specifically organized to provide outreach to bases and stations. They offer regular opportunities for worship, Bible studies, and fellowship. Many also provide weekly or monthly meals and transportation to church activities for those without a car. Their goal is to incorporate military members and families into community church life and all that entails.

A number of evangelical parachurch organizations have arisen to answer the spiritual needs of military members and their families. Usually these organizations arose in areas or situations faraway from local churches and in response to the personal spiritual challenges as well a sense of God's call. Organizations such as the Cadence International, the Navigators, Officers' Christian Fellowship, and Cru Military Ministry (formerly Campus Crusade for Christ) offer Bible studies, discipleship, opportunities for companionship for military members deployed away from home, and even a meal and place to stay in overseas locations (Cadence International). These parachurch organizations are led by central boards and funded by donations from individuals and churches. Their statements of faith reflect the evangelical tradition while avoiding doctrinal distinctives that might cause division. Although they exist to serve the human needs of military members and their families, their core mission is evangelism and Christian discipleship: to evangelize military members and then to help them grow in their faith (discipleship). Hundreds of thousands of military members and their families have benefitted from the ministries of these organizations, both in peace and war.

Dayne E. Nix

See also: Cru; Navigators; Officers' Christian Fellowship; Parachurch Ministries

Further Reading

"Being a Leader That God Can Use." Officers' Christian Fellowship. (n.d). Accessed April 29, 2017. http://www.ocfusa.org.

Cadence International. Accessed April 29, 2017. https://www.cadence.org.

Cru Military. Accessed April 29, 2017. http://crumilitary.org.

Loveland, Anne C. *American Evangelicals and the U.S. Military, 1942–1993.* Baton Rouge: Louisiana State University Press, 1997.

The Navigators. Accessed April 29, 2017. http://www.navigators.org.

MISSIONS, EVANGELICALS AND

World Missions is the practice of taking the message of Christianity and engaging in cross-cultural ministry in order to share the truth of the gospel to those who have not received it. It stands as part and parcel of the evangelical ethos and commitment to evangelism and has been integral in the evangelical experience since the mid-1800s.

However, Protestantism has not always had such strong representation among the missionary community. During the Protestant Reformation, there was little engagement and development in Protestant World Missions. The majority of Christian missionaries were deployed by the Roman Catholic Church as the Protestant world attempted to detangle and defend their doctrinal developments from Roman Catholic dogma. Encouraged by the *Missio Dei*, Catholic priests and missionaries spread across the world in the hope of one day making the entire world Christian. But with the rise of Evangelicalism in the 18th century, a paradigm shift would take place within Protestant Christianity. Seeing the vast number of unbelieving peoples in the world, evangelical Christians began to spread throughout the globe, permeating closed countries and engaging unreached people groups. Evangelicals became students of culture, translating the Bible into multiple languages as the need arose in order to advance the spread of the gospel.

The first missionary society was the Company for Propagating the Gospel in New England and Parts of Adjacent North America (1649) and supported John Eliot's (1604–1690) mission work among Native Americans. Concerned for the salvation of Native Americans and other indigenous populations, mission societies such as the Society for Promoting Christian Knowledge and the Society for the Propagation of the Gospel believed that salvation was impossible apart from faith in Christ. As such, Christians must spread and proclaim the gospel to those who have not heard. William Carey (1761–1834) is understood by many to be the father of modern missions. A British Baptist, his work led to the founding of the Baptist Missionary Society (1792). Carey served as a missionary in India and under his leadership the Bible was translated into 39 languages. He also advocated for the establishment of indigenously led churches, a radical concept in his day. Throughout the 18th and 19th centuries, the primary goal of evangelical world missions was conversion. This began to shift in the 20th century, when a greater emphasis was placed on church planting and equipping indigenous populations to make disciples. Throughout the past few centuries, missionaries ranging from James Hudson Taylor (1832–1905) to James ("Jim") Elliot (1927–1956), Lottie Moon (1840–1912), and David Livingstone (1813–1873) have had a tremendous impact in the global church and have served as exemplars to countless others who have followed in their footsteps. Also, there are Christian thinkers who are described as "missionaries" to the intellectuals, such as Dr. Francis A. Schaeffer (1912–1984) and his wife and lifelong partner in ministry, Edith (1914–2013), who reached out to disenfranchised young people caught in the height of the countercultural revolution of the 1960s and 1970s in the Swiss mountains. Another such is the analytic American philosopher Dr. Alvin Plantinga (1932–), whose philosophical works have motivated atheistic and agnostic philosophers in the last quarter of the 20th century to reconsider the reasonableness of Christian theism. Moreover, Christian apologists such as Dr. William Lane Craig (1949–), Dr. Gary Habermas (1950–), Josh McDowell (1939–), Dr. Norman Geisler (1932–), and Dr. Ravi Zacharias (1946–) have contributed to missions worldwide with their writings and public debates, forums, and presentations held at college and university campuses and cities across the world.

Personality Profile: Arthur Blessitt

Arthur Blessitt (1940–), a Guinness World Record holder for the longest ongoing pilgrimage, has carried a cross more than 41,552 miles. He has walked seven continents and 323 nations, islands, and territories. His testimony about Jesus Christ began when he made a 12-foot, 45-pound cross in 1968 and carried it along the Sunset Strip in Hollywood. He has taken the cross to places like the Antarctica, Athen's Parthenon, Roman Coliseum, Egypt's pyramids, Moscow's Red Square, and Mount Fuji in Japan. He's been attacked by a number of animals (e.g., green mamba, baboon, crocodile, elephant) and arrested or jailed 24 times.

During the 18th century, evangelism was understood to be the primary purpose of evangelical engagement in world missions. However, as time has passed, evangelicals have begun to adopt a perspective called "holistic mission," which seeks to minister to both the spiritual and material components of the human person. In other words, this approach attempts to maintain a central focus on faith in Jesus Christ for salvation while also highlighting the fact that love for God results in a transformed life and an authentic love for one's neighbor by meeting their practical needs. The topic of holistic missions continues to be hotly debated among evangelicals as they endeavor to delineate the relationship between social activism and evangelism.

The impact of evangelical missionaries has not been completely positive. Ethnocentrism and the attempt to "civilize" indigenous populations have contributed to imperialism and left many communities damaged. In some cases, the gospel of salvation is confused with Western or American values. In attempting to convert indigenous populations to Christianity, missionaries have acted as forces of Westernization and have been limited by their own bias. This involves a misunderstanding of the nature of culture, as Christianity is not confined to any singular cultural identity or expression. This misappropriation of the missionary task has impacted the perception of missionaries in China and Latin America, among other countries, where some now view the gospel message with increased skepticism.

Traditionally, evangelical participation in world missions has been fueled by two components: obedience to the Great Commission and the glory of God. Believing that they are called to make disciples of all nations, evangelical Christians have spread across the globe, often being on the forefront of ethnographical and anthropological studies as they strive to communicate the message of the gospel to different people groups. It is the evangelical understanding of sin as well as their commitment to the exclusivity of Christ, the belief that salvation only comes through faith in the Son of God, that continues to stir the hearts of missionaries as they spread throughout the world to plant churches and make disciples.

Throughout the 20th and 21st centuries, evangelical engagement in world missions has reached closed countries with the gospel of salvation. Organizations such as Frontiers, Wycliffe Bible Translators, Service in Mission (SIM), and the International Mission Board (IMB) have worked not only to provide holistic care to desperate communities but also to teach the truth's of Christianity in was that are understandable to that context. Additionally, evangelical missionaries have served as preservers of culture due to their commitment to the Bible and willingness to translate it into multiple languages.

Another more recent development in world missions has been the discussion revolving around the Contextualization Spectrum due to the difficulty of sharing the gospel in traditionally Muslim contexts. Contextualization is the process of crafting and communicating the truth of God in a manner that is receptive to a people group while remaining faithful to God's revelation. The Contextualization Spectrum addresses the extent to which the concepts and teachings of Christianity can be immersed in a cultural context before it loses its distinctively Christian nature.

C1 involves using outsider forms and importing them into a cultural context. C2 involves using a mixture of outsider and insider forms. While still retaining English terms for God, C2 is willing to use the language of the culture. C3 attempts to minimize the foreignness of Christianity and utilize forms of Islamic worship that are culturally neutral such as prayer, music, and ethnically defined clothing. C4 embraces forms of Islamic worship that are acceptable from a Christian standpoint, such as abstaining from pork and using prayer postures. C5 allows members to still attend mosque and remain within the Islamic community. Levels C1 through C3 would still self-identify as Christian, whereas C4 would be known as Christians to its community or followers of Isa. Level C5 would allow an individual to remain culturally Muslim.

Although evangelical missionaries have received considerable criticism from sociologists and anthropologists for their cultural impact, this criticism is often misguided. Culture by nature is organic and dynamic. In other words, culture is always changing. Missiologists, those who study missionary means, method, and history, have put a tremendous amount of effort into ethnographic research in order to ensure that they are accurately communicating and inculturating the gospel message. Organizations such as Wycliffe Bible Translators take things a step further by recording local languages and helping them develop their own hymns and styles of worship in manners that are culturally appropriate. SIM seeks to provide evangelism to unreached people groups and medical aid to those in need. In many cases, evangelical missionaries have helped preserve cultural forms while also presenting the gospel.

Daniel Hill

See also: Christian Apologetics; Elliot, James ("Jim"); Emerging and Emergent Churches; Graham, William F., Jr. ("Billy"); InterVarsity Christian Fellowship/USA; Jews for Jesus; L'Abri Fellowship; Pacific Garden Mission; Parachurch Ministries; Schaeffer, Francis A. and Edith; Wycliffe Global Alliance

Further Reading

Howell, Brian M., and Jenell Williams Paris. *Introducing Cultural Anthropology: A Christian Perspective.* Grand Rapids, MI: Baker Academic, 2010.

Ott, Craig, and Stephen Strauss. *Encountering Theology of Mission: Biblical Foundations, Historical Developments, and Contemporary Issues.* Grand Rapids, MI: Baker, 2010.

Piper, John. *Let the Nations Be Glad! The Supremacy of God in Missions.* Grand Rapids, MI: Baker Books House, 2010.

Pocock, Michael, Gailyn Van Rheenen, and Douglas McConnell. *The Changing Face of World Missions: Engaging Contemporary Issues and Trends.* Grand Rapids, MI: Baker Academic, 2005.

Taylor, William D. *Global Missiology for the 21st Century: The Iguassu Dialogue.* Grand Rapids, MI: Baker Academic, 2001.

Tucker, Ruth A. *From Jerusalem to Irian Jaya: A Biographical History of Christian Missions.* Grand Rapids, MI: Zondervan, 1983.

MOODY, DWIGHT LYMAN (1837–1899)

Dwight Lyman Moody was born on February 5, 1837, in Northfield, Massachusetts, to Edwin J. Moody (1800–1841), a farmer and tradesman, and Betsy (Holton) Moody (1805–1896). Dwight was the sixth of nine children. When he was four years old, his father died of heart complications on May 28, 1841. In 1854, Dwight left home at the age of 17 and traveled to the city of Boston in the pursuit of financial prosperity. Despite having scant financial resources and little more than a fifth-grade education, he found employment in his Uncle Samuel Holton's boot and shoe store. As part of Moody's conditions of employment, he was required to attend the Congregational Church of Mount Vernon. On April 21, 1855, Moody committed himself to the Christian faith through the ministry and encouragement of his Sunday school teacher, Edward Kimball.

In 1856, Moody left Boston for the city of Chicago, where he started a Sunday school class for the youth of Chicago's slums and the local Young Men's Christian Association (YMCA). As the Sunday school grew in both size and notoriety, it was visited by President Abraham Lincoln on November 25, 1860, who delivered some inspiring words at Moody's request. With the onset of the Civil War (1861–1865), Moody offered his service in the form of relief work through an Army and Navy Committee of the YMCA, as well as ministering to both union and confederate soldiers as a chaplain. On August 28, 1862, Moody married Emma Charolette Revell (1843–1903), with whom he had three children: Emma Reynolds Moody (1864–1942), William Revell Moody (1869–1933), and Paul Dwight Moody (1879–1947). To help facility Moody's growing ministry, he established the Illinois Street Church (ISC), which was formally dedicated on December 30, 1864. On October 8, 1871, however, the ISC, along with Moody's home and many other important buildings, was destroyed in the Great Chicago Fire. (*Note:* The ISC was later rebuilt as The Chicago Avenue Church on the corner of Chicago Avenue and LaSalle, and was dedicated in June 1876).

In June 1873, Moody traveled to England with the American gospel singer and composer Ira D. Sankey (1840–1908). Together, they traveled throughout the British Isles, holding Gospel meetings and ministering to millions of people until July 1875. At the conclusion of their visit, Moody and Sankey had become household names across much of Europe, thanks in part to Sankey's songbook titled *Sacred Songs and Solos*, which become one of the most popular English hymn books ever written. On returning to America, Moody and his family settled permanently in his native hometown of Northfield in August 1875. A few months later, in October 1875, Moody began a revival tour of great American cities that included Brooklyn, New York City, and Philadelphia, where President Ulysses S. Grant attended one of the meetings. As news and accounts of Moody's meetings spread, he built a stalwart reputation as an honest and sincere evangelist whose Bible-based messages and dramatic style of storytelling was as dynamic and engaging as it was persuasive and transformative. To aid in his ministry, Moody made great use of the evangelistic teaching tool The Wordless Book, which consisted of four blocks of pure color that represented sin (black), atonement (red), righteousness (white), and heaven (gold; first added by Moody in 1875).

In the late 1870s, Moody focused more and more on ministry education and other related ventures. In 1879, he founded the Northfield Seminary for Young Women. In 1881, he established the Mount Hermon School for Young Men. In 1886, he chartered the Chicago Evangelization Society, and in 1889, he established its corresponding Chicago Bible Institute, which was renamed Moody Bible Institute in 1900. In 1895, Moody established the Bible Institute Colportage Association, a publishing venture, which became Moody Press in 1941. On November 16, 1899, Moody preached his last sermon in Kansas City, Missouri. Roughly a month later, Moody died in Northfield on December 22, 1899. Those who knew Moody described him as compassionate, hardworking, humorous, teachable, personable, loving, honest, and one who's Gospel message appealed to all people of all social classes and Christian denominations. He has since been widely celebrated as one of the most influential American Christian evangelists of the 19th century.

Steve R. Halla

See also: Bible Institutes and Bible Colleges; Evangelism; Moody Bible Institute

Further Reading

Belmonte, Kevin. *D. L. Moody: A Life-Innovator, Evangelist, World Changer.* Chicago: Moody Press, 2014.

Dorsett, Lyle W. *A Passion for Souls: The Life of D.L. Moody.* Chicago: Moody Press, 2001.

Evensen, Bruce J. *God's Man for the Gilded Age: D. L. Moody and the Rise of Modern Mass Evangelism.* New York: Oxford University Press, 2003.

Findlay, J. F., Jr. *Dwight L. Moody: American Evangelist 1837–1899.* Eugene, OR: Wipf & Stock, 2007.

MOODY BIBLE INSTITUTE

Moody Bible Institute (MBI) is a Christian institution of higher education founded in 1886 by evangelist and businessman Dwight Lyman Moody. Since its founding, Moody's main campus has been located in the Near North Side of Chicago, but it maintains an undergraduate campus in Spokane, Washington, and a graduate campus in Plymouth, Michigan.

In 1873, D. L. Moody met Miss Emma Dryer, the principal and a teacher at Illinois State Normal University. As they walked to Moody's church, they became immediate friends. Though Dryer was planning to return to Illinois, Moody persuaded her to remain in Chicago and get involved in the work of the church. Dryer agreed to stay, and the following year, while ministering to the needs of thousands who were left homeless by the Chicago Fire, she began developing a program of Bible study, teaching, and home visitation for young women that soon developed into what she called her "Bible work."

During the next decade, as Moody continued his involvement in global evange-listic work, Dryer further developed her training program among the women of Chicago. But as she labored among women, she took every opportunity to encourage Moody to start a training school for young men and women.

With funding from Moody's Chicago Avenue Church, Dryer invited Dr. W. G. Moorhead (later president of Xenia Seminary) to conduct a short-term Bible institute. In May 1882, the institute opened with 50 students. These "May Institutes" were repeated each year until 1889, when the Training School of the Chicago Evangelization Society initiated year-round classes.

The Chicago Evangelization Society grew out of two special meetings held at Farwell Hall in Chicago to discuss inner-city evangelism. At the first meeting, held in 1885, Moody presented the challenge. A fully equipped training school would require at least $250,000. A little over a year later, Moody met with a group in his room at the Grand Pacific Hotel in Chicago and drafted a constitution for the Chicago Evangelization Society with the express purpose of the training and education of ministers, musicians, missionaries, teachers, and laity to proclaim the message of Christianity. Six men were appointed as the institute's first trustees at this meeting. Following Moody's death in 1899, the Society would be renamed the Moody Bible Institute.

Moody explained the purpose of the Society,

> I tell you what I want, and what I have on my heart. I believe we have got to have gap-men to stand between the laity and the ministers; men who are trained to do city mission work. Take men that have the gifts and train them for the work of reaching the people. (http://www.moody.edu/)

The Moody Correspondence School was established in January 1901 for "the benefit of those of both sexes who cannot, for financial or other reasons, attend the Institute personally. The purpose is to give them, as far as possible, all the advantages

---

Irwin Moon and the Moody Institute of Science Films

Rev. Irwin A. Moon (1907–1986) was famously known for being the producer and host of award-winning science films. Founder and director of the Moody Institute of Science, a division of the Moody Bible Institute, the same school where he graduated from, Moon began using science as illustrations in his sermons when he served as a pastor. Consequently, he spent the remainder of his years using science to teach and illustrate Christian concepts, with his scientific films being his greatest contribution (e.g., *City of the Bees, The God of Creation, Facts of Faith, The God of the Atom, Signpost Aloft, The Red River of Life,* and *Windows of the Soul*). Of the 39 educational films the institute produced under his supervision beginning in the 1940s, 27 of them received national and international prizes, including the Eastman Kodak Gold Medal (1980) for qualitatively advancing education through the use of film.

of the systematic methods of study pursued here." The school started with two courses: Bible Doctrine and Practical Christian Work. Both courses were written by Moody's second president, R.A. Torrey. The number of courses grew steadily from 1901 to 1945, and by the end of 1945, there were 17 courses available.

In January 2000, Moody Distance Learning pioneered a Bachelor of Science in Biblical Studies degree available completely online. Since 2000, an online Associate of Biblical Studies degree and an online Certificate of Biblical Studies for graduate and undergraduate students have also been offered. In 2012, Moody Distance Learning launched a complete online Master of Arts in Applied Biblical Studies.

In October 1903, the Moody's Evening School began offering classes four nights a week. During its first term, it averaged 125 students. Its objective was similar to the day program, but with a greater focus on lay workers instead of students working full-time in the church.

The Evening and Day Schools offered the same programs from 1918–1924. From 1925–1930, the Evening School curriculum was narrowed, offering only one course of study matching the Day School (the General Course). In 1959, a Basic Bible Course was designed for students with academic deficiencies, to receive Bible instruction.

In 1982, the Evening School offered students an Adult Bible Studies Certificate. Two years later, students taking college credit courses could earn an Associate of Arts degree (later changed to the Associate of Science in Biblical Studies degree).

Moody Distance Learning offers almost 70 independent studies for personal enrichment or college credit. In spring 2009, Moody Distance Learning offered Web-based independent studies for the first time. In 1997, Moody Distance Learning began offering a Bachelor of Science in Biblical Studies degree. The Evening School continues through Moody Distance Learning's extension sites. Currently operating in Chicago, Ohio, Florida, and Texas, extension sites offer college credit and continuing education courses to nonresident students during evening hours or Saturday mornings.

In 1985, Moody Bible Institute started the Moody Graduate School to provide biblical leadership training. Two name changes have followed: in 2009, to Moody Graduate School and Seminary; then to Moody Theological Seminary in 2011. Moody Theological Seminary currently offers 10 master's degrees and five graduate certificates.

In 2010, Michigan Theological Seminary merged with Moody Theological Seminary to become Moody Theological Seminary–Michigan. MTS–Michigan trains students to be spiritually and theologically prepared leaders who will serve in churches in Michigan and throughout the world. Since 1993, Moody Bible Institute has offered classes in Spokane, Washington, first as an extension site known as Moody Northwest Center for External Studies. In 2005, Moody Aviation—Moody's program focused on training missionary pilots—was relocated from Tennessee to its current site in Spokane. One year later, Moody Northwest became the first branch campus, Moody Bible Institute–Spokane, offering eight bachelor's degrees and two certificate programs. Spokane's Moody Aviation facility partners with Spokane Community

College and employs faculty from mission aviation agencies to offer a Bachelor of Science in Missionary Aviation with two emphasis options.

Throughout the 20th century Moody Bible Institutes was one of the key institutions of the evangelical movement, and its influence continues into the 21st century. Firmly committed to evangelical theology and the Bible, as an institution it was quick to capitalize on utilizing and educating students on the benefits of mass communication and technology, such as aviation, to further the message of Christianity.

James Menzies

See also: Bible Institutes and Bible Colleges; Moody, Dwight Lyman

Further Reading

George, Timothy. *Guaranteed Pure: Moody Bible Institute, Business, and the Making of Modern Evangelicalism.* Chapel Hill, NC: The University of North Carolina Press, 2015.
Getz, Gene A. *MBI: The Story of Moody Bible Institute.* Chicago: Moody Press, 1986.
Moody Bible Institute. (n.d.). Accessed April 27, 2017. http://www.moody.edu/.
Vincent, James M., and Jerry B. Jenkins. *The MBI Story: The Vision and Worldwide Impact of Moody Bible Institute.* Chicago: Moody Press, 2011.

MOODY CHURCH (CHICAGO)

Moody Church in Chicago, Illinois, is one of America's historic "downtown" churches dating to the mid-1800s and one of the most prominent churches of evangelicalism throughout its history. Like other older churches of evangelicalism, the church dates to an era when the religious vitality in cities took place in churches that were located in the center of the cities rather than in the suburbs. Other similar prominent evangelical churches include Tenth Presbyterian Church (Philadelphia), Fourth Presbyterian Church (Bethesda, Maryland), First Baptist Church (Dallas), and Park Street Church (Boston).

The church grew out of a Sunday school for impoverished children founded by Dwight L. Moody in the 1850s. By 1860, there were more than 1,000 children and parents attending weekly. It was the largest mission of its type, prompting President Abraham Lincoln to visit it in 1860. In 1864, a 1,500-seat auditorium and building had been constructed and dedicated on the corner of Illinois and Wells Streets in Chicago's impoverished North Side, and the ministry became the nondemoninational Illinois Street Church. The facility burned in the great Chicago fire of 1871, and the church relocated to the corner of Chicago and LaSalle Streets; it became known as the Chicago Street Church and was dedicated in 1876. As a result of Moody's evangelistic campaigns in the United States and Great Britain in the 1890s, attendance grew enormously, with as many as 10,000 worshipping inside weekly and 6,000 outside. Moody died in 1899, and the church was renamed Moody Church in 1908. In 1915, the church moved to its present site at the corners of LaSalle and Clark Streets and North Avenue.

Moody Church continues to be a vibrant congregation with an active worship outreach program, including a long-standing radio ministry, global evangelism, and active ministries at Chicago's O'Hare and Midway Airports.

Timothy J. Demy

See also: Fourth Presbyterian Church; Moody, Dwight Lyman; Park Street Church; Tenth Presbyterian Church

Further Reading

Carpenter, Joel A. *Revive Us Again: The Reawakening of American Fundamentalism.* New York: Oxford University Press, 1997. http://www.moodychurch.org/get-to-know-us/history-moody-church/

MOODY MONTHLY

Moody Monthly was a publication of Moody Bible Institute (MBI), produced from 1900 to 2003. It began as a monthly magazine for alumni called *The Institute Tie*, with Dwight L. Moody's brother-in-law A. P. Fitt serving as editor. James Gray and R. A. Torrey assumed editorial duties in 1907 and broadened its target audience beyond Moody alumni, renaming it *The Christian Workers Magazine* in 1910. The name was changed again in 1920, to *Moody Bible Institute Monthly* and then to *Moody Monthly* in 1938. Though featuring religious content, it was targeted at a lay audience and presented consumer-oriented as well as religious advertising. MBI President Will Houghton served as editor, beginning in 1935, and doubled the circulation to 75,000 by 1945.

Responsibility for editing the magazine was transferred from the president's office to a professional editor in the 1940s. Wayne Christianson served as editor through the 1950s and 1960s, bringing improvements to the design and graphics of the publication, and was followed by Jerry Jenkins in the 1970s. It was during the 1970s when a major push was made to increase the number of subscribers, which had reached 100,000 in the previous decade. Subsidized by MBI, promotional mailings were sent to 2.5 million potential readers across the country. This resulted in a growth of subscriptions to around 250,000 by 1974, as well as profitability for the magazine.

In 1990, the magazine was renamed *Moody* and dropped one issue a year. The proliferation of media options and the rise of digital media, which placed increased financial pressure on all Christian publications, led the magazine to become bimonthly in 1996. Declining circulation led to an increased need for subsidization by MBI. Finally, with circulation standing at about 85,000, MBI ceased publication of *Moody* in the summer of 2003.

Joshua Michael

See also: Christianity Today; Mass Media, Evangelicals and; Moody Bible Institute

Further Reading

Board, Stephen. "Moving the World with Magazines: A Survey of Evangelical Periodicals." In *American Evangelicals and the Mass Media*, edited by Quentin J. Schultze. Grand Rapids, MI: Zondervan, 1990.

Flood, Robert. "Moody Monthly: Yesteryear and Today." *Moody Monthly* 86:6 (1986): 62–64.

Vincent, James. *The MBI Story: The Vision and Worldwide Impact of the Moody Bible Institute.* Chicago; Moody Press, 2011.

MORAL MAJORITY

The Moral Majority was an American political organization with deep evangelical roots associated with the Christian Right and the Republican Party. It was founded in 1979 by Baptist minister Jerry Falwell and associates, and dissolved in the late 1980s. It played a key role in the mobilization of conservative Christians as a political force and particularly in Republican presidential victories throughout the 1980s.

The Moral Majority grew out of a series of "I Love America" rallies started by Jerry Falwell in 1976. The purpose of these rallies was to raise awareness of social issues Falwell believed were critical to Western morality and freedoms. Through these rallies, Falwell was able to gauge national support for a formal organization and to raise his profile as a leader. Having already been a part of a well-established network of ministers and ministries, Falwell was favorably positioned to launch the Moral Majority.

The Moral Majority was formally initiated in 1978 as a result of a struggle for control of an American conservative Christian advocacy group known as Christian Voice. The next year, former Christian Voice members Paul Weyrich, Terry Dolan, Richard Viguerie (Roman Catholic) and Howard Phillips (Jewish), following a falling out with Christian Voice President Robert Grant, urged Falwell to found Moral Majority. Joining Falwell in the effort was Ed McAteer, who that same year founded the Religious Roundtable in Memphis, Tennessee. Falwell and Weyrich officially launched the Moral Majority in June 1979. The name Moral Majority was suggested by Weyrich.

The organization's headquarters were located in Lynchburg, Virginia, where Falwell was the presiding minister of the nation's largest independent Baptist church, Thomas Road Baptist Church. Falwell lead the Moral Majority and maintained an advisory board, constituting the organization's primary leadership, drawn mostly from Falwell's fellow members of the Baptist Bible Fellowship. Falwell also insisted the Moral Majority leadership include Roman Catholics and Jews. The Moral Majority believed it imperative for the United State to maintain the Judeo-Christian concept of moral law. They maintained that this attitude represented the opinions of the majority of Americans (hence the movement's name). With a membership of millions, the Moral Majority became one of the largest conservative lobby groups in the United States, and at its height, claimed more than 4 million members and over 2 million donors. These members were spread among about 20 state organizations, of which Washington State's was the largest.

Among the many issues raised by the Moral Majority, some of the better-known included support for Christian prayers in schools, promotion of a "traditional" vision of family life, Opposition to the Equal Rights Amendment (ERA) and Strategic Arms Limitation Talks (SALT), opposition to state recognition or acceptance of homosexual acts, and opposition to abortion.

A number of approaches were used to garner support and raise funds for the Moral Majority, including direct-mail campaigns, telephone hotlines, rallies, and religious television broadcasts. Although the Moral Majority operated for only a decade, it rapidly became a visible political force and was effective in its mobilization goals.

As it grew, the Moral Majority comprised four distinct organizations: Moral Majority Inc. (the organization's lobbying division), Moral Majority Foundation (the organization's educational component), Moral Majority Legal Defense Fund (the organization's legal division), and the Moral Majority Political Action Committee (the organization's mechanism for supporting the candidacy of people whose political platforms reflected Moral Majority values). State chapters were financially independent of the national organization and relied on local resources to conduct their activities.

By the late 1980s, the views of the Moral Majority were being challenged, and the organization started to deteriorate. With its waning support, critics coined the phrase that the Moral Majority was neither moral nor a majority. The organization was incorporated into the Liberty Federation in 1985, remaining a distinct entity but falling under the Liberty Federation's larger jurisdiction. By 1987, Falwell retired as the formal head of the Moral Majority, although he maintained an active and visible role within the organization. With serious cash flow problems, Falwell dismantled the organization in 1989.

In November 2004, Falwell revived the Moral Majority name for a new organization, the Moral Majority Coalition. The intent of the organization is to get conservative politicians to run and be elected. Referring to the Coalition as the resurrection of the Moral Majority, Falwell committed to leading the organization for four years. He died on May 15, 2007. The Moral Majority was one of the first and largest politically oriented evangelical organizations and did much to influence public perceptions of evangelicalism in the 1970s and 1980s and to effect conservative American politics.

James Menzies

See also: Falwell, Jerry L., Sr.; Politics, Evangelicals and

Further Reading

Falwell, Jerry. *Falwell: An Autobiography, The Inside Story.* Lynchburg, VA: Liberty House, 1997.
Liebman, Robert, and Robert Wuthnow. *The New Christian Right.* New York: Aldine, 1983.

Lindsay, D. Michael. *Faith in the Halls of Power.* New York: Oxford University Press, 2007.

Wilcox, Clyde. *God's Warriors.* Baltimore, MD: Johns Hopkins University Press, 1991.

MORRIS, HENRY (1918–2006)

The father of the modern Creationism movement, Henry Madison Morris Jr. was born October 6, 1918, in Dallas, Texas. Morris earned his bachelor's degree in civil engineering from Rice University in 1939, a master's in hydraulics from University of Minnesota in 1948, and a PhD in hydraulic engineering in 1950 from University of Minnesota.

Morris was raised in a Christian home where he was taught the accounts of Genesis, but during his junior high and high school years, he drifted away from those beliefs. On earning his bachelor's degree, he concluded that theistic evolution was the means by which God created the earth. He married Mary Louise Beach in 1940 and continued to be active in church. Morris's perspective on Genesis changed in 1942, when Irwin A. Moon, who was sponsored by Moody Bible Institute, presented his "Sermons from Science." Morris discovered that the geological effects on the earth were consistent with the Biblical account of Noah's Flood. From that point forward, Morris began to study the Bible more consistently and eventually concluded that the book of Genesis affirmed that the universe was created thousands of years rather than the evolutionary view of billions of years ago.

Morris taught from 1951–1957 at University of Southwestern Louisiana as the chair and professor of civil engineering and then from 1957–1970 at Virginia Polytechnic Institute and State University as professor of hydraulic engineering and later chair of the Civil Engineering Department. John Whitcomb, a professor of Old Testament at Grace Theological Seminary in Winona Lake, Indiana, was influenced by Morris's book *That You Might Believe* (1946) while a student a Princeton, and he later coauthored with Morris *The Genesis Flood* in 1961. The book exploded in popularity within the Christian community, and Morris became a sought-after speaker at churches and conferences. This work seeded what grew into a "creationist" movement that may be partly responsible for the high numbers of Americans that polls continue to reveal still believe Genesis teachings, for example, Adam as the first human. Professional controversy followed the book's publication and creationist viewpoint, and Morris agreed to resign from Virginia Polytech Institute with a one-year severance package. Auburn and Le Tourneau Universities offered Morris professorial positions, but Morris wanted to found a college that affirmed young earth creationism.

Morris cofounded with like-minded academics the Creation Research Society in 1963, which produces a quarterly technical journal including original research from all disciplines that present results or conclusions that challenge mainstream origins. In 1970, Morris met San Diego pastor Tim LaHaye, who had a similar vision and together they cofounded Christian Heritage College (now San Diego Christian College) with a firm belief in a young earth, a global flood, and in biblical inerrancy.

For the next 10 years, 1970–1980, Morris taught apologetics and served as vice president for Academic Affairs and, the last two years, served as president.

Morris wanted to develop a research institution in the field of creation science and origins, and in 1980, Morris resigned as the president of Christian Heritage College and focused his attention at Institute of Creation Research (IRC). During his time at IRC, Morris authored 60 books in the area of creation studies, established Master's degrees at IRC in the areas of biology, astro/geophysics, geology, and science education. He also debated more than 100 times against leading evolutionary scientists. After starting the institute in 1970 while still at Christian Heritage College, Morris served as president of the IRC from 1980–1995.

Morris's influence can be seen throughout the world in the subsequent establishment of similar creationist organizations, such as The Creation Research Society (Arizona), Answers in Genesis (Kentucky), and Creation Ministries International (Australia, Canada, New Zealand, United Kingdom, Singapore, and South Africa). Furthermore, Morris founded and was the first president of Transnational Association of Christian Colleges and Schools (TRACS)—a recognized accrediting agency by the U.S. Department of Education (USDOE) and the Council for Higher Education Accreditation (CHEA).

In the early 1940s, when Morris began his interest in creation studies, there were very few colleges that affirmed a young earth position and a global flood during the time of Noah. Since that time, Liberty University, Cedarville University, Truett-McConnell College, Grace College (Winona Lake, Indiana), Pensacola Christian College, The Master's College and Seminary, Summit University, Southern California Seminary, San Diego Christian College, and Bryan College (Dayton, Tennessee), among others, have been founded (or revised) on a firm belief that Genesis communicates a young earth and then a global flood during the time of Noah.

With his annotations in *The New Defender's Study Bible*, the notable works listed below, and his prolific other writings on creation research, Morris continued to write until 2006. He died on February 26, 2006, near San Diego, California. Creationist views are rejected by evolutionists, and there is not unanimity across the evangelical spectrum on matters of science and faith, but Morris's life and work remain at the center of the creationist perspective. A humble but unshakable conviction that Genesis conveys real history of a recent creation rests at the core of Morris's legacy.

David A. McGee and Brian Thomas

See also: Creation Research Society; *The Genesis Flood*; Institute for Creation Research; Intelligent Design Movement; Science, Evangelicals and

Further Reading

Morris, Henry, and John Whitcomb. *The Genesis Flood: The Biblical Record and Its Scientific Implications*. Phillipsburg, NJ: Presbyterian and Reformed Publishing, 1961.
Morris, Henry. *Scientific Creationism*. Green Forest, AR: Master Books, 1974.

Morris, Henry. *The Genesis Record*. Grand Rapids, MI: Baker Book House, 1976.
Morris, Henry. *History of Modern Creationism*. Green Forest, AR: Master Books, 1984.
Numbers, Ronald L. *The Creationists: From Scientific Creationism to Intelligent Design*, expanded ed. Cambridge, MA: Harvard University Press, 2006.

MOUW, RICHARD J. (1940–)

Richard J. Mouw (1940–) is President Emeritus and Professor of Faith and Public Life at Fuller Theological Seminary. A graduate of Houghton College, Mouw studied at Western Theological Seminary before receiving graduate degrees in philosophy at the University of Alberta (MA) and the University of Chicago (PhD). After teaching philosophy at Calvin College (1968–1985) alongside noted colleagues Alvin Plantinga and Nicholas Wolterstorff, Mouw was appointed Professor of Christian Philosophy and Ethics at Fuller. During his time at Fuller, Mouw held the posts of provost and senior vice president before becoming the institution's fourth president—a position he held for 20 years (1993–2013).

Mouw has a wealth of professional service. In addition to leadership roles (including president from 2010–2012) in the Association of Theological Schools, Mouw has performed in various advisory positions on a number of boards and institutions, including the International Center for Religion and Diplomacy, The Council of Civil Society, International Justice Mission, Harvard Divinity School Board of Visitation, and the Institute for Ecumenical and Cultural Research. He has also worked in various editorial roles at *Ethics* (1966–1968), *Reformed Journal* (1972–1991), *Journal of Religious Ethics* (1985–1999), *Laity Exchange* (1977–present) and *Books and Culture* (1996–present). In addition to numerous scholarly articles, Mouw has published 20 volumes on subjects ranging from ethics to interfaith-dialogue, to theology of culture and political theology.

The son of an evangelical pastor and an heir of the evangelical heritage, Mouw is as likely to quote a hymn as to quote a philosopher or theologian. In his volume, *The Smell of Sawdust*, Mouw fondly (though not uncritically) recounts his evangelical upbringing by way of guiding his fellow evangelicals on the importance of retaining an appreciation for the strengths of their heritage. Similarly, in *Consulting the Faithful*, Mouw calls his fellow evangelical intellectuals to approach popular expressions of evangelicalism with a "hermeneutic of charity," recognizing that behind such popular forms of religion are often values central to evangelical scholarship. In his most recent book, *Called to the Life of the Mind*, Mouw carries on his investment in younger evangelical scholars through a discussion of motifs such as "calling," "humility and hope," and "being like Jesus."

Mouw is not only an heir of the evangelical tradition but also a pioneer, as he draws heavily on Dutch theologian and statesman Abraham Kuyper. In his volume *Abraham Kuyper: A Short and Personal Introduction*, Mouw credits Kuyper for giving him a vision of active involvement in public life that allowed him to navigate the complexities he faced in the social upheaval of the 1960s and 1970s—steering between privatized evangelicalism, on one hand, and liberal Protestant approaches, on the other. A number of Kuyper's theological themes make their way into Mouw's corpus, often with Mouw reframing or updating Kuyper. In *He Shines in All That's Fair*, Mouw develops Kuyper's discussion of common grace in light of recent scholarship and the challenges of postmodernity. In *The Challenges of Cultural Discipleship: Essays in the Line of Abraham Kuyper*, Mouw argues for an appreciative updating of Kuyper's doctrines of creation, sphere sovereignty, and the church. And in his *Calvinism in the Las Vegas Airport*, Mouw offers a more winsome "Neo-Kuyperian" approach to Calvinism: taking up Kuyper's vision for bringing all of life under the Lordship of Christ and wedding it to self-giving service embodied by Mother Theresa.

Mouw's desire for evangelicals to be engaged thoughtfully with politics, social concerns, commerce, art, and so on, began early in his career with the publications *Political Evangelism, Politics and the Biblical Drama, Called to Holy Worldliness,* and *When the Kings Come Marching In*. To navigate immersion in the broader cultural and public life, Mouw develops what he sees as Kuyper's dialectic of commonness and antithesis. Although evangelicals are to participate in culture and public life (commonness), they must retain their distinctiveness (antithesis). It is this dialectic that shaped Mouw's responses in the highly publicized debates in the 1970s with Anabaptist theologian John Howard Yoder. For Mouw, Yoder's emphasis on culture as created but *fallen*, only stresses one side of the dialectic. Culture is better understood as *created* but fallen and waiting to be *redeemed*.

As president emeritus of one of the largest evangelical seminaries in the world Mouw serves as an evangelical statesman. In public interactions, Mouw's tone is characteristically undefended, inquisitive, and civil. This posture embodies Mouw's desire to guide evangelicals away from culture wars to a more dialogical approach; a value evident not only in Mouw's engagement with Muslim, Catholic, and Jewish scholars, but also in his books *Uncommon Decency: Christian Civility in an Uncivil World* and *Pluralism and Its Horizons*. In so doing, Mouw seeks to model to other evangelicals a third way: neither abandoning public life nor combatively taking it over, but rather engaging public life with a posture that is gracious yet compelling, humble yet bold.

Robert S. Covolo

See also: Evangelicalism; Fuller Theological Seminary; Reformed Tradition, Evangelicalism and

Further Reading

Mouw, Richard J. *Political Evangelism*. Grand Rapids, MI: Eerdmans, 1973.

Mouw, Richard J. *Uncommon Decency: Christian Civility in an Uncivil World*. Downers Grove, IN: IVP, 1992.

Mouw, Richard. J. *The Smell of the Sawdust Trail: What Evangelicals Can Learn from Their Fundamentalist Heritage*. Grand Rapids, MI: Zondervan, 2000.

Mouw, Richard J. *He Shines in All That's Fair: Culture and Common Grace.* Grand Rapids, MI: Eerdmans, 2001.

Mouw, Richard J. *Abraham Kuyper: A Short and Personal Introduction.* Grand Rapids, MI: Eerdmans, 2011.

Marsden, George M. *Reforming Fundamentalism: Fuller Seminary and the New Evangelicalism.* Grand Rapids, MI: Eerdmans, 1987.

Marsden, George. M. *Fundamentalism and American Culture: The Shaping of Twentieth Century Evangelicalism,* 2nd ed. New York: Oxford University Press, 2006.

NATIONAL ASSOCIATION OF EVANGELICALS

The National Association of Evangelicals (NAE) is a fellowship of member denominations, churches, and organizations with a stated mission "to honor God by connecting and representing evangelical Christians." The association represents more than 45,000 local churches from 40 different denominations and serves a constituency of millions.

The NAE began in April of 1942, when 147 people met in St. Louis hoping to shape the direction of evangelical Christianity in America. If any one individual can be credited with forming the NAE, it is J. Elwin Wright.

Wright's father was a Free Will Baptist minister who later formed a Pentecostal ministry called the First Fruits Harvesters Association in Rumney, New Hampshire. After graduating from the Missionary Training Institute (now Nyack College) at Nyack, New York, in 1921, J. Elwin Wright was ordained by his father to the work in Rumney. When Wright succeeded his father in 1929, he transformed First Fruits Harvesters into the New England Fellowship, seeking to serve a broader constituency throughout New England. In 1934, he was received into the fellowship of Park Street Church in Boston, an affiliation that enhanced his relationship with emerging evangelical leaders, including the influential Harold John Ockenga.

While Wright was working in New England, the then-president of Moody Bible Institute, Will Houghton, called for an exploratory meeting in October 1941 in Chicago. At that meeting, a temporary committee for United Action Among Evangelicals was created, with Wright named as chairman. In April 1942, a national conference was held in St. Louis. The committee opened an office in New York and issued an invitation to the first National Conference for United Action Among Evangelicals. Following the St. Louis meeting, Wright moved the New York office to Boston and launched the official NAE publication, *United Evangelical Action*.

In 1944, the NAE formed the National Religious Broadcasters (NRB) and created two task-specific commissions: the Chaplains Commission and War Relief Commission (later known as World Relief). The following year, NAE created the Evangelical Foreign Missions Association (now The Mission Exchange), the largest missionary association in the world.

Frequent transitions in leadership and cultural upheaval took a toll on NAE. In 1963, black evangelicals formed the National Black Evangelical Association, and in 1972, NAE's third largest denomination, the National Association of Free Will Baptists, pulled out because of internal struggles. By the late 1970s, NAE had experienced a net membership gain of only five denominations in 10 years.

In November 2006, Ted Haggard resigned as president amid allegations of sexual misconduct resulting in a public scandal. The Executive Committee invited Leith Anderson to serve as interim president. Anderson agreed to serve during the search for a new president. Following a search, the Task Force asked Anderson to consider assuming the presidency. Anderson agreed and was formally elected to a three-year term at the October 2007 board meeting. With over 70 years of facilitating evangelical unity, the NAE serves a critical need by providing connectedness for evangelicals while projecting a respected voice for the evangelical movement across America.

James Menzies

See also: Evangelicalism; Neo-Evangelicalism; Ockenga, Harold John

Further Reading

Marsden, George. *Reforming Fundamentalism: Fuller Seminary and the New Evangelicalism.* Grand Rapids, MI: Eerdmans, 1995.

Matthews, Arthur Hugh. *Standing Up, Standing Together: The Emergence of the National Association of Evangelicals.* Washington, D.C.: National Association of Evangelicals, 1992.

National Association of Evangelicals. "History." (n.d.). Accessed April 29, 2017. https://www.nae.net.

Stackhouse, John G. "The National Association of Evangelicals, the Evangelical Fellowship of Canada, and the Limits of Evangelical Cooperation." *Christian Scholar's Review* 25, no. 2 (December 1995).

NATIONAL BLACK EVANGELICAL ASSOCIATION

The National Black Evangelical Association (NBEA) is a multidenominational alliance of black Christians who emphasize a pro-black perspective and unite under conservative evangelical beliefs such as an emphasis on a conversion experience, the authority of the Bible, the centrality of Jesus Christ to salvation, the importance of evangelism, and the integral work of the Holy Spirit. The NBEA's theological roots are fundamentalist in orientation, but its outlook on society has historically mixed various kinds of social engagement and political activity. The NBEA began in 1963 as the National Negro Evangelical Association. Its early vision attempted to create networks and affiliations of black Christians to address pressing matters of the time, particularly at the height of the modern Civil Rights Movement. With a membership of hundreds, if not thousands, the NBEA continues to host an annual meeting and provide spiritual counsel and biblical commentary through its digital presence.

Although the NBEA adheres to conservative, fundamentalist theology, the denominational influences at its founding came from multiple directions. For example, William Pannell, a Fuller Seminary professor, had ties to the black Plymouth Brethren church; Howard Jones, an associate with Billy Graham's ministry, had an affiliation with the Christian and Missionary Alliance Church; and William Bentley represented black Pentecostalism. At the time of the NBEA's genesis, its primary aim was to promote conservative Christianity within black American circles. It also sought to forge alliances in the face of white disregard for the experiences of black Christians, which led some members to sympathize with Black Power philosophy despite retaining conservative theological beliefs. On the one hand, conservative members sought to privilege an evangelical focus on personal sin and individual salvation as a solution to racial conflict. On the other hand, progressive participants emphasized the need to address broader societal structures of racial discrimination and economic justice. During the 1970s, the Black Power and black theology movements affected the direction of the NBEA. Black Power's foundational doctrine of self-determination convinced some members to emphasize black-only alliances, whereas conservative advocates of the NBEA trumpeted black–white Christian unity. Regarding the ascendance of black theology, NBEA progressives found meaningful theological expressions resonant with black culture, even if they contested elements of liberal theology itself. Conservative voices within the NBEA remained skeptical; they questioned whether black theology promoted black culture over and above the Christian gospel. Questions over the relationship between theological precision continued to occupy the NBEA throughout the 1980s and 1990s. In a move that modeled other racial reconciliation initiatives among Pentecostals and Southern Baptists in the 1990s, the National Association of Evangelicals and the NBEA issued a joint declaration that condemned racism and acknowledged white complicity in structures of inequality. It demanded that white Christians collectively repent and urged black Christians to consider extending forgiveness. Moreover, it linked Christianity's—and evangelicalism's—credibility to the successful outcome of racial unity among the nation's conservative Christians. Recent NBEA President Walter McCray acknowledged the organization's role in addressing evangelicalism's increasing ethnic diversity even in the midst of white supremacy's residual presence, tasks vital to the future of both the NBEA and evangelicalism.

Phillip Luke Sinitiere

See also: African American Evangelicalism; Civil Rights Movement, Evangelicals and

Further Reading

Gilbreath, Edward. "Black to the Future." UrbanFaith.com (April 19, 2012). http://www.urbanfaith.com/2012/04/black-to-the-future.html/.

Miller, A. G. "National Black Evangelical Association." In *Encyclopedia of African American Culture and History*, edited by Colin A. Palmer. New York: Macmillan, 1996.

Salzman, Jack, David Lionel Smith, and Cornel West. "The Rise of African-American Evangelicalism in American Culture." In *Perspectives on American Religion and Culture*, edited by Peter Williams. (259–269). Oxford: Blackwell, 1999.

Wadsworth, Nancy D. *Ambivalent Miracles: Evangelicals and the Politics of Racial Healing.* Charlottesville, VA: University of Virginia Press, 2014.

NATIONAL DAY OF PRAYER

The National Day of Prayer is an annual observance held on the first Thursday of May, encouraging people of all faiths to pray individually and collectively for the United States. The observance was created in 1952 during the Korean War by a joint resolution of the United States Congress and signed into law by President Harry Truman after evangelist Billy Graham encouraged such a day. In 1988, the law was amended and signed by President Reagan, permanently setting the day as the first Thursday of every May. Each year, the president signs a proclamation encouraging all Americans to pray on the first Thursday of May. It is coordinated by the National Day of Prayer Task Force, an evangelical nonprofit organization founded in 1983. The annual observance is part of a long tradition in American history of political and religious leaders calling for and observing days of prayer, often during times of national crisis or war.

Hostilities in 1768–1776 between the American colonists and England resulted in American colonies proclaiming days of prayer. Boston declared a day of fasting and prayer in September 1768 as a protest against a British plan to post troops in the city, and the Colony of Virginia's House of Burgesses established a day of fasting and prayer on Wednesday, June 1, 1774, to protest the Boston Port Act. The Provinces of South Carolina, Maryland, and Georgia all observed official days of fasting and prayer during 1774–1775.

A national day of fasting and prayer was established by the Second Continental Congress in 1775 when Congress issued a proclamation recommending "a day of publick humiliation, fasting, and prayer" be observed by the English colonies on Thursday, July 20, 1775. The text, written by John Witherspoon and John Hancock, instructed colonists to pray for a resumption of "the just rights and privileges of the Colonies" in civil and religious matters.

As Commander-in-Chief of the Continental Army, General George Washington acknowledged a day of "fasting, humiliation and prayer," as proclaimed by the Continental Congress, be held on Thursday, May 6, 1779. Washington ordered a one-day cessation of recreation and unnecessary labor. In March 1780, Congress announced a day of "fasting, humiliation and prayer" be held on Wednesday, April 26, 1780.

The practice was abandoned from 1784 until 1789, even though thanksgiving days were observed each fall. On October 3, 1789, President Washington called for a national day of prayer and thanksgiving to be observed on Thursday, November 26, 1789, as an extension of the thanksgiving tradition already common in New England. After James Madison, none of the next 11 presidents issued prayer proclamations.

In 1863 President Abraham Lincoln proclaimed a day of "humiliation, fasting, and prayer." Thomas Jefferson issued a day of prayer and thanksgiving while serving as governor of Virginia, and the Supreme Court affirmed the right of state legislatures to open their sessions with prayer in 1983.

Between 1789 and 2015, there have been 144 national calls to prayer and thanksgiving by the president of the United States. Since 1952, there have been 67 presidential proclamations for a National Day of Prayer, and every president since 1952 has signed a National Prayer Day proclamation.

It is estimated that more than 2 million people attend more than 30,000 observances organized by approximately 40,000 volunteers who meet at state capitols, city halls, and other public venues to pray. The constitutionality of the event was unsuccessfully challenged by the Freedom from Religion Foundation in 2011.

James Menzies

See also: Graham, William F., Jr. ("Billy"); Politics, Evangelicals and

Further Reading

Adams, John (March 6, 1799). "Proclamation—Recommending a National Day of Humiliation, Fasting, and Prayer." The American Presidency Project. University of California, Santa Barbara. http://www.presidency.ucsb.edu/ws/?pid=65675.

Bornschein, John. *A Prayer Warrior's Guide to Spiritual Battle: On the Front Line*, 2nd ed. Bellingham, WA: Kirkdale Press, 2016.

"History of Prayer in America." National Day of Prayer. (n.d.). Accessed April 29, 2017. http://www.nationaldayofprayer.org/history_of_prayer_in_america.

Lincoln, Abraham, and William Seward. "Proclamation Appointing a National Fast Day." Abraham Lincoln Online. (March 30, 1863). http://www.abrahamlincolnonline.org/lincoln/speeches/fast.htm.

Lindsay, D. Michael. *Faith in the Halls of Power: How Evangelicals Joined the Political Elite.* New York: Oxford University Press, 2008.

National Day of Prayer. (n.d.). Accessed June 17, 2016. http://www.nationaldayofprayer.org/.

Uebersax, John S. "National Days of Prayer to Avert War: An Historical Comparison." john-uebersax.com. (April 26, 2012). http://www.john-uebersax.com/plato/proclam.htm.

NAVIGATORS

The Navigators is a worldwide Christian parachurch organization headquartered in Colorado Springs, Colorado. Its purpose is training Christians, with a particular emphasis on enabling them to share their faith with others. The Navigators works alongside local churches by providing resources such as Bible study booklets and study aid materials, Scripture memory aids, and Christian-oriented books. These are produced through the organization's NavPress publishing group, which also offers *The Message Bible* paraphrase. It also supports full-time workers who work mostly within local communities. Currently, more than 4,600 Navigator staff of 69 nationalities minister to college students, military personnel, business and professional people, communities, and churches in 103 countries.

The Navigators ministry began in the 1930s. After seeing the benefits of discipleship in his life, a young California lumberyard worker, Dawson Trotman, wanted to teach the same principles to others. Trotman began teaching high school students and local Sunday school classes, and in 1933, he and his friends extended their work to sailors in the U.S. Navy. There, Dawson taught sailor Les Spencer the foundations of Christian growth. As a result of mentoring Spencer aboard the USS *West Virginia*, 135 additional sailors on Spencer's ship became Christians before it was sunk at Pearl Harbor. By the end of World War II, thousands of men on ships and bases around the world were learning the principles of Christian discipleship.

Since World War II, The Navigators has grown into a worldwide organization with representatives in most countries. In 1949, The Navigators' first overseas missionary left to serve in China; more soon followed to other countries. The Navigators' headquarters moved from southern California to Colorado Springs in 1953 with the purchase of the Glen Eyrie property, former home of city founder General William J. Palmer. Now, that property is home to the U.S. and International offices, Glen Eyrie Conference Center, and our publishing division, NavPress. A few miles away is Eagle Lake Camp.

The collegiate chapter of the Navigators was founded in 1951 at the University of Nebraska–Lincoln. The organization was established by a group of students in the Sigma Nu fraternity house who, along with Trotman, decided to spread the organization onto the college campus. The collegiate organization of the Navigators has since spread to more than 50 different campuses in the United States and many more worldwide.

The Navigators organize and offer more than 100 Christian conferences, retreats, and programs each year at Glen Eyrie. The general public is allowed on its grounds during the day to visit its bookstore and café. Tours of the Castle—originally the home of Colorado Springs founder General William Jackson Palmer—are available to the public for a nominal fee, although advance reservations are required. The Castle also serves as a conference and retreat center available for use by various groups.

On January 1, 2005, Michael W. Treneer succeeded Dr. Jerry White as The Navigators' international president. White had served in that capacity for the previous 18 years. On April 18, 2015, Mutua Mahiaini succeeded Michael Treneer as the fifth international president of The Navigators.

James Menzies

See also: Evangelism; Parachurch Ministries

Further Reading

Foster, Robert. *The Navigator.* Colorado Springs: NavPress, 2014.
The Navigators. (n.d.). Accessed April 29, 2017. http://www.navigators.org/Home.
The Navigators. *Dawson Trotman: In His Own Words.* Colorado Springs, CO: NavPress, 2011.
Skinner, Betty Lee. *Daws: The Story of Dawson Trotman, Founder of the Navigators.* Grand Rapids, MI: Zondervan, 1974.

NEO-EVANGELICALISM

Neo-evangelicalism, or "new evangelicalism," is a term that was coined by the pioneer of the movement, Harold J. Ockenga (1905–1985), in 1947. This term characterizes a group of inclusivist evangelicals in the 1940s who were pro-intellectual and pro-social action while still prioritizing orthodox Protestant tenets consistent with the Evangelical Quadrilateral (or The Bebbington Quadrilateral). This group reacted against the type of fundamentalism that sought to separate Christians from social action and intellectual pursuit. American evangelicalism enjoyed a prominent influence in the latter part of the 20th century as a direct result of the strategic actions taken by the neo-evangelicals from 1942 through the 1960s.

Coming out of 19th-century postmillennial optimism, evangelical Christianity had a comfortable position in American culture. Evangelicals had influenced educational curriculum in both public and private sectors to include moralistic education, and university presidents were typically appointed from clergy, not business or industry. Thus, some of the most respectable evangelical centers for learning—where the Bible was held up as the ultimate authority and where social reform was driven toward helping build a Christian nation—were Princeton Theological Seminary, Harvard Divinity School, and Yale Divinity School. The common attitude of the day regarding biblical authority was synthetic toward science, believing that scientific discovery would always affirm truths found in Scripture and that the scientific method should be used to discover more about the world that was not explicitly revealed in the Bible.

After the Scopes Monkey Trial (*The State of Tennessee v. John Thomas Scopes*) in 1925, evangelicals were fractured as a result of what they considered the "Modernist Problem.' American attitudes toward evolution became more favorable, casting doubt on biblical authority and disillusioning some evangelicals toward science and intellectual pursuits in general. During the period between 1925 and 1945, fundamentalism was observed by scholars such as evangelical historian Robert E. Webber to be (1) anti-intellectual, (2) anti-ecumenical, and (3) antisocial action. Termed *fundamentalists*, many theologically conservative Protestants decried what they thought to be liberal theology and practices in their churches, denominations, and mission boards. As a result of ensuing power struggles, the fundamentalists either left or were forced out of their churches and organizations. They subsequently became denominationally independent or joined other existing groups or formed new alliances, networks, and institutions. Beginning in the 1940s, a small group of theologically conservative religious leaders began an effort to reshape earlier American Protestant fundamentalism.

The theologically conservative centrist Ockenga accused Protestant liberals of losing the center of biblical authority and the fundamentalists of losing the heart of the Gospel. Proponents of neo-evangelicalism, such as Ockenga, Charles Fuller (1887–1968), Wilbur M. Smith (1894–1977), Billy Graham (1918–); Carl F. H. Henry (1913–2003), Edward J. Carnell (1919–1967), and George Eldon Ladd (1911–1982), sought to promote a spirit of evangelicalism that was pro-intellectual, pro-cultural engagement, pro-ecumenical, and pro–social action. Additionally, the pioneers of the movement founded Fuller Theological Seminary in Pasadena, California, to serve as the intellectual base for the Bible-believing neo-evangelical movement. They believed the Gospel needed to be reasserted to prevent it from being diminished by liberal, modernistic theologians and from separatistic fundamentalists. These views were articulated in Carl F. H. Henry's landmark writing *The Uneasy Conscience of Modern Fundamentalism* (1947).

Perhaps one of the most important strategies of neo-evangelicals was to engage the world in a compassionate way while not participating in or conceding to liberal theological positions regarding the prominence of Scripture. In 1942, J. Elwin Wright and Harold J. Ockenga led a meeting of about 200 Christian men and formed the Conference for United Action among Evangelicals (now the National Association of Evangelicals). They also sought to partner across denominations with evangelical churches and Trinitarian Pentacostals, prioritizing "essential doctrines" in accordance with Protestant orthodoxy. Additionally, they began working with the world-renowned evangelist Billy Graham (1918–), who attended conservative schools like Wheaton College and Florida Bible Institute but who was also criticized by fundamentalists for ecumenical work with Roman Catholics and other mainline Protestant denominations.

Neo-evangelicals strategically worked through various media formats to promote their centrist ecumenical dialogue. They established multiple regular print publications such as *Christianity Today* and *Moody Monthly*, which achieved a broad readership. They also used the rise of television through the 1950s and 1960s to broadcast their platform to even wider audiences and to display the ways in which they demonstrated compassion for the world. Eventually, *neo-evangelicalism*, due to the success of their "middle way" between liberalism and fundamentalism, would come to be known simply as *evangelicalism*.

Currently, the term *neo-evangelicalism* has little meaning outside of its historical movement. If it is used at all, the term is generally used pejoratively by fundamentalist critics who want to differentiate their ideas of evangelicalism from another

---

The Five Fundamentals of the Evangelical Christian Faith

1. Verbal-plenary inspiration of the Scripture: Hebrews 1:1–2; 2 Timothy 3:16–17; 2 Peter 1:21; Matthew 5:18; John 10:35.
2. Virgin birth of the Son of God, Jesus Christ: Luke 1:27, 21, 35; Isaiah 7:14; Galatians 4:4.
3. Vicarious substitutionary atonement of Jesus Christ: Matthew 20:28; 1 Peter 3:18; John 6:51; Romans 5:6–8, 8:32; 1 Timothy 2:5; Hebrews 2:9.
4. Bodily resurrection of Jesus Christ from the dead: Romans 4:25; Acts 2:23–24; Matthew 28:5–7; 1 Corinthians 15:4, 14.
5. Physical return of Jesus Christ: Acts 1:11; John 14:1–3; 1 Thessalonians 4:13–17; Revelation 19–20.

view or practice that they regard to be more liberal than their own. Toward the latter part of the 20th century, evangelicalism became characterized by evangelical diversity, an ever-widening expression of intellectual curiosity and social concern. If not for the historical neo-evangelicals, however, American Evangelicalism might have stalled as a result of theological drift or irrelevant Gospel application.

Bryce Hantla

See also: Carnell, Edward John; Evangelicalism; Fuller, Charles E.; Fuller Theological Seminary; Fundamentalism; Graham, William F., Jr. ("Billy"); Henry, Carl F. H.; International Council on Biblical Inerrancy; National Association of Evangelicals; Ockenga, Harold John; Pentecostalism (and Charismatic Movement), Evangelicals and; *The Uneasy Conscience of Modern Fundamentalism*

Further Reading

Henry, Carl F. H. *Confessions of a Theologian: An Autobiography.* Waco, TX: Word Books, 1986.

Marsden, George. *Reforming Fundamentalism: Fuller Seminary and the New Evangelicalism.* Grand Rapids, MI: Eerdmans, 1995.

Noll, Mark A. *Between Faith and Criticism: Evangelicals, Scholarship, and the Bible in America,* 2nd ed. Vancouver, British Columbia: Regent College, 2004.

Rosell, Garth M. *The Surprising Work of God: Harold John Ockenga, Billy Graham, and the Rebirth of Evangelicalism.* Grand Rapids, MI: Baker Academic, 2008.

Smith, Christian, Michael Emerson, Sally Gallagher, Paul Kennedy, and David Sikkink. *American Evangelicalism: Embattled and Thriving.* Chicago: University of Chicago Press, 1998.

Strachan, Owen. *Awakening the Evangelical Mind: An Intellectual History of the Neo-Evangelical Movement.* Grand Rapids, MI: Zondervan, 2015.

Webber, Robert E. *The Younger Evangelicals: Facing the Challenges of the New World.* Grand Rapids, MI: Baker Books, 2002.

NOLL, MARK A. (1946–)

Mark A. Noll is one of the foremost scholars of evangelical history and culture. A native of Iowa, Noll received degrees from Wheaton College (1968), the University of Iowa (1970), Trinity Evangelical Divinity School (1972), and Vanderbilt University (1975). He spent the majority of his academic career teaching history at Wheaton College, and in 2006 assumed the Francis A. McAnaney Professor of History at the University of Notre Dame, a chair once occupied by his mentor and fellow evangelical historian George Marsden (1939–). In addition to professorial work, in the 1980s Noll was integral to the formation of the Institute for the Study of American Evangelicals, and thereafter shaped evangelical intellectual culture through editorial roles in publications such as *Books & Culture, Reformed Journal,* and *Christianity Today.*

Noll's scholarly contributions to the broader field of North American religious history include publications on religion and politics of the Revolutionary Era and antebellum period, theology during the Civil War, the Bible and American culture, evangelicals and modern intellectual life, evangelical ecumenical engagement with Roman Catholics, religion and science, Canadian religious history, Christian higher education, and most recently, global Christianity. His long-standing interest in literary history has also inspired the composition of numerous poems, some of which he published in journals and autobiographical writings.

Although Noll has made signature contributions to the political history of American religion as well as to constructive evangelical–Roman Catholic engagement, his most enduring work in American religious history has been, first, a keen focus on evangelical intellectual life. His *The Scandal of the Evangelical Mind* (1994) explained the historical development of evangelical anti-intellectualism and criticized the relative absence of evangelical intellectual engagement. Noll insisted that Christianity allowed for loving God with the mind and through intellectually responsible scholarship, a message he clarified further in *Jesus Christ and the Life of the Mind* (2011), a prescriptive volume that emphasized more of a theological rationale for Christians pursuing first-order intellectual work. Noll's commitment to critical academic scholarship, even when it did not conform to the ideological wishes of evangelical activists or adhere to uncritical assessments of evangelical history, modeled a version of the evangelical mind toward which he encouraged others to aspire.

Another substantial mark that Noll has made on the history of evangelicalism is an emphasis on world Christianity. Impacted intellectually by the critical cultural work of missionary scholars such as Andrew Walls, Lamin Sanneh, and Dana Robert, Noll's turn to studying Christianity in the non-Western world has provided a set of global lenses through which he has internationalized evangelical history. Books such as *The New Shape of World Christianity: How American Experience Reflects Global Faith* (2009) and *Clouds of Witnesses: Christian Voices from Africa and Asia* (2011) present his commitment to cultivating a global evangelical history. He documents his widening intellectual horizons in *From Every Tribe and Nation: A Historian's Discovery of the Global Christian Story* (2014). Noll's legacy is one of robust and readable intellectual work that places evangelicalism's history in relationship to wider trends in American and world culture.

Phillip Luke Sinitiere

See also: Christianity Today; Counterculture, Evangelicals and; *Evangelicals & Catholics Together*; Fundamentalism; Marsden, George M.; Schaeffer, Francis A. and Edith; Wheaton College

Further Reading

Burch, Maxie B. *The Evangelical Historians: The Historiography of George Marsden, Nathan Hatch, and Mark Noll*. Lanham, MD: University Press of America, 1996.
Noll, Mark A. *The Scandal of the Evangelical Mind*. Grand Rapids, MI: Eerdmans, 1994.

Noll, Mark A. *Jesus Christ and the Life of the Mind.* Grand Rapids, MI: Eerdmans, 2011.

Noll, Mark A. *From Every Tribe and Nation: A Historian's Discovery of the Global Christian Story.* Grand Rapids, MI: Eerdmans, 2014.

NORMAN, LARRY DAVID (1947–2008)

Often called the "Father of Christian Rock," Norman was born in 1947 in Corpus Christi, Texas, but his family soon moved to San Francisco. Growing up, he was much impressed with the music of Elvis Presley, and he began to put Christian words to rock music. Before his death at age 60 in 2008, he had recorded more than 100 albums on a range of labels (Capitol, MGM/Verve, ABC, Word, Solid Rock, & Phydeaux, the last mainly a mail order operation), with his music performed by as many as 300 artists. Among his fans were Bob Dylan, Bono, Van Morrison, Paul McCartney, John Mellencamp, and Sammy Davis Jr.

After high school, in 1965, he joined in a new band calling itself People in reaction to such names as the Beatles, Turtles, Crickets, Byrds, and Animals. They opened for the Doors, Janis Joplin, the Who, and Jimi Hendrix, and their version of "I Love You" traveled well up the pop charts in 1968. When the majority of the members turned to Scientology, Norman left the band.

As a solo performer, Norman wrote and recorded such classics as "I Wish We'd All Been Ready" (from *Upon This Rock*, 1969) and "Why Should the Devil Have All the Good Music?" (from *Only Visiting This Planet*, 1972). He's credited with originating the "One Way" [through Christ] symbol with the raised index finger, a gesture that probably began when, on stage, he gave God the credit for his fans' applause.

At the peak of his popularity, he joined with other Christian musicians for performances at the Carter White House, Moscow's Olympic Stadium, the Sydney Opera House, the Hollywood Bowl, and London's Royal Albert Hall. Still, with his long hair and edgy lyrics, he was an outlier with the majority of churches—more so as upbeat "praise and worship" music moved front and center.

His revolutionary, streetwise songs resonated with the Jesus Movement, which both drew on and contributed to his rise to prominence. Known as a "Jesus freak," he performed at Explo '72 (the "Christian Woodstock"), sponsored by Campus Crusade for Christ. Attendees filled the Cotton Bowl in Dallas, and the resulting album featured Norman's "Sweet Song of Salvation," along with numbers by Johnny Cash and Andrae Crouch.

Norman's landmark album, *Upon This Rock*, was less than a commercial success, and he lost his place on the Capitol label. His recordings were shunned and even denounced by prominent televangelists, disparaged by secular reviewers, and ignored by some Christian retailers, but Norman was unfazed. He simply said his work was too religious for one group and not religious enough for another.

He had little use for the "established church" and disdained the commercialization of contemporary Christian music. He insisted that he was not writing and performing for the comfortably saved, but for the lost. So although his gritty lyrics from "Why Don't You Look Into Jesus?" (e.g., "Gonorrhea on Valentine's Day/Are you still lookin' for the perfect lay?") didn't ingratiate him to most churches, he said they were meant to connect with outsiders.

By the 1990s, he found himself marginalized not only by shifts in musical preferences but also by the emergence of other edgy voices tackling Christian themes, e.g., Bob Dylan and U2. But he was also hurt by his own behavior, which some formerly close friends found off-putting. Perhaps a blow to the head in an airplane accident, to which he attributed bipolar symptoms, or a long string of heart problems, beginning with a damaging attack in 1992, led to his erratic behavior. Whatever the cause, his difficulties resulted in two divorces and the breakdown of professional relationships with fellow musicians Randy Stonehill and the Daniel Amos Band. Later on, he claimed he had been cured by prayer, and some reconciliation was reflected in a joint concert with Randy Stonehill in 2001.

Both early and late in his career, Norman was known for a range of causes, from street evangelism to the purchase of food, clothing, and lodging for new converts, to prison ministry. And testimonials at the time of his death showed an impressive breadth and depth of gratitude from those he'd mentored in the music business.

In 2001, he was inducted into the Gospel Music Association's Hall of Fame, along with Elvis Presley and Keith Green. Along the way, he'd been compared to John Lennon and Bob Dylan in terms of the influence they had on their own genres. In 2013, the Library of Congress added his *Only Visiting This Planet* album to the National Recording Registry, along with 24 other works by such luminaries as Bing Crosby, the Everly Brothers, Creedence Clearwater Revival, Isaac Hayes, Aaron Copland, and U2.

Not long before he died, he prescribed words for his cross-shaped tombstone, which now reads

Larry Norman
Evangelist
Without Portfolio
1947–2008
Bloodstained Israelite

His music influenced an entire generation of young evangelicals in the 1960s and 1970s and did much to influence subsequent popular Christian music.

Mark Coppenger

See also: Contemporary Christian Music; Explo '72; Jesus People Movement

Further Reading

Cusic, Don, ed. *Encyclopedia of Contemporary Christian Music: Pop, Rock, and Worship.* Santa Barbara, CA: Greenwood, an Imprint of ABC-CLIO, LLC, 2010.

McNeil, W. K., ed. *Encyclopedia of American Gospel Music*. New York: Routledge, 2005.

Miller, Steven P. *The Age of Evangelicalism: America's Born-Again Years*. New York: Oxford University Press, 2014.

Powell, Mark Allen. *Encyclopedia of Contemporary Christian Music*. Peabody, MA: Hendrickson, 2002.

NYACK COLLEGE AND ALLIANCE THEOLOGICAL SEMINARY

Nyack College and Alliance Theological Society is a private, nonprofit, church-related academic institution supported by The Christian and Missionary Alliance denomination. Nyack College has two campuses: Nyack, New York; and New York City, New York; as well as an extension site in San Juan, Puerto Rico. The college is divided into three divisions: the Alliance Theological Seminary (the denomination's official seminary), the College of Arts and Sciences, and the College of Graduate and Professional Programs.

The school was founded as the Missionary Training Institute, the first Bible college in North America, in 1882 in New York City by Dr. A. B. Simpson (1843–1919), who had resigned a prestigious New York City pastorate to pursue this goal of crafting an training school. Simpson had been brought up in the United Presbyterian Church on Prince Edward Island, Canada, and later served as pastor of the Chestnut Street Church, Louisville, Kentucky.

Simpson sought to develop an interdenominational fellowship passionate to serving unreached people. This view was shared by a group of leaders from mainline churches and the creation of a training school for missionaries was critical in the process. The Missionary Training Institute first met on the stage of a theater on Twenty-third Street, New York City. In October 1883, the school moved to a new home on Eighth Avenue, and it was then organized as The Missionary Training College for Home and Foreign Missionaries and Evangelists, moving several other times as well as changing its name, until 1897, at which time it was redesignated as The Missionary Training Institute and moved to Nyack, New York.

Attendance continued at around 200 during the years prior to World War I but doubled in size after the war. The Institute had a declared "object" to offer courses of study for the education of Christian workers: to establish students in the fundamental doctrines of the Christian faith; to foster missionary interest and evangelistic zeal; to promote deeper spiritual life; and to aid in the training of a thoroughly evangelical Christian ministry.

The 1950s and 1960s brought expansion and growth: as in 1953, the institution was first authorized to confer the Bachelor of Science degree and then in 1961, the Bachelor of Arts degree. The school changed its name in 1956 to Nyack Missionary College.

The seminary was established in 1960 as the Jaffray School of Missions, a graduate program within the college and emphasized an interdisciplinary encounter between theology and social science. In September 1979, the school was recognized by the Christian and Missionary Alliance as the denomination's official seminary in the U.S., with the name changed to the Alliance Theological Seminary. By the 1990s, the majority of undergraduate students were majoring in liberal arts and professional studies.

In 1997, the college returned to Manhattan by opening a branch campus. Nyack College graduated its first baccalaureates in nursing in spring 2013. Also, through a partnership with the Hudson Link for Higher Education in Prison, Nyack College has a Bachelor of Science degree in Organizational Management for prison inmates at Fishkill Correctional Facilities in Beacon, New York. Nyack College calls its sports teams the Warriors (formerly the Purple Pride and the Fighting Parsons). Nyack is a member of the Central Atlantic Collegiate Conference of the NCAA's Division II as well as The National Christian College Athletic Association (NCCAA).

J. Craig Kubic

See also: Evangelicalism; Evangelism; Missions, Evangelicals and

Further Reading

Niklaus, Robert L. "The School That Vision Built." Centennial Review of Nyack College 1882–1982. *Nyack College Archive.* Retrieved July 27, 2016.
The Official Nyack College. (n.d.). Accessed July 27, 2016. http://nyack.edu.

O

OCKENGA, HAROLD JOHN (1905–1985)

Harold John Ockenga was a generating force behind neo-evangelicalism (and coined the term in 1947), a movement that came about in reaction to the fundamentalist and modernistic or liberal controversies of the first half of the 20th century. Ockenga also established the National Association of Evangelicals, where he served as first president (1942–1944), and was cofounder and first president of Fuller Theological Seminary (1947–1954 and 1960–1963); cofounder of *Christianity Today* magazine; a director of the Billy Graham Evangelistic Association; president of Gordon College and Divinity School (1969–1976); and pastor for 33 years at Park Street Church in Boston, Massachusetts.

Born to Herman and Angie Ockenga in Chicago in 1905, his frail body made him susceptible to illness and injury and thus caused him to live a reclusive life that allowed for extended times of quiet reflection. At the age of 11, in a summer Methodist camp meeting, Ockenga said he believed he was "saved from his sins," but it was not until December 31, 1922, at the age of 17 that he received assurance of his salvation.

Ockenga continued in the heritage of his mother's Methodist influence as he entered Taylor College, a small Methodist college in Upland, Indiana, in 1923. He excelled in every area of his studies but was most comfortable in joining one of the Taylor youth evangelistic teams, where he began his preaching tradition. He believed that in order to preach well, he must actually preach. He also believed that good preaching must be undergirded by not only careful Bible study but also regular seasons of fervent prayer.

On June 15, 1927, Ockenga graduated from Taylor College and in the fall began his theological studies at Princeton Theological Seminary. His main professor, by whom he was influenced more than any another, was New Testament scholar J. Gresham Machen (1881–1937). It was Machen's decision to leave Princeton in 1929 to help establish Westminster Theological Seminary in Philadelphia that led Ockenga to follow his mentor to the new school for the final year of his seminary training. It proved to be a good decision for Ockenga who became an influence on the movement toward the renewal of the evangelical mind that was beginning to emerge in the scholarly world of academia.

One of the early organizational steps to the renewal of evangelical thinking was the establishment of the National Association of Evangelicals (NAE) in 1942. The meeting was held in St. Louis, Missouri, and Harold John Ockenga was the keynote speaker. The name of the new organization signaled a return to the familiar 19th-century term "evangelical" and also a separation from the anti-intellectual and fanatical term "fundamentalists" as used in the earlier 20th-century

Fundamentalist–Modernist Controversy. Yet the preaching of Ockenga sounded much the same. He had come to believe that evangelical Christianity suffered only a series of defeats with the influence of liberalism in organizations, publications, pulpits, seminaries, and other schools, the attractiveness of materialism among young preachers, and the exponential growth of iniquity.

His most notable pastorate was his 33 years as senior pastor of Park Street Church in Boston (1936). From this place of service, he became the face and voice of the New Evangelicalism of the mid-20th century. Ockenga was known for "drawing the line" against what he believed was wrong with the theological movements of the day: modernism (liberalism), neo-Orthodoxy, and fundamentalism. For him, liberalism was a defection from creedal orthodoxy. It repudiated much of the content of historic Christianity as reflected in Scripture, the Nicene Creed, and the Apostles Creed, and substituted a new anti-supernatural content in its place. Neo-Orthodoxy, a German theological movement (introduced into the United States by Reinhold Niebuhr in the 1930s) that criticized liberalism but did not hold strictly to biblical inerrancy, was a subtle perversion of true Christianity. It abandoned the church's historic commitment to the Bible as objective revelation in favor of a more subjective or existential understanding of the Scriptures. Although fundamentalism was essentially correct in its commitment to sound doctrine, its militancy, anti-intellectualism, and cultural withdrawal had to be replaced with Christian charity, the cultivation of the mind, and reengagement with culture.

Harold John Ockenga spearheaded what has been coined the "Mid-Twentieth Century Revival" with his invitation to a young 31-year-old evangelist by the name of Billy Graham (1918–). Graham spoke to more than 6,000 young people at a rally in the city of Boston, December 31, 1949. The overwhelming response of the New Year's Eve rally cemented a lifelong bond between Ockenga and Graham. From their relationship, a new phrase was established for the evangelical movement: "Cooperation without compromise."

Harold John Ockenga's influence on evangelicalism in the 20th century was profound and remains so even today. Those affiliated with the association were interested in maintaining many of the biblical concerns that fundamentalism held to. However they also sought to direct conservative Christianity away from the anticultural and anti-intellectual tendencies that had begun to typify fundamentalists.

J. Denny Autrey

See also: Carnell, Edward John; Fuller Theological Seminary; Gordon-Conwell Theological Seminary; Graham, William F., Jr. ("Billy"); Henry, Carl F. H.; Neo-Evangelicalism; Park Street Church

Further Reading

Autrey, C. E. *The Theology of Evangelism.* Nashville: Broadman Press, 1966.
Carpenter, Joel A. *Revive Us Again: The Reawakening of American Fundamentalism.* New York: Oxford University Press, 1997.

Marsden, George M. *Reforming Fundamentalism: Fuller Seminary and the New Evangelicalism.* Grand Rapids, MI: Eerdmans, 1987.

Rosell, Garth M. "America's Hour has Struck." *Christian History & Biography* 92 (Fall 2006): 48.

Rosell, Garth M. *The Surprising Work of God: Harold John Ockenga, Billy Graham, and the Rebirth of Evangelicalism.* Grand Rapids, MI: Baker Academic, 2008.

Rosell, Garth M. *Boston's Historic Park Street Church.* Grand Rapids, MI: Kregel, 2009.

Strachan, Owen. *Awakening the Evangelical Mind: An Intellectual History of the Neo-Evangelical Movement.* Grand Rapids, MI: Zondervan, 2015.

ODEN, THOMAS C. (1931–2016)

Thomas Clark Oden was known widely in Evangelicalism for his work in the retrieval of the theology of the Church Fathers and championing historic Christian orthodoxy over and against classic Protestant Liberalism. Oden was born in 1931 in Altus, Oklahoma, and received his undergraduate education at the University of Oklahoma. He then carried out his graduate work at Perkins School of Theology at Southern Methodist University before moving on to complete his doctoral research in 1960 at Yale University under the direction of Richard Niebuhr. He taught at several academic institutions, with his longest tenure at Drew University Divinity School, where he joined the faculty in 1970 and served as professor of ethics and theology for 33 years. Following his retirement in the mid-1990s, Oden assumed the director position at the Center for Early African Christianity at Eastern University. Regarding his personal life, Oden married Edrita Pokorny, and they had three children together. He was also ordained into the United Methodist Church in 1954 and was active in revitalizing his church through emphasizing a return to orthodox Christian faith and practice.

Oden's thought and life are marked out by two contrasting trajectories. His early academic training included prestigious institutions of higher education, and his theological research concerned the works of Bultmann, Freud, Nietzsche, and Marx. His interest in these and other classic liberal thinkers developed from the 1940s through the 1960s. His return to Christian orthodoxy began soon after when he became rapidly more disenfranchised in the cultural and political revolutions going on around him. After Oden accepted a tenured position at Drew University, he befriended a Jewish social philosopher named Will Herberg (1901–1977), who would make a lasting impression on him. Herberg became a mentor to Oden, and after a lengthy interchange of ideas, he poignantly remarked that Oden would remain theologically uneducated until he invested himself in the great minds of the Christian tradition such as Athanasius and Augustine. After this encounter, Oden experienced something of a transformation and engrossed himself in the classic writings of the church fathers. As his appreciation for the great thinkers of church history grew, so also did his faith. Eventually he abandoned his idealism and socialism and turned back toward historic Christian orthodoxy. Looking back, he considered himself a prodigal during the first 40 years of his life when he roamed away from home as far as he could go, but returned home as a son during the last 40. Oden confesses that he had been in love with novelty and, consequently, heresy, but the writings of the ancient church called him back home to the communion of the saints and the 2,000-year stable memory of Christian orthodoxy.

Oden published an extensive number of essays, articles, and books that reflect on his journey of faith and the path back to orthodoxy through the theology of the ancient church. Several of these writings are highly critical of mainline Protestant liberalism and plead for a revival of orthodoxy, including: *After Modernity . . . What?: Agenda for Theology* (1992), *Requiem: A Lament in Three Movements* (1995), and *The Rebirth of Orthodoxy: Signs of New Life in Christianity* (2002). He also composed several works that discuss the importance of consensual Christian orthodoxy, or what he calls "paleo-orthodoxy," that runs throughout the history of the Christian tradition, including *One Faith: The Evangelical Consensus* (with J. I. Packer) and his extensive three-volume systematic theology (1987, 1992, 1994). His most recent publications have taken a turn toward the continent of Africa and a recovery of the African theological heritage, including *How Africa Shaped the Christian Mind: The African Seedbed of Western Christianity* (2007), *The African Memory of Mark: Reassessing Early Church Tradition* (2011), and *Early Libyan Christianity* (2011). In certain respects, he considers this work on recovering the theological heritage of Africa his most important positive contribution to scholarship. Among evangelicals, though, Oden is probably best known for his work editing the *Ancient Christian Commentary on Scripture* (1998–2009), which is a massive 29-volume project that provides samplings of patristic commentary on every book of the Bible.

Throughout his research, Oden traveled extensively and met with a number of prominent church leaders and theologians, including Karl Barth and Joseph Ratzinger. Oden died on December 8, 2016.

Finally, Oden's life and thought is a testament to his belief in the theological bankruptcy of liberal Christianity when it abandons a commitment to historic Christian orthodoxy. Although Oden was not educated in evangelical institutions nor taught in any capacity in a distinctively evangelical school, he has garnered a significant following among the evangelical community. Oden's work on the church Fathers has inspired a new generation of evangelical scholars to return to the ancient sources and discover the wisdom in early Christian theological reflection. Those evangelicals that follow his lead have discovered faithful pastors and scholars in the early church who share many of their own cherished theological convictions.

Stephen O. Presley

See also: Theological Controversies within Evangelicalism

Further Reading

Oden, Thomas C. *After Modernity . . . What?* Grand Rapids, MI: Zondervan, 1992.

Oden, Thomas C. *Requiem: A Lament in Three Movements.* Nashville, TN: Abingdon Press, 1995.

Oden, Thomas C. *The Rebirth of Orthodoxy: Signs of New Life in Christianity.* San Francisco: HarperOne, 2002.

Oden, Thomas C. *A Change of Heart: A Personal and Theological Memoir.* Downers Grove, IL: IVP Academic, 2014.

Packer J. I., and Thomas C. Oden. *One Faith: The Evangelical Consensus.* Downers Grove, IL: IVP Academic, 2004.

OFFICERS' CHRISTIAN FELLOWSHIP

Officers' Christian Fellowship (OCF) is a layperson-led organization formed in 1943 to provide Christian fellowship, Bible studies prayer, and discipleship among American military officers and their families. The organization's history dates to the mid-1800s and the time when British military Captain John Trotter was posted in India in 1851 during the tumultuous years of what the British call the Great Mutiny and Indians call the Great Rebellion of 1851. Trotter, in common with many Christian military men and women, felt a deep sense of need for Christian fellowship and prayer during his dangerous deployment. In response, he organized other like-minded Christians to participate in informal lay-led gatherings for prayer and fellowship and mutual encouragement. On his return to England, Trotter organized the Army Prayer Union to continue the activities he had led in India. His organization took root and flourished in England and continues today under the title Armed Forces Christian Union.

The U.S. version of this organization began when U.S. Army Lieutenant Colonel Hayes A. Kroner met with a member of the British Army Prayer Union aboard a ship and participated in its activities. Kroner appreciated the benefits of the informal gatherings and the spiritual benefits he experienced, and decided to establish an American version on his return to the United States. His first meetings were Bible studies that took place in Washington, D.C., in 1939. The American OCU was officially begun in 1943, during the height of the Second World War. The name was officially changed to Officers' Christian Fellowship in 1972.

"OCF exists to glorify God by uniting Christian officers for biblical fellowship and outreach, equipping and encouraging them to minister effectively in the military society . . ." (http://www.ocfusa.org). The organization exists throughout the U.S. military and provides fellowship, spiritual support, and informal Bible studies both at home and while deployed. It has a special focus on building healthy families.

OCF is led by a group of elected military officers who oversee the activities of the organization. They also run two retreat and conference centers, one in Buena Vista, Colorado, and the other in White Sulphur Springs, Pennsylvania. OCF publishes a quarterly magazine, *Command.* OCF groups exist at most major U.S. military installations and on many ships in the U.S. Navy, and lists more than 16,000 active members. OCF illustrates the breadth of evangelical outreach as a parachurch ministry and its participation in every segment of American life.

Dayne E. Nix

See also: Military Ministries; Parachurch Ministries

Further Reading

Loveland, Anne C. *American Evangelicals and the U.S. Military, 1942–1993*. Baton Rouge, LA: Louisiana State University Press, 1997. http://www.ocfusa.org.

OSTEEN, JOEL (1963–)

Joel Osteen is pastor of Lakewood Church in Houston, Texas, the largest megachurch in the United States, with more than 40,000 members. It is one of the nation's most ethnically diverse congregations. After working as Lakewood's television producer for nearly two decades, Osteen became the church's pastor in 1999 on the death of his father and Lakewood's founder, John Osteen (1921–1999). The elder Osteen, a Southern Baptist-turned-Pentecostal influenced by the likes of Oral Roberts (1918–2009) and Kenneth E. Hagin (1917–2003), founded Lakewood in 1959, grew the church numerically over his four-decade ministry in Houston, and played a leading role in the post–World War II neo-Pentecostal movement. From the 1970s to the 1990s, John was one of the most ardent promoters of the prosperity gospel. Building on his father's legacy, Joel has continued to increase Lakewood's size and influence, not least due to hiring a Latin Grammy-winning musician and pastor named Marcos Witt, who worked at the church from 2002 to 2012; musicians Cindy Cruse Ratcliff and Israel Houghton; and Pastor John Gray. At Lakewood, Osteen also ministers alongside his mother, Dodie Osteen; his brother, Paul Osteen; and his sister Lisa Osteen Comes.

Although he never finished college at Oral Roberts University, Osteen has become one of the most popular Christian ministers in contemporary America. Heavily influenced by the prosperity gospel teachings of his father and neo-Pentecostal teacher Joyce Meyer, along with the self-help teachings of leadership consultant John Maxwell, Osteen's prosperity sermons to offer a message of redemption, second chances, and spiritual success. Focused on more than money, his prosperity gospel supports emotional wholeness, psychological well-being, physical fitness, and a healthy lifestyle. Osteen articulates these themes by arranging his sermons and teachings around positive thinking, part of America's culture of self-help individuality, and positive confession, a neo-Pentecostal practice that verbalizes wishes and desires in the hopes of bringing them into material reality.

To disseminate his teachings, Osteen created an innovative and enterprising television ministry while playing a leading role in ushering televangelism into the 21st-century digital frontier. Recognizing the promise of new media, in the early 21st century Osteen was arguably the first televangelist who strategically placed his messages across multiple media modalities such as Facebook, Twitter, iTunes, and YouTube. For Osteen, new media saturation played a central role in catapulting his ministry into a highly visible realm and translated into soaring popularity. Osteen started a radio program, which includes a live call-in component, on his own SiriusXM channel. *Joel Osteen*, his weekly television broadcast, appears to more than 7 million viewers weekly, and millions more visit his Web site, like him on Facebook, and follow him on Twitter. As a prosperity minister with more than 30 years of experience in television production, Osteen produces and edits his sermons before broadcasting them. Osteen has promoted his message on numerous talk-shows, including *Larry King Live*, *The Dr. Oz Show*, and Oprah's *Lifeclass*, and it has also appeared in countless of his books such as his first, *Your Best Life Now: 7 Steps to Living At Your Full Potential* (2004), and thereafter: *Become a Better You: 7 Keys to Improving Your Everyday Life* (2007); *It's Your Time: Activate Your Faith, Achieve Your Dreams, and Increase in God's Favor* (2009); *Every Day a Friday: How to Be Happier 7 Days a Week* (2011); *I Declare: 31 Promises to Speak Over Your Life* (2012); and *You Can, You Will: 8 Undeniable Qualities of a Winner* (2014). Along with his wife and Lakewood's copastor, Victoria, Osteen has edited and published one of the few prosperity gospel reference books, *Hope for Today Study Bible* (2009).

Extraordinarily popular, Osteen has received significant criticism from evangelical pastors and theologians, especially those associated with New Calvinism, a theological movement that prizes academic theology and divine power. Southern Baptist commentator and seminary president R. Albert Mohler first took issue with statements Osteen made in 2005 on *Larry King Live*, in which Osteen reportedly faltered when asked about Christianity's exclusivity on the matter of salvation. More recently, Mohler targeted Osteen's prosperity message of positive thinking and happy living with what he called "theological bankruptcy." Similarly, Westminster Theological Seminary Professor Michael S. Horton decried Osteen's "cotton candy gospel" in a *60 Minutes* interview focused on Osteen's 2007 book *Become a Better You*. A longtime critic of televangelism and the prosperity gospel, Horton's analysis of Osteen in his book *Christless Christianity* (2008) linked the Houston pastor's teachings of "self-salvation" with ancient Gnosticism and Pelagianism. Echoing Mohler and Horton, California minister John MacArthur found theologically problematic Osteen's prosperity gospel, which he called a "religious Ponzi scheme." MacArthur had previously criticized Pentecostalism in publications such as *Charismatic Chaos* (1992), and later in *Strange Fire* (2013), but in Joel Osteen—whose message he also dubbed a "massive swindle" and "a shallow, saccharine variety of universalism"— he found one of the most egregious examples of misapplying the Bible to matters of faith and life. The subject of profuse praise and extended criticism, Osteen is one of America's most consequential evangelical figures.

Phillip Luke Sinitiere

See also: Calvinism; MacArthur, John F., Jr.; Pentecostalism (and Charismatic Movement), Evangelicals and; Vineyard Movement

Further Reading

Bowler, Kate. *Blessed: A History of the American Prosperity Gospel*. New York: Oxford University Press, 2013.

Carney, Charity R. "Lakewood Church and the Roots of the Megachurch Movement in the South." *Southern Quarterly* 50, no. 1 (Fall 2012): 60–78.

"Joel Osteen Answers His Critics." 60 Minutes. (October 11, 2007). http://www.cbsnews .com/news/joel-osteen-answers-his-critics/2/.

MacArthur, John. *Strange Fire: The Danger of Offending the Holy Spirit with Counterfeit Worship*. Nashville: Thomas Nelson, 2013.

Sinitiere, Phillip Luke. *Salvation with a Smile: Joel Osteen, Lakewood Church, and American Christianity*. New York: New York University Press, 2015.

P

PACIFIC GARDEN MISSION (CHICAGO)

Pacific Garden Mission is the oldest continuously operating gospel rescue mission in the United States. Founded in Chicago on September 15, 1873, in a tiny store front at 386 South Clark Street, by Sarah (Dunne) Clarke and her husband, Colonel George Clarke, the mission opened with a seating capacity of 40. In 1880, the Clarkes moved the mission to a building vacated by the Pacific Beer Garden. Evangelist Dwight L. Moody, visiting the Clarkes, suggested they drop the word "Beer" and add the word "Mission" to their name.

PGM's mission is serve the poor and homeless with the compassion of Christ. Their purpose is "[t]o reach the lost with the Gospel of Christ."

In its longer than 140-year history PGM's nine presidents have moved its location and expanded the campus to best serve the poor and homeless. Their current location is 1458 South Canal Street, Chicago. Ministries have increased to include a serviceman's center, woman and children's ministry, medical and dental clinic, Bible Academy program, the Old Lighthouse Redemption choir, prison and hospital ministries, and numerous career development programs. PGM's radio program *UNSHACKLED!*, started in 1950, broadcasts to more than 1,800 stations in English, Spanish, Arabic, Romanian, Russian, and Polish. In 2000, a two-minute radio testimony called "Free Indeed" debuted and is heard on more than 250 stations. Well-known evangelicals associated with PGM include Billy Sunday, D. L. Moody, and Melvin Trotter.

James Menzies

See also: Evangelism; Social Action, Evangelicals and

Further Reading

Adair, James R. *The Old Lighthouse: The Story of the Pacific Garden Mission.* Chicago: Moody Press, 1966.

Henry, Carl F. H. *The Pacific Garden Mission: A doorway to heaven.* Grand Rapids, MI: Zondervan, 1942.

Magnuson, Norris. *Salvation in the Slums: Evangelical Social Work 1865–1920.* Eugene, OR: Wipf & Stock, 2004.

Pacific Garden Mission. "Our Mission." Accessed July 30, 2017. https://www.pgm.org/who -we-are/our-mission/.

PARACHURCH MINISTRIES

Parachurches ministries are voluntary, not-for-profit associations of Christians working outside the oversight and control of religious denominations to provide specific ministry or social service to a specific group or individual. The prefix *para* comes from Greek and means "beside" or "alongside of." Parachurches are not churches, but are an extension of the broader church, tasked with delivery of specific ministries or services. Although most local churches and certainly all Protestant denominations have a calling to a variety of core ministries, parachurch ministries traditionally extend that reach. This emphasis of coming alongside is reflected in the functional goals of these ministries that focus on activities that local churches and individual denominations are unable or unwilling to perform on their own. These organizations often focus on community outreach to colleges, prisons, homeless individuals and families, and other unreached groups. In addition, some groups provide social services, including homeless shelters, child care, disaster relief, and emergency aid. Evangelical Christians donate billions of dollars annually toward humanitarian, political, and evangelistic causes through parachurch ministries.

The significant employment of parachurch organizations and Protestant missions in modern times dates to the late 18th century and is credited to the work of William Carey (1761–1834), a Baptist preacher in England with a vision for world evangelism. This led to the founding of the Baptist Missionary Society. In 1793, Carey sailed to India and spent 41 years evangelizing and translating the New Testament into Bengali and 24 other languages, and portions of it into 209 other languages and dialects. This beginning also shows the overlap that is often found in parachurch ministries with evangelism and mission endeavors.

Contemporary estimates are that there are more than 10,000 groups in the United States. Parachurch ministries can vary from a few unpaid workers relying on donations from the local congregation to very large organizations with hundreds of paid staff and entire departments dedicated to promoting the missionary goals and pursuing funding in support of those goals. Parachurch ministries often operate without governing boards and oversight, which has the potential to lead to problems of governance. Concerns about the financial practices of parachurch agencies led to the formation of the Evangelical Council for Financial Accountability (ECFA). The ECFA was founded in 1979 with the purpose of providing accreditation to leading Christian nonprofit organizations that faithfully demonstrate compliance with established standards for financial accountability, transparency, fundraising, and board governance. The ECFA has nearly 700 affiliated religious organizations, including parachurch ministries.

One of the most well-known parachurch ministries is the Young Men's Christian Association. Founded in London in 1844 by George Williams, the YMCA provided young men with a wholesome alternative to the evils of urban life. Bible classes, Christian fellowship, spiritual development, and athletics were among its earliest goals. Today there are more than 2,700 YMCAs, with 19,000 full-time staff, serving 45 million people in 119 countries.

Evangelist Billy Graham (1918–) is one of the best-known evangelicals of the 20th and 21st centuries. The Billy Graham Evangelistic Association is the nonprofit religious corporation that conducts the ministries of Billy Graham, his associate evangelists, and affiliated agencies. Headquartered in Minneapolis, Minnesota, the BGEA has an operating budget of more than $80 million and hundreds of full-time employees.

According to *Sharefaith* magazine, Samaritans Purse, another ministry, is ranked as the 25th largest NGO in the country and the fourth largest Christian NGO. The organization's president is Franklin Graham (1952–), son of Christian evangelist Billy Graham. Active in more than 100 countries, this organization specializes in emergency relief and has been active in some large-scale disaster relief projects during times of humanitarian crisis events, including Kosovo, Somalia, and Afghanistan conflicts, and emergency relief in times of hurricane Katrina and earthquakes in El Salvador and currently Ecuador. Samaritan's Purse generates over $400 million annually, about 90 percent of which goes directly to evangelism and relief projects.

Other organizations include InterVarsity Christian Fellowship, Cru, Fellowship of Christian Athletes, L'Abri Fellowship, World Vision International, The Navigators, Scripture Union, and Youth with a Mission (YWAM). Parachurch ministries have been a central element in American evangelicalism since its inception, and illustrate the depth and breadth of evangelical commitment to social and cultural causes and to the expansion of evangelical Christianity through evangelism and nurturing the spiritual growth of individuals.

Katherine Pang

See also: Africa Inland Mission; BSF International; Cru; Fellowship of Christian Athletes; Graham, William F., Jr. ("Billy"); InterVarsity Christian Fellowship/USA; L'Abri Fellowship; Ligonier Ministries; Military Ministries; Navigators; Young Life

Further Reading

Anderson, Leith. *Leadership That Works: Hope and Directions for Church and Parachurch Leaders in Today's Complex World.* Bloomington, MN: Bethany House, 1999.

House, Wayne H. *Christian Ministries and the Law: What Church and Para-Church Leaders Should Know.* Grand Rapids, MI: Kregel, 1992, 1999.

Reid, Daniel G., Robert D. Linder, Bruce L. Shelley, and Harry S. Stout. *Dictionary of Christianity in America.* Downers Grove, IL: InterVarsity Press, 1990.

Willmer, Wesley Kenneth. *The Prospering Parachurch: Enlarging the Boundaries of God's Kingdom.* San Francisco: Jossey-Bass, 1998.

PARK STREET CHURCH (BOSTON)

The Park Street Church is one of America's oldest and most influential evangelical churches and congregations. It was built in 1809 in downtown Boston, Massachusetts, at the corner of Tremont and Park Street. The church is a conservative

Congregational church with an active membership of 1,459, a mission budget of $2.1 million, and ministry and operations budget of $3.1 million (2015).

The founding of the church is predated to 1804, when the Religious Improvement Society began weekly meetings with lectures and prayer. On February 27, 1809, 26 former members of the Old South Meeting House, wanting to counter rising Unitarianism, met to form a charter.

By April of 1809, a location had been chosen, and by 1810, the congregation had raised over $100,000 to complete construction. The cornerstone of the building was laid on May 1, 1809, and construction completed by the end of the year under the guidance of architect Peter Banner. The first worship service was held on January 10, 1810. The church's steeple rises 217 feet and remains a landmark visible from several Boston neighborhoods. From 1810 to 1867, the church was the tallest building in the United States.

Park Street Church is known for its emphasis on missions, evangelical doctrine, and the application of Scripture to social issues. In 1816, Park Street joined with Old South Church to form the City Mission Society to serve Boston's urban poor. In 1974, the church built a Church Ministries Building at 1 Park Street beside the main edifice and in the 1990s, the church purchased the 2 and 3 Park Street buildings from Houghton-Mifflin.

In 1949, Billy Graham's first transcontinental crusade began at Park Street. From 1936 to 1969, Harold J. Ockenga was senior pastor and during this time cofounded Gordon-Conwell Theological Seminary with Billy Graham, and cofounded Fuller Theological Seminary, the National Association of Evangelicals, War Relief (now World Relief), and the publication Christianity Today.

James Menzies

See also: Graham, William F., Jr. ("Billy"); Neo-Evangelicalism; Ockenga, Harold John

Further Reading

Howe, Daniel Walker. *What Hath God Wrought: The Transformation of America, 1815–1848.* New York: Oxford University Press; 2007.

Lindsell, Harold. *Park Street Prophet: A Life of Harold John Ockenga.* Salem, OR: Wipf & Stock, 2015.

Old, Hughes Oliphant. *The Reading and Preaching of the Scriptures in the Worship of the Christian Church,* Vol. 6, *The Modern Age.* Grand Rapids, MI: Eerdmans, 2007.

Park Street Church. (n.d.). Accessed April 29, 2017. http://www.parkstreet.org/.

Rosell, Garth M. *Boston's Historic Park Street Church.* Grand Rapids, MI: Kregel, 2009.

PENTECOSTALISM (AND CHARISMATIC MOVEMENT), EVANGELICALS AND

Pentecostalism is a movement that is both inside and outside of evangelicalism. Most American evangelicals are not Pentecostals. Pentecostalism refers to an ecclesiological movement that emphasizes the baptism of the Holy Spirit and his present work in the lives of believers through the expression of spiritual gifts. Some trace the movement's origins to the experiences of the early church as well as some of the mystic practices of Eastern Orthodox churches, Pentecostalism is a 20th-century movement with strong ties to the Wesleyan-Holiness tradition of the 19th century, African American Christianity, and miraculous healing. Emphasizing the person and work of the Holy Spirit, Pentecostalism has found fertile ground in Africa, Latin America, and Asia to the point that some estimate that Pentecostals and Charismatics constitute approximately 18 to 25 percent of the total number of Christians within the global church.

During the first few years of the 20th century, multiple centers of Charismatic and Pentecostal expression were emerging within small pockets in Russia, Brazil, Argentina, South Africa, Korea, and North America, among others. Of particular note is the Azusa Street Revival in Los Angeles in 1907. Led by William Joseph Seymour (1870–1922), an African American preacher who had been allowed to listen to the teaching of Charles Parham, an integrated small group of believers began meeting together for prayer and worship continually. Speaking in tongues and being "slain in the Spirit" were common occurrences, and as the congregation began to grow, it drew interest from churches across America. People from all over the country and world would flock to Los Angeles, receive a "baptism of the Spirit" and return home, carrying the message of Pentecostalism with them.

Since this time, Pentecostalism has exploded throughout the majority world, particularly in Latin America and Sub-Saharan Africa. Pentecostalists reject a rationalistic and dualistic worldview that separates the physical from the spiritual, while also proclaiming the power of God for victory over demonic forces and illness, and embracing the message of a powerful and present God who can heal sickness. This has led to the creation of many independent, inculturated churches that are no longer dependent on their denominations and are better equipped to engage their immediate cultural context. Unfortunately, the emphasis on power and healing can also lead to the exploitation of the poor by some pastors who peddle the promise of hope in desperate times.

Pentecostalism's history has also been marked by denominationalism and schism. From the moment of its birth within the United States, the reality of interracial conflict caused divisions within the church. Additionally, discrepancies in understanding the doctrine of the Trinity as well as the nature of sanctification have led to the emergence of three primary schools of thought: Classical Pentecostals, who believe that sanctification is a second blessing that occurs subsequent to conversion and then believe in a third work of grace in the baptism of the Holy Spirit; Finished Work Pentecostals, who coalesce sanctification and conversion into one work of grace; and Oneness Pentecostals, who reject the Trinity and believe that Father, Son, and Holy Spirit are all names for Jesus, a renewed form of an early church heresy known as modalism. The Church of God in Christ is the largest Pentecostal denomination within the United States, with more than 5 million members. Another significant denomination is the Assemblies of God, founded in 1914, claiming more than 3 million members.

Due to the almost anti-Creedal nature of early Pentecostalism, the movement's rapid spread throughout the majority world, and the relative independence of many of the churches, delineating the doctrinal distinctives of the Pentecostal and Charismatic movement has proven to be a difficult task. Yet, with that said, Pentecostal theology centralizes around the person, work, and baptism of the Holy Spirit. The Holy Spirit is believed to baptize believers post conversion, resulting in the visible expression of spiritual gifts such as prophecy, divine healing, and speaking in tongues (Acts 2). The baptism of the Holy Spirit is viewed as God's act of empowering and equipping the Christian for service, ministry, and mission. As such, it is to be sought and "speaking in tongues," an ecstatic empowerment or blessing, is viewed as one of the primary evidences of the Holy Spirit's presence in the life of the believer.

Pentecostals hold firmly to a literal interpretation of the Scriptures and believe that it is authoritative in all areas of faith in practice. The goal of theological reflection and understanding the Scriptures is to experience the fullness of the Spirit who equips the believer for ministerial service. The Gospels and Luke–Acts play an important role in Pentecostal theology and are used to defend the church's practice of spiritual gifts. Additionally, experience plays an important role in Pentecostal theological method and is an authoritative source. Although many Pentecostal scholars advocate for caution and the supremacy of Scripture in interpreting experience, the authority given to experience creates a certain level of tension in many churches.

Yet Pentecostalism is also ultimately Christo-centric and focused on evangelism and world missions. Though Pentecostals often exhibit a propensity to exalt the work of the Spirit, the movement is fueled by a premillennial eschatology and a belief in the immanency of Christ's return. This belief has caused Pentecostals to train their members for evangelism, world missions, and outreach from the movement's inception. Although Catholic evangelism is rooted in the Mission Dei, and most Protestants emphasize obedience to the Great Commission, Pentecostals engage in world mission and evangelism because of their belief that the Holy Spirit is leading, and has sent and equipped them to proclaim the gospel. Pentecostals have also emphasized church planting and indigenous churches within the populations in which they minister. All of this has contributed to Pentecostalism's pervasive influence and expanding presence within the global church and majority world.

In recent years, Pentecostals engaged in more theological reflection as they have defended their belief system in light of the criticisms from broader evangelicalism. But Pentecostalism remains and will continue to be a dominant force in world Christianity. Pentecostalism is a theology that focuses on the presence of God in the Holy Spirit and his empowerment for Christian service, evangelism, and world missions.

Daniel Hill

See also: Fuller Theological Seminary; Missions, Evangelicals and; Osteen, Joel; Premillennialism; Rapture; Regent University; Vineyard Movement

Further Reading

Anderson, Allan. *An Introduction to Pentecostalism: Global Charismatic Theology.* Cambridge: Cambridge University Press, 2004.

Kalu, Ogbu. *African Pentecostalism: An Introduction.* Oxford: Oxford University Press, 2008.

Macchia, Frank D. *Baptized in the Spirit: A Global Pentecostal Theology.* Grand Rapids, MI: Zondervan, 2006.

Synon, Vinson. *The Holiness-Pentecostal Movement in the United States.* Grand Rapids, MI: Eerdmans, 1971.

Synon, Vinson. *The Century of the Holy Spirit: 100 Years of Pentecostal and Charismatic Renewal.* Nashville, TN: Thomas Nelson, 2001.

Yong, Amos. *The Spirit Poured Out on All Flesh: Pentecostalism and the Possibility of Global Theology.* Grand Rapids, MI: Baker, 2005.

PHILOSOPHY, EVANGELICALS AND

Evangelicals have had a long, difficult, and fruitful interaction with philosophy. In order to elucidate that interaction, it is helpful first to distinguish between the two meanings that the term "philosophy" can have. The first meaning points to an ideal: the pursuit and ardent love for wisdom. The second meaning signifies a specific discipline with its own traditions, vocabulary, and standards for progress. Given Evangelicals' reverence for Scripture, and the many biblical exhortations to seek wisdom, it is not unfair to describe philosophy in the first sense, the ideal, as a biblical commandment. Christians notice passages like Proverbs 4:5, "Get wisdom; get insight; do not forget, and do not turn away from the words of my mouth," and James 1:5, "If any of you lacks wisdom, let him ask God, who gives generously to all without reproach, and it will be given him." This high regard for wisdom in the Bible is emphasized by early theologians. For example, in *De Trinitate* (417 CE) St. Augustine (354–430 CE) argues that 1 Corinthians 1:24 identifies Jesus as the wisdom of God. Thus, following St. Augustine's lead, loving wisdom and loving Jesus are only superficially different loves. They would be, in reality, the same love. Philosophy, then, seems like a Christian duty.

This ideal of philosophy as the love of wisdom, an ideal so consonant with the gospel and Scripture, often comes into conflict with philosophy in the second sense: philosophy as a specific discipline or tradition. Indeed, St. Augustine was no stranger to this conflict, himself writing an early book *Contra Academicos* (386 CE), "Against the Academicians," in order to refute philosophical positions antithetical to Christian beliefs. St. Augustine's works continue to inspire Christian philosophers, as he maintains a lively interplay with the philosophical schools of his time, praising and using some of their arguments and insights, yet also defending Christianity against their attacks. It is a more interactive approach than that of some of his forebears.

Writing *De Praescriptione Haereticorum* some 200 years before St. Augustine's time, Tertullian (160–220 CE) famously asked, "What does Athens have to do with Jerusalem?" He used this now famous rhetorical question to reject philosophy. As he reckons, all the arguments, specialized vocabulary, and mythology that philosophy musters could never be an equal interlocutor with Christianity or a fitting vessel to convey Christian truth. Athens, the world of philosophical reasoning, could have nothing in common with Jerusalem, the world of faith and obedience.

Within the evangelical tradition, one finds both the approaches of Tertullian and Augustine. It is, however, difficult for those following Tertullian to expunge all philosophy from theology. The discipline of philosophy has taken on the task of studying and analyzing argumentation and definition as such, and theology cannot avoid spending a great deal of effort both in argumentation and definition. Thus it is not possible for the discipline of theology to avoid being indebted to the discipline of philosophy. Because theology is concerned with issues of ultimate importance, its argumentation and definition must be of the very highest quality. For that task, the tools of philosophy play an important role.

Even though theology must rely on the tools of philosophy, and Christians must be devoted to philosophy as an ideal, nevertheless it is naïve for an evangelical to see no difference between philosophy as an ideal and as a discipline. This is so primarily because Christianity is a revealed religion, not one founded on reason or discovery. As such, Christians cannot always follow their intuitions about what God would be like, what He would want from His followers, and which divine characteristics are compatible with each other. The revealed tenets of Christianity are not the most obvious, easiest to defend, or most palatable to a non-Christian audience. As one might expect, the history of philosophy is replete with arguments alleging the monstrosity of eternal punishment, the impossibility of a God-man (i.e., the incarnation of Jesus), the incoherence of miracles, the irrationality of faith, the freedom-destroying properties of divine foreknowledge, the self-destructive power of religious temperance, and so on. These arguments against Christian beliefs make it tempting to take St. Paul's warning to believers in as broad a way as possible: "See to it that no one takes you captive by philosophy and empty deceit, according to human tradition, according to the elemental spirits of the world, and not according to Christ" (Colossians 2:8). The temptation is for evangelicals to reject the discipline of philosophy as unsafe and hostile to Christian truth, especially those who have "separatist" from culture-type propensities.

Yet evangelicals thinkers like Francis A. Schaeffer (1912–1984) or Christian philosopher William Lane Craig (1949–) claim that one should not give into this temptation. Although it is true that some philosophy falls under Paul's warning, not all philosophy is "empty deceit" and antithetical to Christ. In fact, many great philosophical works were written as explorations of Christian ideas and reflect deep religious commitment. These Christian interactions with philosophy fall within three general categories: defense of the faith through argumentation, elucidation of theological concepts, and appreciation of intellectual beauty.

First, the rigorous argumentation and clear definition that characterizes philosophy are ideal tools for defending Christianity against those who would seek to discredit its tenets. For example, the arguments purporting to show the freedom-destroying properties of divine foreknowledge are initially plausible, but their intuitive strength diminishes on close analysis. One need not choose between affirming free will or affirming providence, but without that philosophical analysis believers may feel forced to make such a choice. By undertaking that painstaking analysis, Christian philosophers perform an important service to the church.

Second, many of Christianity's teachings are not entirely clear. What, exactly, does it mean that Abraham was an example of faith, given his many strange choices? When Jesus says at the Last Supper, "This is my body," what, exactly, could that mean? The Gospel of John states, "In the beginning was the Word, and the Word was with God and the Word was God," but how, exactly, can the Word *be* God and *be with* God at the same time? Paul states in Romans 1 that those civilizations without written revelation can know that there is a God, yet how they are able to do so is not obvious. Clear and precise argumentation can illuminate these questions, especially when considering how these questions impact other theological positions. The elucidation of these puzzling issues strengthens the faith of Christians.

The Problem of Evil and Suffering and the God of the Bible

Every worldview has to contend with the problem of evil and suffering, and consequently doubt. This problem is not only philosophical but also personal. For evangelicals who experienced evil and suffering yet believe the God of the Bible is all-good, all-knowing, all-powerful, and sovereign, an incredible amount of works have been published on the subject and have proven to be beneficial, including the following 11:

1. *The Problem of Pain* by C. S. Lewis (1940, 1996)
2. *A Grief Observed* by C. S. Lewis (1961, 1996)
3. *God, Freedom, and Evil* by Alvin Plantinga (1974, 1977)
4. *Affliction: A Compassionate Look at the Reality of Pain and Suffering* by Edith Schaeffer (1978, 1993)
5. *The Many Faces of Evil (Revised and Expanded Edition): Theological Systems and the Problems of Evil* by John S. Feinberg (1979, 1994, 2004)
6. *The Roots of Evil* by Norman L. Geisler (1982, 2013)
7. *Unspeakable: Facing Up to the Challenge of Evil* by Os Guinness (2005)
8. *How Long, O Lord? Reflections on Suffering and Evil* by D. A. Carson (2006)
9. *An Act of God? Answers to Tough Questions about God's Role in Natural Disasters* by Erwin Lutzer (2011)
10. *Walking with God through Pain and Suffering* by Timothy Keller (2013)
11. *When There Are No Easy Answers: Thinking Differently about God, Suffering and Evil* by John S. Feinberg (2016)

Third, and finally, the study of philosophy offers a unique intellectual satisfaction. Seeking wisdom is itself a kind of worship. As evangelicals are commanded to love God with all our minds (Luke 10:27), they can obey using philosophy: the most abstract, universal, and timeless discipline. Studying philosophy, examining truth and goodness as such, can be its own reward because it is a way of showing gratitude for the gift of rationality. In these three ways, evangelicals engage philosophy, fruitfully participating in its debates.

Russell Hemati

See also: Christian Apologetics; Geisler, Norman L.; Intelligent Design Movement; L'Abri Fellowship; Plantinga, Alvin C.; Schaeffer, Francis A. and Edith; Walvoord, John F.

Further Reading

Clark, Kelly James, ed. *Philosophers Who Believe: The Spiritual Journeys of 11 Leading Thinkers.* Downers Grove, IL: InterVarsity Press, 1993.

Craig, William Lane, and Moreland, J. P. *Philosophical Foundations for a Christian Worldview.* Downers Grove, IL: InterVarsity Press, 2003.

Gould, Paul M., and Richard Brian Davis, eds. *Four Views on Christianity and Philosophy.* Grand Rapids, MI: Zondervan, 2016.

Morris, Thomas V., ed. *God and the Philosophers: The Reconciliation of Faith and Reason.* Oxford, UK: Oxford University Press, 1994.

Plantinga, Alvin. "Advice to Christian Philosophers." *Faith and Philosophy: Journal of the Society of Christian Philosophers* 1, no. 3 (1984): 253–271.

Schaeffer, Francis A. *The Collected Works of Francis A. Schaeffer.* 5 volumes. Wheaton, IL: Crossway, 1985.

Swinburne, Richard. *The Coherence of Theism,* rev. ed. New York: Oxford University Press, 1977, 1993.

Wolterstorff, Nicholas. *Reason within the Bounds of Religion.* Grand Rapids, MI: Eerdmans, 1984.

PIERARD, RICHARD V. (1934–)

Richard V. Pierard is a historian and Professor Emeritus at Indiana State University, Terre Haute, Indiana. Although an evangelical, he is best known for his critiques of evangelicalism, particularly the collaboration of evangelical leaders and denominations with right-wing politicians and ideologues. He was born in Chicago, Illinois, and raised in Richland, Washington. After service with the U.S. Army, he completed his undergraduate degree in history at California State University–Los Angeles in 1958 and obtained an MA in history at the same institution a year later. He earned a PhD in modern European history from the University of Iowa in 1964. It was while a graduate student at Iowa that he met two other evangelical students, Robert D. Linder and Robert G. Clouse, and this began a scholarly collaboration that continued throughout the careers of all three, but was particularly active in the 1960s and 1970s. Acting on a suggestion from Clouse in 1964, Pierard applied for and obtained an assistant professorship in modern European history at Indiana State University. He remained at Indiana State until retirement in 2000. He then became a scholar in residence and Stephen Phillips Professor of History at Gordon College, Wenham, Massachusetts, until retiring again in 2006. He was one of the founders of the Conference on Faith and History and served as secretary-treasurer from 1967 to 2004.

Along with coauthors Clouse and Linder, Pierard provided an early analysis of evangelicalism set against the backdrop of the turbulent 1960s years of civil and political unrest in the United States through *Protest and Politics: Christianity and Contemporary Affairs*, published in 1968. Pierard was one of the signers of the 1973 Chicago Declaration of Social Action that called for evangelicals to be more involved in issues related to the social and economic rights of the poor and oppressed. The declaration gained little traction with evangelicals at the time, but Pierard became a consistent advocate of its progressivist ideals through his prodigious writing activities through books and periodicals. In that same year, he coauthored with Linder a handbook on political activity for Christian university students, *Politics: A Case for Christian Action*. Pierard was among the first evangelical scholars to explore evangelicalism's relationship to and partnership with the prevailing civil religion in the United States. He and Linder coauthored *Twilight of the Saints: Biblical Christianity and Civil Religion in the United States* in 1978, and historical case studies of civil religion in action in *Civil Religion and the Presidency*, written 10 years later.

Beginning in the 1980s, Pierard's production turned to investigations of global Christianity and Baptist history. An American Baptist layperson, Pierard served as a leading member of the Baptist World Alliance Baptist Heritage and Identity Commission, which sought to create a permanent record of Baptist history throughout the world. Pierard was a frequent critic of Baptists whose conduct he believed to be inconsistent with the historical distinctives of the Baptist movement, with Southern Baptists frequently receiving the brunt of his opinions. He has been a strong voice in evangelical scholarship for decades, influencing colleagues, students, and readers.

Liam J. Atchison

See also: Chicago Declaration of Evangelical Social Concern; Conference on Faith and History; Evangelical Theological Society; Politics, Evangelicals and

Further Reading

Clouse, Robert G., Robert D. Linder, and Richard V. Pierard, eds. *Protest and Politics: Christianity and Contemporary Affairs.* Greenwood, SC: Attic Press, 1968.

Linder, Robert Dean, and Richard V. Pierard. *Politics: A Case for Christian Action.* Downers Grove, IL: InterVarsity Press, 1973.

Linder, Robert Dean, and Richard V. Pierard. *Twilight of the Saints: Biblical Christianity & Civil Religion in America.* Downers Grove, IL: InterVarsity Press, 1978.

Pierard, Richard. *The Unequal Yoke: Evangelical Christianity and Political Conservatism*. Eugene, OR: Wipf & Stock, 2006 [originally published, 1970].

Pierard, Richard V., and Robert Dean Linder. *Civil Religion & the Presidency*. Grand Rapids, MI: Zondervan, 1988.

PLANTINGA, ALVIN C. (1932–)

Alvin C. Plantinga (1932–) is an evangelical Christian philosopher. He was born in Ann Arbor, Michigan and received his undergraduate degree from Calvin College and PhD from Harvard University. He taught at Yale University, Wayne State University, Calvin College, and the University of Notre Dame. His contributions to metaphysics (especially the metaphysics of modality), philosophy of science, philosophical theology, epistemology, and philosophy of religion make him one of the leading Christian philosophers of the last 60 years. His most important contributions concern religious epistemology.

Belief in God Is Properly Basic

According to Plantinga, the primary role of human reason with respect to Christian belief is not to determine whether Christian belief is true, but to rebut criticisms of it and to provide a model that describes how Christian beliefs can be known. On

Other Recent Notable Christian Philosophers

Marilyn McCord Adams	David Bentley Hart
William Alston	Paul Helm
Elizabeth Margaret Anscombe	Richard G. Howe
Francis A. Beckwith	Peter van Inwagen
J. Budziszewski	Peter Kreeft
G. K. Chesterton	John Lennox
Paul Copan	C. S. Lewis
Mark Coppenger	Alasdair MacIntyre
Winfried Corduan	Hugh J. McCann
William Lane Craig	Angus Menuge
C. Stephen Evans	J.P. Moreland
Paul Feinberg	Ronald H. Nash
Bas van Fraassen	Louis Paul Pojman
John Frame	Roger Scruton
Robert K. Garcia	Richard Swinburne
Peter Geach	Dallas Willard
Norman L. Geisler	Nicholas Wolterstorff
Douglas Groothius	

Plantinga's model, a Christian's belief in God and in the great truths of the gospel are known if they are properly basic. That is, one is warranted in believing them because the beliefs have been formed by properly functioning cognitive faculties in the appropriate epistemic environment according to a design plan successfully aimed at the production of true belief. (Plantinga contrasts his view with those that hold that in order to possess knowledge, one must have good reasons to accept one's true beliefs.) A Christian's belief in the existence of God, for example, is properly basic not because it is reached by reasoned argumentation, but because it is produced by what Plantinga, following John Calvin, calls the *sensus divinitatis*: a natural readiness in humans to form theistic beliefs in response to the sort of conditions in which proper beliefs about God arise. (As examples of these conditions, Plantinga often describes human experience of natural beauty.) However, because the Fall corrupted human cognitive faculties (Genesis 3), the *sensus divinitatis* must be accompanied by the internal work of the Holy Spirit to repair those faculties.

Objection and Rebuttals to the Christian Faith

In response to critics of Christianity who claim that Christian belief is somehow irrational (what Plantinga calls a de jure objection), Plantinga argues that this claim cannot be substantiated apart from a successful argument against the truth of Christianity (a de facto objection). Someone with knowledge of such an argument would have a defeater for one's Christian belief, that is, a reason to give up one's Christian belief or, at least, to hold it less firmly. Plantinga, however, thinks that there are no good de facto objections to the truth of Christianity (thus, no good de jure objections either) and has offered rebuttals to many proposed defeaters of Christian belief. Three of his more well-known rebuttals are his free-will defense (which argues that the existence of evil is not logically incompatible with the existence of God); his evolutionary argument against naturalism (which argues that if the neo-Darwinian theory of evolution is true, then there is no good reason to think that human cognitive faculties produce true beliefs); and his account of the relation between science and religion (which holds that any conflict between science and religion is superficial and that contrary to current popular perception, there is deep concord between the two).

Plantinga's example of autonomous and integrated Christian philosophy and his wide-ranging work on the foundations of Christian belief and practice make him a significant figure in the history of philosophy and a leading academic in American evangelicalism. In fact, Plantinga received the 2017 Templeton Prize, which involves a 1.4 million dollar award, for his spiritual contribution to the task of philosophy. Past recipients have included evangelicals like Billy Graham, Charles Colson, and Bill Bright.

Gary Hartenburg

See also: Bright, William R. ("Bill"); Christian Apologetics; Colson, Charles Wendell ("Chuck"); Ethics, Evangelical Theories of; Graham, William F., Jr. ("Billy");

Philosophy, Evangelicals and; Reformed Tradition, Evangelicalism and; Schaeffer, Francis A. and Edith

Further Reading

Plantinga, Alvin. *God, Freedom, and Evil.* Grand Rapids, MI: Eerdmans, 1974.

Plantinga, Alvin. *Warrant: The Current Debate.* New York: Oxford University Press, 1993.

Plantinga, Alvin. *Warrant and Proper Function.* New York: Oxford University Press, 1993.

Plantinga, Alvin. *Warranted Christian Belief.* New York: Oxford University Press, 2000.

Plantinga, Alvin. *Where the Conflict Really Lies: Science, Religion, and Naturalism.* New York: Oxford University Press, 2011.

Sennett, James, ed. *The Analytic Theist: An Alvin Plantinga Reader.* Grand Rapids, MI: Eerdmans, 1998.

Shellnutt, Kate. "Templeton Prize Winner: Alvin Plantinga, Who Proved God's Not Dead in Academia." Christianity Today (April 25, 2017). http://www.christianitytoday.com/gleanings/2017/april/templeton-prize-alvin-plantinga-philosophy-gods-not-dead.html.

POLITICS, EVANGELICALS AND

Evangelicals have been involved in American politics since pre–Revolutionary War days. Their relationship with politicians and the government has often been an uneasy one, but evangelicals have made a lasting mark on the nation. In the process, they have adopted new, non-biblical; ideas as just, such as republican democracy, no taxation without representation, and rule by consent of the governed. They have also promoted closely held ideas that all American now accept, such as the separation of church and state, freedom of religion, and the abolition of slavery. However, because evangelicals have no centralized authority and tend to be independent in their thinking, it would be possible throughout American history to find instances when some evangelicals were in opposition to each of the ideas just mentioned. The frequent lack of an evangelical political consensus has led a handful of historians to wonder whether there is such a thing as an evangelical political position. However, there can be no doubt that evangelicals of the North and South, black and white, conservatives and progressives, Democrats and Republicans, isolationists and internationalists, and hawks and pacifists have always shared much more in common with one another through their faith than their politics have divided them. Whether their belief is justified or not, America would be a very different place without evangelical influence and participation in the civic life of the United States.

The opening of the 18th century in the American colonies was a time of spiritual malaise as many Protestant churches, particularly in "Puritan" New England had become primarily social institutions. These "halfway" churches had departed from the Reformation ecclesiology in permitting a membership that was unconverted, the very antithesis of evangelical doctrine. However, in 1725 a revival began in the Middle Colonies and spread to New England, where Jonathan Edwards (1703–1758) was the instrument of what is now called The First Great Awakening in 1734. The Awakening not only brought about the revitalization of Christianity in New England but spread throughout the colonies and across denominational lines and the borders of countries, where new believers held a high regard for the Bible and personal conversion. These revived Christians, evangelicals, prized religious liberty, which would prove to be an essential basis for a new nation.

Concerns about the potential loss of religious freedom were common throughout the colonies during the French and Indian War (1754–1763). A perceived lack of resolve on the part of England for her colonies created fear among Protestant Christians of the near threat of French Catholicism with its perceived unwavering allegiance to the Pope, considered to be the enemy of their liberty. Religious freedoms were also a concern among evangelicals when the success of the American Revolution (1775–1783) was in doubt at its inception. Many religious leaders played an indispensable part by seeking to preserve liberties through influencing public opinion for the revolution and mobilizing congregants on behalf of the war. This activism on the part of Protestant ministers, particularly New Light evangelicals, represented a collaboration between evangelicals and Real Whig republicans. It is apparent that though the Founders represented an elite group of individuals with power and influence who acted mainly from political and self-interested convictions, their plans for independence could not come to fruition without an alliance with evangelical Protestants motivated by concerns for the preservation of religious liberties. This remarkable accord brought about a successful dissolution of the colonists' political ties to Britain. Evangelicals began to embrace republican ideas that were not necessarily new, but which they were largely indifferent to previously, such as rule by consent of the governed, no taxation without representation, and the importance of citizen armies.

After the birth of the new nation and the close of the Revolution, the impact of the war and the spreading of Enlightenment ideas that influenced leadership, the churches of America went through another period of malaise. Even while churches saw membership dip to the lowest levels of church membership before or after in American history, the seeds of new revival were germinating. The Second Great Awakening, which began around 1800, ushered in a new golden age of evangelicalism that persisted until the Civil War. Although increasingly divided over issues related to slavery, the nation established an evangelical consensus that continued throughout the 19th century. During this time, evangelical Christianity with its impulse to convert the world to Christianity, and democratic idealism, with its mission to bring democracy to the world, became the chief characteristics of America and Americans. Evangelicals were in the forefront of social movements in a politically charged time in American history. Evangelicals advanced political reform, universal free public education, women's rights, temperance and the regulation of alcohol, and the abolition of slavery. Evangelical abolitionists created a new political culture when they settled Kansas to prevent the spread of slavery into that territory, but they could not prevent civil war over the South's peculiar institution.

The Civil War (1861–1865) was a blow to democratic idealism and weakened the nation's moral resolve for decades. Evangelicals once again called for political reform as multiple scandals debilitated the office of president during the administration (1869–1877) of Ulysses S. Grant. Political and business institutions were feeling the first wave of Social Darwinism with its acceptance of the survival of the fittest. Slavery had ended, but injustice and racism kept African Americans from assimilation into the mainstream of American society, while northern evangelicals pressed a Reconstruction that called for an evangelization and Christian enculturation of the defeated South and both blacks and whites. However, renewal once again flourished in a new urban revivalism that had grown out of the Prayer Revival of the late 1850s and revivals in both the Confederate and Union armies during the war. A significant byproduct of postwar Reconstruction was the releasing of African Americans to create religious institutions, which were largely evangelical. These churches became increasingly politically active and gave birth to the Civil Rights Movement in the 20th century.

The 19th century closed with a veneer of stability as the old evangelical consensus had given way to a Protestant establishment, societal leaders and culture shapers who represented a patrician class drawn from mainline churches. Underneath, American society was seething with waves of new immigrants that evangelicals could not readily assimilate and the patricians could not shape. The establishment was further weakened and transformed by the inroads of a theological liberalism spurred on by the influence of German higher criticism in universities and mainline Protestant seminaries. After World War I (1914–1918) ended, the old evangelicals left the mainline churches to the liberal "modernist" newcomers and established churches, seminaries, and mission agencies. Disillusioned and aggrieved, these theological conservatives were reluctant to take part in social action, as the substitution of social and political activism for biblical authority and evangelism had been the hallmark of the modernists. The conservatives called themselves fundamentalists because they committed themselves to the basics, or fundamentals, of the historic Christian faith. The flight of fundamentalists appeared to be a social, cultural, and political victory for the modernists, but their apparent dominance was the beginning of the end of a time when Protestants determined the shared values of the nation.

Later evangelicals, who saw the great error of effectively surrendering to the Modernists in the historic Protestant denominations, criticized the fundamentalist movement because fundamentalists were adverse to concerted political action during a time when the nation needed their involvement. Economic depression, racism, and inequality had fractured the country. Some evangelical historians have blamed this on a pervasive dispensational premillennial eschatology, which they claim made evangelicals pessimistic about earthly institutions and persistent in awaiting Christ's return. This view is untenable because many, if not most, fundamentalists were not dispensational. At the same time, premillennialism was an understandable theological reaction to the bankrupt optimistic eschatology of the old Protestant establishment, destroyed by the horrible realities of inhumanity in World War I. Whatever the cause, evangelicals were conspicuously absent in public affairs in the first decades of the 20th century. In many instances, other

Americans perceived evangelicals to be outside the mainstream of American cultural and political life for the first time, and the dominant mainline churches were not inviting evangelicals to a place at the table of cultural respectability.

World War II (1939–1945) only brought a further religious decline in America, but once again there was a stage-setting. What followed was arguably the greatest revival in American history. It began to stir in the 1940s with the establishment of the National Association of Evangelicals, the ministry of Billy Graham (1918–), and the unprecedented establishment of many missionary and parachurch ministries by American military veterans returning from the war. There was also the emergence of a new generation of African American church leaders such as Martin Luther King Jr. (1929–1968), who joined activism to Christian nonviolence and gained significant political victories. By the mid-1960s, the nation was in the midst of national doubt and rudderless uncertainty, but the Evangelical resurgence brought evangelicals and their institutions into their most influential political position since the 19th century. Evangelicals were particularly united in opposition to atheistic communism and supported the U.S. government in its foreign policy of containment during this period.

In 1947, Carl F. H. Henry (1913–2003) wrote *The Uneasy Conscience of Modern Fundamentalism*. This important book criticized the withdrawal of fundamentalists from social, cultural, and political life, and called on a renewed evangelical movement to engage culture in a meaningful way. In the 1960s, evangelicals fretted about the removal of prayer from public schools, and some advocated an amendment to the U.S. Constitution to restore it. Meanwhile, evangelical professors such as Robert Linder (1933–) and Richard Pierard (1934–) were encouraging evangelical university students to become politically active. In 1973, a small influential group of young and establishment evangelicals signed The Chicago Declaration, a call for co-religionists to be more involved in pursuing political, social, and economic justice.

Evangelicals were brought into the national limelight in 1976, when a Georgia farmer and outspoken evangelical Baptist named James Earl Carter (1924–) was elected the United States' 39th president. Ironically, four years later Carter was defeated when evangelicals overwhelming supported conservative Republican Ronald Wilson Reagan (1911–2004) for the highest office. Some historians mark the 1980s as the high-water mark of Christian political influence, mostly within the sphere of conservative politics. Although evangelicalism is largely politically conservative since the 1980s, there are a significant number of moderates and a small evangelical left-wing movement. In 1979, Virginia Baptist minister Jerry Falwell founded an organization called the Moral Majority, the most conspicuous of a vast number of fundamentalist and evangelical organizations that made up the "Christian Right," and espoused especially conservative social views on issues such as abortion, school prayer, private education, and communism. Despite the meteoric success of the Christian Right, many evangelicals are uneasy about its negative perception in the mind of the public and its tendency to be so mired in earthly concerns that its agenda distracts from the most important distinctive of evangelicalism: the preaching of the Gospel. Another assumption of the Christian Right was that America was a Christian nation, or at least founded on Christian principles, though most Christian historians dispute this. Perhaps the greater ongoing threat to evangelicals lies in the Christian's uneasy relationship to civil religion, the true national faith built on shared beliefs of Americans and designed to create maximum inclusivity for the benefit of the state. Civil religion is expressed through myths, symbols, and rituals and has as much potential for great evil as for great good. It encourages individuals to give their highest allegiance to the nation, and that has always been an intolerable demand for an evangelical.

Liam J. Atchison

See also: Israel, Evangelicals and; Moral Majority; Social Action, Evangelicals and

Further Reading

Atchison, Liam J. "The Biblical Text That Primed the Revolutionary Canon." In Liam J. Atchison, Keith Bates, and Darin D. Lenz, eds. *Civil Religion and American Christianity.* (pp. 239–274). Mountain Home, AR: BorderStone Press, 2016.

Hatch, Nathan O. *The Democratization of American Christianity.* New Haven, CT: Yale University Press, 1989.

Henry, Carl F. H. *The Uneasy Conscience of Modern Fundamentalism.* Grand Rapids, MI: Eerdmans, 1947.

Linder, Robert Dean, and Richard V. Pierard. *Twilight of the Saints: Biblical Christianity & Civil Religion in America.* Downers Grove, IL: IVP Books, 1978.

Lindsay, Michael D. *Faith in the Halls of Power: How Evangelicals Joined the American Elite.* New York: Oxford University Press, 2008.   .

Marsden, George. *The Twilight of the American Enlightenment: The 1950s and the Crisis of Liberal Belief.* New York: Basic Books, 2014.

PREMILLENNIALISM

Premillennialism has been the predominant theological view Bible prophecy and eschatology (the doctrine of future things) among American evangelicals.

Key Term in Evangelicalism: *Second Coming*

The Second Coming refers to Jesus Christ's physical return to earth following the seven-year tribulation to establish the millennial kingdom. Dispensationalists distinguish the Second Coming from the rapture of the Church, seeing both of these as contrastive events separated by seven years of tribulation. The Second Coming is not only an evangelical end-time belief but is also one that is clearly expressed in early church writings: Daniel 2:44–45, 7:9–14, 12:1–3; Zechariah 14:1–15; Matthew 13:41, 24:15–31; Mark 13:14–27, 14:62; Luke 21:25–28; Acts 1:9–11, 3:19–21; I Thessalonians 3:13; II Thessalonians 1:6–10; II Peter 3:1–14; Jude 14–15; Revelation 1:7, 19:11–20:6, 22:7,12, 20.

Overview

Premillennialism is the eschatological view that believes the future physical Second Coming of Jesus Christ to earth is the time when God will establish His physical kingdom on earth for 1,000 years. The general order of the future events are a seven-year Tribulation period (Revelation 6–18), the Second Coming of Jesus Christ (Revelation 19), the millennial Kingdom (Revelation 20), and then a new heaven and earth (Revelation 21–22). Thus, premillennialism understands that the millennial kingdom follows the Second Coming of Jesus Christ. The duration of the kingdom will be a literal 1,000 years. The location of the millennial kingdom is on earth as a theocratic rule by Jesus Christ's personal presence reigning as king. Proponents of premillennialism believe that the millennial kingdom is what is referred to in the Matthew 10:6 phrase "Thy kingdom come" (King James Version [KJV]) from the teaching and words of Jesus in "The Lord's Prayer."

Premillennialism exists with a variety of understandings concerning timing of the event known as the rapture of the church (1 Thessalonians 4:13–18). The different understandings include pretribulationalism, midtribulationalism, posttribulationalism, prewrath, and partial rapture. The most common perspective within premillennialism is pretribulationism.

History

Ancient premillennialism was embraced by many of the early church fathers through most of the third century. Such church fathers as Ignatius (ca. 35–107), Justin Martyr (ca. 100–165), Irenaeus (ca. 130–200), and Tertullian (ca. 160–225) held to a premillennial position. The concept that Israel's promises in the Old Testament (e.g., a future kingdom) are applied to the church as the new or true Israel and not to the nation of Israel is called replacement theology or supersessionism. The source of this belief appears to surface after the Bar Kokhba revolt by the Jews against the Romans (132–135). This theological concept is expressed by Justin Martyr (ca. 160), and solidified in the church by the political-ecclesiastical alliance of Eusebius and Constantine in the early part of the fourth century.

Irenaeus claimed that he derived his view of future things from Papias's writings (ca. 60–130). The view of Irenaeus is representative of ancient premillennialism. He divided history into seven eras of 1000-year increments, where the seventh era would be the reign of Christ in peace. By the end of the third century, premillennialism had declined, and in the fourth century it was no longer the prominent position. The rise of Augustine (354–430) and his view of amillennialism prevailed for many centuries. Amillennialism does not believe in a literal 1000-year kingdom at Christ's Second Coming. Amillennialists usually believe that the kingdom is now present in the Church Age through God's Word, His Spirit, and His church. The view of postmillennialism did not arise until the 17th century. This view also does not believe in a literal 1,000-year kingdom. but holds that the reign of Christ spiritually increases by the triumph of the church and the gospel until the world is Christianized. At the end of this long period of peace and prosperity, Christ will return. Also, in the 17th century, ancient premillennialism rises to prominence, and in the centuries that follow, modern premillennialism is developed.

Modern Premillennialism

The two basic views of premillennialism today are historic (or covenant) premillennialism and dispensational premillennialism. Historic premillennialism does not make a clear distinction between Israel and the church, and thus, it considers the church as spiritual Israel. This view does not demand a consistent literal interpretative method. However, they distinguish themselves from amillennialism by recognizing a literal future for national Israel, which involves Israel's salvation. The future details of national Israel have a variety of views.

Most historic premillennialists are posttribulational; thus, they believe the church will go through the judgment of the tribulation that precedes the Second Coming of Jesus Christ. At the Second Coming of Christ, the believers of all ages will be bodily resurrected to enter the millennial kingdom. At the end of the millennial kingdom, all the unbelieving will be bodily resurrected, judged, and punished eternally in the lake of fire. At Christ's Second Coming, and before the millennial kingdom starts, Satan will be bound and cast into the bottomless pit (the abyss) for the duration of the millennial kingdom. Christ's physical reign in the kingdom on earth will be in perfect peace and righteousness. However, not all historic premillennialists understand the 1000-year kingdom as a literal 1000 years, but some understand it as a symbolic expression for a long period of time. At the end of the millennial kingdom, Satan will be loosed and will gather the unbelievers who have outwardly conformed to Christ's reign but inwardly rebelled against Him. However, the satanic rebellion will be defeated by God. After the resurrection and eternal judgment of all unbelievers at the end of the kingdom, all believers will enter the eternal state.

Key Term in Evangelicalism: *Judgment seat of Christ*

This term used by evangelicals like dispensationalists refers to the future occasion whereby every Christian will stand before Jesus Christ and be evaluated for their faithfulness. Where faithfulness occurred, there will be rewards. Where there was a lack of faithfulness, rewards will be withheld (Romans 14:10–12; 1 Corinthians 3:10–15; 2 John 8; Revelation 22:12). Although evangelicals disagree on the exact nature of and timing of the rewards, they do believe that this judgment is not a loss of salvation, but an experience of rewards. Thus, the need to be faithful in every detail with this anticipation of rewards is to undergird their daily living.

Dispensational premillennialism characterizes their position with two main distinctive features: (1) a clear distinction between Israel and the Church (the Church is not spiritual Israel); and (2) a consistently literal interpretation of Scripture (this view recognizes figurative language, but if the plain sense makes sense, seek no other sense unless contextual evidence leads otherwise). For example, the first coming of Jesus Christ was fulfilled literally, thus the prophecy of the Second Coming of Jesus Christ is expected to be fulfilled literally. Most dispensational premillennialists understand the rapture of the Church to be pretribulational. The rapture of the Church is considered to be an imminent event (it could happen at any time) in the New Testament Church Age. At the moment of the rapture, believers who have died in the New Testament Church Age will be resurrected, and alive Church believers will be changed into their resurrected bodies. Thus, at the rapture, all Church believers (dead and alive) will be caught up to Christ who appears in the sky and will be taken back to heaven with Him (1 Thessalonians 4:13–18). The future seven-year tribulation period (Revelation 6–18) will begin after the rapture. At the end of the seven-year tribulation period, the resurrected Church believers will return to the earth with Jesus Christ at His Second Coming. Christ will literally and bodily return and reign in peace and righteousness on the earth.

After Christ's Second Coming but before the millennial kingdom begins, the Old Testament believers and the tribulation believers will be resurrected and will join the living believers who survived the tribulation (this group will populate the millennium) to enter into the millennial kingdom with Christ. Furthermore, Satan will be bound and cast into the bottomless pit for the duration of the millennial kingdom. The millennial kingdom is taken to be a literal 1,000 years. At the end of the millennial kingdom, Satan will be loosed, and he will gather the unbelievers in the kingdom who have outwardly conformed to Christ's reign but inwardly rebelled against Him. However, this satanic rebellion will be defeated by God, and Satan will be condemned forever in the judgment of the lake of fire. After the millennial kingdom, all unbelievers of all the ages will be resurrected for the final judgment and eternal punishment. All the believers of all the ages will enter the eternal state of the new heaven and earth, where sin and its effect will be eliminated (Revelation 20–22).

In American evangelical history and culture, premillennialism has been the prevailing view and has been widely disseminated through *The Scofield Reference Bible, The New Scofield Reference Bible; The Ryrie Study Bible, The Late Great Planet Earth* (Hal Lindsey), and the *Left Behind* series of novels (Tim LaHaye and Jerry Jenkins), to name a few. The theological writings of authors such as Lewis Sperry Chafer, John MacArthur, J. Dwight Pentecost, Charles C. Ryrie, John F. Walvoord and many others have provided a large collection material. Premillennialism has been a central teaching in many evangelical colleges, Bible colleges, and Bible institutes such as Moody Bible Institute.

Seminaries with a strong history of premillennialism in their doctrinal statements and the teaching of it include Dallas Theological Seminary, Denver Seminary, Grace

Theological Seminary, Talbot School of Theology, The Master's Seminary, and Western Seminary. Prominent pastors, Bible teachers, and evangelists espousing premillennialism include James M. Boice, William R. ("Bill") Bright, Jerry Falwell, Billy Graham, Thomas Ice, Tim LaHaye, J. Vernon McGee, Charles W. ("Chuck") Smith, and Charles R. ("Chuck") Swindoll. Many parachurch ministries, evangelical mass media programs, and mission organizations have also formally or informally been associated with premillennialism. Premillennialism permeated American evangelicalism in the 20th century. Though not as strong as it was earlier, premillennialism remains a major perspective and influence in contemporary American evangelicalism.

Steve P. Sullivan

See also: Dispensationalism; Eschatology; *The Late Great Planet Earth*; Rapture; Ryrie, Charles Caldwell; *Scofield Reference Bible;* Walvoord, John F.

Further Reading

Bock, Darrell L., ed. *Three Views on the Millennium and Beyond.* Grand Rapids, MI: Zondervan, 1999.

Clouse, Robert G., ed. *The Meaning of the Millennium: Four Views.* Downers Grove, IL: IVP, 1977.

Couch, Mal, ed. *Dictionary of Premillennial Theology.* Grand Rapids, MI: Kregel, 1996.

Enns, Paul. *The Moody Handbook of Theology*, rev and expanded ed. Chicago: Moody Press, 2008.

Ryrie, Charles C. *The Basis of the Premillennial Faith.* Neptune, NJ: Loizeaux Brothers, 1953.

Sutton, Matthew Avery. *American Apocalypse: A History of Modern Evangelicalism.* Cambridge, MA: Belknap Press, 2014.

Walvoord, John F. *The Millennial Kingdom: A Basic Text in Premillennial Theology.* Grand Rapids, MI: Dunham, 1959.

PRINCETON EVANGELICAL FELLOWSHIP

Founded in 1931 by Princeton University alumnus Donald B. Fullerton, Princeton Evangelical Fellowship (PEF) remains the oldest evangelical Christian group at the university. The fellowship initially met with five students, and by 1937, the group formally organized, with undergraduate A. G. Fletcher Jr. serving as the first president.

In an open letter to *The Daily Princetonian* editor, Fletcher wrote that there were undergraduates who remained "optimistic enough to feel that the fine tradition on which Princeton was founded is not entirely dead." According to Fletcher, Princeton men formed the group "to enjoy fellowship with one another, to affirm the Bible as the inspired Word of God, and to encourage other students to take a stand for Jesus Christ on campus." Fullerton, a World War I veteran and former missionary to India, remained unwavering in his stance that the Bible served as the "whole foundation" of the fellowship. He led weekly PEF meetings in Murray-Dodge Hall and remained affiliated with the group until his retirement in 1980. Despite the Presbyterian roots of the University, PEF has remained nondenominational since its inception.

Under the leadership of current director and Princeton alumnus Dr. William Boyce, PEF endures as a coed campus ministry that serves both undergraduate and graduate students. The organization exists "to promote among its members a deepening knowledge of Jesus Christ as Lord and Savior and to enable them through yielded lives to make him known on the University campus and around the world." The fellowship not only maintains its tradition of holding weekly group meetings, but it also conducts small group Bible studies and personal mentoring sessions. The organization places members on a four-year biblical and theological study plan for personal growth, and approximately 1,000 PEF alumni serve in various occupations and ministries across the country and the world.

Brittany Burnette

See also: Evangelism; Parachurch Ministries

Further Reading

Fletcher, A. G., Jr. Letter to the Editor "Announces Evangelical Fellowship." *The Daily Princetonian* 62, no. 104 (1937): 2.

Just, Richard. "Evangelical Organizations Strive to Increase Campus Membership." *The Daily Princetonian* 122, no. 54 (1998): 1.

Lindsay, Holland. "Religious Group Opposes Liberalism." *The Daily Princetonian* 90, no. 13 (1966): 1.

"Obituary for Donald Fullerton." *Town Topics*, April 17, 1985, p. 29.

Princeton Evangelical Fellowship. "Purpose of PEF." Accessed May 19, 2017. http://pef.mycpanel.princeton.edu/.

Rusten, Sharon, and E. Michael Ruston. *The Complete Book of When & Where in the Bible and throughout History.* Wheaton, IL: Tyndale House, 2005, 427.

PRISON FELLOWSHIP

Prison Fellowship is a Christian prison ministry and criminal justice reform organization with programs that serve prisoners, former prisoners, and families and friends of prisoners. Its ministry is active throughout the United States and, through Prison Fellowship International, in 112 countries.

Prison Fellowship's mission, posted on its Web site, is that "no life is beyond the reach of God's power, and we envision a future in which countless prisoners, ex-prisoners, and their families, are redeemed, restored, and reconciled through the love and truth of Jesus Christ. We equip local churches and thousands of trained volunteers to spread the Gospel and nurture disciples behind prison walls, so that men and women become new creations in Christ—not repeat offenders. We prepare

Christian inmates to become leaders of their families, communities, and churches once they are released back into the community. We support inmates' families, helping them become reconciled to God and one another through transformative relationships with local churches."

Prison Fellowship was founded in 1976 by Charles "Chuck" Colson. Once known as President Richard Nixon's "hatchet man" and describing himself as "incapable of humanitarian thoughts," Colson gained notoriety at the height of the Watergate scandal, for his involvement with the infamous "Watergate Seven."

Just prior to his arrest, a close friend of Colson's, Raytheon Company Chairman of the Board Thomas L. Phillips, gave him a copy of *Mere Christianity* by C. S. Lewis, and Colson came to faith in Christ. He then joined a prayer group led by Douglas Coe and including Democratic Senator Harold Hughes and Republican congressman Al Quie. Following his release, he founded Prison Fellowship Ministries (1976), fulfilling a promise made to inmates that he would "never forget those behind bars."

Prison Fellowship has a number of ministries under its auspices, including Project Angel Tree, Operation Starting Line, the InnerChange Freedom Initiative, Justice Fellowship, BreakPoint, and the Colson Center. Project Angel Tree ministers to children of inmates and provides opportunities for them to participate in mentoring and summer camps. Project Angel Tree's most popular ministry is Christmas gift-giving projects held in local churches.

Operation Starting Line was started in 2001 as a network of ministries to evangelize and disciple prisoners and their families. Its Web site states, "OSL brings together dozens of Christian organizations to prisons across the country with a simple, life-changing message: that Jesus came to seek and save the lost." PF reports that more than 700,000 prisoners have been reached through OSL.

The InnerChange Freedom Initiative started in 1997 as a voluntary values-based Reentry Program. PF's Web site describes the program as "a reentry program for prisoners based on the life and teachings of Jesus Christ. Inmates begin the program 18 to 24 months before their release date and continue for an additional 12 months once they have returned to the community."

Justice Fellowship was founded by Colson in 1983 and serves as the criminal justice reform arm of Prison Fellowship. JF mobilizes people and state and federal policymakers to reform the criminal justice system. Colson and JF were at the forefront of supporting the Religious Freedom Restoration Act, the Religious Liberty Protection Act, and the Prison Rape Elimination Act.

BreakPoint is a daily 4-minute commentary program providing a Christian perspective on the news via radio, interactive media, and print. BreakPoint airs each weekday on more than 1,200 outlets with an estimated weekly audience of 8 million. The Chuck Colson Center for Christian Worldview Web site states that it "seeks to build and resource a movement of Christians committed to living and defending the Christian worldview."

The Centurions Program was founded by Colson in 2004 as an intensive biblical studies program that equips Christians to engage community and culture with biblical truth. It's Web site states, "The Centurions Program educates people of strong faith with relevant skills, biblical knowledge, and a solid Christian worldview, so you can not only navigate culture, but re-shape it in a way that is pleasing to God." As of 2011, more than 700 individuals have gone through the one-year program. Studies such as *The Faith, ReWired, Wide Angle*, and *Doing the Right Thing* assist believers to understand and apply Scripture to everyday life.

Prison Fellowship is one of the most prominent American evangelical parachurch ministries working in the realms of social action and justice. It continues the long history of social engagement dating back to the 1800s.

James Menzies

See also: Colson, Charles Wendell ("Chuck"); Parachurch Ministries; Social Action, Evangelicals and

Further Reading

Aitken, Jonathan. *Charles W. Colson: A Life Redeemed.* Colorado Springs, CO: WaterBrook Press, 2010.

The Chuck Colson Center for Christian Worldview. (n.d.). Accessed April 30, 2017. http://www.colsoncenter.org.

Colson, Chuck, and Nancy Pearcey. *How Now Shall We Live?* Carol Stream, IL: Tyndale House, 2004.

Perry, John. *God Behind Bars: The Amazing Story of Prison Fellowship.* Nashville, TN: Thomas Nelson, 2006.

Prison Fellowship. (n.d.). Accessed April 30, 2017. https://www.prisonfellowship.org/about/.

PROMISE KEEPERS

Promise Keepers is a nondenominational parachurch ministry founded in 1990 that focuses on building the character of men from what the organization understands to be a biblical perspective. Promise Keepers attempts to challenge, exhort, and inspire men to embrace their biblical masculinity and be wise stewards, servant-leaders, and Christlike empowered disciples in their homes, churches, and communities.

In March 1990, Bill McCartney, then football coach for the University of Colorado, and Dave Wardell traveled to a Fellowship of Christian Athletes banquet in Pueblo, Colorado. They discovered that the key for spiritual maturity is discipleship. Dave and Bill began to meet weekly to seek God's direction concerning large gatherings of men. Chuck Lane, working with Campus Crusade, and Dan Schaffer, who was experienced in men's discipleship, later joined these prayer-planning meetings.

In July 1990, 72 friends and associates of the group gathered at Boulder Valley Christian Church to discuss a conference for the men of Colorado. The name Promise Keepers evolved out of McCartney's messages on personal integrity to a number of Colorado churches. The men also committed to pray and fast on Wednesdays for a men's conference to be held in July 1991. A board of directors was developed, and Promise Keepers was incorporated in the state of Colorado in December 1990.

The first arena conference in 1991 drew 4,200 men to the University of Colorado Events Center. Men who attended were challenged to bring 12 others to the next year's conference. Following this conference, a Field Ministry team was developed to reach out to churches throughout Colorado. Two further ministries were developed: the Point Man (later changed to Key Man) and Ambassador. The Point Man serves his local pastor as the main organizer while the Ambassador volunteers present the concept of Promise Keepers to churches in a particular geographic or cultural area.

In July 1992, Promise Keepers' held a two-day men's conference and a three-day leadership conference. Dr. James Dobson's Focus on the Family aired a radio program on the ministry, resulting in extraordinary growth. That same year 1,500 pastors and lay leaders gathered for the first National Leadership Conference, and 22,000 men from throughout the United States convened at Folsom Field at the University of Colorado for the first National Men's Conference. During this conference, a mandate was issued for men to pursue reconciliation across racial and denominational lines.

In September 2008, Promise Keepers founder Coach Bill McCartney was elected chairman of the board and Rev. Raleigh Washington, DD, was named president/CEO. During the year 2015, events are planned for Phoenix, Arizona; Stockton, California; Baton Rouge, Louisiana; Pittsburgh, Philadelphia; Dallas, Texas; Rochester, Minnesota; and Redmond, Washington.

In essence, Promise Keepers realized that when a husband or father attends church, the rest of the family is likely to follow.

James Menzies

See also: Evangelism; Parachurch Ministries

Further Reading

Abraham, Ken. *Who Are the Promise Keepers?* New York: Doubleday, 1997.

Bright, Bill. *Seven Promises of a Promise Keeper.* Nashville, TN: Thomas Nelson, 1999.

Claussen, Dane. *Standing on the Promises: The Promise Keepers and the Revival of Manhood.* Cleveland, OH: Pilgrim Press, 2000. https://promisekeepers.org/.

McCartney, Bill, T. John Trent, and Gary Smalley. *What Makes a Man? Twelve Promises That Will Change Your Life!* Carol Stream, IL: Navpress, 1992.

RAPTURE

The rapture is what many evangelicals believe to be a yet-future event taught in the Bible and part of Bible prophecy. It is the teaching that Jesus Christ will return to call up into heaven Christians before His Second Coming to earth. Within evangelicalism in the last part of the 20th century, the doctrine was popularized by Hal

The Left Behind Series

The Left Behind series, coauthored by Jerry B. Jenkins (1949–) and Tim LaHaye (1926–2016), founder of the Pre-Trib Research Center and author of more than 60 nonfiction books, sold 62 million copies within 300 weeks on the *New York Times'* bestseller list. LaHaye's decision to create an apocalyptic fictional series, drawing from the events associated with dispensational premillennial eschatology, not only impacted the novel and marketing industry by rethinking the possibilities though Christian novels, but also influenced Christian fiction. What prompted LaHaye's idea to use dispensational doctrines such as the rapture, the Tribulation, and the Second Coming to write this fictional series was sitting on airplanes watching pilots. He asked himself, "What if the rapture occurred on an airplane?" Several years later, LaHaye was introduced to Jenkins, a writer, editor, and publisher. Jenkins has published more than 186 books.

The story-line chronological order of the books is as follows:

The Rising: Antichrist is Born: Before They Were Left Behind (2005)
The Regime: Evil Advances: Before They Were Left Behind (2005)
The Rapture: In the Twinkling of an Eye: Countdown to Earth's Last Days (2006)
Left Behind: A Novel of the Earth's Last Days (1995)
Tribulation Force: The Continuing Drama of Those Left Behind (1996)
Nicolae: The Rise of Antichrist (1997)
Soul Harvest: The World Takes Sides (1999)
Apollyon: The Destroyer Is Unleashed (1999)
Assassins: Assignment: Jerusalem, Target: Antichrist (1999)
The Indwelling: The Beast Takes Possession (2000)
The Mark: The Beast Rules the World (2000)
Desecration: Antichrist Takes the Throne (2001)
The Remnant: On the Brink of Armageddon (2002)
Armageddon: The Cosmic Battle of the Ages (2003)
Glorious Appearing: The End of Days (2004)
Kingdom Come: The Final Victory (2007)

Lindsey's *The Late Great Planet Earth* (1970) and the 1990s Left Behind series of novels by Tim LaHaye and Jerry Jenkins.

Proponents of the doctrine argue that the clearest New Testament passage on the rapture is found in I Thessalonians 4:13–18. Proponents believe that in these verses are found several truths about the rapture. First, because the rapture of the Church is described differently from other passages depicting Christ's Second Advent, it is an event that is distinct from the Second Advent. For example, at the rapture Christ will come in the air (1 Thessalonians 4:16–17), whereas at the Second Advent Jesus Christ will come back to the earth (Zechariah 14:4). Second, the rapture will involve the catching up of every believer to meet the Lord in the air (1 Thessalonians 4:17). "Caught up" is the Greek translation from the verb *harpazō*, which means "to be seized" or "caught up by force." When *harpazō* was translated into Latin in Jerome's Latin Vulgate, the word *repere* was used. When *repere* was then translated into English, the word *rapture* was employed. Third, the rapture will be a reunion. At the point of the rapture, deceased of this age (the Church Age) whose souls are currently in the presence of the Lord (2 Corinthians 5:8) will descend from heaven with the Lord. Then those believers who are living on the earth at the time will be caught up to meet the Lord and these descending saints. The two groups will be reunited together in the clouds to be forever with the Lord (1 Thessalonians 4:15–17).

Proponents also believe several more truths about the rapture can be discerned from 1 Corinthians 15:50–58, which is considered another important New Testament rapture text. First, the rapture represents the time in history when all Church Age believers, both living and deceased (1 Corinthians 15:51–52), will receive their resurrected bodies. Second, the rapture will exempt an entire generation of Christians from death. First Corinthians 15:51 reads, "Behold, I tell you a mystery; we will not all sleep, but we will all be changed." Third, the rapture will take place instantaneously. In 1 Corinthians 15:52, Paul analogizes the speed of the rapture to "the twinkling of an eye." Fourth, the rapture is a mystery (1 Corinthians 15:51). In Greek, "*mystery*" means "a previously unknown truth now disclosed" (Romans 16:25–26; Colossians 1:26). Thus, the rapture is a theological concept unknown in the Old Testament and is barely even hinted at in the Gospels. In fact, it is not just the rapture that is a mystery, but so is the entire Church Age (Ephesians 3:3–6). Paul's special calling was to unfold this unique period of time. Part of this mystery realm doctrine pertains to how the Church Age will end. Thus, God revealed to Paul the termination of the Church's earthly mission through the rapture as part of this new mystery-realm Church Age doctrine. Fifth, the rapture is imminent. When describing the rapture, note Paul's use of the pronoun "*we*" (1 Corinthians 15:51). Thus, as Paul unfolded the concept of the rapture, he anticipated that this event could have taken place in his own lifetime. In other words, Paul maintained that the rapture could happen at any moment. No prophetic sign must first transpire before the rapture can occur.

Finally, the rapture is a traditional doctrine now being recovered. The prevalence of nonliteral methods of interpreting Bible prophecy began to dominate the Church during and following the time of Augustine in the fourth century, thereby causing the rapture doctrine to wane in influence. However, we now have the writings of some who still approached prophecy literally during this era and consequently maintained their steadfast belief in the rapture. One such individual was Pseudo-Ephraem the Syrian (4th–6th centuries CE). It is likely that similar rapture statements will continue to be discovered as scholars diligently explore this area of Christian history.

Among premillennialists (those who believe in a future tribulation period that will be followed by Christ's earthly reign), debate persists concerning the timing of the rapture. Pretribulationalists believe that the rapture will occur before the tribulation begins. Midtribulationalists assert that the rapture will take place in the middle of the tribulation. Posttribulationalism contends that the rapture will take place at the end of the tribulation. Prewrath rapturism maintains that Christians will be present for the three quarters of the tribulation. Partial rapturism contends that only those believers that are earnestly looking for the Lord will be raptured.

However, proponents argue that there are seven reasons that make the pretribulational position the most plausible view. First, the tribulation's ultimate purpose concerns Israel rather than the Church (Jeremiah 30:7). Second, the word "church" is missing not only from Revelation 4–22 but also from all tribulation passages. Third, the Church has been promised an exemption from divine wrath (1 Thessalonians 1:10; 5:9), whereas the tribulation represents an expression of divine wrath (Revelation 6:16–17). Fourth, the rapture is an imminent event, and only the pretribulation view harmonizes with imminency by teaching that the rapture is the very next event on the prophetic horizon. Fifth, only avoidance of the tribulation period in its entirety, as taught by pretribulationalism, is in harmony with the New Testament's presentation of the rapture as a comfort (1 Thessalonians 4:18). Sixth, the rapture must take place before the seven-year tribulation period begins because the Antichrist, who inaugurates the tribulation period (Daniel 9:27a), cannot even come on the world scene until the Holy Spirit's restraining ministry through the Church is first removed (2 Thessalonians 2:6–7). Seventh, the symbolic parallels of the days of Noah and Lot (Luke 17:26–30) mandate that God's people must first be taken out of harm's way before the pouring out of divine judgment (Genesis 7:1, 16–17; 19:22).

The idea of the rapture is prominent throughout American evangelicalism, but it is not the only view held. However, it has strong roots in many evangelical seminaries, churches, and parachurch ministries.

Andrew M. Woods

See also: Eschatology; Premillennialism; Theological Controversies within Evangelicalism; Walvoord, John F.

Further Reading

Boyer, Paul. *When Time Shall Be No More: Prophecy Belief in Modern American Culture.* Cambridge, MA: Harvard University Press, 1992.

Carpenter, Joel A. *Revive Us Again: The Reawakening of American Fundamentalism.* New York: Oxford University Press, 1989.

Demy, Timothy J., and Thomas D. Ice. "The Rapture and an Early Medieval Citation." *Bibliotheca Sacra* 152, no. 607 (July–September 1995): 305–316.

English, E. Schuyler. *Re-Thinking the Rapture: An Examination of What the Scriptures Teach as to the Time of the Translation of the Church in Relation to the Tribulation.* Neptune, NJ: Loizeaux Brothers, 1954.

Showers, Renald. *Maranatha Our Lord, Come!: A Definitive Study of the Rapture of the Church.* Bellmawr, NJ: Friends of Israel, 1995.

Stanton, Gerald. *Kept From the Hour: Biblical Evidence for the Pretribulational Return of Christ.* Grand Rapids, MI: Zondervan, 1956. Reprint, Miami Springs, FL: Schoettle, 1991.

Sutton, Matthew Avery. *American Apocalypse: A History of Modern Evangelicalism.* Cambridge, MA: Belknap Press, 2014.

Walvoord, John F. *The Rapture Question*, rev. ed. Grand Rapids, MI: Zondervan, 1979.

REFORMED TRADITION, EVANGELICALISM AND

The Reformed Tradition within the context of American evangelicalism, also known as Confessional Evangelicalism, is a story of both solidarity with evangelicalism at times and resistance against it. The Reformed Tradition dates back to the very origins of American Evangelicalism, as Puritan separatists migrated to the American Colonies in the 17th century. The general disposition of dissent in the Reformed Church is one thing that makes it a part of American evangelicalism, but it is also what makes the Reformed Church resistant toward what some dissenters reject as a "popular" or noncritical religious movement in the United States. Whereas revivalist evangelicals and Pietists tend to emphasize religious experience, confessional evangelicals prioritize religious orthodoxy.

In his work, *Evangelicalism in Modern Britain* (2003), historian of evangelicalism David W. Bebbington (1949–) identifies four key distinctives of evangelicalism: crucicentrism, conversionism (being "born again"), biblicism, and activism. These four defining characteristics form an organizational matrix under which the Reformed Tradition relates with the development of evangelicalism in the United States, firstly in historical development and secondly in theological alignment.

The historical development of the Reformed Tradition, like many aspects of American history, is eclectic, bringing together many different types of European traditions. Puritans crossed the Atlantic to flee persecution from religious authorities in Europe. Although never formally recognized as an established Christian denomination, Puritans affirmed a Reformed theology and Presbyterian polity and developed what many believe to be the backbone of Congregationalism in America. One line of evangelicalism in the United States is Calvinist Protestantism, which is marked by freedom of religion, freedom of thought, and social action. Another important aspect of the early Reformed Tradition is the Dutch Reformed Church established by Jonas Michaëlius (1577–1638) in New Amsterdam (New York City) in 1628.

However, in the mid-18th century, the Reformed Tradition generally aligned with one of two attitudes toward the First Great Awakening (ca. 1730–1755). One of the most prominent figures during The First Great Awakening was Jonathan Edwards (1703–1758), a Congregationalist Protestant minister. George Whitefield (1714–1770) recruited Edwards to preach to a particularly recalcitrant congregation in Enfield, Connecticut, in 1741, where Edwards preached "Sinners in the Hands of an Angry God," a hell-fire and brimstone sermon that is typical of the Great Awakening–style preaching. "Old Lights," or Congregationalist ministers who were resistant toward colonial revivalism, criticized Edwards and the "Enthusiasm" associated with The Great Awakening (e.g., outcries, swoonings, and convulsions). "New Lights" such as Edwards recognized the benefits of revivalism for the church and partnered with non-Reformed churches in an effort to grow the influence of the church overall. Edwards frequently wrote in defense of revivalism, insisting that charismatic manifestations were not distinguishing marks of the Holy Spirit.

The 19th century saw several developments within the Reformed Tradition that were significant to its evangelical identity. Calvin College and Calvin Theological Seminary were founded by Reformed theologian Egbert Boer in 1876, and the 19th century enjoyed a great deal of intellectual and social growth. Additionally, Princeton Theological Seminary (and its "Princeton Theologians") was strongly aligned with the Reformed Tradition during this period. The Christian Reformed Church in North America, an evangelical split from the Dutch Reformed Church rooted in the Classis Holland, was solidified in 1905. The intellectualism of Reformed Evangelicals prospered during the 19th century, but this became problematic in the face of the modernist problem and rising biblical critical approaches that had begun infiltrating the American Academy.

The 20th century for the Reformed Tradition was marred with division and doctrinal conflict. After the end of the World Wars, at one of the more critical junctures in American evangelicalism, The Reformed Church in America (RCA) aligned itself with the more liberal National Council of Churches and World Council of Church, whereas the Synod of Mid-America was part of the neo-evangelical National Association of Evangelicals. Thus, the Reformed Tradition in the United States has become more fractured along evangelical lines, especially regarding the authority of Scripture as applied in feminist exegesis. One such instance is with the Presbyterian Church (USA)'s "Confession of 1967," which affirms that parts of the Bible that are not "witnesses to Christ" may not be true. Due to the freedom of conscience embraced by the Reformed Tradition, these interpretive differences have been encountered with a degree of tolerance under the Reformed banner, but as culture wars continued to be waged in the United States, these battles have grown more embittered over time.

As a confessional tradition, most Reformed congregations subscribe to ecumenical creeds such as the Apostles' Creed, the Athanasian Creed, and the Nicene Creed; but most also adopt Reformed confessions such as the Heidelberg Catechism, the

Belgic Confession, and the Canons of the Synod of Dordt (including the latter adoption "Our World Belongs to God" [1986]).

Consistent with the Reformed Tradition's emphasis on intellectual freedom, the late 20th century and the early part of the 20th century has seen a great deal of diversity emerge in the United States outside of the tradition's general creeds. Using the Bebbington Quadrilateral as a reference point for Evangelicalism, the Reformed Tradition affirms Christ's redemptive work in terms of three offices—prophet, priest, and king—although they have been reinterpreted from a critical perspective by theologians such as Karl Barth (1886–1968). Reformed evangelicals affirm conversionism but in more extreme instances may affirm Monergism (as opposed to Synergism), a doctrine of irresistible grace that is associated with Calvinism. The Bible has always served as a cornerstone of confessional evangelicalism, but modern Reformed theologians, such as Dawn Devries and Karl Barth, have begun shifting the tradition away from biblical inerrancy. Finally, the Reformed Tradition has a long history of activism, especially in the United States. The Reformed Tradition has fingerprints on a majority of the early settlements in the British Colonies, from the Massachusetts Bay Colony (1628) to the Plymouth Colony (1620). The Reformed Tradition's ideas of freedom of religion have played a prominent role in American politics.

New Calvinism is a recent movement in the evangelical Reformed Tradition that aims to realign the tradition with more of the fundamental Reformed doctrines out of which the tradition began. Figures such as Timothy J. Keller (1950–), Charles Joseph ("C. J.") Mahaney (1953–), John Piper (1946–), Mark Driscoll (1970–), Mark Dever (1960–), and Albert Mohler (1959–), representing a myriad of denominational affiliations, have begun to challenge broader theology within Reformed denominations.

Bryce Hantla

See also: Baptists and Evangelicalism; Calvinism; Carnell, Edward John; Christian Apologetics; Dispensationalism; Emerging and Emergent Churches; Evangelism; Fundamentalism; Graham, William F., Jr. ("Billy"); Henry, Carl F. H.; Inerrancy; Israel, Evangelicals and; Ligonier Ministries; Master's Seminary; Neo-Evangelicalism; Ockenga, Harold John; Premillennialism; Rapture; Theological Controversies within Evangelicalism

Further Reading

Marsden, George. *Understanding Fundamentalism and Evangelicalism.* Grand Rapids, MI: Eerdmans, 1991.

Mohler, R. Albert, Jr., Kevin T. Bauder, John G. Stackhouse Jr., and Roger E. Olson. "Confessional Evangelicalism." In *Four Views on the Spectrum of Evangelicalism*, edited by Stanley N. Gundry, Andrew D. Naselli, and Collin Hansen. (68–96). Grand Rapids, MI: Zondervan, 2011.

Smidt, Corwin. *American Evangelicals Today.* Lanham, MD: Rowman & Littlefield, 2013.

Smith, Christian, Michael Emerson, Sally Gallagher, Paul Kennedy, and David Sikkink. *American Evangelicalism: Embattled and Thriving.* Chicago, IL: University of Chicago Press, 1998.

REGENT UNIVERSITY

Regent University is a private evangelical college founded in 1977 as CBN University (referring to the Christian Broadcasting Network) by Pat Robertson (1930–). It was the third of three prominent new Christian schools in the late 20th century based on a founder's media ministry; the other two are Liberty University (1971—Jerry Falwell) and Oral Roberts University (1965—Oral Roberts).

CBN University initially offered only graduate programs, beginning with the School of Communication and the Arts. Ten years later, there were schools of business and Leadership, Divinity, Education, Government, and Law; followed by the school of Psychology and Counseling. An undergraduate College of Arts and Sciences was added in the 2000s, completing the range of degree programs from BA to PhD.

The name change to Regent came in 1990, explained thusly: "A 'regent' is defined as one who represents a king in his absence. For Regent University, a regent is one who represents Christ, our Sovereign, in whatever sphere of life he or she may be called to serve Him" (http://www.regent.edu).

Robertson, a JD graduate of Yale Law School, strongly emphasizes quality in operations, rigorous academic standards, and esthetic excellence. Regent consistently seeks and acquires the highest possible standards of accreditation and academic practice. Its campus is a showplace of neo-Georgian architecture, displaying consistency of design and beauty of presentation rare in universities. This design, impeccably executed with historicist materials and interior trim, intentionally bespeaks the University's commitment to the core principles of the 18th-century American founding.

Regent indeed seeks a conservative renewal, even revolution, in a nation and world that care little for such principles. Its various schools seek strategic placement of well-trained, effective practitioners of their disciplines who will change the terms of societal thought and life. Regent hosts various alternative institutions and conferences, the American Center for Law and Justice (ACLJ) being the most prominent. Its synergy with CBN includes a worldwide media reach of news, inspiration, and equipping, as well as connection with top-drawer humanitarian services and disaster relief operations that have won over even the most severe critics.

Befitting its founder's media savvy and success, Regent is a pioneer and foremost practitioner of Web-based education that is recognized as among the best such programs in the nation. These programs are constantly revised and updated to maintain currency of technology and quality.

The outreach of CBN and Regent has long featured a highly diverse appeal based on the century-old Holy Spirit renewal movement that is still growing dynamically around the world. Regent's student body, numbering 9,000 in 2015, with plans for great growth, typically consists of about 25% African Americans, Caucasians in the low 50%+ range, and the remainder of other backgrounds. These numbers are the uncommon envy of many universities seeking—unsuccessfully—to express the racial diversity that they proclaim.

Located near the world's largest naval base, Regent has painstakingly built many military-friendly features to make it a leading choice for students of military background, who form about one-quarter of the student body. Regent's forthrightly patriotic bent is an important feature of this partnership.

Regent's strategic mission of "Christian Leadership to Change the World" has seen great cumulative success in terms of its 20,000 graduates (2015) so far sent forth. This University, secure in its explicitly Christian grounding and purpose, seeks to see those graduates leverage their education into genuinely world-changing deeds. Regent University illustrates the broad reach of evangelicalism across America as well as its denominational and theological breadth and its affinity for higher education and mass media in the 21st century.

Mark A. Jumper

See also: Higher Education, Evangelicals and; Mass Media, Evangelicals and; Pentecostalism (and Charismatic Movement), Evangelicals and

Further Reading

Harrell, David Edwin, Jr. *Pat Robertson: A Life and Legacy.* Grand Rapids, MI: Eerdmans, 2005.
Miller, Steven P. *The Age of Evangelicalism: America's Born-Again Years.* New York: Oxford University Press, 2015. http://www.regent.edu.

RYRIE, CHARLES CALDWELL (1925–2016)

Charles Caldwell Ryrie (1925–2016) has been known to be one of the most effective theologians of the 20th century. His impact was experienced not only in America but also across the globe as he authored more than 30 books and contributed numerous articles to theological journals, such as *Bibliotheca Sacra* (1844–present).

The rich content and accessibility that flowed out of Ryrie's works distinguished his work among other evangelical theologians. In other words, Ryrie had a way of writing theology that made it available to any layperson and yet did not leave out any valuable insights or details. Consequently, this type of style set him apart from his contemporaries among the wide array of evangelicals.

Ryrie, who was one of the major advocates of normative dispensationalism in his day, was immensely successful at contending for and engaging significant controversial topics within and beyond evangelicalism. Some of those issues included the nature of dispensationalism, salvation by faith alone, hermeneutics, and Neo-orthodoxy. In fact, his books *Dispensationalism Today* (1965) and *So Great a Salvation* (1989) are a few of those just mentioned. Additionally, being one of the most distinguished and prolific writers of his day, Charles Ryrie was able to accomplish this while maintaining a great sense of humility, as demonstrated through his scholarship and personal life.

Charles C. Ryrie was born on March 2, 1925, in St. Louis, Missouri. Ryrie was raised in Alton, Illinois, where he attended First Baptist Church of Alton and also where his own father, John Alexander (banker), led him to faith in Christ. As a young

---

Covenant Theology versus Dispensational Theology

Covenant theology and dispensational theology are two competing evangelical systems of belief that emerged from Reformation theology. Covenant theology deductively interprets the Scriptures on the basis of two covenants, namely, the covenant of works. Adam failed the covenant of works by disobedience, and thus God then made a covenant to the elect sinner in Christ. As a result, God has one people, namely, the redeemed, throughout history. Dispensationalists inductively contend that if one consistently follows a plain, normal, literal grammatical-literary-historical method of interpretation, one will discover that God has two people, namely, Israel and the Church, with two distinct plans but with one plan of salvation: Himself. Throughout history God has dealt with people differently—hence, dispensations—but with the over-arching theme being to glorify Himself.

---

man, Ryrie was highly competent in school, graduating valedictorian of his high school class at the age of 16. Yet, even with a 98.6 grade point average, he was sent to Stony Brook School on Long Island, New York, for one semester because his father felt he still needed improvement before beginning his college education. Ryrie met the headmaster Frank E. Gaebelein (1899–1983) and, like his older brother, was recommended by Gaebelein to attend Haverford College, a Quaker school in suburban Philadelphia. Young Ryrie had every intention to follow after his father's footsteps and enter the banking business, so he enrolled in the mathematics program at Haverford. Like many students in the past, Ryrie changed his career. There was a man by the name of Dr. Lewis Sperry Chafer (1871–1952) who was one of the founders of the Evangelical Theological College (which later became Dallas Theological Seminary). Ryrie had become acquainted with Dr. Chafer through his maternal grandfather, so on hearing that Dr. Chafer was coming to Philadelphia for a speaking engagement, Ryrie made arrangements for the two of them to meet. Through that conversation that took place on April 23, 1943, Charles Ryrie made a decision to pursue a life in Christian ministry.

Having begun his college career with Haverford, Charles transitioned and applied to a school specifically centered on the field he now wanted to pursue. In the summer of 1944, Charles Ryrie was enrolled at Dallas Theological Seminary (DTS). While enrolled at DTS, Charles requested from Haverford that they grant him a bachelor's degree as a result of his studies at Dallas. In June of 1946, Charles Ryrie received his baccalaureate degree from Haverford College, and the following year on May of 1947, Charles received his ThM from Dallas Theological Seminary. He wrote his thesis on "The Relation of the New Covenant to Premillennialism." After receiving his ThM from DTS, Ryrie intended to further his education under Carl F. H. Henry (1913–2003) at Northern Baptist Theological Seminary. His plan was not realized when Henry received a job at Fuller Seminary, so Ryrie returned to Dallas and received his ThD degree with high honors. His dissertation built on his thesis and was titled, "The Basis of the Premillennial Faith" (1949). Ryrie taught Greek and Bible at Westmont College, and due to unexpected circumstances, he was made dean of men and chairman of the Department of Biblical Studies and Philosophy. After his experience at Westmont College, Charles furthered his studies and received a PhD from the University of Edinburgh. There he studied under liberal and tolerant scholars such as Thomas Torrance (1913–2007) and Matthew Black (1909–1994). His dissertation was later published by Moody as *The Role of Women in the Church* (1970).

On receiving his PhD, Ryrie returned to DTS as a professor of systematic theology but took a pause from teaching in 1958 to serve as president at Philadelphia College of Bible. In 1962, Charles returned to DTS as professor of systematic theology and dean of doctoral studies. In 1983, after many academic achievements and much Christian impact, Charles C. Ryrie retired from Dallas Theological Seminary. Ryrie was also awarded an honorary LittD by Liberty Baptist Theological Seminary for his extraordinary theological depth, discernment, and skills.

In regards to Ryrie's published material, much of it is worth recognizing, including his theological "magnum opus," titled *Basic Theology* (1986, 1999). In this book, Ryrie not only explains the major doctrines of the Bible, both historically and systematically, but he does it in a way that is very understandable and readable for those who have little background in theology. This book quickly sold more than 60,000 copies.

Another major accomplishment by Ryrie was *The Ryrie Study Bible* (1986), perhaps his greatest contribution to the Christian faith. This study Bible provided great exegetical insight to the passages in footnote form and also offered cultural, geographical, historical, political, and theological information in a very accessible way. Moreover, Ryrie explains other positions on certain issues instead of merely giving his view. He gives an introduction to each of the books of the Bible in which he includes information about the author, date of writing, purpose, and so on.

Some of Ryrie's books were written in response to some of the allegations being made against him and the views he was promoting. *Dispensationalism Today* (1965) was written to dispel any misconceptions from people like Oswald T. Allis (1880–1973), Daniel Fuller (1925–), and Clarence Bass, who were attacking dispensationalism and its proponents. In this book, Ryrie succinctly clarifies what makes one a dispensationalist, namely, the sine qua non (1) consistent use of the plain, normal, literal, grammatical, historical, and literary method of interpretation; (2) clear distinction between God's programs for Israel and the Church; and (3) that God's overall purpose is glorify Himself.

Ryrie's *So Great Salvation* (1997) was written in response to John MacArthur's publication of *The Gospel According to Jesus* (1988). In this book, MacArthur attacked proponents of the view that one can accept Jesus Christ as Savior without making him Lord of one's life. His book made a significant impact among evangelicals struggling with the question of what one necessarily needs to know in order to be saved and assured of salvation (e.g., free grace vs. lordship salvation debate).

Among these published books mentioned above, there are many others written by Ryrie that have received credit and recognition for their scholarly contribution to contemporary issues, including *The Miracles of Our Lord* (1984) and, in particular, *So Great Salvation* (1997), which received the Gold Medallion Award from the Evangelical Christian Publishers Association.

Ryrie was also highly recognized for his private Bible collection. According to the Museum of Biblical Art in Dallas, Texas, Ryrie has more than a hundred Bibles, pages, and fragments. He began collecting in 1960 and has one of the most significant Bible collections by a single person, reflecting his deep love and respect for the Scriptures. According to the Museum of Biblical Art, his private collection of ancient Bibles and manuscripts include a page from the Gutenberg Bible (1450s); the first edition of the King James Bible (1611); the Wycliffe New Testament (1430); the Genoa Psalter (1516); Coverdale's first edition (1535) of the first printed English Bible; the very rare Tyndale's Pentateuch (1530); Erasmus's New Testaments; and Eliot's Bible (1663; the first Bible to printed in America, which was written in the Algonquin language).

Ryrie had an enormous impact on evangelicalism. His works, including Ryrie's *Basic Theology* (1986, 1999) and *The Ryrie Study Bible* (1986) with all its study notes, continue to be printed and sold today. His expertise in communicating complex theological ideas in ways that are easy to understand has provided a bridge for many to have a greater appreciation and love for theology. A master in the use of words, his evangelical impact extends beyond the United States; it is global. His reputation among those who know him is that of a careful interpreter of Scripture who presented his works with as much humility as is required in his fields of theological scholarship and teaching ministry.

Matias Perez and Paul R. Shockley

See also: Chafer, Lewis Sperry; Dallas Theological Seminary; Dispensationalism; Hermeneutics; Inerrancy; MacArthur, John F., Jr.; Premillennialism; Rapture; Walvoord, John F.; Women's Ministries

Further Reading

Elwell, Walter A., ed. *Handbook of Evangelical Theologians.* Grand Rapids, MI: Baker Books, 1993.

Enns, Paul P. "Charles Ryrie." In *Handbook of Evangelical Theologians*, edited by Walter A. Elwell. Grand Rapids, MI: Baker Books, 1993.

Hannah, John D. *An Uncommon Union: Dallas Theological Seminary and American Evangelicalism.* Grand Rapids, MI: Zondervan, 2009.

Museum of Biblical Art. (n.d.). "The Charles C. Ryrie Library at the Museum of Biblical Art in Dallas." Biblicalarts.org. Accessed May 30, 2015. https://www.biblicalarts.org/ryrie-library.

Ryrie, Charles C. *The Basis of the Premillennial Faith.* Neptune, NJ: Loizeaux Brothers, 1986.

Ryrie, Charles C. *Basic Theology.* Wheaton, IL: Victor Books, 1986.

Ryrie, Charles C. *So Great Salvation: What It Means to Believe in Jesus Christ.* Wheaton, IL: Victor, 1989.

Weaver, Paul D. "The Theological Method of Charles Caldwell Ryrie." *Journal of Ministry and Theology* 17:2 (Fall 2013): 33–89.

SCHAEFFER, FRANCIS A. AND EDITH (1912–1984 AND 1914–2013)

Francis A. Schaeffer (1912–1984), author of more than 21 books, and Edith Schaeffer (1914–2013), author of over a dozen books, are considered to be two of the most significant evangelical leaders in the 20th century. Francis's influence was far-reaching, speaking to generations of young adults who were finding their personal worldviews to be inadequate, existentially bankrupt, and logically inconsistent in a turbulent era in Western society when people were not finding "final answers" in the political left, atheistic existentialism, the drug scene as an ideology, and affluence. The incompleteness people experienced within the midst of countercultural movements was made even worse by the inadequacies of Christian evangelicals who were unwilling to connect real faith to culture, ask the hard questions, resonate with peoples' difficulties, and truly listen to the questions asked and the concerns raised. But Schaeffer, along with his wife and lifelong partner in ministry, Edith, integrated and modeled in life an authentic passion for God, truth, and people. They connected the dots for those to whom they ministered, to recognize that the Christian faith not only possesses the best answers to the nature of reality, life, meaning, and purpose, but also provides the basis to speak to culture, ranging from the arts to the environment. In essence, this couple introduced Christianity as "total truth," speaking to all aspects of life in the most dynamic and meaningful ways to both Christians and non-Christians alike. The Schaeffers' written works, audio lectures, and videos continue to inspire evangelicals and others in areas of Christian scholarship and even Christian conservative activism. But their call for Christians to take ideas and implications seriously was only matched by their demonstration of authentic faith and its relationship to culture in their home as classical music was played; the arts appreciated, the environment valued; and they made real, practical investments in the lives of people, welcoming friends and strangers alike, no matter their background or baggage. Even as he himself suffered with cancer, Francis ministered to those around him who were hurting and fearful. He died in Rochester, Minnesota, in 1984 leaving behind Edith, his three daughters, and his one son. Edith passed away in Gryon, Switzerland, in 2013 at the age of 98.

Francis A. Schaeffer was born into a blue-collar family in Pennsylvania in 1912. His family was nominally Christian. But at the age of 18 he moved from an agnostic position to becoming a Christian following an intense study of the Bible (1930). He studied at Hampden-Sydney College and later at Faith Theological Seminary. In 1935, he married the love of his life, Edith Seville. Edith was born in Wenzhou,

China. Her parents, who were missionaries, served with China Inland Mission. In 1937, Francis A. Schaeffer was the first to be ordained into the Bible Presbyterian Church after they split from the Orthodox Presbyterian Church. The Bible Presbyterian Church was not only Calvinistic and strongly evangelistic, but it was also premillennial.

From 1938 to 1948, Francis pastored three churches. But when he was sent to Europe following the aftermath of World War II in 1948 to do international missions, he found Switzerland to be his new home. In 1951, however, Francis Schaeffer experienced a spiritual crisis with some of the issues flowing out of the unloving attitude among certain people in the fundamentalist movement. He decided to start again from an agnostic position and reexamined the intellectual, existential, and empirical evidences of Christianity from an honest, open position. After coming to some life-changing conclusions about what "true spirituality" means, he resigned from the mission board in 1955. It was the same year in Huemoz, Switzerland, that L'Abri (which means "shelter") emerged in their home.

Without any advertisement, L'Abri, their actual home, became a Christian community were people could come and find honest answers to honest questions regardless of their appearance, their problems, or their philosophical or religious worldview; the Schaeffers welcomed all. Thus, by word of mouth many young people in Europe and in America began to hear about a place in Switzerland where people could come for intellectual, spiritual, and emotional help. In view of his exceptional interpersonal skills, Francis and the ever-tireless Edith Schaeffer began impacting people, demonstrating to them by proclamation and presence not only what it means to be a mature Christian but also how the Christian faith touches all of life. Francis was someone who understood the art of conversation, and he also took people seriously, meeting them where they were and attempting to take them where the needed to be, whether they were Christians or not. Although he was an intellectual and a theologian, he was also an evangelist who inspired evangelicals to think seriously about other disciplines of study, such as the arts, philosophy, and history, and to see how the Christian faith connected to not only to the believing mind but also to culture with all of its reflective glory (e.g., the arts) and depravity (e.g., abortion). His inspiration for Christians to take philosophical and cultural ideas seriously was contagious among those who sought more from the Christian faith than mere "blind faith." In essence, Francis and Edith moved evangelicals to reconsider their fundamentalist separatism from culture and engage the greater society in which they were already imbedded.

Schaeffer also contributed to contemporary Christian apologetics. Since he took evil very seriously, he recognized that everyone was inherently corrupted by sin. Even though he believed that everyone is fallen, he emphasized that people have the "common grace" ability to reason, test, and verify truth claims—for all are made in God's image, living in God's created universe. For Schaeffer, reason precedes faith. This type of process is not only intuitive but also common as one deals with truth claims in any discipline such as philosophy, history, or science. One looks for reasons and evidences and then places one's trust or faith in that which is verified to be true and trustworthy. Thus, for Schaeffer, faith is reasonable, not a blind leap.

Francis Schaeffer took this verification approach and actually applied it to other disciplines of study (e.g., philosophical or religious truth claims). Moreover, he demanded that evangelicals should seek to understand their own culture, engaging non-Christians in such a way that they too can see the explanatory power, the logical coherence, empirical adequacy, and existential relevance of the Christian worldview with a disposition of Christian love and humility. Once the Christian enters into the worldview of a non-Christian, in what he describes as "taking the roof off," via dialogue, one can show how the non-Christian worldview is not as adequate in substance and in consequence as the Christian worldview by applying this verification-type examination.

Edith Schaeffer, who authored significant works such as *The Hidden Art of Homemaking* (1971) and *What Is a Family* (1975), offered by thought and by example in their home what it means to live out womanhood biblically. It is often said that apart from Edith's contribution, L'Abri would never have been born. Through Edith's efforts, young people across the world found a place, a ministry, and a home where they were taken seriously and, for some, loved authentically for the very first time. Her work, *Affliction* (1978), in particular, speaks to the problem of pain and suffering from the point of view of a mother, a wife, and a Christian servant-leader.

Francis Schaeffer recommended that if one wants to understand his work, one should begin by reading *The God Who Is There* (1968), *Escape from Reason* (1968), and *He Is There and He Is Not Silent* (1972) in consecutive order. His book *True Spirituality* (1971) offers an authentic look into his own spiritual crisis and how he discovered the Christian faith to be authentically viable in both content and lifestyle.

An application of Schaeffer's thought to Western thought and culture is found in his sweeping account of history, *How Should We Then Live: The Rise and Decline of Western Thought and Culture* (1976); *Whatever Happened to the Human Race?* (1979), coauthored with the late surgeon general C. Everett Koop (1916–2013) under President Ronald Reagan's administration, unpacks how human values are in decline in

Significant Evangelical Cultural Apologists

1. Voddie Baucham
2. Harold O. J. Brown
3. Charles Colson
4. Os Guinness
5. Rick and Nancy Pearcey
6. Francis A. and Edith Schaeffer
7. Ravi Zacharias

view of such matters as the legal right to have an abortion and the growing cultural support for euthanasia and infanticide.

Francis and Edith Schaeffer's influence continues today in their multifarious writings and recordings, their daughters' ministries, and in the lives in which they qualitatively invested such as Os Guinness (1941–) and Nancy Pearcey (1952–), and also in the number of L'Abri communities located around the world. Edith's works offers detailed insight into the birth and life of L'Abri, their lives, and their ministries in such books as *The Tapestry: The Life and Times of Francis and Edith Schaeffer*, *L'Abri*, *With Love, Edith: The L'Abri Family Letters: 1948–1960*, and *Dear Family: The L'Abri Family Letters: 1961–1986*.

Though Francis Schaeffer's historical and philosophical insights and political activism are not without sound criticism, even by other evangelicals, he was a servant-leader, a missionary, and an intellectual who loved people passionately. Francis and Edith spoke to evangelicals who were fragmented by fundamental separatism, oppressed by humanistic philosophies, and divided by fact/value splits. Together they sought to demonstrate how the Christian faith, which possesses logical strength, empirical evidences, explanatory power, workability, viability, and existential relevance, is to be integrated into the whole of life (e.g., arts, creativity, the environment, history, home life, imagination, philosophy, politics, spirituality, and work).

Paul R. Shockley

See also: Abortion, Evangelicals and; Calvinism; Christian Apologetics; Colson, Charles Wendell ("Chuck"); Falwell, Jerry L., Sr.; Fine Arts, Evangelicals and; International Council on Biblical Inerrancy; Koop, C. Everett; L'Abri Fellowship; Missions, Evangelicals and; Parachurch Ministries; Premillennialism

Further Reading

Burson, Scott R., and Jerry L Walls. *C. S. Lewis and Francis Schaeffer: Lessons for a New Century from the Most Influential Apologists of Our Time*. Downers Grove, IL: InterVarsity Press, 1998.

Duriez, Colin. *Francis Schaeffer: An Authentic Life*. Wheaton, IL: Crossway, 2008.

Follis, Bryan A. *Truth with Love: The Apologetics of Francis Schaeffer*. Wheaton, IL: Crossway, 2006.

Hankins, Barry. *Francis Schaeffer and the Shaping of Evangelical America*. Grand Rapids, MI: Eerdmans, 2008.

Morris, Thomas V. *Francis Schaeffer's Apologetics: A Critique*. Chicago: Moody Press, 1976.

Parkhurst, Louis G., Jr., and Louis Gifford. *Francis Schaeffer: The Man and His Message*. Wheaton, IL: Tyndale House, 1985.

Schaeffer, Edith. *The Tapestry: The Life and Times of Francis and Edith Schaeffer*. Waco, TX: Word Books, 1981.

Schaeffer, Francis A. *The Complete Works of Francis A. Schaeffer*. 5 volumes. Wheaton, IL: Crossway, 1985.

SCIENCE, EVANGELICALS AND

The relationship between science and evangelicalism, especially in the last 150 years or so, has been wrought with caricatures, confusion, and controversy; there is no widespread agreement about how this relationship should be understood within and beyond evangelicalism. Discoveries continue to be made that advance human understanding of the universe, life, and the various contexts in which people live and function (e.g., ecological systems; forestry; sociology; psychology), which both evangelicals and non-evangelicals are exploring, affirming, and questioning. The tenuous relationship between science and evangelicals is evidenced in at least four ways:

First, for more than 150 years an intellectual and cultural division has occurred between science and historical evangelical thought. The entry of Darwinian thought into the university and seminary, the impact of German Higher Criticism, and the reactionary spirit of fundamentalists led many evangelicals to withdraw from the academy to create a subculture with their own authorities, institutions, personalities, and resources. In some cases, coming out of the Great Awakenings, where personal piety and religious experience were prized, faith was no longer viewed by certain fundamentalists as reliance on that which one has good reasons and evidences to believe. Rather, faith was perceived as an irrational blind leap of faith over and against evidence. Thus, the need and value for logical reasoning and empirical evidences as justifications for belief were displaced by personal feelings and religious experiences.

Yet this dividing mindset was foreign to the Christian pioneers of science such as Francis Bacon (1561–1626), Johannes Kepler (1571–1630), Galileo (1564–1642), Sir Isaac Newton (1643–1727), Blaise Pascal (1623–1662), and even Puritan theologians like Jonathan Edwards (1703–1758) who believed that science was a way to understand and know God better.

Even today certain intelligent design proponents, such as evangelical mathematician and philosopher William Dembski (1960–) and University of California Berkeley law professor Phillip E. Johnson (1940–), affirm and value both science and evangelicalism. Astrophysicist, author, and noted evangelical speaker Hugh Ross (1945–), a progressive creationist and founder of Reasons to Believe (1986), speaks around the world about the compatibility of faith and science. But the enriching relationship between faith and science is also evidenced among scientific creationists with the Institution of Creation Research (1970) and Answers in Genesis (1994), who differ with progressive creationists.

The Discovery Institute (1994) is a secular think tank made up of agnostics, deists, theists, and evangelicals (e.g., mathematician and philosopher David Berlinski (1942–), author of *The Devil's Delusion: Atheism and Its Scientific Pretensions* (2009)). Intelligent Design advocates claim Darwinian evolution is lacking as the best explanation for specified and irreducible complexity that is empirically observed on a molecular level, in biological systems, and on a cosmic level (e.g., Strong Anthropic Principle). Young earth creationists such as Henry Morris (1918–2006), Duane Gish

(1921–2013), and Brian Thomas (1971–) are exclusively evangelicals who affirm a literal interpretation of Genesis and seek to use empirical evidence to support their claims. Although these two movements, namely, intelligent design and scientific creationism, are not be conflated or confused, they both affirm science while rejecting the philosophical presuppositions of a naturalistic worldview and the lack of explanatory power from those who claim a random, blind process of natural selection is the basis for the origins of life.

Second, the call for science and faith to be placed into distinct and non-overlapping categories contributes to the tenuous relationship between some scientists and science. Consequently, some, whether Christian or secular, call for a distinct separation between science and theology into two distinct categories whereby evangelicals will deal only with the spiritual realm (who and why questions) and science will only deal with the physical realm, asking objective facts and making observations (how questions). Those opposing this counter that the underpinnings for both science and theology are philosophical presuppositions about God, reality, truth, ethics, and even aesthetics. This presents ongoing difficulties, disputes, and possibilities as both have to deal with the ontological, epistemological, and ethical consequences that flow from theological and scientific truth claims, pursuits, and experimentations (e.g., biotechnology) that not only affect individuals and society but also impact future generations.

Further, evangelicals believe that the God of the Bible has communicated facts that are in accord with science in the Scriptures (e.g., Genesis 1–2). For evangelicals, the Bible is not only a religious text of faith and spiritual practice but also a book of objective scientific and historical facts inspired by God. Moreover, evangelicals typically affirm the value of natural revelation, that is, information given to all people from God as disclosed by physical creation, human design, human conscience, God-ward longings, and even consequences from volitional choices. But with competing worldviews (e.g., deism, naturalism, theism, pantheism) in a growing secular society that is calling for the privatization of all religious beliefs (reducing them to personal values and preferences), the popular perception that only in the domain of science can objective facts be found (known as the fact/value split) and that all of life is an accidental byproduct of time, energy, and chance, controversies between faith and science continue to find expression. For example, Ben Stein's 2008 documentary *Expelled: No Intelligence Allowed* explored why professors who endorse intelligent design as having greater explanatory power than empirical evidence for evolution are being removed from their tenured positions.

Third, the interrelationships of science, faith, public education, politics, and judicial rulings have contributed to this ongoing tension. For example, the 1925 "Scopes Monkey Trial" (*The State of Tennessee v. John Thomas Scopes*) put evolution and evangelical thought both on the "witness stand" before the public, thus opening the door for further court cases involving controversial topics such as the constitutionality of free speech, religious freedom, what counts as critical thinking, and how science is to be defined.

For example, in the 1968 *Epperson v. State of Arkansas* case, the U.S. Supreme Court struck down an Arkansas statute that prohibited teaching evolution. In 1981, the *Segraves v. State of California* case involved an anti-dogmatic policy that was believed to prohibit free exercise of religion. In 1982, *McLean v. Arkansas Board of Education*, a federal court ruled that creation science is not real science in view of an Arkansas statute affirming the directive that public schools were to give a balanced treatment to both creation science and evolutionary science. In 1987, in *Edwards v. Aguillard*, the U.S. Supreme Court claimed that by teaching creation science, one was affirming a supernatural being, thus sanctioning religion. In 1990, in the *Webster v. New Lenox School District* case, it was ruled that free speech rights were not violated by prohibiting a teacher from teaching creationism because it is endorsing religion. In the 1994 *Peloza v. Capistrano School District* case, the Ninth Circuit Court of Appeals came to the conclusion that the requirement to teach evolution is not a violation of free exercise of religion. In 1997, in the *Freiler v. Tangipahoa Parish Board of Education* case, the court ruled that intelligent design curriculum is comparable to creation science. In *Rodney LeVake v. Independent School District 656*, the teacher claimed that he had the right to teach the evidences for and against the theory of evolution. The school district claimed that all teachers must follow the school's curriculum. The court ruled that LeVake's free speech rights were not violated, and religious discrimination was not found. In 2005, *Kitzmiller et al. v. Dover*, U.S. District Court Judge John E. Jones III ruled, among other things, that Intelligent Design is not science. In each of these cases, the relationship between religion and science was central to the case.

And fourth, there is a lack of unity among evangelicals about faith and science. The "Scopes Monkey Trial" (1925) occurred during a time of religious history where Protestant fundamentalists and modernists were in conflict regarding the Bible and science, Darwinian evolution, German Higher Criticism, and broadening theological trends in many Protestant denominations. The ramifications of this internal division are still experienced today in certain traditions and movements reducing science to mere "human wisdom." Yet, Neo-evangelicals such as Harold J. Ockenga (1905–1985) and cultural apologists such as Francis A. Schaeffer (1912–1984) called for the evangelical reengagement of culture, and Christian scholars today, such as William Lane Craig (1949–), Norman L. Geisler (1932–), John Lennox (1943–), Alister McGrath (1953–), J. P. Moreland (1948–), Nancy Pearcey (1952–), Alvin Plantinga (1932–), Ravi Zacharias (1946–), and many others, have demonstrated how one can affirm science and faith holistically while criticizing the logical coherence, empirical evidences, and existential relevance of naturalism. For example, in his work, *Where the Conflict Really Lies: Science, Religion, and Naturalism* (2011), Alvin Plantinga criticized the logical coherence and epistemological strength of naturalism since there is no way to cognitively know if the theory of evolution by random natural selection is true. Survival of the fittest or maximal reproductive succession does not guarantee complex cognitive abilities for abstract thought. Thus, following the naturalistic position of randomness, there is no good reason to believe that evolution is true.

Moreover, the scientific scholarship of evangelical scientists such as geneticist John Collins (1950–), director of the National Institutes of Health (NIH) and famously known for directing the Human Genome Project (HGP), demonstrate to evangelicals and secular society alike that evangelicals can offer noteworthy contributions where both faith and science, once again, can cohere together. In other words, evangelicals affirm scientific inquiries, investigations, and pursuits. But they reject an exclusively naturalistic, reductionistic, and scientism view of reality, epistemology, and values.

Paul R. Shockley with R. Don Deal and Tom Peeler

See also: Center for Bioethics and Human Dignity; Christian Apologetics; Colson, Charles Wendell ("Chuck"); Environment, Evangelicals and the; Geisler, Norman L.; Institute for Creation Research; Intelligent Design Movement; Morris, Henry; Ockenga, Harold John; Plantinga, Alvin C.; Schaeffer, Francis A. and Edith; Theological Controversies within Evangelicalism

Further Reading

Dembski, William A., and Michael Behe. *Intelligent Design: The Bridge Between Science and Theology.* Downers Grove, IL: InterVarsity Press, 2002.

Gilbert, James. *Redeeming Culture: American Religion in an Age of Science.* Chicago: The University of Chicago Press, 1997.

Livingstone, David N., D. G. Hart, and Mark A. Noll, eds. *Evangelicals and Science in Historical Perspective.* New York: Oxford University Press, 1989.

Meyer, Stephen C. *Signature in the Cell: DNA and the Evidence for Intelligent Design.* New York: HarperCollins, 2009.

Moreland, J. P. *Christianity and the Nature of Science: A Philosophical Investigation.* Grand Rapids, MI: Baker Books, 1989.

National Association of Evangelicals. Washington, DC: National Association of Evangelicals, 2015; also at nae.net.

Pearcey, Nancy R., and Charles B. Thaxton. *The Soul of Science: Christian Faith and Natural Philosophy.* Wheaton, IL: Crossway, 1994.

Plantinga, Alvin *Where the Conflict Really Lies: Science, Religion, and Naturalism.* New York: Oxford University, Press, 2011.

Ross, Hugh. *Improbable Planet: How Earth Became Humanity's Home.* Grand Rapids: Baker Book Press, 2016.

SCOFIELD, CYRUS INGERSON (1843–1921)

The editor of the Scofield Reference Bible, Cyrus I. Scofield's reference Bible, and other writings significantly affected the theological views of 20th-century American evangelicalism. He was the last of seven children born into the family of Elias and Abigail Scofield shortly after their arrived in Lenamee County, Michigan, from New York State, apparently a typical pioneering family seeking land, livelihood, and heritage. Little is known of Scofield in his earliest years. As a teenager, he is found residing with a sister in Lebanon, Tennessee, and subsequently he served in the Confederacy for a single term of enlistment, 1861–1862, but refused a second enlistment, making his loyalties suspect. He deserted the Southern cause and moved to the less politically charged enclaves of St. Louis, Missouri, where an oath to the Union was taken, and he received a parole from the Union Provost Marshal that secured his safety in the city.

In the city, Scofield became well connected both socially and politically, marrying into a Roman Catholic family, the Cerres. In addition, he emerged as a lawyer with Republican sympathies and forged a connection with John J. Ingalls, a Kansas senator. Moving to Atchison, Kansas, with his wife, Leontine, and his daughters, he held the offices of state legislator and district attorney for some time. The opportunities for moral dereliction proved more alluring than the benefits of family and career, and he lost both to drunkenness and illegalities.

Returning to St. Louis, where he lived with a sister and her husband, his career dissolved and his marriage fractured in the murky sludge of divorce proceedings. Shady financial dealings and false pretenses led to incarcerations in Wisconsin and Missouri; the once-promising lawyer proved little more than a swindler, con man, and deceiver. It was at this time, the nadir of his 36 years, that Scofield experienced the grace and mercy of God. The year was 1879 or 1880, and the messenger was a lady from the St. Louis Flower Mission who visited the local jail, where he was serving time, but the message came from heaven.

As is often true, Scofield's life did not match his apparent profession of faith immediately. Lies and deception continued to characterize his conduct, but he joined the Pilgrim Congregational Church in the city and became involved in various church outreaches, particularly in East St. Louis among railroad men. However twisted and corrupted his choices continued to be at times (redemption not curing human nature), Scofield gradually submerged himself into various Christian activities that included being acting secretary of the local YMCA; through his pastor, C. C. Goodell, approval by the St. Louis Association of Congregational Churches for pastoral work; the founding of the Hyde Park Congregational Church in North St. Louis; and an appointment as missionary with the Congregational American Home Missions Board (AHMB) for church planting.

In that capacity, Scofield arrived in Dallas, Texas, in 1882 under the auspices of the AHMB to take a small group of about 13 people and organize the First Congregational Church in the city. Under his faithful labors, Scofield readily evidenced latent pastoral and teaching gifts coupled with an unrelenting zeal to study and teach the Bible. The church grew to hundreds of parishioners; branch churches were organized in the city; and he was eventually formally ordained by a group of Congregational peers. In this context, he married Hettie Hall von Wartz and consequently was given his first son, Noel, the third of his children.

His developing reputation was evidenced by his appointment as superintendent for church extension in the South and Southwest (he was one of the founders of Lake Charles [Louisiana] College at this time, later taking on additional responsibility of church extension in Colorado). In the early 1890s, his passion for Bible study came to fruition in the development of what became the Scofield Correspondence Course, a tool for understanding the Bible. In the same decade, Scofield, with the help of the church, founded the Central American Mission, coalescing his Bible study and mission passions. In 1888, he authored perhaps his most influential work (other than the Bible notes a decade later), "Rightly Dividing the Word of God." In addition, he wrote several books throughout his life and contributed portions to many others.

Scofield's church work gradually led to various conference ministries in the emerging Bible Conference Movement throughout the nation, particularly the Niagara Bible conferences, where he met the leading pastors of the day. As a result of his growing interconnectedness with the broader evangelical movement in America, he was invited to Northfield, Massachusetts, to pastor the local Congregational Church where Dwight L. Moody attended and to serve as the director of the Northfield Training School, an expression of Moody's educational interests. Leaving Dallas in 1895, Scofield became Moody's pastor and a regular speaker at the Northfield Bible Conferences as well as other conferences.

With Moody's death in 1899, Scofield returned to his former pastorate in Dallas, but a project conceived at the Sea Cliff Bible Conference, Long Island, New York, in 1902 would make his time in the pulpit sporadic at best in the decade. The project, what became the notes in the much-celebrated *Scofield Reference Bible*, were completed in 1909 and published by Oxford Press. The Bible became the most important literary production in the defense of the dispensational premillennial approach to understanding Scriptures in the century. The enormous popularity of the Bible allowed a revision of the notes in 1917 and another in 1967.

As the Liberal Movement in American church life became increasingly disruptive, Scofield felt compelled to leave the Congregational churches, and he sought ministerial certification in the Paris (Texas) Presbytery of the Southern Presbyterian Church, holding ministerial credentials in that community for the rest of his life.

Scofield left the church in Dallas shortly after completing his work of the Bible notes and settled in Douglaston, New York, a suburb of New York City, for the remainder of his years, days often characterized by declining health. In those years, he founded the New York Night School of the Bible (a correspondence and extension program) as well as the Philadelphia School of the Bible, Philadelphia, Pennsylvania. Having met Lewis Chafer in his classes at Northfield Training School in 1901, he and his student formed a teaching tandem and traveled extensively throughout the country after 1910, Scofield emphasizing eschatology, and Chafer, the doctrine of the spiritual life.

After 40 years of service to the Lord, Scofield was conducted to heaven in 1921. Scofield was a gifted Bible teacher and articulate writer, most importantly a proponent of the great and grand teaching of divine, redeeming grace through Christ. Dug from a spiritual quagmire by God's unexpected and unmerited, even discriminatory, grace, he was translated from a professional shyster and drunken derelict into a trophy of the mercies of God.

John D. Hannah

See also: Bible Conference Movement; Bible Exposition; Bible Institutes and Bible Colleges; Dispensationalism; Eschatology; Moody, Dwight Lyman; Premillennialism; Rapture; *Scofield Reference Bible*

Further Reading

Canfield, James M. *The Incredible Scofield and His Book.* Vallecito, CA: Ross House Books, 1988.

Hannah, John D. "A Review of The Incredible Scofield and His Book." *Bibliotheca Sacra* 147 (July–September, 1990): 351–364.

Rushing, Jean J. "From Confederate Deserter to Decorated Veteran Bible Scholar: Exploring the Enigmatic Life of C. I. Scofield, 1861–1921." MA thesis, East Tennessee State University, 2011.

Trumbull, Charles. *The Life Story of C. I. Scofield.* New York: Oxford Press, 1920.

SCOFIELD REFERENCE BIBLE (1909)

The *Scofield Reference Bible* (1909) and its successors *The New Scofield Reference Bible* (1967) and *Oxford Scofield Study Bible III* (2003, and other variations from Oxford University Press) is a popular study Bible edited and annotated by American Bible teacher Cyrus Ingerson Scofield (1843–1921) in the early 20th century. It was the first Bible to print notes on the biblical text alongside the text since the publication of the Geneva Bible in 1560.

Popular Bible Translations

10 Popular Bible Translations:
1. *English Standard Version* (2001)
2. *Holman Christian Standard Bible* (2004)
3. *King James Version* (1611)
4. *New American Standard* (1971)
5. *New King James Version* (1982)
6. *New International Reader's Version* (1996)
7. *New International Version* (1978)
8. *New Living Translation* (1996)
9. *Reina Valera 1960* (1569)
10. *The Voice* (2012)

The study Bible contained a cross-reference system of Bible verses in a middle column of the page that allowed readers to follow a biblical theme throughout the Bible, moving from one chapter and book of the Bible to another. The notes on prophetic biblical passages presented a view of future things (the doctrine of eschatology) that was premillennial and dispensational. In its interpretation of biblical history, the study notes followed the chronological calculations of Irish Archbishop James Ussher (1581–1656), who posited a 4004 BCE date for the creation of the universe based on his reading of Genesis 1–3. In the interwar years during the Fundamentalist–Modernist Controversy and the 1925 "Scopes Monkey Trial" in Dayton, Tennessee, conservative Protestant interpretations of the relationship between science and the Bible were in great flux, with many conservative Protestants rejecting Darwinism and favoring what came to be known as Scientific Creationism. Some of this was due to the easy accessibility and acceptance of Scofield's notes that presented what he considered to be a middle-of-the-road approach known as the "gap theory." Internal debates within evangelicalism continue in the present with respect to balancing a high view of the Bible with contemporary science. The study notes and perspective supported study of Bible prophecy that led many evangelicals in the post–World War II years and after the founding of the State of Israel to intensely study the book of Revelation, resulting in various prophetic timetables and attempts to link current events with biblical prophecies.

The original reference Bible was first published in 1909 and revised by Scofield in 1917. Originally aligned with the King James Version of the Bible, revised editions of the study Bible were adapted to other popular Protestant translations such as the New King James Version, New American Standard Bible, and New International Version.

The *Scofield Reference Bible* was the most important publication in spreading the idea of dispensationalism throughout American Protestantism. The work's popularity continued in subsequent editions, and for many evangelicals it was the Bible of choice until at least the 1970s, when a host of study Bibles began to appear; some of these continued the theological perspective of premillennialism (*The Ryrie Study Bible*), and others focused on broader evangelicalism and scholarship or particular themes (*NET Bible, ESV Study Bible, NIV Study Bible, NIV Archaeological Study Bible, Holman Study Bible*). The *Scofield Reference Bible* is also important in that it gave conservative Christians who were serious in their efforts to study the Bible an opportunity to understand the biblical content and grasp conservative Christian doctrine. It provided biblical content and study aids as well as a specific biblical and theological perspective of dispensationalism to laypersons, and it has sold millions of copies and been translated into numerous languages in its more than 100-year history.

Timothy J. Demy

See also: Dispensationalism; Eschatology; Premillennialism; Scofield, Cyrus Ingerson

Further Reading

Crutchfield, Larry V. *The Origins of Dispensationalism*. Lanham, MD: University Press of America, 1992.

English, E. Schuyler. *A Companion to the New Scofield Reference Bible*. New York: Oxford University Press, 1972.

Mangum, Todd R., and Mark S. Sweetnam. *The Scofield Bible: Its History and Impact on the Evangelical Church*. Colorado Springs, CO: Paternoster Press, 2009.

Pietsch, B. M. *Dispensational Modernism*. New York: Oxford University Press, 2015.

SEXUALITY, EVANGELICALS AND

Evangelicals believe sex is a gift from God in which "two become one" (Genesis 2:25; Ephesians 5:31). Throughout the ages, the church has viewed marriage as the only legitimate context for sexual expression.

In some eras, Christians have believed that even sex between married couples was considered valid only if engaged in for the purpose of reproduction. But evangelicals have rarely understood sexuality in this way, seeing in it much broader purposes than to "be fruitful and multiply."

The Ten Commandments include a prohibition against adultery. Fornication, which Jesus cited as an acceptable reason for divorce, has long been understood as a reference to any sexual expression outside of monogamous marriage (e.g., Matthew 5:32; John 8:41–42; 1 Corinthians 5:1, 6:18–20, 7:2; Galatians 5:19–21). Fornicators and adulterers are included on the list of those whom the apostle Paul says will not inherit the kingdom of God.

Most evangelicals believe that God prohibits same-sex sexual expressions. A minority of evangelicals, however, view same-sex marriage as a legitimate means of such intimacy. The latter are more likely, then, to view same-sex marriage as a civil rights issue.

The church across the world is overwhelmingly united around the core theology of sexuality assumed or articulated by the great theologians and Christian philosophers across the Orthodox, Roman Catholic, and Protestant traditions. Their core theology of sexuality is the belief that God created male and female in his image, and the mystery of their unique partnership is reflected in the exclusive male–female covenant. Their union is intended to picture Christ and the church, and sexual intercourse between them is a sacred blessing that physically expresses the ideal that "two shall become one." Christopher West's writings based on the work of Vatican II on sexuality serves as the foundation for most contemporary evangelicals' work on core sexual issues and is closely aligned with contemporary Roman Catholic thought.

Protestants on the left, however, have long argued for the validity of sex outside of marriage and favored same-sex unions. Increasingly, progressives who identify with evangelical mainstream culture are seeking to give evangelicalism a liberal Protestant presence on this issue. American evangelicals continue to address and debate the entire spectrum of gender and sexuality issues without consensus and with all sides contending for what each considers legitimate interpretation and application of the biblical text with respect to the issues.

Sandra Glahn

See also: Gender, Evangelicals and

Further Reading

Lopez, Kathryn J. "When Evangelicals Got Standing Ovations at the Vatican." The Corner. The National Review. November 20, 2014. http://www.nationalreview.com/corner /393088/when-evangelicals-got-standing-ovations-vatican-kathryn-jean-lopez.

West, Christopher. *Theology of the Body*, rev. ed. West Chester, PA: Ascension Press, 2009. http://www.theologyofthebody.net.

SIDER, RONALD JAMES (1939–)

Ronald James Sider (1939–) was a leading theologian and social activist within the progressive evangelical movement, or the evangelical left, from the early 1970s through the second decade of the 21st century. In addition to leading Evangelicals for Social Action, Sider served as professor of theology, holistic ministry, and public policy at Palmer (formerly Eastern Baptist) Theological Seminary until his retirement in 2013. Sider's most popular and debated work, *Rich Christians in an Age of Hunger* (1977, 2005), was ranked by *Christianity Today* as one of the top 10 most influential books shaping modern evangelicalism.

Born in rural southern Ontario, Sider was reared in a conservative Brethren in Christ community dedicated to Anabaptist theology and Wesleyan piety. Around the age of 8, he accepted Jesus as his Savior during a revival service. After excelling as a high school student and athlete, Sider attended Waterloo Lutheran University. Though he wrestled with scientific and historicist challenges to Christianity, the influence of professor John Warwick Montgomery (1931–), who would soon become an influential Christian apologist, fortified Sider's faith and inspired his goal to exercise Christian influence as a professor on a secular campus. At Yale University, he completed his PhD in early modern European and Reformation history. During the course of his studies in the mid-1960s, however, Sider became increasingly concerned with Christians' ethical responsibilities to address social problems—especially racial and economic injustices. His family moved into a predominantly black neighborhood in New Haven, and Sider became active in voter registration drives and other civil rights issues. On completing his graduate work, he accepted a teaching position at Messiah College's urban campus in Philadelphia. In this context, Sider shifted his teaching focus to racism, poverty, and war, which matched his ongoing involvement in social justice activism.

In the early 1970s, Sider became a prominent participant within a small, emerging network of politically progressive evangelical leaders. He helped to organize a quixotic group, Evangelicals for McGovern, during the 1972 presidential election and then served as a primary convener of a 1973 workshop that issued the Chicago Declaration of Evangelical Social Concern. This groundbreaking manifesto challenged the politically conservative majority of evangelicals to combat social injustices as part of their Christian responsibilities of citizenship. To capitalize on the momentum from this workshop, Sider founded Evangelicals for Social Action, an organization that became one of the primary institutional advocates for evangelical progressivism over the coming decades.

The publication in 1977 of *Rich Christians in an Age of Hunger* vaulted Sider into heated debates among evangelicals concerning how to define and how to promote economic justice. He argued that the Bible reveals God's special concern for the poor and that structural injustices cause most poverty. Rejecting the laissez-faire economics promoted by conservative evangelicals, Sider proclaimed that Christians must alleviate economic inequalities not merely through charitable personal acts but also through redistributive public policies and government programs. He also wrote and edited books on the theme of simple living. In the 1990s, however, Sider began moderating his economic views. Later editions of *Rich Christians* and other works acknowledged both the benefits of market-oriented economies and the complex, often personal causes of poverty. Nevertheless, Sider maintained, the state should promote economic justice through "faith-based initiatives" (antipoverty partnerships with private ministries), effective government programs, and progressive tax rates.

As a committed Anabaptist, Sider consistently urged other evangelicals to reject violence and to resist war. He wrote and acted in protest against forms of American militarism such as the Cold War nuclear arms race, intervention in Central America in the 1980s, the 1991 Gulf War, and the 2003 invasion of Iraq. Sider's efforts to promote active nonviolent resistance to evil helped to inspire the formation of Christian Peacemaker Teams in the late 1980s.

Sider portrayed his diverse political commitments as completely pro-life. Along with other politically progressive evangelicals and many Catholic social activists, he insisted Christians must defend the sacred worth and dignity of humans wherever and whenever threatened. Thus, Sider argued, biblically informed pro-life politics includes opposition not only to legalized abortion but also to racism, sexism, family disintegration, economic injustice, war, the death penalty, human rights violations, and other injustices. Based on this perspective, Sider consistently criticized the platforms and priorities of both Republicans and Democrats as insufficiently pro-life.

By the end of his career, Sider became more centrist in his politics, attempting to remain within the evangelical mainstream and to find common ground with conservative evangelicals. He published his books with major evangelical presses, long served as a contributing editor to *Christianity Today*, and continued defending traditional Christian sexual ethics and marriage. Nevertheless, during an era known for the rise and influence of the Religious Right, Sider joined other leaders such as Jim Wallis (1948–) and Tony Campolo (1935–) in promoting more progressive forms of evangelical political engagement. He remains one of the most prominent voices in evangelicalism.

Brantley W. Gasaway

See also: Abortion, Evangelicals and; African American Evangelicalism; Civil Rights Movement, Evangelicals and; Environment, Evangelicals and the; Evangelicalism; *Evangelicals & Catholics Together*; Fundamentalism; Foreign Policy, Evangelicals and; Hispanic American Evangelicals; Human Rights, Evangelicals and; Social Action, Evangelicals and

Further Reading

Gasaway, Brantley W. *Progressive Evangelicals and the Pursuit of Social Justice.* Chapel Hill, NC: University of North Carolina Press, 2014.

Sider, Ronald J. *Completely Pro-Life: Building a Consistent Stance.* Downers Grove, IL: Inter-Varsity Press, 1987.

Sider, Ronald J. *Rich Christians in an Age of Hunger: A Biblical Study.* Downers Grove, IL: Inter-Varsity Press, 1977, 2005.

Sider, Ronald J. *Just Politics: A Guide for Christian Engagement.* Grand Rapids, MI: Brazos Press, 2012.

Sider, Ronald J. *Nonviolent Action: What Christian Ethics Demands but Most Christians Have Never Really Tried.* Grand Rapids, MI: Brazos Press, 2015.

Swartz, David R. *Moral Minority: The Evangelical Left in an Age of Conservatism.* Philadelphia: University of Pennsylvania Press, 2012.

SMITH, CHARLES W. ("CHUCK") (1927–2013)

Charles W. ("Chuck") Smith (1927–2013) was an evangelical pastor known for establishing the Calvary Chapel network of churches beginning with his ministry as pastor of Calvary Chapel of Costa Mesa, California, in 1965 impacting the small congregation that met as a Bible study group in a trailer park. With his dynamic Bible teaching ability, Chuck enabled Calvary Chapel to grow in number. The late minister is known for leading an evangelical revolution in an era that celebrated drug use and sexual promiscuity. This pastor who outreached to hippies, left a lasting legacy that changed the way evangelical churches worshipped God.

Chuck Smith was born in Ventura, California, on June 25, 1927. He graduated from Life Bible College, today known as Life Pacific College, in San Dimas, California, and was known by his parish at Calvary Chapel as a pastor who preached verse by verse and chapter by chapter from Genesis to Revelation. With 17 years of ministry experience, Smith left the Foursquare Gospel denomination, in which he pastored several churches, and joined the 25-member congregation of Calvary Chapel. Within two years of leading Calvary Chapel, the attendance grew up to 200 regularly attending families. Realizing that California was home to a large population of hippie youth and surfers, Chuck and his wife, Kay, found it crucial to begin outreach to these young people. Smith's passion for preaching the Bible to anyone who would listen and discipling those who would believe drove his commitment, despite cultural and religious norms.

The future of Calvary Chapel took a drastic turn in 1971 when Chuck met Lonnie Frisbee, a hippie who understood the hippie culture and mentality, an unorthodox appearance, belief in rejecting moral values, and consuming hallucinogenic drugs. Through Lonnie the fast-growing church of Costa Mesa then began welcoming a diverse group of young people and did not discriminate on style of clothes or length of hair. Because of this warm atmosphere, many young hippies began visiting Calvary Chapel's Bible studies, causing the church's demographic to be largely populated by these free-spirited young people. The change resulted by embracing the diverse group, preaching the Gospel to them, and discipling them as they placed their faith in Jesus Christ. This brought forth the Jesus People Movement, comprised of Jesus-loving hippies who found the love they were hoping to find through salvation in Jesus Christ instead of drug use and sexual promiscuity. They moved away from a hippy mindset to embracing a biblical worldview. Consequently, this changed evangelical worship and church ministry across the United States.

As Calvary Chapel's Bible studies continued to grow, these gatherings converted into churches under Calvary Chapel's umbrella. Of these Bible-study-turned-churches is well-known Pastor Greg Laurie's Harvest Christian Fellowship in Riverside, California. Greg Laurie came to Calvary Chapel when he was 19 years old and was put in charge of a Bible study group that consisted of 30 regular attendees. Furthermore, Chuck Smith's Sunday messages were being recorded on cassette tapes and distributed all across the United States. Word for Today radio began broadcasting the Sunday services, and Smith would eventually create *Maranatha! Music* to promote songs of the Jesus Movement that were written by the young hippies from Calvary Chapel. *Maranatha! Music* is home to artists such as Charles Billingsley, Terry Clark, Tommy Walker, and Kelly Willard.

In more recent years, up to his death, though he never discontinued preaching through the Bible from Genesis to Revelation, Smith's expository sermons consisted of the topics on judgment for what he believed was the nation's depravity, with natural disasters and national catastrophes seen as retaliation from God for forsaking Him. Smith was also a strong proponent of eschatology, believing each year to be the world's last. He incorrectly predicted this event several times in his ministry.

In 2011, Smith was diagnosed with lung cancer, and despite enduring chemotherapy and radiation treatment, he continued to preach weekly. His battle with cancer ended on October 3, 2013. The Sunday before his death he entered the pulpit one final time, with oxygen hose and tank with him, as if to bid his congregation farewell. What began as a small Bible study made up of 25 people, led by Smith, has become a worldwide ministry of more than 1,600 churches. Smith's ministry emphasized expository biblical teaching and preaching and transformed the evangelical music of today.

Samuel Palacios

See also: Calvary Chapel; Counterculture, Evangelicals and; Jesus People Movement

Further Reading

Balmer, Randall. *Encyclopedia of Evangelicalism.* Waco, TX: Baylor University Press, 2004.

Goffard, Christopher. "Pastor Church Smith Dies at 86; Founder of Calvary Chapel Movement." *Los Angeles Times*, October 3, 2013.

Moll, Rob. "Day of Reckoning: Chuck Smith and Calvary Chapel Face an Uncertain Future." *Christianity Today International* (March 2007).

Parrott, Les, III, and Robin D. Perrin. "The New Denominations." *Christianity Today International* (March 11, 1991).

SOCIAL ACTION, EVANGELICALS AND

Evangelical responses to social problems and needs have been varied and without agreement on the nature of the problems or the best course of action for addressing them. Yet, a call to greater involvement in the larger American society was one of the key elements of the rise of postwar evangelicalism. What Carl F. H Henry (1913–2003) in the late 1940s and evangelical scholars today refer to as "social action," secular scholars often refer to as "social welfare," by which they mean any activity that tries to ameliorate human suffering and need in others. Other terms often used include "charity," "alms," "poor relief," "philanthropy," and "social reform."

Since the 1600s, there has been a recurring, doctrinal debate within evangelical communities about how social action fits within the work of the Church and message of Christianity. The principal plank in that debate concerns the prioritization of social action versus evangelism. No one appears to question the primacy of evangelism; the debate centers on the necessity of social action as a complement thereto. Bob Pierce (1914–1978), founder of the international relief organization World Vision, expressed the view of many evangelicals that social action is indispensable to evangelism, contending that one should not give the gospel to people with empty stomachs. Nevertheless, there are some who argue that social action is sufficient as a means of evangelism or as an end unto itself. This argument arose with the advent of modern social work as a profession in the early 20th century and tends to emphasize addressing the material interests, status struggles, or mental pathologies that give rise to human suffering over addressing sin and repentance.

Another plank in the debate among evangelicals concerns whether social action is an imperative for each individual believer or for the corporate church body. Colonial era Methodists and Puritans as well as more modern personalities like Ron Sider (1939–), Jim Wallis (1948–), and John Alexander contended that sin expresses itself socially as well as from person to person, and that the social manifestations of sin—slavery, pornography, human trafficking, injustice—require a corporate response from Christians. Only a few argue that individuals should not be involved with "loving their neighbor" (Matthew 22: 39) in tangible, practical ways. Nevertheless, since at least the 1970 triannual missions conference, *Urbana*, proponents of greater social action have contended with what they refer to as a "middle-class captivity" within U.S. churches that puts such a priority on "peaceful and quiet lives in all godliness and holiness" (1 Timothy 2:2) that crowds out social action if it does not rule out social action altogether, as it is much less peaceful and quiet by nature.

Rounding out the debate among evangelicals on social action is the issue of what exactly concerns the actual activity that qualifies as social action. Secular scholars have focused on the influence of religion on individuals' participation in principally four areas of activity: social work (as a profession), social justice, mass politics, and elite politics. Although there is a long history of evangelical involvement in social work and social justice, there is very little controversy about it. The participation of evangelicals in mass politics has largely split the U.S. evangelical community along both political lines and also partisan lines. Moreover, with Robert Putnam and David Campbell reporting substantial majorities of adults in the United States believing that churches and clergy should stay out of politics, overt evangelical involvement in mass politics and elite politics finds the least amount of approval within the evangelical community. To better understand the nature of this debate, the next section details evangelical involvement in each of these areas.

Evangelicals have a historic relationship with the social work profession. In the United States, social work as a profession began around the turn of the 20th century. It was not birthed out of a vacuum, but rather out of the enormous, though patchy, safety net of charity and benevolence societies operated largely by churches. Evangelicals supplied assistance out of notions of "practical care" to the poor to bring about their personal change and thereby social change. The commonly held belief was that this was the best means, versus government intervention, by which society was to be improved.

The social work profession began to distance itself from its evangelical underpinnings as the profession adopted techniques and theory informed by social science rather than by religious doctrine. In the modern and postmodern eras, social science disciplines, like other schools of thought, decidedly rejected any idea or tradition that argues that a human's worth or value system stems from any source other than the human him- or herself or from humanity collectively. This new ideological underpinning is echoed in social work training programs, which runs afoul

Four Significant Evangelical Agencies Providing Humanitarian Assistance

Compassion International (1952)
Living Water International (1990)
Samaritan's Purse (1970)
World Vision International (1950)

not only of evangelicals' religious doctrine but also their approach toward preparation for social action. Evangelicals then and now generally believe that the qualities necessary for charitable work are almost entirely spiritual. Nevertheless, in response to the labor market demand for professional training, especially in the government's social welfare interventions, many evangelicals pursue social work training, and several evangelical colleges offer such programs. However, the differences in ideology and perspectives on preparation has proven to make it almost impossible for evangelical institutions and associations of social welfare professionals to validate each other's contributions and to make it challenging for individual evangelicals to reconcile this secular ideology with their religious ideology.

Evangelicals have a long history of involvement in social justice efforts. Referred to also as social reform and social movements, social justice efforts generally involve public protests and other coordinated activity by large numbers of people with the goal of correcting something that is wrong in society by means of changing public policy. Notable U.S. examples of such movements that evangelicals have participated in include the colonial-era abolitionist campaign, the turn of the 20th-century temperance/Prohibition movement, the Civil Rights Movement, antiabortion efforts, and modern-day efforts to end human trafficking.

These movements are motivated by a belief that sin sometimes takes on a corporate form, leading to society condoning or even fostering sinful behavior. Depending on the movement, evangelicals have not always agreed on whether the social behavior constituted "sin." Particularly, with abolition and the Civil Rights Movement, a significant portion of the U.S. evangelical community stood against those movements.

It is interesting that U.S. colonial-era evangelicals believed that private action, not government intervention, was the best way to address human suffering due to poverty or illness and such, yet appear not to have hesitated to involve the government to rid the society of its ills. Also interesting is that social justice is the one area of social action that secular U.S. society has largely validated, if not welcomed. Although evangelicals tapered off their social welfare activities, particularly in education and health care, in response to government expansion into that area and to the "Separation of Church and State" doctrine established by the U.S. Supreme Court (*Everson v. Board of Education*, 330 U.S. 1 1947), few in the evangelical community or in the secular culture argue that the Church should stay out of these matters. In fact, the argument is often the opposite—that religious leaders are often called on to use their moral authority and influence over their membership to aid these efforts at social change. Political scientists Edward Carmines and James Stimson point out in their 1989 book *Issue Evolution* that evangelicals are welcomed because these movements center on "valence issues," or issues about which voters usually share a common preference, on which there is a "right" side and a "wrong" side, and public opinion generally agrees on which is which. On nonvalence issues, evangelical agreement and involvement is fraught with much more tension and disagreement.

Some might disagree with the categorization of abortion as a valence issue. Abortion can be considered a valence issue when recognizing that even in 2015 most polls reveals that only 25 percent of U.S. adults support abortion without restrictions; thus, 75 percent consider it "bad" in some sense. The "right" to an abortion specifically splits the country roughly right down the middle, which indicates that many adults who think that abortion is bad nevertheless want it to be legal. Issues with such a 50–50 split in public opinion, tap what researchers call "cleavages," and political parties often use these issues to motivate voters toward their candidates during election season. The social action around these issues is often called mass politics (sometimes terms like "electoral politics" or "partisan politics" are also used). Generally, evangelicals are rarely involved institutionally in mass politics, with notable exceptions, except in providing congregants with basic assistance like helping folks register to vote. Such institutional involvement, though popular in the 1980s and 1990s, has largely fallen out of favor among evangelicals and the larger public.

Robert Putnam and David Campbell, in their 2010 book *American Grace*, point out how U.S. adults are very comfortable with people of differing religious traditions, including those with no religion per se. That comfort disappears even within religious circles when dealing with two political issues—abortion (mentioned above) and gay marriage (as representative of the issues of sexual orientation, gender identity, and gender expression). Because of the Republican and Democratic parties' stances on these two issues, voters, including evangelical ones, readily identify with one political party or the other and tend to relocate themselves geographically and socially into settings where they will be among like-minded individuals, as Bill Bishop points out in 2008 in *The Big Sort*. Granted, there is more agreement on these issues within the evangelical community than between evangelicals and the nonreligious, but evangelicals tend to sort themselves on whether these two issues or issues of social justice should dominate their vote choice. Personalities and movements that affiliate more with the Republican Party and prioritize (against) abortion and sexuality politics include the Ralph Reed Jr. (1961–), Rev. Jerry Falwell (1933–2007), the *Moral Majority*, and the *Christian Coalition*. On the other side, often characterized as the Religious Left or Christian Left, include figures like John Sider and Jim Wallis, who prioritize antipoverty and social justice and tend to affiliate with the Democratic Party.

Sociologist Michael Lindsay is a leading researcher on evangelical involvement in elite politics, which can be understood as the political activities and relationships among individuals whose positions in government imbue them with direct influence over public policy. Research along these lines tends to be very recent and to focus on chronicling and/or quantifying the amount of influence evangelical ideology or institutions has among political elites. It is unquestionable that religion in general, and Christianity in particular, were prominent ideologies among political elites prior to the 1960s. Yet such ideology remains substantially influential today, in spite of the increasing diversity of thought and practice in elite circles. This is particularly true as evangelical institutions (e.g. denominations, ministries, colleges) become both more active and astute at using their large memberships to persuade elected officials.

Marvin McNeese Jr.

See also: Abortion, Evangelicals and; African American Evangelicalism; Civil Rights Movement, Evangelicals and; Environment, Evangelicals and the; Evangelicalism; *Evangelicals & Catholics Together*; Falwell, Jerry L., Sr.; Foreign Policy, Evangelicals and; Fundamentalism; Hispanic American Evangelicals; Human Rights, Evangelicals and; Israel, Evangelicals and; Moral Majority; National Black Evangelical Association; Politics, Evangelicals and; Sider, Ronald James; Southern Bible Institute; Wallis, Jim

Further Reading

Gasaway, Brantley W. *Progressive Evangelicals and the Pursuit of Social Justice.* Chapel Hill, NC: University of North Carolina Press, 2014.

Lindsay, D. Michael. *Faith in the Halls of Power: How Evangelicals Joined the American Elite.* New York: Oxford University Press, 2007.

Putnam, Robert D., and David E. Campbell. *American Grace: How Religion Divides and Unites Us.* New York: Simon & Schuster, 2010.

Swartz, David R. *Moral Minority: The Evangelical Left in an Age of Conservatism.* Philadelphia: University of Pennsylvania Press, 2012.

Young, Michael P. *Bearing Witness Against Sin: The Evangelical Birth of the American Social Movement.* Chicago: University of Chicago Press, 2006.

SOJOURNERS

Sojourners is the leading organization within a minority faction of politically progressive evangelicals, or the evangelical left, that arose in the 1970s. Its eponymous magazine, *Sojourners*, became the most influential progressive evangelical publication while also attracting mainline Protestant and Roman Catholic supporters. Under the leadership of Jim Wallis (1948–), Sojourners has attempted to challenge all Christians—especially conservative evangelicals—to promote social justice as both a religious concern and political priority.

Sojourners began in 1971 with a small group of Trinity Evangelical Divinity School students disillusioned by most evangelicals' support for the Vietnam War and apparent apathy toward racism, poverty, and other social problems. Led by Wallis, they formed the People's Christian Coalition and began publishing a homespun magazine under the title *Post-American*. Articles combined biblical interpretations with leftist critiques of the United States, as authors proclaimed that a holistic understanding of the Christian gospel should produce "radical" disciples committed not only to spiritual renewal but also to social justice. The confrontational style of the People's Christian Coalition and its liberal politics provoked controversy and criticism. But widespread distribution of the *Post-American* and Wallis's speaking engagements increased its following. Members withdrew from seminary, formed an intentional community in Chicago, and dedicated themselves to publicizing their message. In 1975, after internal disagreements fractured the original community, Wallis and some members relocated to Washington, D.C., and renamed both their community and magazine Sojourners. Over the coming decades, members of the Sojourners community engaged in urban ministries, participated in both local and national campaigns and protests, and continued to publish their magazine.

Based on their biblical interpretations of social justice, Sojourners promoted an unusual combination of political positions. Their opposition to systemic racism led them to support affirmative action programs and to condemn American support for South Africa's apartheid regime. Sojourners endorsed the feminist movement and the Equal Rights Amendment, calling for women's full equality in both society and religious ministries. In terms of economic justice, they championed effective state-sponsored welfare programs and redistributive policies while denouncing tax cuts for the wealthy enacted by Presidents Ronald Reagan and George W. Bush. Sojourners' commitments to nonviolence and antinationalism led them to oppose the United States' Cold War militarism, interventions in Central America in the 1980s, the 1991 Gulf War, and the post-9/11 invasion and occupation of Iraq. By the 21st century, Sojourners also promoted environmental regulations and called for protective measures to ensure the rights of immigrants.

Although these more liberal positions estranged their relationship with the Religious Right and other conservatives, Sojourners also frustrated the political left. They identified as "pro-life," viewing abortion as violence against vulnerable unborn children. Though Sojourners defended gay civil rights, leaders long refused to affirm the morality of same-sex relationships. In 2013, however, Wallis endorsed same-sex marriage, and Sojourners began featuring the perspectives of LGBT Christians.

Although the intentional community disbanded in the late 1990s, as an organization Sojourners has remained prominent in inspiring progressive evangelicals and ecumenical allies to pursue social justice as part of their religious calling.

Brantley W. Gasaway

See also: African American Evangelicalism; Civil Rights Movement, Evangelicals and; Environment, Evangelicals and the; Evangelicalism; *Evangelicals & Catholics Together*; Foreign Policy, Evangelicals and; Fundamentalism; Hispanic American Evangelicals; Human Rights, Evangelicals and; Israel, Evangelicals and; National Black Evangelical Association; Politics, Evangelicals and; Sider, Ronald James; Southern Bible Institute; Wallis, Jim

Further Reading

Bivins, Jason. *The Fracture of Good Order: Christian Antiliberalism and the Challenge to American Politics.* Chapel Hill, NC: University of North Carolina Press, 2003.

Gasaway, Brantley W. *Progressive Evangelicals and the Pursuit of Social Justice*. Chapel Hill, NC: University of North Carolina Press, 2014.

Swartz, David R. *Moral Minority: the Evangelical Left in an Age of Conservatism*. Philadelphia: University of Pennsylvania Press, 2012.

Wallis, Jim. *Revive Us Again: a Sojourner's Story*. Nashville, TN: Abingdon Press, 1983.

SOUTHERN BIBLE INSTITUTE

Southern Bible Institute is a nondenominational Bible school, offering certificates, diplomas, and undergraduate degrees (Bachelor of Arts and Bachelor of Science) in Bible and Theology, located in Dallas, Texas. The institute's origins and focus is historical within evangelicalism in view of the racial divide, problems, and tensions that created the need to train African American pastors and laypeople for the ministry.

The school traces its founding to 1927 as the Dallas Colored Bible Institute, when Edmund H. Ironside—at the time a student at Dallas Theological Seminary—noted a desire among African American ministers for formal theological training and academic study of the Bible, and began meeting with three young men preparing for ministry. Classes initially met in Ironside's Dallas home, and he served as its lone professor and first president.

Originally chartered in 1937 as the Southern Bible Training School, the school's stated purpose was to ensure that quality theological education was made available to all persons, though it clearly targeted African American ministers and laypersons, who were not, at that time, admitted to the theological schools in the Dallas–Fort Worth area and were generally underprivileged. Its original charter, therefore, states that its policy is to charge no tuition and to provide textbooks and supplies at cost to students. Since then, the school has admitted students from all nationalities and races and has had an average enrollment of approximately 500, but still focuses on the unique needs of Dallas's African American community and strives to keep costs to a minimum.

Evangelical Statement of Faith and Recent Court Case

Although governed by a self-perpetuating board, the Southern Bible Institute has a strict statement of faith that includes elements that are evangelical, exclusivist, premillennial, and cessationist, and that oppose sinless perfectionism, to which all board members, administrators, and faculty must subscribe.

The school was involved in a successful case (joining Tyndale Theological Seminary in Fort Worth and Hispanic Bible Institute in San Antonio) against the State of Texas Higher Education Coordinating Board, which required accreditation in order to confer degrees. The Texas Supreme Court ruled that the requirement violated the First Amendment rights of the schools. In 2006, Martin E. Hawkins was installed as the school's fourth president and its first African American president.

Notwithstanding, Lester Huber (1941–1945) was installed as "Superintendent," though he could be considered the school's second president, making Hawkins its fifth president. The school illustrates the importance evangelicals place on knowledge of and education in the biblical text and is an example of the Bible institute and Bible college phenomena in American evangelicalism since the early 20th century.

John D. Laing

See also: African American Evangelicalism; Bible Institutes and Bible Colleges; Dallas Theological Seminary; Social Action, Evangelicals and

Further Reading

Anderson, James D. *The Education of Blacks in the South, 1860–1935.* Chapel Hill, NC: University of North Carolina, 1988.

Cooks, Michael J. F. "The Historical Development and Future of the Southern Bible Institute." EdD diss., University of North Texas, 2008.

Daniel, William Andrew. *The Education of Negro Ministers.* New York: Negro Universities Press, 1969.

Mays, Benjamin Elijah. "The Significance of the Negro Private and Church-Related Colleges." *Journal of Negro Education* 29:3 (1960): 245–51.

Mumford, Gordon R. "Southern Bible Institute: The History from 1927 to 1992." PhD diss., Tyndale Theological Seminary, 1998. http://www.southernbible.org.

SWINDOLL, CHARLES R. ("CHUCK") (1934–)

Charles Rozell ("Chuck") Swindoll (1934–) is an evangelical pastor, educator, and popular author. He is most recognized by his founding of the ministry *Insight for Living*, a radio program that is aired currently in all 50 states and across the world in multiple languages. Best known for his exposition and application of the Scriptures, his popular books on Christian living, and his international broadcasts, his 30 years of pastoring congregations equipped him to become both an international radio Bible preacher and also the fourth president of Dallas Theological Seminary (established in 1924). Swindoll's ministry is not only cross-cultural but also cross-generational; he became a fixture of both the study of and personal application of Bible exposition across the spectrum of evangelicalism and beyond. Chuck, and his wife and partner in ministry, Cynthia, have four grown children, 10 grandchildren, and two great-grandchildren.

Swindoll was born in the small town of El Campo, Texas, just southwest of Houston. He attended Milby High School in Houston during his later teenage years. On graduation, he entered military service with the United States Marine Corps. His tour of duty led him to San Francisco and then to the Japanese island Okinawa. Following his honorable discharge in 1959, Swindoll attended Dallas Theological

Seminary, where he graduated magna cum laude. Along with other awards, Swindoll received the prestigious Harry A. Ironside Award for Expository Preaching (1963).

In 1963, Swindoll was ordained into Christian ministry. From 1963 to 1965, he served at Grace Bible Church in Dallas, Texas, as an assistant pastor under Dr. J. Dwight Pentecost (1915–2014), who became renowned for Bible teaching and dispensational scholarship at Dallas Theological Seminary. Then in 1965, Swindoll began his first senior pastorate in Waltham, Massachusetts, at Waltham Evangelical Free Church. He served there two years and then moved to Irving Bible Church in Irving, Texas, where he served till 1971. Swindoll moved from Irving, Texas, to Fullerton, California, to become the senior pastor of First Evangelical Free, where he served from 1971 to 1994. In 1977, Swindoll received an honorary Doctor of Divinity from Talbot Theological Seminary. Then in 1986, he received an honorary Doctor of Humane Letters from Taylor University. Swindoll received a Clergyman of the Year—Religious Heritage of America award in 1988. In 1990, he received an honorary Doctor of Laws from Pepperdine University. In 1998, Swindoll also received an honorary Doctor of Literature from Dallas Baptist University.

In 1994, Swindoll moved back to Dallas, Texas, to become the fourth president of the Dallas Theological Seminary, and now serves as the school's chancellor. Unlike his predecessors, Dr. Lewis S. Chafer (1871–1952), the seminary's founding president, and Dr. John F. Walvoord (1910–2002), the seminary's longest serving president, Swindoll became the first president without an earned undergraduate degree on July 1, 1994. He had received a certificate of graduate studies after he completed the ThM program because he never earned an undergraduate degree. His leadership style as president is described as people centered, with traditional theological convictions but open-minded in view of considering and reflecting on other arguments, positions, and challenges. Though Swindoll brought both numerical growth and financial stability to Dallas Theological Seminary, perhaps his greatest impact was his repeated emphasis and exhortation to the student body, faculty, and alums to be people of virtue, possessing moral excellence and spiritual integrity. In 1998, Swindoll established Stonebriar Community Church in Frisco, Texas, where he continues to serve as senior pastor.

Key Term in Evangelicalism: *Identity in Christ*

Evangelicals believe that Christian living is allowing Jesus Christ by means of the Holy Spirit to live in and through their lives. On receiving the gift of salvation by means of placing their faith in Christ, evangelicals believe Christians receive a "new self," which is historically termed as a "new nature." Consequently, they contend that Christians are spiritually and dynamically related to Christ in such a way that they are capable of true, authentic spirituality, growth, and spiritual maturity (Galatians 2:20; John 15; Romans 6:4–5; 2 Corinthians 4:10–11).

Swindoll's popularity and influence with a wide range of audiences results from his style of biblical exposition whereby he is able to reach people where they are in a very comprehensible way; in addition, he also often teaches about the biblical teachings of grace, namely, the nature and value of God's undeserved favor and the importance of extending God's grace to others as people seek to live life with all of its tragedies, obstacles, and successes. He also uses dramatic storytelling techniques, wisdom, and personal accounts to illustrate practical applications that resonate cross-culturally. As a result of the form, content, and delivery of his messages, Swindoll was named one of the top 12 preachers in the nation by the Effective Preachers Program of Baylor University and George W. Truett Theological Seminary in 1997.

Insight for Living, Swindoll's radio ministry, founded in 1979, launched Swindoll into the national and then international spotlight and is now heard on more than 2,000 stations as well as webcasts, and is translated into several different languages. The ministry was moved from California to Texas when he accepted the ministry position at Stonebriar. Swindoll's radio ministry has received other awards such as Program of the Year, National Religious Broadcasters (1994), the Religious Broadcaster of the Year, National Religious Broadcasters (1999), and Hall of Fame Award, National Religious Broadcasters (2000). His wife, Cynthia, serves as president and CEO for *Insight for Living*.

Swindoll has also authored more than 60 books. His first book, *You and Your Child*, was published in 1977. Some of his later works include *The Grace Awakening* (1990), *Hope Again* (1996), and *Hear Me When I Call: Learning to Connect with a God Who Cares* (2013). Swindoll has also taught Bible commentary series such as *Insights on Romans* (2010), *Insights on James and 1 & 2 Peter* (2010), and *Insights on Luke* (2012). He also has taught Bible character profiles series such as *David: A Man of Passion & Destiny* (1997), *Paul: A Man of Grace and Grit* (2002), and *Jesus: The Greatest Life of All* (2008). Consequently, Swindoll received the Gold Medallion Lifetime Achievement Award by the Evangelical Press Association in 1997. Swindoll has been awarded 12 Gold Medallion Awards.

Christianity Today celebrated his 50th anniversary in ministry by publishing an article naming Swindoll as one of the top 25 most influential preachers of the past 50 years from 1956–2006. In 2009, Swindoll received a Lifetime Achievement Award at the Catalyst Conference. Dr. Swindoll was ranked only second to the Reverend Billy Graham in a 2009 survey that asked 800 Protestant pastors to name the living Christian preachers who most influenced them.

In sum, Dr. Swindoll's ministry spans more than five decades of service while reaching countless listeners through both national and international media outlets. Swindoll attributes his time in the military to be a major factor in his writing as well as his experience in pastoral ministry. He also credits as a major influence his theological training from Dallas Theological Seminary and the men who served on the faculty who deeply invested their time and skill into him.

Tracy L. Winkler

See also: Bible Exposition; Chafer, Lewis Sperry; Dallas Theological Seminary; Dispensationalism; Ryrie, Charles Caldwell; Walvoord, John F.

Further Reading

Hannah, John D. *An Uncommon Union: Dallas Theological Seminary and American Evangelicalism.* Grand Rapids, MI: Zondervan, 2009. http://www.insight.org/about/chuck-swindoll.html?ga=topnav-about-L2.

Mauldlin, Michael G. "Dallas' New Dispensation: An Interview with Charles Swindoll." *Christianity Today* 37 (25 October 1993).

TADA, JONI EARECKSON (1949–)

Joni Eareckson Tada, founder of Joni and Friends International Disability Center, is a world-renowned author, speaker, and radio host. Born October 15, 1949, in Baltimore, Maryland, Joni enjoyed a quiet childhood. At age 17, she miscalculated the depth of water while diving into the Chesapeake Bay, which resulted in a fracture of her spinal cord between the fourth and fifth cervical levels. Completely paralyzed, including no use of her hands, Joni became a quadriplegic on July 30, 1967.

Initially, she experienced anger, depression, suicidal thoughts, and doubt. Struggling to find purpose in her injury, Joni turned to the Lord for understanding. She emerged from rehabilitation with a greater belief in the sovereignty of God and his purpose to use her disability to reach others with the gospel.

In 1979, Joni founded Joni and Friends, an advocacy center for people with disabilities. The organization legally changed its name to Joni and Friends International Disability Center in 2006. The vision of Joni and Friends International Disability Center is to "to accelerate Christian ministry in the disability community." Their mission is "to communicate the gospel and equip Christ-honoring churches worldwide to evangelize and disciple people affected by disabilities."

Joni and Friends accomplishes its mission through a variety of ministries, which assist local and international churches as well as communities. These ministries include the following:

- *Wheels for the World* shares the gospel while providing mobility to disabled children and adults by distributing free wheelchairs around the globe. Joni and Friends Radio shares biblical insight, hope, and encouragement through five- and one-minute radio spots.
- *Christian Institute on Disability (CID)* seeks to educate, train, and write public policy relating to disability and the disabled. CID serves to advocate for the sanctity of human life in concord with the value and dignity to the unborn and born.
- *Cause 4 Life* seeks to educate, train, and activate the next generation of global leaders to advocate for the world's disabled, primarily through global missions and internship programs.
- *Total Access* functions to make everyday environments more accessible to the disabled, whether through building ramps, widening doors, or constructing homes. Total Access joins Wheels for the World in sharing the gospel through meeting daily mobility needs.

- *Team MED* offers outreach opportunities to medically trained professionals, including therapists, to offer a better quality of life for those with disabilities. Team MED works alongside community leaders and other individuals to share the love of Christ tangibly with medical care. Family and International Retreats serve families around the globe who live with and care for the disabled.

Eareckson married Ken Tada in 1982, 16 years after her accident. In 2013, they cowrote the book *Joni and Ken: An Untold Love Story*, chronicling their love story and the realities about marriage to a quadriplegic.

Tada's bestselling autobiography, *Joni*, recounts her journey through quadriplegia. From this book came a feature film by the same title. It has been translated into numerous languages. Joni has also authored more than 70 additional books related to suffering, healing, faith, and Christian living.

She holds a Bachelor of Letters from Western Maryland College. Many institutions have awarded her honorary doctorates including the following: Doctor of Humanities from Gordon College; Doctor of Humane Letters from Columbia International University (the first honorary degree given in their 75-year history); Doctor of Divinity from Westminster Theological Seminary; Doctor of Divinity from Lancaster Bible College; Doctor of Laws from Biola University; and Doctor of Humane Letters from Indiana Wesleyan University.

Tada's ministry extends beyond the walls of Joni and Friends and is globally recognized. She served on the National Council on Disability and the Disability Advisory Committee to the U.S. State Department in 2005, as well as under the Reagan and first Bush administrations. She accepted a position as Senior Associate for Disability Concerns for the Lausanne Committee for World Evangelism. In 1993, Tada became the first woman chosen for Layperson of the Year by the National Association of Evangelicals. Her voice has been heard on Larry King Live and ABC World News Tonight, and her writings have appeared in *Christianity Today* and *World* magazine. In 2010, Joni received a new diagnosis, breast cancer. She underwent chemotherapy treatments and is now in remission.

Joni is also a singer. She performed "Alone Yet Not Alone," composed by Bruce Broughton and lyricist Dennis Spiegel, for the same-titled feature film. The film depicts a German family and their immigration to the Americas in the mid-1700s. The song received an Oscar nomination, which the Academy later rescinded.

Tada's life echoes her words: "Sometimes God uses what he hates to accomplish what he loves." She believes that her choice to remain faithful in the midst of continual suffering points the disabled and abled toward the truth of God's sovereignty in the midst of all things. As an individual with disabilities, she has been an advocate and leader in evangelicalism for the integration of evangelical theology with bioethics and social concerns.

Sandra Glahn and Marnie Blackstone Legaspi

See also: Ethics, Evangelical Theories of

Further Reading

Bailey, Sarah Pulliam, Joni Eareckson Tada, and Ken Tada. "Suffering Servants: Chronic Pain and Depression Taught Joni Eareckson and Ken Tada to Put Each Other's Needs First." *Christianity Today* 57:3 (April 1, 2013): 69.

"About Us." Joni and Friends. (n.d.). Accessed April 20, 2017. http://www.joniandfriends .org/about-us/.

Tada, Joni Eareckson. *Joni: An Unforgettable Story.* Grand Rapids, MI: Zondervan, 1976.

Tada, Joni Eareckson. *The God I Love: A Lifetime of Walking with Jesus.* Grand Rapids, MI: Zondervan, 2003.

Tada, Joni Eareckson. "God Permits What He Hates." Joni and Friends. (May 15, 2013). http://www.joniandfriends.org/radio/5-minute/god-permits-what-he-hates1/.

Tada, Joni Eareckson, and Sarah Pulliam Bailey. "Something Greater Than Healing: Joni Eareckson Tada, Now Facing Breast Cancer and Chronic Pain, Talks about the Blessings of Suffering." *Christianity Today* 54:10 (October 1, 2010): 30–33.

Tracy, Kate. "Academy Disqualifies Joni Eareckson Tada's Oscar-Nominated Song from Christian Movie." *Christianity Today* (blog), January 30, 2014. http://www.christianitytoday .com/gleanings/2014/january/oscar-best-song-alone-yet-not-alone-joni-eareckson -tada.html?paging=off.

TALBOT SCHOOL OF THEOLOGY

The Talbot School of Theology (Talbot) is a nondenominational seminary located in La Mirada, California. The school is a leading evangelical seminary with an orthodox and theologically conservative premillennial theology. The doctrinal statement of the school affirms biblical inerrancy, Trinitarianism, salvation by faith in Christ alone, that life begins at conception, and marriage as between a man and woman only. The stated mission of Talbot is "the development of disciples of Jesus Christ whose thought processes, character and lifestyles reflect those of our Lord, and who are dedicated to disciple making throughout the world." Talbot focuses on the spiritual development of its students, consistent with biblical doctrine, and defines its purpose as "to develop in the lives of its students a spiritual life which is in harmony with the great doctrines taught, in order that they may grow in the grace as well as in the knowledge of our Lord and Savior Jesus Christ." Specifically, the seminary's goal is to educate and graduate students characterized by practical Christian service, missionary and evangelistic zeal, and an adequate knowledge of the Scriptures.

Talbot grew out of Biola University, which was founded in 1908 to equip men and women to be effective ministers of the gospel in a world that was becoming increasingly secular. In 1952, during his last year as Biola's president, Talbot worked to establish a fully accredited theological seminary. The seminary's first dean was noted Christian scholar Charles Feinberg, who, along with his colleagues, unanimously voted to name the seminary "Talbot Theological Seminary." Talbot has approximately 1,200 students, 70 full-time faculty members, and 50 part-time faculty. The school is accredited by the Western Association of Schools and Colleges. Talbot first became accredited in 1978 by Association of Theological Schools (ATS) in the United States. ATS is an organization of seminaries and other graduate schools of theology that provides graduate schools of theology with accreditation. Master of Arts, Master of Divinity, Master of Theology, and three doctoral (PhD) programs are offered in areas of study that include Bible exposition, New Testament and Old Testament, philosophy, theology, Christian education, pastoral care, evangelism and educational studies. Talbot offers online courses, and students may complete up to 50 percent of degree programs online. Notable faculty members include New Testament scholar Clinton T. Arnold (1958–) and philosopher William Lane Craig (1949–), both of whom are well regarded Christian theologians with a great number of books and scholarly articles in the area of Christian theology and apologetics. Arnold is the current dean of Talbot.

Katherine Pang

See also: Bible Exposition; Biola University; Christian Apologetics; Ethics, Evangelical Theories of; Evangelicalism; Inerrancy; Neo-Evangelicalism; Philosophy, Evangelicals and

Further Reading

Craig, William Lane, and Moreland, J. P. *Philosophical Foundations of a Christian Worldview.* Downers Grove, IL: InterVarsity Press, 2003.

Craig, William Lane. *Reasonable Faith*, 3rd ed. Grand Rapids, MI: Crossway, 2008.

Rae, Scott B. *Moral Choices: An Introduction to Ethics*, 3rd ed. Grand Rapids, MI: Zondervan, 1995, 2009.

Talbot School of Theology, Biola University. (n.d.). Accessed April 30, 2017. http://www.talbot.edu.

TENTH PRESBYTERIAN CHURCH (PHILADELPHIA)

Tenth Presbyterian Church is one of America's historic evangelical churches. It has a congregation of 1,500 members and is located in downtown Philadelphia, Pennsylvania. It is a biblical, confessional, and Presbyterian Church with a faith statement that affirms as their source for everything they believe to be inspiration, inerrancy, and authority of the Scripture (2 Timothy 3:16–17).

The church is located in Philadelphia's Rittenhouse Square neighborhood. Tenth Presbyterian Church of Philadelphia grew out of the Sixth Church in March 1829. It later merged with its daughter church, the West Spruce Street Church, in 1895 and retained its name. The Tenth Presbyterian Church is a member of the Presbyterian Church in America (PCA), which is in the Reformed and Calvinistic tradition. As a church of the PCA, it affirms the infallible and inerrant authority of the Bible as outlined in the distinctive doctrines of the Westminster Standards and Reformed tradition.

During the Fundamentalist–Modernist Controversy of the 1920s and 1930s, the Philadelphia Presbytery (PCUSA) was a center of conservative Presbyterianism. Tenth Presbyterian became the conservative Presbyterian Church in Center City of

Philadelphia, and this distinction persists. The membership embraced conservative Reformed theology under the leadership of Senior Pastors Donald G. Barnhouse (1927–1960) and James Montgomery Boice (1968–2000). Post–World War II saw a growth in ministry. The United Presbyterian Church in the United States of America in 1979 ruled that all congregations elect both men and women to the office of ruling elder. Tenth Presbyterian withdrew from the UPCUSA in 1980 and subsequently aligned itself with the Reformed Presbyterian Church, Evangelical Synod. Three years later, that denomination merged with the Presbyterian Church in American, taking Tenth Church as well. The congregation pursued a lengthy property battle that allowed it to leave the denomination yet retain its facilities. The churches ministries include a wide missions program and a medical campus outreach to area neighborhoods with doctors from nearby medical schools. Philip G. Ryken (1966–) served as senior pastor from 1995–2010 and is now president of Wheaton College. Liam Goligher currently serves as senior minister, beginning May 22, 2011, to present. It remains a vital worshiping congregation with a history of influencing evangelicals in America from within the Reformed tradition.

J. Craig Kubic

See also: Bible, Authority of; Boice, James Montgomery; Calvinism; Fuller Theological Seminary; Gordon-Conwell Theological Seminary; Henry, Carl F. H.; Inerrancy; Neo-Evangelicalism; Reformed Tradition, Evangelicalism and

Further Reading

Boice, James Montgomery, Allen C. Guelzo, and Timothy Clark Lemmer. *Making God's Word Plain: One Hundred and Fifty Years in the History of Tenth Presbyterian Church of Philadelphia.* Philadelphia: The Church, 1979.

Ryken, Philip, ed. *Tenth Presbyterian Church of Philadelphia: 175 years of Thinking and Acting Biblically.* Phillipsburg, NJ: P&R, 2004.

White, William P. "Presbyterian Churches of Philadelphia: Their Organization and Changes of Location and Name." *Journal of the Presbyterian Historical Society.* Vol. VII, No. 6 (June 1914): 257–273.

THEOLOGICAL CONTROVERSIES WITHIN EVANGELICALISM

American evangelicalism is not monolithic with respect to theology. Evangelicals have a theologically conservative framework with core beliefs, but within that framework there have been and are ongoing theological disagreements as well as controversies that have affected the movement as a whole.

General Background

Controversies in theology, like any discipline, augment, clarify, compel, define, and impact particular ideas, institutions, movements, critics, and contributors. Sources for controversies within evangelicalism are the same as for other theological perspectives (e.g., Roman Catholicism, liberalism, or neo-liberalism): the amalgamation of or separation from certain cultural, philosophical, political, psychological, sociological, or religious ideas, institutions, movements, and personalities. Central to theological controversies are personal biases and moldable influences, contextual setting, and personal experiences.

Theological controversies tend to mirror or follow contemporary currents in metaphysics, epistemology, ethics, and aesthetics. Thus, theological controversies emerge out of certain assimilations, moods, reactions, and consequences ranging from hermeneutics to criteria for justification, to theological truth-claims (e.g., direct realism; moderate realism; Kantian metaphysics and epistemology; modernism; postmodern critique; deontological ethics; virtue ethics).

Like philosophers, evangelical theologians discern, deliberate, and engage provocative beliefs, problems, and perplexities about death, decision-making, ethics, humanity, life, meaning, origins, purposes, the supernatural, values, and evil. They deal with worldview systems, sublime experiences, and historical events that shape people's lives and impact the way they look at the world and those things for which life is worth living. They consider the relationships of those controversies to individuality, the arts, the present state and future of society, and the preservation of what is good and beneficial.

Theological controversies deal with challenging questions and answers, motivating people to think, act, and reflect in various ways, bringing about the best and worst in people, congregations, institutional authorities, and subcultures. Theological controversies can be valuable, for they can expose implicit beliefs people possess, what assumptions they make about Scripture and their applicability to life, church, and other contexts in which people are embedded. But they can also be detrimental, for they can create sharp disunity, divisions, and displacement, existentially, physically, or collectively. Theological ideas have consequences. Therefore, some of the most notable theological controversies, perennial and contemporary, are evidenced in major evangelical doctrines.

Historically, evangelicals differ in the areas of what is called prolegomena—how theology should be done. Prolegomena refers to preliminary remarks that should be considered before one practices theology (e.g., hermeneutics, sources of theology, worldview systems, criteria for justifying truth claims, the art and science of doing theology). For example, conservative evangelicals, also known as traditionalists, contend that biblical doctrine is the essence of Christianity. Consequently, the Bible offers a collection of divine truths or facts within various literary genres that can be placed into theological systems of coherence, hence, biblical, systematic theology. What one believes in one doctrine will affect other doctrines. Yet evangelicals are criticized for not recognizing their own situatedness as heirs of the Enlightenment, ignoring the cultural, historical context in which those biblical truth claims are given and assimilated.

Fundamentalist–Modernist Controversy of the 1920s–1930s

Given the contextual challenges and tensions that were taking place intellectually, socially, and religiously with the rise of Darwinian thought, historical criticism, social sciences immigration, technological innovations, and economic transition from an agriculture base to industrialized urbanization, New Theology, liberal Protestantism, or "modernistic" theology found pertinent expression. Rather than rejecting ideas like evolutionary thought and German Higher Criticism, mainline Protestantism accommodated it, embracing the cultural mood of progress and believing in the goodness of humanity, the moral example of Jesus Christ, and the immanence of God. In contrast, conservative Christians believed that secularization was claiming a foothold in the United States, especially after World War I. The camps continued to form until they divided in 1922 following a liberal message by Harry Emerson Fosdick (1878–1969), who argued that conservatives should tolerate liberalism (theological pacifism). Following a keen response by Clarence E. Macartney (1879–1957), who asserted that one should contend against liberalism, not only for the sake of the church but also to preserve the influence of Christianity on society, a united front against modernistic liberalism arose with decades of controversies between the two parties. J. Gresham Machen (1881–1937), who authored the famous work, *Christianity and Liberalism* (1923), claimed liberal theology was devoid of the distinctives of the Christian faith, that it was an altogether different faith and that only the rebirth of Christianity can save the church and society.

Others known as reformists value envisioning and constructing theology in insightful ways without forsaking the larger evangelical paradigm of beliefs. Reformism (not the same as Reformed theology) has also been labeled as "postconservative evangelicalism." Reformism values the critique of authority structures as delineated in continental philosophy in order to free evangelicals from the vices of modernism. Thus, they welcome the deconstructive insights of postmodern thought, in various degrees, into their theological constructions.

Yet other reformists believe that the amalgamation of postmodernism, like modernism, is not only wrong but also detrimental to Christianity. Instead, they turn to the teachings and practices of the early years of Christianity in the hope of a purer orthodox theology. This type of approach is seen in terms of how certain emerging and emergent churches are redefining the nature of corporate worship by their ideas and practices.

Doctrinal Categories of Controversies

In bibliology (the study of the Bible), theological controversies involve the extent of the Bible's inspiration. Evangelicals have historically affirmed that the Bible in its original manuscripts is totally true and free from error, whether cultural, doctrine, ethics, geography, social, physical, or life sciences. Thus, inerrancy means that the Bible tells the truth even with the use of approximations, free quotations, and languages of appearances. This view of the Bible was affirmed by mainstream evangelicalism as late as 1978 with the International Council on Biblical Inerrancy.

But some have sought to distinguish inspiration from inerrancy. While believing the original manuscripts were divinely inspired, inerrancy is modified or restricted to matters of faith and practice. The errors remaining, though perhaps argued to be inconsequential by some, are in areas such as geography, history, or social, physical, and life sciences. Thus, the Bible is inspired but errant.

In theology proper (study of God and God's activities), three controversies are perennial in evangelicalism: the value of natural theology for the non-Christian and whether God has a specific will or divine design or purpose for each Christian or a general will or precepts for every believer to follow, and the Arminian-Calvinist debate that considers topics such as God's divine sovereignty, human freedom, pretemporal election, and predestination.

One of the most contentious debates in recent years is over evangelicals identifying with open theism (e.g., proponents such as Gregory Boyd, Clark Pinnock, Richard Rice, John Sanders). Akin to process theology and largely flowing from Arminian theology, open theism is the belief that since God's love involves care, commitment, sensitivity, and response, and humans can engage and influence God in that, history involves both God's will and human free will. Consequently, God grows in knowledge of events as events occur, thus dependent on our actions in some ways. God values libertarian freedom in view of God's love, for forced love is perceived as not true love. In part, open theism comes out of an Arminian dilemma, namely, if God foreknows everything, there can be no libertarian freedom. Rather than turning to the strict Calvinistic solution (the denial of human libertarian free will), open theists deny God's infinite, exhaustive divine foreknowledge.

Theology proper is often extended to science and creationism with evangelicals differing as to how Genesis 1–3 should be interpreted and how the teachings of Scripture relate to science (e.g., scientific creationism or young earth creationism, progressive creationism or day-age creationism, or theistic evolution). Moreover, the intelligent design movement (e.g., Michael Behe, William Dembski) with the Discovery Institute; the scholarship of evangelical scientist Francis Collins, both author of *The Language of God: A Scientists Presents Evidence for Belief* (2006) and founder of the BioLogos Foundation; the coherence of a biblical and holistic worldview (e.g., John Lennox, J. P. Moreland, Nancy Pearcey, Hugh Ross, Francis A. Schaeffer); the Veritas Forum across American colleges and universities; and the theistic critiques of naturalism by analytic evangelical philosophers such as Alvin Plantinga (*Where the Conflict Really Lies: Science, Religion, and Naturalism* [2011]) have redirected evangelicals to reconsider the compatibility between Christian faith and science, contending that faith is not an irrational leap, but a reliance on that which one has good reasons to believe are true and reliable. In other words, faith is not an irrational leap against evidences, but reliance on that which is compatible to what is factual and probable.

In Christology (the study of Christ), three prominent theological controversies stand out: the meaning of Christ's life sufferings (vicarious or non-atoning view), the impeccability versus peccability debate (whether or not Jesus Christ was able to sin), and the present and future ministry of Jesus Christ. Recent attention by evangelical New Testament theologians, historians, and philosophers to historical methodology (historiography), thus treating the New Testament as historical documents, and the exploration of other ancient evidences (e.g., Jewish, Gnostic, Roman) have caused a shift among many scholars to reconsider the historicity, the empty tomb, and post-resurrection appearances of Jesus Christ (e.g., Gary Habermas; N. T. Wright) given the historical impact of European theologians Rudolf Bultmann (1884–1976) and Karl Barth (1886–1968).

In pneumatology (the study of the Holy Spirit), controversies largely revolve around the meaning and timing of the Holy Spirit's baptism (1 Corinthians 12:12–13), the use of the "sign gifts" of the Holy Spirit, and the role of the Holy Spirit in sanctification (the ongoing spirituality of the individual Christian). Perhaps most controversial is whether the "sign gifts" of the Holy Spirit, namely, healings, miracles, prophecies, and *glossolalia* ("speaking in tongues") are present today. There are at least six views: (1) hyper-cessationism: nonuse of all the gifts of the Holy Spirit (e.g., Gene Getz); (2) cessationism: nonuse of the "sign gifts only"; all other gifts are operative for today (e.g., evangelism, giving, teaching). The "sign gifts" ceased with both the death of the Apostles and the complete writing of the Scriptures (e.g., John F. MacArthur Jr., Charles C. Ryrie, John F. Walvoord); (3) soft cessationism: the "sign gifts" of the Holy Spirit are practiced where the church is not yet established, for example, with "unreached people groups" or in a particular tribal area; (4) open-but-cautious viewpoint: the "sign gifts" are operative for today but are not to be emphasized (e.g., Robert Saucy). The other gifts of the Holy Spirit such as evangelism, teaching, and giving, as well as the biblical mandate to love other, are to be stressed. The open-but-cautious view takes into account critiques made or abuses observed by both cessationists and charismatics; (5) charismatic theology: this affirms all gifts of the Spirit are valid for today, just as they were on the day of Pentecost (Acts 2) (e.g., John Wimber). But charismatics differ on whether the baptism of the Holy Spirit is subsequent of salvation and if tongues are required for evidence for that special event. (6) Pentecostal: the gifts of the Holy Spirit are not only valid for today, as they were on the Day of Pentecost, but are subsequent to personal salvation. The baptism of the Holy Spirit will be evidenced by the speaking of tongues (e.g., Pentecostal denominations such as the Assemblies of God).

In sanctification, that is, the setting apart of people to God and their positional and ongoing spiritual conformity or maturity to Jesus Christ, evangelicals differ on how Christians grow in spiritual maturity. The debate typically centers on the nature of both God's work and the Christian's work in sanctification (e.g., Wesleyan model, Keswick model, Reformed model, Chaferian or Augustinian-dispensational model).

In angelology (study of angels), demonology (study of demons), and Satanology (study of Satan), the identity of the Sons of God in Genesis 6:2, the "Spirits in Prison" in 1 Peter 3:19, the fall and sin of Satan in Isaiah 14:12–20 and Ezekiel 28:15, and whether demons can possess Christians in view of passages such as 1 Samuel 16:13–14; Luke 13:11–16; Acts 5:4; 1 Corinthians 5:5; 2 Corinthians 11:4, 12:7 are all widely debated.

One of the most significant controversies where evangelicals hold polarizing views involves the doctrine of creation as it relates to the origins of humanity (guided theistic evolution; directed theistic evolution; direct and immediate creation by God by His command (e.g., Genesis 2:7; Psalm 33:6–9; Hebrews 11:3), the nature of humans (dichotomy vs. trichotomy), the transmission of the immaterial aspects of humanity (creationism or traducianism), and how sin spreads from Adam to humanity (federal headship vs. seminal headship) in view of Romans 5:12–21.

The perennial controversies are perhaps not as difficult as recent ones that involve the nature and roles of biblical masculinity and femininity; women in ministry; homosexuality and God, the Bible, and the church; sexual fluidity; cohabitation and premarital sex; abortion; selective genetic engineering; and natural moral law. These issues affect church–state relations, evangelical models of ethics, and evangelical engagement with culture and the political domain.

Within soteriology (the study of salvation), there are a number of debatable issues: (1) the nature of election: divine election (whether pretemporal, particular, and unconditional; particular, but not conditional; or corporate election of church body); (2) the extent of the atonement, whether limited, particular, or unlimited; (3) whether one can lose salvation (eternal security); (4) what is essential for salvation (e.g., Free Grace vs. Lordship Salvation); (5) What assurances one needs to have in order to know one is genuinely a Christian; (6) the salvation of the unborn, infants, and those who cannot believe (also titled as "infant salvation"); (7) The evidence of salvation and/or the relationship between faith and works. The recent debate known as Free Grace vs. Lordship Salvation is significant and has involved evangelical scholars such as Wayne Grudem, Zane Hodges, Robert P. Lightner, John F. MacArthur Jr., Charles Ryrie, Charles Swindoll, and Bob Wilkin.

In ecclesiology (the study of the church), controversies include the denial of the universal church, the beginnings of the Church, the plurality of elders in every local church, the office of deaconesses, the mode of Christians' baptism, the Lord's Table, and the government of the local church. Particularly controversial is the nature and methodology of corporate church worship given the contemporary emergence of a post-Christian society with various models identified as being traditional, seeker-sensitive, emerging, and emergent.

Lastly, in eschatology (the study of the end times), certain controversies are long-standing: the nature and meaning of the biblical covenants (e.g., Abrahamic Covenant, Genesis 12:1–3; Land Covenant, Deuteronomy 30:1–10; Davidic Covenant, 2 Samuel 7:12–16, and New Covenant, Jeremiah 31:31–34), and the nature and timing of the rapture, whether midtribulational (e.g., Gleason Archer), partial

---

Evangelical Views on Hell

Based on biblical terms like *Sheol* (used 65 times) in Biblical Hebrew and *Hades* (10 times) and *Gehenna* (12 times) in New Testament Greek, there are four major views among evangelicals about the final destiny of those who reject the gospel of Jesus Christ:

1. *Literal:* Hell is both a literal place and state that is forever punitive, never redemptive.
2. *Figurative:* Hell is real but expressed in figurative language; hell is indefinable.
3. *Annihilation:* The soul is ultimately extinguished out of existence (no eternal conscious suffering).
4. *Purgatorial:* The soul experiences a beneficial healing effect through the prayers of the living for the dead, prayer, and charitable effects.

---

rapture (e.g., Robert Govett, Ray Brubaker), pretribulational (e.g., J. Dwight Pentecost, John F. Walvoord), or posttribulational (e.g., Douglas Moo). Further, the nature and timing of the Millennium from Revelation 20, whether amillennialism (e.g., Robert Strimple), premillennialism (e.g., Craig Blaising), or postmillennialism (e.g., Kenneth L. Gentry Jr.); types of eternal rewards; and the doctrine of hell (e.g., annihilationism, figurative vs. literal language, degrees of eternal punishment) are ongoing debates.

Preterism, in particular, has made recent inroads into evangelicalism. Preterism, whether in its forms known as moderate preterism or full preterism, states that the events described by Jesus Christ in Matthew 24 and 25 and Revelation 6–18 have already been fulfilled in history. Moderate preterists, such Kenneth Gentry, Hank Hanegraaff, and R. C. Sproul, believe that those biblical passages and prophecies were fulfilled with the fall of Jerusalem in 70 CE with only the resurrection of the dead and the Second Coming of Jesus Christ remaining. Full preterists, such as Max King, John Noe, and Ed Stevens, assert all prophecies were fulfilled in the first century.

Paul R. Shockley

See also: The Battle for the Bible; Calvinism; Christian Apologetics; Dispensationalism; Emerging and Emergent Churches; Fundamentalism; Hermeneutics; Inerrancy; International Council on Biblical Inerrancy; Pentecostalism (and Charismatic Movements), Evangelicals and; Philosophy, Evangelicals and; Rapture; Reformed Tradition, Evangelicalism and; Science, Evangelicals and

Further Reading

Elwell, Walter A., ed. *Handbook of Evangelical Theologians*. Grand Rapids, MI: Baker Books, 1993.

Enns, Paul. *The Moody Handbook of Theology*. Chicago: Moody Press, 1989, 2008.

Geisler, Norman L. *Systematic Theology: In One Volume.* Minneapolis, MN: Bethany House, 2002, 2011.

Lightner, Robert P. *Handbook of Evangelical Theology: A Historical, Biblical, and Contemporary Survey and Review.* Grand Rapids, MI: Kregel, 1995.

Ryrie, Charles C. *Basic Theology: A Popular Systematic Guide to Understanding Biblical Truth.* Chicago: Moody Press, 1986, 1999.

TRINITY EVANGELICAL DIVINITY SCHOOL

Trinity Evangelical Divinity School (TEDS) is an evangelical seminary located in Deerfield, Illinois, and is affiliated with the Evangelical Free Church of America denomination. It is part of Trinity International University and is one of the largest seminaries in the world, enrolling more than 1,200 graduate students in professional and academic programs, including more than 150 in its PhD programs. The Master of Divinity degree, the school's most popular degree, prepares pastors, teachers, and missionaries for a wide variety of ministries. The school also offers a range of Master of Arts programs in counseling, Christian thought, New Testament, Old Testament, and other disciplines. TEDS is affiliated with the Evangelical Free Church of America and is accredited by the Association of Theological Schools in the United States and Canada. It is evangelically broad in its doctrine and community life. The school also publishes the *Trinity Journal*, an academic theological journal for pastors and those in academia.

Trinity's beginnings are traced to 1897, when the Swedish Evangelical Free Church began a 10-week Bible course in the basement of a Chicago church. The seminary was christened Trinity Evangelical Divinity School in 1963 and began conferring the Master of Divinity degree in 1969. During the 1960s, the seminary moved to its present Deerfield campus (just north of Chicago). In 1995, Trinity College (located on the same campus); Trinity College at Miami; Trinity Law School in Santa Ana, California; and Trinity Evangelical Divinity School were united to form Trinity International University. TEDS also offers degrees through the University's South Chicago regional center as well as extension sites around the United States. Their broad online programs bring educational opportunities anywhere an Internet connection exists.

Trinity identifies itself as follows: "As an institution committed to inerrant Scripture, given by God as our final authority for faith and life, we hold ourselves accountable to it and to each other with regard to these values as we cultivate academic excellence, Christian faithfulness, and lifelong learning" (http://divinity.tiu.edu/). It identifies its four core values as Christ Centered, Community Focused, Church Connected, and Culturally Engaged.

TEDS faculty represents diverse cultural and ethnic backgrounds as well as diverse evangelical theological traditions, all united by a broadly evangelical ethos centered on the life, death, and resurrection of Jesus and the inerrancy and authority of Scripture. Included among its notable faculty are Gleason Archer, Constantine R. Campbell, D. A. Carson, John Warwick Montgomery, Kevin J. Vanhoozer, and

John Woodbridge. Prominent alumni include Craig Blomberg, New Testament scholar at Denver Seminary; William Lane Craig, apologist and professor of philosophy at Biola University's Talbot School of Theology; Bill Hybels, founding and senior pastor of Willow Creek Community Church; Douglas J. Moo, New Testament scholar and theologian; and Mark A. Noll, noted Christian historian and professor of history at The University of Notre Dame.

In his inaugural address in October 2014, Trinity President David S. Dockery called for a fresh commitment to biblical orthodoxy, a historical Christianity shaped by the pattern of Christian truth, and a faithful intercultural, multigenerational, multiethnic, and transcontinental evangelicalism that stands or falls on first-order issues.

James Menzies

See also: Higher Education, Evangelicals and

Further Reading

Manetsch, Scott. *Trinity Evangelical Divinity School: The Early Years.* Deerfield, IL: Trinity International University, May 1, 2014. Free download ebook at http://tinyurl.com/h48kcsq.
Trinity Evangelical Divinity School. (n.d.). Accessed April 30, 2017. http://divinity.tiu.edu/.

THE UNEASY CONSCIENCE OF MODERN FUNDAMENTALISM (1947)

The Uneasy Conscience of Modern Fundamentalism was a short book authored by evangelical theologian and spokesperson Carl F. H. Henry (1913–2003). Henry was one of the founding leaders and architects of post–World War II American evangelicalism. The volume was an introspective look at the state of Fundamentalism out of which evangelicalism emerged. Although Henry's work rejected liberal Protestant theology, it also criticized Protestant fundamentalism for being too rigid and for largely disengaging from social activism and "its growing silence on pressing global problems."

Henry argued in the book that Fundamentalism had self-marginalized, declaring: "It was the failure of Fundamentalism to work out a positive message within its own framework, and its tendency instead to take further refuge in a despairing view of world history that cut off the pertinence of evangelicalism to the modern global crisis." His works were a strong rebuke to the Fundamentalist movement of the prewar years. He applauded Fundamentalism's steadfastness in doctrinal orthodoxy but believed that they should be more engaged in the social, political, and cultural life of the United States. Theological critique of Western civilization and culture and a positive presentation of evangelicalism's social and theological values was to become a central focus of many of Henry's later writings in works such as *The Drift of Western Thought* (1951), *Aspects of Christian Social Ethics* (1964), *A Plea for Evangelical Demonstration* (1971), and *Twilight of a Great Civilization* (1988).

The volume became a manifesto for young evangelical scholars and leaders, many of whom had come under the influence of Boston Park Street Church Pastor Harold John Ockenga and who were earning doctorates at Boston area schools such as Boston University and Harvard Divinity School. Known as "the Harvard Evangelicals," these students went on to become some of the major leaders of evangelicalism and neo-evangelicalism in the last half of the 20th century and early 21st century. The themes Henry wrote of in *Uneasy Conscience* were ones that remained part of his work and legacy. Extremely prolific, his magnum opus is the six-volume work *God, Revelation and Authority* (1976–83).

Timothy J. Demy

See also: Chicago Declaration of Evangelical Social Concern; Harvard Evangelicals; Henry, Carl F. H.; Neo-Evangelicalism; Social Action, Evangelicals and

Further Reading

Doyle, G. Wright. *Carl Henry: Theologian for All Seasons*. Eugene, OR: Wipf & Stock/Pickwick, 2010.

Henry, Carl F. H. *The Uneasy Conscience of Modern Fundamentalism*. Grand Rapids, MI: Eerdmans, 1947.

Henry, Carl F. H. *Confessions of a Theologian: An Autobiography*. Waco, TX: Word, 1986.

Marsden, George M. *Reforming Fundamentalism: Fuller Seminary and the New Evangelicalism*. Grand Rapids, MI: Eerdmans, 1987.

Miller, Steven P. *The Age of Evangelicalism: America's Born-Again Years*. New York: Oxford University Press, 2014.

Strachan, Owen. *Awakening the Evangelical Mind: An Intellectual History of the Neo-Evangelical Movement*. Grand Rapids, MI: Zondervan, 2015.

VINEYARD MOVEMENT

The Vineyard Movement is a neo-charismatic, or Third Wave evangelical association of more than 1,500 churches worldwide. Though their roots are in the Pentecostal-charismatic tradition, there are some doctrinal distinctives that set them apart as what has been termed the Third Wave of the Holy Spirit in the 20th century. The founding of the movement is generally credited to John Wimber and C. Peter Wagner. This movement has also been called the Signs and Wonders movement, the Wimber movement, and Empowered Evangelicals.

The term "first wave" refers to the classic Pentecostal movement, which was characterized by identifying the baptism of the Holy Spirit with glossalia (speaking in tongues or ecstatic utterance) as a necessary second work of grace for sanctification and separation into distinct Pentecostal denominations. The "second wave" described the modern charismatic movement that began in 1960 when Dennis Bennett, rector of St Mark's Episcopal Church in Van Nuys, California, admitted to his congregation that he spoke in tongues, but remained in his denomination. Theologically the second wave was like the first, but its adherents stayed within their denominations. The "third wave" attempted to take a less doctrinaire approach to tongues, healings, and miracles by reducing the connection between the baptism of the Holy Spirit, the universal expectation of speaking in tongues, and elevating the expectation of the miraculous and power from the Holy Spirit.

The first Vineyard-named church was pastored by Kenn Gulliksen and was founded in Hollywood in 1974. However, it was when John Wimber, the pastor of the former Calvary Chapel of Yorba Linda, joined Gulliksen's association of six churches in 1982 that the movement exploded.

Wimber, a former pianist with the Righteous Brothers and credited with bringing them together, became a Christian in 1962 and was initially part of a Quaker church. At this earlier stage, he rejected charismatic doctrines while adhering to dispensational beliefs. In 1974, he became the director of the department of Church Growth at Fuller Theological Seminary that led to his close association with C. Peter Wagner. In the following years, they co-taught a course on Signs and Wonders which led to some experimentation trying to perform miracles, healings, and exorcisms. Wimber's views on the so-called charismatic gifts and the Holy Spirit underwent change due to the influence of personal experience, testimonies from the mission field, and various counterculture figures such as Lonnie Frisbee, a founder of the so-called Jesus Movement. It was during this period that Wimber founded Calvary Chapel of Yorba Linda, a moderately charismatic church.

In 1982, Wimber was asked to leave the Calvary Chapel Association because of views considered to be on the fringe—specifically his views that assumed the veracity of any claimed miracle as being from the Holy Spirit until it was proved otherwise, his rejection of dispensational theology, and his acceptance of Kingdom Now theology. In 1982, his church associated with Gulliksen's Vineyard Association.

In 1986, Wimber published *Power Evangelism*, and then *Power Healing* in 1987. These books set forth his theology that miracles and healing must accompany the true proclamation of the gospel for it to be effective. During the 1980s, the ministry continued to evolve, and in 1988 a controversial, faith-healing evangelist named Paul Cain, who initially came to prominence in the faith-healing revivals of the late 1940s, become associated with the Vineyard. During this time, Mike Bickel, pastor of the Kansas City Vineyard, also came to prominence. Together Bickel and Cain led the Vineyard movement into new areas of prophecy, healing, evangelism, and—to many—heresy. This eventually led to a disassociation for a brief time between the Vineyard and the newly named Kansas City Prophets due to some controversial practices.

Vineyard theology is similar to charismatic theology in that it advocates glossolalia, prophecies, "words of knowledge," visions, and miracles. Unlike the earlier Pentecostal-charismatic theology, however, these are not theoretically normative, though they do become expected in practice. Similar to Pentecostal-charismatic theology, critics accuse the Vineyard of having an experience-based theology, which is borne out by statements in their "Core Values and Beliefs." Vineyard theology also emphasizes a view of spiritual warfare similar to that developed within the healing movements of the late 1940s, believing that Christians can become demon possessed and that exorcism should be practiced and more normative. Their view of "power" evangelism is that miracles as well as signs and wonders should be expected to accompany and validate the presentation of the Gospel. Critics argue that the clarity of their gospel is somewhat opaque. Additionally, they point out that seldom in Scripture did miracles produce belief; even Christ's miracles were often followed by unbelief and rejection.

John Wimber died November 17, 1997. Following his death, the Vineyard association continued to flourish and to expand throughout the world. Following their separation from Calvary Chapel, they, like Calvary Chapel, formed their own music label that is one of the top contemporary worship labels today.

Robert L. Dean Jr.

See also: Contemporary Christian Music; Evangelism; Pentecostalism (and Charismatic Movement), Evangelicals and

Further Reading

Jackson, Bill. *The Quest for the Radical Middle: The History of the Vineyard.* Cape Town: Vineyard International, 1999.

Miller, Steven P. *The Age of Evangelicalism: America's Born-Again Years.* New York: Oxford University Press, 2014.

Noll, Mark. *A History of Christianity in the United States of America.* Grand Rapids, MI: Eerdmans, 1992.

Sweeney, Douglas A. *The American Evangelical Story: A History of the Movement.* Grand Rapids, MI: Baker Academic, 2005.

Synon, Vinson. *The Century of the Holy Spirit: 100 Years of Pentecostal and Charismatic Renewal.* Nashville, TN: Thomas Nelson, 2001.

W

WALLIS, JIM (1948–)

James E. ("Jim") Wallis Jr. has served as editor of *Sojourners* magazine and is the most prominent leader of the progressive evangelical movement, or the evangelical left, since the 1970s. Through his social activism, magazine commentaries, public speaking, popular books, and media appearances, Wallis has challenged the conservative political tendencies of most evangelicals by arguing that the Bible calls Christians to make social justice and peace their foremost political goals. Although the Evangelical Left has remained less visible and influential than the Religious Right, Wallis has played a central role in promoting the theological interpretations and political goals of a progressive faction within contemporary evangelicalism.

Born and reared outside of Detroit, Wallis had an evangelical conversion at age 6 and was baptized within his family's Plymouth Brethren congregation. As a teenager, however, he became disillusioned with the suburban conservatism and apolitical attitudes of his church. Wallis was particularly troubled by the apathy of the white Christians he knew toward the plight of African Americans whom he met in Detroit. Their stories of suffering and oppression galvanized his concerns for social justice. As Wallis studied at Michigan State University, involvement in the antiwar movement further alienated him from his childhood faith. The evangelicals he encountered on campus seemed indifferent toward pressing political issues such as war, racism, and poverty, and thus Wallis abandoned the church and channeled his passion into radical student protests. But by the end of his undergraduate studies, Wallis also grew disenchanted with the secular New Left. Searching for a foundation for both political and spiritual transformation, he reread the New Testament—especially Jesus's identification with the poor and suffering in Matthew 25—and embraced a new understanding of Christian discipleship that entailed not only personal piety but also public responsibilities for combating social problems.

To further his theological education, Wallis enrolled in Trinity Evangelical Divinity School in 1970. Within a short time, he and a small group of like-minded seminarians, who called themselves the People's Christian Coalition, stirred debates and backlash on campus by condemning most evangelicals' support for the Vietnam War and insensitivity to other injustices. The self-styled "radical evangelical" group began publishing a tabloid, the *Post-American*, in order to publicize their conviction that Christians' cultural conformity rendered them unable to challenge the sinfulness of American nationalism, militarism, racism, sexism, and economic inequality. Wallis and other members soon left seminary, moved into an intentional community in Chicago, and devoted themselves full-time to publishing and spreading their message. The reputation and influence of the *Post-American* grew under Wallis's leadership, and in late 1975 Wallis and the magazine's staff relocated to Washington, D.C., and renamed both their community and periodical Sojourners.

Throughout his public career, Wallis has promoted a broad range of political positions that alternately put him at odds with the Religious Right and the secular left. As an advocate for nonviolent peacemaking, he campaigned for nuclear disarmament and criticized America's military intervention in Central America in the 1980s, the 1991 Persian Gulf War, and the 21st century "war on terror." Wallis consistently supported redistributive economic policies and governmental programs intended to empower the poor. He also endorsed left-leaning strategies to redress racial injustice; further the feminist goal of women's equality; combat global warming and environmental destruction; and defend the dignity and rights of immigrants. At the same time, Wallis alienated political and religious liberals by identifying as pro-life. In addition, even as he criticized conservative Christians' efforts to curtail gay civil rights, for most of his career Wallis refused to affirm the moral legitimacy of homosexual relationships. He modified this stance in 2013, however, by expressing public support for same-sex marriage.

Wallis and other evangelical progressives such as Ron Sider and Tony Campolo have consistently attempted to combat the perception—popular among many Christians, the media, and the public at large—that evangelicalism is inherently politically conservative. As alternatives to the Religious Right, these leaders formed groups such as Call to Renewal in the mid-1990s and Red Letter Christians in the early 21st century. A breakthrough came in 2005 with the success of Wallis's *New York Times* bestselling book, *God's Politics: Why the Right Gets It Wrong and the Left Doesn't Get It.* His recognizability grew among evangelical and ecumenical audiences, and Wallis gained increased media attention and opportunities to advise politicians and policymakers at events such as the World Economic Forum in Davos, Switzerland. Wallis also became part of a small group of "spiritual advisors" to President Barack Obama, building on their relationship that began in the late 1990s. His more liberal political sympathies and support for Democratic politicians made him a frequent target of conservative evangelicals' criticism. Nevertheless, Wallis helped to sustain a small but viable movement of contemporary evangelical Christians dedicated to progressive politics.

Brantley W. Gasaway

See also: Politics, Evangelicals and; Social Action, Evangelicals and; Sojourners

Further Reading

Gasaway, Brantley W. *Progressive Evangelicals and the Pursuit of Social Justice.* Chapel Hill, NC: University of North Carolina Press, 2014.

Swartz, David R. *Moral Minority: The Evangelical Left in an Age of Conservatism.* Philadelphia: University of Pennsylvania Press, 2012.

Wallis, Jim. *God's Politics: Why the Right Gets It Wrong and the Left Doesn't Get It*. San Francisco: HarperSanFrancisco, 2005.

Wallis, Jim. *The Great Awakening: Reviving Faith & Politics in a Post-Religious Right America*. New York: HarperOne, 2008.

Wallis, Jim. *On God's Side: What Religion Forgets and Politics Hasn't Learned about Serving the Common Good*. Grand Rapids, MI: Brazos Press, 2013.

Wallis, Jim. *Revive Us Again: a Sojourner's Story*. Nashville, TN: Abingdon Press, 1983.

WALVOORD, JOHN F. (1910–2002)

John F. Walvoord is considered one of the most significant evangelical scholars in the 20th century. He was not only the second and longest president of Dallas Theological Seminary (1952–1986) where he began serving on faculty as a professor of systematic theology in 1936, but Walvoord perhaps is also considered the foremost scholar on Bible prophecy from Genesis to Revelation. He was the author of over thirty books including *Armageddon: Oil and the Middle East Crisis*, a *New York Times* bestseller. He was a strong proponent of and defender of dispensationalism, premillennialism, and the doctrine of the rapture.

John Flipse Walvoord, was born on May 1, 1910, in Sheboygan, Wisconsin, to John Garrett Walvoord, a school teacher, and Mary Flipse Walvoord. In view of Mary's complicated pregnancy, her doctors recommended she abort her unborn baby. But because his parents were Christians, believing every life possesses inherent value and is truly a gift from God, they decided to keep their child. Thus, John F. Walvoord, the youngest of three, was born into a Christian family that attended First Presbyterian Church. His father, who served as an elder and Sunday school superintendent, along with his mother, not only committed their children to the memorization of Scripture, but also the Westminster Shorter Catechism. At the age of 15, the Walvoord family moved to Racine, Wisconsin (1925), after his father accepted a principal position at a school. There in Racine, John became an outstanding athlete and student. His family became church members of Union Gospel Tabernacle (now Racine Bible Church).

Though raised in a committed Christian home, John Walvoord's attitude toward the Christian faith was nominal. However, in 1922, following a message he heard by a retired Baptist preacher, he responded to an altar call, committing himself to full-time ministry. Although he thought he was a Christian, it was not until he attended a class on Galatians led by William McCarrell, who later become one of the founding leaders of the Independent Fundamental Churches of America (1930), that he truly converted to Christianity. It was in that study that he realized he could never be good enough for salvation. He discovered that salvation was a free gift of grace, something entirely undeserved.

In 1928, he enrolled in Wheaton College, where he majored in Greek and minored in Latin. He not only continued to excel in both his academic studies and athletics, but he also joined a debate team that won state championship twice in a row (1930,

35 Significant Evangelical Theological Texts

1. Louis Berkhof, *The History of Christian Doctrine* (1937)
2. Louis Berkhof, *Systematic Theology* (1939)
3. Lewis S. Chafer, *Systematic Theology*, 8 vols. (1947, 1948)
4. *Counterpoints Theological Studies Collection One: 9-Volume Set: Resources for Understanding Controversial Issues in Theology* (2015)
5. Walter A. Elwell, ed., *Evangelical Dictionary of Theology* (1984, 2001)
6. Paul Enns, *The Moody Handbook of Theology* (1989, 2008)
7. Millard J. Erickson, *Christian Theology* (1983, 2013)
8. John M. Frame, *Salvation Belongs to the Lord: An Introduction to Systematic Theology* (2006)
9. Normal Geisler, ed., *Inerrancy* (1979)
10. Norman Geisler, *Systematic Theology: In One Volume* (2011)
11. Stanley J. Grenz, *Theology for the Community of God* (2000)
12. Wayne Grudem, *Systematic Theology: Introduction to Bible Doctrine* (1995)
13. John D. Hannah, *Our Legacy: The History of Christian Doctrine* (2001)
14. Charles Hodge, *Systematic Theology*, 3 vols. (1973)
15. H. Wayne House, *Charts of Christian Theology and Doctrine* (1992)
16. Elliot E. Johnson, *A Dispensational Biblical Theology* (2016)
17. George Eldon Ladd, *The Blessed Hope* (1956)
18. Robert P. Lightner, *Sin, Savior, and Salvation* (1996)
19. Roger E. Olson, *The Story of Christian Theology: Twenty Centuries of Tradition & Reform* (1999)
20. J. Dwight Pentecost, *Things to Come* (1959)
21. Clark H. Pinnock, *Biblical Revelation: The Foundation of Christian Theology* (1971)
22. Alvin Plantinga and Nicholas Wolterstorff, eds. *Faith and Rationality* (1991)
23. Robert L. Reymond, *A New Systematic Theology of the Christian Faith* (1998)
24. Charles C. Ryrie, *Basic Theology* (1986, 1999)
25. Charles C. Ryrie, *Dispensationalism: Revised & Expanded* (2007)
26. Thomas R. Schreiner, *The King in His Beauty: A Biblical Theology of the Old and New Testaments* (2013)
27. William G. T. Shedd, *Dogmatic Theology* (1907)
28. Augustus Strong, *Systematic Theology* (1903)
29. Geerhardus Vos, *Biblical Theology* (1948, 2014)
30. Daniel B. Wallace, *Revisiting the Corruption of the New Testament: Manuscript, Patristic, and Apocryphal Evidence (Text and Canon of the New Testament)* (2011)
31. John F. Walvoord, *Jesus Christ Our Lord* (1969)
32. John F. Walvoord, *Millennial Kingdom* (1959)
33. John F. Walvoord, *The Rapture Question* (1954)
34. B. B. Warfield, *The Inspiration and Authority of the Bible* (1948)
35. B. B. Warfield. *The Plan of Salvation* (1935)

1931). It was also at Wheaton that that John Walvoord became the president of Christian Endeavor, whereby he committed himself to foreign missions; he was passionate in wanting to see the gospel be extended into China. John Walvoord completed his Bachelor of Arts degree with honors in 1931.

Following his graduation from Wheaton, he attended Evangelical Theological College (which later became Dallas Theological Seminary) after hearing Dr. Lewis Sperry Chafer (1871–1952) speak at Union Gospel Heritage and on the recommendation of Dr. J. Oliver Buswell (1895–1977), a systematic theologian and president of Wheaton College. Dr. Chafer was Dallas Theological Seminary's president. Dr. Buswell personally recommended to John Walvoord Evangelical Theological College over Princeton Theological Seminary. At Dallas Theological Seminary, John Walvoord earned a bachelor's (ThB) and master's of theology (ThM), magna cum laude in 1934, and a doctorate in theology (ThD) in 1936.

While at Dallas Theological Seminary, he studied under Dr. Lewis Sperry Chafer (1871–1952). Following his graduation in 1934 with his ThM, he began his doctoral studies at the same seminary and became pastor of Rosen Heights Presbyterian Church in nearby Fort Worth, Texas, where he served for 16 years. In 1936, he was asked to step in and assist Dallas Theological Seminary as a temporary registrar and faculty member. In view of his success there, he became an assistant to Dr. Chafer until the latter man passed away in 1952. Dr. Chafer mentored Dr. Walvoord; the two men were kindred spirits. From 1952 to 1986, Dr. John F. Walvoord served as president of Dallas Theological Seminary.

Interestingly, as a theologian teaching systematic theology, Dr. Walvoord discovered he needed to formally study philosophy. Consequently, he attended Texas Christian University, where he earned a master's degree in philosophy in 1945, writing his thesis on existential philosopher Soren Kierkegaard. Then in 1960, Dr. Walvoord received an honorary doctor of divinity (DD), and in 1984, Liberty University awarded him the Doctor of Letters (LittD).

On June 28, 1939, John married Geraldine Delores Lundgren (1914–2012). Geraldine was from Geneva, Illinois, one of six children born and raised by Swedish parents. John met Geraldine through a mutual friend who also attended Dallas Theological Seminary. After their meeting, they cultivated a friendship; a deep, abiding love; and a partner in ministry that would last a lifetime. Geraldine served as a pianist as Rosen Heights and later became an organist at Reinhardt Bible Church in Dallas, Texas. They were married for 63 years. Together they ministered not only all over the United States, but also on five continents. including both Australia and New Zealand. As first lady of Dallas Theological Seminary, Geraldine established, organized, and led the Dallas Seminary Wives' Fellowship, beginning in 1953. As a couple they had four sons: John Edward, James Randall, Timothy Peter, and Paul David. Though they faced certain personal tragedies and difficulties in their family, they were unwavering in their commitment to God, His goodness, and His sovereignty.

Walvoord's tall stature, striking intellect, and poise, made him quite a formidable figure. He possessed natural leadership skills and a tender heart. Under his direction, the seminary grew from 300 to more than 1,700 people. Under his tenure as president, the degree programs expanded from three to six programs, and four major buildings were added to the campus, which is located in east Dallas between downtown and Texas State Fair Park.

In the classroom, the pulpit, and writings, Walvoord truly loved the God of the Bible. He became a leading scholar not only in eschatology, that is, the study of end times, but also in both Christology (the doctrine of Christ) and Pneumatology (the doctrine of the Holy Spirit). He had a deep appreciation for systems of thought and was able to think abstractly at a very high level. His mind was so sharp that he could dictate his work into a tape recorder, and his secretary would listen and transcribe book manuscripts. Walvoord had a passion for systematic theology, particularly, dispensationalism, but he also loved students and was concerned about their integrity and calling to proclaim and live out in the most practical ways the whole counsel of Scripture.

In 1986, Walvoord became chancellor and held the post until 2001. Even after his retirement as chancellor, he continued his teaching and preaching ministry until he passed away in 2002 at the age of 92. Though Walvoord published over 30 books and numerous articles, his book, *Armageddon, Oil, and Middle East Crisis*, particularly his second revised edition (1990), sold more than 2 million copies and was printed in 16 languages. Copies of this book were requested by the White House under the United States Presidency of George H. W. Bush and read by his staff. A subsequent edition was published in 2007.

Walvoord's contribution to dispensation theology is historic in leading one of the most rigorous and largest evangelical seminaries in the United States. His contribution to evangelical theology cannot be overemphasized, especially in the area of eschatology in how it shaped individuals and mass culture as people, movements, and denominations examined end-time events and saw certain events take place, such as Israel becoming a nation in 1948; the establishment of the United Nations; and the constant political, social, and religious upheaval in the Middle East. Walvoord's theological studies on the Holy Spirit and Jesus Christ continue to be published. He was a charter member of the Evangelical Theological Society and served as the society's president in 1954. He also participated on the revision committee for the *New Scofield Reference Bible* for 12 years of its existence.

Some of Walvoord's most popular writings include *The Holy Spirit*, which is his first published book (1954); *Jesus Christ our Lord* (1969); *The Rapture Question* (1979); *The Millennial Kingdom* (1983); *Daniel, the Key to Prophetic Revelation* (1971); *Major Bible Themes* (coauthor) (1974); *Matthew: The Kingdom Come* (1974); *Major Bible Prophecies* (1999); *The End Times: An Explanation of World Events in Biblical Prophecy* (1998); *Four Views on Hell* (coauthor) (1996); and *Every Prophecy of the Bible* (1990; 2011). He also served as coeditor of popular *Bible Knowledge Commentary* (1983). His autobiography is titled *Blessed Hope: The Autobiography of John F. Walvoord* (2001).

Paul R. Shockley

See also: Chafer, Lewis Sperry; Dallas Theological Seminary; Dispensationalism; Premillennialism; Rapture; Ryrie, Charles Caldwell; *Scofield Reference Bible*; Swindoll, Charles R. ("Chuck"); Wheaton College

Further Reading

Elwell, Walter A., ed. *Handbook of Evangelical Theologians.* Grand Rapids, MI: Baker Book House, 1993.

Hannah, John D. *An Uncommon Union: Dallas Theological Seminary and American Evangelicalism.* Grand Rapids, MI: Zondervan, 2009.

Walvoord, John F., with Mal Couch. *Blessed Hope: The Autobiography of John F. Walvoord.* Chattanooga, TN: AMG Publishers, 2001.

WARREN, RICHARD DUANE ("RICK") (1954–)

Rick Warren (1954–) is the founder and senior pastor of Saddleback Church in Lake Forest, California, one of America's largest evangelical megachurches. The megachurch has 13 church campuses in the Southern California area, from Hollywood to San Clemente, to South Bay, to Corona. It also has four international sites in places such as Berlin, Germany; Buenos Aires, Argentina; Hong Kong; and South Manila, Philippines. Warren is the author of the second most translated book in the world and most popular Christian nonfiction book, aside from the Bible, *A Purpose Driven Life.* He has also been called the next Billy Graham (1918–) among evangelicals.

Warren was born on January 28, 1954, in San Jose, California. He achieved a Bachelor of Arts from California Baptist College, a Master of Divinity from Southwestern Baptist Theological Seminary, and a Doctor of Ministry from Fuller Theological Seminary. During his sophomore year at California Baptist College, Warren heard the famous and late Baptist preacher W. A. Criswell (1909–2002) charge pastors to commit themselves to their congregations. This changed Warren's focus from wanting to be a worldwide evangelist to deciding to remain at a single church and serve his parish as a pastor. In 1980, at the age of 26, Warren and his wife, Kay, planted Saddleback Church in Lake Forest, California. This church, which began as a Bible study with a small group of people in an apartment living room, has become one of the biggest evangelical churches in the United States over the last 36 years.

The model by which Warren led Saddleback Church is found in the dissertation he wrote for his Doctor of Ministry degree at Fuller Theological Seminary. On applying this formula that he had written, Warren turned his material into a manual of church-growing for pastors entitled *The Purpose Driven Church* (1995). Seven years later, his book *The Purpose Driven Life* (2002) was published by Zondervan and became one of the most popular Christian books ever written, with more than 30 million copies sold by 2007. In more recent years, he has rereleased the book in order to target a younger generation who were children when the original version of the book was released and are now in their 20s. The book is entitled *The Purpose Driven Life: What on Earth Am I Here for?* (2012).

Since the beginning of Saddleback Church, Warren said he would retire after 40 years of pastoring. Warren has set a plan for the church to engage the 3,400 unreached people groups via world missions. The said plan is referred to as PEACE plan by the Saddleback Church congregation and serves as a platform for people to become involved in missions to plant churches in unchurched locations; equip leaders to serve these churches around the world; assist and care for the poor and sick with food, water, and medical care; and teach preschool-level education as well as English as second language classes. This plan also includes translating most of the Bible to the languages of people groups who have not been exposed to its teachings.

Although Warren has been successful in his church ministry and in writing books, the Warren family has also experienced tragedy. In 2013, the Warren's 27-year-old son, Matthew, ended his life after struggling with mental illness all of his life. Although they knew about Matthew's struggles enduring the disorder of constantly feeling depressed, the death was unexpected.

Warren has been pastoring Saddleback Church for 36 years and has authored many popular books such as *God's Power to Change Your Life* (1990), *The Hope You Need* (2009), and several study resources to complement his *The Purpose Driven Life*. His ministry is that of one who is passionate about evangelism and the spiritual development of individuals. He has become one of the most popular American evangelicals of the era and has shown many people that their lives have purpose.

Samuel Palacios

See also: Baptists and Evangelicalism; Calvary Chapel; Emerging and Emergent Churches; Graham, William F., Jr. ("Billy"); Theological Controversies within Evangelicalism

Further Reading

Balmer, Randall. *Encyclopedia of Evangelicalism.* Waco, TX: Baylor University Press, 2004.

Morgan, Timothy C. "Rick Warren's Final Frontier." *Christianity Today International* (April 2013).

Sommerville, Raymond R. "The Prophetic-Driven Life: Martin Luther King, Jr. and Rick Warren." *Encounter* (Spring 2011).

WESTERN SEMINARY

Western Seminary is a conservative, evangelical seminary in Portland, Oregon, founded by Walter B. Hinson in 1925 as Portland Baptist Bible Institute. It was officially dedicated as Western Baptist Theological Seminary in 1927. In 1949, it joined with the Conservative Baptist Association of Oregon when the Baptists started leaning toward a more liberal stance.

At one time, the seminary was called Western Conservative Baptist Seminary. However, the school removed "Conservative Baptist" from its name to be more inclusive of other evangelical denominations. It has two extension campuses in

California, at Santa Clara and Rocklin, in addition to a campus in Bellevue, Washington. It also has an expansive online program. Western Seminary is accredited by the Northwest Commission on Colleges and University and the Association of Theological Schools.

The seminary offers master's degrees in divinity, counseling, biblical and theological studies, marital and family studies, ministry and leadership, and global studies. It also offers a Master of Theology (ThM), doctor of ministry, and doctor of intercultural studies, and it provides certificates in transformational coaching and lay leadership. Prestigious alumni from this school include Tim LaHaye (1926–2016), Bruce A. Ware (1953–), and Craig Evans (1952–). Western Seminary also offers individual, family, and relationship counseling at A New Day Counseling Center. The counseling center is staffed with prelicensed interns along with experienced clinicians. Additionally, Western Seminary has a Center for Leadership Development that issues certificates for business, theological studies, woman studies, and elder training for the general public. These classes are taught online.

The seminary also publishes the *Spurgeon Fellowship Journal*, which focuses on pastoral theology. Furthermore, an annual conference called the Spurgeon Fellowship Shepherd's Symposium is hosted by the school. Western Seminary also has a Women's Center on Ministry. The purpose of the center is to train women in ministry, prepare them to disciple other women, and get them involved in local ministries.

J. Craig Kubic

See also: Baptists and Evangelicalism; Bible Exposition; Dallas Theological Seminary; Evangelicalism; Evangelical Theological Society; LaHaye, Tim and Beverly; Premillennialism; Rapture

Further Reading

Laney, J. Carl. "Western Seminary." *The Oregon Encyclopedia.* Accessed July 20, 2018. http://www.oregonencyclopedia.org/articles/western_seminary/.

Western Seminary. "Western Seminary Homepage." Western Seminary. Accessed August 1, 2016. https://www.westernseminary.edu/.

WESTMINSTER THEOLOGICAL SEMINARY

Westminster Theological Seminary is a Presbyterian and Reformed graduate educational institution formed in 1929 and located in Glenside, Pennsylvania, with a satellite location in London, England. The school's motto is "The Whole Counsel of God" (Lillback, 2008).

Westminster Seminary started in reaction to a reorganization at the Theological Seminary of the Presbyterian Church at Princeton, New Jersey. Founded by the General Assembly of the Presbyterian Church in the United States of America in 1812, the seminary at Princeton originally subscribed to the Westminster Confession of Faith and Catechisms as its doctrinal standards.

The seminary at Princeton excelled under distinguished teachers who devoted themselves to the propagation of the Reformed faith. Among the best known were its earliest professors: Archibald Alexander, Charles Hodge, J. A. Alexander, B. B. Warfield, and J. Gresham Machen. But in 1929, a movement ended Princeton's adherence to scriptural theology, and Princeton Seminary was reorganized under what was then called "modernist influences," including an emphasis on the Bible's human origins and questions concerning inerrancy.

Immediately after Princeton's reorganization, Princeton faculty Robert Dick Wilson, J. Gresham Machen, Oswald T. Allis, and Cornelius Van Til founded Westminster Theological Seminary in Philadelphia and, with others who were invited to join the teaching staff, continued the defense and tradition of the Reformed faith.

Though the school remains independent, it maintains a close relationship with the Orthodox Presbyterian Church, which J. Gresham Machen helped found in 1936. The first president of the Seminary was Edmund Clowney (1966–1984). He was followed by George C. Fuller (1982–1991), who was followed by Samuel T. Logan (1991–2005). The current president is Peter Lillback (2005), who also serves as a professor of historical theology. In 1982, the California branch of Westminster became an independent institution, Westminster Seminary California, and in 2009, the Dallas, Texas, branch was established as Redeemer Theological Seminary.

Westminster received accreditation in 1954 by the Middle States Association of Colleges and Schools and was accredited in 1986 by the Association of Theological Schools in the United States and Canada.

According to the school Web site, the vision of Westminster Theological Seminary is "to serve with excellence in global reformed theological education." Its mission is explained as "through a world-class faculty with a faithfully Reformed and confessional curriculum, train[ing] students to serve in roles of the global church in the 21st century, including pastors and theologians, to the glory of God" (http://www.wts.edu/).

Westminster Seminary is committed to the systematic exposition of the Reformed faith. In addition to the Westminster Confession of Faith and Catechisms, the Seminary appreciates the diversity of creeds and confessions within the historic Reformed tradition. In particular, it recognizes that the system of doctrine contained in Scripture is also confessed in the Three Forms of Unity (the Belgic Confession, the Heidelberg Catechism, and the Canons of Dort).

The "Westminster Distinctives" listed on their Web site are the study of Scriptures in the original languages; exegetical theology and redemptive historical/conventional hermeneutics; systematic theology grounded in biblical theology; presuppositional apologetics; Reformed confessionalism; Christ-centered preaching; biblical counseling; spiritual formation for ministry in the Church; contextual missiology and urban ministry; and Presbyterian polity.

The Seminary offers the following degrees: Master of Divinity, Master of Arts in Religion, Master of Arts in Counseling, Master of Theology, Doctor of Philosophy, and Doctor of Ministry. It also offers a Certificate in Christian Studies, Mastering Theological English, and an Anglican Partnership for Anglican students preparing for licensure.

The focus of the Seminary's curriculum includes a Christian-theistic defense of the faith; languages of the Bible, biblical introduction, biblical exegesis, biblical history, biblical theology, systematic theology, church history, homiletics, church government, liturgics, pastoral theology, missions, urban ministry, biblical counseling, and Christian education, all of which concern the presentation and application of the Gospel to the modern world.

In brief, the seminary's seven core values are (1) The triune God, Father, Son, and Holy Spirit, is worthy of the worship of all people; (2) Scripture, as the "very Word of God written," is absolutely authoritative and without error; (3) Reformed orthodoxy represents faithfully and accurately what Scripture teaches; (4) biblical exegesis and theology in symphony with systematic theology and presuppositional apologetics are among the crucial methods to be used in interpreting Scripture and in developing a biblical worldview; (5) a learned ministry set in the lifestyle of humble and "holy affection" for Jesus Christ is essential in today's church; (6) a fundamental mandate of the church, discipling the nations for the glory of Christ, requires culturally sensitive, theologically competent ministers who have both the ability and the passion to apply "the eternal word" of Scripture to "the changing world" in which God has placed us; (7) because there is "one body and one Spirit," all who would "build up the whole body of Christ" must "make every effort to keep the unity of the Spirit in the bond of peace" (http://www.wts.edu/).

The seminary is governed by a self-perpetuating board consisting of at least 15 but not more than 30 trustees, of whom at least one-half, but not more than three-fifths, must be ministers of the Gospel. Each member of the board is required by the charter to subscribe to a pledge of a character similar to that required of the faculty, and is required to be a ruling or teaching elder in a church that shares the Seminary's commitments and Presbyterian and Reformed heritage. The president of the Seminary is charged with administrative responsibility and serves as moderator of the Administrative Cabinet. Academic policies are established by the faculty, subject to review by the board; three members of the faculty, chosen by the faculty, sit with the board in an advisory capacity. All trustees and faculty members are required to affirm their agreement with the theological perspective presented in the Westminster Confession of Faith and the Larger and Shorter Catechisms.

The semiannual publication *Westminster Theological Journal* (*WTJ*) is a highly respected conservative theological journal specializing in all aspects of theology, church history, and biblical interpretation. The journal's inaugural issue appeared in 1938, making it one of America's oldest continuous-running theological journals. The journal was "founded upon the conviction that the Holy Scriptures are the word of God and the only infallible rule of faith and practice, and that the system of belief commonly designated the Reformed Faith is the purest and most consistent formulation and expression of the system of truth set forth in the Holy Scriptures" (*WTJ*, 1938, vol. 1, p. 1).

Firmly committed to Reformed theology, Westminster Theological Seminary is one of American evangelicalism's historic seminaries that continues to have a worldwide influence through its faculty and alumni.

James Menzies

See also: Calvinism; Reformed Tradition, Evangelicalism and

Further Reading

Carpenter, Joel A. *Revive Us Again: The Reawakening of American Fundamentalism*. New York: Oxford University Press, 1997.

Lillback, Peter A. "The President's Welcome." 80th Convocation of Westminster Theological Seminary, Philadelphia, PA, September 4, 2008. https://students.wts.edu/stayinformed /view.html?id=209.

Marsden, George M. *Reforming Fundamentalism: Fuller Seminary and the New Evangelicalism*. Grand Rapids, MI: Eerdmans, 1988.

Westminster Theological Seminary. (n.d.). Accessed April 30, 2017. http://www.wts.edu/.

WHEATON COLLEGE

Wheaton College is a private, nonprofit, four-year evangelical Christian liberal arts college located on 80 acres in Wheaton, Illinois, a suburb 25 miles west of Chicago and one of the nation's oldest evangelical colleges. Founded in 1860, its predecessor, the Illinois Institute, had been founded in 1853 by Wesleyan Methodists as a college and preparatory school.

Wheaton's first president was Jonathan Blanchard, a former president of Knox College in Galesburg, Illinois. Blanchard, a committed abolitionist, took on the role as president in 1860. He officially separated the college from any denominational support and was responsible for its new name, given in honor of trustee and benefactor Warren L. Wheaton, who founded the town of Wheaton after moving to Illinois from New England. Following the Civil War, Blanchard campaigned against Freemasonry, resulting in a national presidential campaign on the American Anti-Masonic Party ticket in 1884. Under Blanchard's leadership, the college was a stop on the Underground Railroad.

Blanchard lobbied for universal coeducation and was a proponent of reform through public education for all. At the time, Wheaton was the only school in Illinois with a college-level women's program. Wheaton saw its first graduate of color in 1866, Edward Breathitte Sellers, who is also the first African American college graduate in the state of Illinois. The first woman graduate was Adeline Collins, who remained at the school to become the Lady Principal for the next three years.

Following the Civil War, women outnumbered men in the student body. Of the 51 students in 1870, 29 were women and only 22 were men. In 1882, Charles A. Blanchard succeeded his father as president of the college.

In 1925, Presbyterian J. Oliver Buswell delivered a series of lectures at Wheaton College. Shortly thereafter, Charles Blanchard died, and Buswell was called to be the third president. On his installation in April 1926, he became the nation's youngest college president at age 31. Buswell's tenure was characterized by expanding enrollment (from approximately 400 in 1925 to 1,100 in 1940), a building program, and strong academic development. By the late 1940s, Wheaton was emerging as a standard-bearer of Evangelicalism.

Drawing 2,500 undergraduates from 50 states, 50 countries, and more than 55 denominations, Wheaton offers 40 majors in the arts, humanities, literature, foreign languages, social sciences, and natural sciences. The school was ranked eighth in "Best Undergraduate Teaching" by the *U.S. News & World Report* for national liberal arts colleges in 2016 and 57th overall among national liberal arts colleges by *U.S. News & World Report* for 2016. *Forbes* listed Wheaton among the Top 100 Colleges and Universities in its 2015 rankings.

Wheaton College is home to a conservatory of music, fully accredited by the National Association of Schools of Music. The Conservatory offers two professional music degrees: the Bachelor of Music and the Bachelor of Music Education.

The Wheaton College Graduate School was founded in 1937. Both the college and graduate school are a 45-minute train ride west of downtown Chicago. There are approximately 550 graduate students enrolled, with a 14:1 student/faculty ratio.

Buswell Memorial Library's collection contains more than 1 million items, making it the largest library collection of liberal arts colleges in the state of Illinois. The Library, named after college trustee Robert E. Nicholas, opened in January 1952. In 1975, Buswell Memorial Library, named for the college's third president, was built adjacent to the Nicholas Library, and an interior corridor linked the two, creating the college's main library.

The Marion E. Wade Center, formerly housed in Buswell Library, moved to a new purpose-built site in September 2001. The Center, established in 1965 by Professor of English Clyde S. Kilby, is a research library and museum of the books and papers of seven British writers: C. S. Lewis, G. K. Chesterton, J. R. R. Tolkien, Owen Barfield, Dorothy L. Sayers, George MacDonald, and Charles Williams. The Center has memorabilia of the Inklings, including C. S. Lewis's writing desk and a wardrobe from his childhood home, constructed by his grandfather and widely thought to have inspired the Chronicles of Narnia series; Charles Williams's bookcases; J. R. R. Tolkien's writing desk, where he wrote the entirety of *The Hobbit* and worked on *The Lord of the Rings*; and illustrator Pauline Baynes's original map of Narnia.

The Billy Graham Center, named after one of the college's most well-known graduates, opened in September 1980. The Center itself, as the repository of the evangelist's corporate records, has existed since 1974. The BGC houses several evangelism institutes, a museum of the history of evangelism, and the college's Archives and Special Collections as well as the Wheaton College Graduate School and the school radio station. Over the decades, Wheaton College has graduated many students who went on to become evangelicalism's prominent leaders, authors, pastors, theologians, and educators, and it remains an academic center of American evangelicalism.

James Menzies

See also: Elliot, James ("Jim"); Henry, Carl, F. H.; Higher Education, Evangelicals and; Walvoord, John F.

Further Reading

Bechtel, Paul M. *Wheaton College: A Heritage Remembered, 1860–1984.* Wheaton, IL: H. Shaw, 1984.

Maas, David E. *Marching to the Drumbeat of Abolitionism: Wheaton College in the Civil War.* Wheaton, IL: Wheaton College, 2010.

Wheaton College. (n.d.). Accessed April 30, 2017. http://www.wheaton.edu.

Willard, W. W. *Fire on the Prairie: The Story of Wheaton College.* Wheaton, IL: Van Kampen Press, 1950.

WILLOW CREEK COMMUNITY CHURCH (SOUTH BARRINGTON, ILLINOIS)

Willow Creek Community Church is a nondenominational Christian church located in the Chicago suburb of South Barrington, Illinois. The church has become a model and example of the megachurch phenomenon in the last few decades in evangelicalism. It was founded on October 12, 1975, by Bill Hybels, who is currently the senior pastor. The church's three weekend services at six regional campuses average 24,000 attendees, and it is often listed in national polls as the most influential church in America. The church states that its mission is to "turn irreligious people into fully devoted followers of Jesus Christ."

Willow Creek started in 1972 when a 20-year-old Bill Hybels heard New Testament Professor Dr. Gilbert Bilezikian of Trinity College (Deerfield, Illinois) discuss the early church as described in Acts 2:42–47. Consequently, this type of church was foreign to his soul.

The first Willow Creek service met on October 12, 1975, in the Willow Creek Theatre in Palatine, Illinois. The church quickly outgrew the space, and in 1977, they purchased 90 acres in South Barrington, Illinois—the site of the central church campus today—and construction began. In February 1981, the church met for the first time in its new building. Since opening, the building has doubled in size, and the property has expanded to 155 acres.

In 1992, the Willow Creek Association was created to link together churches for the purpose of "reaching increasing numbers of lost people." The WCA develops training and leadership conferences and resources for member churches. Currently there are more than 13,000 member churches, which come from 90 denominations and 45 different countries.

Since 1995, Willow Creek Association has held an annual Leadership Summit, with speakers such as former Presidents Bill Clinton and George W. Bush; Texas pastor T. D. Jakes; and Rick Warren, author of *The Purpose Driven Life*. The 2007 Summit served 80,000 leaders in more than 130 cities.

Willow Creek launched its first regional campus in 2001. Today, there are seven campuses, making it possible to find a church within 30 minutes of anywhere in the Chicago area.

Willow Creek's principles are divided into Core Values and Core Beliefs. According to their Web site, "Ten core values bring clarity to the things that matter most at Willow." These values include teaching for life change; the truth that lost people matter to God and to the church; that the church should be culturally relevant while remaining doctrinally pure; and that loving relationships should permeate every aspect of church life.

Willow Creek's Core Beliefs describes their theological positions on central beliefs of the Christian faith. These beliefs include the church's position on the inspiration of the Bible; the nature and character of God; the process of salvation; the person and work of Jesus Christ; the person and work of the Holy Spirit; the eternal destiny of humanity; purpose of the local church; daily faith and practice; and the ordinances of baptism and communion.

James Menzies

See also: Contemporary Christian Music; Emerging and Emergent Churches

Further Reading

Ellingson, Stephen. *The Megachurch and the Mainline: Remaking Religious Tradition in the Twenty-first Century.* Chicago: University of Chicago Press, 2007.

Hawkins, Greg, and Cally Parkinson. *Move: What 1,000 Churches Reveal about Spiritual Growth.* Grand Rapids, MI: Zondervan, 2011.

Hybels, Bill. *Courageous Leadership: Field-Tested Strategy for the 360° Leader.* Grand Rapids, MI: Zondervan, 2012.

Hybels, Bill. "From the Beginning, Part 4: Become Fully Devoted followers." (2000). Willow Creek Association. http://www.willowcreek.com/store/prodinfo.asp?invtid=PR03884.

Hybels, Bill, and Lynn Hybels. *Rediscovering Church.* Grand Rapids, MI: Zondervan, 1997.

Miller, Steven P. *The Age of Evangelicalism: America's Born-Again Years.* New York: Oxford University Press, 2014.

WOMEN'S MINISTRIES

Evangelicals have a long history of women ministering both to men and women and advocating for women. From evangelicalism's beginnings, women have served through marriage, motherhood, and community service. One of the core teachings of the Reformation, "the priesthood of all believers," led women who had previously taken monastic vows, such as Katherine von Bora Luther, to leave monasticism to join the Reform Movement. Also, as women later pursued formal education, their participation grew.

Women pioneered midweek prayer gatherings, developed fellowship and community activities, and nurtured the church. They joined the Puritan and Quaker separatist movements and found new equality, even though they served mostly in private settings. Key figures were Anne Hutchinson, who, despite opposition, was and is considered one of the most well-known preachers in colonial New England, and Susanna Wesley, whose instruction to her sons John and Charles Wesley was influential in the Wesleyan Revival—which included the preaching of women such as Mary Fletcher.

In 1848, a Quaker spearheaded the first women's rights convention in America. Men and women in New York drafted the Seneca Falls Declaration of Sentiments, addressing the inequality of women. The event focused on employment, rights of married women, and educational opportunities. The convention marked the start of first-wave feminism.

As opportunities came available, women taught in and pursued higher education. Oberlin, founded as an evangelical college in 1833, became the first institution of higher education in the United States to accept women students. When Wheaton College opened (1860), it was the first to open all courses and programs to women. From its foundation, women served on the faculty, and homiletics classes were open to females. Its first full-time Bible teacher, Edith C. Torrey, taught men such as John F. Walvoord, founder of Dallas Theological Seminary. Coed from its beginning (1879) and founded by A.M.E. Zion ministers to train clergy, Livingstone

Recent Rise of Women Apologists

Houston Baptist University not only offers the first cultural apologetics program in the United States, which is an apologetic approach and way of life pioneered by thinkers like Dr. Francis A. and Edith Schaeffer, but is also one that is being taught by a number of significant evangelical scholars who are women. Among the Department of Apologetics faculty are Kristen Davis, Mary Jo Sharp, Holly Ordway, Nancy Pearcey, and Melissa Travis. In fact, Nancy Pearcey is not only director for the Center for Christian Worldview at HBU, but also Scholar-in-Residence. She is author of *Total Truth: Liberating Christianity From Its Cultural Captivity*, which received both *Christianity Today* Award of Merit winner and ECPA Gold Medallion winner. She, along with Charles Colson and Harold Ficket, also received the same awards with *How Now Shall We Live?* Her most recent works include *Saving Leonardo: A Call to Resist the Secular Assault on Mind, Morals, and Meaning* and *Finding Truth: 5 Principles for Unmasking Atheism, Secularism & Other God Substitutes*.

College/Hood Theological Seminary graduated in its first class the first two African American women to earn college degrees in North Carolina.

Since the late 1800s, the Bible Women Program, a Methodist initiative, has trained women across the world in Bible study, literacy, economic development, human rights advocacy, and nutrition awareness. Organizations such as The Salvation Army, along with Pentecostals and Methodists, have had strong participation from women in offering humanitarian aid and restorative justice. One arm of evangelicalism, the Holiness Movement—which included Phoebe Palmer and the Azusa Street Revival of 1906—saw the full participation of women in public ministry.

Mission movements offered unparalleled opportunities for women. Whether single or married, doctor or translator, women freely served overseas. The 20th century also ushered in a new era as women began speaking, organizing, leading, and launching their own ministries. Through the gifts of women such as Christabel Pankhurst, who took the stage at Bible gatherings alongside evangelicals like Dwight L. Moody, many heard the gospel.

Public opinion shifted after World War II, as men returned home from war needing jobs, and women who remained employed were told they were unfeminine. Rural churches viewed female itinerant preachers as a sign of lower economic status. And Freudian ideas about women's roles suggested that employed women were underdeveloped sexually. Betty Friedan's bestselling book, *The Feminine Mystique*, challenged such thinking, as well as questioned some women's decisions to stay home with children. Its release marked the beginning of second-wave feminism, against which the church strongly reacted. Consequently, views of women's ministry became more conservative, and Bible translations have treated the verses about women with more conservative renderings.

Today, women with the gift of teaching often use their spiritual gifts by leading segregated women's Bible studies. Such ministries, especially popular in Bible and Baptist churches, typically include Bible teaching, marriage support, and mentoring for mothers. Organizations such as MOPS (Mothers of Preschoolers), Precept Ministries, and Women of Faith, as well as women such as Beth Moore, Nancy Leigh DeMoss, and Priscilla Shirer, are popular with these audiences. Women such as Elizabeth Eliot and Anne Graham Lotz are also popular speakers, often speaking to mixed audiences. Joyce Meyer, whose ministry is popular with both male and female charismatics, has an international television and writing outreach.

A growing number of women hold clergy positions. Many evangelicals, especially in the Southern states, limit the role of senior pastor to men. As more women receive seminary training, an increasing number of churches, however, have hired females to shepherd women and children, and use all but the gift of teaching for mixed audiences. Additionally, the number of female educators within Christian universities, Bible colleges, and seminary settings continues to rise.

Sandra Glahn and Marnie Blackstone Legaspi

See also: Missions, Evangelicals and; Parachurch Ministries

Further Reading

Larsen, Timothy. "Women in Public Ministry: A Historical Evangelical Distinctive." In *Women, Ministry and the Gospel*, edited by Mark Husbands and Timothy Larsen. (pp. 213–235). Downers Grove, IL: InterVarsity Press, 2007.

MacHaffie, Barbara. *Her Story.* Minneapolis, MN: Fortress Press, 2006.

Noll, Mark. *A History of Christianity in the United States of America.* Grand Rapids, MI: Eerdmans, 1992.

Tucker, Ruth, and Walter Liefeld. *Daughters of the Church.* Grand Rapids, MI: Zondervan, 1987.

WORLD VISION INTERNATIONAL

World Vision International (WVI) is an independent Christian relief, development, and advocacy organization focused on children, families, and communities and their efforts to overcome poverty and injustice. It is comprised of a federation of interdependent partnership offices headquartered in Monrovia, California; Geneva, Switzerland; Nairobi, Kenya; Nicosia, Cyprus; Bangkok, Thailand; and San José, Costa Rica. WVI is a private voluntary organization that is not affiliated with any government, church denomination, foundation, or corporation. It is one of the largest international nongovernment humanitarian organizations in the world. With revenue of more than $2.8 billion USD (2014), WVI operates in more than 90 countries and employs more than 40,000 staff and volunteer members.

World Vision International began as World Vision Inc., founded by Bob Pierce in 1950. Pierce was a Christian pastor who had worked in the late 1940s for the missionary organization Youth for Christ in China and the Republic of Korea. While working as a war correspondent for the United Nations, Pierce was able to raise awareness and funds for the plight of orphans, widows, and refugees of the Korean War. He established World Vision Incorporated, which received donations and channeled them to existing missionary and humanitarian organizations in South Korea. In 1966, World Vision Inc. expanded its work to other parts of Asia, with its primary focus as a child sponsorship program. In 1967, Pierce resigned, and under new leadership the organization enlarged its mission to include community development and advocacy. It also began to receive government aid and grants. Because of increased international participation in its relief and development work, and to overcome the perception that World Vision Inc. was solely an American entity, the organization took a global approach and became transnational. In 1977, World Vision International was established along with World Vision U.S. and other national partner offices in several countries. WVI became the coordinating body to its partner offices and provided an internal forum for strategy and policy decisions while serving as the single public voice of the organization.

The mission of WVI is rooted in its religious beliefs. The organization's mission is to follow Christian teaching in working with the poor and oppressed and to promote human transformation, seek justice, and bear witness to a Christian message. WVI activities can be categorized into three main groups: short-term relief for victims of natural or human-made disasters; long-term community development projects such as water purification, education, agricultural reform, and sanitation; and advocacy work with policy makers and public awareness efforts at the national, regional, and global levels on issues pertaining to poverty and unjust systems that perpetuate it. WVI's subsidiary, VisionFund, provides microloans to business owners in local communities and is integrated into its community development programs. WVI is a signatory to the International Red Cross Code of Conduct and provides aid regardless of the religion, race, creed, or nationality of the recipients and without adverse distinction of any kind. Additionally, priorities for aid are calculated on the basis of need alone. WVI is a member of International NGO Charter of Accountability (INGO Charter) and has partnered with the International Aid Transparency Initiative (IATI) to make applicable data available on their Web site for public review. WVI is one of many evangelical organizations working on a global scale for human rights and the alleviation of poverty and disease, believing that to do so is integral to Christianity.

Judy Malana

See also: Human Rights, Evangelicals and; Missions, Evangelicals and; Parachurch Ministries; Social Action, Evangelicals and

Further Reading

Dunker, Marilee Pierce. *Man of Vision: The Candid, Compelling Story of Bob and Lorraine Pierce, Founders of World Vision and Samaritan's Purse.* Waynesboro, GA: Authentic Media, 2005.

King, David P. "Word Vision: Religious Identity in the Discourse and Practice of Global Relief and Development." *Review of Faith & International Affairs* 9, no. 3 (September 2011): 21–28.

Lindsay, Drew. 2015. "Firm Center, Soft Edges: World Vision Maintains Religious Identity as It Broadens Its Mission." *Chronicle of Philanthropy* 28, no. 2 (2015): 4.

McCleary, Rachel M. *Global Compassion Private Voluntary Organizations and U.S. Foreign Policy since 1939.* New York: Oxford University Press, 2009.

World Vision International Web site. (n.d.). Accessed April 30, 2017. http://www.wvi.org.

World Vision US. (n.d.). Accessed April 30, 2017. http://www.worldvision.org.

WYCLIFFE GLOBAL ALLIANCE

Wycliffe Global Alliance, formerly Wycliffe Bible Translators, is an alliance of organizations whose purpose is to translate the Bible for every language group that needs it. It describes itself as "multicultural, multinational, creative and facilitative." Wycliffe Global Alliance has its headquarters in Singapore. The Global Leadership Team is a virtual team spread across Africa, Asia, Australia, Europe, and North and Central America.

Wycliffe was founded in 1942 by William Cameron Townsend, who was a missionary distributing Spanish Bibles to the Cakchiquel Indians of Guatemala.

Townsend caught the vision for translation when Cakchiquel-speaking men expressed their surprise and concern that God did not speak their language. As a result, Townsend resolved that every man, woman, and child should be able to read God's Word in his or her own language. Wycliffe's philosophy regards the intercultural and multilinguistic spread of Christianity as a divine command and regards Biblical texts as the authoritative and infallible word of God.

To make his vision a reality, Townsend founded a linguistics training school called Camp Wycliffe in 1934. The school was named after John Wycliffe (c. 1330–1384), the man responsible for the first complete English translation of the whole Bible into Middle English. By 1942 Camp Wycliffe became Wycliffe Bible Translators and later Wycliffe Bible Translators and the Summer Institute of Linguistics (now SIL International).

Until 1991, Wycliffe was a single organization with divisions in various countries. It has been restructured so that the Wycliffe organizations in each country became fully independent, causing Wycliffe International to become an association of organizations. In February 2011, Wycliffe International took on a "doing business as" name, Wycliffe Global Alliance. There are currently more than 100 Wycliffe member organizations from more than 60 countries.

The mission of Wycliffe USA is to see a Bible translation program in progress in every language needing one by the year 2025. The organization's vision is to see God's Word accessible to all people in their language. Wycliffe personnel are involved in translation projects that affect more than 90 countries worldwide. Members work on every continent except Antarctica. Wycliffe states its focus is participating with Christian churches to encourage them to minister to minority languages so that every language community can have access to the Bible.

Wycliffe USA partners with churches both overseas and within the United States, and supports missionaries through finances and prayer. Many churches also send short-term teams to work alongside Wycliffe members. These workers often serve through Wycliffe Associates, one of Wycliffe USA's ministry partners. Wycliffe Associates recruits and mobilizes laypeople to offer practical assistance that frees up Wycliffe missionaries to focus on their own work.

Wycliffe USA offers training in a variety of skills, vocations, and areas of spiritual growth. Rather than expecting individuals to come to Wycliffe with the "complete package," the organization strives to equip people for the work God has called them to do.

Training for linguistic work often takes place at SIL or at the Graduate Institute of Applied Linguistics (GIAL). A limited amount of training for other positions, such as managerial positions or computer support positions, is offered at various Wycliffe locations. In addition to Wycliffe Associates, Wycliffe USA has many ministry partners, including OneStory, Faith Comes by Hearing, North American Forum of Bible Agencies, The JESUS Film Project, and Oak Cliff Bible Fellowship.

Wycliffe's work is not limited to translation. Without literacy or some other provision—such as audio recordings of Scripture—a completed translation may fail to move from the page to the human heart. So Wycliffe trains literacy workers and promotes mother-tongue literacy programs. People who learn to read the Scriptures find their new literacy skills offer benefits such as better jobs to provide for families, access to a variety of information, and increased participation in the broader culture.

Additionally, Wycliffe translates health information such as "Kande's Story," the true-life story of an AIDS orphan and how she and her siblings found help and healing through her church community. It is now available in more than 190 languages in more than 20 countries.

Wycliffe has made great strides since its inception, but more than 209 million people—representing almost 2,000 languages—still do not have any Scripture in a language they can understand. Additionally, there are more than a billion more people who have projects started in their language but that will take years to finish. Wycliffe offers such people opportunity, freedom, and hope through Bible translation. As of November 2012, translations of either portions of the Bible, the New Testament, or the whole Bible exist in more than 2,800 of the 6,877 languages.

James Menzies

See also: Missions, Evangelicals and

Further Reading

Anderson, Neil, and Hyatt Moore. *In Search of the Source: A First Encounter with God's Word.* Portland, OR: Multnomah Books, 1992.

Hefley, James C., and Marti Hefley. *Uncle Cam: The Story of William Cameron Townsend.* New York: Hodder & Stoughton, 1975.

Steven, Hugh. *Wycliffe in the Making: The Memoirs of W. Cameron Townsend, 1920–1933.* Wheaton, IL: Harold Shaw, 1995.

Tucker, Ruth A. *From Jerusalem to Irian Jaya: A Biographical History of Christian Missions.* Grand Rapids, MI: Zondervan, 1983.

Wycliffe Bible Translators. Revolvy. (n.d.). Accessed April 30, 2017. https://www.revolvy.com/main/index.php?s=Wycliffe Bible Translators&item_type=topic.

Wycliffe Global Alliance. (n.d.). Accessed April 30, 2017. http://www.wycliffe.net/.

Y

YOUNG LIFE

Young Life is an international organization of evangelical persuasion that seeks to introduce adolescents to the person and work of Jesus Christ, also known as the Christian gospel. Young Life has an almost 80-year history and is one of several evangelical parachurch ministries that directs its efforts to pre–college age students.

The organization was started in October 16, 1941, by recently graduated seminarian Jim Rayburn, in collaboration with four other seminarians. The beginnings of the organization also included a board of trustees. The headquarters moved from Dallas, Texas, to Colorado Springs, Colorado, in 1946, where it remains as of this writing. At the center of Young Life, is the Young Life Club. The "Club" was developed in Texas, and a Club includes appropriate popular and Christian songs, a skit or two, and a talk by a qualified leader about both the Person and work of Jesus Christ and how one might receive salvation by faith alone in Him.

The goal of a club is to show that Christianity can be fun, active, and life transforming. A Club is the first of the five "C's" of Young Life.

Young Life additionally has Wyldlife (for middle school students), Capernaum (for kids with disabilities), a small town/rural initiative (for kids in towns with populations under 25,000), Young Lives (for pregnant teens and young mothers), Young Life College (for students on college campuses), Young Life Military (for kids located with their families on military installations), Young Life International (for adolescents in every culture—with divisions in Africa, Russia, and the Northern and Southern hemispheres), and Amicus (for international adolescents who live with Christian host families).

Young Life wants adolescents everywhere and in any situation to hear of the hope centered on Jesus Christ. Young Life's hope is to have touched 2 million kids with the love of Christ and the gospel by the year 2016, and to connect with people through their *Reaching a World of Kids* initiative with some 80,000 volunteers in 8,000 ministry locations. Young Life even desires people to travel the globe to minister in Christ's service in Young Life expeditions.

Campaigners (the second "C") is Young Life's weekly Bible study on a variety of Christ-centered topics. The name "Campaigners" is based on the original name of the entire group, called The Young Life Campaign.

The entire Young Life program is reinforced by multiple summer and weekend *Camps* (the third "C"), scattered around the world. The camping program includes a weeklong family camp—Trail West—near Buena Vista, Colorado (weekend family camps are also an option).

Contact work (the fourth "C") is relationship-building time. Through registering many, many hours with kids (by going to students' games, playing sports, going to school lunches, or just hanging out, etc.), Young Life leaders win the right to be heard in order for them to tell the good news or gospel about Jesus Christ to their adolescent students.

A local *Committee* (the fifth and final "C") supports a Young Life team. The Young Life committee is comprised of parents, Young Life alumni, and public heads who support the efforts of Young Life leaders in financial, administrative, spiritual, and moral ways.

Young Life also publishes a magazine three times a year, in the spring, fall, and winter. It's called *Relationships* and has many different kinds of articles, including a featured one. The magazine is appropriately named because the whole of Young Life revolves around developing *relationships* with kids. The incarnation of Jesus as the eternal Son of God who become flesh and dwelt among us, of course, is the model (theologians would call Christ's coming among us in the flesh the "Incarnation"). After all, Jesus bought a house and "moved into the neighborhood" as *The Message* paraphrases (John 1: 14).

David Naugle

See also: AWANA Clubs International; Cru; Evangelism; Parachurch Ministries; Youth for Christ International

Further Reading

Miller, John. *Back to the Basics on Young Life*, 3rd rev., updated ed. Colorado Springs, CO: Young Life, 2008.

Mitchell, Bob. *Letters to a Young Life Leader.* Houston, TX: Whitecaps Media, 2012.

Sublett, Kit, ed. *The Diaries of Jim Rayburn.* Houston, TX: Whitecaps Media, 2008.

YOUTH FOR CHRIST INTERNATIONAL

Youth for Christ International (YFC) is an evangelical, nondenominational youth organization focused on evangelism and discipleship and headquartered in Denver, Colorado. YFC arose in the mid-1940s out of evangelistic urban youth rallies that occurred in the United States as well as Canada and Great Britain. New York City had been an early locus for youth rallies in the 1930s by Lloyd Bryant and by Jack Wyrtzen and Percy Crawford in 1940s. These in turn spawned other rallies in major American cities, particularly in the Midwest. Torrey Johnson, a Baptist pastor in Chicago, had organized large youth rallies there, culminating in a 70,000-person rally at Soldier Field in 1945. Johnson, Charles Templeton, and other rally leaders met at the Winona Lake Bible Conference in July 1945 in Indiana and established an organization, Youth For Christ, to coordinate and administer these efforts, and named Johnson as chairman.

Over its first two years, YFC organized more than 900 Saturday-night meetings across the country, targeting youth audiences through evangelistic preaching and singing and a revival atmosphere. Johnson hired Billy Graham as an evangelists and the first full-time YFC staff member. Graham traveled extensively across North America, and soon he and other leaders were holding rallies around the world, covering 46 countries by 1947. Graham and other early leaders in YFC soon left to establish their own ministries and organizations; YFC served as a launching point for many Christian leaders over the next decades.

Bob Cook followed Johnson as chairman in 1948, and under his leadership YFC expanded its emphasis beyond youth rallies to Bible clubs, which promoted evangelism without the revival setting of the rallies. These clubs were known first as Youth for Christ Clubs and then as Campus Life. He also initiated the Youth Guidance Program (later renamed as Juvenile Justice Ministries), a summer camp ministry for delinquent teenagers.

YFC ministries continued to expand in the following decades while attempting to remain a relevant voice in the changing world of youth culture. Expansion included periodicals (such as *Campus Life*), service organizations (Project Serve), training programs, short-term missions work, and witnessing materials. In 1968, it established the International Council of Youth for Christ to serve as the worldwide coordinating body, with Sam Wolgemuth as president. Youth For Christ International is the worldwide body, with Youth For Christ, USA serving as the United States ministry. As of 2013, Youth For Christ worked in 133 nations, had more than 36,000 paid and volunteer staff, operated 550 ministry centers, and claimed nearly 250,000 youth responded to its evangelistic appeals that year.

The development of YFC was similar to the evangelical movements in the 1940s and 1950s that de-emphasized theological separatism and denominational ties for greater social impact (though it was initially more separatist in its initial years); its immediate and long-term success is reflective of the rising importance of youth culture in mid-20th-century America. The emphasis on evangelism and its sustained global outlook testify to the importance of gospel proclamation and cross-cultural ministry in evangelicalism.

Joshua Michael

See also: Evangelism; Graham, William F., Jr. ("Billy"); Parachurch Ministries; Young Life

Further Reading

Carpenter, Joel A. *Revive Us Again: The Reawakening of American Fundamentalism.* New York: Oxford, 1997.

Shelley, Bruce. "The Rise of Evangelical Youth Movements." *Fides et Historia* 18:1 (1986): 47–63.

Primary Documents

NATIONAL ASSOCIATION OF EVANGELICALS STATEMENT OF FAITH (1942)

Founded in 1942, the National Association of Evangelicals is an umbrella organization of more than 45,000 local churches and 40 Protestant denominations with a constituency of millions. The organization works to strengthen its members, influence public policy, endorse military chaplains, and provide world relief and development assistance. Recognizing the theological diversity within evangelicalism, the NAE provides a brief and straightforward statement of faith.

Statement of Faith

We believe the Bible to be the inspired, the only infallible, authoritative Word of God.

We believe that there is one God, eternally existent in three persons: Father, Son and Holy Spirit.

We believe in the deity of our Lord Jesus Christ, in His virgin birth, in His sinless life, in His miracles, in His vicarious and atoning death through His shed[ding of] blood, in His bodily resurrection, in His ascension to the right hand of the Father, and in His personal return in power and glory.

We believe that for the salvation of lost and sinful people, regeneration by the Holy Spirit is absolutely essential.

We believe in the present ministry of the Holy Spirit by whose indwelling the Christian is enabled to live a godly life.

We believe in the resurrection of both the saved and the lost; they that are saved unto the resurrection of life and they that are lost unto the resurrection of damnation.

We believe in the spiritual unity of believers in our Lord Jesus Christ.

Source: As adopted by the National Association of Evangelicals. Available at http://www.nae.net/statement-of-faith/.

"CHICAGO DECLARATION OF EVANGELICAL SOCIAL CONCERN" (1973)

The Chicago Declaration of Evangelical Social Concern arose out of a meeting of evangelicals who shared a common socially oriented perspective regarding the teaching of the Bible with respect to social issues. Although not all of the participants and signatories of the document were on the political left, the document did become a foundational item in the development of the evangelical left throughout the 1970s and 1980s, and its influence remains to the present.

As evangelical Christians committed to the Lord Jesus Christ and the full authority of the Word of God, we affirm that God lays total claim on the lives of his people. We cannot, therefore, separate our lives from the situation in which God has placed us in the United States and the world.

We confess that we have not acknowledged the complete claim of God on our lives.

We acknowledge that God requires love. But we have not demonstrated the love of God to those suffering social abuses.

We acknowledge that God requires justice. But we have not proclaimed or demonstrated his justice to an unjust American society. Although the Lord calls us to defend the social and economic rights of the poor and oppressed, we have mostly remained silent. We deplore the historic involvement of the church in America with racism and the conspicuous responsibility of the evangelical community for perpetuating the personal attitudes and institutional structures that have divided the body of Christ along color lines. Further, we have failed to condemn the exploitation of racism at home and abroad by our economic system.

We affirm that God abounds in mercy and that he forgives all who repent and turn from their sins. So we call our fellow evangelical Christians to demonstrate repentance in a Christian discipleship that confronts the social and political injustice of our nation.

We must attack the materialism of our culture and the maldistribution of the nation's wealth and services. We recognize that as a nation we play a crucial role in the imbalance and injustice of international trade and development. Before God and a billion hungry neighbors, we must rethink our values regarding our present standard of living and promote a more just acquisition and distribution of the world's resources.

We acknowledge our Christian responsibilities of citizenship. Therefore, we must challenge the misplaced trust of the nation in economic and military might—a proud trust that promotes a national pathology of war and violence which victimizes our neighbors at home and abroad. We must resist the temptation to make the nation and its institutions objects of near-religious loyalty.

We acknowledge that we have encouraged men to prideful domination and women to irresponsible passivity. So we call both men and women to mutual submission and active discipleship.

We proclaim no new gospel, but the Gospel of our Lord Jesus Christ who, through the power of the Holy Spirit, frees people from sin so that they might praise God through works of righteousness.

By this declaration, we endorse no political ideology or party, but call our nation's leaders and people to that righteousness which exalts a nation.

We make this declaration in the biblical hope that Christ is coming to consummate the Kingdom and we accept his claim on our total discipleship until he comes.

November 25, 1973, Chicago, Illinois

Source: Evangelicals for Social Action. (n.d.). Accessed April 30m 2017. http://www .evangelicalsforsocialaction.org/.

"CHICAGO STATEMENT ON BIBLICAL INERRANCY" (1978)

Debates surrounding the issues of the authority, inspiration, and inerrancy of the Bible were the primary theological controversies within American evangelicalism during the 1970s and 1980s, and the ramifications of those debates continue to the present. Evangelicals affirming the inerrancy of the biblical text created the International Council on Biblical Inerrancy in 1977 to be a organization that would hold summits and coordinate publishing on the topic of inerrancy for 10 years. In 1978, a summit was held in Chicago, with the following document being the resulting declaration:

Preface

The authority of Scripture is a key issue for the Christian church in this and every age. Those who profess faith in Jesus Christ as Lord and Savior are called to show the reality of their discipleship by humbly and faithfully obeying God's written Word. To stray from Scripture in faith or conduct is disloyalty to our Master. Recognition of the total truth and trustworthiness of Holy Scripture is essential to a full grasp and adequate confession of its authority.

The following Statement affirms this inerrancy of Scripture afresh, making clear our understanding of it and warning against its denial. We are persuaded that to deny it is to set aside the witness of Jesus Christ and of the Holy Spirit and to refuse that submission to the claims of God's own Word which marks true Christian faith. We see it as our timely duty to make this affirmation in the face of current lapses from the truth of inerrancy among our fellow Christians and misunderstandings of this doctrine in the world at large.

This Statement consists of three parts: a Summary Statement, Articles of Affirmation and Denial, and an accompanying Exposition. It has been prepared in the course of a three-day consultation in Chicago. Those who have signed the Summary Statement and the Articles wish to affirm their own conviction as to the inerrancy of Scripture and to encourage and challenge one another and all Christians to growing appreciation and understanding of this doctrine. We acknowledge the limitations of a document prepared in a brief, intensive conference and do not propose that this Statement be given creedal weight. Yet we rejoice in the deepening of our own convictions through our discussions together, and we pray that the Statement we have signed may be used to the glory of our God toward a new reformation of the Church in its faith, life, and mission.

We offer this Statement in a spirit, not of contention, but of humility and love, which we purpose by God's grace to maintain in any future dialogue arising out of what we have said. We gladly acknowledge that many who deny the inerrancy of Scripture do not display the consequences of this denial in the rest of their belief and behavior, and we are conscious that we who confess this doctrine often deny it in life by failing to bring our thoughts and deeds, our traditions and habits, into true subjection to the divine Word.

We invite response to this statement from any who see reason to amend its affirmations about Scripture by the light of Scripture itself, under whose infallible authority we stand as we speak. We claim no personal infallibility for the witness we bear, and for any help which enables us to strengthen this testimony to God's Word we shall be grateful.

—The Draft Committee A Short Statement

1. God, who is Himself Truth and speaks truth only, has inspired Holy Scripture in order thereby to reveal Himself to lost mankind through Jesus Christ as Creator and Lord, Redeemer and Judge. Holy Scripture is God's witness to Himself.

2. Holy Scripture, being God's own Word, written by men prepared and superintended by His Spirit, is of infallible divine authority in all matters upon which it touches: it is to be believed, as God's instruction, in all that it affirms: obeyed,

as God's command, in all that it requires; embraced, as God's pledge, in all that it promises.

3. The Holy Spirit, Scripture's divine Author, both authenticates it to us by His inward witness and opens our minds to understand its meaning.

4. Being wholly and verbally God-given, Scripture is without error or fault in all its teaching, no less in what it states about God's acts in creation, about the events of world history, and about its own literary origins under God, than in its witness to God's saving grace in individual lives.

5. The authority of Scripture is inescapably impaired if this total divine inerrancy is in any way limited or disregarded, or made relative to a view of truth contrary to the Bible's own; and such lapses bring serious loss to both the individual and the Church.

Articles of Affirmation and Denial

Article I

WE AFFIRM that the Holy Scriptures are to be received as the authoritative Word of God.

WE DENY that the Scriptures receive their authority from the Church, tradition, or any other human source.

Article II

WE AFFIRM that the Scriptures are the supreme written norm by which God binds the conscience, and that the authority of the Church is subordinate to that of Scripture.

WE DENY that Church creeds, councils, or declarations have authority greater than or equal to the authority of the Bible.

Article III

WE AFFIRM that the written Word in its entirety is revelation given by God.

WE DENY that the Bible is merely a witness to revelation, or only becomes revelation in encounter, or depends on the responses of men for its validity.

Article IV

WE AFFIRM that God who made mankind in His image has used language as a means of revelation.

WE DENY that human language is so limited by our creatureliness that it is rendered inadequate as a vehicle for divine revelation. We further deny that the corruption of human culture and language through sin has thwarted God's work of inspiration.

Article V

WE AFFIRM that God's revelation within the Holy Scriptures was progressive.

WE DENY that later revelation, which may fulfill earlier revelation, ever corrects or contradicts it. We further deny that any normative revelation has been given since the completion of the New Testament writings.

Article VI

WE AFFIRM that the whole of Scripture and all its parts, down to the very words of the original, were given by divine inspiration.

WE DENY that the inspiration of Scripture can rightly be affirmed of the whole without the parts, or of some parts but not the whole.

Article VII

WE AFFIRM that inspiration was the work in which God by His Spirit, through human writers, gave us His Word. The origin of Scripture is divine. The mode of divine inspiration remains largely a mystery to us.

WE DENY that inspiration can be reduced to human insight, or to heightened states of consciousness of any kind.

Article VIII

WE AFFIRM that God in His work of inspiration utilized the distinctive personalities and literary styles of the writers whom He had chosen and prepared.

WE DENY that God, in causing these writers to use the very words that He chose, overrode their personalities.

Article IX

WE AFFIRM that inspiration, though not conferring omniscience, guaranteed true and trustworthy utterance on all matters of which the Biblical authors were moved to speak and write.

WE DENY that the finitude or fallenness of these writers, by necessity or otherwise, introduced distortion or falsehood into God's Word.

Article X

WE AFFIRM that inspiration, strictly speaking, applies only to the autographic text of Scripture, which in the providence of God can be ascertained from available manuscripts with great accuracy. We further affirm that copies and translations of Scripture are the Word of God to the extent that they faithfully represent the original.

WE DENY that any essential element of the Christian faith is affected by the absence of the autographs. We further deny that this absence renders the assertion of Biblical inerrancy invalid or irrelevant.

Article XI

WE AFFIRM that Scripture, having been given by divine inspiration, is infallible, so that, far from misleading us, it is true and reliable in all the matters it addresses.

WE DENY that it is possible for the Bible to be at the same time infallible and errant in its assertions. Infallibility and inerrancy may be distinguished, but not separated.

Article XII

WE AFFIRM that Scripture in its entirety is inerrant, being free from all falsehood, fraud, or deceit.

WE DENY that Biblical infallibility and inerrancy are limited to spiritual, religious, or redemptive themes, exclusive of assertions in the fields of history and science. We further deny that scientific hypotheses about earth history may properly be used to overturn the teaching of Scripture on creation and the flood.

Article XIII

WE AFFIRM the propriety of using inerrancy as a theological term with reference to the complete truthfulness of Scripture.

WE DENY that it is proper to evaluate Scripture according to standards of truth and error that are alien to its usage or purpose. We further deny that inerrancy is negated by Biblical phenomena such as a lack of modern technical precision, irregularities of grammar or spelling, observational descriptions of nature, the reporting of falsehoods, the use of hyperbole and round numbers, the topical arrangement of material, variant selections of material in parallel accounts, or the use of free citations.

Article XIV

WE AFFIRM the unity and internal consistency of Scripture.

WE DENY that alleged errors and discrepancies that have not yet been resolved vitiate the truth claims of the Bible.

Article XV

> WE AFFIRM that the doctrine of inerrancy is grounded in the teaching of the Bible about inspiration.
>
> WE DENY that Jesus' teaching about Scripture may be dismissed by appeals to accommodation or to any natural limitation of His humanity.

Article XVI

> WE AFFIRM that the doctrine of inerrancy has been integral to the Church's faith throughout its history.
>
> WE DENY that inerrancy is a doctrine invented by scholastic Protestantism, or is a reactionary position postulated in response to negative higher criticism.

Article XVII

> WE AFFIRM that the Holy Spirit bears witness to the Scriptures, assuring believers of the truthfulness of God's written Word.
>
> WE DENY that this witness of the Holy Spirit operates in isolation from or against Scripture.

Article XVIII

> WE AFFIRM that the text of Scripture is to be interpreted by grammatico-historical exegesis, taking account of its literary forms and devices, and that Scripture is to interpret Scripture.
>
> WE DENY the legitimacy of any treatment of the text or quest for sources lying behind it that leads to relativizing, dehistoricizing, or discounting its teaching, or rejecting its claims to authorship.

Article XIX

> WE AFFIRM that a confession of the full authority, infallibility, and inerrancy of Scripture is vital to a sound understanding of the whole of the Christian faith. We further affirm that such confession should lead to increasing conformity to the image of Christ.
>
> WE DENY that such confession is necessary for salvation. However, we further deny that inerrancy can be rejected without grave consequences, both to the individual and to the Church.

Source: Alliance of Confessing Evangelicals. Available at http://www.alliancenet.org /the-chicago-statement-on-biblical-inerrancy.

SELECTIONS FROM *EVANGELICALS & CATHOLICS TOGETHER* (1994)

In 1994, prominent American Roman Catholic and Evangelical leaders and scholars joined together to craft a statement of concern as Christians approached the 21st century. It was received within both communities with a mix of approval and disapproval. Within the 6,800-word document there were affirmations of common faith and common hope. There were also acknowledgements that Evangelicals and Roman Catholics have significant theological differences. It is that portion of the document that is presented here.

We Search Together

Together we search for a fuller and clearer understanding of God's revelation in Christ and his will for his disciples. Because of the limitations of human reason and language, which limitations are compounded by sin, we cannot understand completely the transcendent reality of God and his ways. Only in the End Time will we see face to face and know as we are known. (1 Corinthians 13) We now search together in confident reliance on God's self-revelation in Jesus Christ, the sure testimony of Holy Scripture, and the promise of the Spirit to his church. In this search to understand the truth more fully and clearly, we need one another. We are both informed and limited by the histories of our communities and by our own experiences. Across the divides of communities and experiences, we need to challenge one another, always speaking the truth in love building up the Body (Ephesians 4).

We do not presume to suggest that we can resolve the deep and long-standing differences between Evangelicals and Catholics. Indeed these differences may never be resolved short of the Kingdom Come. Nonetheless, we are not permitted simply to resign ourselves to differences that divide us from one another. Not all differences are authentic disagreements, nor need all disagreements divide. Differences and disagreements must be tested in disciplined and sustained conversation. In this connection we warmly commend and encourage the formal theological dialogues of recent years between Roman Catholics and Evangelicals.

We note some of the differences and disagreements that must be addressed more fully and candidly in order to strengthen between us a relationship of trust in obedience to truth. Among points of difference in doctrine, worship, practice, and piety that are frequently thought to divide us are these:

- The church as an integral part of the Gospel or the church as a communal consequence of the Gospel.
- The church as visible communion or invisible fellowship of true believers.
- The sole authority of Scripture (*sola scriptura*) or Scripture as authoritatively interpreted in the church.
- The "soul freedom" of the individual Christian or the magisterium (teaching authority) of the community.
- The church as local congregation or universal communion.

- Ministry ordered in apostolic succession or the priesthood of all believers.
- Sacraments and ordinances as symbols of grace or means of grace.
- The Lord's Supper as eucharistic sacrifice or memorial meal.
- Remembrance of Mary and the saints or devotion to Mary and the saints.
- Baptism as sacrament of regeneration or testimony to regeneration.

This account of differences is by no means complete. Nor is the disparity between positions always so sharp as to warrant the "or" in the above formulations. Moreover, among those recognized as Evangelical Protestants there are significant differences between, for example, Baptists, Pentecostals, and Calvinists on these questions. But the differences mentioned above reflect disputes that are deep and long standing. In at least some instances, they reflect authentic disagreements that have been in the past and are at present barriers to full communion between Christians.

On these questions, and other questions implied by them, Evangelicals hold that the Catholic Church has gone beyond Scripture, adding teachings and practices that detract from or compromise the Gospel of God's saving grace in Christ. Catholics, in turn, hold that such teachings and practices are grounded in Scripture and belong to the fullness of God's revelation. Their rejection, Catholics say, results in a truncated and reduced understanding of the Christian reality.

Again, we cannot resolve these disputes here. We can and do affirm together that the entirety of Christian faith, life, and mission finds its source, center, and end in the crucified and risen Lord. We can and do pledge that we will continue to search together-through study, discussion, and prayer-for a better understanding of one another's convictions and a more adequate comprehension of the truth of God in Christ. We can testify now that in our searching together we have discovered what we can affirm together and what we can hope together and, therefore, how we can contend together.

Source: First Things, 2017. All rights reserved. Available at https://www.firstthings.com/article/1994/05/evangelicals-catholics-together-the-christian-mission-in-the-third-millennium.

"THE CORNWALL DECLARATION ON ENVIRONMENTAL STEWARDSHIP" (2000)

The Cornwall Declaration arose out of the evangelical Christian public policy organization called the Cornwall Alliance, although signatories include prominent Jewish and Roman Catholic leaders as well as evangelicals. It also approaches issues of climate change from a free-market approach and argues that human beings should be regarded as "producers and stewards" as opposed to "consumers and polluters." In 2006, the Cornwall Alliance published an open letter response to the Evangelical Climate Initiative cited above, and in so doing established an evangelical perspective that is at odds with the Christians and Climate organization. The document below shows a different starting point and line of theological reasoning and also illustrates the diversity of opinion among evangelicals as well as the larger American population on topics of the environment and climate change.

The past millennium brought unprecedented improvements in human health, nutrition, and life expectancy, especially among those most blessed by political and economic liberty and advances in science and technology. At the dawn of a new millennium, the opportunity exists to build on these advances and to extend them to more of the earth's people.

At the same time, many are concerned that liberty, science, and technology are more a threat to the environment than a blessing to humanity and nature. Out of shared reverence for God and His creation and love for our neighbors, we Jews, Catholics, and Protestants, speaking for ourselves and not officially on behalf of our respective communities, joined by others of good will, and committed to justice and compassion, unite in this declaration of our common concerns, beliefs, and aspirations.

Our Concerns

Human understanding and control of natural processes empower people not only to improve the human condition but also to do great harm to each other, to the earth, and to other creatures. As concerns about the environment have grown in recent decades, the moral necessity of ecological stewardship has become increasingly clear.

At the same time, however, certain misconceptions about nature and science, coupled with erroneous theological and anthropological positions, impede the advancement of a sound environmental ethic. In the midst of controversy over such matters, it is critically important to remember that while passion may energize environmental activism, it is reason—including sound theology and sound science—that must guide the decision-making process. We identify three areas of common misunderstanding:

- Many people mistakenly view humans as principally consumers and polluters rather than producers and stewards. Consequently, they ignore our potential, as bearers of God's image, to add to the earth's abundance. The increasing realization of this potential has enabled people in societies blessed with an advanced economy not only to reduce pollution, while producing more of the goods and services responsible for the great improvements in the human condition, but also to alleviate the negative effects of much past pollution. A clean environment is a costly good; consequently, growing affluence, technological innovation, and the application of human and material capital are integral to environmental improvement. The tendency among some to oppose economic progress in the name of environmental stewardship is often sadly self-defeating.
- Many people believe that "nature knows best," or that the earth—untouched by human hands—is the ideal. Such romanticism leads some to deify nature or oppose human dominion over creation. Our position, informed by

revelation and confirmed by reason and experience, views human steward-ship that unlocks the potential in creation for all the earth's inhabitants as good. Humanity alone of all the created order is capable of developing other resources and can thus enrich creation, so it can properly be said that the human person is the most valuable resource on earth. Human life, therefore, must be cherished and allowed to flourish. The alternative—denying the pos-sibility of beneficial human management of the earth—removes all rationale for environmental stewardship.

- While some environmental concerns are well founded and serious, others are without foundation or greatly exaggerated. Some well-founded concerns focus on human health problems in the developing world arising from inadequate sanitation, widespread use of primitive biomass fuels like wood and dung, and primitive agricultural, industrial, and commercial practices; distorted resource consumption patterns driven by perverse economic incentives; and improper disposal of nuclear and other hazardous wastes in nations lacking adequate reg-ulatory and legal safeguards. Some unfounded or undue concerns include fears of destructive manmade global warming, overpopulation, and rampant species loss. The real and merely alleged problems differ in the following ways:

    The former are proven and well understood, while the latter tend to be speculative.
    The former are often localized, while the latter are said to be global and cata-clysmic in scope.
    The former are of concern to people in developing nations especially, while the latter are of concern mainly to environmentalists in wealthy nations.
    The former are of high and firmly established risk to human life and health, while the latter are of very low and largely hypothetical risk.
    Solutions proposed to the former are cost effective and maintain proven benefit, while solutions to the latter are unjustifiably costly and of dubious benefit.

Public policies to combat exaggerated risks can dangerously delay or reverse the economic development necessary to improve not only human life but also human stewardship of the environment. The poor, who are most often citizens of develop-ing nations, are often forced to suffer longer in poverty with its attendant high rates of malnutrition, disease, and mortality; as a consequence, they are often the most injured by such misguided, though well-intended, policies.

Our Beliefs

Our common Judeo-Christian heritage teaches that the following theological and anthropological principles are the foundation of environmental stewardship:

- God, the Creator of all things, rules over all and deserves our worship and adoration.

- The earth, and with it all the cosmos, reveals its Creator's wisdom and is sustained and governed by His power and loving kindness.
- Men and women were created in the image of God, given a privileged place among creatures, and commanded to exercise stewardship over the earth. Human persons are moral agents for whom freedom is an essential condition of responsible action. Sound environmental stewardship must attend both to the demands of human well being and to a divine call for human beings to exercise caring dominion over the earth. It affirms that human well being and the integrity of creation are not only compatible but also dynamically interdependent realities.
- God's Law—summarized in the Decalogue and the two Great Commandments (to love God and neighbor), which are written on the human heart, thus revealing His own righteous character to the human person—represents God's design for shalom, or peace, and is the supreme rule of all conduct, for which personal or social prejudices must not be substituted.
- By disobeying God's Law, humankind brought on itself moral and physical corruption as well as divine condemnation in the form of a curse on the earth. Since the fall into sin people have often ignored their Creator, harmed their neighbors, and defiled the good creation.
- God in His mercy has not abandoned sinful people or the created order but has acted throughout history to restore men and women to fellowship with Him and through their stewardship to enhance the beauty and fertility of the earth.
- Human beings are called to be fruitful, to bring forth good things from the earth, to join with God in making provision for our temporal well being, and to enhance the beauty and fruitfulness of the rest of the earth. Our call to fruitfulness, therefore, is not contrary to but mutually complementary with our call to steward God's gifts. This call implies a serious commitment to fostering the intellectual, moral, and religious habits and practices needed for free economies and genuine care for the environment.

Our Aspirations

In light of these beliefs and concerns, we declare the following principled aspirations:

1. We aspire to a world in which human beings care wisely and humbly for all creatures, first and foremost for their fellow human beings, recognizing their proper place in the created order.
2. We aspire to a world in which objective moral principles—not personal prejudices—guide moral action.
3. We aspire to a world in which right reason (including sound theology and the careful use of scientific methods) guides the stewardship of human and ecological relationships.

4. We aspire to a world in which liberty as a condition of moral action is preferred over government-initiated management of the environment as a means to common goals.

5. We aspire to a world in which the relationships between stewardship and private property are fully appreciated, allowing people's natural incentive to care for their own property to reduce the need for collective ownership and control of resources and enterprises, and in which collective action, when deemed necessary, takes place at the most local level possible.

6. We aspire to a world in which widespread economic freedom—which is integral to private, market economies—makes sound ecological stewardship available to ever greater numbers.

7. We aspire to a world in which advancements in agriculture, industry, and commerce not only minimize pollution and transform most waste products into efficiently used resources but also improve the material conditions of life for people everywhere.

Source: The Cornwall Alliance for the Stewardship of Creation. Available at http://cornwallalliance.org/landmark-documents/the-cornwall-declaration-on-environmental-stewardship/.

WORLD EVANGELICAL ALLIANCE STATEMENT OF FAITH (2001)

Encyclopedia Editors' Introduction:
Evangelicalism is a global phenomenon with theological and ideological roots dating to the 18th and 19th centuries and with transatlantic connections between the United States and United Kingdom. Part of that long-standing relationship is through the work of the World Evangelical Alliance that began in 1846 in England as the Evangelical Alliance. It is a global alliance seeking to strengthen evangelical churches around the world, and it offers a short and clear statement of evangelical faith.

We Believe

. . . in the **Holy Scriptures** as originally given by God, divinely inspired, infallible, entirely trustworthy; and the supreme authority in all matters of faith and conduct . . .

One **God**, eternally existent in three persons, Father, Son, and Holy Spirit . . .

Our **Lord Jesus Christ**, God manifest in the flesh, His virgin birth, His sinless human life, His divine miracles, His vicarious and atoning death, His bodily resurrection, His ascension, His mediatorial work, and His Personal return in power and glory . . .

The **Salvation** of lost and sinful man through the shed blood of the Lord Jesus Christ by faith apart from works, and regeneration by the Holy Spirit . . .

The **Holy Spirit**, by whose indwelling the believer is enabled to live a holy life, to witness and work for the Lord Jesus Christ . . .

The **Unity** of the Spirit of all true believers, the Church, the Body of Christ . . .

The **Resurrection** of both the saved and the lost; they that are saved unto the resurrection of life, they that are lost unto the resurrection of damnation.

Source: World Evangelical Alliance Statement of Faith (2001). Available at http://www.worldea.org/whoweare/statementoffaith.

THE GOSPEL COALITION FOUNDATION DOCUMENTS (2005)

Created in 2005, The Gospel Coalition is a broadly Reformed evangelical network of pastors, leaders, churches, and individuals committed to the encouragement and education of "current and next-generation Christian leaders" (www.thegospelcoalition.org/about/overview). Its Web site receives millions of "hits" per year, and they have formulated three interrelated "Foundation Documents" articulating Evangelicalism from within the Reformed tradition—A Preamble, Confessional Statement, and Theological Vision for Ministry.

Preamble

We are a fellowship of evangelical churches in the Reformed tradition deeply committed to renewing our faith in the gospel of Christ and to reforming our ministry practices to conform fully to the Scriptures. We have become deeply concerned about some movements within traditional evangelicalism that seem to be diminishing the church's life and leading us away from our historic beliefs and practices. On the one hand, we are troubled by the idolatry of personal consumerism and the politicization of faith; on the other hand, we are distressed by the unchallenged acceptance of theological and moral relativism. These movements have led to the easy abandonment of both biblical truth and the transformed living mandated by our historic faith. We not only hear of these influences, we see their effects. We have committed ourselves to invigorating churches with new hope and compelling joy based on the promises received by grace alone through faith alone in Christ alone.

We believe that in many evangelical churches a deep and broad consensus exists regarding the truths of the gospel. Yet we often see the celebration of our union with Christ replaced by the age-old attractions of power and affluence, or by monastic retreats into ritual, liturgy, and sacrament. What replaces the gospel will never promote a mission-hearted faith anchored in enduring truth working itself out in unashamed discipleship eager to stand the tests of kingdom-calling and sacrifice. We desire to advance along the King's highway, always aiming to provide gospel advocacy, encouragement, and education so that current- and next-generation church leaders are better equipped to fuel their ministries with principles and practices that glorify the Savior and do good to those for whom he shed his life's blood.

We want to generate a unified effort among all peoples—an effort that is zealous to honor Christ and multiply his disciples, joining in a true coalition for Jesus. Such a biblically grounded and united mission is the only enduring future for the church. This reality compels us to stand with others who are stirred by the conviction that the mercy of God in Jesus Christ is our only hope of eternal salvation. We desire to champion this gospel with clarity, compassion, courage, and joy—gladly linking hearts with fellow believers across denominational, ethnic, and class lines.

Our desire is to serve the church we love by inviting all our brothers and sisters to join us in an effort to renew the contemporary church in the ancient gospel of Christ so that we truly speak and live for him in a way that clearly communicates to our age. As pastors, we intend to do this in our churches through the ordinary means of his grace: prayer, the ministry of the Word, baptism and the Lord's Supper and the fellowship of the saints. We yearn to work with all who, in addition to embracing the confession and vision set out here, seek the lordship of Christ over the whole of life with unabashed hope in the power of the Holy Spirit to transform individuals, communities, and cultures. You will find attached both our Confessional Statement and our Theological Vision for Ministry—a vision rooted in the Scriptures and centered on the gospel.

Confessional Statement

For more about our confessional statement, check out our series of 14 booklets written by the Council and edited by cofounders D. A. Carson and Timothy Keller.

- **The Triune God** We believe in one God, eternally existing in three equally divine Persons: the Father, the Son, and the Holy Spirit, who know, love, and glorify one another. This one true and living God is infinitely perfect both in his love and in his holiness. He is the Creator of all things, visible and invisible, and is therefore worthy to receive all glory and adoration. Immortal and eternal, he perfectly and exhaustively knows the end from the beginning, sustains and sovereignly rules over all things, and providentially brings about his eternal good purposes to redeem a people for himself and restore his fallen creation, to the praise of his glorious grace.
- God has graciously disclosed his existence and power in the created order, and has supremely revealed himself to fallen human beings in the person of his Son, the incarnate Word. Moreover, this God is a speaking God who by his Spirit has graciously disclosed himself in human words: we believe that God has inspired the words preserved in the Scriptures, the sixty-six books of the Old and New Testaments, which are both record and means of his saving work in the world. These writings alone constitute the verbally inspired Word of God, which is utterly authoritative and without error in the original writings, complete in its revelation of his will for salvation, sufficient for all that God requires us to believe and do, and final in its authority over every

domain of knowledge to which it speaks. We confess that both our finitude and our sinfulness preclude the possibility of knowing God's truth exhaustively, but we affirm that, enlightened by the Spirit of God, we can know God's revealed truth truly. The Bible is to be believed, as God's instruction, in all that it teaches; obeyed, as God's command, in all that it requires; and trusted, as God's pledge, in all that it promises. As God's people hear, believe, and do the Word, they are equipped as disciples of Christ and witnesses to the gospel.

- **Creation of Humanity** We believe that God created human beings, male and female, in his own image. Adam and Eve belonged to the created order that God himself declared to be very good, serving as God's agents to care for, manage, and govern creation, living in holy and devoted fellowship with their Maker. Men and women, equally made in the image of God, enjoy equal access to God by faith in Christ Jesus and are both called to move beyond passive self-indulgence to significant private and public engagement in family, church, and civic life. Adam and Eve were made to complement each other in a one-flesh union that establishes the only normative pattern of sexual relations for men and women, such that marriage ultimately serves as a type of the union between Christ and his church. In God's wise purposes, men and women are not simply interchangeable, but rather they complement each other in mutually enriching ways. God ordains that they assume distinctive roles which reflect the loving relationship between Christ and the church, the husband exercising headship in a way that displays the caring, sacrificial love of Christ, and the wife submitting to her husband in a way that models the love of the church for her Lord. In the ministry of the church, both men and women are encouraged to serve Christ and to be developed to their full potential in the manifold ministries of the people of God. The distinctive leadership role within the church given to qualified men is grounded in creation, fall, and redemption and must not be sidelined by appeals to cultural developments.

- **The Fall** We believe that Adam, made in the image of God, distorted that image and forfeited his original blessedness—for himself and all his progeny—by falling into sin through Satan's temptation. As a result, all human beings are alienated from God, corrupted in every aspect of their being (e.g., physically, mentally, volitionally, emotionally, spiritually) and condemned finally and irrevocably to death—apart from God's own gracious intervention. The supreme need of all human beings is to be reconciled to the God under whose just and holy wrath we stand; the only hope of all human beings is the undeserved love of this same God, who alone can rescue us and restore us to himself.

- **The Plan of God** We believe that from all eternity God determined in grace to save a great multitude of guilty sinners from every tribe and language and people and nation, and to this end foreknew them and chose them. We believe that God justifies and sanctifies those who by grace have faith in Jesus, and that he will one day glorify them—all to the praise of his glorious grace. In love God commands and implores all people to repent and believe, having set his saving love on those he has chosen and having ordained Christ to be their Redeemer.

- **The Gospel** We believe that the gospel is the good news of Jesus Christ—God's very wisdom. Utter folly to the world, even though it is the power of God to those who are being saved, this good news is christological, centering on the cross and resurrection: the gospel is not proclaimed if Christ is not proclaimed, and the authentic Christ has not been proclaimed if his death and resurrection are not central (the message is: "Christ died for our sins . . . [and] was raised"). This good news is biblical (his death and resurrection are according to the Scriptures), theological and salvific (Christ died for our sins, to reconcile us to God), historical (if the saving events did not happen, our faith is worthless, we are still in our sins, and we are to be pitied more than all others), apostolic (the message was entrusted to and transmitted by the apostles, who were witnesses of these saving events), and intensely personal (where it is received, believed, and held firmly, individual persons are saved).

- **The Redemption of Christ** We believe that, moved by love and in obedience to his Father, the eternal Son became human: the Word became flesh, fully God and fully human being, one Person in two natures. The man Jesus, the promised Messiah of Israel, was conceived through the miraculous agency of the Holy Spirit, and was born of the virgin Mary. He perfectly obeyed his heavenly Father, lived a sinless life, performed miraculous signs, was crucified under Pontius Pilate, arose bodily from the dead on the third day, and ascended into heaven. As the mediatorial King, he is seated at the right hand of God the Father, exercising in heaven and on earth all of God's sovereignty, and is our High Priest and righteous Advocate. We believe that by his incarnation, life, death, resurrection, and ascension, Jesus Christ acted as our representative and substitute. He did this so that in him we might become the righteousness of God: on the cross he canceled sin, propitiated God, and, by bearing the full penalty of our sins, reconciled to God all those who believe. By his resurrection Christ Jesus was vindicated by his Father, broke the power of death and defeated Satan who once had power over it, and brought everlasting life to all his people; by his ascension he has been forever exalted as Lord and has prepared a place for us to be with him. We believe that salvation is found in no one else, for there is no other name given under heaven by which we must be saved. Because God chose the lowly things of this world, the despised things, the things that are not, to nullify the things that are, no human being can ever boast before him—Christ Jesus has become for us wisdom from God—that is, our righteousness, holiness, and redemption.

- **The Justification of Sinners** We believe that Christ, by his obedience and death, fully discharged the debt of all those who are justified. By his sacrifice, he bore in our stead the punishment due us for our sins, making a proper, real, and full satisfaction to God's justice on our behalf. By his perfect obedience he satisfied the just demands of God on our behalf, since by faith alone that perfect obedience is credited to all who trust in Christ alone for their acceptance with God. Inasmuch as Christ was given by the Father for us, and his obedience and punishment were accepted in place of our own, freely and not for anything in us, this justification is solely of free grace, in order that both the exact justice and the rich grace of God might be glorified in the justification of sinners. We believe that a zeal for personal and public obedience flows from this free justification.

- **The Power of the Holy Spirit** We believe that this salvation, attested in all Scripture and secured by Jesus Christ, is applied to his people by the Holy Spirit. Sent by the Father and the Son, the Holy Spirit glorifies the Lord Jesus Christ, and, as the other Paraclete, is present with and in believers. He convicts the world of sin, righteousness, and judgment, and by his powerful and mysterious work regenerates spiritually dead sinners, awakening them to repentance and faith, and in him they are baptized into union with the Lord Jesus, such that they are justified before God by grace alone through faith alone in Jesus Christ alone. By the Spirit's agency, believers are renewed, sanctified, and adopted into God's family; they participate in the divine nature and receive his sovereignly distributed gifts. The Holy Spirit is himself the down payment of the promised inheritance, and in this age indwells, guides, instructs, equips, revives, and empowers believers for Christ-like living and service.

- **The Kingdom of God** We believe that those who have been saved by the grace of God through union with Christ by faith and through regeneration by the Holy Spirit enter the kingdom of God and delight in the blessings of the New Covenant: the forgiveness of sins, the inward transformation that awakens a desire to glorify, trust, and obey God, and the prospect of the glory yet to be revealed. Good works constitute indispensable evidence of saving grace. Living as salt in a world that is decaying and light in a world that is dark, believers should neither withdraw into seclusion from the world, nor become indistinguishable from it: rather, we are to do good to the city, for all the glory and honor of the nations is to be offered up to the living God. Recognizing whose created order this is, and because we are citizens of God's kingdom, we are to love our neighbors as ourselves, doing good to all, especially to those who belong to the household of God. The kingdom of God, already present but not fully realized, is the exercise of God's sovereignty in the world toward the eventual redemption of all creation. The kingdom of God is an invasive power that plunders Satan's dark kingdom and regenerates and renovates through repentance and faith the lives of individuals rescued from that kingdom. It therefore inevitably establishes a new community of human life together under God.

- **God's New People** We believe that God's New Covenant people have already come to the heavenly Jerusalem; they are already seated with Christ in the heavenlies. This universal church is manifest in local churches of which Christ is the only Head; thus each "local church" is, in fact, the church, the household of God, the assembly of the living God, and the pillar and foundation of the truth.

The church is the body of Christ, the apple of his eye, graven on his hands, and he has pledged himself to her forever. The church is distinguished by her gospel message, her sacred ordinances, her discipline, her great mission, and, above all, by her love for God, and by her members' love for one another and for the world. Crucially, this gospel we cherish has both personal and corporate dimensions, neither of which may properly be overlooked. Christ Jesus is our peace: he has not only brought about peace with God, but also peace between alienated peoples. His purpose was to create in himself one new humanity, thus making peace, and in one body to reconcile both Jew and Gentile to God through the cross, by which he put to death their hostility. The church serves as a sign of God's future new world when its members live for the service of one another and their neighbors, rather than for self-focus. The church is the corporate dwelling place of God's Spirit, and the continuing witness to God in the world.

- **Baptism and the Lord's Supper** We believe that baptism and the Lord's Supper are ordained by the Lord Jesus himself. The former is connected with entrance into the New Covenant community, the latter with ongoing covenant renewal. Together they are simultaneously God's pledge to us, divinely ordained means of grace, our public vows of submission to the once crucified and now resurrected Christ, and anticipations of his return and of the consummation of all things.

- **The Restoration of All Things** We believe in the personal, glorious, and bodily return of our Lord Jesus Christ with his holy angels, when he will exercise his role as final Judge, and his kingdom will be consummated. We believe in the bodily resurrection of both the just and the unjust—the unjust to judgment and eternal conscious punishment in hell, as our Lord himself taught, and the just to eternal blessedness in the presence of him who sits on the throne and of the Lamb, in the new heaven and the new earth, the home of righteousness. On that day the church will be presented faultless before God by the obedience, suffering and triumph of Christ, all sin purged and its wretched effects forever banished. God will be all in all and his people will be enthralled by the immediacy of his ineffable holiness, and everything will be to the praise of his glorious grace.

Theological Vision for Ministry

This is not an outline of our doctrinal beliefs (see the Confessional Statement), but a statement of how we intend to discharge Christian ministry and interact with our culture in biblical and theological faithfulness.

I. How should we respond to the cultural crisis of truth? (The epistemological issue)

For several hundred years, since the dawning of the Enlightenment, it was widely agreed that truth—expressed in words that substantially correspond to reality—does indeed exist and can be known. Unaided human reason, it was thought, is able to know truth objectively. More recently, postmodernism has critiqued this set of assumptions, contending that we are not in fact objective in our pursuit of knowledge, but rather interpret information through our personal experiences, self-interests, emotions, cultural prejudices, language limitations, and relational communities. The claim to objectivity is arrogant, postmodernism tells us, and inevitably leads to conflicts between communities with differing opinions as to where the truth lies. Such arrogance, they say explains, in part, many of the injustices and wars of the modern era. Yet postmodernism's response is dangerous in another way: its most strident voices insist that claims to objective truth be replaced by a more humbly "tolerant" and inclusively diverse subjective pluralism—a pluralism often mired in a swamp that cannot allow any firm ground for "the faith that was once for all entrusted to the saints." Such a stance has no place for truth that corresponds to reality, but merely an array of subjectively shaped truths. How shall we respond to this cultural crisis of truth?

1. We affirm that truth is correspondence to reality. We believe the Holy Spirit who inspired the words of the apostles and prophets also indwells us so that we who have been made in the image of God can receive and understand the words of Scripture revealed by God, and grasp that Scripture's truths correspond to reality. The statements of Scripture are true, precisely because they are God's statements, and they correspond to reality even though our knowledge of those truths (and even our ability to verify them to others) is always necessarily incomplete. The Enlightenment belief in thoroughly objective knowledge made an idol out of unaided human reason. But to deny the possibility of purely objective knowledge does not mean the loss of truth that corresponds to objective reality, even if we can never know such truth without an element of subjectivity. See CS–(2).

2. We affirm that truth is conveyed by Scripture. We believe that Scripture is pervasively propositional and that all statements of Scripture are completely true and authoritative. But the truth of Scripture cannot be exhausted in a series of propositions. It exists in the genres of narrative, metaphor, and poetry which are not exhaustively distillable into doctrinal propositions, yet they convey God's will and mind to us so as to change us into his likeness.

3. We affirm that truth is correspondence of life to God. Truth is not only a theoretical correspondence but also a covenantal relationship. The biblical revelation is not just to be known, but to be lived (Deuteronomy 29:29). The purpose of the Bible is to produce wisdom in us—a life wholly submitted to God's reality. Truth, then, is correspondence between our entire lives and God's heart, words and actions, through the mediation of the Word and Spirit. To eliminate the propositional nature of biblical truth seriously weakens our ability to hold, defend, and explain the gospel. But to speak of truth only as propositions weakens our appreciation of the incarnate Son as the Way, the Truth,

and the Life, and the communicative power of narrative and story, and the importance of truth as living truly in correspondence to God.

4. How this vision of truth shapes us.

We adopt a "chastened" correspondence–theory of truth that is less triumphalistic than that of some in the older evangelicalism. But we also reject a view of truth that sees truth as nothing more than the internally coherent language of a particular faith–community. So we maintain, with what we hope is appropriate humility, the principle of sola Scriptura.

Though truth is propositional, it is not only something to be believed, but also to be received in worship and practiced in wisdom. This balance shapes our understanding of discipleship and preaching. We want to encourage a passion for sound doctrine, but we know that Christian growth is not simply cognitive information transfer. Christian growth occurs only when the whole life is shaped by Christian practices in community—including prayer, baptism, the Lord's Supper, fellowship, and the public ministry of the Word.

Our theoretical knowledge of God's truth is only partial even when accurate, but we nevertheless can have certainty that what the Word tells us is true (Luke 1:4). It is through the power of the Holy Spirit that we receive the words of the gospel in full assurance and conviction (1 Thessalonians 1:5).

II. How should we read the Bible? (The hermeneutical issue)

1. Reading "along" the whole Bible. To read along the whole Bible is to discern the single basic plot–line of the Bible as God's story of redemption (e.g., Luke 24:44) as well as the themes of the Bible (e.g., covenant, kingship, temple) that run through every stage of history and every part of the canon, climaxing in Jesus Christ. In this perspective, the gospel appears as creation, fall, redemption, restoration. It brings out the purpose of salvation, namely, a renewed creation. As we confess in CS–(1), [God] providentially brings about his eternal good purposes to redeem a people for himself and restore his fallen creation, to the praise of his glorious grace.

2. Reading "across" the whole Bible. To read across the whole Bible is to collect its declarations, summons, promises, and truth–claims into categories of thought (e.g., theology, Christology, eschatology) and arrive at a coherent understanding of what it teaches summarily (e.g., Luke 24:46–47). In this perspective, the gospel appears as God, sin, Christ, faith. It brings out the means of salvation, namely the substitutionary work of Christ and our responsibility to embrace it by faith. As we confess in CS–(7), Jesus Christ acted as our representative and substitute, so that in him we might become the righteousness of God.

3. How this reading of the Bible shapes us

Many today (but not all) who major in the first of these two ways of reading the Bible—that is, reading along the whole Bible—dwell on the more corporate aspects of sin and salvation. The cross is seen mainly as an example of sacrificial service and a defeat of worldly powers rather than substitution and propitiation for our sins. Ironically, this approach can be very legalistic. Instead of calling people to individual conversion through a message of grace, people are called to join the Christian community and kingdom program of what God is doing to liberate the world. The emphasis is on Christianity as a way of life to the loss of a blood–bought status in Christ received through personal faith. In this imbalance there is little emphasis on vigorous evangelism and apologetics, on expository preaching, and on the marks and importance of conversion/the new birth.

On the other hand, the older evangelicalism (though not all of it) tended to read across the Bible. As a result it was more individualistic, centering almost completely on personal conversion and safe passage to heaven. Also, its preaching, though expository, was sometimes moralistic and did not emphasize how all biblical themes climax in Christ and his work. In this imbalance there is little or no emphasis on the importance of the work of justice and mercy for the poor and the oppressed, and on cultural production that glorifies God in the arts, business, etc.

We do not believe that in best practice these two ways of reading the Bible are at all contradictory, even though today, many pit them against each other. We believe that on the contrary the two, at their best, are integral for grasping the meaning of the biblical gospel. The gospel is the declaration that through the death and resurrection of Jesus Christ, God has come to reconcile individuals by his grace and renew the whole world by and for his glory.

III. How should we relate to the culture around us? (The contextualization issue)

1. By being a counter–culture. We want to be a church that not only gives support to individual Christians in their personal walks with God, but one that also shapes them into the alternative human society God creates by his Word and Spirit. (See below, point 5c.)

2. For the common good. It is not enough that the church should counter the values of the dominant culture. We must be a counter–culture for the common good. We want to be radically distinct from the culture around us and yet, out of that distinct identity, we should sacrificially serve neighbors and even enemies, working for the flourishing of people, both here and now, and in eternity. We therefore do not see our corporate worship services as the primary connecting point with those outside. Rather, we expect to meet our neighbors as we work for their peace, security, and well–being, loving them in word and deed. If we do this we will be "salt" and "light" in the world (sustaining and improving living conditions, showing the world the glory of God by our patterns of living; Matt 5:13–16). As the Jewish exiles were called to love and work for the shalom of Babylon (Jeremiah 29:7), Christians too are

God's people "in exile" (1 Peter 1:1; James 1:1). The citizens of God's city should be the best possible citizens of their earthly city (Jeremiah 29:4–7). We are neither overly optimistic nor pessimistic about our cultural influence, for we know that, as we walk in the steps of the One who laid down his life for his opponents, we will receive persecution even while having social impact (1 Peter 2:12).

3. How this relationship to culture shapes us.

We believe that every expression of Christianity is necessarily and rightly contextualized, to some degree, to particular human culture; there is no such thing as a universal a–historical expression of Christianity. But we never want to be so affected by our culture that we compromise gospel truths. How then do we keep our balance?

The answer is that we cannot "contextualize" the gospel in the abstract, as a thought experiment. If a church seeks to be a counter–culture for people's temporal and eternal good, it will guard itself against both the legalism that can accompany undue cultural withdrawal and the compromise that comes with over–adaptation. If we seek service rather than power, we may have significant cultural impact. But if we seek direct power and social control, we will, ironically, be assimilated into the very idolatries of wealth, status, and power we seek to change.

The gospel itself holds the key to appropriate contextualization. If we over–contextualize, it suggests that we want too much the approval of the receiving culture. This betrays a lack of confidence in the gospel. If we under–contextualize, it suggests that we want the trappings of our own sub–culture too much. This betrays a lack of gospel humility and a lack of love for our neighbor.

IV. In what ways is the gospel unique?

This gospel fills Christians with humility and hope, meekness and boldness, in a unique way. The biblical gospel differs markedly from traditional religions as well as from secularism. Religions operate on the principle: "I obey; therefore I am accepted," but the gospel principle is: "I am accepted through Christ; therefore I obey." So the gospel differs from both irreligion and religion. You can seek to be your own "lord and savior" by breaking the law of God, but you can also do so by keeping the law in order to earn your salvation.

Irreligion and secularism tend to inflate self-encouraging, uncritical, "self-esteem"; religion and moralism crush people under guilt from ethical standards that are impossible to maintain. The gospel, however, humbles and affirms us at the same time, since, in Christ, each of us is simultaneously just, and a sinner still. At the same time, we are more flawed and sinful than we ever dared believe, yet we are more loved and accepted than we ever dared hope.

Secularism tends to make people selfish and individualistic. Religion and morality in general tend to make people tribal and self-righteous toward other groups (since their salvation has, they think, been earned by their achievement). But the gospel of grace, centered on a man dying for us while we were his enemies, removes self-righteousness and selfishness and turns its members to serve others both for the temporal flourishing of all people, especially the poor, and for their salvation. It moves us to serve others irrespective of their merits, just as Christ served us (Mark 10:45).

Secularism and religion conform people to behavioral norms through fear (of consequences) and pride (a desire for self-aggrandizement). The gospel moves people to holiness and service out of grateful joy for grace, and out of love of the glory of God for who he is in himself.

V. What is gospel-centered ministry?

It is characterized by:

1. Empowered corporate worship.

   The gospel changes our relationship with God from one of hostility or slavish compliance to one of intimacy and joy. The core dynamic of gospel-centered ministry is therefore worship and fervent prayer. In corporate worship God's people receive a special life–transforming sight of the worth and beauty of God, and then give back to God suitable expressions of his worth. At the heart of corporate worship is the ministry of the Word. Preaching should be expository (explaining the text of Scripture) and Christ–centered (expounding all biblical themes as climaxing in Christ and his work of salvation). Its ultimate goal, however, is not simply to teach but to lead the hearers to worship, individual and corporate, that strengthens their inner being to do the will of God.

2. Evangelistic effectiveness.

   Because the gospel (unlike religious moralism) produces people who do not disdain those who disagree with them, a truly gospel-centered church should be filled with members who winsomely address people's hopes and aspirations with Christ and his saving work. We have a vision for a church that sees conversions of rich and poor, highly educated and less educated, men and women, old and young, married and single, and all races. We hope to draw highly secular and postmodern people, as well as reaching religious and traditional people. Because of the attractiveness of its community and the humility of its people, a gospel-centered church should find people in its midst who are exploring and trying to understand Christianity. It must welcome them in hundreds of ways. It will do little to make them "comfortable" but will do much to make its message understandable. In addition to all this, gospel-centered churches will have a bias toward church planting as one of the most effective means of evangelism there is.

3. Counter–cultural community.

   Because the gospel removes both fear and pride, people should get along inside the church who could never get along outside. Because it points us to a man who died for his enemies, the gospel creates relationships of service rather than of selfishness. Because the gospel calls us to holiness, the people of God live in loving bonds of mutual accountability and discipline. Thus the gospel creates a human community radically different from any society around it. Regarding sex, the church should avoid both the secular society's idolization of sex and traditional society's fear of it. It is a community which so loves and cares practically for its members that biblical chastity makes sense. It teaches its members to conform their bodily being to the shape of the gospel—abstinence outside of heterosexual marriage and fidelity and joy within. Regarding the family, the church should affirm the goodness of marriage between a man and a woman, calling them to serve God by reflecting his covenant love in life–long loyalty, and by teaching his ways to their children. But it also affirms the goodness of serving Christ as singles, whether for a time or for a life. The church should surround all persons suffering from the fallenness of our human sexuality with a compassionate community and family. Regarding money, the church's members should engage in radical economic sharing with one another—so "there are no needy among them" (Acts 4:34). Such sharing also promotes a radically generous commitment of time, money, relationships, and living space to social justice and the needs of the poor, the oppressed, the immigrant, and the economically and physically weak. Regarding power, it is visibly committed to power–sharing and relationship–building among races, classes, and generations that are alienated outside of the Body of Christ. The practical evidence of this is that our local churches increasingly welcome and embrace people of all races and cultures. Each church should seek to reflect the diversity of its local geographical community, both in the congregation at large and in its leadership.

4. The integration of faith and work.

5. The good news of the Bible is not only individual forgiveness but the renewal of the whole creation. God put humanity in the garden to cultivate the material world for his own glory and for the flourishing of nature and the human community. The Spirit of God not only converts individuals (e.g., John 16:8) but also renews and cultivates the face of the earth (e.g., Genesis 1:2; Psalm 104:30). Therefore Christians glorify God not only through the ministry of the Word, but also through their vocations of agriculture, art, business, government, scholarship—all for God's glory and the furtherance of the public good. Too many Christians have learned to seal off their faith–beliefs from the way they work in their vocation. The gospel is seen as a means of finding individual peace and not as the foundation of a worldview—a comprehensive interpretation of reality affecting all that we do. But we have a vision for a church that equips its people to think out the implications of the gospel on how we do carpentry, plumbing, data–entry, nursing, art, business, government,

journalism, entertainment, and scholarship. Such a church will not only support Christians' engagement with culture, but will also help them work with distinctiveness, excellence, and accountability in their trades and professions. Developing humane yet creative and excellent business environments out of our understanding of the gospel is part of the work of bringing a measure of healing to God's creation in the power of the Spirit. Bringing Christian joy, hope, and truth to embodiment in the arts is also part of this work. We do all of this because the gospel of God leads us to it, even while we recognize that the ultimate restoration of all things awaits the personal and bodily return of our Lord Jesus Christ (CS–[13]).

6. The doing of justice and mercy.

7. God created both soul and body, and the resurrection of Jesus shows that he is going to redeem both the spiritual and the material. Therefore God is concerned not only for the salvation of souls but also for the relief of poverty, hunger, and injustice. The gospel opens our eyes to the fact that all our wealth (even wealth for which we worked hard) is ultimately an unmerited gift from God. Therefore the person who does not generously give away his or her wealth to others is not merely lacking in compassion, but is unjust. Christ wins our salvation through losing, achieves power through weakness and service, and comes to wealth through giving all away. Those who receive his salvation are not the strong and accomplished but those who admit they are weak and lost. We cannot look at the poor and the oppressed and callously call them to pull themselves out of their own difficulty. Jesus did not treat us that way. The gospel replaces superiority toward the poor with mercy and compassion. Christian churches must work for justice and peace in their neighborhoods through service even as they call individuals to conversion and the new birth. We must work for the eternal and common good and show our neighbors we love them sacrificially whether they believe as we do or not. Indifference to the poor and disadvantaged means there has not been a true grasp of our salvation by sheer grace.

Conclusion

The ministry we have outlined is relatively rare. There are many seeker–driven churches that help many people find Christ. There are many churches seeking to engage the culture through political activism. There is a fast–growing charismatic movement with emphasis on glorious, passionate, corporate worship. There are many congregations with strong concern for doctrinal rigor and purity and who work very hard to keep themselves separate from the world. There are many churches with a radical commitment to the poor and marginalized.

We do not, however, see enough individual churches that embody the full, integrative gospel balance we have outlined here. And while, in God's grace, there is an encouraging number of bright spots in the church, we see no broad movement yet of this gospel-centered ministry. We believe such a balance will produce churches with winsome and theologically substantial preaching, dynamic evangelism and apologetics, and church growth and church planting. They will emphasize repentance, personal renewal, and holiness of life. At the same time, and in the same congregations, there will be engagement with the social structures of ordinary people, and cultural engagement with art, business, scholarship, and government. There will be calls for radical Christian community in which all members share wealth and resources and make room for the poor and the marginalized. These priorities will all be combined and will mutually strengthen one another in each local church.

What could lead to a growing movement of gospel-centered churches? The ultimate answer is that God must, for his own glory, send revival in response to the fervent, extraordinary, prevailing prayer of his people. But we believe there are also penultimate steps to take. There is great hope if we can unite on the nature of truth, how best to read the Bible, on our relationship to culture, on the content of the gospel, and on the nature of gospel-centered ministry. We believe that such commitments will drive us afresh toward Scripture, toward the Christ of Scripture, toward the gospel of Christ, and we will begin to grow in our ability, by God's grace, as churches, to "act in line with the truth of the gospel" (Galatians 2:14). We are ashamed of our sins and failures, grateful beyond measure for forgiveness, and eager to see afresh the glory of God and embody conformity to his Son.

Source: The Gospel Coalition. Available at https://www.thegospelcoalition.org/about/foundation-documents.

"STATEMENT OF THE EVANGELICAL CLIMATE INITIATIVE, CLIMATE CHANGE: AN EVANGELICAL CALL TO ACTION" (2006)

The American public is divided on the degree to which global climate change is accepted as being a long-term reality and challenge to human security on earth. So too are evangelicals divided on the subject. As with many areas of concern and public policy, there are areas of overlapping agreement among evangelicals and areas where there is ideological dissent. The following document, signed by more than 300 senior evangelical leaders, strongly affirms global climate change. Their work also included a set of principles for federal policy on climate change and addressed concerns of enhancing national security by reducing U.S. reliance on foreign oil, creating jobs, and keeping the environment clean.

As American evangelical Christian leaders, we recognize both our opportunity and our responsibility to offer a biblically based moral witness that can help shape public policy in the most powerful nation on earth, and therefore contribute to the well-being of the entire world. Whether we will enter the public square and offer our witness there is no longer an open question. We are in that square, and we will not withdraw.

We are proud of the evangelical community's long-standing commitment to the sanctity of human life. But we also offer moral witness in many venues and on many issues. Sometimes the issues that we have taken on, such as sex trafficking, geno-cide in the Sudan, and the AIDS epidemic in Africa, have surprised outside observ-ers. While individuals and organizations can be called to concentrate on certain issues, we are not a single-issue movement. We seek to be true to our calling as Christian leaders, and above all faithful to Jesus Christ our Lord. Our attention, therefore, goes to whatever issues our faith requires us to address.

Over the last several years many of us have engaged in study, reflection, and prayer related to the issue of climate change (often called "global warming"). For most of us, until recently this has not been treated as a pressing issue or major priority. Indeed, many of us have required considerable convincing before becoming per-suaded that climate change is a real problem and that it ought to matter to us as Christians. But now we have seen and heard enough to offer the following moral argument related to the matter of human-induced climate change. We commend the four simple but urgent claims offered in this document to all who will listen, beginning with our brothers and sisters in the Christian community, and urge all to take the appropriate actions that follow from them.

CLAIM 1: Human-Induced Climate Change Is Real

Since 1995 there has been general agreement among those in the scientific com-munity most seriously engaged with this issue that climate change is happening and is being caused mainly by human activities, especially the burning of fossil fuels. Evidence gathered since 1995 has only strengthened this conclusion.

Because all religious/moral claims about climate change are relevant only if cli-mate change is real and is mainly human-induced, everything hinges on the scien-tific data. As evangelicals we have hesitated to speak on this issue until we could be more certain of the science of climate change, but the signatories now believe that the evidence demands action:

- The Intergovernmental Panel on Climate Change (IPCC), the world's most authoritative body of scientists and policy experts on the issue of global warm-ing, has been studying this issue since the late 1980s. (From 1988–2002 the IPCC's assessment of the climate science was Chaired by Sir John Houghton, a devout evangelical Christian.) It has documented the steady rise in global temperatures over the last fifty years, projects that the average global tempera-ture will continue to rise in the coming decades, and attributes "most of the warming" to human activities.
- The U.S. National Academy of Sciences, as well as all other G8 country sci-entific Academies (Great Britain, France, Germany, Japan, Canada, Italy, and Russia), has concurred with these judgments.
- In a 2004 report, and at the 2005 G8 summit, the Bush Administration has also acknowledged the reality of climate change and the likelihood that human activity is the cause of at least some of it.

In the face of the breadth and depth of this scientific and governmental concern, only a small percentage of which is noted here, we are convinced that evangelicals must engage this issue without any further lingering over the basic reality of the problem or humanity's responsibility to address it.

CLAIM 2: The Consequences of Climate Change Will Be Significant, and Will Hit the Poor the Hardest

The earth's natural systems are resilient but not infinitely so, and human civilizations are remarkably dependent on ecological stability and well-being. It is easy to forget this until that stability and well-being are threatened.

Even small rises in global temperatures will have such likely impacts as: sea level rise; more frequent heat waves, droughts, and extreme weather events such as torrential rains and floods; increased tropical diseases in now-temperate regions; and hurricanes that are more intense. It could lead to significant reduction in agricultural output, especially in poor countries. Low-lying regions, indeed entire islands, could find themselves under water. (This is not to mention the various negative impacts climate change could have on God's other creatures.)

Each of these impacts increases the likelihood of refugees from flooding or famine, violent conflicts, and international instability, which could lead to more security threats to our nation.

Poor nations and poor individuals have fewer resources available to cope with major challenges and threats. The consequences of global warming will therefore hit the poor the hardest, in part because those areas likely to be significantly affected first are in the poorest regions of the world. Millions of people could die in this century because of climate change, most of them our poorest global neighbors.

CLAIM 3: Christian Moral Convictions Demand Our Response to the Climate Change Problem

While we cannot here review the full range of relevant biblical convictions related to care of the creation, we emphasize the following points:

- Christians must care about climate change because we love God the Creator and Jesus our Lord, through whom and for whom the creation was made. This is God's world, and any damage that we do to God's world is an offense against God Himself (Genesis 1; Psalms 24; Colossians 1:16).
- Christians must care about climate change because we are called to love our neighbors, to do unto others as we would have them do unto us, and to protect and care for the least of these as though each was Jesus Christ himself (Matthew 22:34–40; 7:12; 25:31–46).
- Christians, noting the fact that most of the climate change problem is human induced, are reminded that when God made humanity he commissioned us

to exercise stewardship over the earth and its creatures. Climate change is the latest evidence of our failure to exercise proper stewardship, and constitutes a critical opportunity for us to do better (Genesis 1:26–28).

Love of God, love of neighbor, and the demands of stewardship are more than enough reason for evangelical Christians to respond to the climate change problem with moral passion and concrete action.

CLAIM 4: The Need to Act Now Is Urgent. Governments, Businesses, Churches, and Individuals all have a Role to Play in Addressing Climate Change—Starting Now.

The basic task for all of the world's inhabitants is to find ways now to begin to reduce the carbon dioxide emissions from the burning of fossil fuels that are the primary cause of human-induced climate change.

There are several reasons for urgency. First, deadly impacts are being experienced now. Second, the oceans only warm slowly, creating a lag in experiencing the consequences. Much of the climate change to which we are already committed will not be realized for several decades. The consequences of the pollution we create now will be visited upon our children and grandchildren. Third, as individuals and as a society we are making long-term decisions today that will determine how much carbon dioxide we will emit in the future, such as whether to purchase energy efficient vehicles and appliances that will last for 10–20 years, or whether to build more coal-burning power plants that last for 50 years rather than investing more in energy efficiency and renewable energy.

In the United States, the most important immediate step that can be taken at the federal level is to pass and implement national legislation requiring sufficient economy-wide reductions in carbon dioxide emissions through cost-effective, market-based mechanisms such as a cap-and-trade program. On June 22, 2005 the Senate passed the Domenici-Bingaman resolution affirming this approach, and a number of major energy companies now acknowledge that this method is best both for the environment and for business.

We commend the Senators who have taken this stand and encourage them to fulfill their pledge. We also applaud the steps taken by such companies as BP, Shell, General Electric, Cinergy, Duke Energy, and DuPont, all of which have moved ahead of the pace of government action through innovative measures implemented within their companies in the U.S. and around the world. In so doing they have offered timely leadership.

Numerous positive actions to prevent and mitigate climate change are being implemented across our society by state and local governments, churches, smaller businesses, and individuals. These commendable efforts focus on such matters as energy efficiency, the use of renewable energy, low CO_2 emitting technologies, and the purchase of hybrid vehicles. These efforts can easily be shown to save money, save energy, reduce global warming pollution as well as air pollution that harm human health, and eventually pay for themselves. There is much more to be done, but these pioneers are already helping to show the way forward.

Finally, while we must reduce our global warming pollution to help mitigate the impacts of climate change, as a society and as individuals we must also help the poor adapt to the significant harm that global warming will cause.

Conclusion

We the undersigned pledge to act on the basis of the claims made in this document. We will not only teach the truths communicated here but also seek ways to implement the actions that follow from them. In the name of Jesus Christ our Lord, we urge all who read this declaration to join us in this effort.

Source: Christians and Climate: An Evangelical Call to Action. Available at http://www.christiansandclimate.org/.

NATIONAL ASSOCIATION OF EVANGELICALS RESOLUTION ON IMMIGRATION (2009)

Throughout its history, the National Association of Evangelicals has produced many resolutions, statements, and position papers on issues facing the nation and the world. In 2009, a statement was drafted on immigration and presented in English and Spanish. This was not the first time the NAE had spoken on the topic, but the statement presented here reflects how one large evangelical organization understands the issue:

The significant increase in immigration and the growing stridency of the national debate on immigration compel the National Association of Evangelicals to speak boldly and biblically to this challenging topic. The complexity of immigration issues provides an opportunity to mine Scripture for guidance. A biblically informed position provides a strong platform for the NAE to make a contribution in the public square that will be explicitly Christian. Out of commitment to Scripture and knowledge of national immigration realities comes a distinct call to action.

Biblical Foundations

Discussion of immigration and government immigration policy must begin with the truth that every human being is made in the image of God (Genesis 1:26–28). Immigrants are made in the image of God and have supreme value with the potential to contribute greatly to society. Jesus exemplifies respect toward others who are different in his treatment of the Samaritans (Luke 10:30–37; John 4:1–42).

The Bible contains many accounts of God's people who were forced to migrate due to hunger, war, or personal circumstances. Abraham, Isaac, Jacob and the families of his sons turned to Egypt in search of food. Joseph, Naomi, Ruth, Daniel and his friends, Ezekiel, Ezra, Nehemiah, and Esther all lived in foreign lands. In the New Testament, Joseph and Mary fled with Jesus to escape Herod's anger and became refugees in Egypt. Peter referred to the recipients of his first letter as "aliens" and "strangers," perhaps suggesting that they were exiles within the Roman Empire. These examples from the Old and New Testaments reveal God's hand in the movement of people and are illustrations of faith in God in difficult circumstances.

Migration was common in the ancient world. Outsiders were particularly vulnerable. They stood outside the kinship system that regulated the inheritance of property. They did not have extended family to care for them in case of need. The Law recognized their helplessness and stipulated measures that served as a safety net. The motivations behind this generous spirit were that the people of God were not to forget that they had been strangers in Egypt (Exodus 22:21; Leviticus 19:33–34) and that God loved the foreigner (Deuteronomy 10:18–19). The New Testament adds that all believers are spiritual sojourners on earth (Philippians 3:20; 1 Peter 2:11). Christians should show compassion and hospitality to outsiders (Romans 12:13; Hebrews 13:2).

The Bible does not offer a blueprint for modern legislation, but it can serve as a moral compass and shape the attitudes of those who believe in God. An appreciation of the pervasiveness of migration in the Bible must temper the tendency to limit discussions on immigration to Romans 13 and a simplistic defense of "the rule of law." God has established the nations (Deuteronomy 32:8; Acts 17:26), and their laws should be respected. Nevertheless, policies must be evaluated to reflect that immigrants are made in the image of God and demonstrate biblical grace to the foreigner.

National Realities

Immigration is a worldwide phenomenon. People migrate due to economic globalization, armed conflicts, and a desire to provide for their families. The United States of America is a country founded by immigrants, and its history has been characterized by waves of immigrants from different parts of the world. Immigrants will continue to be an essential part of who we are as a country. Our response to immigration must include an understanding of this immigrant history and an awareness of the positive impact of multiple cultures on national life over the last 250 years. The challenge today is to determine how to maintain the integrity of national borders, address the situation with millions of undocumented immigrants, devise a realistic program to respond to labor needs, and manifest the humanitarian spirit that has characterized this country since its founding.

The problems related to immigration are many and complicated. In many instances the arrival of a large number of immigrants has compromised the border. Some communities now struggle with significant stress on infrastructures in education, health care, social services, and the legal system. At the same time, many jobs and industries rely on immigrant workers. Current quotas do not grant enough visas to meet these needs, nor does federal immigration law provide sufficient opportunities to others who also come seeking gainful employment. Many immigrants who obtain legal entry yearn to be reunited with families, but backlogs under family-based immigration law result in excessive periods of family separation.

Due to the limited number of visas, millions have entered the United States without proper documentation or have overstayed temporary visas. While these actions violate existing laws, socioeconomic, political, and legal realities contribute to the problematic nature of immigration. Society has ignored the existence of an unauthorized work force due to the economic benefits of cheap immigrant labor. Without legal status and wary of reporting abuses, immigrants can be mistreated and underpaid by employers. Deportation of wage-earners has separated families and complicated the situation for many. Most undocumented immigrants desire to regularize their legal status, but avenues to assimilation and citizenship are blocked by local, state, and federal laws. This has generated an underground industry for false documentation and human smuggling.

These quandaries offer fresh opportunities for the church. Immigrant communities offer a new, vibrant field for evangelism, church planting, and ministry. Denominations have launched efforts to bring the gospel to these newcomers, establish churches, and train leaders for immigrant believers. Millions of immigrants also come from Christian backgrounds. These brothers and sisters in Christ are revitalizing churches across the country and are planting churches and evangelizing. Their presence is a blessing of God. These spiritual realities remind evangelicals that an evaluation of recent immigration cannot be reduced to economics and national security issues.

Call to Action

Motivated by the desire to offer a constructive word for the country's complicated immigration situation and guided by the Scripture, the National Association of Evangelicals calls for the reform of the immigration system. We believe that national immigration policy should be considerate of immigrants who are already here and who may arrive in the future and that its measures should promote national security and the general welfare in appropriate ways. Building upon biblical revelation concerning the migration of people and the values of justice and compassion championed in "For the Health of the Nation: An Evangelical Call to Civic Responsibility," we urge:

- That immigrants be treated with respect and mercy by churches. Exemplary treatment of immigrants by Christians can serve as the moral basis to call for government attitudes and legislation to reflect the same virtues.
- That the government develop structures and mechanisms that safeguard and monitor the national borders with efficiency and respect for human dignity.
- That the government establish more functional legal mechanisms for the annual entry of a reasonable number of immigrant workers and families.

- That the government recognize the central importance of the family in society by reconsidering the number and categories of visas available for family reunification, by dedicating more resources to reducing the backlog of cases in process, and by reevaluating the impact of deportation on families.
- That the government establish a sound, equitable process toward earned legal status for currently undocumented immigrants, who desire to embrace the responsibilities and privileges that accompany citizenship.
- That the government legislate fair labor and civil laws for all residing within the United States that reflect the best of this country's heritage.

That immigration enforcement be conducted in ways that recognize the importance of due process of law, the sanctity of the human person, and the incomparable value of family.

Source: National Association of Evangelicals. Available at http://www.nae.net /immigration-community-serving-churches/.

NATIONAL ASSOCIATION OF EVANGELICALS RESOLUTION ON PREDATORY LENDING (2014)

The 2008 banking crisis in the United States sent a seismic shock through financial institutions, the government, and the citizens of the nation. It also exposed the deep interrelated nature of the nation's economy. In the following document, the National Association of Evangelicals addressed the debt trap in which many Americans, young and old, find themselves. The resolution is one example of an evangelical organization speaking out on contemporary social concerns:

When used responsibly, credit can be a blessing. Banks, credit unions and other financial institutions play a vital role in the efficient functioning of a modern economy, contributing to the common good.

Scripture upholds principles of just and honest commerce, while prohibiting usury, exploitation and oppression of those in need. This includes predatory lending in which vulnerable people with immediate financial needs are lured into short-term, high interest loan agreements that are rolled over from paycheck to paycheck. In many cases annual interest and fees may exceed 300 percent of the loan amount. What starts as a one-time need quickly grows into a long-term debt trap.

Most families experience emergency needs from time to time. Churches, charities and employers can and do help with gifts or loans in times of personal crisis. They can also offer financial literacy classes and model the virtues of disciplined saving, delayed gratification and investment for future needs.

The NAE calls on lenders to design loan products that do not exploit poor and vulnerable borrowers. We call on the Consumer Financial Protection Bureau to investigate predatory lending abuses and to establish just regulations that protect consumers, particularly the most poor and vulnerable among us, from exploitation.

Source: National Association of Evangelicals. Available at http://www.nae.net/new
-rules-small-dollar-loans/.

"WHAT IS AN EVANGELICAL?" NATIONAL ASSOCIATION OF EVANGELICALS (2017)

Precise definitions of evangelicals are difficult to find and as a result, there is often confusion and misrepresentation by those studying evangelicalism, those observing it, and even those participating in it and self-identifying as evangelicals. In 1989 historian David Bebbington of the University of Stirling in Scotland identified four qualities in his book Evangelicalism in Modern Britain: A History from the 1730s to the 1980s *that he contends are central to any understanding of evangelicals. Known today at Bebbington's Quadrilateral or the Evangelical Quadrilateral, it was quickly and widely accepted and continues to be used. In the document below the National Association of Evangelicals builds upon his quadrilateral and provides a broad definition:*

Evangelicals take the Bible seriously and believe in Jesus Christ as Savior and Lord.

The term "evangelical" comes from the Greek word *euangelion*, meaning "the good news" or the "gospel." Thus, the evangelical faith focuses on the "good news" of salvation brought to sinners by Jesus Christ.

Evangelicals are a vibrant and diverse group, including believers found in many churches, denominations and nations. Our community brings together Reformed, Holiness, Anabaptist, Pentecostal, Charismatic and other traditions.

Our core theological convictions provide unity in the midst of our diversity. The NAE Statement of Faith offers a standard for these evangelical convictions.

Historian David Bebbington also provides a helpful summary of evangelical distinctives, identifying four primary characteristics of evangelicalism:

- Conversionism: the belief that lives need to be transformed through a "born-again" experience and a life long process of following Jesus
- Activism: the expression and demonstration of the gospel in missionary and social reform efforts
- Biblicism: a high regard for and obedience to the Bible as the ultimate authority
- Crucicentrism: a stress on the sacrifice of Jesus Christ on the cross as making possible the redemption of humanity

These distinctives and theological convictions define us—not political, social or cultural trends. In fact, many evangelicals rarely use the term "evangelical" to describe themselves, focusing simply on the core convictions of the triune God, the Bible, faith, Jesus, salvation, evangelism and discipleship.

Source: National Association of Evangelicals. Available at https://www.nae.net/what
-is-an-evangelical/.

Further Reading

Amstutz, Mark R. *Evangelicals and American Foreign Policy.* New York: Oxford University Press, 2014.

Balmer, Randall. *The Making of Evangelicalism: From Revivalism to Politics and Beyond.* Waco, TX: Baylor University Press, 2010.

Balmer, Randall. *Evangelicalism in America.* Waco, TX: Baylor University Press, 2016.

Bebbington, David. *Evangelicalism in Modern Britain: A History from the 1730s to the 1980s.* Grand Rapids, MI: Baker Books, 1989.

Bebbington, David W. *The Dominance of Evangelicalism: The Age of Spurgeon and Moody.* Downers Grove, IL: InterVarsity Press, 2005.

Bock, Darrell L. *How Would Jesus Vote?* New York: Howard Books, 2016.

Borg, David. "The End of Evangelical Support for Israel?" *The Middle East Quarterly* 21:2 (Spring 2014) at http://www.meforum.org/3769/israel-evangelical-support.

Boyer, Paul. *When Time Shall Be No More: Prophecy Belief in Modern American Culture.* Cambridge, MA: Harvard University Press, 1992.

Burch, Maxie B. *The Evangelical Historians: The Historiography of George Marsden, Nathan Hatch, and Mark Noll.* Lanham, MD: University Press of America, 1996.

Bustraan, Richard. *The Jesus People Movement: A Story of Spiritual Revolution among the Hippies.* Eugene, OR: Pickwick Publications, 2014.

Carpenter, Joel A. *Revive Us Again: The Reawakening of American Fundamentalism.* New York: Oxford University Press, 1997.

Chute, Anthony L., and Michael A. G. Haykin. *The Baptist Story: From English Sect to Global Movement.* Nashville, TN: B&H Academic, 2015.

Craig, William Lane, and J. P. Moreland. *Philosophical Foundations for a Christian Worldview.* Downers Grove, IL: InterVarsity, 2003.

Cusic, Don, ed. *Encyclopedia of Contemporary Christian Music: Pop, Rock, and Worship.* Santa Barbara, CA: Greenwood Press, an Imprint of ABC-CLIO, LLC, 2010.

Elwell, Walter A., ed. *Handbook of Evangelical Theologians.* Grand Rapids, MI: Baker Books, 1993.

Elwell, Walter A., ed. *Evangelical Dictionary of Theology.* Grand Rapids, MI: Baker Books, 2001.

Eskridge, Larry. *God's Forever Family: The Jesus People Movement in America.* New York: Oxford University Press, 2013.

FitzGerald, Frances. *The Evangelicals: The Struggle to Shape America.* New York: Simon & Schuster, 2017.

Gasaway, Brantley W. *Progressive Evangelicals and the Pursuit of Social Justice.* Chapel Hill, NC: University of North Carolina Press, 2014.

Geisler, Norman. *Inerrancy.* Grand Rapids, MI: Zondervan, 1980.

Geisler, Norman, and William C. Roach. *Defending Inerrancy: Affirming the Accuracy of Scripture for a New Generation.* Grand Rapids, MI: Baker Books, 2012.

George, Timothy. *Guaranteed Pure: Moody Bible Institute, Business, and the Making of Modern Evangelicalism.* Chapel Hill, NC: The University of North Carolina Press, 2015.

Getz, Gene A. *MBI: The Story of Moody Bible Institute.* Chicago, IL: Moody Press, 1986.

Goldberg, Louis, ed. *How Jewish Is Christianity? Two Views on the Messianic Movement.* Grand Rapids, MI: Zondervan Publications, 2003.

Gould, Paul M., and Richard Brian Davis, eds. *Four Views on Christianity and Philosophy.* Grand Rapids, MI: Zondervan Publishing, 2016.

Hangen, Tona J. *Redeeming the Dial: Radio, Religion, and Popular Culture in America.* Chapel Hill, NC: The University of North Carolina Press, 2002.

Hankins, Barry. *Fundamentalism and Evangelicalism: A Documentary Reader.* New York: NYU Press, 2008.

Hannah, John D. *The Uncommon Union: Dallas Theological Seminary and American Evangelicalism.* Grand Rapids, MI: Zondervan, 2009.

Hart, D. G. *Deconstructing Evangelicalism: Conservative Protestantism in the Age of Billy Graham.* Grand Rapids, MI: Baker Academic, 2004.

Hartman, Andrew. *A War for the Soul of America: A History of the Culture Wars.* Chicago, IL: The University of Chicago Press, 2015.

Hatch, Nathan O. *The Democratization of American Christianity.* New Haven, CT: Yale University Press, 1989.

Henry, Carl F. H. *The Uneasy Conscience of Modern Fundamentalism.* Grand Rapids, MI: Eerdmans, 1947.

Henry, Carl F. H. *God, Revelation, and Authority.* 6 vols. Waco, TX: Word Books, 1976–1983.

Henry, Carl F. H. *Confessions of a Theologian: An Autobiography.* Waco, TX: Word Books, 1986.

Kantzer, Kenneth S. *Applying the Scriptures.* Dulles, VA: Academie Books, 1987.

Lindsay, Michael D. *Faith in the Halls of Power: How Evangelicals Joined the American Elite.* New York: Oxford University Press, 2008.

MacLeod, A. Donald. *C. Stacey Woods and the Evangelical Rediscovery of the University.* Downers Grove, IL: IVP Academic, 2007.

Marsden, George. *Reforming Fundamentalism: Fuller Seminary and the New Evangelicalism.* Grand Rapids, MI: Eerdmans, 1988.

Marsden, George. *Understanding Fundamentalism and Evangelicalism.* Grand Rapids, MI: Eerdmans, 1990.

Marsden, George M. *Fundamentalism and American Culture*, 2nd ed. New York: Oxford University Press, 2006.

McDermott, Gerald R., ed. *The New Christian Zionism: Fresh Perspectives on Israel and the Land.* Downers Grove, IL: IVP Academic, 2016.

Miller, Steven P. *The Age of Evangelicalism: America's Born-Again Years.* New York: Oxford University Press, 2014.

Morris, Thomas V., ed. *God and the Philosophers: The Reconciliation of Faith and Reason.* Oxford, UK: Oxford University Press, 1994.

Morrison, Douglas. *Has God Said? Scripture, the Word of God, and the Crisis of Theological Authority.* Eugene, OR: Wipf & Stock Publishers, 2006.

Mouw, Richard J. *The Smell of the Sawdust Trail: What Evangelicals Can Learn from Their Fundamentalist Heritage.* Grand Rapids, MI: Zondervan, 2000.

Noll, Mark. *A History of Christianity in the United States of America.* Grand Rapids, MI: Eerdmans, 1992.

Noll, Mark A. *The Scandal of the Evangelical Mind.* Grand Rapids, MI: Eerdmans, 1994.

Noll, Mark A. *Between Faith and Criticism: Evangelicals, Scholarship, and the Bible in America,* 2nd ed. Vancouver, Brit. Col.: Regent College Publishing, 2004.

Noll, Mark A. *Jesus Christ and the Life of the Mind.* Grand Rapids, MI: Eerdmans, 2011.

Noll, Mark A. *From Every Tribe and Nation: A Historian's Discovery of the Global Christian Story.* Grand Rapids, MI: Eerdmans, 2014.

Plantinga, Alvin. "Advice to Christian Philosophers." *Faith and Philosophy: Journal of the Society of Christian Philosophers* 1, no. 3 (1984): 253–271.

Radmacher, Earl, and Robert Preus. *Hermeneutics, Inerrancy, and the Bible: Papers from ICBI Summit II.* Dulles, VA: Academie Books, 1984.

Rah, Soong-Chan, and Gary Vanderpol. *Return to Justice: Six Movements that Reignited Our Contemporary Evangelical Conscience.* Grand Rapids, MI: Brazos Press, 2016.

Rosell, Garth M. *The Surprising Work of God: Harold John Ockenga, Billy Graham, and the Rebirth of Evangelicalism.* Grand Rapids, MI: Baker Academic, 2008.

Rosell, Garth M. *Boston's Historic Park Street Church.* Grand Rapids, MI: Kregel Publications, 2009.

Rudolph, David, and Joel Willetts, eds. *Introduction to Messianic Judaism: Its Ecclesial Context and Biblical Foundations.* Grand Rapids, MI: Zondervan Publications, 2013.

Ryrie, Charles C. *Dispensationalism Today.* Chicago, IL: Moody Press, 1966.

Ryrie, Charles C. *Dispensationalism,* revised and expanded. Chicago, IL: Moody Press, 1995.

Schaeffer, Francis A. *The Collected Works of Francis A. Schaeffer.* 6 vols. Wheaton, IL: Crossway Publishers, 1985.

Schafer, Axel R., ed. *American Evangelicals and the 1960s.* Madison, WI: The University of Wisconsin Press, 2013.

Schultze, Quentin J. *Televangelism and American Culture: The Business of Popular Religion.* Eugene, OR: Wipf & Stock Publishers, 2003.

Schultze, Quentin J., and Robert H. Woods, Jr., eds. *Understanding Evangelical Media: The Changing Face of Christian Communication.* Downers Grove, IL: InterVarsity Press, 2008.

Shelley, Bruce. "The Rise of Evangelical Youth Movements." *Fides et Historia* 18:1 (1986): 47–63.

Smith, Christian, et al. *American Evangelicalism: Embattled and Thriving.* Chicago, IL: University of Chicago Press, 1998.

Stanley, Brian. *The Global Diffusion of Evangelicalism: The Age of Billy Graham and John Stott.* Downers Grove, IL: InterVarsity Press, 2014.

Stowe, David W. *No Sympathy for the Devil: Christian Pop Music and the Transformation of American Evangelicalism.* Chapel Hill, NC: University of North Carolina Press, 2011.

Strachan, Owen. *Awakening the Evangelical Mind: An Intellectual History of the Neo-Evangelical Movement.* Grand Rapids, MI: Zondervan Publishing, 2015.

Sutton, Matthew Avery. *American Apocalypse: A History of American Evangelicalism.* Cambridge, MA: Belknap Press, 2014.

Swartz, David R. *Moral Minority: The Evangelical Left in an Age of Conservatism.* Philadelphia, PA: University of Pennsylvania Press, 2012.

Sweeney, Douglas A. *The American Evangelical Story: A History of the Movement.* Grand Rapids, MI: Baker Academic, 2005.

Sweet, Leonard I., ed. *The Evangelical Tradition in America.* Macon, GA: Mercer University Press, 1997.

Synon, Vinson. *The Holiness-Pentecostal Movement in the United States.* Grand Rapids, MI: Eerdmans, 1971.

Synon, Vinson. *The Century of the Holy Spirit: 100 Years of Pentecostal and Charismatic Renewal.* Nashville, TN: Thomas Nelson, 2001.

Thornbury, Gregory. *Recovering Classic Evangelicalism: Applying the Wisdom and Vision of Carl F. H. Henry.* Wheaton, IL: Crossway, 2013.

Wacker, Grant. *America's Pastor: Billy Graham and the Shaping of a Nation.* Cambridge, MA: Belknap Press, 2014.

Walvoord, John F. *The Rapture Question.* Rev. ed. Grand Rapids, MI: Zondervan, 1979.

Ward, Mark Sr. *Air of Salvation: The Story of Christian Broadcasting.* Grand Rapids, MI: Baker Books, 1994.

Watson, William C. *Dispensationalism before Darby: Seventeenth-Century and Eighteenth-Century English Apocalypticism.* Silverton, OR: Lampion Press, 2015.

Webber, Robert E. *The Younger Evangelicals: Facing the Challenges of the New World.* Grand Rapids, MI: Baker Books, 2002.

Weber, Timothy P. *Living in the Shadow of the Second Coming: American Premillennialism, 1875–1982*, enlarged edition. Chicago, IL: The University of Chicago Press, 1987.

Wright, Doyle G. *Carl Henry: Theologian for All Seasons.* Eugene, OR: Wipf & Stock/Pickwick, 2010.

Web Sites

Billy Graham Center Archives: http://www2.wheaton.edu/bgc/archives/archhp1.html.
CBE International (Christians for Biblical Equality): www.cbeinternational.org.
The Center for Bioethics & Human Dignity: https://www.cbhd.org.
Christian Legal Society: www.clsnet.org.
Christian Medical & Dental Associations: https:www.cmda.org.
Conference on Faith & History: www.faithandhistory.org.

Corwnall Alliance: For the Stewardship of Creation: www.cornwallalliance.org.

MW: A Coalition for Biblical Sexuality: www.cbmw.org.

Evangelical Environmental Network: www.creationcare.org.

Evangelical Manifesto: www.evangelicalmanifesto.com.

Evangelical Philosophical Society: www.epsociety.org.

Evangelicals for Social Action: www.evangelicalsforsocialaction.org.

The Evangelical Theological Society: www.etsjets.org.

The Gospel Coalition: www.thegospelcoalition.org.

Henry Institute for the Study of Christianity and Politics: http://henry.calvin.edu /about-the-institute/paul-b-henry.html.

Institute for the Study of American Evangelicals: www.wheaton.edu/ISAE.

National Association of Evangelicals: https://www.nae.net.

Pew Research Center: Religion & Public Life: www.pewforum.org.

Records of the International Council on Biblical Inerrancy: http://library.dts.edu /Pages/TL/Special/ICBI.shtml.

About the Editors and Contributors

The Editors

Timothy J. Demy is Professor of Military Ethics at the U.S. Naval War College, Newport, Rhode Island He previously served as a U.S. Navy chaplain for 27 years, holding assignments afloat and ashore with the Navy, Marine Corps, and Coast Guard. He received the BA in History from Texas Christian University, the ThM and ThD in Historical Theology from Dallas Theological Seminary, and the MA and PhD in Humanities from Salve Regina University. Additionally, he earned the MA in National Security and Strategic Studies from the Naval War College, the MSt in International Relations from the University of Cambridge, and the MA in European History from the University of Texas at Arlington. He has authored and edited more than 20 books on ethics, theology, and current issues, and contributed to numerous journals and encyclopedias.

Paul R. Shockley is Professor of Bible & Theology at the College of Biblical Studies-Houston and adjunct faculty (philosophy) at Stephen F. Austin State University's division of Multidisciplinary Programs in Nacogdoches, Texas. He received his BA in History from Stephen F. Austin State University; ThM in both Bible Exposition and Systematic Theology from Dallas Theological Seminary; an MA in Humanities in History of Ideas from the University of Texas-Dallas; and a PhD in Philosophy from Texas A&M University in College Station, Texas. His dissertation centered on John Dewey's aesthetics. His philosophical interests include aesthetics, history of philosophy, moral philosophy, and philosophy of religion. His theological interests include hermeneutics, biblical exposition, systematic theology, and historical theology. Paul has also taught at Texas A&M University, Prairie View A&M University, Houston Baptist University, and Southwestern Baptist Theological Seminary's J. Dalton Havard School of Theological Studies. He has lectured in Ghana, Indonesia, Israel, Liberia, and Scotland. He is currently chairman of the theological aesthetics study group for the Evangelical Theological Society. His personal Web site is www.prshockley.org.

The Contributors

Liam J. Atchison	Global Scholars
J. Denny Autrey	Southwestern Baptist Theological Seminary's J. Dalton Havard School of Theological Studies (Houston)

Brittany Burnette	College of Biblical Studies-Houston
Mark Coppenger	Southern Baptist Theological Seminary
Robert S. Covolo	Fuller Theological Seminary & VU Amsterdam
R. Don Deal	Southern Evangelical Seminary
Robert L. Dean Jr.	West Houston Bible Church
Timothy J. Demy	U.S. Naval War College
Brantley W. Gasaway	Bucknell University
George Gatgounis	Cummins Memorial Theological Seminary
Sandra Glahn	Dallas Theological Seminary
Jeffrey Gutterman	Ariel Ministries
Steve R. Halla	Union University
John D. Hannah	Dallas Theological Seminary
Bryce Hantla	University of Houston
Gary Hartenburg	Houston Baptist University
Russell Hemati	Houston Baptist University
Daniel Hill	Wheaton College
Dennis Hillman	Kregel Publications
H. Wayne House	Faith Evangelical Seminary
Thomas D. Ice	Tyndale Seminary
J. Craig Kubic	Southwestern Baptist Theological Seminary
Mark A. Jumper	Regent University
John D. Laing	Southwestern Baptist Theological Seminary's J. Dalton Havard School of Theological Studies (Houston)
Stefana Dan Laing	Southwestern Baptist Theological Seminary's J. Dalton Havard School of Theological Studies (Houston)
Marnie Blackstone Legaspi	Dallas Theological Seminary
Israel P. Loken	College of Biblical Studies–Houston
Judy Malana	Salve Regina University
Louis Markos	Houston Baptist University
Thomas McCuddy	Southern Evangelical Seminary
David A. McGee	Liberty University
Marvin McNeese Jr.	College of Biblical Studies–Houston
James Menzies	Salve Regina University
Joshua Michael	Cedarville University

David Naugle	Dallas Baptist University
Dayne E. Nix	U.S. Naval War College
Samuel Palacios	Dallas Theological Seminary
Katherine Pang	Criswell College
Tom Peeler	Reasons to Believe (Houston chapter)
Matias Perez	Dallas Theological Seminary
Benjamin Blair Phillips	Southwestern Baptist Theological Seminary's J. Dalton Havard School of Theological Studies (Houston)
Stephen O. Presley	Southwestern Baptist Theological Seminary
Jason Runnels	Southwestern Baptist Theological Seminary
Jeffrey M. Shaw	U.S. Naval War College
Paul R. Shockley	College of Biblical Studies & Stephen. F. Austin State University
Phillip Luke Sinitiere	College of Biblical Studies–Houston
Shawn Smith	University of Oklahoma
R. Alan Streett	Criswell College
Steve P. Sullivan	College of Biblical Studies–Houston
Brian Thomas	Institute of Creation Research
James Towns	Stephen F. Austin State University
Tracy L. Winkler	College of Biblical Studies–Houston
Andrew M. Woods	College of Biblical Studies–Houston

Index

Note: Page numbers in **bold** indicate the location of main entries.

National Association of Evangelicals
and, 313–314
neo-evangelicalism and, 142, 173, 304,
305–306, 313
Park Street Church and, 313, 314, 324
science and faith and, 365
*Uneasy Conscience of Modern
Fundamentalism, The* (1947) and, 400
Wright and, 299
O'Connor, John, 144
Oden, Thomas C. (1931–2016), **315–317**
Drew University and, 315
Herberg and, 315
historic Christian orthodoxy and,
315–316
publications, 316
Oecolampadius, Johannes, 43
Officers' Christian Fellowship, **317–318**
American version, 317
British version, 317
leadership, 315
purpose, 315
Ohio Association of Christian Schools, 12
Old Fashioned Revival Hour (radio
program), 166–167, 168, 270
Old Testament studies, Kaiser and, 239,
240
Old Time Gospel Hour, 151
On Old Testament Ethics (Kaiser), 240
"One Way" symbol, 309
Oneness Pentecostals, 325
Open Bible Hour (radio program), 276
Open theism, 44, 137–138, 394
Operation Carelift, 275
Operation Starting Line, 344
Oral Roberts University, 11, 353
Ordway, Holly, 157, 420
Origen, 145
Origin of Species (Darwin), 94, 141
Orthodox Presbyterian Church (OPC), 28
Westminster Theological Seminary and,
414
Ortlund, Ray, 103, 186
Orwell, George, 275
Osteen, Dodie, 318
Osteen, Joel (1963–), **318–320**
books, 319
criticism of, 319

Lakewood Church and, 318
neo-Pentecostalism and, 318
prosperity gospel and, 318–319
television and social media ministry,
318–319
Osteen, John, 318
Osteen, Paul, 318
Our Daily Bread, 68
Oxford Scofield Study Bible III, 369

Pacific Garden Mission (Chicago), **321**
Pacific Justice Institution, 63
Packer, J. I., 137
Packer, James I., 144
Pagitt, Doug, 120
Palau, Luis, 208
Palmer, Phoebe, 421
Palmer, William J., 304
Pankhurst, Christabel, 421
Pannell, William, 72, 300
Pantheism, 123
Parachurch ministries, 105, 193, **322–323.**
See also L'Abri Fellowship
Billy Graham Evangelistic Association,
323
Carey and, 322
establishment post-World War II, 337
financial practices of, 322
Ligonier Ministries, 257–259
military ministries, 280–281
Navigators, 303–304
premillennialism and, 342
Princeton Evangelical Fellowship,
342–343
Prison Fellowship, 343–345
Promise Keepers, 345–346
Samaritans Purse, 323
significant, 246
YMCA, 322
Young Life, 427–428
Youth for Christ International, 428–429
Parham, Charles, 325
Park Street Church (Boston), **323–324**
founding of, 323–234
Graham and, 324
Ockenga and, 313, 314, 324
Parker, Jim, 157
Partial Rapturism, 127, 349